Verified Victories

Top JG 52 Aces Over Hungary 1944-45

Daniel & Gabor Horvath

Helion & Company

Helion & Company Limited
Unit 8 Amherst Business Centre
Budbrooke Road
Warwick
CV34 5WE
England
Tel. 01926 499 619
Email: info@helion.co.uk
Website: www.helion.co.uk
Twitter: @helionbooks
Visit our blog at blog.helion.co.uk

Published by Helion & Company Limited 2022
Designed and typeset by Farr out Publications, Wokingham, Berkshire
Cover designed by Paul Hewitt, Battlefield Design (www.battlefield-design.co.uk)

ISBN 978-1-915070-87-6

British Library Cataloguing-in-Publication Data.
A catalogue record for this book is available from the British Library.

Contents

Acknowledgements

Before the Respected Reader pages through the aerial victories, the Authors would like to express their thanks and gratitude to all of those fellow researchers, friends, officials and especially our family members, without whose support this book would have never been written. Special thanks goes out to:

- First and foremost to our family who not only endured, but also encouraged our father-son authorship of this book. We thank you and we love you.
- Boris Vladimirovich Davidov, Russian aviation-historical researcher, who over the past decade enthusiastically and selflessly helped to complete the list and documentation of all lost Soviet warplanes in Hungary during the Second World War for the Szolnok Aircraft Museum. This gigantic database was not only essential in the identification of the crashed Soviet aircrafts that have been recovered in the past years, but it was also the key to test and analyse all Axis aerial victory claims against Soviet planes, including the ones of the JG 52 aces.
- Magó Károly, secretary of the Hungarian Wreck Research Association and project manager of the Szolnok Aircraft Museum for his continued support.
- Andrew Johannes Matthews, writer-consultant and Luftwaffe-expert and Luftaffe claims expert for his ongoing support, assistence and advice.
- Matti Salonen, Luftwaffe-expert for his help with the planes of the JG 52 aces as well as the loss records of the Luftwaffe over Hungary.

We also wish to commend the following individuals who through their selfless support have contributed to this work, your time and assistance is much appreciated:

Andrey Evgenevich Nikolaev (aviation researcher)
Bernád Dénes (Romanian Air Force expert)
Bernd Barbas (JG 52 historian, Luftwaffe expert)
Brian Cameron Webb (researcher)
Carl-Fredrik Geust (aviation historian)
Christer Bergström (aviation historian)
Horváth Péter (researcher, local historian of the Seregélyes area)
Legrády Lajos (Hungarian Wreck Research Association)
Maria Horvath (illustrator)
Dr. Markus Reisner (Austrian aerial-warfare historian)
Pálffy Sándor (archaeologist, restorer – Laczkó Dezső Museum)
Punka György (aviation historian)
Dr. Stenge B. Csaba (military historian)
Dr. Számvéber Norbert (military/armour historian)
Dr. Theo Boiten (aviation historian)
Vitaly Olegovich Mamedov (aviation researcher)

Abbreviations and Glossary

Abbreviation / Term	Native Translation	English Translation
Ia		Operations Officer
Ic		Intelligence Officer
Absch.	Abschuss (plural. -üsse)	Shoot Down
Abt.	Abteilung	Department or Battalion
Acc.		Accident
Az.	Aktenzeichen	File Mark/Sign
A.Bo.	Am Boden	(Destruction) On the Ground
ADD	АДД – Авиация Дальнего Действия	Long-Range Aviation
BAD	БАД – Бомбардировочная Авиационная Дивизия)	Bomber Air Division
BAO	БАО – Баталон Аеродромного Обслуживания	Aerodrome Service Battalion
BAP	БАП – Бомбардировочный Авиационный Полк	Bomber Air Regiment
Bes.	Besondere	Special
Br. B. Nr.	Briefbuch Nummer	Letter Book or File
Capt.	Капитан	Captain (rank)
Chef d. Pers. Rüstung u. NS-Führung d. Luftwaffe	Chef der Personellen Rüstung und Nationalsozialistischen Führung der Luftwaffe	Head of Personnel Armaments and National Socialist Air Force leadership
Chef f. Ausz. u. Diszpl.	Chef für Auszeichnungen und Disziplinarangelegenheiten	Chief of Awards and Disciplinary Matters
CL		Crash-landed
CO		Commanding Officer
C/N*		Construction Number
Dav.	Davon	From that / of which
Dep.		Deputy
Fhdgy.	Főhadnagy (Hungarian rank)	First Lieutenant (1Lt)
Furniture Van		Enemy Light Bomber/Sturmovik
Garden Fence		Base Airfield
Gv	Гвардии	Guards
GVF	ГВФ – Гражданский Воздушный Флот	Civil Air Fleet
Hanni		Altitude
Hdgy.	Hadnagy (Hungarian rank)	Second Lieutenant (2Lt)
HSU	Герой Советского Союза	Hero of the Soviet Union (title)

Abbreviation / Term (*continued*)	Native Translation	English Translation
Hydr.		Hydraulics
IAD	ИАД – Истребительная Авиационная Дивизия	Fighter Air Division
IAK	ИАК – Истребительный Авиационный Корпус	Fighter Air Corps
IAP	ИАП – Истребительный Авиационный Полк	Fighter Air Regiment
Indians		Enemy Fighters
IP		Initial Point (for bomb runs)
JG	Jagdgeschwader	Fighter Wing
-KA	-КА – Красная Армия	Red Army
KIA		Killed In Action
KIFA		Killed in Flying Accident
KTB	Kriegstagebuch	War Diary
Kurfürst		Rear HQ of the Luftwaffe, different locations indicated by numbers
LAC		Landing Accident
LP	Luftwaffenpersonalamt	Air Force Personnel Office
LT		Local Time
L.V. Blatt	Luftwaffenverordnungsblatt	Air Force Regulation Sheet
LW	Luftwaffe	Air Force (German)
Maj.	(in Russian) Майор	Major (rank)
Ml.Lt.	Младший лейтенант	Junior, or Second Lieutenant (2Lt., rank)
MACR		Missing Air Crew Report (USA)
MK	Механизированный Корпус	Mechanized Corps
MKHL	Magyar Királyi Honvéd Légierő	Royal Hungarian Air Force (RHAF)
MT		Moscow Time
NARA		National Archives & Records Administration (USA)
NBAD	НБАД – Ночная Бомбардировочная Авиационная Дивизия	Night Bomber Air Division
NBAP	НБАП – Ночная Бомбардировочная Авиационная Полк	Night Bomber Air Regiment
NKAP	НКАП – Народный комиссариат авиационной промышленности СССР	People's Commissariat of the Aviation Industry of the USSR
No.		Number
Nr.	Nummer	Number
OAE	ОАЭ – Отдельная Авиационная Эскадрилья	Separate Air Squadron
OAES	ОАЭС – Отдельная Авиационная Эскадрилья Связи	Separate Air Communications Squadron
OTER	ОТЭР – Отдельной Технической Эвакуационной Роты	Separate Technical Evacuation Company

Abbreviation / Term (*continued*)	Native Translation	English Translation
OTTR	ОТТР – Отдельной Техническая Трофейная Роты	Separate Technical Trophy Company
OVNOSRB	ОВНОСРБ – Отделъный Воздушное Наблюдение, Оповешение и Связь Радио Баталиьон	Separate Aerial Surveillance Alert and Radio Communications Battalion
OKL	Oberkommando der Luftwaffe	Air Force High Command
OKRAP	ОКРАП – Отдельный Корректировочно-Разведывательный Авиационный Полк	Separate Observation and Reconnaissance Air Regiment
OKW	Oberkommando der Wehrmacht	Wehrmacht High Command
ORAP	ОРАП – Отдельный Разведывательный Авиационный Полк	Separate Reconnaissance Air Regiment
OUTAP	ОУТАП – Отдельного Авиационного Учебно-Тренировачного Полк	Separate Training School Air Regiment
O.Z (O.Zg.)	Ohne Zeugen	Without Witness
Őrm.	Őrmester (Hungarian rank)	Sergeant (Sgt.)
Picnic Ground		Airfield
PV		Potential Victory
PVO	ПВО – Противовозду́шная Оборо́на	Anti-Air Defense
Recon.		Reconnaissance
RK	Ritterkreuz	Knights Cross
RLM	Reichsluftfahrtministerium	Reich Ministry of Aviation
Robinson		Forward HQ of the Luftwaffe at the Führer HQ, different locations indicated by numbers
RR		Railroad
ShAD	ШАД – Штурмовая Авиационная Дивизия	Assault Air Division (Il-2)
ShAK	ШАК – Штурмовой Авиационный Корпус	Assault Air Corps (Il-2)
ShAP	ШАП – Штурмовой Авиационный Полк	Assault Air Regiment (Il-2)
S/N		Serial Number
STAVKA	Ставка – Штаб Верховного Главнокомандующего	Headquarters of the Supreme Commander-in-Chief
St.Lt.	Старший лейтенант	Senior, or First Lieutenant (1Lt., rank)
Szds.	Százados (Hungarian rank)	Captain (Capt.)
TA	Танковая Армия	Tank Army
Taran	Таран	The deliberate act of aerial ramming considered a legitimate tactic by the VVS
TAP	ТАП – Тренировка Авиационная Полк	Training Air Regiment
TBr	ТБр – Танковая Бригада	(Soviet) Tank Brigade (~65 tanks)

Abbreviation / Term (*continued*)	**Native Translation**	**English Translation**
TOA		Take Off Accident
TP	ТП – Танковый Полк	(Soviet) Tank Regiment (~35 tanks)
TsAMO RF	ЦАМО РФ – Центральный Архив Министерства Обороны Российской Федерации	Central Archives of the Ministry of Defense of the Russian Federation
V		Victory
VA	ВА – Воздушная Армия	(Soviet) Air Army – one for each Front
VMF	ВМФ – Военно-Морского Флота	Military Maritime Fleet
VOL	Verbindungsoffizier des Luftschutzes	Air Defense Liaison Officer
VVS	ВВС – Военно-Воздушные Силы	Air Force
Wahrsch.	Wahrscheinlich(er)	Probable
ZAP	ЗАП – Зенитный Артиллерийский Полк	Anti-Aircraft Artillery Regiment
ZAP	ЗАП – Запасной Авиационный Полк	Reserve Air Regiment
Zls.	Zászlós (Hungarian rank)	Ensign (Ens.)
ZShAP	ЗШАП – Запасного Штурмового Авиационного Полка	Reserve Assault Air Regiment

* Construction number as well as serial number both represent the aircraft's unique identification number, with the Soviets numbers being c/n while the American-built planes using S/N. In Soviet reporting, the American Serial number was deemed equivalent to their use of their construction number, therefore it was retained.

Introduction

Jagdgeschwader 52. As Germany's most decorated and successful Fighter-Wing during World War II, it contained some of the most prominent Luftwaffe fighter pilots such as Erich Hartmann, Gerhard Barkhorn, Günther Rall, Hermann Graf, Helmut Lipfert and many others. The Geschwader's total victory tally stood over an astounding 10,000 claims by the end of the war, a tally that is higher than the entire wartime aircraft production of many countries. Throughout the final year of the war JG 52's second group, II./JG 52, fought over the Hungarian skies and saw action in the desperate campaigns against the 5th and 17th Air Armies of the Soviet 2nd and 3rd Ukrainian Fronts. Some of the pilots survived the war and lived long lives, passing on their memoires and experiences to new generations; others did not. Their military careers with the Thrid Reich's Luftwaffe remains known because of surviving wartime documents, letters, personal/official records and interviews collected and combined then put into the chronicles and books. These pieces of World War II historiography are the achievements of those authors who collected, organized, wrote and published the unit's stories during the post-war decades.

This massive and necessary work however reflects the limitations of available sources, which in many cases are incomplete and may stay as such for some time to come. However one area of this unit's history has yet to be written, namely the real wartime material damage JG 52 managed to inflict on the opposing enemy. With the opening of the Russian military archives to the greater public after the 1990s, a detailed analysis of wartime documents made it possible to accurately verify not only the losses suffered by the Soviet Air Force, but also the accuary of any opposing Air Force's claims, including that of the Luftwaffe's JG 52, even II./JG 52 over Hungary. It is the intent of the Authors of this book to compaire the victory claims of a select group of II./JG 52 pilots over Hungary against the Soviet Air Force (VVS) losses.

Owning to the facts that late war Soviet VVS documents were preserved from destruction, their contents cross-referenceable on many levels and written in great detail, such a project of verifying victory claims against verifiable losses over Hungary has become a reality. As the volunteer historian and researchers of the Szolnok Aircraft Museum (RepTár), having been able to obtain records of all lost Soviet warplanes in Hungary during the war, having partaken in the archeological digs of destroyed aircrafts to physically unearth history and by being in connection with a large and ever-growing group of passionate, knowledgable and willing-to-help researchers the Authors of this book felt confident to undertake this project to accurately verify the victories of the top Jagdgeschwader 52 aces over Hungary. In this book the Respected Reader will see the comparision of the German and Soviet records, which will reshape the knowledge and understanding of aerial victory claims these eight JG 52 fighter pilots made over Hungary in 1944-45.

Although this analysis uses numbers, charts and statistics, let us keep in mind that these numbers represent the real tragedies of real people, who had names, faces, families, pasts and plans for the future that were often ended by the terror

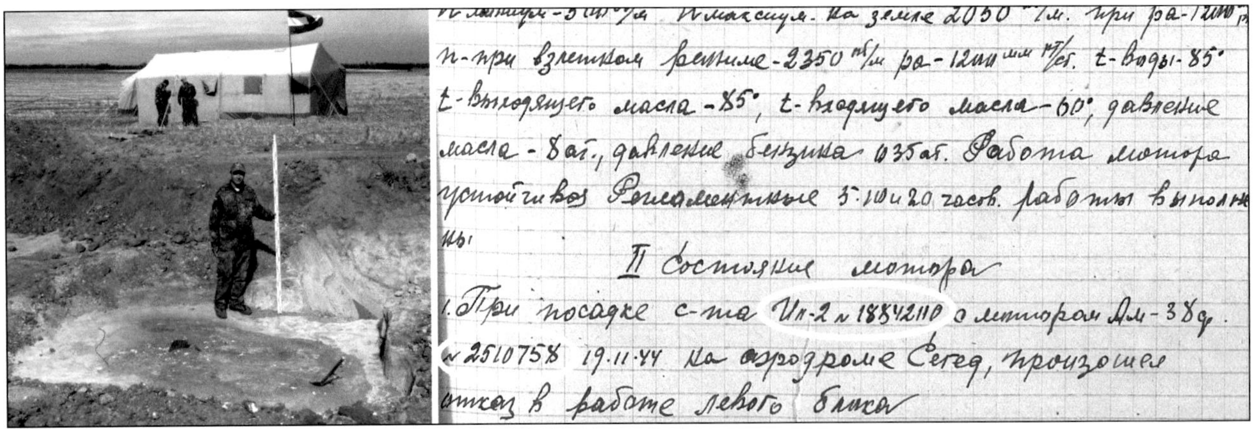

The impact point in 2013 and details of the Soviet mechanical report on the left cylinder-row repair of 210 ShAP Il-2m3 (c/n: 18842110, AM-38F engine: 2510758, white '30') on 19 November 1944 on the airfield of Szeged. This Il-2 was lost to flak on 14 March 1945 at Seregélyes-SW with Ml.Lt. Lev Constantinovich Vorobiev's crew. Beside the matching location mentioned in the combat report, the recovered and matching AM-38F engine-number helped to positively identify the remains of the pilot whose personal belongings were returned to his relatives 68 years after the war. (Photos: Magó Károly and TsAMO RF via Boris Vladimirovich Davidov)

of the war. Those who survived the long war had to live with the consequences of their injuries, both mental and physical, for the rest of their lives. The Soviet Union alone lost around ten million servicemen and servicewomen during the Great Patriotic War, not to mention the millions of their civilian population. While the research and preservation of the past is necessary, the Authors do it in a hope that the terror, destruction and the unmeasurable human suffering of World War II will never happen again.

Daniel and Gabor Horvath

SECTION I

1

What is a Victory?

The Second World War produced the greatest number of aces with the highest number of claims from nearly every participating nation. Scoring five victories or more to become an 'ace' became somewhat normal rather than exceptional, in turn requiring the creation of more prestigious achievements and awards to both incentivizes and reward fighter pilots. In the Luftwaffe 94 'aces' were credited with over one hundred aerial victories,[1] all who later were grouped by postwar literature into 'clubs' named after the number of victories they made: the 100, 200 and 300 clubs. Thankfully unable to top these achievements in our current world, many have marveled over how these pilots could have achieved such incredible military feats and wondered how they were able to do it. While the title 'ace' is commonly applied to all air crewmembers who shot down and destroyed five or more enemy planes, the term was not consistently used by all nationalities,[2] moreover the term was never officially used by Luftwaffe who preferred the term 'Experte' to describe their successful pilots.

Yet the blinding glamour of such flashy achievements often overshines historical fact and may lead to inaccurate perceptions about the aerial war. The quantity of victories claimed by a pilot is universally used to demonstrate their success, however a closer look at each individual claims may tell a different story. We wish to verify these victories, offering an answer to the question of 'was this pilot really that successful?' Yet before any victory verification may begin, it is necessary to define under what circumstances a pilot's claim may be deemed a victory. Certain language used when discussing aerial victories should be defined in order to remove any possible confusion. In addition, the criteria and definitions used to verify victories should also be outlined, paving a solid foundation for the verification which will take place later chapters.

Claims

A claim is nothing more than one pilot's personal account of what happened. In aerial combat, the term claim is most commonly used referring to a pilot shooting down/destroying an enemy aircraft. Commonly used by pilots to demonstrate their personal combat abilities, claims were tallied for comparison purposes, intelligence purposes, and for the distribution of awards. Pilots of the Luftwaffe would make their claims for Abschüsse (shoot downs). According to a translation of a *RLM* directive from 1939: *'An Abschuss is understood to be, that an enemy aircraft goes down as a result of being struck by ammunition and is destroyed by crashing into the ground and subsequently made of no further use by the enemy.'*[3] Directive Az. 29 Nr. 55270/41 issued on 16 April 1941 titled 'Ziffer 431. Anerkennung von Abschüssen, Zerstörungen und Schiffsvernichtung' also offers insight into what is meant by the term Abschuss: '[an enemy aircraft is considered destroyed] *if it has burnt or been sunk or damaged to the point where its use is no longer possible by the enemy or if following a combat, its use is denied the enemy (for example, internment in a neutral country).'*[4]

Claims could be officially made over select types of targets. Directives Az. 29 Nr. 55270/41 along with Az. 29 Nr. 55270/41 III. Ang. (5, VII) made it clear what the LP of the RLM considered for recognition. According to these directives: *The shooting down of enemy aircraft and manned tethered balloons, destruction of enemy aircraft on the ground and of barrage balloons as well as ship destructions (warships of the combat value of a battleship, heavy crusier or aircraft carrier) are to be recognized by the air force and flak artillery for the unit, not for the individual crew or protection service.*[5] Directive Az. 29 Nr. 55270/41 III. Ang. (5, VII) stated that the submission for recognition of armored vehicles, trains and artillery will not be accepted by the LP of the RLM.[6] According to directive Az. 29 Nr. 55270/41, there were only seven ways successes in the air could be

1 Andrew-Johannes, Mathews and John Foreman, *Luftwaffe Aces: Biographies and Victory Claims*, Vol. 4 (Surrey: Red Kite, 2014), pp. 1534-1535.
2 Hugh Morgan, Jürgen Seibel, *Combat Kill: The Drama of Aerial Warfare in World War 2 and the Controversy Surrounding Victories* (Somerset: PSL, 1997), p.10.
3 Theo Boiten, *Nachtjagd Combat Archive: 1 January-22 June 1943* Part 1, (Surrey: Red Kite, 2018), p. 9.
4 Jean-Yves Lorant, Richard Goyat, *Jagdeschwader 300 "Wilde Sau": A Chronicle of a Fighter Arm Geschwader in the Battle for Germany*, Vol. 1 (Hamilton, Montana: Eagle Edition Ltd., 2005), pp. vi-vii.
5 Karl Pawlas, *Luftfahrt International: Blohm & Voss BV 138*, Vol. 11 (Publizistisches Archiv: *Nürnberg, 1975)*, pp. 1649-1650, 1661-1662.
6 Pawlas, *Luftfahrt International*, p. 1662.

made.[7] The first was the aircraft shootdown, requiring the enemy aircraft to crash and burn after being attacked either from the air or from Flak and subsequently destroyed upon impact. The second was the forced landing, explicitly stating that this could only be deemed successful if the enemy aircraft landed on German held territify or could not be repossessed and used by the enemy. The third was dismantling, requiring that vital parts of the enemy aircraft (wings or tail unit) become detached so that the plane is unable to fly or bursts apart; non-vital parts (canopy) would not fullfill this category. The fourth was the buring crash requiring that the enemy aircraft be burning while airborne before crashing and becoming destroyed upon impact. The fifth and sixth were dependent on what color (light or dark) of trailing material the enemy aircraft spewed after an attack, however these were explicitly stated to be non-definiative ways of identifying success. The seventh was through the abandonment of the enemy plane by its entire crew. Directive Az. 29 Nr. 55270/41 also stated that sucesses on the ground (am Boden) were possible through two ways, the first being setting grounded aircraft on fire, while the second method required that the landing gear to have been collapsed or vital areas of the aircraft to be destroyed.[8]

A pilot may choose to personally record all types of victorys alongside his aerial scores, with examples found on victory tallies painted onto aircraft rudders such as those flown by Maj. Wilhelm Balthasar or Lt. Hans Dammers. Indeed, there could be many different types of claim lists for each pilot such as personal lists, his unit's list as well as officially confirmed lists issued by the higher Luftwaffe authorities. Often all three lists are found by researchers to be incomplete, therefore a reliance on all original lists are used to construct the pilot's claiming total.

Yet with all the information available suggesting a pilot made a certain number of claims, it is important to note that at the time of making an Abschuss, the pilot's claim is only supported on his word, that is to say the claim has little to substantiate it. With this in mind, the conflict of interest or likelihood for error by taking any pilot's personal Abschussliste (shoot down list) at face value becomes immediately apparent, therefore additional evidence to support the claim is required; the Luftwaffe recognized this and used a confirmation system to address the issue.

The counting of claims served multiple purposes such as estimating the successes of the the war effort, assisting the intelligence departments, and to distinguish individual pilots by issuing awards and decorations. Within the Luftwaffe, awards were issued relative to the total number of confirmed claims a fighter pilot made, with the number of claims required for an award itself being relative the war situation. As such, medals and awards including the Ritterkreuz (RK, Knight's Cross) would be issued to fighter pilots who reached a specific number of claims. From the outbreak of the war up until June 1941, the number of successful claims for the RK was set at around 20,[9] yet this number increasingly began to fluctuate with the sudden successes by many German fighter pilots. By September 1943 the number required for just the RK rose to 100 in the East, yet by the end of the year the victories requirement was brought down to around 75. This number was kept for 1944 and most likely until the end of the war.[10] A more prestigious RK with Oak Leaves and Swords reserved a post war estate for the recipient,[11] and by the end of 1943 the requirement for this award was 200-225 in the East and 100 in the West.[12] The origin for the differences between the two Fronts stemmed from the relative 'ease' at which a fighter pilot could obtain claims in the East, therefore an additional measure was taken by the Luftwaffe to even out the requirements for pilots fighting on the Western Front. The *'Punktzahl'* (points system) was put into place in 1943 for the purpose of defining and legislating how specific combat actions which did not necessarily lead to the final destruction of enemy aircraft could be eligible for awards.[13] The system worked such that the accumulation of points would be converted and equated based on its usefulness to the war effort, thereby allowing pilots the opportunity to achieve awards through a second route. Additional Abschuss types were also introduced so that fighter pilots could take advantage of the system. The points system was generally only used on the Western Front as pilots faced different air threats posed by heavily defended Allied bombers and were less likely to make the number of claims possible in the East.

The coveting of awards was rather common among fighter pilots, and the term *'Halsschmerz'* (throat pain) referring to the friction caused by wearing awards around one's neck was used to describe such desires. *Reichsmarschall* Hermann Göring's ObdL explicitly encouraged such activity in his order 582/42 to *General der Jagdflieger* Adolf Galland, not in the least as a selfish method to elevate his Luftwaffe: *The personal ambition of the pilot to get enemy kills and decorations is all to the good – as is the competition between pilots, flights, groups and squadrons. This inter-unit and pilot competition furthers the achievements of fighter command.*[14] In the quests for awards, some pilots would take less than honest routes in order to receive them: *Among fighter pilots there were some who tried to 'swipe' every victory – the others had a dramatic expression for this,*

7 Pawlas, *Luftfahrt International,* p. 1654.
8 Pawlas, *Luftfahrt International,* pp. 1654-1655.
9 Morgan, Seibel, *Combat Kill,* p. 189.
10 Morgan, Seibel, *Combat Kill,* p. 191.
11 Patrick Eriksson, *Alarmstart East: The German Fighter Pilot's Experience on the Eastern Front 1941-1945,* Kindle, chapter 10.
12 Morgan, Seibel, *Combat Kill,* p. 191.
13 Erik Mombeeck, Maciej Gòralczyk, *Luftwaffe Gallery 6: Luck Fate and Destiny* (La Porte d Hoves, Belgium: ASBL La Porte d Hoves, 2020), p. 26.
14 Hugh, Seibel, *Combat Kill,* p. 180.

referring to such persons as 'horny for victories'. Sometimes a pilot 'pocketed' a victory which had in fact been scored by someone else, for instance when a pilot was a few victories short of the number required for a coveted decoration.[15]

Confirmed/Unconfirmed Claims

A confirmed claim refers to an Abschuss for which an upper level of authority has accepted the documented claim as genuine based on the additional gathered supporting evidence. To achieve a confirmed claim, Luftwaffe pilots would have to file their Abschüsse to the respective authorities in order to gain official recognition. The RLM was the overarching governing body responsible for the ultimate confirmation of each individual claim, however as the RLM's structure changed so did the claiming system it operated. Lt. Heinz Ewald briefly describes the claiming process: At this time I must point out that an aerial victory had to be recognized by an aerial or ground witness. A file was created at the group command post for each Abschuss made beginning with a sketch, the location of the Abschuss, the combat report of the fighter pilot, witness reports and a statement from the commander with the request for recognition by the RLM.[16] To become familiar with the details of this system, the Authors outline the processes that were required below in greater detail.

Once a pilot has made an Abschuss, he would be required to fill out an Abschussmeldung (shoot down form). Usually containing 21 points, the completed Abschussmeldung would contain questions such as location, time, altitude, aircraft type, enemy aircraft type, witnesses, and expelled ammunition among other areas of interest; there were many occasions were some of the questions would be left blank. Alongside the Abschussmeldung a pilot would need to file his supportive Gefechtsbericht (combat report), while his listed air witnesses would be required to support the claim by writing and signing a Luftkampfzeugenbericht (air witness combat report). Once these documents were complied, the claim could be passed forward to the respective authorities, with officers able to authorize the forwarding of Abschussmeldung (these officers were usually Staffelkapitäns).[17] From then on the Abschussmeldung and descriptions of the aerial engagement would be passed up the chain of command with the attachment of the unit commander's (Staffelkapitän, Gruppenkommandeur, Geschwaderkommodore etc.) own Stellungnahme (statement). The next few processes required the Abschussmeldung package to pass through the greater levels of authorities such as Geschwader, Jagddivision and Fliegerkorps whereafter it would pass through the respective Luftflotte then onto the Aussenstelle Abschusskommission (Shoot down commission branch office) within the RLM. Directive Az. 29 Nr. 55270/41 stated that the rise up to the Luftflotte should take a maximum of three days.[18] The levels below the RLM mainly ensured that the claim was not duplicated and that all the necessary paperwork was in order, while levels within the RLM mainly conducted checks to assess the validity of the claim. The Abschusskommission was the official victory credit board of the OKL/RLM whose sole purpose was to assess the validity of the claim based on existing regulations,[19] however its exact structure is loosely known due to the loss of its archives during the war while surviving employees could remember few details about the organization.[20] Many different branches existed such as those in Berlin and Vienna,[21] yet the most notable was the Wiesbaden branch. If a claim had been deemed genuine by any of the branches, then claimant's Abschuss package would be sent further into the RLM. At this stage, the claim would be recorded and included into the Luftwaffe's overall tally by the LP. The LP was the sole organization with the authority to reward each successful claim with recognition. These successful claims would receive an Anerkennung (recognition) number and certificate.[22] The Anerkennung certificate, officially called the Abschussbestätigung (shoot down confirmation sheet), would be the physical receipt of confirmation by the Luftwaffe and would document the pilot's claim within the cumulative number of confirmed claims by unit, most commonly by Staffel. A key point is outlined in Luftgautagesbefehl Nr. 5/44 dated 2 February 1944, inferring that the recognition number on the Abschussbestätigung is the recognition number given by the LP (OKL/RLM) not the number the claimed by the Gruppen or Staffel.[23]

Abschuss with corresponding Abschussbestätigung were fully confirmed by the OKL/RLM. The final confirmed or witnessed ultimate destruction of an aircraft in the air as a result of an Abschuss which usually resulted in the death of the enemy pilot was called a Luftsieg (aerial victory). The term Luftsieg used to describe claims was apparently unpopular with fighter pilots who preferred the term Abschuss when discussing their combat achievements, while Luftsiege was used more for propaganda purposes.[24] Claims which were rejected were labeled as Abgelehnt (rejected), while those which did not receive approval at one of the many levels in this system were classified as nicht bestätigt (n.b. – not recognized) and

15 Jochen Prien, *Jagdeschwader 53: A History of the "Pik As" Geschwader, January 1944–May 1945*, Vol. 3 (Atglen, Pennsylvania: Schiffer Publishing, 1998), p. 789.
16 Heinz Ewald, *ESAU: Heinz Ewald Als Jagdflieger Im Erfolgreichsten Jagdeschwader 1943-1945*, (Coburg: Self-Published, 1980) p. 103.
17 Erik Mombeeck, Maciej Gòralczyk, *Luftwaffe Gallery 6: Luck Fate and Destiny* (La Porte d Hoves, Belgium: ASBL La Porte d Hoves, 2020), p. 25.
18 Karl Pawlas, *Luftfahrt International*, p. 1653.
19 Boiten, *Nachtjagd Combat Archive*, p. 9.
20 Correspondence with Dr Theo Boiten (25 April 2021)
21 NARA T971/R11/000742, 000849
22 Patrick Eriksson, *Alarmstart East: The German Fighter Pilot's Experience on the Eastern Front 1941-1945*, Kindle, chapter 10.
23 NARA T405/R43/4880872
24 Mombeeck, Gòralczyk, *Luftwaffe Gallery 6*, p. 23.

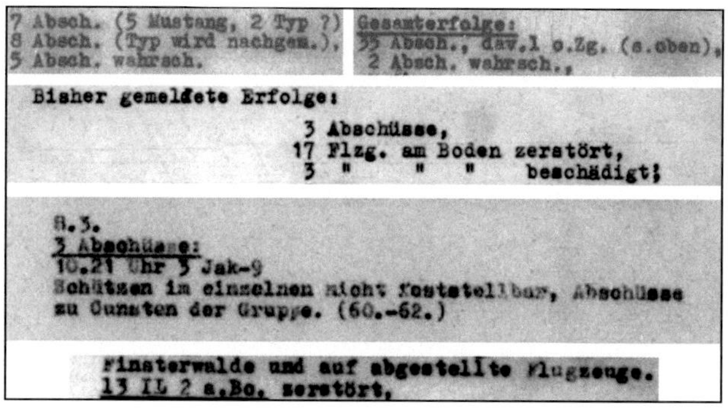
7 Absch. (5 Mustang, 2 Typ ?)
8 Absch. (Typ wird nachgem.),
5 Absch. wahrsch.

Gesamterfolge:
35 Absch., dav.1 o.Zg. (s.oben),
2 Absch. wahrsch.,

Bisher gemeldete Erfolge:
3 Abschüsse,
17 Flzg. am Boden zerstört,
3 " " " beschädigt;

8.3.
3 Abschüsse:
10.21 Uhr 3 Jak-9
Schützen im einzelnen nicht feststellbar, Abschüsse zu Gunsten der Gruppe. (60.-62.)

Finsterwalde und auf abgestellte Flugzeuge.
13 IL 2 a.Bo. zerstört,

Examples of probable, damaged, ground, without-witness and shared Abschüsse

the pilot in question would not be rewarded with the victory.[25] L.V. Blatt Nr. 18/41 also states a few conditions to receive confirmation. '*Conditions: a flawless eyewitness report, if possible, with photo. Aircraft shot down this side of our own lines: look for and find aircraft wreckage.*'[26] Directive Az. 29 Nr. 55270/41 stated that the witness report could be replaced with film taken by a gun camera in instances where the technology was present and required that the wreckage of the enemy aircraft be located if combat took place over German held territory.[27]

Now while the above outlined formula for claiming requires several authorizations in order for a pilot to be rewarded with a victory, such complexity should not be taken to equate to rigidity or soundness of operation. Dated literature often asserted that due to its complexity, the Luftwaffe claiming system was superior to all others and that there was little room for error: *the terms 'probable' and 'damaged' were not known in the Luftwaffe. If the 'kill' was uncertain it was not reported at all.*[28] This misjudgment is unfortunately still prevalent today. The Luftwaffe claiming system, contrary to the dated notions of its rigidity, had multiple areas of questionable soundness. Contrary to the above quoted statement, *the terms 'probable' and 'damaged' were not known in the Luftwaffe*, probable claims did exist within both Luftwaffe aviation and flak units and were less infrequent than contemporary literature would have one believe. Claims which lacked full convincing evidence yet were 'felt' to be genuine Abschuss were allowed Abschussmeldungs and were often subtitled as Wahrscheinlicher Abschuss (probable shoot down);[29] Wahrscheinlicher Abschuss implied that the claimant successfully engaged the enemy though did not whitness the impact or crash.[30]

Problematic *Abschüsse* were also accepted into the confirmation system. The *Abschusskommission* classified *Abschussmeldungs* with all sorts of problems in the multiple ways listed below:

ASM – *Anerkennung Später Möglich (confirmation possible later)*
VNE – *Vernichtung Nicht Erwiesen (destruction not proven)*
VNE.ASM – *Vernichtung Nicht Erwiesen, Anerkennung Später Möglich (destruction not proven, confirmation possible later)*
X – *Returned Abschussmeldung back to respective unit as the documents package was incomplete (ie. the Gefechtsbericht, Luftkampfzeugenbericht, Stellungnahme, and other supportive documents were not attached)*

With the introduction of the '*Punkzahl*' additional types of *Abschuss* were institutionalized to be used primarily in the West, usually for the damaging of aircraft:

W.B. – *Wirklich Beschossen (effectively shot up)*
E.V. – *Endgültige Vernichtung (final destruction of damaged aircraft)*
H.S.S – *Herausschuss (the damaging of a 'Viermot' causing it to leave formation)*
O.Z. – *Ohne Zeugen (without witness, used on all fronts throughout the war)*

Furthermore, several crediting options were in place contrary to notions that claims could not be allocated to multiple recipients. Below are some of the crediting options for claims:

Gruppen/Staffel abschuss – *Victory allotted to the unit and divided amongst the pilots that were involved.*[31] *Alternatively the abschuss may be allotted to the unit rather than to the pilots.*
i.Zus.Arb *abschuss* – *im Zusammenarbeit (in collaboration with, commonly involving searchlight and flak units)*

25 Eriksson, *Alarmstart East*, Kindle, chapter 10.
26 Morgan, Seibel, *Combat Kill*, p. 181.
27 Lorant, Goyat, *Jagdeschwader 300 "Wilde Sau*, p. vi.
28 Green William, Gordon Swanborough, *Flying Review International 1965-66*, Volume 21 (London: Purnell & Sons, 1965), p. 245.
29 Eriksson, *Alarmstart East*, Kindle, chapter 10.
30 Theo Boiten, *Nachtjagd Combat Archive*, p. 9.
31 Boiten, *Nachtjagd Combat Archive: 1 January-22 June 1943,* Part 1, p. 37.

im Zus. ***abschuss*** – *im Zusammenwirken (in cooperation with, commonly involving searchlight and flak units)*

Directive Az. 29 Nr. 55270/41 addressed the sharing of claims: *where different units have destroyed enemy material in a joint military engagement, a global accreditation will be accorded to the parent formation which will specify the units taking part. Where these are from different branches of the armed forces, for example the flak and fighter arms, each unit or parent formation will receive a confirmation which will indicate where other units have participated.*[32]

Abschussbestätigung would be issued for claims label with any of the problematic titles. Claims for different Abschuss types could receive confirmation either in full or as outlined by one of the many credit options depending on the circumstance. By 1944 the air war situation over continental Europe was completely against the Axis' favor, increasing the tempo at which the Reich could be assaulted while in the East the Soviets had long recovered from the far-reaching German victories and were now flying aircraft models in larger numbers which equally rivaled what the Axis were operating. The OKL reporting directly to DRdLuObdL, both of which were positions headed by Reichsmarschall Hermann Göring, decided that a restructuring of command was the correct path towards reversing the losing position they so clearly were in. Due to these restructuring events, the claiming system underwent considerable changes from 1944 until the end of the war. As the cause of many questionable developments in the confirmation process, developments which contribute of the faulty recording of victories, a few structural changes along with many other regulatory events are outlined below. Far from being perfect, the Luftwaffe claiming system seems to have been the victim of a constant shifting of goalposts throughout its use, and as such cracks began to appear which could be exploited by those able and willing to for the sake of statistics. This overview offers enough information to substantiate the position that many flaws were present.

1) The overall top-level structure of the Luftwaffe saw increased overlap of responsibility between its departments from 1943 onwards, and its first major reorganization starting in 1944 began a vicious cycle of restructuring and clearing out of personnel which would not stop until the war was lost the following year.[33] This intensifying activity most likely had negative effects on the recording and confirmation of claims submitted by fighter pilots. By 1943 the Chief-of-Staff found himself and his office increasingly responsible for both military and ministerial matters signing both 'on behalf' and as a 'representative of' Göring, therefore the head of the legal department recommended keeping the double designation of DRdLuObdL in its letter headings unless the Göring was specifically required.[34] As such, on any original Abschussbestätigung predating the second half of 1944 had this double heading printed at the top of the certificate. As a close friend of Göring, Gen. Oberst Bruno Loerzer became the head of the LP on 23 February 1943 under which lied the LP (A) 5 responsible for the organization and final signing of all Abschussbestätigung.[35] As a power grab move, Göring began to divide up and reorganize the existing command structure of the Luftwaffe in order to benefit his authority. As a result the LP which previously reported directly to the DRdLuObdL was then placed under the Chef d. LP under the OKL by 1944, shortly thereafter entrusted under the newly created Chef d. Pers. Rüstung u. NS-Führung d. Luftwaffe on 30 May 1944 which was coincidentally also now commanded by Loerzer.[36] The move to incorporate Nazi political training was ordered upon the OKW and subsequently the Luftwaffe at the turn of the year, and thus many departments within the RLM and OKL had to put up with the struggle of forced political indoctrination into their work; the 8. Abt. (historical department) of the Chef d. Generalstabes which worked on the historiography/teaching of personnel/literature within the Luftwaffe struggled as the new political command threatened the ideologization of its war and aerial warfare histories.[37]

After 30 May 1944 the LP (A) 5 was redesignated Chef f. Ausz. u. Diszpl., retaining the duties it previously held but was now under the direct authority of the Chef d. Pers. Rüstung u. NS-Führung d. Luftwaffe.[38] The Chef d. Pers. Rüstung u. NS-Führung d. Luftwaffe was subordinate to the OKL which reported to the DRdLuObdL. In June office group (A) containing LP (A) 1-5 was dissolved and reorganized under new administration with the exception of the late LP (A) 5 which was now named Chef f. Ausz. u. Diszpl.[39] As such Abschussbestätigung dated around June of 1944 no longer bore the subheading of LP (A) 5, rather they had Chef f. Ausz. u. Diszpl. printed on the certificates. To complicate matters further, the tripart responsibility structure of the Luftwaffe comprised of the Chef d. Gerneralstabes, Chef d. Pers. Rüstung u. NS-Führung d. Luftwaffe, and the Chief of Aviation had simply too much on its hands to effectively operate; in November 1944 the OKL/Chef d. Generalstabes d. Lw had swollen sevenfold in personnel since the outbreak of war yet the managerial situation was at a point where no one in the LwFüSt Ia was able to tell Chef d. Generalstabes d. Lw

32 Lorant, Goyat, *Jagdeschwader 300 "Wilde Sau*, p. vii.
33 Horst Boog, *Die Deutsche Luftwaffenführung 1935 – 1945. Führungsprobleme, Spitzengliederung, Generalstabsausbildung* (Stuttgart: Deutsche Verlags-Ansalt, 1982), p. 282.
34 Boog, *Die Deutsche Luftwaffenführung 1935-1945*, p. 281.
35 Boog, *Die Deutsche Luftwaffenführung 1935-1945*, p. 280.
36 Boog, *Die Deutsche Luftwaffenführung 1935-1945*, pp. 291, 581-583.
37 Boog, *Die Deutsche Luftwaffenführung 1935-1945*, pp. 290, 291.
38 Boog, *Die Deutsche Luftwaffenführung 1935-1945*, p. 292.
39 Boog, *Die Deutsche Luftwaffenführung 1935-1945*, p. 293.

Gen. Werner Kreipe the overall strength of the Luftwaffe.[40] Kreipe was shortly thereafter sacked and replaced with Gen Lt. Karl Koller. On 9 November 1944 outgoing Chef d. Generalstabes Werner Klosinski was asked by Göring to clean out the Luftwaffe, affecting about 200 Generals and 2000 Oberste and Oberstleutnants, though this number seems to be inflated.[41] Klosinski refused stating that such a cleaning out was far overdue and owing to the disastrous war situation such a move would only further cripple the Luftwaffe, though he did recommend that Gen.Oberst Loerzer be sacked.[42]

As of 12 December 1944, the tripart high command structure was broken with the dissolving of the Chef d. Pers. Rüstung u. NS-Führung d. Luftwaffe which returned under the LP,[43] and the departure of Gen.Oberst Loerzer later on.[44] Göring then took direct control over the LP including the Abt. Ausz. u. Diszpl. (the title Chef f. was dropped as a separate Chef Abt. was created) and all other offices and departments which were previously under the Chef d. Pers. Rüstung u. NS-Führung d. Luftwaffe.[45] The Abt. Ausz. u. Diszpl. was now under the LP/OKL which reported directly to the DRdLuObdL and would stay this way until the final week of March 1945 which then would regain the title Chef f.;[46] this reorganization in structure is again showcased in the headings printed on original Abschussbestätigung. Late March of 1945 saw the complete crumbling of the Luftwaffe top-structure due to the constant downsizing of staff and emplacement of special representatives to control various administrational offices and by April the system was all but collapsed.[47] The Luftwaffe was split in two by 15 April 1945 with Luftflotte Reich in the north under Gen.Oberst. Stumpff and Luftflotte 6 in the South under Gen.Oberst. Ritter von Greim.[48] What all these developments from 1944 – 1945 meant for the confirmation of claims is largely unknown, though it is certain that the constant reshuffling of offices, departments and reduction in staff likely had a negative impact on the confirmation capabilities of the Luftwaffe.

2) On 16 April 1942, order 582/42 from *Reichsmarschall* Hermann Göring's office issued to *General der Jagdflieger* Adolf Galland for JG 54 on the Eastern Front stated that: *If the pilot can find no eyewitness for the destruction of the aircraft, his report will be marked as probable and will be passed on for further review … Claims for shot down aircraft without witnesses will only be passed on as probables if the pilot has achieved at least three previously reliable claims. Where there are follow-on claims without witnesses, it is better to pass the report on, marked as probable, than to waste time looking for witnesses whose testimonies will be, at the least, doubtful. On different fronts, and with the tactics used by ourselves and the enemy, we will always get satisfactory claims with, or without, witnesses.*[49] This new regulation effectively elevated claim status for Abschüsse which lacked concrete evidence at least initially, exclusively on the basis that eligible pilots had previously reported sound claims. Incidentally the regulation would also allow for the overall number of claims submitted to suddenly increase, thereby restoring the tarnished image of Göring's Luftwaffe. This allowed the possibility of questionable claims to enter the confirmation system, all on the onus that a pilot had reported his claims honestly in the past!

3) Oblt. Gerhard Barkhorn's LaGG claim for 30 November 1942 was sent up to the OKL/RLM but did not receive an Anerkennung number as it was missing certain documentation, and thus was noted with and X.[50] Many years later on 7 February 1945, by now promoted to a Major, Gerhard Barkhorn had this very same claim confirmed.[51] Moreover, this particular claim was made *Ohne Zuegen* and an explanation written on the claim read that *'In accordance with existing regulations, pilots with more than 30 victories could submit victory claims without witnesses.'*[52] Once again, the burden of proof was not placed on supportive evidence, but rather the pilot's previous accomplishments.

4) As a comment to his description of Maj. Walter Nowotny' 250 claims by the fall of 1944, *General der Jagdflieger* Adolf Galland stated that *The Luftwaffe employed a more liberal system of certifying 'kills'. Both the USAAF and the R.A.F required witness of: (1) the crash of enemy aircraft or (2) the bailing out of pilot and/or crew. Thus many kills registered by enemy German pilots would be listed as 'probables by the Allies.'*[53] His comment shows that even those who held authoritative positions within the Luftwaffe hierarchy during the war were well aware of the limitations brought in by fresh regulations.

40 Boog, *Die Deutsche Luftwaffenführung 1935-1945*, p. 313.
41 Boog, *Die Deutsche Luftwaffenführung 1935-1945*, p. 315.
42 Boog, *Die Deutsche Luftwaffenführung 1935-1945*, p. 315.
43 Boog, *Die Deutsche Luftwaffenführung 1935-1945*, p. 313.
44 Boog, *Die Deutsche Luftwaffenführung 1935-1945*, p. 313.
45 Boog, *Die Deutsche Luftwaffenführung 1935-1945*, p. 318.
46 Boog, *Die Deutsche Luftwaffenführung 1935-1945*, pp. 585, 586.
47 Boog, *Die Deutsche Luftwaffenführung 1935-1945*, pp. 332-336.
48 Boog, *Die Deutsche Luftwaffenführung 1935-1945*, p. 337.
49 Morgan, Seibel, *Combat Kill*, p. 180.
50 Tony Woods, O.K.L. Fighter Claims, Eastern Front [Ostfront] August-December 1942, Issue I.
51 Bernd Barbas, *Das Vergessene As: Der Jagdflieger Gerhard Barkhorn* (Osnabrück: Luftfahrtverlag-Start, 2019), p. 204.
52 Barbas, *Das Vergessene As*, pp. 62-63.
53 Adolf Galland, *The First and the Last: the Rise and Fall of the German Fighter Forces, 1938-1945*, (New York: Ballantine Books, 1969), p. 266.

5) Initial confirmation of claims at the stage of writing the Abschüssemeldung could be got not only through witnesses or the observations of wrecks littering the earth, but also through the radio. Hptm. Emil Clade of JG 27 explains: *In fact confirmation of a claim could be got even during the combat phase, or within a day or two, just by listening to the British radio traffic ... I would say that half of the claims were confirmed over the radio.*[54] War correspondent Heinz Eckert recalled that in the afternoon on 24 August 1944, the date when Oblt. Erich Hartmann leaped from 291 to 301 claims, himself and many others left on the airfield were huddled around a radio set listening to what Hartmann and his wingman talked about over the frequency.[55] Five claims were heard over the radio, after which those listening on the ground went 'crazy' with excitement.[56] Wreaths were braided, shields and inscriptions were painted, banners were fashioned, champagne and glasses were procured, all while Hartmann was still in the air![57] Upon landing the victor was raised up over the solders of his comrades and cheered on throughout the evening. Within 24 hours Erich Hartmann was asked to travel to the Wolf's Lair a few days later to receive the Diamonds to his RK with Oak Leaves and Swords, meaning that the confirmation process was fast-tracked for this special occasion, with the radio confirmation playing a large part of the process. Hptm. Helmut Lipfert also recalled similar events: *My wingman landed after me. He had seen everything and confirmed my 84th victory. His confirmation was unnecessary however, as the command post was already well aware of my battle. ... Our listening post had discovered the frequency being used by the two enemy fighters and had overheard the following scraps of conversation ...* [58]

6) As a very critical point of fact, due to successful night raids on Berlin throughout November 1943 by RAF Bomber Command, a large majority of the claims documentation were actually destroyed leaving the records-departments of the OKL/RLM without this information.[59] As the result of such an informational loss, OKL/RLM requested on 25 November 1943 that all Luftwaffe units send in their summary victory claims lists for the periods of 1940-1943,[60] and that by 1 April 1944 these summarized lists (lists of those claim confirmed or rejected) including copies of claims submitted before 25 November 1943 which had not yet been confirmed must be handed over to the DRdLuObdL.[61] Nearly all victory claims documented by the OKL/RLM covering this time period which remain today are therefore not original, rather they are reconstructions of original summary documents that remained in possession of the individual Luftwaffe units. This is also the reason why the time for confirmation of claims suddenly grew exponentially as the documentation units, including the LP (A) 5, had to start almost from scratch. It must also be noted that claiming information made prior to 25 November 1943 was still being sent in as late as December 1944![62] The reconstruction of old/copied data presents another crack in the system increasing the chances of clerical error and opportunities for the inclusion of erroneous entries.

Beyond this event, another bombing raid on 3 February 1945 conducted by some 950 B-17s of the 8th USAAF also contributed to the destruction of many documents.[63] Kept in the archive building on Kronenstraße, some 15,000 RLM files dating from 1933 onwards were lost on top of which some 80,000 additional documents from various other branches were also lost.[64] Later another batch of around 80,000 files held in Karlsbad (Karlovy Vary) in addition to those held in Herwegen were shipped to Heldburg between 21 February and 8 March 1945.[65] Most of these 80,000+ documents were then shipped by rail back to Karlovy Vary in April then to Hohenburg (where presumably some were left) then experienced nomadic travels as a final destination for the archival shipment could not be sorted out.[66] Around this same time on 19 March 1945 the Führer ordered his 'Zerstörungsmaßnahmen im Reichsgebiet' to begin, the systematic destruction of all military, traffic, news, industry, supply systems and material assets which could fall into enemy hands and be used to against the Reich.[67] With the quickly approaching Western Allied forces an order was given out, Operation Feuertod,[68] to burn these archives including that of the 8.Abt. (historical department) which was completed by 3 May 1945.[69] The estimated 50-60 tons of paper took 100 men 44 hours to destroy, leaving only those documents remaining in Heldburg

54 Morgan, Seibel, *Combat Kill*, p. 183.
55 Raymond Toliver, Trevor Constable, *The Blond Knight of Germany* (Blue Ridge Summit, Pennsylvania: Aero, 1985), p. 138.
56 Toliver, Constable *The Blond Knight of Germany*, p.139.
57 Toliver, Constable, *The Blond Knight of Germany*, p.140.
58 Helmut Lipfert, Werner Gribig, *The War Diary of Hauptmann Helmut Lipfert: JG 52 on the Russian Front 1943-1945*, (Atglen, Pennsylvania: Schiffer Publishing, 1993), p. 85.
59 Boiten, *Nachtjagd Combat Archive*, p. 4.
60 Theo Boiten, *Nachtjagd Combat Archive: 1 January – 22 June 1943*, Part 1 (Surrey: Red Kite, 2018), p. 4.
61 Lorant, Goyat, *Jagdeschwader 300 "Wilde Sau"*, p. 42.
62 Lorant, Goyat, *Jagdeschwader 300 "Wilde Sau"*, p. 42.
63 Lorant, Goyat, *Jagdeschwader 300 "Wilde Sau"*, p. 217.
64 Noack von Wulf-Dietrich, *Die Schließung von Überlieferungslücken am Beispiel des Schriftgutes der Luftwaffe 1933-1945*, (2003) <http://www.lwag.org/reference/fla001.pdf> (accessed 26 April 2021).
65 Von Wulf-Dietrich Noack, *Die Schließung von Überlieferungslücken am Beispiel des Schriftgutes der Luftwaffe 1933-1945* <http://www.lwag.org/reference/fla001.pdf >
66 Von Wulf-Dietrich Noack, *Die Schließung von Überlieferungslücken am Beispiel des Schriftgutes der Luftwaffe 1933-1945* <http://www.lwag.org/reference/fla001.pdf >
67 NARA T971/R11/000887-000888
68 Theo Boiten, *Nachtjagd Combat Archive: 1 January-22 June 1943,* Part 1 (Surrey: Red Kite, 2018), p. 4.
69 Von Wulf-Dietrich Noack, *Die Schließung von Überlieferungslücken am Beispiel des Schriftgutes der Luftwaffe 1933-1945,* (2003) < http://www.lwag.org/reference/fla001.pdf >, accessed 26 April 2021.

and Hohenburg unscathed.[70] The majority of unit and Luftgaukommando KTB papers were also destroyed in April 1945 through Operation Feuertod while the archives of the Abschusskommission also disappeared.[71] 97 percent of all Luftwaffe files and documents relating to personnel (claims information included) were destroy at the end of the war.[72] Most of the fighter claims from the OKL/RLM which survive today are captured on eighteen hurriedly produced microfilm rolls, documenting summaries of claims titled the Chef für Ausz. und Dizsiplin Luftwaffen-Personalamt L.P. [A] V Films and are the basis for most Luftwaffe fighter claims research. Supplemental surviving information such as those discovered by Soviet forces and preserved (some 28,000 files partially on the Luftwaffe) along with surviving copies of unit documents are therefore relied upon to reconstruct claims.

7) By the end of 1944, the Wiesbaden Abschusskommission was ordered to dissolve. Gen.Maj. Homburg was ordered to disband the branch in November, and this was completed by 15 December 1944.[73] After its dissolution, units were required to send their claims to their respective Luftgaukommandos who would forward them directly to the Luftflottekommand Reich Adjutant II.[74] Such dissolution most likely occurred for all Abschusskommission branches approaching the end of the war.

8) No official OKL/RLM records for claims in 1945 appear on the Chef für Ausz. und Dizsiplin Luftwaffen-Personalamt L.P. [A] V microfilm rolls, one of the main surviving sources for Luftwaffe claims. Whether additional rolls of film were made on which the 1945 claims were documented is unclear, however certain interesting patterns do appear on the existing films which shed light onto the deteriorating nature of claiming confirmation. The most intact period of claims appears between 1943 and most of 1944, with dates prior to 1943 less complete as to be expected from the need to reconstruct data through archived unit level data after the bombings in November 1943. The fall of 1944 as documented in the films shows a sudden reduction of recorded data, with a complete stop in Anerkennung numbers by the end of October. The last Anerkennung numbers were for claims made by 5./JG 52 on 31.10.44 in the East, and 15./JG 3 on 28.9.44 in the West.[75] Beyond these dates only the claims themselves are listed without any notice of confirmation number. It is possible that beyond this date confirmation for claims were made through the respective Luftflotten then sent for archiving in the Reich. Here too it is also perceivable that because of the sudden decentralization, any new regulations pertaining to claiming were issued by individual Luftflotten such as the acceptance of claims made O.Z. by claimants who have previously demonstrated 30 confirmed victories.

Victories

What constitutes an aerial victory? An aerial victory can only occur when an enemy aircraft is irrecoverably destroyed in combat, anything less must be considered as damaged. The victory must meet two main destruction criteria: the claimed aircraft must have destroyed to the point where it is unable to fly and subsequently crashes/explodes/disintegrates or is no longer able to be put back into operational service. Claims over aircraft on the ground in a ground strike need to follow the exact same destruction criteria to be deemed a legitimate victory. In instances where the claimed aircraft meets the above criteria however its destruction was caused by multiple sources (aircraft or anti-aircraft fire or other combat means), the final source of additional damage to the aircraft prior to its destruction or disintegration or irreparability is the ultimate cause for the loss. Destruction to the levels specified above due to non-combat related occurrences such as wear-and-tear, weather, maintenance mishaps, non-combat related accidents, retirement from service and intentional strategic destruction by aircrews all exclude the lost aircraft from being claimed by an enemy. It is important to once again stress the critical difference which divides a claim from a victory: a victory requires permanent combat damage to be suffered which results in a loss, damage on its own is not enough for a victory. Damages are not enough because all planes needed some amount of service time before they could be flown into combat. Larger and more complex aircraft needed additional service time, while returning damaged or belly-landed aircraft needed even more. The length of time spent on the ground while under repair does not matter so long as the aircraft is operational once again. Expressed in a more tangible way, if your vehicle suffers a flat tire is it written off? Obviously not. Once the tire is changed or repaired your vehicle is fully functional again.

70 Wulf-Dietrich, *Die Schließung von Überlieferungslücken am Beispiel des Schriftgutes der Luftwaffe 1933–1945,* (2003) <http://www.lwag.org/reference/fla001.pdf>

71 Boiten, *Nachtjagd Combat Archive*, p. 4.

72 Boiten, *Nachtjagd Combat Archive*, p. 4.

73 Erik Mombeeck, Maciej Gòralczyk, *Luftwaffe Gallery 6: Luck Fate and Destiny* (La Porte d Hoves, Belgium: ASBL La Porte d Hoves, 2020), p. 26

74 Mombeeck, Gòralczyk, *Luftwaffe Gallery 6*, p. 26

75 Tony Woods O.K.L Fighter Claims Reich, West & Südfront August-December 1944, Issue 1; *Eastern Front,* Vol 4. 1944. Jul-Dec, Issue 1

Overclaims

An overclaim occurs when a plane is attacked and claimed as a victory though not actually destroyed. The Authors assume that the majority of overclaims were made as a result of poor observation rather than a dishonest action by a pilot. Visibility and level of focus may be causes for overclaims, along with delayed documentation of an aerial encounter leading to incorrect statements. The delay of confirmation may also play some part in this (claims left unconfirmed before the November 1943 reconstruction efforts could have been submitted leading to overclaims). Three main events may lead to overclaiming, namely poor observation, faulty award allocation and dishonest intent. Throughout this book the term overclaim will be used to describe claims which have been submitted by the claimant yet cannot be proven to have been irrecoverably lost. One should always be cautious of accepting a claim and should strive to use methods which further check the permanent damage done to the opposing aircraft.

As an example of overclaiming most probably due to the confusing nature of combat, on 1 January 1945 during Operation Bodenplatte the Germans claimed *'about 70 enemy aircraft shot down in air combat'*.[76] Another source states that the Germans *'reported 79 aerial victories'*.[77] Original documents dated 3 January and 25 February 1945 report 55 destroyed with 11 probably destroyed, and 65 destroyed with 12 probably destroyed respectively.[78] Unfortunately the original German claims themselves are scares, inconsistent and swell as time progresses. Allied accounts detail that around ten planes were damaged in the air while no greater than 15 of their own aircraft were shot down in aerial combat.[79] When this is compared to the lowest German claim figures from 3 January (fully destroyed only), the overclaiming ratio becomes greater than 3.6:1. Such examples theoretically could have all been avoided by maintaining visual contact with the damaged opponent until it exploded upon crashing into the ground. Lt. Schenk of 2./JG 300 stated the following on the realities of observing one's victim: *As a rule, an aerial combat lasted only a matter of a few seconds, although brining down a bomber took a few seconds longer; only rarely would it prove possible to observe the destruction of one's victim during the actual combat ... In the majority of instances we would only see that our opponent had been damaged, sometimes seriously so. Assessing what had happened realistically required real self-discipline on the part of the fighter pilot.*[80]

Examples of overclaiming due to dishonest intent can be found in Oblt. Kurt Welter who made many claims against RAF 'Mosquito' while serving as a night fighter pilot,[81] yet when these claims were compared against RAF records a large portion can be conclusively proven to have been little more than *pure fantasy* and *largely fictious.*[82] According to one publication only six of his 'Mosquito' claims are backed by surviving documentary evidence.[83] Welter was also unpopular within his units both during and after the war most likely because his comrades knew the ingenuine nature of his claims.[84] In a different case, Lt. Stahlschmidt of JG 27 once noticed Bf 109s firing their guns into the sand dunes of the Western desert, the culprits had a reputation of finding and claiming British aircraft when others could not, and he immediately reported the pilots to the higher authorities.[85]

Overclaiming may also occur through the misallocation of victories between pilots as a result of incorrectly processing/awarding claims or even post-war research. In these cases, the individual pilots cannot to be blamed for the overstatements. Alfred Grislawski's 133rd victory was for a P-38 'Lightning' on 26 September 1944,[86] however Grislawski himself refutes shooting down such a plane on such a date or the fact that he ever made that claim.[87] Lt. Hans Santler of Stab I./JG 2 recalled that after an air battle the Kommandeur spoke to his men saying that the day's successes consisted of seven claims, he claimed two while another three could be properly allocated but the remaining two victories were left unclaimed, and after many pilots expressed that they had achieved successes the Kommandeur randomly chose two pilots out of the group to close the ordeal.[88] In post-war research the exact number of victory claims has been at times based on the awards pilots received and were photographed with, not actual lists: *Proof that successes continued to be recorded is found in photos of the*

76 Jochen Prien, *Jagdeschwader 53: A History of the "Pik As" Geschwader, January 1944-May 1945*, Vol. 3 (Atglen, Pennsylvannia: Schiffer Publishing, 1998), p. 1019.
77 John Manrho, Ron Putz, *Bodenplatte The Luftwaffe's Last Hope: The Attack on Allied Airfields New Year's Day 1945* (Sussex: Hikoki Publications, 2004), p. 272.
78 John Manrho, Ron Putz, *Bodenplatte The Luftwaffe's Last Hope: The Attack on Allied Airfields New Year's Day 1945* (Sussex: Hikoki Publications, 2004), p. 287.
79 Manrho, Putz, *Bodenplatte*, p. 273.
80 Jean-Yves Lorant, Richard Goyat, *Jagdeschwader 300 "Wilde Sau": A Chronicle of a Fighter Arm Geschwader in the Battle for Germany*, Vol. 2 (Hamilton, Montana: Eagle Edition Ltd., 2005), p. 352.
81 25 Mosquitos according to Mathews and Foreman and 35 according to Aders.
82 Andrew-Johannes Mathews, John Foreman, *Luftwaffe Aces: Biographies and Victory Claims*, Vol. 4 (Surrey: Red Kite, 2014), pp. 1397-1398, 1541.
83 Gebhard Aders, *History of the German Night Fighter Force 1917-1945* (London: Jane's Publishing Company, 1997), p. 245.
84 Mathews, Foreman, *Luftwaffe Aces*, p. 1397.
85 Mathews, Foreman, *Luftwaffe Aces*, p. 2.
86 Tony Woods O.K.L Fighter Claims Reich, West & Südfront August-December 1944, Issue 1. This particular claim was labeled as VNE: ASM.
87 Christer Bergström, *Graf and Grislawski: A Pair of Aces* (Hamilton, Montana: Egales Editions Ltd., 2003), pp. 237, 300.
88 Erik Mombeeck, Maciej Gòralczyk, *Luftwaffe Gallery 6: Luck Fate and Destiny* (La Porte d Hoves, Belgium: ASBL La Porte d Hoves, 2020), p. 25.

Geschwader's young pilots wearing decorations … [89] Additional overclaiming may result from accepting 'officially unclaimed claims' found within a few pilot's memories. These claims are written about however do not appear in any claim lists for the pilot in question; it is necessary for these claims to be thoroughly check before they are accepted.

In other cases, overclaiming comes as a result of post war intervention into records, purposefully tampering with data for a host of reasons; author Jean-Yves Lorant has come across these *suspicious additions in different coloured inks* during his research.[90] Sometimes there are risks with 'original' claim documents as they have been altered after the war. Author Johannes Matthews has noted that he has come across an original logbook of a Luftwaffe pilot which had entries written into it after the war,[91] and only after cross checking with other data could he conclude the false nature of these entries. In another case, author Dr. Theo Boiten obtained a copy of an 'original' claims list from a collector and found that the claims have been allegedly tampered with through the inclusion of falsified entries. Again, only after consulting with other primary sources and loss data could he conclude that these additional entries (roughly 5 percent of the list) were indeed false.[92] Such cases highlight the risk of accepting claims as victories without verifying them against multiple sources, especially against opposing losses. Similar to claims, victories need to be verified, and to do this one should review the recorded losses suffered by the opposing side. Only from the use of this method can a claim be proven to be fully accurate and to have resulted in the destruction of an enemy aircraft, something with the OKL/RLM nor any other confirmation organization can guarantee every time.

Verified Victories/Potential Victories

Verified victories represent those victory claims which can be traced and matched from the claim entry to the corresponding loss report. This is the ultimate check any claim may face. If both the victory claim and the loss report match, then one may be sure that the actions of the claimant resulted in the ultimate destruction of an enemy aircraft. A potential victory occurs when the loss documentation does not oppose any information in a claim, however there is little information from the claim which supports a connection to the available loss documentation. Potential victories are liable to turn into victories/overclaims if new original information is discovered. One should keep in mind that both claims and verified/potencial victory lists may exist at the same time for the same pilot, this is because they represent two fundamentally different things.

Process of Verifying Victories

Contemporary authors writing in the early 1990s such as Werner Girbig have stated that: *Unfortunately Soviet historical writings do not include detailed information on their own material losses from which one could make a comparison of successes and losses.*[93] With access to the Russian archives possible in the 21st century, this above statement can be proven to be very far from the truth. For the 21st century military researcher or author, he/she is blessed to live in a 'post-archive' era. The process of verifying victories requires the gathering of all available losses for a period/location of interest, every permanent and irrecoverable loss must be gathered before verification may begin. Once this information has been gathered all claims of interest may be compared against the loss documentation. Though simple in principle, such an exercise requires large quantities of accurate information. The scope of this book's analysis, six months over the Hungarian skies, relies upon a large quantity of archival information containing all Soviet irrecoverable wartime aircraft losses over the country.

The framework for victory verification in this book relies on many different types of documents to achieve success, with most documentation originating from the Soviet units which fought over Hungary. These Soviet documents are necessary as the Luftwaffe documentation is rather incomplete and lacks detail in many areas for various reasons; the Soviet documentation is much more complete and very detailed. Soviet loss documentation, contrary to the dated 'Cold war mentality', is trustworthy as these were internal documents prepared for the successful operation of a unit. Without accurate loss documentation the VVS intelligence and the resupply of units (men and material) could not function effectively. Moreover, the details found within the Soviet VVS loss documentation accurately correspond to the archaeological discoveries made after the war, pointing to their trustworthiness. Information on the Luftwaffe claims are derived from both archival and published sources, in some cases supported by pilot memoirs and accounts.

However as with all accounts (VVS or Luftwaffe) they must not be taken at face value but rather used in conjunction to and compared against surviving documentation from all sides. The heat of battle required pilots to make split-second observations which were prone to manifest into what the observer wanted to see. All sides displayed a tendency to misidentify

89 Willi Reschke, *Jagdgeschwader 301/302 'Wilde Sau': In Defense of the Reich with the Bf 109, Fw 190 and Ta 152* (Atglen, Pennsylvania: Schiffer Millitary History, 2005), p. 219.

90 Falkeeins, *Hartmann's Claims Disputed: An Over-view of Dimitri Khazanov's article in Le Fana with comments by Jean-Yves Lorant and Hans Ring*, *The Way Back Machine* (2007), <https://web.archive.org/web/20070209153845/http://members.aol.com/falkeeins/Sturmgruppen/hartmannclaims.html> (accessed 24 July 2021).

91 Johannes Mathew, *Hartmann: claims vs. victories*, 12 O'Clock High.net (6 July 2020). <http://forum.12oclockhigh.net/showthread.php?t=55840&page=14>, post# 131 accessed 27 April 2021

92 Theo Boiten, *Nachtjagd Combat Archive: 1 January – 22 June 1943*, Part 1 (Surrey: Red Kite, 2018), p. 6.

93 Lipfert, Gribig, *The War Diary of Hauptmann Helmut Lipfert*, p. 10.

opposing aircraft and report inaccurate aircraft types due to bias/preference over their opponents. An example from the Battle of Britain highlights such a bias. *Group Captain Peter Townsend, who flew Hurricanes in the battle* [of Britain], *wrote that the Luftwaffe put so much store in being shot down by Spitfires, rather than Hurricanes, that they suffered from 'Spitfire Snobbery.'*[94] *'The 109 pilots claimed a total of 1,017 Spitfires destroyed, whereas 216 were actually destroyed by them. This represents an over-claim of 4.7. The 109s claimed 660 Hurricanes but destroyed 249 – an over-claim of only 2.6. The predominance of Spitfire claims is again immediately apparent – even though there were thirty-three less Spitfires actually destroyed.*[95] On the Eastern Front the Soviets held a tendency to report Focke-Wulf Fw 190 aircraft over the Messerschmitt Bf 109. This could be due to preference stemming from the fact that the Soviet doctrine of aerial warfare centered around supporting the ground forces,[96] an area where the Fw 190 posed a larger threat then the Bf 109. Soviet pilots repeatedly claimed Fw 190 fighters when the only airborne aircrafts were Bf 109s. Soviet planes misidentified or labeled under proprietary terminology over Hungary by German pilots include the Yak-11 (a trainer first flown after the war), the LaGG-5 (none flew over Hungary, though the name indicated the La-5) the Yak-7 (of which only four examples were lost in combat over Hungary) and the MiG-3 (not a single MiG-3 is known to have flown over Hungary). For Hungarian civilian eyewitnesses, nearly every Soviet plane was a 'Rata', every American plane was a 'Liberator' and every German plane was a 'Messerschmitt' or 'Stuka'. German ground force reports also misidentified planes, occasionally claiming to have seen 'Spitfires' when in fact the correct model of aircraft was the P-51 'Mustang' while Flak units also misreported aircraft types.

Therefore, original documentation from all sides must be used to verify what actually took place in the sky, and for II./JG 52 victory verification it is precisely the VVS documents which are required. The most important pieces of information for verifying victories are hereby listed in order of importance: the date/time and location of the claim, the claimed aircraft's type, and the altitude at which the claim was made. Aircraft model type is not necessarily useful in many cases due to misidentification, while the loss documentation will specify the aircraft lost in much greater detail anyway. Altitude information is the least important, especially on the Eastern Front, as date/time/location/type data provides ample information to verify if a claim is a victory; altitude information is a nice-to-have in nearly all cases and rarely becomes the deciding factor in verification. For verifying victories, the Authors of this book rely on five main types of Soviet documents:

1. Regiment-, Division-, Corps- and Air Army-level combat reports, unit diaries
2. Mechanical/maintenance reports, aircraft inventory reports
3. Aircraft loss reports
4. Personnel loss reports
5. Personnel achievement records

These five types of documentation overlap in terms of content to a certain degree, however for a full picture multiple types of reports should be used to better understand each aerial encounter. Throughout the eight large-scale operations and offensives Hungary endured within six months,[97] all of which requiring aerial support, the individual claims of eight II./JG 52 pilots will be assessed and verified utilizing archival data to best understand the events over the Hungarian skies.

Finally, the Respected Reader should keep a few things in mind while reviewing the text and lists in the following chapters. All Soviet claims included within the text are unverified unless a specific loss has been assigned as corresponding to the claim; these are included to offer a well-rounded picture of the aerial combats pertaining to each day. The tables contain all permanent Soviet aircraft losses for the specific day which satisfy the claimed aircraft type, i.e. single-engine fighter, twin-engined bomber, Il-2 Sturmovik etc. Beside the losses, the Authors also list a few damaged aircraft as well to see if they could be potential opponents in the observed events. The lists of the damaged planes are certainly incomplete, since almost all planes received some (usually smaller) damages during their sorties. As damaged planes cannot be considered victories, their non-exhaustive inclusion into the lists is permissible. In the 'Details' column the aircraft types indicate the attacking planes that were mentioned in the Soviet combat reports. Note the large number of 'Fw 190s', while in reality most of the attackers were Bf 109s; the questionable aircraft IDs are represented in *Italics*. Aircraft which were later repaired are also listed in *Italics*. Finally, in the 'Details' column the listed 'numbers' indicate the known tactical marking(s).

94 Sarkar, Dilip, *How the Spitfire Won the Battle of Britain*, Kindle Edition. Introduction.
95 Sarkar, Dilip, *How the Spitfire Won the Battle of Britain,* Kindle Edition. Conclusion.
96 Hans, Seidl, *Stalin's Eagles: An Illustrated Study of the Soviet Aces of World War II and Korea.* (Atglen, Pennsylvania: Schiffer Publishing, 1998), p. 21.
97 Soviet Debrecen Offensive, Soviet Budapest Offensive, German Operation *Konrad* (I-III), German Operation *Südwind* (Southwind), German Operation *Frühlingserwachen* (Spring Awakening), Soviet Vienna Offensive.

2

Situation, Organization, Location

The Opponents

During their six month stay over Hungary between October 1944 – March 1945, the pilots of II./JG 52 faced air units of the Soviet 5 and 17 Air Armies (VA), the recently defected Romanian Air Force subordinated to the Soviet 5 VA and the strategic formations of the 15th AF heavy bombers along with their fighter escorts operating from Southern-Italy.

The Soviet 5 VA provided aerial support for the ground forces of the 2nd Ukrainian Front advancing across Northern-Hungary. This Soviet Front reached Hungary's current border with Romania near Battonya on 23 September 1944 and gradually migrated towards Czechoslovakia between December 1944 and April 1945. The Soviet 17 VA provided aerial support to the ground forces of the 3rd Ukrainian Front advancing across Southern Hungary, entering the country from Yugoslavia at the end of November 1944 and later migrated to Austria in April 1945. The linkages to the ground Fronts are very important because they reveal which Soviet air units could have fought against the pilots of JG 52 over Hungary during certain months.

Beside the Soviet 5th and 17th Air Armies, units of the Soviet 8th and 18th Air Armies and the 9 PVO corps also fought in Hungary between November 1944 and April 1945, but their actions were very minimal and rarely engaged in air combat with II./JG 52. The 8 VA which covered the ground forces of the 4th Ukrainian Front operated over Czechoslovakia just North of the 2nd Ukrainian Front. Their operational area was mostly separated from the 5 VA and there was only a very small overlap between their operations. Some of their known actions included the 8 ORAP's Pe-2R reconnaissance sorties in the Csap, Miskolc, Sátoraljaújhely and Nyíregyháza areas in October 1944 and some ground attack missions flown by 227 ShAD Il-2 Sturmoviks in November-December 1944 in the Kassa (Košice) region; they lost several Il-2m3 Sturmoviks here.[1] One Il-2 fell in the forest on the Hungarian side of the border near the castle of Füzér.[2] Yet despite neighboring operational area, there are no known 8 VA aircraft downed by German daytime fighters over Hungary, therefore they do not play a part in the aerial history this book describes.

The 18 VA was formed on 6 December 1944 from the units of the former Soviet Long-Range Air Army (VVS ADD) and contained the 4 GvBAK whose aircrafts were long-range transports and bombers such as the Il-4 (DB-3F), Li-2, C-47, and B-25 Mitchell. By the last day of 1944 the 4 GvBAK's 15 GvBAD was in Kalynivka, Ukraine and the 53 BAD was in Lvov, Ukraine,[3] these units would eventually fly a number of missions into Hungary. The 15 GvBAD would be stationed in Hungary later in 1945 at the Csepel airfield. The 15 GvBAD operated primarily at dusk and at night while the 53 BAD only lost three aircraft in Hungary, all to accidents.[4] Therefore these units did not engage with German daytime fighters of II./JG 52 and as such do not play in the aerial history this book describes.

The Soviet Air Defense Forces (PVO) 9 corps, part of the South-Western PVO Front stationed behind the Red Army's offensive Air forces (VVS), was also active in Hungary by the closing weeks of 1944 throughout the end of the war. In its main debut over in Hungary, the unit was ordered to create and maintain an air blockade around Budapest on 26 December 1944.[5] A direct link with the 2nd Ukrainian Front only occurred by 10 January 1945 after a liaison officer was sent to establish the connection from the 9 PVO corps.[6] The corps did not possess any aircraft at the time, rather it held only a

1 On 13 November 1944 the 8 VA, 227 ShAD, 525 ShAP lost three Il-2s (c/n: 9547, 9950, 303505), while a fourth one (c/n: 10944) received combat damages.; it was repaired, then on 13 December 1944 it was lost again – this time permanently. The 208 ShAP lost two (c/n: 1872292, 1882202) and the 637 ShAP lost one additional Il-2 Sturmovik (c/n: 11180).

2 This plane was probably Il-2m3 of 525 ShAP, c/n: 302686, lost to flak on 13 December 1944. The other 525 ShAP Il-2m3 lost on the Slovak side of the post-war border near Kelecsenyborda (Košický Klečenov) was also downed by flak, while Il-2m3, c/n: 11017 of the 208 ShAP crashed at Petőszinye (Svinica).

3 Combat log of the 4th GvBAK. TsAMO RF: fu. 20516, inv. 1, f. 34, p. 216.

4 53 BAD losses were all from the 239 GvBAP. Li-2 (c/n: 18410610) on 8.1.1945 at Madocsa to LAC, Li-2 (c/n: 18411903) on 24.3.1945 at Kiskunlacháza to TOA, and Li-2 (c/n: 18414910) on 26.4.1945 at Szombathely to LAC with a 39 ORAP Pe-2PF (c/n: 8/228).

5 Kamen Nevenkin, *Fortress Budapest: The Siege of the Hungarian Capital, 1944–45*, Vol. 1 (Keszthely: PeKo Publishing, 2020), p. 1022.

6 Combat log of the 9th PVO corps, entry for 9.1.1945. TsAMO RF, fu. 13607, inv. 20368, f. 797, p. 8.

few anti-aircraft units.[7] By 1 February 1945 the 9 PVO corps had three aircraft in Hungary,[8] and by the first of March its inventory had grown to 27.[9] The involvement of the 9 PVO corps in the aerial blockade over Budapest was only more pronounced after mid/late January 1945 when the ground units consisting of the 583 ZAP partially equipped with RAP-150 radar-guided searchlights and the 43 OVNOSRB equipped with RUS-2 radar systems for aircraft detection arrived.[10] The only known PVO aircraft lost over Hungary was a Yak-9M form 586 IAP flown by female pilot Lt. Maria Semenovna Batrakova who lost her life on 12 July 1945 (post-war) in a flight-accident at the Vecsés (Ferihegy) airport. As such despite the presence of the 9 PVO corps in Hungary, the corps plays no part in the aerial history this book describes. All of this means that the II./JG 52 aces over Hungary fought Soviet planes only from the Soviet 5 VA and 17 VA.

According to German intelligence estimates calculated for 1 January 1945, the opposing enemy forces were comprised of 1,400 aircraft of the 5 VA, 900 aircraft of the 17 VA, and 350 aircraft of the 1st Romanian Air Corps for a total of 2,650 aircraft.[11] The Authors have listed to the best of their abilities the total number of aircraft within the 5 and 17 Air Armies. The total of 2,675 aircraft is the minimum number of aircraft available on New Year's Day (the total for the 17 VA is complete, whereas the 5 VA is not). It should be noted that the Soviet Army would have held a handful of miscellaneous aircraft including small single engine planes such as the Po-2. The Po-2 owing to its excellent and robust design was very capable at completing a number of tasks and could be found sprinkled around many units, even among the ground forces. As an example, on 22 January 1945 the 3rd Ukrainian Front's 1st Guards Mechanized Corps had two Po-2s in its Independent Communications Air Detachment stationed at Baracska.[12] There were also several miscellaneous aircraft used for transportation and communications which are not calculated.

<table>
<tr><th colspan="5">The main air units of the Soviet 5 VA, October 1944 – March 1945</th></tr>
<tr><th>Division</th><th>Regiment</th><th>Main type</th><th colspan="2">Main airfields</th></tr>
<tr><td rowspan="3">4 GvShAD</td><td>90 GvShAP</td><td>Il-2m3</td><td rowspan="10">5 ShAK</td><td>Kölső-kiritó, Nádudvar, Detk, Gyöngyös</td></tr>
<tr><td>91 GvShAP</td><td>Il-2m3</td><td>Földes, Nádudvar, Detk, Horpács</td></tr>
<tr><td>92 GvShAP</td><td>Il-2m3</td><td>Püspökladány, Nádudvar, Jászberény</td></tr>
<tr><td rowspan="3">264 ShAD</td><td>235 ShAP</td><td>Il-2m3</td><td>Debrecen, Karácsond, Tóalmás, Tolmács</td></tr>
<tr><td>451 ShAP</td><td>Il-2m3</td><td>Debrecen, Karácsond, Tóalmás, Vadkert</td></tr>
<tr><td>809 ShAP</td><td>Il-2m3</td><td>Tolmács, Rétság, Visznek</td></tr>
<tr><td rowspan="3">331 IAD</td><td>122 IAP</td><td>Yak-1,-9</td><td>Külső-Kiritó, Nádudvar, Jászberény</td></tr>
<tr><td>179 IAP</td><td>Yak-1,-9</td><td>Földes, Kunmadaras, Detk, Hatvan, Sándorhalma</td></tr>
<tr><td>513 IAP</td><td>Yak-1,-9</td><td>Debrecen, Kunmadaras, Füzesabony, Horpács</td></tr>
<tr><td>N/A</td><td>423 OAES</td><td>Po-2, UT-2</td><td>Unknown, linked to the 5 ShAK HQ.</td></tr>
<tr><td rowspan="3">279 IAD</td><td>92 IAP</td><td>La-5, La-7</td><td colspan="2">Szarvas, Tószeg, Örkény, Vecsés (Ferihegy)</td></tr>
<tr><td>192 IAP</td><td>La-5, La-7</td><td colspan="2">Tótkomlós, Tószeg, Kecskemét, Ecser (Ferihegy)</td></tr>
<tr><td>486 IAP</td><td>La-5, La-7</td><td colspan="2">Nagylak, Kecskemét, Pozsonyszőllős</td></tr>
<tr><td rowspan="3">7 GvShAD</td><td>130 GvShAP</td><td>Il-2m3</td><td rowspan="6">3 GvShAK</td><td>Kisszénás, Kondoros, Szarvas, Ferihegy</td></tr>
<tr><td>131 GvShAP</td><td>Il-2m3</td><td>Szarvas, Ferihegy, Csákvár, Győr</td></tr>
<tr><td>132 GvShAP</td><td>Il-2m3</td><td>Szarvas, Tiszavezseny, Ferihegy (Vecsés)</td></tr>
<tr><td rowspan="3">12 GvShAD</td><td>187 GvShAP</td><td>Il-2m3</td><td>Pitvaros, Kecskemét, Örkény, Mátyásföld</td></tr>
<tr><td>188 GvShAP</td><td>Il-2m3</td><td>Pitvaros, Kecskemét, Mátyásföld</td></tr>
<tr><td>190 GvShAP</td><td>Il-2m3</td><td>Kecskemét, Mátyásföld, Pozsony</td></tr>
</table>

7 Combat log of the 9th PVO corps, entry for 1.1.1945. TsAMO RF, fu. 13607, inv. 20368, f. 797, p. 2.

8 The 141 IAD had 1 Airacobra, 1 Yakovlev UT-2, and 1 Po-2. Combat Log of the Air Force South-Western Front PVO, 1.2.1945. TsAMO RF, fu.13067. inv. 20368, f. 774, p. 12.

9 The 141 IAD had 1 P-39 Airacobra, 1 Yakovlev UT-2, and 1 Po-2, its 586 IAP had 14 Yak-9 and 2 Po-2 and the 822 IAP had 8 La-5s stationed in Debrecen. Combat log of the Air Force headquarters of the South-Western Front PVO. TsAMO RF, fu. 13067, inv. 20368, f. 775, pp. 11-13.

10 Nevenkin, *Fortress Budapest*, Vol. 1, pp. 1034-1035.

11 NARA T78/R561/000193,000200 via Dr. Markus Reisner

12 TsAMO RF: fu. 33, inv. 686196, storage unit. 2990, record number. 24990848; and TsAMO RF: fu. 33, inv. 686196, storage unit. 284, record number. 22601632. Interestingly the peculiar use of 'unorthodox' equipment was also practiced in the Air Armies as can be found in the 5 VA which held a company of T-34 tanks in a security unit in its HQ.

The main air units of the Soviet 5 VA, October 1944 – March 1945 *(continued)*				
6 GvIAD	31 GvIAP	Yak-1,-9-3	3 GvIAK	Mezőtúr, Aszód, Vecsés, Budaörs
	73 GvIAP	Yak-1,-9-3		Békéscsaba, Tószeg, Erdőtarcsa, Vecsés
	85 GvIAP	Yak-1,-9-3		Tószeg, Tápiószentmárton, Vértesboglár
13 GvIAD	149 GvIAP	Yak-1,-9-3		Kocsér, Hatvan, Mátyásföld
	150 GvIAP	Yak-1,-9-3		Kecskemét, Horpács, Alagivilla
	151 GvIAP	Yak-1,-9-3		Kunmadaras, Kecskemét, Hatvan, Alagivilla
14 GvIAD	177 GvIAP	La-5, La-7		Tóalmás-N, Alagivilla
	178 GvIAP	La-5, La-7		Szeghalom, Túrkeve, Tóalmás, Alagivilla
	179 GvIAP	La-5, La-7		Gyoma, Kiskunlacháza, Tóalmás-S
N/A	8 GvOAES	Po-2 (U-2)		Rákóczifalva, Nagykáta, linked to 3 GvIAK
218 BAD	48 BAP	A-20G	Arad, Tiszavezseny, Ferihegy (Vecsés)	
	452 BAP	A-20G	Debrecen, Szolnok, Kecskemét, Ferihegy (Vecsés)	
	453 BAP	A-20G	Debrecen, Szolnok-S, Bábolnapuszta	
312 NBAD	392 NBAP	Po-2 (U-2)	Szeghalom, Kunhegyes, Irsa, Mohora	
	930 NBAP	Po-2 (U-2)	Kőrösladány, Jánoshida, Érsekvadkert	
	992 NBAP	Po-2 (U-2)	Szeghalom, Kunhegyes, Csány, Érsekvadkert	
	714 OAPS	Po-2 (U-2)	Debrecen, Nyíregyháza, with the 312 NBAD HQ.	
5 VA HQ. or unknown	18 TAP	Po-2 (U-2)	Debrecen	
	44 OAVP GVF	Po-2, Li-2	Debrecen (supporting the Pliev-group)	
	62 OAES	Po-2 (U-2)	*Kecskemét*, linked to the 2 GvMK	
	154 OAES	Po-2 (U-2)	Kunszentmárton	
	207 GOAPS	Po-2 (U-2)	Vác-SE, linked to the 6th Guards Tank Army	
	207 OKRAP	Il-2, Yak-9	Vezseny, Tápiószentmárton, Tóalmás, Alagivilla	
	511 ORAP	Pe-2, Yak-9	Székudvar, Kecskemét, one Sq. in Vecsés	
	1001 OSANAP	Po-2 (U-2)	Mezőberény (Medevac S-2, S-4 versions)	

The front-line 5 VA aircraft inventory on 1 January 1945 as per individual unit documentation, comprised of corps and divisional reports			
Yak-1	(a)	83	All models, serviceable and under repair
Yak-7		-	
Yak-9		109	
Yak-3		16	
La-5		130	
La-7		20	
Il-2	(b)	261	
A-20 Boston	(c)	74	
Pe-2	(d)	25	
Po-2	(e)	91	
Miscellaneous	(f)	1	Li-2, S-2, S-4, UT-2, etc.
1st Romanian Air Corps	(g)	172	Subordinate to 5 VA, serviceable and under repair. Mainly Bf 109, Ju 87, Hs 129, Fi 156, Ju 52 and IAR-38/39/80/81
Soviet Total:		**810**	All Soviet aircraft both serviceable and under repair
Final Total:		**982**	All aircraft both serviceable and under repair

(a) Horváth Gábor, *Bostonok a Magyar Égen és Földben 1944-1945* (Self-published: Szolnok, 2013), p. 24.

(b) (I) Combat report of the 5 ShAK, entry for 1.1.1945. TsAMO fu. 20525, inv. 1, f. 39, pp.146, 212; (II) Combat log of the 264 ShAD, 1.1.1945. TsAMO fu. 22444, inv. 0383419s, f. 1, p.1; (III) Combat log of the 207 OKRAP, entry for 1.1.1945. TsAMO fu. 20177, inv. 1, f. 46, p.4; (IV) Combat log of the 12 GvShAD, entry for 1.1.1945. TsAMO fu. 20057, inv.

1, f. 55, p.346; (V) Combat log of the headquarters of the 7 GvShAD, entry for 1.1.1945. TsAMO fu. 20039, inv. 1, f. 22, p. 266.

(c) Horváth Gábor, *Bostonok a Magyar Égen és Földben 1944-1945*, pp. 29-31.

(d) Медведь Александр Николаевич, Хазанов Дмитрий, Пикирующий бомбардировщик Пе-2. "Пешка", ставшая ферзем (Эксмо: Москва, 2007), p. 153.

(e) (I) Combat log of the 207 OKRAP, entry for 1.1.1945. TsAMO RF: fu. 20177, inv. 1, f. 46, p. 4; (II) Review of the combat work of units 312 NBAD for the month of December 1944, entry for 1.1.1945.

(f) Combat report of the 5 ShAK. TsAMO RF: fu. 20525, inv. 1, f. 39, p. 212.

(g) MApN Microfilm 3.1618. Inventory for 31.12.1944. The C1A also had a number of non-combat ex-Luftwaffe aircraft which are not included. This Information was kindly provided by Bernád Dénes.

The main air units of the Soviet 17 VA, October 1944 – March 1945

Division	**Regiment**	**Main type**	**Main airfields**	
136 ShAD	210 ShAP	Il-2m3	10 ShAK	Szabadszállás, Kiskunlacháza, Veszprém
	715 ShAP	Il-2m3		Bugac puszta, Tököl, Börgönd, Várpalota
	989 ShAP	Il-2m3		Bugac puszta, Kiskunlacháza, Tököl, Pápa
306 ShAD	672 ShAP	Il-2m3		Szabadszállás, Kiskunlacháza, Tököl
	951 ShAP	Il-2m3		Szabadszállás, Bugyi, Tököl, Nagycenk
	995 ShAP	Il-2m3		Madaras, Érsekcsanád, Szabadszállás
295 IAD	31 IAP	La-5, La-7		Kiskunlacháza, Csákvár, Tököl
	116 IAP	La-5, La-7		Kiskunlacháza, Tököl, Veszprém, Pápa
	164 IAP	La-5, La-7		Csanád, Kiskunlacháza, Tököl, Veszprém
N/A	418 OAES	Po-2 (U-2)		Kiskunlacháza-SE, linked to 10 ShAK
189 ShAD	615 ShAP	Il-2m3	Mainly together	Taszár, Madocsa, Őcsény, Cece
	639 ShAP	Il-2m3		Őcsény, Madocsa, Taszár, Szombathely
	707 ShAP	Il-2m3		Decs, Őcsény, Székesfehérvár, Taszár
194 IAD	56 IAP	La-5, La-7		Madocsa, Öcsény, Jánoshalma, Orci
	530 IAP	La-5, La-7		Öcsény, Madocsa, Bugac puszta, Tököl
	848 IAP	La-5, La-7		Öcsény, Jánoshalma
288 IAD	611 IAP	Yak-1,-9,-3	Mainly together	Taszár, Székesfehérvár, Kiskunlacháza
	659 IAP	Yak-1,-9,-3		Madocsa, Székesfehérvár, Kiskunlacháza
	866 IAP	Yak-1,-9,-3		Taszár, Börgönd, Kiskunlacháza, Pápa
	897 IAP	Yak-1,-9,-3		Decs, Madocsa, Börgönd, Kiskunlacháza
244 BAD	260 BAP	A-20 Boston		Sombor, Öcsény, Tököl, Veszprém, Pápa
	449 BAP	A-20 Boston		Madocsa, Sombor, Tököl, Pápa
	861 BAP	A-20 Boston		Őcsény, Sombor, Tököl, Veszprém, Pápa
10 GvShAD	165 GvShAP	Il-2m3	Mainly together	Krnesevci, Nadalj, Kenyeri – May, 1945
	166 GvShAP	Il-2m3		Novi Sad, Bela Crkva, Rábakecskéd
	167 GvShAP	Il-2m3		Ruma, Novi Sad, Csönge – May, 1945
236 IAD	267 IAP	Yak-1,-9,-3		Ruma, Vaszar – May, 1945
	117 GvIAP	Yak-1,-9,-3		Novi Sad, Mandelos, Vaszar – May, 1945
	168 GvIAP	Yak-1,-9,-3		Zemun, Magyarmecske, Vaszar
262 NBAD	370 NBAP	Po-2 (U-2)	Perkáta, Felsőbabad, Makád, Nyírespuszta	
	371 NBAP	Po-2 (U-2)	Perkáta, Kerekegyháza, Berki, Ságvár	
	993 NBAP	Po-2 (U-2)	Tomoripuszta, Berki, Csákvár, Vaszar	
	97 GvNBAP	Po-2 (U-2)	Mélykút, Peszéradács, Makád, Újmalomsok	

The main air units of the Soviet 17 VA, October 1944 – March 1945 (*continued*)			
17 VA HQ or unknown	3 OSANAP	Po-2 (U-2)	Biatorbágy, Ercsi (Medevac S-2, S-4 versions)
	18 OUTAP	La-5, Yak-7	Kovin
	26 OAVP GVF	Po-2, C-47A, R-5	Csanád, Madocsa, Pápa, Budapest
	39 ORAP	Pe-2R, Yak-9	Szabadszállás, Madocsa, Bugac puszta
	48 GvORAP	A-20, Pe-2, Pe-3, Yak-9D	Kecskemét
	95 OAAE	Po-2 (U-2)	Bánd (Veszprém-NW)
	96 OKRAP	Il-2, Yak-9D	Bugac puszta, Szabadszállás, Börgönd
	124 OAE	Po-2 (U-2)	Unknown
	282 OAPS	Po-2 (U-2)	Soltszentimre, Homok(puszta)

The front-line 17 VA aircraft inventory on 1 January 1945 [13]		
Yak-1	117	All models, serviceable and under repair (In combat service and in the 17 VA reserve)
Yak-7	13	
Yak-9	147	
Yak-3	58	
La-5	273	
La-7	1	
Il-2	601	
A-20 Boston	117	
Pe-2	23	
Po-2	292	
Miscellaneous	51	Chuchuliga, Li-2, S-2, S-4, SB-2, Shche-2, UT-1, UT-2, Yak-6
Total:	**1693**	All aircraft both serviceable and under repair

The combined minimum aerial force the 5 and 17 VA could muster by the start of the new year was no less then was 2,675 aircraft. Non-VVS units such as the civilian GVF would only increase this number.[14] It should be noted the both the 10 GvShAD and 236 IAD were positioned in Yugoslavia, so the total number of 17 VA aircraft stationed exclusively in Hungary was 258 aircraft lower.[15] A portion of the above mentioned combined aircraft inventory of both the 5 VA and 17 VA was kept in reserve, and as such the 17 VA had 244 aircraft in its reserve ready to be deployed upon command. For example, 46 Yak-3s were held in the 17 VA reserve, soon to be distributed to operating units such as the 288 IAD which received over 19 from the reserve throughout January 1945.[16]

The German Luftflotte 4 was operational over Hungary and covered the geographical area of the entire country. By 1 January 1945, the MKHL had long been subordinated under Luftflotte 4, flying alongside them with some level of independence. II./JG 52 underwent many structural reorganizations while in Hungary which has led to some confusion. Originally, 4./JG 52 was taken from the Gruppe to fight in the Defense of the Reich in mid- 1944. By the fall of that same year a newly created 4./JG 52 was set up and in late January 1945 another new staffel, 8./JG 52, was created.[17] By the first of March 1945 5./JG 52 became 6./JG 52 while 6./JG 52 became 7./JG 52; by the 8 March 1945 8./JG 52 was disbanded.[18]

The total aircraft inventory of Luftflotte 4 operational in Hungary on 31 December 1944 was at least 802 aircraft (this figure appears to be missing many light-support aircraft and reserve aircraft) of which 211 were Hungarian, while II./JG 52 possessed 21 Bf 109s at this time:[19]

13 17 VA quarterly inventory report for 1.1.1945. TsAMO RF: fu. 35, inv, 11258, f. 349. p. 37b.

14 For example, the 26 OAVP GVF had 66 aircraft on 1.1.1945 (C-47A, Il-2, R-6, R-5 and Po-2). TsAMO RF: fu. 370, inv. 6518, f. 207, p. 181.

15 126 Yak, 119 Il-2, 10 Po-2, 1 Ut-1, 2 Ut-2. 17 VA quarterly inventory report for 1.1.1945. TsAMO RF: fu. 35, inv, 11258, f. 349. pp. 25-37b.

16 The 19 Yak-3 c/n were between 310011-310233. TsAMO RF: fu. 20257, inv. 1, f. 95, p. 42.

17 Bernd Barbas, *Die Geschichte der II. Gruppe des Jagdgeschwaders 52: Offizielle Ausgabe der Traditionsgemeinschaft JG 52* (Überlingen: Self-published, 2003), p. 160.

18 Barbas, *Die Geschichte der II. Gruppe des Jagdgeschwaders 52,* p. 286.

19 Nevenkin, *Fortress Budapest*, Vol. 1, pp. 981-982, 991. DFS 230 gliders are excluded from this calculation.

II./JG 52 Messerschmitt Bf 109 aircraft inventory for 31 December 1944*					
G-6	G-6/U4	G-14	G-14/U4	G-10	Total
2	**4**	**3**	**10**	**2**	**21**

* Peter Düttmann, *Itärintaman hävittäjäsotaa* (Helsinki: Koala-Kustannus, 2002), p. 133.

Soviet aerial reconnaissance estimates for the aircraft strengths opposing their 2nd and 3rd Ukrainian Fronts on 25 December 1944 recorded 846 aircraft of which roughly 150 were in Hungarian service.[20] Though estimated before the turn of the new year, the 25 December 1944 estimation loosely corelated to what the new-year estimation may have been and demonstrates that the Soviets slightly overestimated their opponent's air power. It is interesting to note that the Soviet aviators were incorrect in another category, namely the identification of opposing enemy aircraft in the air; Fw 190 fighters were consistently overreported due to poor identification. The number of Bf 109 aircraft on 31 December was 249, while the number of Fw 190 aircraft was only 154.[21] Comparing these numbers against what the Soviet air force pilots in the air, it is plainly evident why Soviet pilots overreported the number of Focke-Wulf aircraft sighted in aerial combat. Fw 190s were primarily employed in the close-support role over Hungary, occasionally even as air transports to resupply Budapest flying 55 such missions.[22] Their use as fighter aircraft was very limited and the situation on the ground required their close-support capabilities, the fragility of the Bf 109 made it unsuitable for this role. The Focke-Wulfs and Messerschmitts had different airfields, flew different missions and had different tasks. Occasionally both types of aircraft would fly together where the Bf 109s would be the escort. By mid-February 1945, the usefulness of such Bf 109 escorts came into question, whereafter they were dispensed with.[23] When Soviet aerial reports record encounters with a limited number of mixed aircraft, frequently reporting a few Fw 190s flying alongside a larger number of Bf 109s, it is a good indication that the reporting witness misidentified the opposing flight, possibly confusing the different camouflage patterns present on Hungarian Bf 109's for Fw 190s. Only on the rare occasion did such a bizarre and unplanned flight occur between the Focke Wulfs and Messerschmitts, primarily happening spontaneously when a damaged aircraft was found heading for home and needed protection.

Soviet Aircraft Construction Numbers

The Soviet aircraft construction numbers, recorded carefully in the Soviet Air Force documents, might look confusing at first sight but are well structured. They reveal the aircraft model, the factory in which they were built, their batch number and their individual aircraft number within the given batch. The following list will help the Respected Reader understand how the Soviet aircraft construction numbers reported in the battles over Hungary should be 'translated':

7, later 8 = Code of the two-seater Il-2 Sturmoviks in Factory No.18 in Samara, Russia[24]
18 = Factory No.18 in Samara, Russia
21 = Factory No.21 in Nizhny Novgorod (former Gorky), Russia
30 = Factory No.30 in Moscow, Russia
31 = Factory No.31 in Tbilisi, Georgia
39 = Code of La-5 in factory No.21 in Nizhny Novgorod (former Gorky), Russia
41 = Code of the metal winged La-5s in factory No.21 in Nizhny Novgorod, Russia
45 = Code of La-7 in factory No.21 in Nizhny Novgorod (former Gorky), Russia
153 = Factory No.153 in Novosibirsk, Russia
166 = Factory No.166 in Omsk, Russia
292 = Factory No.292 in Saratov, Russia
381 = Factory No.381 in Moscow, Russia
x = Digits of Batch Number
y = Digits of the Individual Aircraft Number within that batch.

Yakovlev Yak-1B:
yy-xxx eg.: 48162 from Saratov, Factory No.292. (Full c/n is displayed.)

20 Diagram of the grouping and basing of enemy aircraft in front of the 3rd Ukrainian Front and the flank of the 2nd Ukrainian Front, 25.12.1944. TsAMO RF: fu. 20193, inv. 1, f. 30, p. 10.
21 Nevenkin, *Fortress Budapest,* Vol. 1, pp. 981-982.
22 LVO b Chef GenStdH Br.b.Nr. 1454/45 geh. vom 25.2.1945 via Dr. Markus Reisner
23 Helmut Lipfert, Werner Gribig, *The War Diary of Hauptmann Helmut Lipfert: JG 52 on the Russian Front 1943-1945* (Atglen, Pennsylvania: Schiffer Publishing, 1993), p. 163.
24 For the old single-seater Il-2s it was number 6, eg: 1863807. None flew over Hungary.

Yakovlev Yak-9:
xx-166-yyy eg.: 07166017 from Omsk, Factory No.166.
xx-153-yy eg.: 1615302 from Novosibirsk, Factory No.153.

Yakovlev Yak-3:
yy-292-xx eg.: 1229217 from Saratov, Factory No.292.
31-xx-yy eg.: 310305 from Tbilisi, Factory No.31.

Lavochkin La-5F, La-5FN:
381-xx-yy eg.: 3811329 from Moscow, Factory No.381.
39-21-xx-yy eg.: 39212776 from Nizhny Novgorod, Factory No.21.
41-21-xx-yy eg.: 41210115 from Nizhny Novgorod, Factory No.21.

Lavochkin La-7FN:
45-21-xx-yy eg.: 45210208 from Nizhny Novgorod, Factory No.21.
381-xxx-yy eg.: 38100256 from Moscow, Factory No.381.

Petlyakov Pe-2:
yy / xxx eg.: 12 / 248 from Kazan, Factory No.22.

Ilyushin Il-2 Sturmovik:
xx-yy, or xxx-yy eg.: 9957, or 11551 from Samara, Factory No.1.
30-xx-yy eg.: 305015 from Moscow, Factory No.30.
18-7-yy-xx, or 18-8-yy-xxx eg.: 1875397 or 18867106 from Samara, Factory No.18.

On late-war La-5/7 and Yak-3 fighters the white tactical numbers were factory-applied onto the fuselage according to the digits of the plane-in-batch number. For instance La-5FN, c/n: 39212776 was marked white '76'. In combat diaries the Soviet aircraft construction numbers were often recorded only in a short form, meaning that only the batch number and the aircraft number were written down. As such La-5FN c/n: 39212776 could be recorded as La-5, No.2776 and Yak-3 c/n: 310305 as Yak-3 No.0305. On American-built aircraft the Soviets kept the original U.S. Army serial numbers and recorded them as they were painted on the vertical stabilizers; A-20G, S/N: 42-53901 was recorded in Soviet documents as 253901.

Geographical Names

Prior to diving into the aerial events this book describes, a few notes about geographical names are necessary as many found in wartime combat reports and victory claims are difficult to locate on modern maps. It is completely understandable that foreign armies in an unknown land often recorded geographical names with all kinds of errors making it nearly impossible to locate them on modern maps. Thus one primary goal of this book is to correct these names so that the Respected Reader may easily locate them on modern maps or in GIS applications such as Google Earth. One good example for this is Hptm. Lipfert's Yak-7 victory claim over the settelment of 'Pakozol' on 13 March 1945, this is in fact the village of Pákozd on the Northern shore of Lake Velence. Another example is Hptm. Sturm's Yak-7 victory claim on 18 October 1944 near 'Miki Peres' which was in fact the village of Mikepércs South of Debrecen. As during the verification process time and location details are the most critical, it must make be made sure that one can locate these places correctly.

But beside the incorrectly spelled –and therefore ficticious– geographical names, there are many locations in wartime diaries which have completely changed names or simply disappeared after the war. One reason was due to border changes. Between the First and Second World Wars in Europe, new countries were created by the Antant such as Czechoslovakia and Yugoslavia, partially from the historical territory of the Hungarian Kingdom. Between 1938 and 1941 as a result of the First Vienna Award, some of these native territories returned to Hungary. Thus in the Soviet 1945 wartime reports some of these settlements are once again called by their original Hungarian names which cannot be found in today's maps. A good example is the village name of Köbölkút, first mentioned in 1233 A.D. as 'Cubulcut'. In Hungarian the name 'Kőből-kút' literally means 'well made of stone', referring to the old stone-well where the village was founded in the 12th century. The village of Köbölkút is now called 'Gbelce', a very different name located in Southern-Slovakia just North of the Danube near Esztergom. Settlement names changed after the war due to political pressure as well. The Soviet supported Communist/Socialist regime preferred location names without any religious and/or outdated political associations. For example, the village name of Kajászószentpéter ('Kajászó-Saint-Peter') simply became 'Kajászó', or Szolgaegyháza ('Slave's Church') became Szabadegyháza ('Free-Church').

A brief note on Hungarian pronounciation. While reading Hungarian settlement names, one must keep in mind that in the Hungarian language there are several diagraph letters, such as cs, sz, gy, ty, ly, ny and zs; these are pronounced as single sounds.

3

The Main Military Campaigns in Hungary during 1944-1945

In order to understand the circumstances of the JG 52 aerial victories and the battles in which they were claimed, the main ground campaigns in which their missions were flown should be briefely reviewed. The first such major campaign was the Armoured Battle of the Hungarian Plain. The second, third, fourth and fifth campaigns were the 108-day long Battle of Budapest and its three relief attempts called the Konrad Operations. The next was Operation Südwind or South Wind which will not be discusses as it took place on what is now mainly Slovakia, the seventh was Frühlingserwachen or Spring Awakening launched between the Lakes of Balaton and Velence; it is also called the Battle of Lake Balaton. And finally the eighth was the Vienna Offensive which was launched as a prepared counterattack immediately after the failure of Operation Spring Awakening.

The Armoured Battle of the Hungarian Plain (*The Battle of Debrecen, the Armoured Battle of Hortobágy*)

First mentioned in 1235 A.D. as 'Debrezun', Debrecen is the largest city in Eastern Hungary and served as the temporary capital during the 1848-1849 war of independence fought against the Habsburgs. It is the main centre of the Calvinist Church in the country, often called the 'Calvinist Rome' of Hungary. After three American air raids, starting on 2 June 1944 (Operation Frantic), Soviet long-range Il-4/DB-3F, Li-2 and B-25 night-bombers bombed the city multiple times in mid-September 1944. The Armoured Battle of the Hungarian Plain, including the Battle of Debrecen was the first main Soviet Operation on the territory of modern Hungary conducted between 6-29 October 1944 carried out by forces of the 2nd Ukrainian Front under the command of Marshal Rodion Yakovlevich Malinovsky (1898-1967). Axis participants included the German 6th Army and the Hungarian VII Army Corps. After 23 August and 8 September 1944 when Romania and Bulgaria armies switched alliances to the Allied war efforts the Axis forces in the Carpathians were faced with a very dangerous situation, and in order to avoid encirclement the commander of Army Group South Ukraine Generaloberst Johannes Friessner (1892-1971) was ordered to attack Malinovsky's 27th Army and 6th Guards Tank Army. On 23 September 1944 parts of the Soviet 18th Tank Corps arriving from Romania reached Hungarian territory near Battonya, soon thereafter engaging with the Hungarian 7th Assault Gun Battalion. Both sides suffered heavy losses especially in the Királyhegyes and Hódmezővásárhely areas.[1] The Soviet Offensive started on 6 October 1944 and rapidly moved to the North towards Debrecen. During the first day the Soviets advanced about 60 km when they ran into the strong resistance of the German 1st and 23rd Panzer Divisions. On 9 October 1944 Lt.Gen. Issa Aleksandrovich Pliyev's Cavalry-Mechanized Corps took Hajdúszoboszló. On 10 October 1944 the Soviet troops occupied several bridgeheads on the western bank of the Tisza River. On 11 October 1944 Pliyev's 4th GvKK reached the outskirts of Debrecen. II./JG 52 was active during this Soviet offensive with many of its top aces who had returned from either leave or hospitalization. Their return was plagued with ammunition shortages to the point where Lt. Düttmann recalled that there were times when only the Staffel leaders and flight leaders were privileged to be allotted ten pieces of 30mm cannon ammunition per sortie, while the other pilots had to suffice with only their machine gun ammunition.[2] As a way to relieve their combat stress many II./JG 52 visited the nearby world famous Tokaj Wine Region and regained their spirits through the consumption of some of the world's best dessert wines.

Although by 19 March 1944 Hungary was officially under German occupation, on 15 October 1944 in Budapest Miklós Horthy de Nagybánya (1868-1957) as *'Regent of the Kingdom of Hungary'* saw a favourable time to announce an armistice and did so in his radio address, immediately requiring harsh repercussions from the German forces who removed him from power and forced him to keep the alliance by threatening to murder his abducted son. The pro-German Szálasi Ferenc (1897-1946) and leader of the Hungarian Arrow Cross Party was then emplaced as prime minister of Hungary. Five days later on 20 October 1944 Debrecen was taken by the Soviets. The following day Pliyev's forces took Nyíregyháza, which was

1 The Soviet 170th and 110th TBr lost several T-34/85s (such as No. 461, 460, 466 and 470), while on the Hungarian side assault gun ace Kőszeghy Barnabás fhdgy. was killed in his StuG III Ausf. G (No.700).
2 Peter Düttmann, *Itärintaman hävittäjäsotaa* (Helsinki: Koala-Kustannus, 2002), p. 122.

re-captured by the 23rd Panzer Division on 26 October 1944 in order to provide an escape route to General Otto Wöhler's 8th Army. By 29 October 1944 approximately one fifth of today's Hungary was taken by the Soviet 2nd Ukrainian Front, which almost immediately received orders directly from Stalin to prepare for the taking the Hungarian capital, Budapest.

The Battle of Budapest and the relief attempts (Konrad Operations) (29 October 1944 / 24 December 1944-13 February 1945)

Budapest is the largest city of Hungary, serving as the capital since 1873. It was created by joining three independent cities: Buda, Pest and Óbuda. Óbuda literally translates to Old-Buda, which in antiquity was called Aquincum and served as the capital of the ancient Roman province of Pannonia. Buda and Óbuda are situated on the Western mountianous side of the city, while Pest is on the flat Eastern side. The two sides of the city were connected by eight bridges over the Danube river which divided the capital, running almost directly from the North to the South. The first Soviet bombs fell on the city on the night of 4/5 September 1942.[3] Later, when the war reached Hungary, Budapest was taken by the ground forces of the Soviet 2nd Ukrainian Front in an extremely fierce, house-to-house, room-to-room style of siege. On 28 October 1944 at 22:00 MT Stalin ordered Marshal Rodion Malinovsky of the 2nd Ukrainian Front through STAVKA directive Nr. 220251 that on 29 October he should begin the Budapest Offensive and take the Hungarian capital within seven days,[4] however the campaign would last over 15 times longer than planed! The 108-day epic battle for the capital was characterised by house to house and floor to floor combat. Since the Führer ordered Budapest to become a stonghold, Festung Budapest, the surrender of its protecting garrison was strictly prohibited. The Waffen SS General Karl Pfeffer-Wildenbruch was in charge of the city's defenses.

At the same time ground forces of the Soviet 3rd Ukrainian Front with strong armored support crossed the Danube at multiple locations South of Budapest and rapidly pushed to the North cutting the final corridor between Budapest and Western Hungary on Christmas Day of 1944, encircling the city from the West. By this Soviet move, approximately 79,000 Axis troops and about 125 Axis tanks became trapped in the Hungarian capital.

The German forces of the garrison had Pz.IVs ('Feldherrnhalle'), JPz.IVs (Pz.Rgt.4), Panthers (Pz.Rgt.4 and 'Feldherrnhalle' – all of them coated in zimmerit!), Hummels with Pz.Beob.Wg. III (Pz.Art.Rgt. 'Feldherrnhalle'), Hetzers (SS-Pz.Jg.Abt.8) and some Italian-built M13/40s in SS Police units. Tiger IIs of s.Pz.Abt.503 seen in many pictures in Budapest had already left the City therefore they did not participate in the battle. The Hungarians had Zrínyi II. (1st Assault Art. Div.), Turán, Nimród in rifle-unit support roles and some Fiat-Ansaldo vehicles in the 'Galánta' Police unit.

Soon after this encirclement, on 29 December 1944 two Soviet truce envoys carrying white flags were sent to Budapest with the proposition of surrender in which the Soviets – among many other details – guaranteed the life of the surrendering forces and promised immediate medical treatment for the wounded. On the Pest side from the direction of Vecsés, 2nd Ukrainian Front officer Capt. Miklós Steinmetz approached the first defensive line but his vehicle ran over a mine and blew up. In Buda Capt. Ilya Afanasevich Ostapenko, officer of the 3rd Ukrainian Front's 316th Rifle Division approached the German first line successfully with two other Soviet officers. Blindfolded, they were taken up to the 8th SS Cavalry Division's headquarters in the Citadel Fort on Gellért Hill. After removing the blindfold Ostapenko handed the proposition of surrender over to the Germans. In about an hour, while they were offered soda water and had a brief conversation with German officers,[5] they received Karl Pfeffer-Wildenbruch's refusal to the proposition. After being blindfolded again they were led back to the first line on the Budaörsi road. Here their blindfolds were removed, yet when they tried to return they received mortar fire from an uninformed Soviet mortar unit and Capt. Ostapenko was killed as well.

These tragic events determined the fate of Budapest and its German-Hungarian garrison. Although the main reason for the unfolding siege of the Hungarian capital was the refusal of surrender, the Soviet propaganda immediately used these events as an opportunity to blame the Germans of additional war crimes, purposely murdering the defenseless Soviet truce envoys which was not the case.

The 29th of December also marks the start date of the Budapest air supply effort which would last until 15 February 1945 for a total of 49 days;[6] the final few days were flown to supply the garrison escapees.[7] As the food, fuel, medical

3 Budapest was first bombed by Soviet planes on the night of 4/5 September 1942. Four Pe-8 heavy bombers of the 45 AD DD (two from the 746 AP DD, 1st Sq. and two from the 890 AP DD) bombed the central districts of Buda. Maj. Endel Karlovich Puusepp's famous 746 AP DD Pe-8 (c/n: 42066, red '1'), the very same plane that he flew to Washington, D.C. on 29 May 1942 with Vyacheslav Molotov's delegation, dropped two large FAB-1000TGA bombs from 7000m, which – based on the two largest explosions – hit and destroyed the villa of writer Zilahy Lajos (1891-1974) on Rose Hill and damaged the R.C. Church in the Városmajor Park. The other three Pe-8s (c/n: 42015/red '5'/Ponomarenko, 42037/blue '2'/St.Lt. Mihail V. Rodnih and 42048/blue '?'/Capt. Pavel M. Arharov) dropped eight FAB-250TGA bombs which also fell on the Városmajor Park and on Rose Hill. The Il-4/DB-3F bombers dropping smaller FAB-100TGA and ZAB-100CK bombs attacked the Eastern side of the city. Planes of the 17 and 24 AD DD bombed downtown Pest along the Danube while the 3 and 36 AD DD bombed the South-Eastern industrial area of Budapest, including the financially poor workers' districts at Kispest. After the attack Capt. Vihorev's Il-4 (17 AD DD, 3 GvAP DD) went missing near Lvov, en route home.

4 Kamen Nevenkin, *Take Budapest!: The Struggle for Hungary, Autumn 1944* Kindle, Chapter 5.

5 Capt. Ostapenko was fluent in German. His fellow officers survived the mission and reported the events.

6 LVO b Chef Gen StdH Br.b.Nr. 1454/45 geh. vom 25.2.1945 via Dr. Markus Reisner

7 Kamen Nevemkin, *Fortress Budapest: The Siege of the Hungarian Capital, 1944-45*, Vol. 1 (Keszthely: PeKo Publishing, 2020), p. 1019.

Capt. Ostapenko's memorial at the edge of Budapest along the Balaton Highway (M7) which marked the spot of his death for decades after the Second World War. (Photo: Fortepan / UVATERV, 1968)

supply and ammunition situation was swiftly approaching a critical stage, and since resupplying the garrison directly was impossible due to the strong Soviet blockade around the city, the MKHL and Luftwaffe launched a joint air supply and airlift operation. Although this action helped, the volume of equipment supplied would ultimately never be enough. Throughout the entire airlift 1,975.3 tons of various supplies were sent,[8] while a smaller quantity reached the garrison due to the drops falling into Soviet hands. On one of the final days in December the garrison spent 133 tons of ammunition alone,[9] therefore supplying these forces by an airlift never stood a chance. In a situation conference on the afternoon of 10 January 1945 held in the Führer's HQ in Adlerhorst, a discussion was held around how to better supply the trapped Axis garrison left within Budapest. Hitler questioned whether such operations could be carried out with the use of Junkers seaplanes that would land on the Danube, Göring voiced the potential use of 'mistel' planes, while the final option of using gliders was later chosen.[10]

German and Hungarian Ju 52/3ms, as well as German He 111s and DFS 230 gliders towed by Ju 87 Stukas were mainly used for delivering supplies to Budapest with many shot down by Soviet flak and fighters before reaching the city. The glider pilots joined the defenders as regular troops after their successful landings. The very last operational airfield in Budapest was the large flat city park 'Vérmező' at the foot of the Buda Royal Castle which offered shelter from the wind but otherwise was surrounded by appartment buildings on all other sides, this was the final drop off/landing zone for the German-Hungarian cargo planes. After the war the 'Vérmező' was used as a depot for the ruins of Buda and as such the elevation of the park was raised above the original ground level by about two metres. The airlift missions sucessfully rescued 1,446 personell.[11] The airlift planes were often escorted by Bf 109 fighters of JG 52 and JG 53 with Helmut Lipfert vividly remembering one such mission: *At this time another so-called 'lunatic mission' fell on our lot. In spite of poor weather with visibility of no more than 300 meters, the corps ordered an escort mission. We were to take He 111s to Budapest.*[12] In a Führer situation briefing on the night of 4/5 February 1945, Hitler made serious accusations against the air force for allegedly inadequate air supplies flown into Budapest, however the complaints expressed by the ground units in the capital often stemmed from the fact that the army

8 LVO b Chef Gen SdH Br.b.Nr. 1454/45 geh. vom 25.2.1945 via Dr. Markus Reisner
9 Nevemkin, *Fortress Budapest*, Vol. I, p. 997.
10 Nevemkin, Fortress Budapest, Vol.1, pp. 1000-1004. Those in attendance were Hitler, Reichsmarschall Göring, Generalfeldmarchall Keitel, Generaloberst Jodl, Generalmajor Christian, Oberstleutnant Hermani, and Oberstleutnant Weiss.
11 LVO b Chef Gen StdH Br.b.Nr. 1454/45 geh. vom 25.2.1945 via Dr. Markus Reisner
12 Helmut Lipfert, Werner Gribig, *The War Diary of Hauptmann Helmut Lipfert: JG 52 on the Russian Front 1943-1945* (Atglen, Pennsylvania: Schiffer publishing, 1993), pp. 157-158.

was unable to transport the necessary supplies to the supply airfields and many cases there was a lack of fuel for the planes.[13] The table below provides the scale of this the airlift.

29.12.1944 – 15.02.1945*			
Aircraft model	**Sorties**	**Fulfilled**	**Losses**
Ju 52	1,193	877	38
He 111	1,740	1,484	14
Gliders (DFS 230)	73	41	11**
Fw 190	55	55	–
Fi 156	13	10	10
ALL	**3,074**	**2,467**	**73*****

* LVO b Chef Gen StdH Br.b.Nr. 1454/45 geh. vom 25.2.1945 via Dr. Markus Reisner

** These were lost enroute to Budapest, total glider losses are therefore 52: 11 lost en-route and 41 which fulfilled their missions with no attempt made to extrat them.

*** This total represents transport aircraft which were lost in the air while attempting to supply Budapest. Final total losses, including the ones which were abandoned in Budapest after the siege, are at least 114.

On the ground the Soviets knew very well that for city combat their strong armored forces would become vulnerable targets and mobility would be greatly limited by the narrow streets, barricades, and rubble of destroyed buildings. For this reason the Soviets used only a very limited number of tanks inside the city. In Pest only 21 T-34/85s of the 3 and ten T-34/85s of the 39 Tank Brigades fought along with some SU-76M self-propelled guns. In Buda T-34/85s of the 3 TBr, the 23 and 25 GvTPs, the 21 and 37 Guards Tank Brigades fought along with some SU-76Ms of the 112, 432 OSADs, the 1505, 1897 SAPs, some IS-2s of the 30 GvOTTP and eight SU-85s of the 251 GvSAP. Most of these tanks however were lost, withdrawn in a few days, or were seriously damaged by the end of the siege.[14] Therefore, instead of using large tank-forces during the battle the Soviets turned to using the larger 'flying-tank' (Il-2 Sturmovik) forces. Their actions were very effective as they could fly up to four sorties a day over the city from their nearby airfields. Their 23mm cannons, wing-launched rockets, fragmentation or general purpose bombs dropped during low passes over the target objects could effectively neutralize any stronghold or resistance. During and after the siege the VVS used several airfields around Budapest: Vecsés (now the Ferihegy International Airport), Mátyásföld and Dunakeszi were used by the 5 VA, while Tököl, Kiskunlacháza and Budaörs were used by the 17 VA. For their actions over the city, the Soviet ground attack Il-2m3 Sturmovik regiments paid a serious price, especially in air crews:

Soviet Il-2 Sturmovik losses over the City of Budapest in 1944-1945				
Date:	**Regiment:**	**c/n:**	**Pilot:**	**Details:**
31.12.	615 ShAP	1887103	A. N. Sivohov+	Flak at Újpest, Northern RR-bridge
01.01.	91 GvShAP	9924	P. L. Masalov+	Flak over downtown Pest at 9:27 LT
02.01.	707 ShAP	18710106	A. K. Maltsev+	Flak, fell on targeted factory building
02.01.	92 GvShAP	1871399	A. T. Timchenko+	Flak, in the Danube at Óbuda-N, '77'
04.01.	210 ShAP	12052	N. I. Sokolov	Bf 109, Csepel-N, 1 km, CL, '7'
06.01.	132 GvShAP	1877379	G.V. Vinogradov+	Flak, Keleti RR Station in downtown
06.01.	188 GvShAP	1874679	P. M. Potapov+	Flak, Pest at 15:05 LT to Csepel-N
11.01.	130 GvShAP	1876971	M. A. Timofeev+	Flak, Gellért Hill at Elisabeth Bridge
13.01.	210 ShAP	10159	B. V. Gureev	Flak, Budafok-N, '1', eng.: 256166

13 Horst Boog, *Die Deutsche Luftwaffenführung 1935-1945. Führungsprobleme, Spitzengliederung, Generalstabsausbildung* (Stuttgart: Deutsche Verlags-Ansalt, 1982), p. 330.

14 For example, the 5 GvTK, 21 GvTBr ('51 x/x'), 1st Tank Battalion lost five burned out T-34/85 tanks in their battle for Buda. Chassis# 406532 and 4110064 were lost on 30.01.1945 on Bimbó Rd. on Rose Hill. 411210 and 4110071 were lost on 03.02.1945, while 4100519 was lost on 04.02.1945 in the Ibrahim-Karolina Rd., Lenke (now: Kosztolányi Dezső) Square areas. T-34/85, '51 3/2' on the corner of Ibrahim St. had the white inscription 'За Сталина! За Родину!' on its main gun. It was hit by artillery and was finished off by a Hungarian magnetic 43M 'LőTAK' mine which exploded on the upper glacis. The 1505 SAP lost two burned out SU-76M SPGs to artillery fire in Buda. Coming from Budakeszi, SU-76M Л-407531 was lost in Hűvösvölgy (Lipótmező-W, 0.5km) on 27.12.1944. SU-76M 408209 (with its two GAZ-70 engines: 45012, 44991) burned out at Vérhalom near the intersection of Fillér St. and Bimbó Rd. on 30.12.1944. A 25 GvTP T-34/85 ('C 219') and Gv.Ml.Lt. Pavel Adolfovich Zaharyanu's 30 GvOTTP IS-2 was lost in the ambush of a German 88mm gun while descending on the Budakeszi Rd. near the tram garages.

Soviet Il-2 Sturmovik losses over the City of Budapest in 1944-1945 (*continued*)				
14.01.	130 GvShAP	9902	P. D. Rizhkov+	Flak, downtown Buda at the Danube
14.01.	187 GvShAP	18817109	G. I. Makarov+	Flak to Gellért Hill, Rudas Bath, '69'
15.01.	951 ShAP	18848100	G. D. Pogudin+	Flak, in the Tabán Park, at Citadel-N
17.01.	989 ShAP	11439	V. L. Kravchuk+	Nagytétény-Budafok in LAC, '29'
23.01.	130 GvShAP	12628	A. T. Kozlov+	Fw 190s, in the Danube at the Castle
23.01.	187 GvShAP	10841	V. I. Ribalchenko+	2./SG 10 into the side of Castle Hill
30.01.	131 GvShAP	18844115	V. N. Provalinskii	TOA at Vecsés, Ferihegy airport, '8'
04.02.	130 GvShAP	18834114	N. I. Zarubin+	Flak, Pest-S, fell on the Acid-factory

Lost 17 and 5 VA Il-2 Sturmovik pilots over Budapest. (L-R:) Lt. Vsevolod Leontyevich Kravchuk (989 ShAP), Lt. Gennadiy Dmitrievich Pogudin (951 ShAP), Gv.St.Lt. Pyotr Matveevich Potapov (188 GvShAP), Gv.Maj. Victor Mihailovich Samodelkin (130 GvShAP), Gv.Ml.Lt. Aleksandr Timofeevich Timchenko (92 GvShAP) and Lt. Aleksandr Nikolaevich Sivohov (615 ShAP). All except for Samodelkin were killed during their crash in the city. (Photos: Boris V. Davidov)

The scattered wreck of St.Lt. Fyodor Pavlovich Momot's and C-a Dmitriy Ivanovich Noskov's downed Il-2 (639 ShAP, c/n: 11306) in Tata, during the Konrad operations on 14 January 1945, right after its crash into a local backyard along the Újhegyi road. The bodies of the two killed crewmen (shown in other pictures of the series) were buried on site the same day. (Photos: Karai Sándor, Hungarian war correspondent via Laborc Péter and Katona József)

Resupplying the Axis garrison through the Danube also failed as only a few barges could reach the city. For all of these reasons the Germans decided to launch mainland relief attempts to liberate the sieged capital, supported by strong armoured forces across the Buda Hills. The first such attempt called Operation Konrad was launched on 1 January 1945 from the Tata area led by the IV SS Panzer Corps. It advanced to Bicske where it was halted by strong Soviet resistance. After the failure of Operation Konrad, Operation Konrad II was launched on 7 January 1945 from the direction of Esztergom. This time they reached Pilisszentkereszt where they were halted by the Soviets again. Finally on 17 January 1945 Operation Konrad III was launched from the Székesfehérvár area.[15] Székesfehérvár is the largest City between Budapest and Lake Balaton and has been the settlement of peoples before the beginning of written history. In antiquity the ancient settlement called Gorsium-Herculia (now Tác, Székesfehérvár-SSW) was the religious centre of the Roman province Pannonia. Later in the medieval period it was a Royal residence, the coronation and burial place of the Hungarian Kings between 1038-1540 A.D. First mentioned in 1009 A.D. as Alba Civitas, its Latin name was Alba Regia/Regalis (White Palace). During World War II due to its key geographical location and transportation junction it was the area of heavy battles for about four months. Its Northern region, including the village of Zámoly, become a nightmare for both the Axis and the Soviet forces. In January 1945 during Operation Konrad III a month long tank battle tore up the region, 64 out of the original 66 new M4A2(76)W Sherman tanks of the 1 GvMK, 9 GvTBr were lost here! In German combat reports it is mentioned as Stuhlweißenburg, in the Soviet combat reports it is called Секешфехервар; in this book the Authors use its proper Hungarian name Székesfehérvár as this is how it can be found in modern maps.

The plan of Operation Konrad III was to break through the multiple Soviet defence lines South of Budapest, then by following the Danube North to reach and liberate the city. This final attempt failed near Ercsi. A day after the start of Operation Konrad III, after losing approximately 22,000 fallen or captured defenders, Pest was taken by the Soviets. Operation Konrad III would come to close on 27 January 1945 in a failure for the Germans. The Luftwaffe support duing this initially sucessful counter-offensive was limited by poor weather conditions as expressed by Luftflotte 4 Conander-in-Chief Generaloberst Deßloch: ... *the weather situation west of the Balkony* [sic] *Woods was considerably more unfavorable than that east of the mountians under the influence of the Russian winter high. This explained why the Russians could often get in the air, while the Luftwaffe could barely get off its airfileds west of the Balkony* [sic!] *Woods.*[16] Indeed the sucess of the German ground forces may be traced almost directly to poor weather conditions which limted the air activity of both sids; once the weather cleared up they were hounded and destroyed by VVS assault aircraft and bombers.

Meanwhile in Budapest, when the Eastern bridgehead of Pest was completely evacuated, the Germans destroyed the last standing bridges of the capital. The battle continued on the Buda side, which – due to the hilly and fortified landscape – was drawn out until 11 February 1945.[17] By this time the defending garioson ran out of supplies and, despite Hitler's strict order, gave up Budapest and broke out with their remaining forces to the West. The total personell strenght reported by the trapped garison on 9 February 1945 included 23,926 German soldiers of which 9,624 were wounded, 20,000 Hungarian soldiers of which 2,000 were wounded, and between 80,000-100,000 civillians of which 500 were from the Arrow Cross Party.[18] A break out was launched from the area of the Buda Royal Castle on 11 February 1945 by German and Hungarian military personell (43,900 able-bodies and 11,600 wounded) which soon turned into a terrible slaughter-nightmare and a merciless manhunt.[19] Thousands fell in the streets and city parks to concentrated Soviet machine gun, mortar and artillery fire in just a few hours, while others were liquidated alone or in smaller groups at the spot of their capture. All armour, artillery, transport and personal equipment of the defenders was left behind in Budapest and fell in Soviet hands.[20] As usually, there was no mercy for the members of the Waffen SS and as such many lost their minds due to fear, hunger, cold, sleep deprivation before completely giving up. Some, before committing suicide, cursed Hitler for sending them into such a living hell, showed photos of their children to the local starving residents and gave their final morsels of food away as they knew they did not need it anymore.[21] The manhunt continued in the Hűvösvölgy/Nagykovácsi regions up to the Pilis

15 The name of the city of Székesfehérvár refers to its royal role throughout the centuries: 'Throne-White-Castle', in German: Stuhlweißenburg, as it is written in the German combat reports.

16 Georg Maier, *Drama Between Budapest and Vienna; The Final Battles of the 6. Panzer-Armee in the East – 1945* (Winnipeg, Manitoba: J.J. Fedorowicz Publishing, 2004). p. 66.

17 In the final hours of the siege the connection between the last two German strongholds (the Citadel Fort on Gellért Hill and the Buda Royal Castle on the Castle Hill) was lost. On Gellért Hill Soviet rifle units and Capt. Német's Allied Hungarian troops kept the unapproachable walls of the Citadel under fire from the West, while selected Marines of Maj. Martinov's and Lt. Kasheev's 83 OSBr MP, 305th battalion climbing the cliffs from the Danube side entered the fort through the rubbles of a blown up section of the Southern wall and crushed the remaining resistance in close combat. At this time all of the remaining Axis forces in Budapest gathered in the Buda Royal Castle area from where they launched their desperate break-out to Northwest through the Széna and Széll Kálmán Squares at the foot of the hill, led by their last three zimmerited Panther Ausf. G tanks. The two Pz.Rgt.4 Panthers were lost in the Retek Street at Széna Square (Hptm. Herbert Mittasch's '615' and Hptm. Walter Bonnwetsch's 'I101'), while the FHH Panther was lost at 18 Városmajor Street (Correspondence with Ungváry Krisztián, 14 November 2021).

18 NARA T311/162/7213723

19 Ungváry Krisztián, *Budapest ostroma* (Budapest: Corvina, 2005), 5th Ed., p. 215.

20 At Dobogókő an abandoned Puch 350 GS (Fgst.Nr.: 15386, or 115.386) military motorcycle was saved and restored by motorcycle enthuziast Herl Károly in 1945 which today remains in a private collection.

21 From the wartime memoires of local resident Zsembery Ilona (1910-1996), who in February 1945 lived along the main path of the breakout on Margit Boulevard in Buda near the Franciscan Church.

Budapest, 1945. The Széchenyi Chain Bridge (1849) and the Buda Royal Castle (Est. 1265 AD, 1749-1769) in ruins. The Chain Bridge (along with the Elisabeth Bridge) was one of the last two bridges that the Germans blew up in the dawn of 18 January 1945 after evacuating the Pest bridgehead. (Photo: Fortepan / Vörös Hadsereg)

Mountains. The snowy forests of the Buda Hills echoed with the sounds of single shots during the next few days. Only about 700 men, not even 1 percent of the original garrison, reached the German front lines in terrible conditions.

The total number of civilian casualties during the siege of Budapest was approximately 76,000 people.[22] SS General Pfeffer-Wildenbruch (1888-1971) and his staff escaped the city through the underground sewage-system into the Buda Hills where they hid in a villa along the Budakeszi Road. Soon they were discovered and Soviet troops surrounded the building sending a Hungarian civilian into the house to order the Germans surrender. Pfeffer-Wildenbruch and his group replied they would surrender if the Soviets could guarantee their lives and an officer (at least a Major in rank) took them prisoner.[23] The Soviets agreed and the German Command of Budapest surrendered to Maj. Vladimir Nikolaevich Skripkin (46th Army, 68th Rifle Corps, 297th Rifle Division) without any further fighting.

The Siege of Budapest was disastrous not only for the humans, but for the animals as well. Military horses leashed up in staircases chewed the wooden railings in starvation before they were slaughtered for food. Almost all animals of the city zoo perished, only 14 out of the original 2,500 survived the war.[24] It is also said that one 'liberated' and terrified lion wondered in the subway tunnels for days eating remains of dead horses until he was caught and returned by Soviet troops to the zoo.

The devastation to buildings and the city infrastructure was terrible as well. In 1945 Budapest had about 40,000 buildings (including 27,000 residential apartment buildings). During the siege approximately 5 percent were completely destroyed (mainly in the Buda Castle area), about 25 percent were seriously damaged and about 50 percent were damaged to various degrees. 14,000 homes were lost and all bridges connecting the two sides of the city went down into the Danube, cutting the city literally in half. The siege of Budapest officially ended on 13 February 1945.

Operation Spring Awakening (Frühlingserwachen) (6-15 March 1945)

By the spring of 1945 the Third Reich has lost most of its oil sources which were essential for running Hitler's war machine. After the loss of the Ploesti oilfields in Romania in August 1944 the importance of the remaining oilfields in Western Hungary and in Austria increased greatly. At this time these two oil regions alone provided about 80 percent of all oil supplies of the Axis forces.[25] Without this last oil reserve Germany could not continue the war. Therefore, securing the oil in Hungary and in Austria was the key to the successful defense of Germany and Berlin itself which is why the rapid advance of Marshal Fedor Ivanovich Tolbukhin's 3rd Ukrainian Front in South-Western Hungary created an extremely dangerous situation that had to be addressed immediately. It was obvious that Germany could not afford a failure in this situation

22 Ungváry Krisztián, *Budapest ostroma* (Budapest: Corvina, 2005), 5th Ed., p. 307.
23 Krisztián, *Budapest ostroma*, pp. 195-196.
24 Unfortunately, the city zoo was located right beside the Western Railway station, which was a prime target for both the Soviet and the American Air Forces. Bombs falling off target often fell on animal shelters. The two young giraffes of Budapest ('Sidi' and 'Sahib') and 'Siam', the Indian elephant, for example perished in such a Soviet bombardment in the night of 13/14 September 1944. By the end of the siege in 1945 only fourteen animals survived starvation and the war including a zebra, two birds, a lama, 'Malah' the elephant, five hippos and a donkey amongst others.
25 Maier, *Drama Between Budapest and Vienna,* p. 113.

therefore they collected all available armoured divisions (even divisions fighting on the Western Front) to push the Soviets back to the Danube and the Drava in Yugoslavia. This top-secret operation was called 'Operation Spring Awakening' ('Frühlingserwachen'), which turned into the very last major German offensive of the Second World War. The backbone of this Operation was the 6th SS-Panzer Army with its four SS-Panzer Divisions: 1., 2., 9. and 12. SS-Pz.Div. The attack was launched on 6 March 1945 between Lake Balaton and Lake Velence. The Soviet air regiments moved back to the Eastern side of the Danube as the advancing Panther columns systematically broke through the Soviet defense lines before their airfields. The Germans managed to push the Soviets back to Cece and Simontornya along the Sárvíz canal in the South, where their campaign was finally exhausted. Ones might ask what was the reason for the failure of this powerful German offensive? The answer is probably the Soviet 17th Air Army as their ground attack Il-2 Sturmovik and A-20 Boston bomber formations systematically hunted for the German supply lines and blocked all road-traffic behind the front.[26] Open fields were wet and soggy which greatly limited the mobility of the heavy tank forces on alternative routes. Without reliable fuel, ammunition, or food supplies, all of the powerful SS-Panzer Divisions were forced to their knees just in a few days. Fighter units of Luftflotte 4, including fighters of JG 52 (along with JG 51, JG 53 and the MKHL) held the task of destroying all possible Soviet planes over the region; this is also why many dogfights and victory claims were reported along the Sárvíz canal, over Székesfehérvár, Seregélyes, Káloz, Soponya, Sárkeresztúr and Simontornya. Operation 'Spring Awakening' finally collapsed on 15 March 1945 and on the very next day, 16 March 1945, the Soviets began their delayed Vienna Offensive. Hundreds of Soviet trophy-tank photographs show the terrible losses of the destroyed, self-destructed and abandoned Axis armour around Lake Balaton from which the Thrid Reich could never recover.

The Vienna Offensive (16 March – 15 April 1945)

After the failure of Operation Spring Awakening at Simontornya, Soviet forces launched a massive counterattack to begin their offensive for the Austrian capital, Vienna. It was a joint operation of the 2nd and 3rd Ukrainian Fronts as well as the 1st Bulgarian Army, which was advancing along the Drava river. The fights were still deep inside of Hungary in the Lake Balaton area, but other than some local strongholds, there was no major organized resistance left before the advancing Soviet forces. In the South, parts of the 1 Guards-Mechanized Corps crossed the Sárvíz canal and started their push to the North to Polgárdi and Lake Balaton. This movement broke through the 'Margit' defence-line and reached the SE-corner of Lake Balaton. This Soviet action was extremely dangerous to the defenders of Székesfehérvár, who abandoned the city on 23 March 1945 as they did not want to be encircled. The rapid evacuation of Székesfehérvár was followed by a hurried and unorganized, sometimes chaotic, retreat on the Northern shore of Lake Balaton. Il-2 formations of the 17 VA were everpresent in the air, making sure that the retreating forces could not stop to stabilize their positions along their way towards Austria. As the organized German resistance collapsed, losses of the Soviet 17 VA decreased significantly as well. Most were downed by flak as the MKHL and Luftwaffe fighter units were busy resupplying and relocating to Western Hungary, or Austria, instead of challenging them in the air.

Sample Soviet aircraft losses during the Vienna Offensive in 1945					
1945	Regiment:	Type:	c/n:	Pilot:	Details:
23.03.	707 ShAP	Il-2m3	1888303	N.P.Mironov+	In Lake Balaton at Alsóörs to flak
23.03.	861 BAP	A-20G	43-9582	O.Dzhanzhutov	Enying-N to Hun. Fekete Ottó zls.
27.03.	707 ShAP	Il-2m3	18825124	S. A. Kosarev	Somogyvár, CL to Tapolca flak
29.03.	238 GvBAP	B-25D	42-87375	N. Pronnikov+	Thomasberg, Austria, fighters, '58'
31.03.	260 BAP	A-20B	41-3626	F. I. Larin+	Fertőrákos, Hungary in the forest
01.04.	611 IAP	Yak-3	310118*	A. I. Salnikov+	Sopron-N, in Austria to Bf 109s
03.04.	707 ShAP	Il-2m3	18873108	P. I. Orlov+	Čakovec RR, Croatia to flak (HSU)
03.04.	615 ShAP	Il-2m3	18843111	L.Y.Nazadze+	Taszár-S, TOA, reductor problem
04.04.	131 GvShAP	Il-2m3	1881401	F.I. Strelnikov	Friedrichsdorf-S, Austria, CL, flak
04.04.	951 ShAP	Il-2m3	18879107	I. A. Yefimov	Nagycenk AB, LAC, hit a tree**
04.04.	951 ShAP	Il-2m3	13447	A. Baboshin	Nagycenk AB-W, CL, 4 Fw 190s
05.04.	56 IAP	La-5FN	39211001	K.V. Kuvabin	Vienna, Austria, MIA to fighters
07.04.	951 ShAP	Il-2m3	10721	V. E. Baranov	Groß-Zistersdorf-SW, 4 Fw 190s
07.04.	951 ShAP	Il-2m3	1878886	M. Magidman	Schwadorf-N, 2km, CL, 4 Fw 190s

26 Due to the bad weather in mid-March 1945 ground forces of the 3rd Ukrainian Front were occasionally covered by the 2nd Ukrainian Front's 5th Air Army, whose Northern airfields were not disabled by fog.

Sample Soviet aircraft losses during the Vienna Offensive in 1945 (*continued*)					
08.04.	116 IAP	La-5FN	39212105	M.Koledziev+	Purkersdorf, Austria, CL, to flak
08.04.	486 IAP	La-7FN	45212064	A.Spiridonov+	Hainburg, Austria to Hptm. Lipfert
08.04.	951 ShAP	Il-2m3	11659***	V. Kutsenko	Sauerbrunn, Au., engine problem
10.04.	615 ShAP	Il-2m3	11233	V. A. Guk+	Prater-SE, Vienna, Austria to flak
10.04.	715 ShAP	Il-2m3	18898119	V.Meshaninov	Kappeln, Austria to flak, '14'
10.04.	715 ShAP	Il-2m3	18810117	G. Melnikov	Götzendorf, '25', 11:10 to fighters
10.04.	715 ShAP	Il-2m3	12965	A. M. Lebedev	Kappeln, Austria to flak, '22'
10.04.	951 ShAP	Il-2m3	13558	N. Kuznetsov	Vienna-NW, flak, CL in orchard
11.04.	130 GvShAP	Il-2m3	1871980	I.V. Zhuravlev	Parndorf, Austria, 12:25 LT, TOA
12.04.	190 GvShAP	Il-2m3	12356	G.I. Nemchin+	Baumgarten, Austria to flak
12.04.	672 ShAP	Il-2m3	11221	M. Kuznetsov	Hintersdorf-NW, 2 km, CL to flak
12.04.	707 ShAP	Il-2m3	18835121	I. D. Zubarev	Vienna, Austria to flak
13.04.	707 ShAP	Il-2m3	13448	I. V. Sedov	Domanjševci forest, Slovenia, flak
13.04.	210 ShAP	Il-2m3	18822124	S. S. Elohov+	Floridsdorf, Austria to flak
14.04.	897 IAP	Yak-3	310292	D. A. Ermak+	Kornienburg, 15:45 LT to *Fw 190s*
14.04.	951 ShAP	Il-2m3	1880702	M.Satanovskii	Brodersdorf to Hun. Tóth Lajos h.
14.04.	989 ShAP	Il-2m3	18802121	V. G. Dranga	Mödling, Au., CL to fighters, '23'
15.04.	31 IAP	La-5FN	39211853	N.Cherepanov	Absdorf, Au., 16:15LT, 12 Bf 109s
15.04.	282 OAPS	Po-2/U-2	9286	I. I. Zamotaev	Harka, Hu. to *Fw 190s* near Vienna
15.04.	951 ShAP	Il-2m3	1877498	S.Manuylenko	Melk-E, Austria to flak****

* This Yak-3 was in 17 VA reserve on 01.01.1945. On 17.02.1945 it was assigned to the 611 IAP.
** The two 23mm cannons of this Il-2m3 were c/n: ГМ-91, ВП-299, AM-38F engine: 254369.
*** One of the 23mm cannons of this Il-2m3 was c/n: ГП-204. (Factory 66, 1944), engine: 254534.
**** Between 14:25-14:35 LT eight 951 ShAP Il-2s escorted by two 116 IAP La-7s attacked a barge and a ship heading for Melk, Austria on the Danube. The tail of Il-2, c/n: 1877498 was blown off by flak at 400m. Although one crewman bailed out successfully before it crashed at Melk-E, 1km, the crew of Ml.Lt. Sergei Izotovich Manuylenko and C-a Stephan Yakovlevich Otstavnih went missing. The plane arrived in the 951 ShAP in March 1945 from the reserve of the 17 VA.

Várpalota fell on 21 March 1945 after a fierce tank battle in its downtown, right beside the local synagogue, between Jagdpanthers of s.H.Pz.Jg.Abt.560, Panthers of SS-Pz.Reg.1 'LSSAH' and T-34/85s of the 5 GvTK, 20 GvTBr. Due to the severe fuel shortage at this point, a mass self-destruction of the German armour had begun. It is stagering to understand that between 24 March and 20 April 1945, 239 axis armoured fighting vehicles were self-destructed due to lack of fuel and the cahotic retreat.[27] Veszprém and Zirc fell on 23 March 1945, Pápa on 26 March 1945, Sárvár, Komárom, Csorna and Győr on 28 March 1945, Kőszeg, Szombathely on 29 March 1945 and Sopron on 1 April, 1945. Although Hungary's territory was officially taken by the Soviets on 4 April 1945 (a force-celebrated day after the war for decades), the outskirts of Nemesmedves and some smaller areas still resisted until as late as 11 April 1945.

27 Archer, Nevenkin, *Panzerwrecks 20: Ostfront 3*, p. 5.

Planes of the II./JG 52 aces over Hungary

Messerschmitt Bf 109G-14, white '1'. This plane was flown by Hptm. Erich Hartmann in the newly created 4./JG 52 in the late fall of 1944. Hartmann's personal red heart emblem bearing his sweetheart's name is visible under the canopy. (Colour artworks by Daniel Horvath)

Messerschmitt Bf 109G-6, black '<<'. This plane was flown by Hptm. Erich Hartmann from Veszprém, Hungary in February, 1945 as the temporary Gruppenkommandeur of I./JG 53. A note in Erich Sommavilla's logbook mentions this machine as being a G-6 variant. Note the short tail wheel, the Erla canopy, the battery box cover protruding from the cockpit wall behind the pilot's seat and the lack of an air ventilation scoop under the port windshield, all common features of Bf 109G-6 machines manufactured by Erla in the 412-xxx and 413-xxx WNr. ranges. (Colour artworks by Daniel Horvath)

Messerschmitt Bf 109G-10/U4 of 6./JG 52, WNr.: 610533, black '1' in 1945. According to Düttmann he flew this plane until the end of the war. Note the red spinner color was commonly used by the 6./JG 52. (Colour artworks by Daniel Horvath)

The same plane as above. According to a 7 March 1945 regulation, aircraft of Luftflotte 4 were to be painted in new identification colors. Note that the old identification markings have been overpainted in dark colors. (Colour artworks by Daniel Horvath)

WNF-built Messerschmitt Bf 109G-14/U4, yellow '1'. This aircraft, WNr.510915, is a potential candidate for one of Hptm. Helmut Lipfert's personal planes, however it was lost on 22 January 1945 in Hungary. (Colour artworks by Daniel Horvath)

Diana-built Messerschmitt Bf 109G-10/U4, black '<<'. This was the plane in which Hptm. Helmut Lipfert overturned on the Vát I. airfield near the Western border of Hungary on 24 March 1945 as the Gruppenkommandeur of I./JG 53. Note the spiral outlines on the spinner and the small '2' in the inner chevron; this personal emblem harkens back to Lipfert's first Messerschmitt. (Colour artworks by Daniel Horvath)

Regiment markings of the Soviet 3rd Ukrainian Front, 17th Air Army, 10th Assault Aviation Corps in Hungary and Austria in 1944-1945

136 ShAD (Ilyushin Il-2m3) – white diagonal tail stripe(s)

210 ShAP

715 ShAP[(a)]

989 ShAP[(b)]

306 ShAD (Ilyushin Il-2m3) – white diagonal tail cap with short stripe(s)

672 ShAP

951 ShAP[(c)]

995 ShAP[(d)]

(a) Known 2nd squadron inscription on their fuselages: Чернигорский Комсомолец with the tactical numbers painted on the tail. Known locations of some 715 ShAP tactical numbers: 6, 9 and 12 were on the fuselage between the cockpit and the fuselage red star, 29 and 38 were on the tail.

(b) The 989 ShAP was one of the Soviet air regiments where several Spanish aviators served in 1944-1945.

(c) Known 2nd squadron inscription on their fuselages: Колхозник Ошской Области.

(d) In early February, 1945 this regiment was withdrawn from combat service for re-arming with the brand-new Ilyushin Il-10 model. Their used Il-2 Sturmoviks were left behind and handed over to the regiments of the 136 and 306 ShAD.

295 IAD (La-5, La-7) – lightning bolt on the fuselages plus diagonal tail stripe(s)

31 IAP

116 IAP

164 IAP

Regiment markings of the Soviet 5th and 17th Air Armies in 1944-1945 in Hungary, Austria and Czechoslovakia

5 VA, 218 BAD (Douglas A-20G Boston) – tail cap in regiment's color, tactical number on the rudder in the squadron's red, yellow, or white color[a]		

48 BAP	452 BAP	453 BAP
Various 5 and 17 VA regiment markings in 1944-1945		
	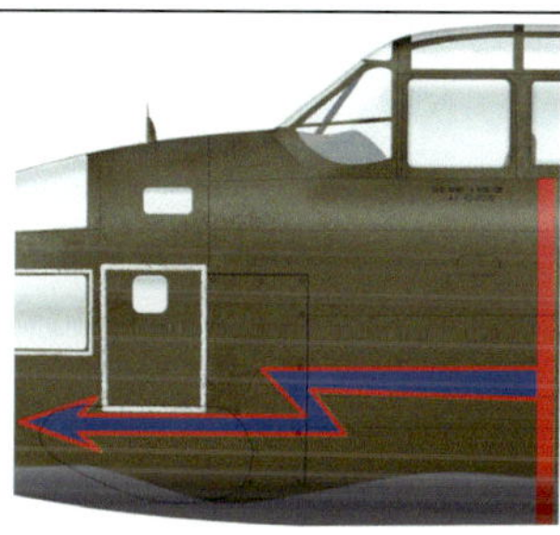	
449 BAP[b]	260 BAP[c]	235 ShAP

187 GvShAP[d]	190 GvShAP[e]	809 ShAP

(a) A-20G, S/N: 42-54202 was shot down by flak over Brno on 25 April 1945 with St.Lt. Bongard's crew. 42-53942 was shot down by flak over Budapest on 1 January 1945 with Lt. Lazarev's crew. 42-53873 crash-landed on the Debrecen airfield on 21 December 1944 with S. Lt. Petrunko's crew.

(b) The regiment marking of the 449 BAP A-20 Bostons was a bomb-dropping seagull. This example is the common one, while some planes bore very artistic and unique detailing.

(c) The 260 BAP lightning-bolt regiment markings were painted on in Squadron colors.

(d) Known 187 GvShAP 2nd squadron fuselages inscription: Смоленск.

(e) The 17 VA, 189 ShAD, 707 ShAP had similar white tail marking without fuselage band.

Various 5 and 17 VA regiment markings in 1944-1945

96 OKRAP

90 GvShAP

611 (& 267) IAP*

85 GvIAP**

31 GvIAP

150 GvIAP's 'Sword Group'

* The white inscription of one of the 267 IAP's squadrons was *Освобожденный Донбасс*. The tail markings of the 17 VA, 236 IAD, 267 IAP and the 17 VA, 288 IAD, 611 IAP was the same.

** Regiment marking of the 5 VA, 6 GvIAD, 85 GvIAP seems to have been a two digit medium or small-sized rudder number in addition to the standard fuselage number, while some Yaks also carried the shark-mouth on their nose.

Yakovlev Yak-9T (c/n: 0815353, white '53') of 17 VA, 288 IAD, 659 IAP, built in Novosibirsk, Factory No.153. Note the white arrow, the regiment marking of the 659 IAP. This plane was flown by Capt. Andrey Antonovich Kopichenko twenty times between 2 March and 2 May 1944. On 2 May 1944 it was transferred to the 288 IAD, 897 IAP where it was lost, since it was missing from the 288 IAD's 1 October 1944 quarterly aircraft inventory report.

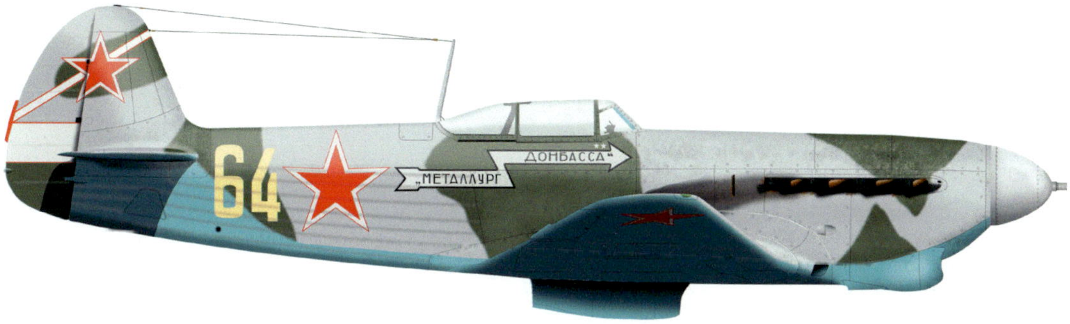

Reconstruction of Soviet 17 VA, 288 IAD, 611 IAP, 3rd Sq. Yakovlev Yak-9T (c/n: 1115364, engine: 345-253), built in Novosibirsk, Factory No.153, lost on 25 December 1944 in combat with II./JG 52 Bf 109s over Zámoly with the inscription of 'Металлург Донбасса' (Metallurgist of Donbass). The pilot, Ml.Lt. Dmitrii Gavrilovich Kirichenko (№7981, 1918-1944), Maj. Aleksei Pavlovich Churilin's wingman probably fell to the guns of Hptm. Helmut Lipfert.

Soviet 17 VA, 194 IAD, 530 IAP Lavochkin La-5FN (c/n: 39211399, ASh-82FN engine: 82111418, white '99') lost on 4 January 1945 over Tardos-Tarján. The pilot, Ml.Lt. Aleksei Stephanovich Suhorukhov (№1235, 1921-1945) was killed in the crash. His plane was also downed by Hptm. Helmut Lipfert. Note the 530 IAP's white rudder and red trim markings.

Soviet 17 VA, 295 IAD, 164 IAP Lavochkin La-5FN (c/n: 39211637, ASh-82FN engine: 8211279, white '37'), lost on 14 March 1945 near Székesfehérvár to Hptm. Helmut Lipfert. The pilot, Lt. Anatolii Victorovich Yozhitskii (№111809, 1922-) bailed out successfully and was taken prisoner of war.

1. A-20G (S/N: 321519) and Helmut Lipfert's 8 January 1945 victim (S/N: 321588) in the 17 VA's inventory for 1.1.1945 (TsAMO RF: fu. 35, inv. 11258, f. 349, p.30)
2. The most important recovered relic: a data plate with the Boston's 43-21519 Serial number.
3. Recovered data plate of the Boston's D-6A battery.
4. Recovered data plate of the R-2600 engines' Stromberg carburetor.
5. Small data plate of the A-20G Boston from Detroit, Michigan, U.S.A.
6. Inside corner of the Soviet National Insignia, the white edged Red Star.
7. Recovery of one of the Boston's main wheels in a corn field in 2006.

(Photos: Authors' collection)

(L) Ml.Lt. Aleksei Stepanovich Suhorukov (№4235, KIA), whose 530 IAP La-5FN was shot down by Helmut Lipfert at Tarján-S, on 4 January 1945. Suhorukov, a brave and skilled 24-year-old Soviet fighter pilot, made the ultimate sacrifice this day. (R) Remains of a red La-5 spinner found in the Tarján forest in 2012. Also, see original color sample of the Lavochkins' factory applied, dark blue edged white tactical numbers. (Photos: pamyat-naroda.ru and Katona József, (MRE) and TsAMO RF: fu. 35, inv. 11258, f. 349, p. 70)

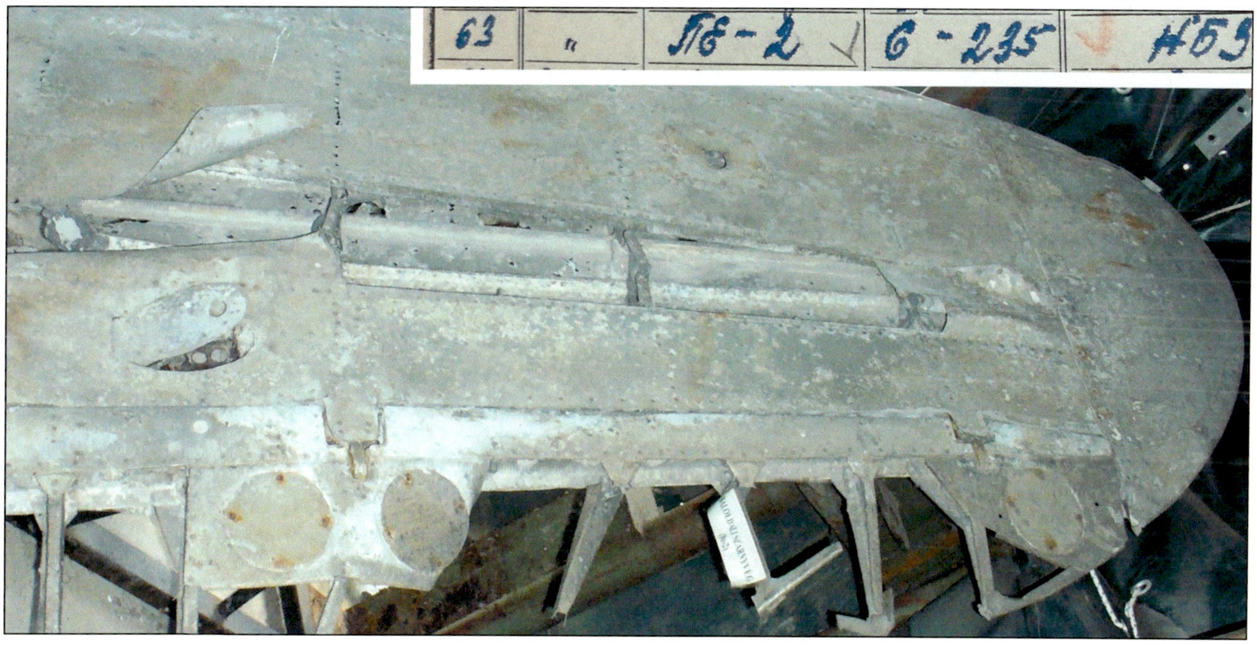

Left wingtip of the 17th Air Army, 39 ORAP Petlyakov Pe-2 (c/n: 6/235) lost on 11 December 1944 over Lake Balaton near Balatonkenese. This Soviet reconnaissance plane, piloted by Lt. Vladimir Radionovich Elohov was downed by Hptm. Helmut Lipfert as his 158th victory claim. The plane exploded in mid-air and fell in the shallow water near the shore, being dangerous to boats and fishermen. The left wing, which was too close to the surface, was recovered in September, 1994 soon after its discovery. (Photo: authors' collection, 2006 and TsAMO RF: fu. 35, inv. 11258, f. 349, p. 13b)

A Soviet Il-2m3 wing-panel with original colors from one of the two lost 5th Air Army, 131 GvShAP Il-2s, downed by Hptm. Helmut Lipfert on 23 October 1944 at Szolnok. (Photo: Authors' collection)

202	"	А-20-Б.	13564	Н.Б.З.
203	"	"	12807	— " —
204	"	А-20-Ж	253865	— " —
205	"	А-20-Ж-20у	321264	— " —

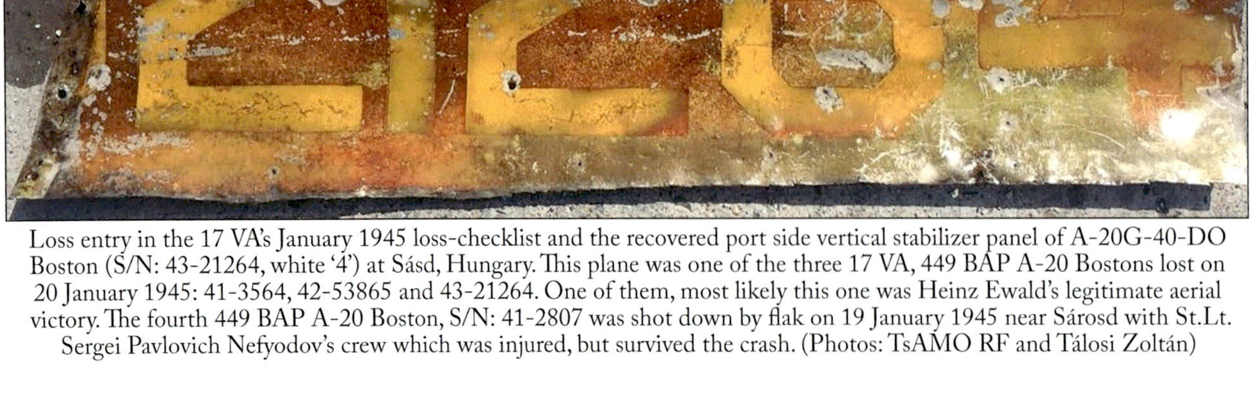

Loss entry in the 17 VA's January 1945 loss-checklist and the recovered port side vertical stabilizer panel of A-20G-40-DO Boston (S/N: 43-21264, white '4') at Sásd, Hungary. This plane was one of the three 17 VA, 449 BAP A-20 Bostons lost on 20 January 1945: 41-3564, 42-53865 and 43-21264. One of them, most likely this one was Heinz Ewald's legitimate aerial victory. The fourth 449 BAP A-20 Boston, S/N: 41-2807 was shot down by flak on 19 January 1945 near Sárosd with St.Lt. Sergei Pavlovich Nefyodov's crew which was injured, but survived the crash. (Photos: TsAMO RF and Tálosi Zoltán)

The prime trophy of Ilyushin Il-2m3 Sturmovik (672 ShAP, c/n: 1877788) after recovery from Lake Velence in 2003. Below recovered live 23mm (VYa-23) Il-2 wing cannon ammunition from the very same plane that was lost in Lake Velence on 14 March 1945 with Ml.Lt. Nikolai Dmitrievich Botin's crew in combat with two Bf 109s. This Il-2m3 Sturmovik was a potential aerial victory for II./JG 52 ace, Maj. Wilhelm Batz. (Photos: Ozsvát Zoltán)

Mementos of the 'Konrad' and 'Spring Awakening' Operations in which pilots of II./JG 52 flew countless support missions in 1945

1. A Soviet machine gun bullet in 2006, still stuck in a steel fence in Kajászó, Budapest-W. It was probably fired around 26-27 January 1945 by the Soviet 1./105 Guards Rifle Regiment from the distance of 300m along the main road, where they lost at least sixteen of their infantrymen in combat with forces of the 3rd SS-Panzer Division 'Totenkopf' attacking from the West. In the battle all five encircled 18 GvTP M4A2(76)W Shermans (Bondar+, Korostelev, Serebrennikov, Stolpnik+, etc.) defending Kajászó were also lost, three of them to Müller's Panther (I./Pz.Rgt.24).
2. A German SS helmet after a Soviet artillery strike. Sárosd-Seregélyes area, 1945.
3. The yellow 'V' marking of Luftflotte 4, painted between black pencil lines on the remains of probably Lt. Eduard Hille's crashed Fw 190F-8/R1, lost on 7 March 1945 to Soviet anti-aircraft artillery near Sárosd (7./SG 10, WNr.: 932715, white '4'). This wing-marking was also applied to II./JG 52 Bf 109s in the fall of 1944 till the beginning of March 1945. (Photos: Authors' collection via Horváth Péter)

1. The harsh reality of tank battles: a completely burned out Soviet 170th Tank Brigade T-34/85 tank's own 85mm shells sunken into the melted aluminum gearbox casting of its transmission. T-34/85, either No.536, 544, 545, or 575, lost on 14 March 1945 near Seregélyes in combat with Oblt. Albert Blaich's Panther Ausf. G tanks. (I./Pz.Rgt. 6)
2. Steel track of one of the six 110th Tank Brigade T-34/85s (No.406, 407, 409, 412, 414, or 447), overrun by Panthers of SS-Pz.Rgt.9 'Hohenstaufen' in their defense positions at Sárosd-W on 8 March 1945, during 'Operation Spring Awakening'. Initially the 18 TK, 110 TBr marked their T-34/85 tanks between '401-465', the 18 TK, 170 TBr between '501-565' and the 18 TK, 181 TBr between '601-665'. With new replacements further numbers were added to the patterns, such as '575', or '668'.
3. The deformed remain of a 75mm Panther shell, found inside the wrecks of this 110th TBr T-34/85. It is entirely possible that this shell was fired by SS-Ostuf. Bauer's famous Panther Ausf. G ('AJ9'), since his Panther was one of the lead SS-Pz.Rgt.9 vehicles that broke through the defense lines of the 110th Tank Brigade on 8 March 1945. In two short weeks 'AJ9' was also lost (self-destructed) in Vilonya during their rapid retreat near Lake Balaton. After the war its wreck was towed to the nearby scrapping yard on the Balatonfűzfő railway station. (Photos: Authors' collection via Horváth Péter)

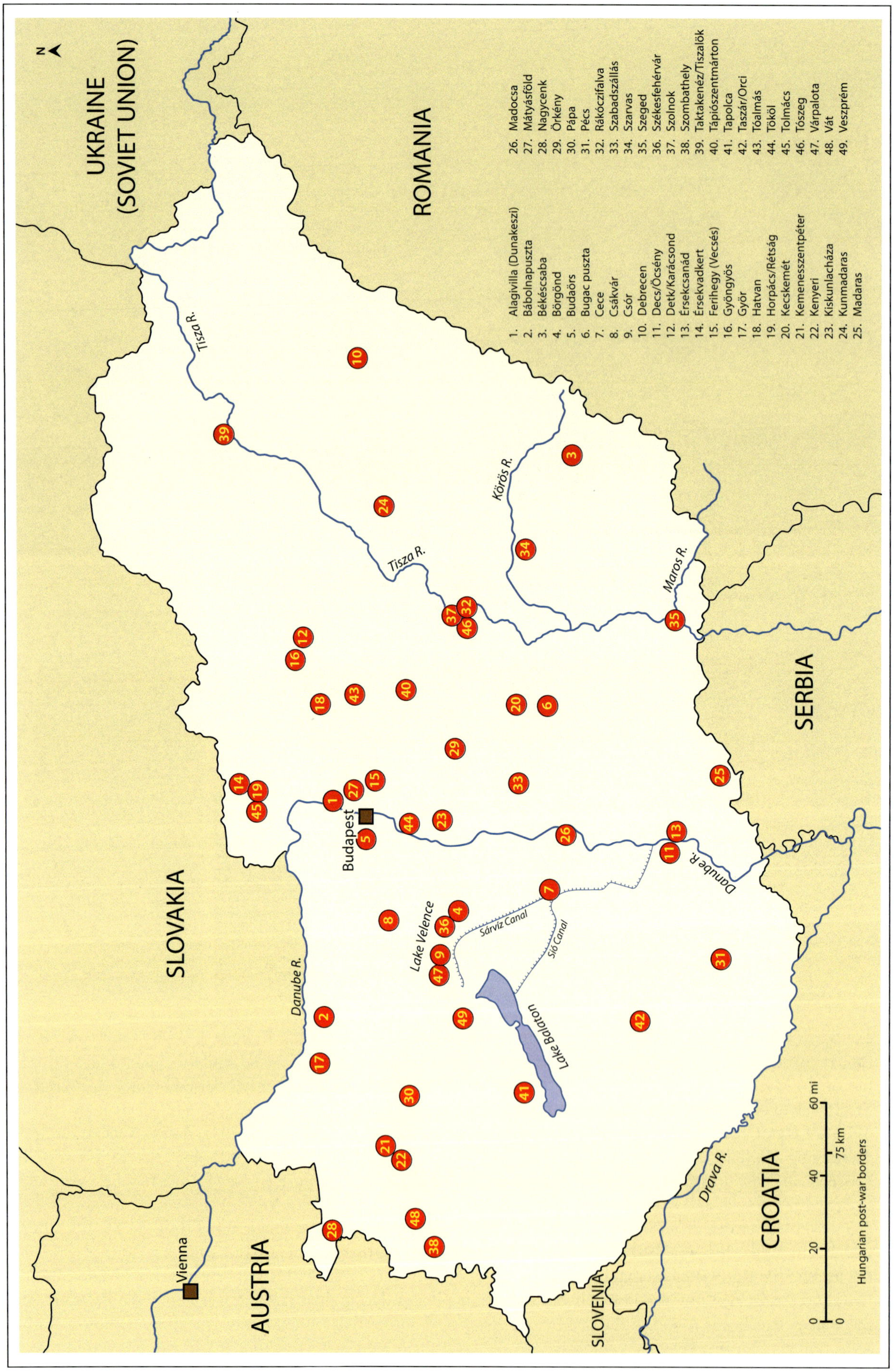

The main German, Hungarian and Soviet airfields in Hungary in 1944–1945.

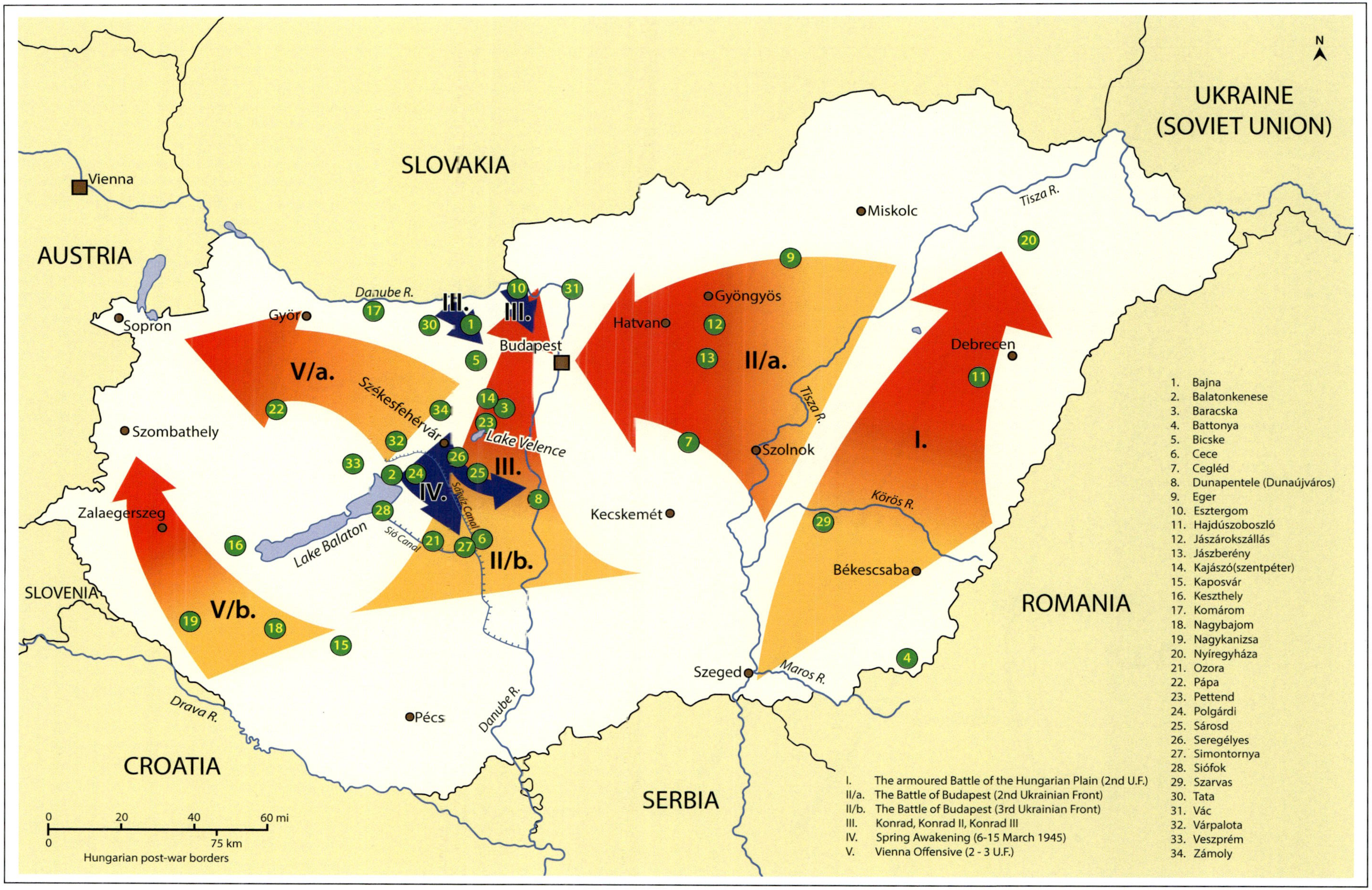

The main campaigns in Hungary in 1944-1945.

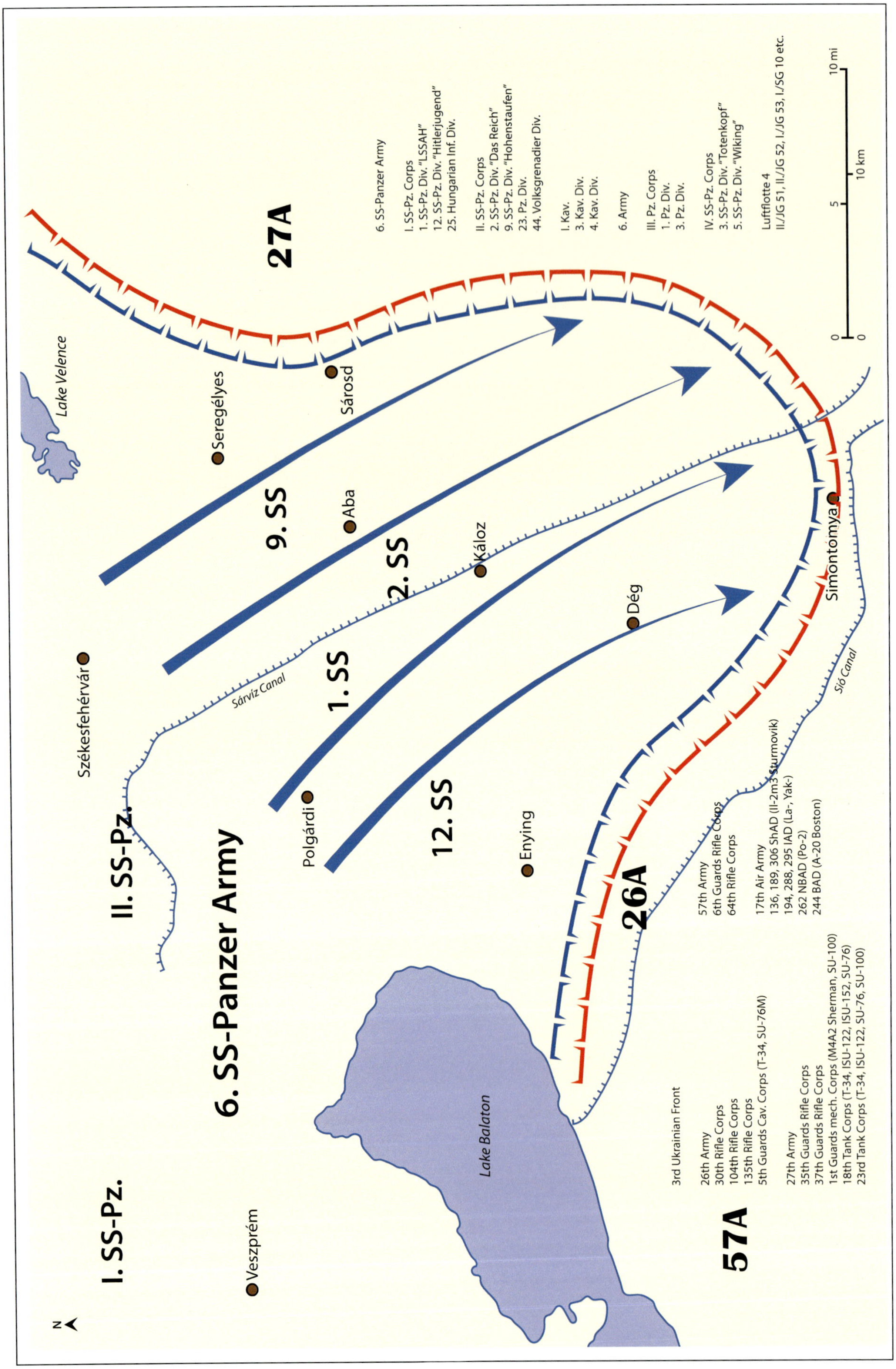

Operation Spring Awakening (6–15 March 1945)

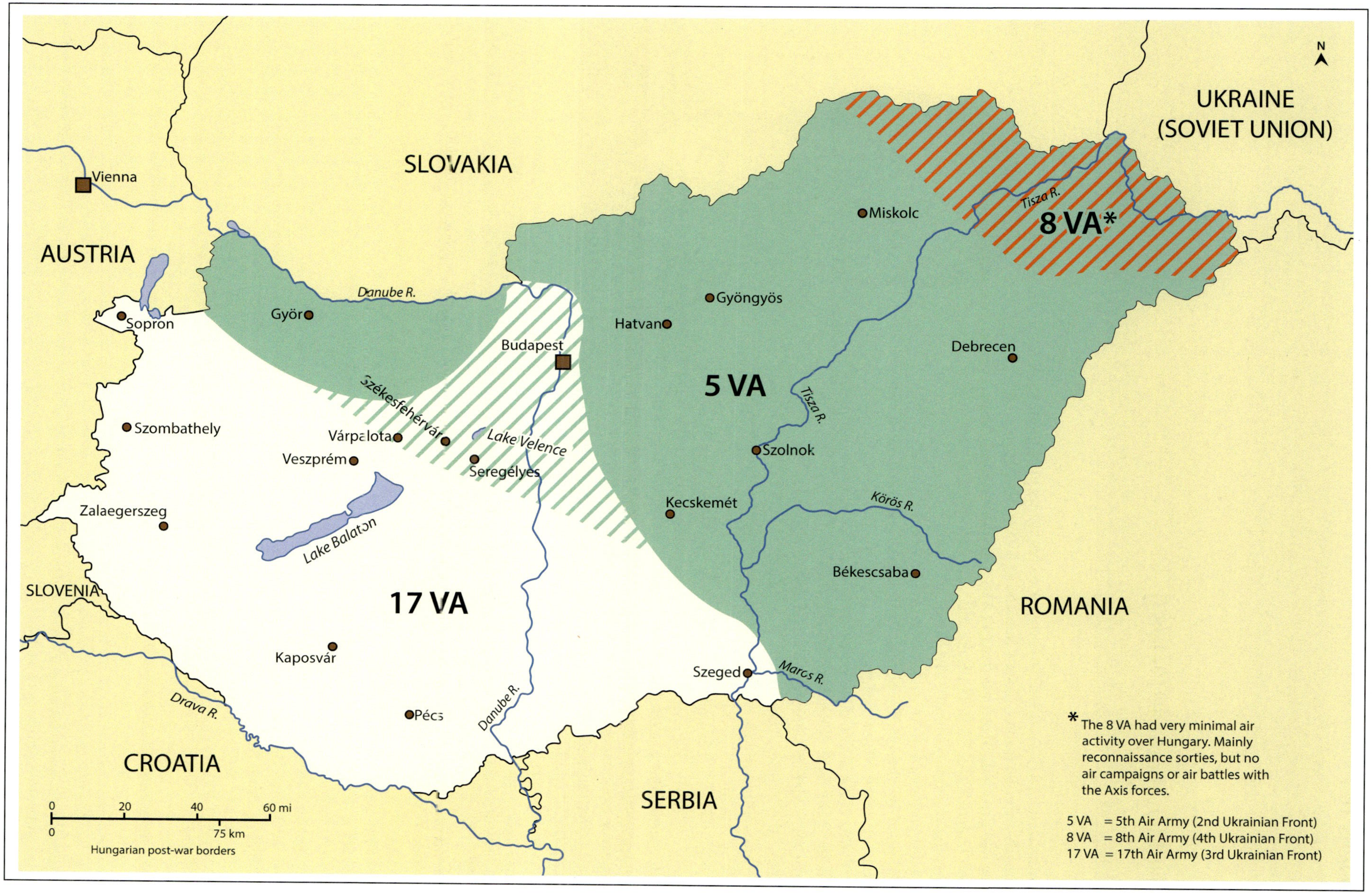

The approximate operational areas of the Soviet 5th, 8th and 17th Air Armies over Hungary in 1944-1945.

SECTION II

4

Gerhard Barkhorn (1919-1983)

Born on 20 March 1919, Gerhard Barkorn started his fighter pilot training a few months after he turned 20 on 1 September 1939.[1] Throughout the war he would eventually rise to the rank of Major. Barkhorn commanded the much famed II./JG 52 in Hungary and claimied 28 aerial victories. With an official claim count of 301,[2] Barkhorn would be the only other fighter pilot besides Maj. Erich Hartmann to enter the so called '300 club'. Admired by those with whom he flew and respected by those he commanded, the Major was not only able to have a distinguished military career but was also able to survive the war. Long term fortunes aside, many short-term adversities limited Barkhorn's ability to claim additional aerial victories during the war. Crash-landing no fewer than four times,[3] the injuries Maj. Barkhorn sustained kept him bedridden and thus away from combat. In hindsight this could be one of the reasons why he was able to survive the war.

Returning from a hospitalization back into combat service late in October of 1944, Maj. Barkhorn once again took command of II./JG 52. As the Eastern Front enclosed onto the Reich, the Gruppe conducted a slow retreat into the Western Hungarian lands. From Taktakenéz to Ferihegy, Csór to Budaörs to Veszprém, Maj. Barkhorn was able to tour the country over the course of his stay. He would later join JG 6 around 23 January 1945,[4] and finish the war having flown 1,104 flights.[5]

Gerhard Barkhorn's claims are compiled from the following sources listed in order of heaviest reliance:

- Luftwaffe Aces: claims and bibliographies, Vol. 1
- Das vergessene As: Der Jagdflieger Gerhard Barkhorn
- Die Geschichte der II. Gruppe des Jagdgeschwaders 52: Offizielle Ausgabe der Traditionsgemeinschaft JG 52
- Tony Woods – Eastern Front Vol 4. 1944. July-Dec, Issue 1

The claim numbering as found in the Mathews & Foreman publication has been used. After returning for his hospitalization in October 1944, Barkhorn's claims were not documented with the same rigor they had been before. His claims over Hungary are comprised of a combination of records in the OKL/RLM microfilms and two other lists put together by Hans Ring and Adolf Galland. Published versions of Barkhorn's claims over Hungary as found in the book sources listed above originate from the combination of the OKL/RLM microfilms and these two lists. There is a possibility that the claims made later in 1944 – early 1945 are partially incorrect as an official document found in the TsAMO RF archives captured from the Germans offers different information on when certain claims were made. Using what is available now, Gerhard Barkorn's known claims will be verified in this chapter.

1 Bernd Barbas, *Das vergessene As: Der Jagdflieger Gerhard Barkhorn* (Osnabrück: Luftfahrtverlag-Start, 2019), p. 6.
2 A 300 plus 1 unconfirmed claim. Andrew-Johannes Mathews and John Foreman, *Luftwaffe Aces: Biographies and Victory claims*, Vol. 1 (Surrey: Red Kite, 2014), pp. 40-46.
3 Andrew-Johannes Mathews and John Foreman, *Luftwaffe Aces: Biographies and Victory claims*, Vol. 1 (Surrey: Red Kite, 2014), p. 40.
4 Barbas, *Das vergessene As*, p. 193.
5 Mathews and Foreman, *Luftwaffe Aces*, Vol 1, p. 40.

26 October 1944 (Thursday)

Barkhorn's 273rd: OVERCLAIM, Yak-3 at 14:25 LT at Nyíregyháza-S, 15 km at 1000m, Anerk. 417

Soviet 5 VA single-engine fighter losses on 26 October 1944

Regiment:	Type:	c/n:	Pilot:	Details:
513 IAP	Yak-9D	19166075	N. M. Botvinov	16:15 LT, lost orientation, CL
151 GvIAP	Yak-9	*Unknown*	V. I. Muratov	*Nyíregyháza, 2 Bf 109s, repaired*

On 26 October between 12:00-12:30 LT and 14:10-14:40 LT, groups of four to six Yak-9s of 151 GvIAP from Mezőberény covered the Pliev combat-group in the Nyíregyháza-Biri-Hajdúsámson area when two Bf 109s attacked them. One Yak-9 was hit but could still reach the Kisszénás airfield where it landed safely. Pilot Gv.Lt. Vladimir Ivanovich Muratov was unhurt and his plane was later repaired. Maj. Barkhorn claimed this Yak victory right in the middle of the second 151 GvIAP mission, however because the Yak-9 was later repaired this was not an actual victory but rather an overclaim.[6]

14 November 1944 (Tuesday)

Barkhorn's 274th: VICTORY, Yak-9 at 11:45 LT Jászberény-SW at 2500m

Barkhorn's 275th: VICTORY, Yak-9 at 12:00 LT at Jászberény-S at 1000m

Soviet 5 VA single-engine fighter losses on 14 November 1944				
Regiment:	Type:	c/n:	Pilot:	Details:
122 IAP	Yak-1B	121xx	I. T. Blagoder	Il-2 escort, later returned, '12'
179 IAP	Yak-1B	xx1xx	V. N. Bocharov	Földes, CL, 08:40LT, 6 Bf 109s
151 GvIAP	Yak-1B	18199	N. V. Rogatin	Jászberény, 2500m, Bf 109s
151 GvIAP	Yak-9T	1715339	L. I. Toropov	Jászberény, 1000m, Bf 109s
151 GvIAP	Yak-9T	xx153xx	A. A. Morozov	*Tápiógyörgye to 6 fighters, repaired*
92 IAP	La-5FN	39213519	S. A. Matveev WIA	Jászberény-NW, 4-5 km, flak
92 IAP	La-5FN	39211212	N.A. Lopatkin MIA	*Repaired, lost on 23 January 1945*
92 IAP	La-5FN	39212944	V.M. Vihlyaev MIA	*Repaired, stayed in service*
92 IAP	La-5FN	39213431	A.F. Kuprianov MIA	*Repaired, lost on 24 March 1945*

On 14 November 1944 Gerhard Barkhorn downed two 151 GvIAP Yakovlev fighters in the Jászberény-S area. The pilots, Gv.Ml.Lt. Nikolai Vasilevich Rogatin and Gv.Ml.Lt. Lev Ivanovich Toropov bailed out successfully and returned to their unit.

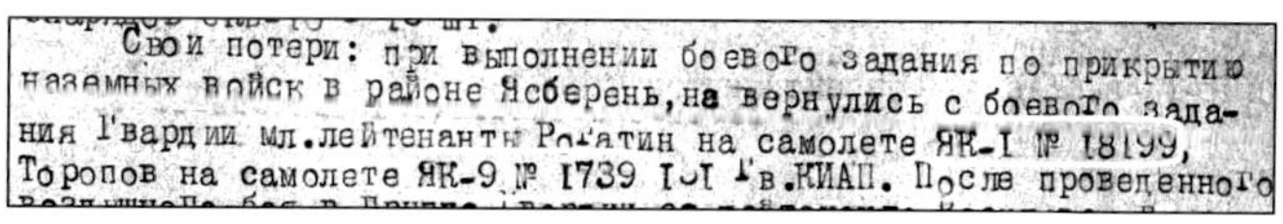
Свои потери: при выполнении боевого задания по прикрытию наземных войск в районе Ясберень, на вернулись с боевого задания Гвардии мл.лейтенанты Рогатин на самолете ЯК-I № 18199, Торопов на самолете ЯК-9 № 1739 I51 Гв.КИАП. После проведенного

Loss entries of Gv.Ml.Lt. Rogatin and Toropov in the Operations journal of 13 GvIAD on 14 November 1944. Both Yakovlev c/n were specified as permanent losses. Yak-9T, c/n: 1715339 and Yak-1B, c/n: 18199. (TsAMO RF: fu. 20511, inv. 1, f. 82, p. 554)

Soviet Soyuz-3 cosmonaut Georgii Timofeevich Beregovoy in 1968 and in 1945 with his 90 GvShAP Il-2m3 Sturmovik. Based on the camouflage pattern and the suspension of the tail wheel, his Il-2 No.'22' was built in Factory №1 with a c/n: 1xxxx. (Photos: astronaut.ru, modelavia.ru)

6 TsAMO RF: fu. 20511, inv. 1, f. 82, p. 491, Operations journal of 13 GvIAD, entry for 26 October 1944. List of permanent losses does not contain Muratov's Yak-9, therefore its c/n is unknown.

16 November 1944 (Thursday)
Barkhorn's 276th: POTENTIAL VICTORY, Il-2
Barkhorn's 277th: POTENTIAL VICTORY, Il-2
Barkhorn's 278th: POTENTIAL VICTORY, Il-2
Barkhorn's 279th: VICTORY, Yak-3 at 13:40 LT in the Jászberény area at 2000m7
Barkhorn's 280th: POTENTIAL VICTORY, La-5 at 13:45 LT at Hatvan-SE[8]

Soviet 5 VA Il-2 and single-engine fighter losses on 16 November 1944				
Regiment:	**Type:**	**c/n:**	**Pilot:**	**Details:**
31 GvIAP	Yak-9D	2015370	V. A. Koptelov	Jászkisér-E, 12:20 LT, 6 Bf 109s
73 GvIAP	Yak-9D	2015315	A. S.Shuvalov MIA	Jászárokszállás, 4000 m, – missing
85 GvIAP	Yak-9D	2015329	Ismail S. Rulev +	Jászberény, 10:10,4000 m,8 Bf 109
122 IAP	Yak-1B	22183	M. I. Sapa, unhurt	Külső-Kiritó, LAC at 15:20 LT
122 IAP	Yak-1B	06179	P. G. Artemev +	Hatvan-S, 12:00, 8 Fw 190, Bf 109
122 IAP	Yak-9M	2715305	B. A. Horkin WIA	Törökszentmiklós-SE at 12:00 LT
122 IAP	Yak-9T	2515332	A. M. Znamenev	Jászfényszaru-E at 12:30, 6 Bf 109
122 IAP	Yak-9T	2515396	I. C. Babanin MIA	Jászfényszaru-E at 12:20, Bf 109s
179 IAP	Yak-1B	12152	M. V. Meshkov	Tiszapüspöki, LAC at 13:55 LT
513 IAP	Yak-9T	1015328	G. D. Yarovoy +	Hatvan, 10:52 LT, 4 *Fw 190s*
149 GvIAP	Yak-9M	3615389	V. A. Ustich WIA	Alsódabas-NE, ~09:10 LT, flak
150 GvIAP	Yak-3	1229217	S. G. Yefimenkov	Pécel, 15:15LT, 6 Bf 109,8 Fw 190
150 GvIAP	Yak-3	3429214	A. N. Agdantsev	Isaszeg, 13.42LT, 8 Yak – 4 Bf 109
150 GvIAP	Yak-9D	2315371	G. Y. Bekkerman	Dogfight at Kóka, landing accident
177 GvIAP	La-5	*3921xxxx*	A. D. Dogadailo	*Damaged by Hungarian 101/3. FS*
177 GvIAP	La-5	*3921xxxx*	G. M. Pyatakov	*Damaged by German Bf 109s*
178 GvIAP	La-5FN	39212952	B. V. Zhigulenkov +	Besenyszög-SE, 6 Bf 109, *~10:10*
192 IAP	La-5F	39214932	V. M. Olnev WIA	Nagykáta-NE, 14:00LT, 6 *Fw 190s*
92 GvShAP	Il-2m3	10294	R. L. Kovalev	*Farmos, Bf 109s, repaired, '71'*
92 GvShAP	Il-2m3	303933	V. E. Bizhko	Farmos, 3 km, Bf 109s, '74'
92 GvShAP	Il-2m3	303925	M. P. Sadokhin	*Kun.., Bf 109s, returned, '75'*
92 GvShAP	Il-2m3	10618	N. P. Konyukhov +	Kóka, 12:28 LT, Bf 109s, '83'
92 GvShAP	Il-2m3	11360	V. A. Bocharov	Tóalmás-E, 4 km, CL, Bf 109s,'99'
188 GvShAP	Il-2m3	11091	N. P. Aleksandrov	Jászberény-W
188 GvShAP	Il-2m3	1878963	Unknown, 3rd Sq.	*Combat damage, repaired at base*
190 GvShAP	Il-2m3	1875556	*Nemchin/Valyuk?*	LAC, Bekkerman's Yak-9 ran in it
207 OKRAP	Il-2KR	*Unknown*	N. A. Voronin WIA	*~150 hits from a Bf 109, repaired*

On 16 November 1944 heavy aerial battles took place during the Battle of Budapest. The 5 VA lost 22 planes including six Il-2s and 16 fighters. Despite of the heavy losses on both sides, this was a lucky day for both Maj. Gerhard Barkhorn and Gv.Capt. Georgii Timofeevich Beregovoy (1921-1995), a 90 GvShAP Il-2m3 pilot and Squadron Commander. Barkhorn claimed five aerial victories while Beregovoy led his six 90 GvShAP Il-2 Sturmoviks against ground targets around Tura twice this day,[9] and successfully manuvered his planes back home under the repeated attacks of four *'Fw 190'* and two Bf 109 fighters without suffering any combat losses.[10] Decades after the war in late October 1968 as the summit of his extremely

7 Yak-9 according to Barbas, *Das vergessene As*, p. 206.
8 Yak-9 according to Barbas, *Das vergessene As*, p. 206.
9 The six Il-2m3s over Tura between 12:25-13:45 LT were piloted by Beregovoy, Kurilov, Averyanov, Novikov, Halin and Ivlev. They were escorted by three 122 IAP Yak-9s. (Source: TsAMO RF: fu. 22219, inv. 0161835c, f. 1, p. 26, Operations journal of 90 GvShAP for 1944, entry for 16 November 1944.)
10 TsAMO RF: fu. 33, inv. 690306, storage 1374, record 41342942, p. 319, Front Order, entry for Gv.Capt. *Georgii Timofeevich* Beregovoy, signed by Gv.Lt.Col. Mihail Arsenevich Ishenko, commander of 90 GvShAP on 21 November 1944.

eventful career he flew the Soviet Soyuz-3 space mission as a cosmonaut, completing eighty-one orbits around our Planet in approximately four days.

On 16 November 1944 at around 08:45 LT eight 190 GvShAP Il-2m3 Sturmoviks escorted by four La-5s attacked ground targets in the Cegléd area, when two Bf 109s ambushed them twice from the altitude of 1400m. Although both attacks were repelled by the aerial gunners it is possible that Il-2m3 c/n: 1875556 suffered tire damages during the dogfight and thus became stuck on the wet landing strip of the Kecskemét airfield, unable to leave the landing area fast enough to avoid a collision with Gv.St.Lt. Bekkerman's landing Yak-9D, a collision in which the Sturmovik was ultimately lost. Later, 190 GvShAP Il-2s were attacked by enemy fighters without losses, such as at 11:30 LT over Atkár (7 Il-2s and 4 La-5s vs. 2 *Fw 190s*), at 13:28 LT over Karácsond (7 Il-2s and 4 La-5s vs. 6 *Fw 190s*) and at 13:40 LT over Hatvan where four *Fw 190s* attacked the Il-2s unsuccessfully. Accordig to the memoires of Gv.Ml.Lt. Victor Alekseevich Matveev (190 GvShAP) in this last engagement with four Fw 190s, three of their four 486 IAP La-5s left the battle (probably due to combat damages) when the commander of the Il-2s ordered the last 'faithful' La-5 (probably Ml.Lt. Andrey Gavrilovich Sheglov) to join the Sturmovik formation so that the aerial gunners could effectively protect him on the way home. Flying alone -even as a fighter- was not recommended in those days.

At 11:40 LT a 207 OKRAP Il-2KR escorted by three Yak-9D fighters flew a photo-reconnaissance mission for the Soviet 7th Guards-Army to the Hatvan area when a Bf 109 attacked. The persistent fighter opened fire no less than eight times and scored about 150 hits which seriously injured the crew and damaged the plane. Pilot Lt. Nikolai Alekseevich Voronin and his observer St.Lt. Ivan Ivanovich Kovalev were able to get back to their airfield where their plane was withdrawn from service and sent to Kirovograd for a major repair. Athough the identity of their surviving plane is unknown, on 26 December 1944 the 207 OKRAP still had two Il-2KRs under major repair in Kirovograd (c/n: 7414 and 302360) while the rest were in combat service in Hungary.

Soon after this incident at around 11:45 LT five Il-2m3s of 92 GvShAP led by Sq. commander Gv.St.Lt. Pyotr Lukich Shmigol, escorted by four Yak-9s of the 122 IAP, attacked the Hatvan railway station area. Near the target the Soviet planes were attacked by six Bf 109s *and Fw 190s*. The fighters managed to shoot down all of the Il-2s except for flight leader Shmigols' plane which returned to the base alone. Gv.Lt. Roman Lukich Kovalev with aerial gunner Gv.Ml.Sgt. Georgii Nikolaevich Pichugin was hit and crash-landed at Farmos. Gv.Lt. Vladimir Yegorovich Bizhko with aerial gunner Gv.C-a. Mihail Nikolaevich Ermachenko was hit and crash-landed three kilometers from Farmos and the pilot returned to his unit the next day. Gv.Ml.Lt. Mihail Petrovich Sadohin with aerial gunner Gv.Sgt. Georgii Mihailovich Lapshin was hit and landed at Kun (an abrevate term for *Kunság?)*. After being refuelled, they flew back to their base unhurt. Gv.St.Lt. Vladimir

Gv.Lt. Aleksandr Nikolaevich Agdantsev

Gv.Lt. Aleksandr Nikolaevich Agdantsev. His 150 GvIAP Yak-3 (c/n: 3429214) was downed by Maj. Gerhard Barkhorn on 16 November 1944 near Dány, Hungary. (Photo: Units and planes, http://ava.org.ru/iap/150g.htm (accessed 4 September 2021)

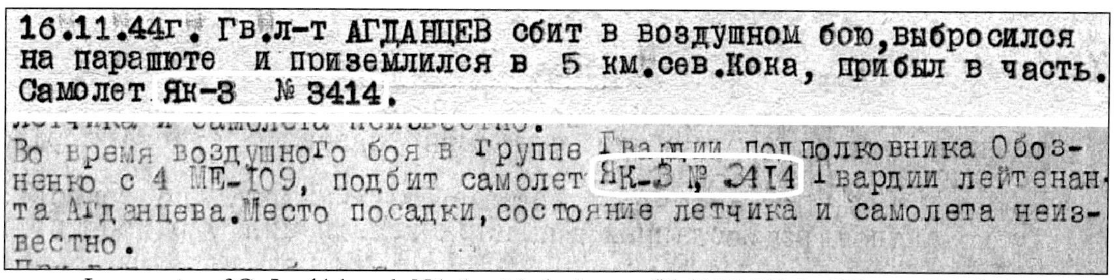

16.11.44г. Гв.л-т АГДАНЦЕВ сбит в воздушном бою,выбросился на парашюте и приземлился в 5 км.сев.Кока, прибыл в часть. Самолет Як-3 № 3414.

Во время воздушного боя в группе Гвардии подполковника Обозненко с 4 МЕ-109, подбит самолет ЯК-3 № 3414 Гвардии лейтенанта Агданцева. Место посадки, состояние летчика и самолета неизвестно.

Loss entries of Gv.Lt. Aleksandr Nikolaevich Agdantsev. (TsAMO RF: fu. 327, inv. 4999, f. 178, p. 35, Operations review of 3 GvIAK, entry for 16 November 1944 and TsAMO RF: fu. 20511, inv. 1, f. 82, p. 556, Operations journal of 13 GvIAD, entry for 16 November 1944.)

Andreevich Bocharov with aerial gunner Gv.C-a Vladimir Ivanovich Mihailov was hit, crossed the frontline and crash-landed four kilometers East of Tóalmás. The pilot returned to his unit on 18 November 1944, but the seriously wounded aerial gunner was rushed to hospital. Later, at 12:28 LT the 92 GvShAP lost a fifth Il-2 during their following six plane mission to Hatvan to 16 Bf 109s. St.Sgt. Nikolai Pavlovich Konyuhov with aerial gunner Ml.Sgt. Anatolii Petrovich Petrov was hit by four Bf 109s over Tura at 600m and went down in flames near Kóka; the entire crew perished. In the dogfight the fighter escort of four 122 IAP Yak-9s flying at 1200m at 12:30 LT lost St.Lt. Anatolii Mihailovich Znamenev who went missing. The Yaks' commander was Ml.Lt. Yosif Dmitrievich Nabeda.

The exact details of Maj. Barkhorn's three Il-2 victories are unknown, but he most likely downed Il-2s of the 92 GvShAP described above. After his Il-2 victories, Gerhard Barkhorn shot down a Yak-3 at 13:40 LT which crashed at Dány, Budapest-E. Flying at 13:42 LT between 2000-3500m, eight 150 GvIAP Yak-3s covered Soviet troops in the Isaszeg-Dány area where they met four Bf 109s. Gv.Lt. Aleksandr Nikolaevich Agdantsev was covering his leader when his Yak-3 was hit.

The Soviet pilot bailed out successfully at five kilometers North of Kóka and returned to his unit. Finally, at 13:45 LT Barkhorn downed a La-5F (c/n: 39214932, engine: 65031326, white '32') whose pilot, Ml.Lt. Vladimir Mihailovich Olnev, bailed out. At 14:00 LT at 2400m, four 192 IAP La-5s covered nine 187 GvShAP Il-2s in the Hatvan area.[11] Over Nagykáta-NE, 2-3 km they met six *'Fw 190s'*. Olnev was hit he left his plane injured at 2000m and on November 20, 1944 returned to his unit. During the fierce dogfights East of Budapest, individual A-20 Bostons of the 17 VA, 260 BAP entered Hungary from the South and flew photo-reconnaissance sorties in the Pécs, Nagykanizsa, Székesfehérvár, Paks and Budapest regions where Ml.Lt. Fyodor Ivanovich Larin's Boston went missing, but later returned to his unit. Over Paks at 2000m St.Lt. Hainov's Boston was attacked by a Fw 190, which unsuccessfully pursued the Soviet bomber to Szeged.

17 November 1944 (Friday)
Barkhorn's 281st: POTENTIAL VICTORY, La-5 at 10:23 at Tápiószecső at 1500m
Barkhorn's 282nd: VICTORY, Yak-3 at 15:00 LT at Tóalmás-SE at 3500m

Soviet 5 VA permanent single-engine fighter losses on 17 November 1944				
Regiment:	**Type:**	**c/n:**	**Pilot:**	**Details:**
122 IAP	Yak-9M	2715306	V. M. Boltachev+	Hort, 08:50 LT, 400 m, 2 Fw 190s
122 IAP	Yak-9M	2615394	V. N. Gaponov+	Hort, to Lipfert at 13:20 LT
179 IAP	Yak-1B	02162	S. G. Purgin MIA	Csány-SE, 12:50 LT, 8 Bf 109s
149 GvIAP	Yak-1B	37191	V. P. Isupov	Kóka-E, 15:00LT, 4 *Fw*, 2 Bf 109s
151 GvIAP	Yak-1B	17139	A. V. Noskov MIA	Dány-Tura, 9:40-10:50LT, 3500 m
178 GvIAP	La-5FN	39212821	Lt. Myakinin MIA	Missing, 4 La-5s covering airfield

On 17 November 1944 La-5s of 178 GvIAP were returning from a combat mission when over Szolnok-N, 10-15 km Lt. Myakinin separated from his group and failed to return to his airfield. This was the sole La-5 loss of the 5 VA during the day.

In the afternoon at 15:00 LT at 3000m eight Yak-1Bs of 149 GvIAP led by Gv.Maj. Aleksei Fedorovich Gorelov patrolled the Kóka-NE area where they met four Fw 190s and two Bf 109s. Ml.Lt. Vladimir Petrovich Isupov's Yak-1B (c/n: 37191, engine: 516-41, 2nd Sq.) was hit, he bailed out East of Kóka and returned to his unit on 19 November 1944. The exact time of Myakinin's loss is unknown, however Isupov's loss perfectly matches Barkhorn's 'Yak-3' victory at 15:00 LT. These two planes are Maj. Gerhard Barkhorn's potential and legitimate aerial victories of the day.

23 November 1944 (Thursday)
Barkhorn's 283rd: OVERCLAIM, Il-2

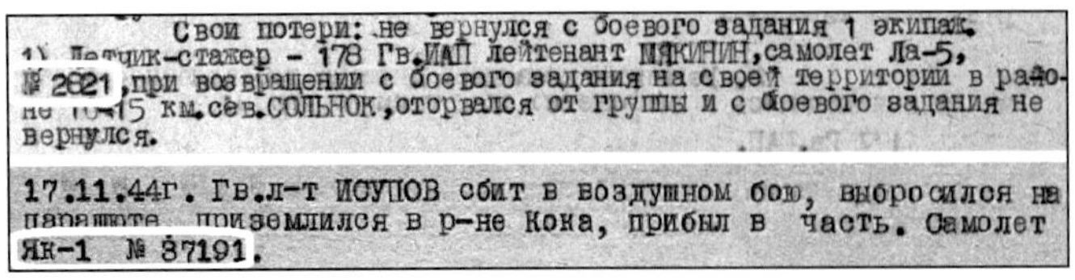
Свои потери: не вернулся с боевого задания 1 экипаж.
1) Летчик-стажер - 178 Гв.ИАП лейтенант МЯКИНИН, самолет Ла-5, № 2821, при возвращении с боевого задания на своей территории в районе 10-15 км.сев.СОЛЬНОК, оторвался от группы и с боевого задания не вернулся.

17.11.44г. Гв.л-т ИСУПОВ сбит в воздушном бою, выбросился на парашюте, приземлился в р-не Кока, прибыл в часть. Самолет ЯК-1 № 37191.

Myakinin's and Isupov's loss entries in the 17 November 1944 combat reports. TsAMO RF: fu. 20511, inv. 1, f. 82, p. 602, Operations journal of 14 GvIAD, entry for 17 November 1944 and TsAMO RF: fu. 327, inv. 4999, f. 178, p. 35 and Operations review of 3 GvIAK for November 1944, entry for 17 November 1944.

11 The nine 187 GvShAP Il-2s (white '65'-CO Lozorenko, 68, 76, 79, 69, 74, 75, 98, 89) flew their mission over Hatvan between 13:05-14:37 LT under the cover of four 192 IAP La-5s. TsAMO RF: fu. 22416, inv. 0222544c, f. 2, p. 81.

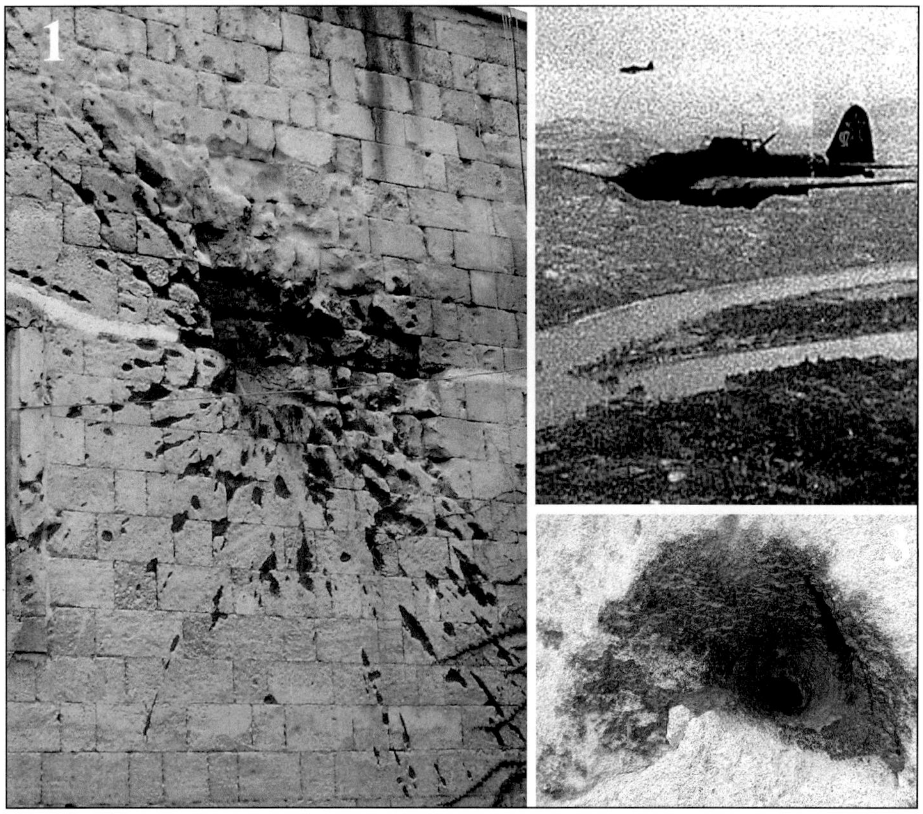

1: Impact point showing the shrapneling effect of a Soviet aerial bomb dropped in January-February 1945, probably by a low flying 187 or 188 GvShAP Il-2m3 onto the 8th SS Cavalry Division 'Florian Geyer' defenders of the Citadel Fort on Gellért Hill in Budapest. (Photo: Authors' collection)
2: Il-2m3, white '97' of 187 GvShAP, piloted by Gv.St.Lt. Vladimir Vladimirovich Fedorenko with aerial gunner Gv.Sgt. Pyotr Lvovich Ikonnikov over downtown Pest on 26 January 1945. Six Il-2s (Feoktistov/60, Makarov/99, Nechiporuk/54, Afanasev/52, Fedorenko/97 and Zhukovskii/55) flew a mission against target object No.32, 35 and 92 in Buda between 10:55-11:45 LT. This photograph was taken by Zhukovskii's aerial gunner, Gv.Sgt. Magusum Arduvanovich Gaisin, who flew on the left edge of their formation. (TsAMO RF, fu. 22416, inv. 222545c, f. 3, p. 26.)
3: A Soviet 23mm Il-2m3 aircraft armor-piercing projectile drilled into the limestone wall of the Citadel Fort on Gellért Hill in Budapest. The tip of the 59.7mm long hard steel core which hit the wall at approximately 20-25 degrees penetrated into the limestone block about 15 cm. (Photo: Authors' collection)

Soviet 5 VA Il-2 Sturmovik losses on 23 November 1944				
Regiment:	**Type:**	**c/n:**	**Pilot:**	**Details:**
187 GvShAP	Il-2m3	12260	B. D. Grilev POW	*Hatvan-NE,* Bf 109, 11:20 LT, '57'
187 GvShAP	Il-2m3	*Unknown*	V. M. Afanasiev	*Nagykőrös, Bf 109s, '59', repaired*
187 GvShAP	Il-2m3	*Unknown*	V. V. Fedorenko	*Zsámbok-NE, flak, '98', repaired*

On 23 November 1944, between 10:43-12:20 LT, nine 187 GvShAP Il-2s of the first squadron led by Gv.Capt. Sergei Alekseevich Feoktistov, escorted by four 279 IAD La-5s attacked ground targets in the Apc, Gyöngyöspata (Hatvan-N) areas. During the approach to Hatvan at 900m at 11:20 LT the nine Il-2s were attacked by two Bf 109s and six *'Fw 190's*.[12] During the twelve minute dogfight with the German fighters the Il-2m3 Gv.Ml.Lt. Boris Dmitrievich Grilev and aerial gunner Gv.St.Sgt. Fedor Nikolaevich Kaftan was hit, left the formation and went missing. As it was later learned, Grilev flew with his hit and failing (AM-38F No.2512489) engine and eventually belly landed on enemy held territory, was captured by the Germans but escaped from captivity and with the help of local resistance returned to the Soviet side.[13] Gv.Ml.Lt. Vasilii Mihailovich Afanasev's Il-2m3 (white '59') was also hit by the enemy fighters and they belly landed near Nagykőrös. The crew was unhurt the plane was later repaired and returned into combat service. One *'Fw 190'* attacked the Nichiporuk – Volkov crew in white '96', but Gv.Sgt. Ivan Stepanovich Volkov managed to shoot the attacker down. This was confirmed by the Gv.Lt. Vladimir Ivanovich Ribalchenko crew in white '71'.[14] Gv.St.Lt. Vladimir Vladimirovich

12 TsAMO RF: fu. 22416, inv. 222544c, f. 1, p. 241, Operative report of 187 GvShAP, entry for 23 November 1944. The nine white tail numbers were: 60 (Feoktistov), 50, 96, 57, 51, 59, 52, 98 and 71.
13 TsAMO RF: fu. 33, inv. 686196, storage 7650, rec. 29952723, p. 281, written by 9 September 1945.
14 The Ribalchenko-Udalov crew was shot down and killed by 2./SG 10 Fw 190Fs on 23.01.1945 over the Royal Castle of Buda in Il-2 c/n: 10841, AM-38F engine: 257716, white '83'. Their plane fell among the buildings of the hillside under the Magdolna Tower with Uffz. Fritz Wachtmann's Fw 190F-8 also downed (WNr.: 583622, black '6', 2./SG 10, KIA).

Fedorenko's Il-2m3 (white '98') was hit by flak over the target and they belly landed at Zsámbok-NE, 4 km. Their plane was also later repaired and returned into combat service.

At 11:38 LT over Gyöngyöspata at 1000m, Il-2s of the 12 GvShAD were attacked by four *'Fw 190's*. The attacks were repelled by the fire of the Soviet aerial gunners and their fighter escort. Hptm. Heinrich Sturm (5./JG 52) claimed two Il-2s at 11:21 LT and 11:22 LT, while Lt. Friedrich Haas claimed one Il-2 at 11:46 LT. The time of Maj. Barkhorn's Il-2 claim is unfortunately not known. Since Hptm. Sturm's first Il-2 claim is only one minute apart from the single verified 5 VA Il-2 loss of the day, this suggests that Gv.Ml.Lt. Boris Dmitrievich Grilev's Il-2m3 was actually Hptm. Sturm's aerial victory. Afanasev's and Fedorenko's damaged and belly-landed Il-2s were both repaired and later returned to combat service therefore they cannot be considered losses. It is possible that these planes could have been damaged by Maj. Barkhorn or Hptm. Sturm, yet because they were later repaired this Il-2 must be deemed an overclaim.

24 November 1944 (Sunday)

Barkhorn's 284th: OVERCLAIM, Pe-2

On 24 November 1944 not a single twin-engined Pe-2 was lost over Hungary. As potential Pe-2 users, neither the 39 and 511 ORAPs, nor the mixed 48 GvORAP lost a Pe-2 on this day. If in Barkhorn's records the month was mistaken and his victory was scored on 24 December 1944, then it could be a legitimate aerial victory. On 24 December 1944 Pe-2 (c/n: 19/296) of 48 GvORAP, 1st squadron was pursued by an enemy fighter to the South, until it crash-landed due to fuel shortage near Martonos, Hungary (now Martonoš, Serbia). Lt. Pyotr Maximovich Ukranskii's crew was unhurt, but the plane was written off. However as there is no proof that this claim was actually made in December it must be considered as an overclaim.

25 December 1944 (Monday)

Barkhorn's 285th: VICTORY, Yak-9 ~ around noon
Barkhorn's 286th: VICTORY, Yak-9 ~ around noon

<table>
<tr><th colspan="5">Soviet 17 Air Army permanent single-engine fighter losses on 25 December 1944*</th></tr>
<tr><th>Type:</th><th>c/n:</th><th>Mission(LT)</th><th>Pilot:</th><th>Details:</th></tr>
<tr><td rowspan="3">Yak-9M
611 IAP</td><td>2715376</td><td rowspan="2">11:05-11:55
Zámoly,
Moha</td><td>G. Alaverdov WIA</td><td>Székesfehérvár-N, crash-landed,
Bf 109s</td></tr>
<tr><td rowspan="2">2715372
2715374</td><td>A. T. Fadeev</td><td>Dinnyés, Batarov's 7 Yak, vs. 4 Bf 109</td></tr>
<tr><td rowspan="3">11:40-12:30
Csákvár,
Moha, Zámoly</td><td>Ivan I. Aleshkin</td><td>Székesfehérvár-N, crash-landed,
Bf 109s</td></tr>
<tr><td>Yak-9T
611 IAP</td><td>1115364</td><td>Dmitrii Gavrilovich
Kirichenko+</td><td>Csákvár-Zámoly, Churilin's wingman
Engine: 345-253, written off by 27th</td></tr>
<tr><td rowspan="3">Yak-1B
611 IAP</td><td rowspan="2">05193
14177 15150</td><td>N.N. Kutsenko WIA</td><td>Zámoly, Bf 109, bailed out, burned</td></tr>
<tr><td rowspan="2">14:55-15:45
Székesfehérvár</td><td>Boris Aleksandrovich
Yavlyukhin</td><td>Székesfehérvár-N, 8km, CL to 4 Bf 109s,
returned on 27 December 1944</td></tr>
<tr><td>44172</td><td>Capt. Konstantin L.
Chernogor KIA</td><td>Csala, led by Capt. Batarov, 8 Yak, vs. 4 Bf 109,
Maj. Isaenko flew 41 times</td></tr>
<tr><td>Yak-9D
659 IAP</td><td>16166065</td><td>Mór, Il-2 escort</td><td>Pavel A. Gorlach MIA</td><td>Vértesszőlős, during 189 ShAD Il-2 escort to
Mór, missing</td></tr>
<tr><td>Yak-9D</td><td>16166092</td><td>Börgönd</td><td>?, 96 OKRAP</td><td>Later returned, engine: 415-124</td></tr>
<tr><td rowspan="2">La-5FN
56 IAP</td><td>39211251</td><td rowspan="2">A-20 escort
13:06-07 LT</td><td>A.V. Rogachev+</td><td rowspan="2">Smederevo-S, Serbia. The A-20 lost orientation,
the two La-5s force landed</td></tr>
<tr><td>39211606</td><td>F. I. Romanenkov</td></tr>
<tr><td>La-5
164 IAP</td><td>39214786
41210113</td><td>18 Il-2 escort
13:00-14:00</td><td>R. I. Alekseenko
B. I. Shilov</td><td>4 La-5s, led by Capt. Zaitsev. Separated from
the group, went missing. No flak.</td></tr>
</table>

* On 25 December 1944 the 17 VA also removed 14 old Yak-1Bs from combat service due to wear and tear (02176, 03170, 05158, 09171, 13150, 14180, 19157, 32152, 33151, 35157, 40152, 41166, 47147, 48158). These planes were not repaired due to the large number of incoming Yak-3s, waiting for being distributed among the fighter regiments in the 17 VA reserve.

A captured Soviet Yakovlev Yak-9D fighter (white '120') with German and Hungarian airfield personnel. Note the intentionally damaged antenna on the fin. (Photos: Benkó Béla, Hungarian long-range recce. airman via Punka György)

On 25 December 1944 around noon Maj. Gerhard Barkhorn participated in a very intense dogfight with Soviet Yakovlev fighters of the 611 IAP in the Székesfehérvár-N, Zámoly area. During the battle he claimed two 'Yak-9's shot down. Analyzing the Soviet loss reports, both of Maj. Barkhorn's Yak-9 claims seem to be legitimate aerial victories. The 611 IAP flew two missions around noon: one between 11:05 and 11:55, the other one between 11:40 and 12:30 LT. They lost two planes during the first and three planes during the second mission to German Bf 109s.[15] Since Helmut Lipfert who also claimed two Yak-9s (Aleshkin and Kirichenko) during the second mission provided more specific time and location information, it might have been that Maj. Barkhorn downed one Yak during the first and the other Yak during the second

15 Operations journal of 288 IAD (incl. 611 IAP), entry for 25 December 1944. TsAMO RF: fu. 20257, inv. 1, f. 42, p. 440.

mission. His victims were probably Ml.Lt. Georgii Artemovich Alaverdov and Lt. Nikolai Nikolaevich Kutsenko in his Yak-1B. Ml.Lt. Alaverdov crash-landed 2 kilometers North of the Székesfehérvár airfield with injuries to his right leg. The engine of his crash-landed Yak-9M remained in good condition and was probably reused later. Lt. Kutsenko bailed out from his burning Yak-1B and landed among his own troops near Zámoly with severe burns of his face and hands. The identity of his Yak-1B is still uncertain but was probably one of these three planes: c/n: 14177, 05193, or 15150. The fourth lost 611 IAP Yak-1B (c/n: 44172) on this day was most likely flown by Capt. Constantin Leontievich Chernogor during the third mission, because c/n: 44172 was a commander's plane. Earlier in the year the regiment commander of 611 IAP Maj. Nikolai Fedorovich Isaenko flew this same plane 41 times in 1944. After the loss of 44172, he flew two new Yak-3s until 15 April 1945: 310123 (28 times) and 2235 (11 times).

It is interesting to note that a report written by a Luftflotte laision office attached to 6 A.O.K documented that Maj. Barkorn achieved four victories on 25 December 1944, propelling his *Luftseig* tally up to 289.[16] The cause for the difference in the tally is unknown and unfortunately no aircraft details are recorded which would assit in matching the claims to Soviet losses.

29 December 1944 (Friday)
Barkhorn's 287th: OVERCLAIM, Il-2
Barkhorn's 288th: OVERCLAIM, Boston

Soviet 5 and 17 VA Il-2 and A-20 Boston losses on 29 December 1944				
Regiment:	Type:	c/n:	Pilot:	Details:
210 ShAP	Il-2m3	12058	Ilya A. Balakin	Missed airfield, CL, 15:15 LT,'22'
N/A	A-20	N/A	N/A	No losses on 29 December 1944

This day Maj. Gerhard Barkhorn reported two aerial victories over an Il-2 Sturmovik and an A-20 Boston bomber. Unfortunatelly neither their times, nor their locations are known, therefore it is very difficult to compare them to the detailed soviet loss reports. What is known is that no Il-2s were lost to enemy fighters over Hungary, only a single returning 210 ShAP Il-2 (c/n: 12058, AM-38F engine: 2511731, No.'22') when it deviated from its twelve-plane flight between 14:35-15:40 LT through navigational error.[17] The crew missed their airfield and crash-landed at Pusztaszentimre around 15:15 LT. The plane burned but Ml.Lt. Ilya Abramovich Balakin's crew was unhurt. The 5 VA scrapped three Il-2s (Il-2m3, c/n: 9883, 1870169 and 1872180 from 131 GvShAP) due to wear and tear.

According to the multiple level combat, mechanical, and personnel reports of the two Soviet A-20 Boston bomber divisions (218 and 244 BAD), none of their regiments lost a bomber on 29 December 1944. The result is the same with the mixed 48 GvORAP, which operated some A-20B and A-20C Bostons beside their Yak-9D, Yak-9R, B-25C, Pe-2 and Pe-3 reconnaissance planes, therefore this claim also must be considered an overclaim.

2 January 1945 (Tuesday)
Barkhorn's 289th: POTENTIAL VICTORY, Il-2
Barkhorn's 290th: POTENTIAL VICTORY, Il-2
Barkhorn's 291st: POTENTIAL VICTORY, Yak-9

On 2 January 1945 very heavy air battles took place in the Budapest-W,-NW area in order to cover and secure the Soviet blockade around Budapest. Luftflotte 4 flew 360 day-time sorties while the 17 VA alone flew 671.[18] During the constant aerial battles the 17th Air Army suffered serious fighter and ground attack losses around the capital, while the 5th Air Army was concentrating their efforts on Budapest itself.

Maj. Barkhorn participated in the heavy dogfight at Budapest-W and claimed two Il-2 and one Yak-9 victory. From this day on it is extremely difficult to analyze his victories over Hungary, because only the claim dates and aircraft types are recorded; this is not enough information to accurately compare them to the detailed Soviet loss reports. It is known when other JG 52 pilots claimed victories (~12:00 LT, +/- 1 hour),[19] so it can be assumed that Barkhorn's claiming times and locations were similar to other JG 52 claims. As a very high number of Il-2s and Yak-9s were lost to enemy fighters this day, it is acceptable to assume that Barkhorn's claims were legitimate aerial victories even if they cannot be explicitly proven based on the records that were reviewed.

16 VOL, Luftlage 25.12.1944. TsAMO, fu. 500, inv. 12472, f. 382, p. 394b.
17 TsAMO RF: fu. 20541, inv. 1, f. 103, p. 10., Operations journal of 136 ShAD (incl. 210 ShAP) for December 1944, entry for 29 December 1944 and TsAMO RF: fu. 20541, inv. 1, f. 195., Aircraft losses of 136 ShAD (210 ShAP), entry for 29 December 1944.
18 The 5 VA flew 982 sorties. Dr. Számvéber Norbert, *Kard a pajzs mögött* (Veszprém: PeKo Publishing Kft., 2013), p. 57.
19 Lt. Heinz Ewald and Hptm. Helmut Lipfert made two claims each.

Aircraft losses of the Soviet 5 and 17 VA on 2 January 1945				
Regiment:	**Type:**	**c/n:**	**Pilot:**	**Details:**
615 ShAP	Il-2m3	*23xxx441*	L. G. Kiselev	Tata, dogfight at 7:40 LT, CL at base
615 ShAP	Il-2m3	1879399	N. G. Milto	Tarján, 08:15 LT, 12-15 Bf 109s
615 ShAP	Il-2m3	*Unknown*	V. P. Voronin WIA	Tata, escort was late, lost to fighters
639 ShAP	Il-2m3	1878997	I. Y. Tarabrin	Budapest flak, CL at base, repaired
672 ShAP	Il-2m3	1872982	P. A. Kuzmin MIA	Tata, flak, AM-38F engine: 256589
707 ShAP	Il-2m3	18710106	A. K. Maltsev+	Budapest, flak at 09:25 LT
707 ShAP	Il-2m3	1870699	I. V. Kryukov	Madocsa airfield, CL upon return
989 ShAP	Il-2m3	11520	E. A. Gorshunov	Felcsút, Bf 109s at Vértesacsa, '31'
989 ShAP	Il-2m3	11517	I. A. Tkachev	Kecel, CL to flak at 08:41LT, '10'
989 ShAP	Il-2m3	11361	A. A. Sidorenko	Vértesacsa, 13:07 LT, Bf 109s, '4'
31 IAP	La-5FN	39211844	D. S. Kravtsov WIA	Dág, after 10:45 LT, 4 *Bf 109s*
116 IAP	La-5F	*Unknown*	A. I. Roy returned	Tata, 8 La-5, Bf 109s, crash-landed
116 IAP	La-5	*Unknown*	A. N. Belkin WIA	*Damaged in dogfight, returned*
611 IAP	Yak-9T	2515318	G. S. Gladkii WIA	Bánhida, 12:20LT, 6-8 *Fw 190s*
611 IAP	Yak-9T	2515334	P. Y. Dimov+	Tata-SE, 2 km, 10:55 LT
659 IAP	Yak-9T	2515315	Y. A. Vinogradov	Makád-S, 2 km, 08:05 LT, 1500m
659 IAP	Yak-9D	16166093	I. P. Trusin WIA	Tata, 08:05LT, 1500 m, 8 Bf 109s
897 IAP	Yak-9T	0815352	V. E. Novikov+	Vereb-W, 11:30, 2000 m, 4 Bf 109s
897 IAP	Yak-9T	0815357	V. M. Gorbunov	Tata, 12:20LT, 8 Bf 109s, on airfield
861 BAP	A-20G-20	42-86881	G. I. Lashin	*Vienna rec., damaged by 8 Fw, '29'*
452 BAP	A-20G-15	42-54186	P. A. Zhalibo KIFA	Debrecen, engine failure at take-off *
611 IAP	Po-2/U-2	4744	R. N. Volkov	Pusztaszabolcs, pilot pickup accident
930 NBAP	Po-2/U-2	8266	R. F. Pahilkin KIFA	Budapest, mid-air collision over central Pest at night, all killed**
930 NBAP	Po-2/U-2	127103	S. D. Ulyahin KIFA	
3 OSANAP	Po-2/S-2	942617	Dmitrichev WIFA	Ercsi, accident, medivac plane
331 IAD	Yak-1B	26174	N/A	Scrapped due to wear and tear
122 IAP	Yak-1B	04168	V. A. Kuznetsov	08:50 LT, 4 'Fw 190s' to Tinnye, CL
122 IAP	Yak-9T	1615361	E. S. Titov+	08:50, 2 'Fw 190s' to Vácrátót***
131 GShAP	Il-2m3	12315	V. F. Salnikov	Budapest flak to Tápiószentmárton
132 GShAP	Il-2m3	1873476	K. P. Levshunov	Kispest flak to Isaszeg-S, 08:35 LT
177 GvIAP	La-5FN	41210115	N. L. Vereshak WIA	Lost A-20 group, CL at Kecskemét
187 GShAP	Il-2m3	12116	A. V. Chuvakin	Budapest flak to Gyálpuszta, 8:55LT
187 GShAP	Il-2m3	1879273	B. I. Lozorenko	Örkény, ran into a La-5, *repaired*
188 GShAP	Il-2m3	11094	*Unknown*	*Combat damage, repaired at base*
188 GShAP	Il-2m3	1878573	*V. I. Machikin?*	*Combat damage, repaired at base*
92 GShAP	Il-2m3	1871399	A. T. Timchenko+	Budapest flak into river Danube '77'
92 IAP	La-5UTI	39215298	G. I. Rodionov+	Örkény, training, KIFA in the forest

* Right R-2600-23 engine (c/n: 42-155219) of Capt. Pyotr Arsentevich Zhalibo's A-20G Boston stopped over Debrecen right after take-off. Capt. Zhalibo could not jettison his 15 FAB-100 bombs on the captured city, rather, he returned to his airfield where at landing his bomb load went off, killing his entire crew.

** 23 Po-2s dropped 267 FAB-50 bombs and 1.1 million leaflets on Budapest on the night of 01/02.01.45.

*** At 2000m 08:50 LT the Kuznetsov-Titov reconnaissance pair was photographing the Nová Vieska railway station where six 'Fw 190s' attacked them. Four attacked Kuznetsov, two Titov. Capt. Vasilii Andreevich Kuznetsov (Yak-1B, '4') was hit, he quit the battle with a steep dive and crash-landed near Tinnye in a ravine. Ml.Lt. Yevgenii Semyonovich Titov was also hit, he headed for home and bailed out over Vácrátót. Tragically he hit the vertical stabilizer and fell to the ground without opening his parachute. The wreck of his Yak-9T ('61') was still in the warehouse of the 10 RAB on 27 February 1945.

3 January 1945 (Wednesday)
Barkhorn's 292nd: POTENTIAL VICTORY, Il-2
Barkhorn's 293rd: POTENTIAL VICTORY, Il-2
Barkhorn's 294th: POTENTIAL VICTORY, Yak-9
Barkhorn's 295th: POTENTIAL VICTORY, Yak-9

Aircraft losses of the Soviet 5 and 17 VA on 3 January 1945				
Regiment:	**Type:**	**c/n:**	**Pilot:**	**Details:**
210 ShAP	Il-2m3	18713106	V. A. Tyulenev	Bicske-NE, Hill 305, Bf 109s, '17'
210 ShAP	Il-2m3	11913	V. I. Lemeshkin	Esztergom-SW to Bf 109s, '29'
210 ShAP	Il-2m3	10111	V. A. Bashkirov	Hill 305-W, 11:02LT, Fw 190,'19'
210 ShAP	Il-2m3	9647	V. K. Mihailyuk	Kiskunlacháza, LAC, La-5FN, '9'
615 ShAP	Il-2m3	11293	F. D. Ponomarev	Bicske, 13:30 LT, lost to fighters
615 ShAP	Il-2m3	305190	A. L. Sepelev	Pusztaszabolcs, flak, crash-landed
639 ShAP	Il-2m3	1871597	G. P. Zaharov	Airfield accident, scrapped.
672 ShAP	Il-2m3	1877488	V. F. Derbishev	Tarján, 12:00 LT to 8 Bf 109s
672 ShAP	Il-2m3	1876488	A. N. Udalov	Felcsút-N, 12:00, 6 '*Fw 190's*, '35'
672 ShAP	Il-2m3	8404	A. F. Yakovenko	Süttő, 09:20 LT, 2 '*Fw 190's*
672 ShAP	Il-2m3	1871885	M. I. Kuznetsov	Tabajd-E, 14:10 LT, '*Fw 190's*
715 ShAP	Il-2m3	11878	M. K. Imedosvili	Bajna, 12:22 LT, 15 fighters
989 ShAP	Il-2m3	10214	A. G. Dobrikov	Gyermely, 11:34 LT, fighters, '13'
989 ShAP	Il-2m3	11426	N. G. Medvedev	Nagysáp, 11:34 LT, fighters, '12'
989 ShAP	Il-2m3	11532	E. A. Gorsunov	*Combat damages, repaired, '27'*
116 IAP	La-5	*Unknown*	V. M. Boltyan	Zsámbék, Bf 109s, CL Kakucs-NE
116 IAP	La-5F	39214687	V. N. Schwarz+	Zsámbék, 13:50 LT to 10 Bf 109s
116 IAP	La-5F	39214952	V. P. Popov	Tata, 6 Fw 190s, CL at Kakucs
116 IAP	La-5F	392150100	V. Novikov KIFA	Kiskunlacháza, TOA at 08:25 LT
116 IAP	La-5FN	3810811	I. D. Plankevich	Délegyháza RR station-E, repaired
116 IAP	La-5FN	39211114	*Unknown, returns*	Szalkszentmárton-S, 1.5 km, CL
116 IAP	La-5FN	39211713	N/A, *parked La-5*	Landing 210 ShAP Il-2 ran into it
116 IAP	La-5FN	39211873	A. A. Radchenko	Tata, flak, CL at Vértesacsa-W
164 IAP	La-5FN	3921*xxxx*	N. Dolnikov MIA	Bajót, 8 La-5s vs. 18 Bf 109s
56 IAP	La-5FN	39211604	A. I. Zlatoverhii	Ferry fl. LAC at Szabadka-E, 2km
530 IAP	La-5FN	39210830	N. F. Belov	Székesfehérvár, ferry LAC, 15:20
611 IAP	Yak-1B	22167	P. M. Belyaev	Héreg flak, 10:10 LT, 5 '*Fw 190s*'
611 IAP	Yak-9T	1115372	N. A. Verbovitskii	Bajna flak, Dunaszekcső, 15:10 LT
611 IAP	Yak-9T	1315342	Oleg I. Shetinkin	Engine c/n: 415-1300, returned
659 IAP	Yak-9D	16166064	M. G. Achitkov	Bicske area, CL on return
659 IAP	Yak-9D	17166003	N/A	Scrapped due to wear and tear
659 IAP	Yak-9D	17166040	N/A	Transferred to the 'NKAP'
659 IAP	Yak-9D	2015365	D. D. Kostin	Székesfehérvár, ferry flight acc.
897 IAP	Yak-9D	17166023	P. P. Karavai	Agostyán, returned on 6 January
39 ORAP	Pe-2PF	14/216	D. V. Pizhik MIA	Single recconassiance sortie, MIA
122 IAP	Yak-9M	2715378	M. A. Nesterov	Heréd, LAC crater, 10:25 LT, '78'
91 GvShAP	Il-2m3	8897	L. I. Rogachev	Süttő, flak, 09:55 LT, missing
91 GvShAP	Il-2m3	11441	V. A. Volkov	Süttő, Bf 109s, Fw 190s, missing
91 GvShAP	Il-2m3	*Unknown*	V. A. Simanchuk	Süttő, fighters, crash-landed at base

Aircraft losses of the Soviet 5 and 17 VA on 3 January 1945 (*continued*)				
130 GvShAP	Il-2m3	303764	B. N. Isaev	Budapest-SE, Ferihegy airport, ground collision
130 GvShAP	Il-2m3	9770	B. E. Gaidash	
130 GvShAP	Il-2m3	305214	B. V. Prihodko	Naszály, flak, Ju 87s, 2 *'Fw 190's*
130 GvShAP	Il-2m3	302978	M. N. Lahtanov	Ferihegy, CL, broken
131 GvShAP	Il-2m3	1878973	*Unknown*	*Combat damages, repaired, 3rd Sq.*
131 GvShAP	Il-2m3	9941	A. I. Budnov	*Combat damages, repaired, 3rd Sq.*
132 GvShAP	Il-2m3	11826	N. V. Grigorev	Tiszavezseny, take off accident
150 GvIAP	Yak-3	1829217	Y. N. Verginskii	13:50 LT to 2 Bf 109s near Kirva
178 GvIAP	La-5F	39214789	V. F. Mudretsov	Tóalmás-SW, 12:17 LT, 2 Bf 109s
178 GvIAP	La-5F	39215236	A. N. Proskurin	Fót-S, 8:55-9:50, Bajna-Esztergom
179 IAP	Yak-9T	1515326	V. A. Alekseev	Süttő area, 09:40 LT, 2 *'Fw 190's*
187 GvShAP	Il-2m3	18842111	M. V. Hramushin	*Right cannon damaged, white '87'*
188 GvShAP	Il-2m3	1878979	V. V. Shavrukov+	Budapest, Kispest-S, 14:10LT, flak
282 OAPS	Po-2/U-2	3984	A. N. Danilushkin	Tarján, burned by 2 Fw 190s
452 BAP	A-20G-15	42-54250	A. D. Kovalevskii	Debrecen, hydraulics failure at RR

* At 13:50 LT eight 150 GvIAP Yak-3s (Yegorov, Konovalov, Tabakov, Ryabtsev, Ovsyannikov, Sergeev, Shamenkov, Verginskii) covered ground troops in the Bajna-Sárisáp area where they engaged in air combat with approximately ten Fw 190s and 12 Bf 109s. Gv.Lt. Yurii Nikolaevich Verginskii repelled the attack on his leader when two Bf 109s hit him. His Yak-3 (c/n: 1829217, engine: 422-501, white '18') caught fire and he bailed out with his parachute near Karva. While descending four Bf 109s opened fire, seriously wounding him. After a hard landing he was rushed to field hospital No.5258.

On 3 January 1945 the aerial war was in full swing over the Budapest-W, -NW area. Luftflotte 4 flew 300 sorties while the Soviet 5 and 17 VA committed all their available resources to provide aerial support to their ground forces in the Budapest, Bicske, Süttő, Bajna, Agostyán, Esztergom areas.[20] At Bajna a very intense tank-battle unfolded between the tank brigades of the Soviet 18th Tank Corps and the German 3rd SS-Pz. Division Totenkopf. Between 13:55-14:55 LT nine 90 GvShAP Il-2s led by Gv.Capt. Georgii Timofeevich Beregovoy attacked the German forces in the Bajót-Süttő area along the Danube at Budapest-NW.[21] Upon leaving the target the Soviet planes were engaged by two *Fw 190s* and two Bf 109s, but again, the very experienced flight-leader Gv.Capt. Beregovoy (HSU, later cosmonaut) lost no Il-2s. Their fighter escort was provided by six Yak-7s [*sic*!] of the 122 IAP.[22]

This day Maj. Gerhard Barkhorn was credited with two Il-2 and two Yak 9 victories. Although neither their times nor their locations are known and the Soviet fighter/Sturmovik losses to enemy fighters are great, these claims can be considered potential victories.

On 1 January 1945 the Germans led by the IV SS Panzer Corps launched their powerful and secretive Operation Konrad to liberate the encircled German-Hungarian garrison of Budapest. The otherwise very accurate and detailed late war Soviet Air Army documentation suddenly became somewhat backlogged, contradictive, or inconsistent. For instance on 3 January 1945 in the rapidly changing critical situation the 17 VA reported six La-5s missing, while one La-5 was lost in air combat.[23] At the same time the 10 ShAK of the 17 VA reported that their 116 IAP lost three La-5s in dogfights, one La-5 to flak and two La-5s in airfield accidents, while the 164 IAP lost one La-5 missing.[24] The 295 IAD reported that its 116 IAP lost three La-5s in dogfights (Ml.Lt. Schwarz, Popov, Boltyan), one La-5 went missing (Ml.Lt. Radchenko) and

20 The Soviets flew 1,886 sorties in total (5 VA: 1,154, 17 VA: 732). Dr. Számvéber Norbert, *Kard a pajzs mögött* (Veszprém: PeKo Publishing Kft., 2013), p. 68.

21 The nine Il-2m3s over Bajót-Süttő were piloted by Beregovoy, Prazhennikov, Fesenko, Gusev, Osipov, Ivanov, Sudorgin, Sadohin and Lopatin. Operations journal of 90 GvShAP for 1945, entry for 3 January 1945TsAMO RF: fu. 22219, inv. 0161830c, f. 3, p. 3.

22 The six Yak-7s mentioned in the 90 GvShAP war diary is probably a clerical error. On 1 January 1945 the 122 IAP had no Yak-7s, only five Yak-9T (c/n: 0815305, 0915396, 1015336, 1615361, 1715327), six Yak-9M (c/n: 2515349, 2615390, 2715378, 2815366, 3215349, 3215389) and six Yak-1B (c/n: 04168, 22172, 31180, 38179, 45170, 50160) fighters. The fighter escort on 3 January 1945 was most likely provided by six Yak-9s.

23 TsAMO RF: fu. 370, inv. 6518, f. 437, p. 22, Operations journal of 17th Air Army units for January 1945, entry for 3 January 1945, incl. combat losses.

24 TsAMO RF: fu. 370, inv. 6518, f. 210, p. 519, Operations review of 10 ShAK (incl. 295 IAD) for January 1945, incl. 116 and 164 IAPs for the month of January 1945.

one La-5 (Ml.Lt. Plankevich) crash-landed near the base due to engine failure. This plane was later repaired and returned into combat service.[25] These reports described the losses of the very same regiment from different levels within the 17 VA.

According to a mechanical record written on 4 January 1945, La-5F c/n: 39214687 was lost in a dogfight. Further records written on 5 January 1945 state that four 116 IAP La-5s (c/n: 3810811, 39214952, 39211114, 39211873) were lost in combat related crash-landings, while La-5FN (c/n: 39211446) was lost in a dogfight as well. Finally, a mechanical record written on 7 January 1945 states that La-5F (c/n: 392150100) was lost in a fatal airfield accident (Capt. Vladimir Alkseevich Novikov, KIFA).[26] Regardless of the documentation backlog resulting from the sudden onslaught of the German operation, all of these events took place on 3 January 1945.

4 January 1945 (Thursday)
Barkhorn's 296th: POTENTIAL VICTORY, La-5
Barkhorn's 297th: POTENTIAL VICTORY, La-5
Barkhorn's 298th: POTENTIAL VICTORY, La-5
Barkhorn's 299th: POTENTIAL VICTORY, Yak-9

Soviet 17 and 5 VA aircraft losses on 4 January 1945				
Regiment:	**Type:**	**c/n:**	**Pilot:**	**Details:**
530 IAP	La-5F	39215048	M. Y. Yefimov	Felsőgalla-E, 14:55 LT to Bf 109
530 IAP	La-5FN	39211920	F. F. Orlovskii	Bicske to Bf 109, crashed at Cece
530 IAP	La-5FN	39211023	A. P. Dyakov+	Vasztély, 09:30 LT, 8 '*Fw 190s*'
530 IAP	La-5FN	39211488	I. P. Vashenko	Martonvásár, 10:30 LT, 8 Bf 109s
530 IAP	La-5FN	39211399	A. S. Suhorukhov+	Tardos-Tarján, 11:12LT to Lipfert
611 IAP	Yak-1B	33192	M. F. Batarov WIA	Székesfehérvár, 08:20 LT, crashed
897 IAP	Yak-9T	0915316	P. M. Krugov	Börgönd, accident at 09:00 LT
897 IAP	Yak-9D	1615391	N. K. Konovalov	Bicske, after 12:10LT, 4 Bf 109s
897 IAP	Yak-9D	1615396	E. L. Samohvalov	Bicske, pilot returned on the 6th
210 ShAP	Il-2m3	18704106	I. A. Balakin	Bajna, downed by Bf 109s, '36'
210 ShAP	Il-2m3	12054	S. M. Kolobkov	Bia-W, Bf 109s, flak, '5'
210 ShAP	Il-2m3	10967	L. A. Philippovich	Bicske-W, '30', Bf 109s, Fw 190s
210 ShAP	Il-2m3	12052	N. I. Sokolov	Csepel-N, 1 km, flak, '7'
210 ShAP	Il-2m3	10987	L. K. Vorobiev	Kiskunlacháza, flak, CL, '15'
210 ShAP	Il-2m3	304836	V. V. Ivanov	Mány-N, CL, Bf 109s, '2'
210 ShAP	Il-2m3	18853106	I. A. Pavlov	Mány-NW, crash-landed, '35'
210 ShAP	Il-2m3	11425	N. P. Ivanov	Bajót-E, to Bf 109s at Bajna, '24'
210 ShAP	Il-2m3	10930	*V. K. Mihailyuk*	*Combat damages, repaired, '210'*
639 ShAP	Il-2m3	1870197	I. Y. Tarabrin	*Tarján, flak, – repaired*
639 ShAP	Il-2m3	*Unknown*	K. A. Gusev	Bánhida, flak, crash at Börgönd
639 ShAP	Il-2m3	*Unknown*	A. I. Kozhin	Bánhida, flak to Székesfehérvár
672 ShAP	Il-2m3	1871398	*Unknown*	*Damaged in combat, – repaired*
707 ShAP	Il-2m3	304822	S. V. Pigalev	Bánhida, 3 Fw 190s, CL 13:55 LT
715 ShAP	Il-2m3	11511	N. I. Soroka MIA	Budapest-SW, flak, '15'
715 ShAP	Il-2m3	11536	N. D. Moskvitchev+	Sárisáp-W, 08:22 LT, '21', Bf 109
951 ShAP	Il-2m3	1874287	N. A. Samoilov	Héreg-NW, 08:00LT, MIA
951 ShAP	Il-2m3	1870194	M. P. Petrakov	Héreg-NW, 08:05LT, flak at 200m
989 ShAP	Il-2m3	10430	I. A. Dzhanaev	Bajna, Bf 109, Herceghalom, '20'
989 ShAP	Il-2m3	11413	M. K. Artazian	Kiskunlacháza, Bf 109, '38'
989 ShAP	Il-2m3	12515	N. A. Bachurin	*Combat damages, repaired, '28'*
166 GvShAP	Il-2m3	1873995	A. P. Dudkin+	Bačka Palanka, flak at 10:36 LT, crash in mid-air collision
166 GvShAP	Il-2m3	*Unknown*	P. I. Buzrukov+	

25 TsAMO RF: fu. 20541, inv. 1, f. 83, pp. 80-81, Combat diary of 295 IAD, entry for 3 January 1945.
26 TsAMO RF: fu. 17 VA, inv. 6531, f. 36, p. 576, Fatal accident entry for Capt. Vladimir Alkseevich Novikov of 17th Air Army, 116th Fighter Regiment, 3rd Squadron at Kiskunlacháza airbase.

260 BAP	A-20G-25	43-9141	N. F. Semyonchuk	Bölcske-S, 11:46 LT, 2 Bf 109s
39 ORAP	Pe-2 82F	10/229	K. A. Smirnov	Madocsa, 1.2 km, engine failure
188 GvShAP	Il-2m3	11065	P. P. Nikolaev	*Combat damages, repaired, 1st Sq.*
188 GvShAP	Il-2m3	1877224	*Unknown*	*Combat damages, repaired, 1st Sq.*
92 IAP	La-5FN	39213325	V. F. Panov	*Ferihegy airport, LAC, repaired*

On 4 January 1945 the intense dogfights continued over the Budapest-NW area. The air was full of aircraft as Luftflotte 4 put in 500 sorties while the Soviets managed over 900.[27] Maj. Barkhorn was credited with three La-5s and one Yak-9 fighter at unspecified times in unspecified locations. The problem this day is the same, too many Soviet fighters were lost in Barkhorn's operational area to be able to accurately specify their exact identity. It is clear however, that if he correctly observed their types, his La-5 oppenents belonged to the 194 IAD's 530 IAP[28], while his Yak-9 belonged to the 288 IAD.[29]

5 January 1945 (Friday)
Barkhorn's 300th: OVERCLAIM, La-5

Soviet 17 and 5 VA (including Romanian) aircraft losses on 5 January 1945				
Regiment:	**Type:**	**c/n:**	**Pilot:**	**Details:**
116 IAP	La-5F	392149100	I. Kochetkov MIA	Missing at Nagykovácsi-WSW
611 IAP	Yak-9T	0815381	Oleg I. Shetinkin	Pusztaszabolcs, CL, Bicske: Bf 109
611 IAP	Yak-9T	0815355	N. A. Verbovitskii	Dunavecse, flak, CL, repaired*
639 ShAP	Il-2m3	1871598	M. I. Risev+	Tarján, flak, 'taran'on German tank
659 IAP	Yak-9D	0815393**	I. A. Stolyarov	Madocsa, LAC, Bf 109s
989 ShAP	Il-2m3	11559	I. Onikinenko WIA	Dorog, Bf 109s,'18', crew returned
989 ShAP	Il-2m3	18802121	M. S. Luchkovskii	Combat damages, repaired, '23'
131 GvShAP	Il-2m3	10752	Unknown	Combat damage, repaired at base
10 GvShAD	Po-2	9891	Unknown	CL, write-off by 5.1.1945
96 OKRAP	Po-2	7242	Unknown	CL, combat, write-off by 5.1.1945
331 IAD	Po-2	5580	N/A	Scrapped due to wear and tear
Escadrilla 41	Hs 129B	Unknown***	Adj. Const. Boghian	Losonc-S flak, damaged, repaired

* Ml.Lt. Nikolai Andreevich Verbovitskii was shot down in his Yak 9T (c/n: 0815355) on 22 January 1945 near Bugyi by Máthé László fhdgy. (Hungarian 102/1. FS Bf 109 ace) and was killed. It is entirely possible that he flew this exact aircraft on 5 January 1945 as well.

** The airframe was scrapped on 24 January 1945 without its engine.

*** Correspondence with Bernád Dénes (25 July 2021)

On 5 January 1945 due to poor weather conditions Luftflotte 4 could only put up 140 sorties this day.[30] The Luftwaffe only reported a few sightings of enemy aircraft which were mostly of the reconassiance type although a few fighters and attack planes were also seen,[31] thus explaining the sudden reduction in enemy aircraft losses. Maj. Barkhorn claimed a La-5 fighter without specifying any time or location details though only one La-5 was lost over Hungary: Ml.Lt. Ivan Yakovlevich Kochetkov's La-5F from the 116 IAP,[32] which went missing during a mission to the Nagykovácsi (Budapest-NW) area.[33] Hungarian Bf 109 fighter ace, Füleky Béla fhdgy. (CO of Hungarian 101/4. FS) approaching with his flight of four Bf 109s claimed a La-5 near Bicske at Nagykovácsi-W,-SW after attacking it from an approximately 1000m altitude advantage.[34] His claim was confirmed by his wingman, Lója Géza fhdgy. Yet more importantly, because Füleky's claim contains information which is comparable to the information found in the Soviet loss report, it is most likely that Maj. Gerhard Barkhorn's final documented claim of the war was an overclaim.

27 Norbert, *Kard a pajzs mögött*, p. 78.
28 TsAMO RF: fu. 17 VA, inv. 6531, f. 37, pp. 145, 173, Combat losses of 194 IAD (incl. 530 IAP), entry for 4 January 1945.
29 TsAMO RF: fu. 370, inv. 6518, f. 340, pp. 640-641., Operations journal of 288 IAD, entry for 4 January 1945.
30 Weather reported as hazy with obstructed visibility conditions. NARA T311/R160/7211987, 7211990.
31 NARA T311/R160/7211987
32 TsAMO RF: fu. 20541, inv. 1, f. 83, p. 87., Operations journal of 295 IAD, entry for 5 January 1945.
33 TsAMO RF: fu. 33, inv. 11458, f. 713, p. 26., Report of permanent 17th Air Army aircrew losses, entry for 5 January 1945.
34 Stenge Csaba, *Elfelejtett Hősök* (Budapest: HM Zrínyi kiadó, 2016), 2nd Ed, pp. 312-313.

Conclusion

Maj. Gerhard Barkhorn claimed 28 aerial victories during his service time over Hungary. He claimed his first victory on 26 October 1944 and the last one on 5 January 1945 which covers his combat career between his 273rd and 300th confirmed claims. Out of these 28 claims he had 22 victories and potential victories meaning that his claiming accuracy was around 80%. This percentage is remarkable not just because of the very high number itself, but because he achieved these victories in the late fall/early winter months in usually poor visibility conditions. His highest daily score of victories and potential victories was five planes on 16 November 1944. His six overclaims are spread among his victories evenly without following any specific pattern. Furthermore, in two cases of overclaiming the Soviet reports verify the damages made by enemy fighter to those exact planes that he claimed. This fact makes his claims reliable.

5

Wilhelm Batz (1916-1988)

Born on 21 May 1916, Hptm. Wilhelm Batz became the final Kommandeur of II./JG 52 on 1 February 1945. Batz arrived at Veszprém at the end of January to take up his new position much to the satisfaction of the other II./JG 52 pilots,[1] and during his time in Hungary made eight victory claims. It is possible that Hptm. Batz piloted the only Bf 109 K-4 aircraft to fly over Hungary as he crashed this plane shortly after relocating to Austria on the 1 April 1945.[2] He finished the war with 237 claimed victories,[3] flew 445 combat sorties,[4] was promoted to the rank of Major and went on to serve in the Bundeswehr.[5] Batz passed away on 11 September 1988.[6]

Wilhelm Batz's claims are compiled from the following sources listed in order of heaviest reliance:

- Luftwaffe Aces: claims and bibliographies, Vol. 1
- Die Geschichte der II. Gruppe des Jagdgeschwaders 52: Offizielle Ausgabe der Traditionsgemeinschaft JG 52
- Major Wilhelm Batz: Vom Fluglehrer zum Schwerterträger

Shot down 3rd Ukrainian Front, 17th Air Army Il-2m3 Sturmovik pilots in March 1945 over Hungary. (L-R:) St.Lt. Nikolai Anisimovich Pribilov (672 ShAP), crash-landed near Baracska on 13 March 1945 due to flak damages, unhurt. Ml.Lt. Lev Constantinovich Vorobiev (210 ShAP), lost to flak on 14 March 1945 near Seregélyes, KIA. Gv.Ml.Lt. Ivan Kirillovich Buryakovskii (989 ShAP), lost to flak and probably Fábián István zls., Hungarian Bf 109 ace on 19 March 1945 near Nádasdladány, KIA. Ml.Lt. Gennadiy Nikolaevich Pirogov (715 ShAP), lost to four 'Fw 190s' on 19 March 1945 at Csór-SE, MIA/KIA. (Photos: B. V. Davidov)

1 Franz Kurowski, *Major Wilhelm Batz: Vom Fluglehrer zum Schwerterträger* (Würzburg: Verlagshaus Würzburg GmbH & Co. KG, 2008), p. 144.
2 Kurowski, *Major Wilhelm Batz:*, p. 146.
3 Kurowski, *Major Wilhelm Batz*, p. 157. Batz's four claims against USAAF aircraft do not however appear on the microfilms, therefore his confirmed total is realistically 233.
4 Kurowski, *Major Wilhelm Batz*, p. 150.
5 Andrew-Johannes Mathews and John Foreman, *Luftwaffe Aces*, Vol. 1, p. 53.
6 Mathews and Foreman, *Luftwaffe Aces*, Vol. 1, pp. 52-53.

All the lists agree on claim dates and aircraft types. The claim number appearing in the Mathews & Foreman publication has been used. Batz made four unconfirmed claims over Allied aircraft hence the discrepancy in the final tally of the Mathews & Foreman listing.[7]

13 March 1945 (Tuesday)
Batz's 224th: POTENTIAL VICTORY, Il-2, Székesfehérvár
Batz's 225th: POTENTIAL VICTORY, Il-2, Székesfehérvár

Soviet 5 and 17 VA Il-2 losses on 13 March 1945 over Hungary				
Regiment:	**Type:**	**c/n:**	**Pilot:**	**Details:**
210 ShAP	Il-2m3	11584	V. T. Harchenko	Öregmajor-NW, flak, 15:10 LT, '33'
210 ShAP	Il-2m3	1887403	I. M. Mitrahovich	Rácalmás-SW, 12:00 LT, CL, No.'3'
639 ShAP	Il-2m3	18858106, 11503	P. F. Vorobiev WIA	Őcsény, flak at 14:20 LT
639 ShAP	Il-2m3		I. E. Geiher MIA	Balatonszabadi, flak, 14:20 LT
672 ShAP	Il-2m3	18870106	N. A. Pribilov	*Baracska, flak, 17:30 LT, CL, rep.*
672 ShAP	Il-2m3	1875499	E. V. Vaitsitskii	*Gárdony, flak, CL, repaired.*
672 ShAP	Il-2m3	11221	N. M. Barsuk	*Agárd, flak, 13:00 LT, CL, repaired*
951 ShAP	Il-2m3	1877483	S. F. Tumashev+	Agárd flak, Agárd-E, 08:00 LT
951 ShAP	Il-2m3	18854106*	A. P. Pulnii+	Agárd flak to Csiribpuszta, 14:00 LT
989 ShAP	Il-2m3	*Unknown*	V. I. Biryukov	*Combat damages, repaired, '3'*
989 ShAP	Il-2m3	*Unknown*	V. A. Vasilevskii	*Combat damages, repaired, '29'*
989 ShAP	Il-2m3	*Unknown*	I. K. Buryakovskii	*Combat damages, repaired, '24'*
130 GShAP	Il-2m3	18836115**	A. I. Proligin	Sárosd-SE at 11:20 LT, *Flakvierling*
131 GShAP	Il-2m3	12036	N. A. Titomirov	Nadap-NE, 10:26 LT, Bf 109s, CL
131 GShAP	Il-2m3	12206	F. I. Strelnikov	*Flak, CL at airbase, repaired*
131 GShAP	Il-2m3	12049	A. I. Zenin	Flak, *Fw 190s*, CL at base, scrapped
131 GShAP	Il-2m3	12632	V. N. Provalinskii	*Flak, CL at airbase, repaired*
131 GShAP	Il-2m3	1876367	I. P. Tsukanov	*Flak, CL at airbase, repaired*
190 GShAP	Il-2m3	*Unknown*	P. A. Davidov	Agárd flak, returned, later written-off
92 GvShAP	Il-2m3	*Unknown*	A. P. Kukovyakin	*Szolnok-NW, 10 km, CL, repaired*
92 GvShAP	Il-2m3	*Unknown*	V. S. Prusakov	*Tóalmás-E, 5 km, CL, repaired*

* This Il-2 with AM-38F engine: 258637 arrived in the 951 ShAP on 6 March 1945 from the reserve of the 17 VA. On 7 March 1945 Maj. A. I. Zabolotnov Deputy Reg. CO ordered the installation of an SCH-3 (c/n: 50618) IFF transponder on it. The plane was lost to flak on 13 March 1945 from a ten-plane flight led by Lt. Ivan Vasilevich Primakin and Capt. Aleksei Manuilovich Vephvadze, escorted by six 164 IAP La-5s.

** No. of one of its VYa-23 cannons was 'ИТ113' (Armament maintenance report on 25 February 1945).

On 13 March 1945 Hptm. Wilhelm Batz claimed two Il-2 Sturmoviks shot down over Hungary. The Soviet 5th and 17th Air Armies suffered twelve Sturmoviks permanently lost mainly to ground based anti-aircraft fire while many planes returned with serious combat damages and were later repaired. One of the Il-2s brought down by enemy fighters was shot down by Lt. Heinz Ewald. Hungarian Bf 109 ace Fábián István zls. (101/2. FS, Bf 109G-10/U4, WNr.: 613107, yellow '5') and Szentteleky Géza hdgy. (101/8. FS) also claimed Il-2s in the Lake Velence area. Although Hptm. Batz's opponents this time cannot be positively identified, it is possible that his Il-2 claims were potential aerial victories (131 GvShAP, c/n: 12036 and 12049).

14 March 1945 (Wednesday)
Batz's 226th: POTENTIAL VICTORY, Il-2
Batz's 227th: POTENTIAL VICTORY, Il-2
Batz's 228th: POTENTIAL VICTORY, Boston

7 Mathews and Foreman, *Luftwaffe Aces*, pp. 53, 56.

Soviet 17 VA Douglas A-20 Boston and Il-2 losses on 14 March 1945				
Regiment:	**Type:**	**c/n:**	**Pilot:**	**Details:**
260 BAP	A-20B	41-3626	F. I. Larin	*Repaired on airfield, lost on 31 March*
260 BAP	A-20G	43-21603	P. T. Zaharov WIA	Tatárszentgyörgy, HUN Bf 109 victory
260 BAP	A-20G	43-9274	N. P. Pavlov	Sombor, 3 km, CL, tail No.: red '4'
260 BAP	A-20G	42-86706	K. A. Tsallagov	Sárosd-NE, CL, exploded after 35 sec.
260 BAP	A-20G	43-21904	A. K. Morozov	*Kiskunlacháza, air-combat, repaired*
449 BAP	A-20B	41-3643	Appolon P. Pavlov	CL at Szabadszállás, tail No.: white '8'
861 BAP	A-20G	42-53664	Ivan Y. Isachenko	*Gunners bailed out, plane returned, '7'*
861 BAP	A-20G	42-86876	E. I. Kropanev+	Sárosd-SE to JG 52 Bf 109s
861 BAP	A-20G	43-21519	V. N. Bahvalov+	Pálinkaházpuszta-W to Lt. Düttmann
210 ShAP	Il-2m3	*Unknown*	S. S. Elohov	*AC not lost, flak damage, repaired, '10'*
210 ShAP	Il-2m3	18886107	V. I. Lemeshkin	'29', LAC with an 897 IAP Yak-9
210 ShAP	Il-2m3	18842110	Lev K. Vorobiev+	Seregélyes-SW, flak, 15:00 LT, '30'
210 ShAP	Il-2m3	11813	V. P. Godyaev	*AC not lost, flak damage, repaired, '39'*
210 ShAP	Il-2m3	12046	V. A. Leonov	*AC not lost, flak damage, repaired, '15'*
210 ShAP	Il-2m3	*18886119*	V. A. Tulenev	*AC not lost, flak damage, repaired, '17'*
210 ShAP	Il-2m3	11082	P. A. Taranovich	*AC not lost, flak damage, repaired, '8'*
615 ShAP	Il-2m3	11521	T. B. Kukacv+	Csiribpuszta, flak. 12 Il-2s, 6 La-5s
615 ShAP	Il-2m3	1874596	Ivan F. Brankov	Csiribpuszta-S, flak, 12 Il-2s, 6 La-5s
615 ShAP	Il-2m3	18801107	A. I. Zhigailo+	Csiribpuszta, flak. 12 Il-2s, 6 La-5s
672 ShAP	Il-2m3	12571	F. T. Mamontov+	Agárd-SE, 2 km , 17:25 LT, flak
672 ShAP	Il-2m3	1875688	P. S. Radchenko	Dinnyés, 2 Fw 190s, 14:35 LT, broken
672 ShAP	Il-2m3	1876788	Y. S. Makkoveev	Sukoró, dogfight, 17:10 LT
672 ShAP	Il-2m3	1877788	N. D. Botin+	Pákozd-S, in Lake Velence, 17:25 LT
672 ShAP	Il-2m3	1889203	M. Golobokov+	Dinnyés-SE, 2 km, flak, 17:25 LT
707 ShAP	Il-2m3	18827109	V. I. Markov+	Őcsény airfield, accident, 16:44 LT
715 ShAP	Il-2m3	18881124	V. I. Kochergin	Sárosd-SE, 3.5 km, flak, white '4'
715 ShAP	Il-2m3	12332	Pirogov-Statsenko	Detric flak, 15:00 LT, CL at Ercsi, '33'
715 ShAP	Il-2m3	12293	I. V. Krasnoperov	Pusztaszabolcs-S, 3 km, white '18'
96 OKRAP	Il-2KR	11933	L. S. Kulikovskii+	Pákozd, 11:56 LT, lost to Lipfert
165 GvShAP	Il-2m3	1871xxx	K. Sidelnikov	Drávaszabolcs-NE, 4 Il-2s, 4 Bf 109s
989 ShAP	Il-2m3	18874124	N. M. Zaharov WIA	Vértesacsa-NW, 4 km , flak, '100'
989 ShAP	Il-2m3	*Unknown*	Leoncio V. Hernans	*Spanish pilot, damaged, white '26'*
989 ShAP	Il-2m3	*Unknown*	N. I. Pahai	*AC not lost, flak damage, repaired, '16'*
989 ShAP	Il-2m3	*Unknown*	V. A. Kabelkov	*AC not lost, flak damage, repaired, '27'*
989 ShAP	Il-2m3	12293	I. P. Krasnoperov	Pusztaszabolcs-S, dogfight, '18'
Unknown	Il-2m3	*Unknown*	*Unknown*	Seregélyes to 210 ShAP Il-2, No.'13'*

* This previously force landed and abandoned Il-2 was discovered and destroyed from the air by the crew of pilot Ml.Lt. Boris Mihailovich Troitskii and aerial gunner Sgt. Kirill Kalinovich Dibrov flying 210 ShAP Il-2m3, No.'13' near Seregélyes over German held territory.

This day Hptm. Batz claimed two Soviet Il-2 Sturmoviks and an A-20 Boston bomber. Unfortunately neither time nor location details are known for his claims, yet because there are at least three Il-2m3 (c/n: 1875688, 1876788, 1877788) and two A-20G (S/N: 42-86706 and 42-86876) losses among the Soviet records which could match his claims, Wilhelm Batz's claims can be considered potential victories.

On 14 March 1945 very heavy air battles took place over the Southern shore of Lake Velence and in the wider Seregélyes areas. At 14:35 LT between 700-800m after their first attack on Dinnyés, Ml.Lt. Prokofii Spiridonovich Radchenko's Il-2m3 fell behind his formation and was immediately attacked by two *'Fw 190s'*. The pilot, Ml.Lt. Radchenko was injured, but his aerial gunner Constantin Nikolaevich Naumov could repel all further attacks of the fighters. The crippled Il-2 managed to return to the Tököl airbase South of Budapest where he conducted a successful belly landing. Since after crash landing their engine was still in good condition, it was later salvaged therefore its c/n was not recorded in the 672 ShAP's mechanical report as a permanent loss, only the plane's broken airframe (No.1875688).[8]

Later at 17:10 LT 11 Il-2s of 672 ShAP, escorted by six La-5s, met eight Bf 109s over Dinnyés around the Southern end of Lake Velence. Ml.Lt. Evgenii Sergeevich Makkoveev's Il-2m3 was hit, he turned to the right over the lake and crash-landed at Sukoró-S. The plane was a complete loss and repairs were not attempted.

At 17:25 LT at 1000m twelve other 672 ShAP Il-2s attacked Agárd and Csiribpuszta areas at Lake Velence-S. During their approach to the target Lt. Fedor Timofeevich Mamontov's Il-2m3 was hit by flak over Gárdony. The plane left its formation and crashed at Agárd-SE killing its entire crew.[9]

The other plane lost from this formation was Ml.Lt. Nikolai Dmitrievich Botin's Il-2m3 Sturmovik (c/n: 1877788, with original AM-38F engine: 255462),[10] which was built on 20 January 1944 and was assigned to the 672 ShAP by 1 October 1944 at the latest. During their attack on Dinnyés, flying between 600-400m, the plane was attacked by two Bf 109s which quickly shot it down. The Il-2 caught fire, turned to the right over the lake and fell in a steep dive towards Pákozd into the reeds of Lake Velence. Hegedűs József, then 14 years old and a former Pákozd resident, wittnessed the tragedy and could recall in details about the event even several decades afterwards:

> I have also seen the crash of this Il-2 from the Pákozd hillside. The planes bombed the railway line on the opposite shore of the lake. They received very heavy defensive fire, since many shells were exploding all around them. The burning Il-2 started to lose altitude from approximately 1 km towards the swamp. When it crashed, it spun around and splashed water and mud 15-20 meters into the sky. It sank within seconds. The crew did not bail out with parachutes and it was obvious right away that nobody could survive such a fatal fall and impact.

Since the tail section and some other parts of the wreck were still visible after the war, local residents regularly visited it during the winters when they could approach it on the frozen swamp in order to remove some useful parts for their houses until it became forgotten. Later it was re-discovered and everything that was accessible in the water under the rhizomes of the floating reed was recovered with the remains of the killed crew (Ml.Lt. Nikolai Dmitrievich Botin pilot [1922-1945] and Nikolai Petrovich Novikov aerial gunner) in April 2003.

For Hptm. Wilhelm Batz's A-20 Boston claim on 14 March 1945 there were two potential planes lost from the 17th Air Army's 244th Bomber Division:

861 BAP, A-20G-20-DO (S/N: 42-86876, R-2600-23 engines: 43-103292, 43-103250)
Ml.Lt. Evgenii Ivanovich Kropanev pilot (wounded, +)
Ml.Lt. Nikolai Ivanovich Stephanov navigator (+)
Sgt. Pavel Fedorovich Lopuhov radioman (wounded, +)
Sgt. Mamed Alekberovich Guseinov aerial gunner (returned)

On 14 March 1945 at 12:50 LT at 2400m sixteen A-20 Bostons of the 861 BAP led by Capt. Aleksandr Semyonovich Zolotarev and escorted by two 288 IAD Yak-9 fighters bombed Seregélyes. Upon leaving the target, the bombers were ambushed by a massive German fighter attack. The attackers consisting of approximately sixteen Bf 109s, Fw 190s and *Bf 110s* [*sic*!] hit Ml.Lt. Kropanev's left engine which immediately burst into flames. The wounded pilot belly landed his burning plane at Perkáta-W. His navigator/bombardier, Ml.Lt. Stephanov, was killed still in the air. According to some records aerial gunner Sgt. Guseinov survived the crash and returned to his unit, while others say the entire crew perished. This plane was possibly destroyed by Hptm. Wilhelm Batz. This A-20G Boston (S/N: 42-86876) was removed from the 244 BAD aircraft inventory in the 18 March 1945 mechanical report. The plane was built in Santa Monica, California, U.S.A. on 18 September 1943 and was delivered to the Soviet Union through Daggett and Nashville, USA.[11]

260 BAP, A-20G-20-DO (S/N: 42-86706, R-2600-23 engines: 43-102911, 43-103123)
Ml.Lt. Kazbek Aleksandrovich Tsallagov pilot (unhurt)
Lt. Pavel Efimovich Silin navigator (unhurt)

8 This mechanical report was created four days later on 18 March 1945.
9 Il-2, c/n: 12571 arrived to the 672 ShAP on 1 February 1945 from the main reserve of the 17 VA.
10 Ml.Lt. Botin's Il-2 was built on 20 January 1944 in Factory No.18 and was lost with its original engine.
11 Individual Aircraft Record Card: AAIR – Aviation Archaeological Investigation & Research, USA.

Lost 17 VA, 244 BAD, 260 BAP A-20G-25-DO Boston (S/N: 43-9274, R-2600-23 engines: 103897, 103769, red '4' near Sombor on 14 March 1945. (Photo: B. V. Davidov)

St.Sgt. Nikolai Ivanovich Mayorov aerial gunner/radioman (+)
C-a. Tihon Ivanovich Astredinov aerial gunner (unhurt)

Later this same day at 17:11 LT at 2000m thirteen A-20 Bostons of the 260 BAP led by St.Lt. Fedor Ilyich Kizim bombed Seregélyes as well. During the approach to the target over Dinnyés the Soviet formation received heavy anti-aircraft fire which hit Ml.Lt. Tsallagov's Boston's right engine and instantly killed the radioman, St.Sgt. Nikolai Ivanovich Mayorov. The crippled bomber left its formation and turned back to its own territory when three *Fw 190s* attacked it. Their attacks were repelled by the accurate defense fire of aerial gunner Tihon Ivanovich Astredinov, who later was promoted for his heroic action. The pilot, Ml.Lt. Tsallagov, finally belly landed at Sárosd-NE on Soviet controlled territory. The surviving crew members left the plane containing its full bomb load still onboard which blew up in a huge detonation only 30-35 seconds later. The plane was completely destroyed and the remains of St.Sgt. Mayorov were buried at Andormajor. This A-20G Boston was removed from the 244 BAD aircraft inventory in the 18 March 1945 mechanical report. The plane was built in Santa Monica, California, U.S.A. on 23 August 1943 and was flown to the Soviet Union through the South-Atlantic delivery route: Daggett, Memphis, Florida, the Caribbean, Brazil, Ascension Island, Nigeria, Egypt, Palestine, Iran and Baku, Azerbaijan.[12]

16 March 1945 (Friday)
Batz's 229th: OVERCLAIM, Il-2

Soviet 17 VA Il-2 Sturmovik losses on 16 March 1945				
Regiment:	**Type:**	**c/n:**	**Pilot:**	**Details:**
167 GvShAP	Il-2m3	*1871190*	I. F. Ivanov MIA	Felsőmiholjác area in Croatia, MIA
210 ShAP	Il-2m3	12229	I. M. Maksimov+	Csór, flak, Il-2m3, No.'38'
615 ShAP	Il-2m3	9958	G. A. Sibiryakov	Székesfehérvár-W, flak, 15:00 LT
672 ShAP	Il-2m3	1871494	*Unknown, 3rd Sq.*	*Combat damages, repaired at base.*
672 ShAP	Il-2m3	1871988	*Unknown, 3rd Sq.*	*Combat damages, repaired at base.*
672 ShAP	Il-2m3	1872787	*Unknown, 3rd Sq.*	*Combat damages, repaired at base.*
951 ShAP	Il-2m3	1874487	V. K. Botov+	Fehérvárcsurgó-Sárkeresztes, Hungarian Bf 109s (Tobak-Pintér) at 15:30 LT
951 ShAP	Il-2m3	11345*	V. I. Gladkii+	
989 ShAP	Il-2m3	1889701	I. K. Buryakovskii	Flak, No.'*24*'
989 ShAP	Il-2m3	11531	M. S. Luchkovskii	Flak, CL behind frontline, No.'15'
989 ShAP	Il-2m3	18874124	N. M. Zaharov WIA	Vértesacsa-NW, 14:20 LT, No.'100'

* According to the January 1945 weapon inspection report the numbers of the installed weapons of Il-2m3 c/n: 11345 were ЖН-38, ЖН-33 (23mm VYa-23s), КГ-146 (7.62mm ShKAS). (TsAMO RF)

12 Individual Aircraft Record Card: AAIR – Aviation Archaeological Investigation & Research, USA.

On 16 March 1945 Hptm. Batz claimed an Il-2m3 Sturmovik destroyed. Since all of the lost Il-2s this day were downed by flak, allocated to somebody else, or after being repaired on their base they returned to combat service, the 16 March claim of Hptm. Batz is most likely an overclaim.

19 March 1945 (Monday)
Batz's 230th: POTENTIAL VICTORY, Il-2
Batz's 231st: POTENTIAL VICTORY, La-5

Soviet 17 VA Il-2 and single-engine fighter losses on 19 March 1945				
Regiment:	**Type:**	**c/n:**	**Pilot:**	**Details:**
116 IAP	La-5F	39215049	A. N. Sidorovskii+	Szigetcsép, 6 La-5s, 4 *'Fw 190s'*
116 IAP	La-5FN	39211166	V. Ozhiganov MIA	Székesfehérvár, 6 La-5s, 4 *'Fw 190s'*
166 GvShAP	Il-2m3	9873	V. S. Philippov+	*Brčko*-E, ~5 km, flak over the target
267 IAP	Yak-1B	35169	D. D. Tormahov	Matty-Illocska, missing in combat
31 IAP	La-5FN	39211550	A. Chebakov WIA	Székesfehérvár, flak, 4 Bf 109s, CL
615 ShAP	Il-2m3	18735100	I. F. Brankov MIA	Székesfehérvár-SW, 08:05 LT, flak
639 ShAP	Il-2m3	11530	A. N. Zharov+	Őcsény, KIFA, hit electrical wires
672 ShAP	Il-2m3	1885503	U. H. Haidarov	*Zámoly, 8:00 LT, 8 Bf 109s, repaired*
715 ShAP	Il-2m3	18819118	P. T. Grebenko+	Nádasdladány-N, Hungarian Bf 109s
715 ShAP	Il-2m3	11485	G. N. Pirogov MIA	Csór-SE, 16:56 LT, 4 *'Fw 190s'*
848 IAP	La-5FN	39211860	E. A. Ruhovets+	Óhodos-puszta, 10:00 LT to flak,'60'
866 IAP	Yak-3	310062	V. S. Lukyanov	Székesfehérvár-N, 7:40 LT, 8 Bf 109
866 IAP	Yak-3	310167	I. F. Chernii+	Csór-S to flak. Koldunov's 8 Yak-3s
951 ShAP	Il-2m3	1878187	V. A. Fomin MIA/+	Bodajk area, hillside in low clouds
951 ShAP	Il-2m3	1871783	E. T. Bragin	*Szigetcsép-N, flak, 08:00 LT, repair.*
989 ShAP	Il-2m3	18835124	I. K. Buryakovskii+	Nádasdladány-N, Hungarian Bf 109s

On 19 March 1945 Hptm. Wilhelm Batz claimed one Il-2 and one La-5 fighter shot down. This day the Soviet 31 IAP lost one La-5FN, the 116 IAP lost two La-5 fighters in dogfights near Székesfehérvár. St.Lt. Aleksei Matveevich Chebakov's La-5FN was hit by flak. As he turned back for home over Székesfehérvár his plane was attacked and shot down by four Bf 109s. The crash-landing plane was destroyed, but its engine was salvaged. Pilot Chebakov was slightly injured. Over Szabadbattyán between 600-800m while escorting 306 ShAD Il-2 Sturmoviks, the La-5 pair of Ml.Lt. Victor Vasilevich Ozhiganov and Lt. Andrey Nazarovich Sidorovskii of 116 IAP were suddenly ambushed by four 'new model *Fw 190s*'. Ozhiganov's La-5FN was hit, went into a diving spin and crashed at Szabadbattyán. Lt. Andrey Nazarovich Sidorovskii's La-5F was also hit but he could return to the Tököl airbase area where his M-82F engine (c/n: 65033144) quit. Crash-landing near Szigetcsép, he died later of his wounds and was buried in Tököl. One of these three La-5s and one of the lost Il-2m3 Sturmoviks could be Hptm. Wilhelm Batz's legitimate aerial victories for 19 March 1945.

Conclusion

Maj. Wilhelm Batz was a very skilled and successful German fighter pilot and fighter instructor. He had over 230 aerial victory claims of which only a very small portion were over Hungary. Since the details of these claims (other than their dates and the aircraft types) are unknown, this makes his victory analysis very challenging. Despite most of these claims being potential victories, since no documents refute the possibility that Batz actually destroyed these aircrafts due to the lack of detail specifying the locations and/or times of Batz's claims, there is insufficient evidence for a detailed investigation for our current analysis.

6

Peter Düttmann (1923-2001)

Born on 23 May 1923 Peter Düttmann joined JG 52 in 1943 at the appointment of Hermann Graf.[1] Altough he was shot down several times he became one of the top scoring aces of 5./JG 52, he was thus awarded the Ritterkreuz on 9 June 1944 shortly after his 21st birthday. On 13 November 1944 he was 'shot down' by an Il-2 Sturmovik around 12:40 LT which forced him to use his parachute and returned to his unit on 28 January 1945. He flew 1570 flights, 398 combat sorties, was hit/ downed by enemy fire no less than 22 times,[2] and personally claimed 152 aerial victories including two tanks![3] Moreover, he also claimed 43 unconfirmed victories including another tank.[4] Peter Düttmann passed away on 9 January 2001.

Heinz Ewald's claims are compiled from the following sources listed in order of heaviest reliance:

- Luftwaffe Aces: claims and bibliographies, Vol. 1
- Die Geschichte der II. Gruppe des Jagdgeschwaders 52: Offizielle Ausgabe der Traditionsgemeinschaft JG 52
- Tony Woods – Eastern Front Vol 4. 1944. Jul – Dec, Issue 1

The claim numbering as found in the Mathews & Foreman publication has been used.

16 October 1944 (Monday)
Düttmann's 104th: VICTORY, LaGG-5 at Derecske-SW at 15:50 LT, at 2500m, Anerk Nr. 436
Düttmann's 105th: OVERCLAIM, LaGG-5 at Derecske-S at 15:54 LT, at 2000m, Anerk Nr. 437

Soviet 5 VA single-engine fighter losses on 16 October 1944				
Regiment:	**Type:**	**c/n:**	**Pilot:**	**Details:**
178 GvIAP	La 5FN	392121142	Y. Y. Gukalin+	Szeghalom-SW, LAC to '*Fw 190*'
179 IAP	Yak-9M	2715334	D. Maksimenkov+	Torda-S, LAC due to flak damage

On 16 October 1944 at 15:50 and 15:54 LT Lt. Peter Düttmann claimed two La-5s shot down in the Derecske (Debrecen-S) area, where severe battles took place during the day.

16.10.44г. Гв.л-т ГУКАЛИН подбит в воздушном бою, тянул на свой аэродром. сорвался в штопор и упал в 6 км.с.з.Шереш. Самолет Ла-5 № 21142 разбит, летчик погиб.

Gv.Ml.Lt. Yevgenii Yefremovich Gukalin's loss entry in the 3 GvIAK records as Peter Düttmann's confirmed aerial victory. (TsAMO RF: fu. 327, inv. 4999, f. 177, p. 27, Operations rewiev of 3 GvIAK for October 1944, entry for 16 October 1944).

1 Christer Bergström, *Graf and Grislawski: A Pair of Aces* (Hamilton, Montana: Egales Editions Ltd., 2003), p. 167.
2 Mathews and Foreman, *Luftwaffe Aces*, p. 248.
3 Falk Klinnert, *Peter Düttmann, "Bonifazius": Wir Kämpften In Einsamen Höhen* (Leipzig: Fips-Druck, 2002), p. 235.
4 Klinnert, *Peter Düttmann, "Bonifazius*, p. 235.

Capt. Boris Ivanovich Lozorenko's Il-2m3 Sturmovik, white '65' of the 5 VA, 568 ShAP (after 27 October 1944: 187 GvShAP), 2nd Squadron that he flew on 16 October 1944 over Derecske. This time his aerial gunner was Gv.Sgt. Stepan Fedorovich Ryabov. Note the attractive 'Smolensk' logo of the 2nd Squadron planes and the regiment's general, red marking on the tail's leading edge. (Photo: Units and planes: <http://ava.org.ru/shap/187g.htm>)

Between 15:10-16:20 LT La-5s of 178 GvIAP led by Gv.St.Lt. Pyotr Romanovich Setinin patrolled in the Berettyóújfalu area where at 15:45 LT they became involved in aerial battles with four Bf 109s. The Bf 109s hit and injured Gv.Ml.Lt. Yevgenii Yefremovich Gukalin whose plane did not crash immediately but turned back for home. Just before reaching the airfield, his La-5 fell into a spin and crashed at Szeghalom-SW, 1.5 km, killing its pilot, or crashed with him alraeady dead or unconscious. Since Gukalin's La-5 was the only lost 5 VA La-5 of this battle, Peter Düttmann's second La-5 claim of the day is an overclaim.

Soon after this between 16:23-16:28 LT, nine Il-2 Sturmoviks of the 568 ShAP 2nd 'Smolensk' Squadron led by Capt. Boris Ivanovich Lozorenko, escorted by two 279 IAD La-5s attacked the Derecske-SE area.[5] Almost at the same time between 16:26-16:30 LT eight Il-2 Sturmoviks of the 568 ShAP 1st Sq. led by Capt. Sergei Alekseevich Feoktistov, escorted by two 279 IAD La-5s attacked the Derecske-N area.[6] They destroyed two vehicles and caused six large fires. The attacks were repeated by flights of seven and eight Il-2s of the 873 ShAP.[7] Capt. Vladimir Stephanovich Palagin's eight Il-2s with four La-5s of the 192 IAP attacked enemy vehicles from 1000m on the Eastern and Northern edge of Derecske. During their strike Ml.Lt. Polikarp Polikarpovich Nikolaev's Il-2 (c/n: 11065) was attacked by two *'Fw 190s'*, but his aerial gunner, Sgt. Mihail Aleksandrovich Baranov managed to repell both of their attacks. As they left Derecske to the South their Il-2 was attacked again by two patrolling Bf 109s. This time the fighters were very persistent, and they struck the Il-2 four times. Although Sgt. Baranov was seriously injured, the crew could return to their airbase where they successfully belly landed. The damaged plane was repaired by Gv.Ml.Mech.Lt. Gavriil Matveevich Yagodzinskii's mechanic team and later as part of the 188 GvShAP, recieved further damages during its 4, 22 January and 27 March 1945 missions and eventually survived the war. Several Il-2 pairs of the 231 ShAD escorted by La-5s of the 192 IAP flew reconnaissance sorties in the Derecske, Szolnok, Újszász, Jászladány, Törökszentmiklós, Abony, Kecskemét, Kiskundorozsma and Kiskőrös areas. During one of these sorties 192 IAP La-5 pilot St.Lt. Nikolai Vasilevich Smirnov shot down a *Fw 190* at Kocsér-S, Kecskemét-NE. The 231 ShAD Il-2 ground attack formations over Derecske were escorted by La-5 pairs of the 192 and 486 IAPs, while the 92 IAP was relocating to their new airfield at Szarvas and flew no combat mission during the day. One 279 IAD La-5 went missing, but later was repaired and returned to its airbase.

18 October 1944 (Wednesday)
Düttmann's 106th: OVERCLAIM, Yak-9 at Mikepércs-N at 13:30 LT, at 2200m, Anerk Nr. 439
Düttmann's 107th: OVERCLAIM, Yak-9 at Mikepércs-NE at 13:34 LT, at 2300, Anerk Nr. 440

Soviet 5 VA single-engine fighter losses on 18 October 1944				
Regiment:	**Type:**	**c/n:**	**Pilot:**	**Details:**
149 GvIAP	Yak-7B	5315329	A. A. Sokolov	Hajdúszoboszló-S, Szeghalom-SW, 14:10 – 15:15 LT, in dogfight
149 GvIAP	Yak-9D	17166057	R. I. Kolechkin	
149 GvIAP	Yak-9D	17166071	P. I. Kozlov WIA	Derecske-W, 14:40 – 16:10 LT
486 IAP	La-5F	39214770	F. I. Nikonorenkov+	Nagylak, KIFA at 14:13 LT

5 The nine 568 ShAP, 2nd Squadron Il-2s were white 65, 68, 70, 75, 73, 60, 72, 74 and 69. Lozorenko flew in Il-2 No.65. TsAMO RF: fu: 22416, inv. 222544c, f. 2, p. 66, Combat register of 187 GvShAP, entry for 16 October 1944. The 568 ShAP was re-organized as 187 GvShAP on 27 October 1944.

6 The eight 568 ShAP, 1st Squadron Il-2s were white tail No.60, 51, 52, 59, 56, 54, 57 and 50. Feoktistov flew in Il-2 No.60. TsAMO RF: fu: 22416, inv. 222544c, f. 2, p. 68, Combat register of 187 GvShAP, entry for 16 October 1944.

7 TsAMO RF: fu. 20512, inv. 1, f. 90, pp. 227-228, Operations journal of 231 ShAD, entry for 16 October 1944.

178 GvIAP	La-5F	39214628	G. E. Karnauhov	*Damaged in dogfight, repaired*

On 18 October 1944 Lt. Peter Düttmann claimed two Yak-9 fighters shot down in the area North of Mikepércs – both of which turn out to be overclaims as their reported times were too early compared to the verified losses of the 5 VA. One of them, Gv.Ml.Lt. Aleksandr Antonovich Sokolov's Yakovlev Yak-7B (2nd Sq., c/n: 5315329, engine: 33-1506) at around 14:40 LT was one of the last combat losses of the Yak-7 model in Hungary.

19 October 1944 (Thursday)

Düttmann's unconfirmed: OVERCLAIM, La-5 at Szolnok at 08:00 LT[8]

Düttmann's 108th: OVERCLAIM, Yak-7 at Debrecen-W,-NW at 09:21 LT, at 2900m, Anerk Nr. 441

Soviet 5 VA single-engine fighter losses on 19 October 1944				
Regiment:	**Type:**	**c/n:**	**Pilot:**	**Details:**
178 GvIAP	La-5FN	39212311	F.G. Semenov MIA	Debrecen-W, 11:25 LT to fighters
92 IAP	La-5FN	39211101	G. G. Tokarev MIA	Debrecen-N, 13:10 LT, 4 Bf 109s

On 19 October 1944 Lt. Peter Düttmann claimed a La-5 and a Yak-7 fighter at 08:00 and 09:21 LT, which can be verified as overclaims due to the large differences from the time reported by the 5 VA for the day.[9] Note, that the 3 GvIAK summary report gives the wrong c/n for Gv.Capt. Fedor Georgievich Semenov's lost La-5FN: 39212331.[10]

21 October 1944 (Saturday)

Düttmann's 109th: OVERCLAIM, Yak-11 at Szolnok-S,-SE at 10:56 LT, at 3500m, Anerk Nr. 443

Düttmann's 110th: POTENTIAL VICTORY, Yak-11 at Szolnok-S at 10:58 LT, at 3500m, Anerk Nr. 444

Soviet 5 VA single-engine fighter losses on 21 October 1944				
Regiment:	**Type:**	**c/n:**	**Pilot:**	**Details:**
192 IAP	La-5F	39214225	A. S. Sukoviants	Szentes-SE, CL, 10:25 LT, 8 *Fw 190s*
486 IAP	La-5FN	39213343	V. Grushkin WIA	Gyoma-NW, CL, 11:05LT, 6 *Fw 190s*

On 21 October 1944 Lt. Peter Düttmann claimed two 'Yak-11' fighters at 10:56 and 10:58 LT in the Szolnok area. According to their records, the Soviet 5 VA lost no Yakovlev fighters this day only two La-5s. One of them piloted by Ml.Lt. Vasilii Mihailovich Grushkin, white '43', was lost during a reconnaissance mission between Mezőtúr and Túrkeve (Szolnok-SE) when six *'Fw 190s'* attacked their flight at 11:05 LT. At this time four La-5s were escorting two Il-2s. Grushkin's plane was hit, he was slightly injured and crash-landed at Gyoma(endrőd)-NW, 6 km. The plane was written off and the pilot was taken to the hospital of the 442 BAO. This incident took place only seven minutes after Düttmann's reported victory time, just a few kilometres East of his reported area. This La-5FN could be a misidentified, but potential victory for Peter Düttmann, however the other claim must have been an overclaim as the time gap between the two lost La-5s was fourty minutes, not two, as documented in Düttmann's claim.

It is however possible that the two escorted 'Il-2s' were in fact the pair of one Il-2KR and one Yak-9D of the 207 OKRAP which patrolled over the Tisza river-crossing at Szolnok at 10:50 LT.[11] It is also possible that Lt. Peter Düttmann claimed this 207 OKRAP Yak-9D shot down as a 'Yak-11' over Szolnok-S,-SE at 10:56 LT, however this plane successfully returned to its base.

Beside these actions there was another big aerial battle in the area during the day: six Yak-1B and Yak-9D fighters of the 85 GvIAP led by Gv.Capt. Anatolii Ustinovich Constantinov covering Soviet ground troops in the Szarvas-Túrkeve area. North of Szarvas they met a large group of Fw 190s, which were about to bomb their Szarvas-S airfield. In the unfolding and wild defensive dogfight the Yaks (Constantinov, Ryabov and Mazan) downed three Fw 190s without a single loss of their own.[12]

23 October 1944 (Monday)

Düttmann's 111th: OVERCLAIM, Il-2 at Szolnok-SE at 15:34 LT, at 600m, Anerk Nr. 448

8 18:00 LT according to Bernd Barbas, *Die Geschichte der II. Gruppe des Jagdgeschwaders 52: Offizielle Ausgabe der Traditionsgemeinschaft JG 52* (Überlingen: Self-published, 2003), p. 369.

9 TsAMO RF: fu. 20062, inv. 1, f. 33, p. 174, Operations journal of 178 GvIAP, entry for 19 October 1944.

10 TsAMO RF: fu. 327, inv. 4999, f. 177, p. 27, Operations review of 3 GvIAK for October 1944, entry for 19 October 1944.

11 TsAMO RF: fu. 22444, inv. 383420c, f. 2, p. 13, Operations journal of 207 OKRAP, entry for 21.10.44.

12 Gv.Capt. Mihail Semyonovich Mazan (HSU) was killed on 12 December 1944 at 10:43 LT at Tápiószentmárton in his Yak-1B (c/n: 05173). This time the Mazan-Minin pair took off to identify some unknown multi-engined planes near their airfield and during return in the cloudy, foggy weather Mazan hit the ground and was killed instantly. It is also possible that he was downed by enemy bombers.

Soviet 5 VA Il-2 losses on 23 October 1944				
Regiment:	**Type:**	**c/n:**	**Pilot:**	**Details:**
131 GvShAP	Il-2m3	10620	A. Lapinskii POW	Szolnok-E, 15:32 LT to Lipfert
131 GvShAP	Il-2m3	302820	V. I. Kralkin KIA	Szolnok-E, 15:31 LT to Lipfert
131 GvShAP	Il-2m3	1873563	V. P. Zubov	*Returned to airbase, major repair*
132 GvShAP	Il-2m3	18753100	S. D. Pilipets KIFA	14:35LT, take off accident, burned

On 23 October 1944 Lt. Peter Düttmann claimed an Il-2 at 15:34 LT at Szolnok-SE. The time of his claim matches Hptm. Helmut Lipfert's double attack on the flight of six 131 GvShAP Il-2 Sturmoviks, in which two Il-2s were lost while a third one required a major repair after limping back to its airbase. Since Htpm. Lipfert's victory exploded and the disintegrated victims did not survive his strikes, Lt. Peter Düttmann had to attack the third plane which returned to its airbase with serious damages and was repaired afterwards. This plane was Gv.Lt. Victor Petrovich Zubov's aircraft from the 2nd Squadron of the 131 GvShAP, which returned to its base with serious combat damages and without the aerial gunner, Gv.Ml.Sgt. Nikolai Mihailovich Gusev, who bailed out with his parachute and went missing. Although Lt. Peter Düttmann seriously hit and damaged this aircraft, his Il-2 is an overclaim.[13] The two 188 GvShAP reconnaissance Il-2s which were attacked by six Fw 190s and four Bf 109s over Tószeg at 300m at 13:25 LT both returned to their airfields. From there two escorting 192 IAP La-5s Lt. Nikolai Vasilevich Smirnov (La-5FN, c/n: *39212274*) was shot down and bailed out with his parachute, while Ml.Lt. Afanasii I. Kudryavtsev returned to his airfield successfully.

30 October 1944 (Monday)

Düttmann's 112th: OVERCLAIM, MiG-3 at Nyíregyháza-W at 13:21 LT, at 1000m
Düttmann's 113th: OVERCLAIM, MiG-3 at Nyíregyháza-S, -SE at 13:24 LT, at 200m

Soviet 5 VA aircraft losses on 30 October 1944				
Regiment:	**Type:**	**c/n:**	**Pilot:**	**Details:**
279 IAD	La-5FN	39211362	*Unknown*	Szolnok area, CL after a dogfight
31 GvIAP	Yak-1B	21151	E. V. Yerofitskii	Kunszentmárton-NE, flak, CL, 13:50
151 GvIAP	Yak-9T	1415399	A. V. Kozlov	Tiszaföldvár-E, Bf 109, ~11:40LT, CL
132 GvShAP	Il-2m3	301476	M. F. Borisenko+	Jászkarajenő, 15:20 LT to 5 Bf 109s
451 ShAP	Il-2m3	9971	N.Myagkostupov+	In mid-air collision over their airfield after return. Only Dodashev bailed out.
451 ShAP	Il-2m3	1874978	V. F. Artemin+	
48 BAP	A-20G	42-53856	I. M. Frolov+	MIA, lost to Gefr. Wagner (5./JG 52)
48 BAP	A-20G	42-54197	L. L. Nikolaev	Kisköre to Pottyondy szds.,14:00 LT

On 30 October 1944 Lt. Peter Düttmann claimed two 'MiG-3' fighters at 13:21 and 13:24 LT in the Nyíregyháza area. Since the 5 VA had no MiG-3s in service by October 1944 and the lost Yakovlevs crashed at different times, both misidentified 'MiG-3's of Lt. Peter Düttmann appear to be overclaims. What is known is that the Soviet 5 VA initially reported the following losses at the end of the day: two La-5s, two Yaks, one Il-2 and two A-20G Bostons failed to return from combat missions.[14] The 279 IAD reported the loss of a single La-5, while the other La-5 which belly landed has no supporting documentation suggesting it was permanently lost. As such it currently must be considered an overclaim. It is possible that they were those two 192 IAP La-5s (including Ml.Lt. Afanasii Ivanovich Kudryavtsev's), which were escorting two 188 GvShAP reconnaissance Il-2s in the Kecskemét-Sári area and got into a dogfight with ten Bf 109s. The exact reason why Lt. Düttmann claimed MiG-3 fighters is unknown, this type of fighter was outdated by the later stages of the war, the VA's over Hungary did not use them, moreover the VVS-KA did not loose a single MiG-3 in combat for the year 1944.[15] There is some indictation that Lt. Peter Düttmann enjoyed adding new models of aircraft to his tally, possibly being the reason why he claimed MiG fighters.[16] During the day the 48 BAP lost two A-20G Bostons which were flying alone. St.Lt. Ivan Mihailovich Frolov's Boston was lost to Gefr. Wagner (5./JG 52) at 10:09 LT at 1500m. This crew (Frolov, Soroka, Kuharev and Slonyaev) was flying in the Nyíregyháza, Miskolc, Losonc, Eger areas. At 09:19 LT they reported the weather conditions to their base. Later at 09:40 LT they transmitted unintelligible radio messages as the background gunfire noises overpowered the signal. The connection was lost and the plane went missing.

13 TsAMO RF: fu. 20039, inv. 1, f. 22, p. 181, Operations journal of 7 GvShAD staff, entry for 23 October 1944.
14 TsAMO RF: fu. 327, inv. 4999, f. 225, p. 43, Operations journal of 5 VA for October 1944, entry for 30 October 1944.
15 Carl-Fredrik Geust, Gennadiy Petrov, *Lend-Lease aircraft in Russia: Red Stars,* Vol. 4 (Tampere, Finland: Apali Oy, 2002), p. 186.
16 Klinnert, *Peter Düttmann "Bonifazius": Wir Kämpften In Einsamen Höhen*, p. 185.

31 October 1944 (Tuesday)
Düttmann's 114th: OVERCLAIM, Il-2 at Szolnok-SE at 08:21 LT
Düttmann's unconfirmed: POTENTIAL VICTORY, Il-2 at Cegléd-E at 14:15 LT[17]
Düttmann's 115th: POTENTIAL VICTORY, Il-2 at Cegléd-SE at 14:17 LT
Düttmann's 116th: POTENTIAL VICTORY, Il-2 at Nagykőrös-N at 14:19 LT

Soviet 5 VA Il-2 losses on 31 October 1944				
Regiment:	**Type:**	**c/n:**	**Pilot:**	**Details:**
130 GvShAP	Il-2m3	8280	D. S. Popov MIA	Nagykőrös, flak, 14:00 LT, 8 Il-2s
130 GvShAP	Il-2m3	9788	A. N. Yeremeev+	Nagykőrös, flak, 14:00 LT, 8 Il-2s
131 GvShAP	Il-2m3	10752	A. N. Korchagin	Nagykőrös-S, 13:50 LT to 4 *Fw190s*
187 GvShAP	Il-2m3	12172	A. G. Lubishev MIA	Kecskemét-SE, lost to fighters, '56'
190 GvShAP	Il-2m3	11035	A. F. Berezhovskii	Gyoma, LAC, flak, Bf 109s, 13:55 LT
190 GvShAP	Il-2m3	1871479	N. A. Bachurin MIA	Kecskemét-SE, 13:55 LT, 18 Bf 109s
190 GvShAP	Il-2m3	303830	P. D. Suhodolskii+	Kecskemét-SW, 13:55 LT, 18 Bf 109s

On 31 October 1944 Lt. Peter Düttmann claimed one Il-2 at Szolnok at 08:21 LT in the morning and three other Il-2s in only four minutes between 14:15-14:19 LT in the Cegléd-Nagykőrös area. This day the Soviet 5 VA reported eleven missing Il-2 Sturmoviks, however only a few of them became permanent losses as the rest later returned to their airfields and into combat service.[18] During the day German and Soviet planes battled several times with losses on both sides.

At 13:50 LT eight 131 GvShAP Il-2s led by Gv.Capt. Mihail Yegorovich Nikitin escorted by four La-5s were attacked by four *'Fw 190s'* at six kilometers South from Nagykőrös. The German fighters hit the rudder of Gv.Ml.Lt. Andrey Nilantevich Korchagin's Il-2m3 (c/n: 10752, AM-38F engine: 257472) which crash-landed and was later repaired. Aerial gunner Gv.Ml.Sgt. Yurii Arhipovich Melnikov was wounded.

Just before 14:00 LT eight 190 GvShAP Il-2s led by CO of 2nd Sq. Gv.Capt. Aaron Savelevich Dubnov flew a combat mission in the Izsák-Fülöpszállás-Solt-Akasztó area. Over Kecskemét-SW, 300m at 13:55 LT, the Soviet planes were attacked by eighteen Bf 109s. This time the Il-2s had no fighter escort which turned out to be a fatal mistake. The Bf 109s attacked the first group of four first led by Ml.Lt. Davidov and downed pilot Gv.Ml.Lt. Pavel Dmitrievich Suhodolskii's and aerial gunner Sgt. Dmitrii Ivanovich Savchuk's Il-2m3 which crashed at Kecskemét-SW. Both crewmen perished. Two aerial gunners, St.Sgt. Adov and Ml.Sgt. Volkov each claimed a Bf 109 shot down. The Bf 109s gained altitude and attacked the Il-2s again. This time they strucked the second four and downed Gv.Lt. Nikolai Aleksandrovich Bachurin Il-2m3 with aerial gunner Sgt. Nikolai Grigorevich Sushkov which left the formation and disappeared over Soviet controlled territory. They then attacked Gv.Ml.Lt. Aleksandr Philippovich Berezhovskii's Il-2 which was previously damaged by flak over Ballószög, Kecskemét SW. In order to avoid further hits, the pilot put his plane into a steep dive. At this point his aerial gunner Ml.Sgt. Constantin Constantinovich Temerev, thinking that his pilot was dead, bailed out from their plane and was killed. Gv.Ml.Lt. Berezhovskii finally recovered from the dive and flew his damaged plane home alone and crash-landed at Gyomaendrőd. He was injured and his Il-2m3 (c/n: 11035, AM-38F engine: 258843) was written off. The remaining five Il-2s returned and landed safely on their airfield.[19]

At 14:00 LT eight Il-2s of 130 GvShAP, led by Gv.Capt. Aleksandr Ivanovich Proligin flew info intense anti-aircraft fire over Nagykőrös. Two Il-2s piloted by Gv.Ml.Lt Dmitrii Stepanovich Popov and Gv.Ml.Lt. Anton Nikolaevich Yeremeev were hit by flak, shot down and went missing. The Germans reported Il-2 and LaGG [*sic!*] activity around this location throughout the day, with 6.-8./ Flak.Abt. 24 spotting fourteen Il-2s and ten LaGG-3s between the hours of 07:00-14:00 LT.[20] These spottings must have included the 130/131 GvShAP flights along with their escorts.

Eight Il-2s of the 188 GvShAP led by Gv.Capt. Vladimir Stepanovich Palagin, escorted by four 177 GvIAP La-5s, attacked ground targets in the Nagykőrös-Cegléd area between 15:10 and 16:20 LT. Here the Soviet planes met several Bf 109s and Fw 190s, but despite the wild unfolding dogfight and three badly damaged planes (Suchkov, Tsukerov, Mayorov) none of the Il-2s were lost.[21]

Confirming exactly which Il-2s were destroyed by Lt. Peter Düttmann is difficult. His morning Il-2 is an overclaim and none of his afternoon claims match the Soviet Il-2 losses by time and location either. However, we can suppose that he was involved in the destruction of some Il-2s within the 20-30 minutes timeframe around 14:00 LT. Ironically, his

17 This is not unconfirmed in *Die Geschichte der II. Gruppe des Jagdgeschwaders 52: Offizielle Ausgabe der Traditionsgemeinschaft JG 52.*
18 TsAMO RF: fu. 327, inv. 4999, f. 225, p. 118, Operations journal of 5 VA for October 1944, entry for 31 October 1944.
19 TsAMO RF: fu. 20057, inv. 1, f. 55, pp. 247-248, Operations journal of 231 ShAD, 5 VA, 2nd Ukr. Front, entry for 31 October 1944.
20 15. Flakdivision (mot) Abt. Ia op 2, Flaklagemeldung vom 31.10.1944. TsAMO RF: fu. 500, inv. 12472, f. 345. pp. 141a/b.
21 The eight 188 GvShAP Il-2 pilots were: Palagin, Bolotaev, Mayorov, Tsukerov, Gurzhii, Prokofiev, Suchkov and Shavrukov. TsAMO RF: fu. 20057, inv. 1, f. 55, pp. 248-249, Operations journal of 231 ShAD, 5 VA, 2nd Ukr. Front, entry for 31 October 1944.

claiming times were closer to those 130 GvSAP Il-2s which went down to anti-aircraft artillery at Nagykőrös not to fighters. Although downed before his claims, the three lost 190 GvShAP Il-2s could have been shot down by him with a four-minute window after 13:55 LT, therefore these are potential aerial victories.

1 November 1944 (Wednesday)
Düttmann's unconfirmed: OVERCLAIM, Yak-9 at Kecskemét-E at 14:02 LT[22]
Düttmann's 117th: OVERCLAIM, Yak-9 at Kecskemét-N at 14:03 LT, at 2000m
Düttmann's 118th: OVERCLAIM, Yak-9 at Abony-S,-SW at 14:05 LT, at 3500m
Düttmann's 119th: POTENTIAL VICTORY, Yak-9 at Nagykőrös-S at 14:06 LT, at 2500m
Düttmann's 120th: OVERCLAIM, Il-2 at Kecskemét-E at 14:09 LT, at 1000m

Soviet 5 VA Il-2 and single-engine fighter losses on 1 November 1944				
Regiment:	**Type:**	**c/n:**	**Pilot:**	**Details:**
177 GvIAP	La-5F	39215336	E. I. Batyunya WIA	Szolnok, to Hungarian Bf 109
177 GvIAP	La-5	*Unknown*	M. V. Danshin	*Later returned, AC not lost!*
73 GvIAP	Yak-9D	18166046	Unknown, 1st Sq.	*Damaged, repaired on its airfield*
73 GvIAP	Yak-1B	08175	A. S. Andrianov	Lakitelek-NW to 8 Bf 109s
85 GvIAP	Yak-1B	*Unknown*	B. I. Gelkin	*Later returned, AC not lost!*
235 ShAP	Il-2m3	10472	V. I. Astahov MIA	Zagyvarékas flak to Törtel, 12:50LT

On 1 November 1944, in a four-minute window, Lt. Peter Düttmann claimed four 'Yak-9' victories in the Abony-Kecskemét area. This day eight Yaks led by Gv.Maj. Zuev and two of his flight-leaders, Gv.Lt.Col. Boris Nikolaevich Yeryomin and Gv.Lt. Aleksandr Semyonovich Andrianov of the 6 GvIAD, covered the Soviet ground forces in the Kecskemét-N, Méntelek area at 4500-6000m. Over Nagykőrös they met eight Bf 109s which missed the leading Yak-3 but hit Andrianov's Yak-1B (c/n: 08175, engine: 345-2353). The seriously injured pilot bailed out, landed on enemy territory and was taken prisoner but later returned to his unit. The dogfight area matches Lt. Peter Düttmann's victories, not to mention that Andrianov's 73 GvIAP had another fighter damaged in air combat during the day. This suggests that Andrianov's Yak-1B could be Düttmann's authentic aerial victory, however his other three were definitely overclaims, as was his Il-2 claim at 14:09 LT.

7 November 1944 (Tuesday)
Düttmann's 121st: OVERCLAIM, La-5[23] at Abony-N,-NE at 16:05 LT, at 1700m

Soviet 5 VA permanent single-engine fighter losses on 7 November 1944				
Regiment:	**Type:**	**c/n:**	**Pilot:**	**Details:**
150 GvIAP	Yak-3	3229214	E. A. Pyankov WIA	Lajosmizse, 12:19 LT, 1400m, 4 Fw
92 IAP	La-5FN	39211227	M. A. Kazanovskii	Szarvas-SE, 15:00 LT, 800m

Düttmann went on to claim a La-5 victory at Abony-N,-NE at 16:05 LT. This day at 15:00 LT four 92 IAP La-5s escorted two Il-2s on their reconnaissance mission to Szarvas. Over the city at 800m Capt. Mihail Afanasevich Kazanovskii's La-5FN burst into flames and crashed in the SE outskirts of Szarvas. Capt. Kazanovskii bailed out and landed safely. Since neither Düttmann's reported claim time (an hour later), nor his reported area (over 50km NE of Kazanovskii's crash site) matches the Soviet fighter losses of the day, this victory is an overclaim. If the reported aircraft type of Yak-9 found in the microfilm list is examined, the end result is also an overclaim.

13 November 1944 (Monday)
Düttmann's 122nd: POTENTIAL VICTORY, Yak-11 at Tápiószele-S,-SW at 09:02 LT, at 4000m
Düttmann's 123rd: OVERCLAIM, Yak-11 at Tápiószele-S,-SW at 09:05 LT, at 4000m
Düttmann's 124th: OVERCLAIM, Il-2 at Jászberény-N at 12:20 LT, at 1500m

22 This is not unconfirmed in *Die Geschichte der II. Gruppe des Jagdgeschwaders 52: Offizielle Ausgabe der Traditionsgemeinschaft JG 52*.
23 Yak-9 according to Tony Woods O.K.L. Fighter Claims: Eastern Front Eastern Front Vol 4. 1944. Jul – Dec, Issue 1.

Soviet 5 VA aircraft losses on 13 November 1944				
Regiment:	**Type:**	**c/n:**	**Pilot:**	**Details:**
122 IAP	Yak-9M	2715382	N. M. Grishaev	Take-off accident (Külső-Kiritó)
149 GvIAP	Yak-1B	11186	A. T. Kotlyar POW	Jászberény, 13:55-14:50 LT
149 GvIAP	Yak-1B	*42178*	Stepanov, returned	Abony-N, 12:55 LT, 6 Bf 109s
149 GvIAP	Yak-9D	3615390	O. D. Kadagidze	Ferry flight accident near Karcag
150 GvIAP	Yak-3	3529218	N. A. Kireev, WIA	Ócsa, 8:41LT, 6 Yak-3, 13 Bf 109s
150 GvIAP	Yak-9D	1815358	Nikolai S. Yegorov	Nagykáta, 11:54 LT, 8 Fw 190s
179 IAP	Yak-9M	2715317	Svistkov, returned	Újszász-E (flak at Jászberény)
179 IAP	Yak-9T	0215354	E. I. Teplishev MIA	Zsámbok-SW, 13:50 LT, 8 Bf 109s
177 GvIAP	La-5FN	41210201	B. G. Kalinin+	Újszász, Hun. Bf 109 (Halasi S.)
187 GvShAP	Il-2m3	18827113	A. D. Bukanov+	Zsámbok-S, 13:45 LT, '88'
235 ShAP	Il-2m3	10454	N. F. Burkanov+	Jászberény, flak in a house, 10:30L
451 ShAP	Il-2m3	1873177	M. S. Chechenev	Besenyszög-E, flak at 12:50 LT
809 ShAP	Il-2m3	9947	S. I. Vasilevich	Kunmadaras, CL, ferry flight acc.
207 OKRAP	Il-2KR	1xxxx	S. I. Gromov	*6 fighters at 15:15 LT, repaired*
48 GvORAP	Pe-2	12/278	N. N. Shukin	Mezőtúr-N, lost to friendly-fire*
13 GvIAD	Po-2/U-2	640808	*Unknown*	13 GvIAD HQ, to enemy fighter

* While returning over the front line at 6000m this 48 GvORAP Pe-2 was downed by a 73 GvIAP Yak-9D by error. Radio operator Ibrahimov's parachute failed to open, while aerial gunner Potamonov went down with the plane. Pilot Shukin landed successfully with his parachute and returned to his unit.

On 13 November 1944 Lt. Peter Düttmann flew as an escort for Hs 129 ground attack aircraft when he claimed two 'Yak-11' and one Il-2 victory.[24] At 08:41 LT over Ócsa at 3500m six Yak-3s of the 150 GvIAP met thirteen 'yellow-nose' Bf 109s. While protecting his leader, Gv.Lt. Nikolai Aleksandrovich Kireev's Yak-3 was hit by a pair of Bf 109s and caught fire, the pilot bailed out with parachute and landed among his own troops who rushed him to hospital. This Yak-3 ('Yak-11') could be Lt. Peter Düttmann's legitimate aerial victory. But because the other 5 VA fighter losses of the day do not match Peter Düttmann's second fighter claim, it was an overclaim along with his Il-2. Interestingly, Düttmann was 'downed' by an Il-2 which deployed its PTAB bombload into the oncoming attaker.[25] Later during the day the 150 GvIAP engaged again in air combat with German fighters over Jászberény. This time eight Yak-3s led by regiment commander Gv.Lt.Col. Anton Dmitrievich Yakimenko fought with 16 Fw 190s and six Bf 109s. The Soviet pilots claimed seven enemy planes shot down without suffering any combat losses. Yakimenko himself claimed a Bf 109 shot down by firing at it from between 200m and 50m in the Nagykáta area.[26]

8 March 1945 (Thursday)
Düttmann's 125th: OVERCLAIM, Yak-3 at Aba-SW, 3 km at 16:24 LT
Düttmann's 126th: OVERCLAIM, Yak-3 at Aba-S, 4 km at 16:27 LT

Soviet 17 VA single-engine fighter losses on 8 March 1945				
Regiment:	**Type:**	**c/n:**	**Pilot:**	**Details:**
31 IAP	La-5F	39215012	I. P. Kapustyanskii	Tököl airfield collision at landing
866 IAP	Yak-3	310099	V. V. Yablochkin+	Zichyújfalu, ~14:30 LT, Bf 109s
897 IAP	Yak-9T	0815354	G. Kondratev WIA	Dömsöd, 14:45 LT, HUN Bf 109
117 GvIAP	Yak-1B	xx1xx	B. V. Fyodorov	*Donji Miholjac, Croatia, returned*

On 8 March 1945 Lt. Peter Düttmann claimed two Yak-9 fighters, though the Soviet combat reports do not support his claims. One La-5F was lost in an airbase landing accident, one Yak-3 and one Yak-9T were lost in dogfights, but at

24 Klinnert, *Peter Düttmann "Bonifazius*, p. 173.
25 Klinnert, *Peter Düttmann "Bonifazius*, p. 173.
26 TsAMO RF: fu. 33, inv. 690306, storage 1293, record 41994126, p. 296, Front Order, entry for Gv.Lt.Col. Anton Dmitrievich Yakimenko, signed on 14 May 1945.

Wrecks of a 150 GvIAP Yak-3 (c/n: 310305, white '05', engine: 432-652) in the forest at Horpács on 25 March 1945 after a take-off accident with Yak-3, c/n: 4629227. Pilot, Gv.Lt. Boris Vladimirovich Smirnov seriously injured in the crash. (Photos: Boris V. Davidov)

A 897 IAP Yak-3 (c/n: 6529233, '65') with typical smaller, 'Saratov-style' digits in Austria. This plane arrived in May 1945 and was listed in the 1 July 1945 quarterly aircraft inventory report of its unit. (Photo: Units and planes, http://ava.org.ru/iap/897.htm (accessed 22 November 2021)

different times and locations. At 14:20 LT eight Yak-3s led by Capt. Ivan Fedorovich Panin covered Soviet ground troops in the Seregélyes-NE area where they met eight Bf 109s. In the dogfight Lt. Victor Vasilevich Yablochkin's Yak-3 was hit, his plane trailed white smoke, lost altitude and went out of sight. After the battle Capt. Panin saw a big, unidentified explosion on the ground. It is believed that Yablochkin's Yak-3 crashed near the railway station of Zichyújfalu, East of Seregélyes.

At 14:40 LT over Börgönd an 897 IAP reconnaissance pair (St.Lt. Georgii Ivanovich Kondratev and Ml.Lt. Georgii Semyonovich Eliseenkov) were attacked by four, presumably Hungarian, Bf 109s. Kondratev's Yak-9T was hit and he crash-landed two kilometers South of Kiskunlacháza with some bruises. His Yak-9T was written off. His plane was probably downed by Hungarian Bf 109 ace Kálmán István zls. (101/7. FS) at 14.45 LT at Dömsöd-NE, or South of Kiskunlacháza airfield, where Kondratev tried to return to. At this time Kondratev's 897 IAP was stationing on the Kiskunlacháza airfield.

As we could see in these events, the Soviet 17 VA's fighter losses on 8 March were not related to Düttmann's actions. But between 16:05 and 17:00 LT, six 866 IAP Yak-3s led by Maj. Aleksandr Ivanovich Koldunov covered Soviet troops in the Sárosd area where heavy dogfight developed between the Yak-3s and Bf 109s.

At 16:20 LT at 2200 m, the Soviet fighters (Koldunov, Rabinov, Polosenko, Patsiba, etc.) ambushed twelve Bf 109s near Káloz and downed many of them. Although they could also have made overclaims, three opening parachutes indicated that at least three planes were downed/claimed. The attacked Bf 109s most likely belonged to 6./JG 52, including Lt. Peter Düttmann, but Hungarian Bf 109s were also present in the area. The Hungarians lost, as one example, Bf 109G-10 (WNr: 610571, white '4', 101/8. FS) piloted by Inkey Viktor hdgy. who went missing in the Káloz-Soponya area.

The timeframe and the location of this big dogfight at Aba-W,-SW definitely matches Peter Düttmann's two Yak-3 'victories', yet this time the Soviet fighters suffered no permanent losses.[27] This means that both of Düttmann's 125th and 126th victories were overclaims.

Interestingly, Maj. Aleksandr Ivanovich Koldunov (1923-1992) was one of the most famous and successful Soviet fighter aces of the Second World War. He received the title of the 'Hero of the Soviet Union' (HSU) twice and became the Chief Marshal of Aviation and commander of the Soviet Air Defence Force. His long and colourful career abruptly ended in 1987 when a German teenager, Mathias Rust with his Cessna F172P (c/n: F17202087, registered: D-ECJB) landed illegally on the Red Square in Moscow, bypassing the entire Soviet air defence system.

9 March 1945 (Friday)

Düttmann's 127th: OVERCLAIM, La-5 at Káloz-E, 12 km at 13:51 LT
Düttmann's 128th: POTENTIAL VICTORY, Il-2 at Káloz-E, 18 km at 13:53 LT

Soviet 5 and 17 VA losses on 9 March 1945				
Regiment:	**Type:**	**C/N:**	**Pilot:**	**Details:**
452 BAP	A-20G-15	42-54225	V. I. Tulskii	Csór to Málik József, Bf 109 ace*
452 BAP	A-20G	*Unknown*	Y. V. Suhov	*Damaged by Hung. fighter, repaired*
453 BAP	A-20G-15	42-54189	V. G. Kochanov+	Missing, perhaps in Lake Balaton**
453 BAP	A-20G-10	*42-53927*	Y. P. Prokofiev	*CL at Alcsút, evacuated, repaired****
453 BAP	A-20G-15	*42-54221*	M. L. Kakulia	*Landed at Dunaföldvár*****
453 BAP	A-20G	*Unknown*	M. I. Guberman	*Returned on its left engine, repaired*
453 BAP	A-20G	*Unknown*	V. K. Yurchenko	*CL on Soviet fighter airfield, repaired*
260 BAP	A-20G-20	42-86687	M. P. Roi	Sombor-SW, TOA, exploded, '5'
449 BAP	A-20C-10	42-33326	N. S. Avdoshin	Polgárdi flak to Bácsbokod,13:50 LT
861 BAP	A-20G-36	43-10085	V. I. Lesnichii	*Polgárdi flak damage, CL, rep.*, '30'
715 ShAP	Il-2m3	11928	A. Y. Zabludovskii	Sárosd-N, '1', 14:15 LT, 12 Bf 109s
715 ShAP	Il-2m3	18805120	G. N. Pirogov	*Combat damages, repaired, '36'*
210 ShAP	Il-2m3	11610	P. A. Taranovich	Dunapataj, 08:00LT, repaired, then Hatvanpuszta, 14:55 LT, Bf 109,'27'
210 ShAP	Il-2m3	11610	V. A. Indyushkin+	
210 ShAP	Il-2m3	1875098	Sergei S. Elohov	Sárkeresztúr-W, 2 km, flak, '51'
639 ShAP	Il-2m3	11545	H. M. Musin+	Taszár-N, flak into forest, 12:00 LT
672 ShAP	Il-2m3	1871494	U. H. Haidarov	Hippolit, 08:20 LT, flak at 400 m
672 ShAP	Il-2m3	18889114	N. M. Barsuk	Seregélyes flak, 08:40 LT to Tököl-S
951 ShAP	Il-2m3	1874888	I. V. Golubev+	Belsőbáránd-SE, flak, 07:33 LT

27 TsAMO RF: fu. 20257, inv. 1, f. 46, pp. 358-359, Operations journal of 288 IAD, entry for 8 March 1945.

Soviet 5 and 17 VA losses on 9 March 1945 (*continued*)				
951 ShAP	Il-2m3	1871794	S. T. Karpachev	Perkáta-W, flak, 15:35 LT
951 ShAP	Il-2m3	11076	B. G. Iutin unhurt	Seregélyes flak to Taksony,13:05 LT
989 ShAP	Il-2m3	11477	G. Nelazhskii MIA	Káloz, flak,11:20, '32', ex-995 ShAP
989 ShAP	Il-2m3	10586	C. Martínez Fierros+	Káloz, flak, Spanish pilot, '19'
989 ShAP	Il-2m3	11395	S. S. Tereshin	Pusztaszabolcs, 10:15 LT, ~flak
989 ShAP	Il-2m3	*Unknown*	L. V. Lipnitskii	*Combat damages, repaired, '6'*
166 GShAP	Il-2m3	1875895	I. M. Abdulin	*Repaired, to Yugoslavia by 27.04.45*
131 GShAP	Il-2m3	9726	F. I. Strelnikov	*Combat damage, repaired, 1st Sq.*
131 GShAP	Il-2m3	1875776	A. N. Dotsenko+	Adony, mid-air-collision, 13:30 LT
131 GShAP	Il-2m3	1877953	I. P. Tsukanov	*Mid-air-collision, 13:30 LT, repaired*
131 GShAP	Il-2m3	1873774	A. M. Skleptchuk	*Flak damage, repaired, 3rd Sq.*
187 GShAP	Il-2m3	1879273	I. D. Harchenko	Pusztavacs, '92', gunner killed
188 GShAP	Il-2m3	18896112	A. M. Mayorov	*Flak damage, repaired*
6 GvIAD	Yak-7B	821224	N/A	*Scrapped due to wear and tear*
73 GvIAP	Yak-9D	18166051	G. K. Chuiko MIA	Börgönd, ~12:25 LT to Bf 109s

* On 9 March 1945 A-20G Bostons of the 218 BAD bombed Várpalota, the repair and logistics-base of the 'Spring Awakening' offensive. The 48 BAP still suffered no losses, but the 452 BAP was attacked by Hungarian Bf 109 fighters. Málik József hdgy. (Bf 109G-14 (WNr.: 512644, 'W-1+71') downed St.Lt. Vasilii Ivanovich Tulskii's A-20G at Csór, which crossed the Danube and burned at Tételalja.

** The 453 BAP's 17 (Prokofiev's eight and Lozovenko's nine) Bostons received very intense anti-aircraft fire near Várpalota which damaged most of their planes. Seeing this, flight leader St.Lt. Storchilo left his group and headed home. Flight leader St.Lt. Victor Gavrilovich Kochanov (2nd Sq., Lozovenko's group) was attacked by three Bf 109s and went missing after a wide descending turn to the left at Várpalota-NE. Since Kochanov's grave is now located in Balatonfüred, it is possible that after his turn he crashed in Lake Balaton and his body was later washed ashore. Perhaps the 'American bomber' in the lake at Tihany-E was his A-20G. After an investigation, St.Lt. Storchilo was locked up for three days for breaking formation which resulted the loss of St.Lt. Kochanov, who probably became the victim of the Bf 109s.

*** Lt.Col. Prokofiev's lead-bomber was also seriously damaged by flak over Fehérvárcsurgó. He left the group and his place in the formation was taken over by Maj. Perederii. Soon after this Prokofiev landed his Boston at Alcsút with over 600 shrapnel holes in its airframe. When the Germans approached the area, the local Soviet commander gave the mechanics an hour to evacuate their plane otherwise it would have to be blown up. Lt. V. P. Aloshenko's mechanics disassembled the plane, put it on trailers right on time and left the scene. The Boston was repaired in ten days and returned to combat service.

**** St.Lt. Mihail Levanovich Kakulia's plane was damaged by Bf 109s and landed at Dunaföldvár for repair, later returning to Rákóczifalva. It was ultimately lost near Brno on 25 April 1945 when Bf 109s of I./JG 52 shot down three 453 BAP A-20G Bostons: 42-53953, 42-54221 and 43-9781. S/N 43-9781 was received as a replacement on 20 April 1945 from the 7 VA, 114 GvBAP in the North.

On 9 March 1945 Lt. Peter Düttmann was credited a La-5 and an Il-2 in the Káloz area. His La-5 victory is obviously an overclaim, since the 17 VA did not lose any fighters on 9 March. His Il-2 victory is however unclear. The 17 VA lost twelve Il-2s this day, interestingly losing one of them twice! Out of these twelve losses, three 136 ShAD Il-2s are potential candidates for his victory based on the reported locations and/or times.[28]

The 210 ShAP Il-2m3 (c/n: 1875098, AM-38F engine: 258066, white '51'), piloted by Ml.Lt. Sergei Stepanovich Elohov was hit by flak over the Soponya-Káloz road, and crash-landed at Sárkeresztúr-W, 2 km. The aerial gunner, Nikolai Dmitrievich Gritsenko was wounded. No fighters were reported lost.

Between 14:15-14:28 LT eight 715 ShAP Il-2s led by Maj. Aleksandr Ilevich Zabludovskii, escorted by Capt. Pantelkin's eight 116 IAP La-5s, attacked enemy vehicles in the Guja-Bodakajtor-Felsőszentiván-Tác-Soponya area. Leaving the target, Maj. Zabludovskii was attacked by *'Fw 190s'*. The plane was shot down and crash-landed at Sárosd-N, 4km. His aerial gunner, Nikolai Nikolaevich Zastavnoi was wounded. Earlier this plane was transferred from the disbanded 995 ShAP. Il-2 piloted by Ml.Lt. Gennadii Nikolaevich Pirogov was also hit, but successfully returned to their airbase.[29]

28 TsAMO RF: fu. 370, inv. 6518, f. 440, pp. 62-78, Operations journal of the 17th Air Army units for March 1945, entry for 9 March 1945.
29 Pilots/Il-2 markings: Zabludovskii/1, Murashko/5, Terehov/2, Godyaev/11, Korolev/33, Philippov/31, Pirogov/36 and Kochergin/39. TsAMO RF: fu. 22926, inv. 188593c, f. 2, p. 14, Combat report of 715 ShAP staff, 2nd entry for 9 March 1945.

Spanish pilot Lt. Celestino Martínez Fierros of 17 VA, 989 ShAP in front of his Il-2m3 Sturmovik. His plane was marked '19' on its fuselage, having white spinner color, just like this 989 ShAP Il-2m3 seen beside. The white squadron color was repeated on the front side of the main wheels' housing too. Note the 989th regiment's standard, three stripes tail marking. The long, flat tail wheel fairing indicates this Il-2 was also built in Factory No.1, having c/n something like 1xxxx, just like the three lost 989 ShAP planes on 9 March 1945, including Lt. Martínez's, which was shot down by flak near Soponya, Hungary, where his crew is buried in the Soviet military cemetery. (Photos: Authors' collection)

Finally, five Il-2s of 989 ShAP, led by St.Lt. Anatolii Alekseevich Ievskii attacked the Soponya, Pinkócpuszta, Rózsamajor (Káloz-S,-SW) areas, when Il-2m3 (c/n: 10586, AM-38F engine: 256838, white '19') was hit by flak. The plane ran into the ground among the German flak batteries near Soponya and exploded on impact. The crew of Spanish aviator Lt. Celestino Martínez Fierros and Ml.Sgt. Vasilii Kuzmich Velmezov perished.[30] No enemy fighters were involved in their loss.[31]

Based on this information, the only remaining option for Düttmann's Il-2 victory on 9 March 1945 is 715 ShAP Il-2m3 (c/n: 11928, AM-38F engine: 2510625, white '1'), piloted by Maj. Aleksandr Ilevich Zabludovskii. The area was near to Düttmann's reported location, however there is a time difference of between 22 and 35 minutes and twelve '*Fw 190s*' reportedly downed them, which was a regular size formation for the JG 52 fighters. We can consider this Il-2 as a potential victory for Peter Düttmann.

11 March 1945 (Sunday)
Düttmann's 129th: OVERCLAIM, Yak-9 at Káloz-SE, 6 km at 13:21 LT[32]
Düttmann's unconfirmed: OVERCLAIM, Yak-9 at Szabadbattyán-SW at 13:23 LT
Düttmann's unconfirmed: OVERCLAIM, Yak-9 at Polgárdi-S at 13:26 LT

Soviet 5 and 17 VA single-engine fighter losses on 11 March 1945				
Regiment:	Type:	c/n:	Pilot:	Details:
92 IAP	La-5FN	39213272	P. I. Orlov	Vecsés, LAC, repaired in 2 hrs
179 IAP	Yak-1B	47163	V. K. Korol	Vecsés, 2 km, 10:05 LT CL, '47'
177 GvIAP	La-5F	39214627	F. M. Telnih+	Dunakeszi, 16:00 LT, LAC, KIFA
611 IAP	Yak-9M	3315386	N. N. Kutsenko+	Simontornya-SE, 14:25 LT to Bf 109
866 IAP	Yak-3	310233	A. D. Piorunskii	Sárbogárd, 3000 m, to Hptm. Lipfert
866 IAP	Yak-3	310xxx	N. G. Surnev	Simontornya, damaged by Lipfert
866 IAP	Yak-3	310xxx	T. K. Gatitskii	Dogfight at 15:00 LT, later returned
164 IAP	La-5FN	39214947	P. M. Taikov	Burned on its airfield due to flak
530 IAP	La-5FN	39211581	G. F. Lesniak	Bugac puszta-NW in take-off accident
56 IAP	La-5FN	39211638	G. I. Dunaev	Őcsény, lost in a ferry-flight accident

On 11 March 1945 Lt. Peter Düttmann claimed three Yak-9 victories, which all turn out to be overclaims due to location/time and cause of destruction differences.

30 Lt. Celestino Martínez Fierros (1915-1945) was trained in the 4th (and last) Spanish aviator class of the Azerbaijan Aviation School at the end of the Spanish Civil War and stayed in the Soviet Union, where he later joined the Soviet Air Force among many Spanish aviators.
31 TsAMO RF: fu. 20174, inv. 1, f. 37, p. 276, Summary of operations of 989 ShAP, entry for 9 March 1945.
32 15:21 LT according to Die Geschichte der II. Gruppe des Jagdgeschwaders 52: Offizielle Ausgabe der Traditionsgemeinschaft JG 52, p. 372.

14 March 1945 (Wednesday)
Düttmann's 130th: VICTORY, A-20 Boston at Aba-N, 8 km at 12:55 LT

Soviet 17 VA Douglas A-20 Boston losses on 14 March 1945				
Regiment:	**Type:**	**S/N:**	**Pilot:**	**Details:**
260 BAP	A-20B	41-3626	F. I. Larin	*Landed on right wheel, field repair*
260 BAP	A-20G	43-21603	P.T. Zaharov WIA	Tatárszentgyörgy to Hungarian Bf 109G
260 BAP	A-20G	43-9274	N. P. Pavlov WIA	Zombor, 3 km, CL, red '4'
260 BAP	A-20G	42-86706	K. A. Tsallagov	Sárosd-NE, 17:11 LT, CL & blown up
260 BAP	A-20G	43-21904	A. K. Morozov	Engine damage in dogfight, returned OK
449 BAP	A-20B	41-3643	Appolon P. Pavlov	CL at Szabadszállás to Lt. Heinz Ewald
861 BAP	A-20G	42-53664	I. Y. Isachenko	*Gunners bailed out, plane returned, '7'*
861 BAP	A-20G	42-86876	E. I. Kropanev +	Sárosd-SE to JG 52 Bf 109s at 12:55 LT
861 BAP	A-20G	43-21519	V. N. Bahvalov +	Pálinkaházpuszta-W to Lt. Düttmann

On 14 March 1945 at 12:55 LT 8 km North of Aba, Lt. Peter Düttmann claimed an aerial victory over a Soviet A-20 Boston bomber. According to his logbook he was involved in a 'free hunt' in the Veszprém area and fought against 15 Bostons and two '*Yak-9*'s. This day at 12:50 LT at 2400m 16 A-20 Boston bombers of the 861 BAP led by Capt. Aleksandr Semyonovich Zolotarev bombed the approximately 80 trucks from the German transport vehicle concentration in the village of Seregélyes. The purpose of this attack was to cut the fuel and ammunition supply line of the German panzer divisions fighting South of Seregélyes in the Sárosd-Cece-Simontornya-Ozora areas which were frustrating the ground forces of the 3rd Ukrainian Front. The Bostons' fighter escort consisted of six 659 IAP Yak-3 fighters led by flight-leader Lt. Fyodor Vasilevich Sergeev.[33] Over the target the Soviet formation received very intense anti-aircraft fire which hit Lt. Vladimir Nikolaevich Bahvalov's A-20G-35-DO Boston (S/N: 43-21519, R-2600-23 engines: 43-105954 and 43-105698, built on 18 March 1944 in Santa Monica, CA, USA).[34] As the bomber formation left the target, approximately sixteen JG 52 Bf 109 fighters attacked. Lt. Peter Düttmann, flying his Bf 109G-10 (WNr.: 610533, black '1') opened fire on Lt. Bahvalov's crippled A-20G Boston and finished it off. The plane exploded in mid-air and covered the fields stretching below with spinning, burning debris just West of Seregélyes. Although one crew member bailed out, the entire crew perished:

Lt. Vladimir Nikolaevich Bahvalov pilot (No.65332, +)
Lt. Pyotr Constantinovich Mayorov navigator (No.9503, +)
C-a Pavel Mihailovich Zolotov radioman/gunner (+)
Cpl. Ivan Fedorovich Solyanik gunner (+)

The Yak-3s intercepted the attackers and Ml.Lt. Vasilii Aleksandrovich Korotkevich claimed one, Ml.Lt. Aleksandr Afinogenovich Fyodorov claimed two Bf 109s in the Seregélyes area. One of Ml.Lt. Fyodorov's claims was Düttmann's Bf 109, which was an obvious overclaim since Düttmann was not shot down, rather he left Bahvalov's destroyed Boston with a dive. The aerial gunners of the Bostons also claimed one Bf 109 shot down. The dogfight continued and near Sárosd the remaining Bf 109s hit the right engine of Ml.Lt. Evgenii Ivanovich Kropanev's A-20G-20-DO Boston (S/N: 42-86876, R-2600-23 engines: 43-31292, 43-103250), which caught fire and crash-landed at Perkáta-W, 6 km.[35] Kropanev's Boston was perhaps downed by Hptm. Wilhelm Batz (II./JG 52). The other famous JG 52 ace, Lt. Heinz 'Esau' Ewald, downed St.Lt. Appolon Petrovich Pavlov's 449 BAP A-20B-DL Boston (S/N: 41-3643, R-2600-11 engines: 57124, 57359, white '8') near Székesfehérvár. The damaged plane successfully escaped by losing altitude, while both of their gunners (Aleksandr Andreevich Sitnikov and Vasilii Mihailovich Bolotov) bailed out with their parachutes. The crippled Boston finally crossed the Danube, crash-landed near Szabadszállás and burned.[36]

Yak-3 pilots Lt. Fedor Vasilevich Sergeev and Ml.Lt. Mihail Dmitrievich Shekolenko downed two more *'Fw 190s'* near Sárosd. The Soviet fighter escort suffered no losses.[37]

33 On 1 March 1945 (beside their 24 Yak-9D,M,T,DDs) the 659 IAP had six Yak-3s: 1515, 1711, 2015, 310055, 310081 and 310220. During the month they received another six Yak-3s, but because -for various reasons- they lost five of them, they finished the month with four combat-ready and three non-operational Yak-3s. By 1 April 1945 they also had 39 combat-ready and four non-operational Yak-9s.
34 TsAMO RF: fu. 20224, inv. 2, f. 61, pp. 108, 109, 158, 162, Combat diary (losses) of 244 BAD, entries for 14 March 1945.
35 TsAMO RF: fu. 20224, inv. 2, f. 61, pp. 158, 162, 187, 188, Combat diary (losses) of 244 BAD, entries for 14 March 1945.
36 TsAMO RF: fu. 20224, inv. 2, f. 61, pp. 148, 152, 153, 162, Combat diary (losses) of 244 BAD, entries for 14 March 1945.
37 TsAMO RF: fu. 20257, inv. 1, f. 46, pp. 372, 373, Operations journal of 288 IAD, entry for 14 March 1945. Ml.Lt. Mihail Dmitrievich Shekolenko flew his Yak-3 (c/n: 2015) between 24 December 1944 and 23 March 1945, when it was finally broken.

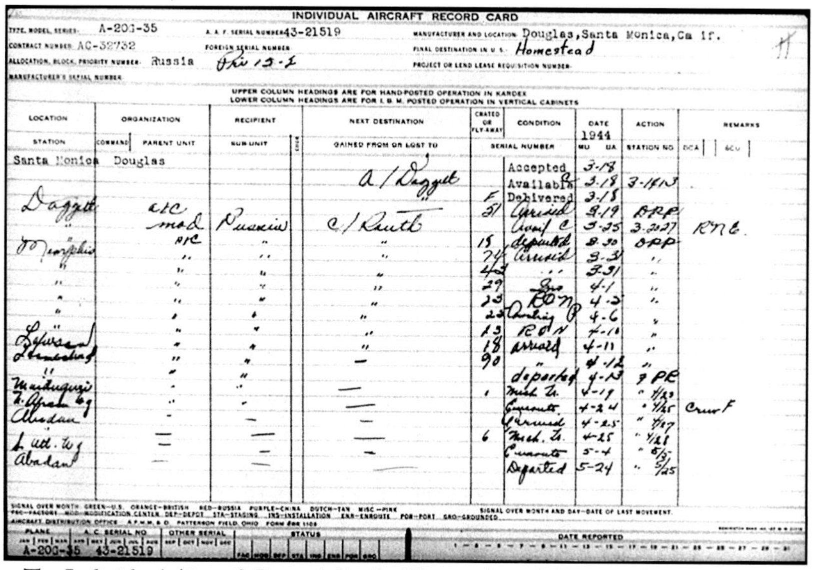
INDIVIDUAL AIRCRAFT RECORD CARD

Type, model, series: A-20G-35 — A.A.F. serial number: 43-21519 — Manufacturer and location: Douglas, Santa Monica, Calif.

Contract number: AC-32732 — Final destination in U.S.: Homestead

Allocation: Russia

Santa Monica — Douglas — Accepted 3-18 — Available 3-18 — Delivered 3-18

1944

A-20G-35 43-21519

The Individual Aircraft Record Card of Soviet A-20G Boston, S/N: 43-21519 (AAIR – Aviation Archaeological Investigation & Research)

The remains of Bahvalov's exploded Boston were recovered in 2006 by local researcher, Horváth Péter. Fortunately, a small data plate was recovered among the debris with the plane's A.A.F. serial number (321519), the key evidence in identifying the plane and its lost crew. The plane was built by Douglas in Santa Monica, California, U.S.A. on 18 March 1944 and was delivered to the Soviet Union via the South-Atlantic delivery route (Florida, Caribbean, Brazil, Ascension Island, Nigeria, Egypt, Palestine and Iran). This 861 BAP A-20G Boston was Lt. Peter Düttmann's confirmed aerial victory over Seregélyes-W in Hungary on 14 March 1945. Its tactical number is unknown however tail numbers 1, 10, 13 and 17 were still missing from the 861 BAP at the end of the war so it could possibly be one of them.

16 March 1945 (Friday)

Düttmann's unconfirmed: OVERCLAIM, Il-2 at Pákozd at 13:55 LT
Düttmann's unconfirmed: OVERCLAIM, Il-2 at Székesfehérvár-N at 13:56 LT
Düttmann's 131st: OVERCLAIM, Il-2 at Pákozd-SW at 13:58 LT
Düttmann's 132nd: OVERCLAIM, Il-2 at Pákozd-NW, 3 km at 13:59 LT
Düttmann's 133rd: POTENTIAL VICTORY, Il-2 at Pákozd-NE, 6 km at 14:01 LT

Soviet 17 VA Il-2 Sturmovik losses on 16 March 1945				
Regiment:	**Type:**	**c/n:**	**Pilot:**	**Details:**
167 GvShAP	Il-2m3	*1871190*	I. E. Ivanov MIA	Felsőmiholjác area in Croatia, MIA
210 ShAP	Il-2m3	*12229*	I. M. Maximov+	Csór, flak, '38'
615 ShAP	Il-2m3	9958	G. A. Sibiryakov	Székesfehérvár-W, flak, 15:00 LT
672 ShAP	Il-2m3	1871494	*Unknown, 3rd Sq.*	*Combat damages, repaired at base.*
672 ShAP	Il-2m3	1871988	*Unknown, 3rd Sq.*	*Combat damages, repaired at base.*
672 ShAP	Il-2m3	1872787	*Unknown, 3rd Sq.*	*Combat damages, repaired at base.*
951 ShAP	Il-2m3	1874487	V. K. Botov+	Fehérvárcsurgó-Sárkeresztes, Hungarian Bf 109s (Tobak-Pintér) at 15:30 LT
951 ShAP	Il-2m3	11345	V. I. Gladkii+	
989 ShAP	Il-2m3	1889701	I. K. Buryakovskii	Székesfehérvár-NW, flak, '*24*'
989 ShAP	Il-2m3	11531	M. S. Luchkovskii	Flak, CL behind frontline, '15'
989 ShAP	Il-2m3	18874124	N. M. Zaharov WIA	Vértesacsa-NW, 14:20 LT, '100'

* The 951 ShAP Il-2s this day were downed by a flight of Hungarian 101/3. FS Bf 109s: Lt. Pintér Gyula (blue '1') and Lt. Tobak Tibor (blue '11'). Lt. Dániel László (blue '9', ex-'W-0+32', WNr.: 760392) along with Szűcs Ferenc (blue '5') damaged a third one. Pintér's victim crashed in a steep dive from ~50 m, while the tail section of Tobak's victim was blown off upon receiving 30mm cannon hits into its fuselage.

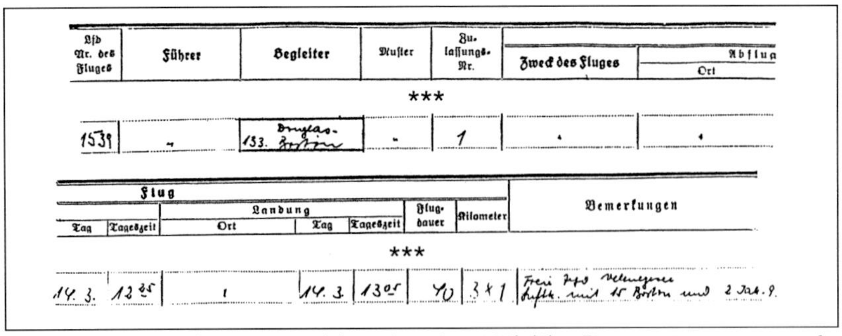

Peter Düttmann's logbook entry for 14.3.1945 (numbered as 133). This Boston victory was made on his 1539th operational sorite, 381st combat sortie (written in the kilometer column). The claim time given in many publicatons assumes that this Boston was shot down in the middle of the 40-minute sortie. (Photo: Authors' collection)

On 16 March 1945 between 13:55 and 14:01 LT in window of only six minutes(!) Lt. Peter Düttmann claimed five Il-2 Sturmoviks shot down in the Northern area of Lake Velence. This is an increadable and at the same time unbelievable combat result. By checking the Soviet 17 VA Il-2 loss reports, only one of his claims could be considered as a potencial aerial victory. Upon leaving the target area within the flight of the 210 ShAP, Ml.Lt. Nikolai Mihailovich Zaharov and aerial gunner Ml.Sgt. Vladimir Petrovich Yashin of 989 ShAP flying in white '100' were attacked by three Bf 109s. It is not clear if the plane, or only the crew, was 'borrowed' from the 989 ShAP for this 210 ShAP mission. Some control cables were damaged and the aerial gunner's machine gun was shot out from the plane. The pilot suffered injuries to the head and the aerial gunner suffered injuries to his left hand. The injured crew crash-landed at 14:20 LT at Vértesacsa-NW, 4 km (in other reports 1-2 km).[38] The plane was salvaged for spare parts, its AM-38F engine (c/n: 2514496) was used for a trainer UIl-2. The other 210, 989 ShAP planes this day were downed by flak. Three planes of the 672 ShAP, 3rd Squadron suffered combat damages, perhaps from Lt. Peter Düttmann's weapons however these were later repaired.

18 March 1945 (Sunday)

Düttmann's unconfirmed: OVERCLAIM, Yak-3 at Káloz-SE at 14:05 LT

Soviet 5 and 17 VA permanent single-engine fighter losses on 18 March 1945				
Regiment:	Type:	c/n:	Pilot:	Details:
92 IAP	La-5FN	39213358	S. A. Matveev	Vecsés, 3 km, engine fire, CL
150 GvIAP	Yak-3	310310	N. V. Alekseev	Alagivilla, 12:25 LT, LAC
177 GvIAP	La-5F	39214848	N. I. Bondar+	Kecskéd-E, 16:15 LT, 6 *Fw 190s*
164 IAP	La-5F	39213879	M. I. Demin+	12:40 LT, 4 La-5s, vs. 8 Bf 109s
164 IAP	La-5FN	39211479	N.V. Mozgov MIA	12:30 LT, 8 La-5s, vs. 22 Bf 109s
18 OUTAP	Yak-7B	822112	N/A, *trainer*	Scrapped due to wear and tear
18 OUTAP	Yak-7V	2615323	Unknown, training	Crash-landed, broken
288 IAD	Yak-9D	1615371	N/A	Scrapped due to wear and tear
659 IAP	Yak-9D	17166077	N. S. Nikitenkov	Csákvár, KIFA after dogfight
848 IAP	La-5FN	39213139	A. M. Golovashev	Enying-Dég, 10:04 LT

On 18 March 1945 the battles continued along the Sárvíz canal at Székesfehérvár-S. The 1 GvMK M4A2(76)W Sherman tank units were struggeling to breaking apart the German resistance in the Sárkeresztúr-Henrikmajor area. Since the nearby bridges were destroyed over the canal, first they had to move down to Felsőtöbörzsök in the South in order to cross the canal at Káloz-SE.[39] As they got over to the West shore, they lost three Shermans (including Gv.St.Lt. A. P. Komarov's '316'), and they immediately turned back North and aimed the Polgárdi railway station en route to Lake Balaton. During their fights Yakovlev and Lavochkin fighters of the 288 and 194 IADs provided aerial support to them in which they frequently confronted flights of Bf 109s and Fw 190s.

38 TsAMO RF: fu. 20174, inv. 1, f. 37, p. 277, Summary of operations of 989 ShAP, entry for 16 March 1945.

39 The Soviet 1 GvMK, 20 GvTP advanced on the Henrikmajor-Felsőtöbörzsök-Káloz-Polgárdi-Balatonfőkajár route towards Lake Balaton. Along their way (especially at the railway station of Polgárdi) they met strong German resistance in which they suffered heavy losses. At Henrikmajor they lost four (No.306, 307, 311, 327), at Polgárdi railway station five (No.310, 312, 318, 320, 324), at Balatonfőkajár another three (No.302, 315, 326) knocked out M4A2(76)W Sherman tanks. On the 21st at Balatonaliga the 19 GvTP lost Sherman No.228, visible in some famous pictures with Soviet trophy Hummels. Hummel No.53 finished its Soviet career at the Vienna Arsenal in April 1945 in Austria.

At 14:05 LT Lt. Peter Düttmann claimed an aerial victory over a Yak-3 fighter at Káloz-SE, right in the airspace of the Soviet canal-crossing. This time, however, the Soviets lost no fighters at all, only a Yak-9D earlier at 08:00 LT near Székesfehérvár. Between 07:20-07:50 LT ten Yak-9s of the 659 IAP, led by Capt. Nikolai Vasilevich Salamatov were covering the attack of the 260 BAP A-20 Bostons on German artillery positions at Mór-SE. After leaving the target around 08:00 LT the Soviets met up to twenty Bf 109s near Székesfehérvár. Two attacked Ml.Lt. Nikolai Stepanovich Nikitenkov's Yak-9D which left the battle and crash-landed near Csákvár. During landing his plane hit a big tree and crashed. The body of the pilot was thrown out of the cockpit and was found approximately fourty meters from his plane. With a time difference of six hours and different combat areas, Lt. Peter Düttmann's Yak-3 claim was rightlyfully left as unconfirmed. It is interesting to note that post-war Düttmann beleived he made this claim on 20 March 1945.[40]

19 March 1945 (Monday)

Düttmann's 134th: OVERCLAIM, Il-2 at Székesfehérvár-NW at 11:52 LT

Düttmann's 135th: OVERCLAIM, Yak-3 at Székesfehérvár-N at 14:56 LT

Düttmann's 136th: POTENTIAL VICTORY, La-5 at Székesfehérvár-S,-SW at 15:03 LT

Soviet aircraft losses over Hungary on 19 March 1945				
Regiment:	**Type:**	**c/n:**	**Pilot:**	**Details:**
91 GvShAP	Il-2m3	9641	I. S. Klimov+	Almásfüzitő, flak, 08:10 LT
92 GvShAP	Il-2m3	13021	M. Chekurin POW	Agostyán, flak, 08:15 LT, '77'
92 GvShAP	Il-2m3	13025	S. I. Ryabov POW	Tatatóváros-S, flak, 13:00 LT, '87'
130 GvShAP	Il-2m3	1870380*	V. N. Kurepin+	Vértesszőlős, flak, 14:40 LT, 2nd Sq.
130 GvShAP	Il-2m3	1870476	A. Y. Timohin+	Vértesszőlős-SW, flak, 09:38 LT
131 GvShAP	Il-2m3	12318	M. P. Lazarev	*Combat damage, repaired, 1st Sq.*
131 GvShAP	Il-2m3	12632	V. N. Provalinskii	*Combat damage, repaired, 1st Sq.*
131 GvShAP	Il-2m3	1877953	I. P. Tsukanov	*Combat damage, repaired, 1st Sq.*
131 GvShAP	Il-2m3	1879973	A. I. Zenin	*Combat damage, repaired, 1st Sq.*
131 GvShAP	Il-2m3	1873774	A. M. Skleptchuk	*Combat damage, repaired, 2nd Sq.*
166 GvShAP	Il-2m3	9873	V. S. Filippov+	Brčko-E, 5 km in Croatia, ~flak
451 ShAP	Il-2m3	1872171	I. F. Grigoryev+	Dad, 09:27 LT. 12 Il-2s, 6 Yaks of 513 IAP vs. 14 *'Fw 190s'* at 300m
451 ShAP	Il-2m3	1878985	P. A. Ermolaev+	
451 ShAP	Il-2m3	1876394	S. V. Vershinin	Dad, damaged by fighter, CL at base
615 ShAP	Il-2m3	18735100	I. F. Brankov MIA	Székesfehérvár-SW, 08:05 LT, flak
639 ShAP	Il-2m3	11530	A. N. Zharov+	Őcsény airfield, hit a powerline
672 ShAP	Il-2m3	1885503	U. H. Haidarov	*Zámoly-W, 08:00 LT to 8 Bf 109s***
715 ShAP	Il-2m3	11485	G. N. Pirogov	Csór-SE, 16:56 LT to 4 *Fw 190s*, '7'
715 ShAP	Il-2m3	18819118	P. T. Grebenko	Nádasdladány, 13:15, Hun., '31'
951 ShAP	Il-2m3	1878187	V. A. Fomin	Bodajk flak, could not be repaired
951 ShAP	Il-2m3	1871783	E. T. Bragin	Szigetcsép-N, 08:00 LT, flak, *repair*
989 ShAP	Il-2m3	18835124	I. K. Buriakovskii	Nádasdladány, 14:18, Hung. Bf 109
989 ShAP	Il-2m3	*Unknown*	N. F. Bakanov	*Combat damages, repaired, '2'*
989 ShAP	Il-2m3	*Unknown*	D. S. Koval	*Combat damages, repaired, '9'*
989 ShAP	Il-2m3	18733102	G. G. Andreev	*Combat damages, repaired, '43'*
73 GvIAP	Yak-1B	01174	N/A	Scrapped due to wear and tear
73 GvIAP	Yak-9M	4515315	I. V. Starikov WIA	Pátka-E, CL to 4 *Fw 190s*, 09:10 LT
73 GvIAP	Yak-9M	4515357	I. H. Kichin	*Martonvásár-NE, repaired next day*
31 IAP	La-5FN	39211550	A. Chebakov WIA	Székesfehérvár flak, 4 Bf 109s, CL
31 IAP	La-5FN	*Unknown*	A. I. Berezin	*Damaged by Bf 109s, repaired*
116 IAP	La-5F	39215049	A. N. Sidorovskii+	Szigetcsép, ~700m to 4 *'Fw 190's*

40 Klinnert, *Peter Düttmann "Bonifazius*, p. 194.

Soviet aircraft losses over Hungary on 19 March 1945 (*continued*)				
116 IAP	La-5FN	39211166	V. Ozhiganov MIA	Székesfehérvár, ~700m, 4 *'Fw 190's*
164 IAP	La-5	*Unknown*	N. D. Goncharenko	*Damaged by Bf 109s, repaired*
848 IAP	La-5FN	39211860	E. A. Ruhovets+	Enying-SE, flak at 10:00 LT, 12 ILs
267 IAP	Yak-1B	35169	D. D. Tormakhov	Matty-E,-NE, CL, near Croatia
866 IAP	Yak-3	310167	I. F. Chernii+	Csór-S to flak, 8 Yak-3s
866 IAP	Yak-3	*310062*	V. S. Lukyanov	Zámoly, CL, 07:40 LT, 8 Bf 109s
861 BAP	A-20G	43-10099	V. V. Stirkov***	*Berhida, flak damage, repaired, '23'*
930 NBAP	Po-2	9065	D. M. Litvinov+	Komárom, flak during night mission

* This aircraft had its four damaged factory installed wing mounted RS-132 rocket-launchers (No.3074, 2088, 21226, 20188) replaced with the smaller, RS-82 type launchers in March 1945.

** Around 08:00 LT 13 Il-2s and 4 La-5s attacked the Csetény area. Upon leaving the target the Soviets were attacked by eight Bf 109s. Two hit Ml. Lt. Ulmas Halmatovich Haidarov's Il-2m3 (c/n: 1885503, AM-38F engine: 255861) which crash-landed three kilometers West of Zámoly and was later repaired.

*** On 19 March 1945 around 15:50 LT from 2000m three 244 BAD A-20 Boston groups bombed about 100 military vehicles at Berhida. The first group (9 A-20s of 861 BAP, 1st Sq.) was led by Capt. Zolotarev, the 2nd group (8 A-20s of 861 BAP, 3rd Sq.) was led by Capt. Petuhov and the 3rd group (9 A-20s of 449 BAP) was) was led by Capt. Yegorkin. The fighter escort was provided by six Yak-9s of the 659 IAP, led by Lt. Sergeev and six Yak-3s of the 866 IAP, led by St.Lt. Surnev. In the target area the Soviet planes were attacked by several Bf 109s, including fighters of the Hungarian 101 FG which after leaving the target chased the bombers back to the South. Over Siófok Máthé László fhdgy. (101/7. FS) damaged one of the bombers, but according to the Soviet reports the fuel tank of 861 BAP, 3rd Sq. A-20G-36-DO Boston (S/N: 43-10099, No.'23') was damaged by flak.

On 19 March 1945 Lt. Peter Düttmann claimed an Il-2, a Yak-3 and a La-5 all shot down in the Székesfehérvár area. Both of his Il-2 and Yak-3 claims turn out to be overclaims, but his La-5 claim at 15:03 LT near Székesfehérvár at 700m is a potential aerial victory over a 116 IAP La-5F, or FN.

This day the 116 IAP has lost two La-5 fighters in a dogfight near Székesfehérvár. Over Szabadbattyán between 600-800m, while escorting 306 ShAD Il-2 Sturmoviks, La-5 pair of Ml.Lt. Victor Vasilevich Ozhiganov and Lt. Andrey Nazarovich Sidorovskii was suddenly ambushed by four 'new model *Fw 190's*. Ozhiganov's La-5FN (white '66') was hit, went into a diving spin and crashed at Szabadbattyán. Lt. Andrey Nazarovich Sidorovskii's La-5F (white '49') was also hit, but he could return to the Tököl airbase area where his engine quit. Crash-landing near Szigetcsép, he later died due to his wounds and was buried in Tököl. One of these two La-5s could be Lt. Peter Düttmann's potential aerial victory.

20 March 1945 (Tuesday)

Düttmann's unconfirmed: OVERCLAIM, P-51 at Veszprém-W,-SW 10 km at 14:05 LT

15th AF permanent single-engine fighter losses on 20 March 1945				
Regiment:	**Type:**	**S/N:**	**Pilot:**	**Details:**
332 FG	P-51B-5	43-7068	Newman C. Golden	Wels, Austria, 11:32 LT

On 20 March 1945 at 14:05 LT Lt. Peter Düttmann claimed an American P-51 Mustang shot down at Veszprém-W,-SW 10 km. The American mission was noted in the KTB of Army Group South as over-flights of large bomber groups near the 2nd Panzer Army.[41] According to his recolections, the following series of events played out during this encounter. Spotting a swarm of P-51 Mustangs returning from their mission, Lt. Düttmann along with his swarm were bounced by the Americans, but by turning on their methonal boost systems they were able to climb away from the attakers.[42] The Mustangs followed them up though they peeled off one-by-one with Düttmann's flight also leveling out.[43] A single persistent Mustang followed Düttmann up to a height of around 6000m, whereafter the JG 52 pilot bounced the American from a thousand-meter height advantage and supposedly shot it down without witnesses.[44] Lt. Peter Düttmann then reveals that this claim was incorrectly marked in his flight log and that he believes that the Abschuss took place two days earlier on 18 March 1945; he categorizes this mix-up in dates as a 'classic case'.[45] Düttman believed that his claim occurred when

41 NARA T311/R162/7214671
42 Klinnert, *Peter Düttmann "Bonifazius*, p. 192.
43 Klinnert, *Peter Düttmann "Bonifazius"*, p. 192.
44 Klinnert, *Peter Düttmann "Bonifazius"*,p. 194.
45 Klinnert, *Peter Düttmann "Bonifazius*, p. 194.

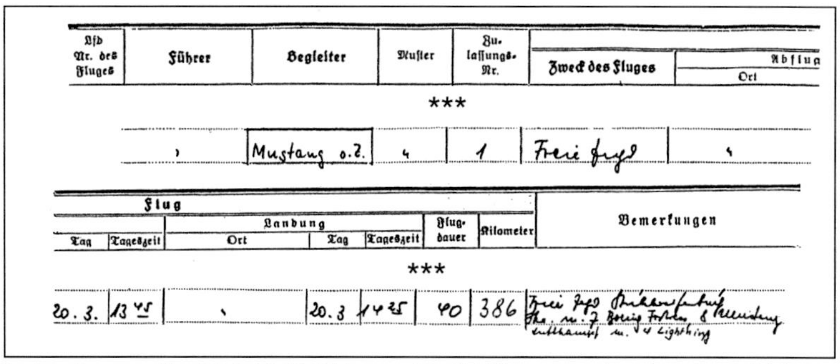

Peter Düttmann's logbook entry for 20.3.1945. This was his 1545th operational sorite, 386th combat sortie. Notice the very strange description: 'Free hunt in the Stuhlweißenburg area sighting 7 Boeing Fortress, air combat with 8 Mustang and 4 Lightning'. There were no such aircraft near Székesfehérvár on 20 March 1945, while again such events did not occur on Düttmann's 'alternative date', 18 March 1945. The claim time given in many publicatons assumes that this event occured in the middle of the 40-minute sortie. (Photo: Authors' collection)

Obfhr. Peter Esser (1./JG 53) shot down a P-51 and managed to talk to the American pilot who was taken prisoner; after the war Esser was able to talk to the American pilot again in the 1980s to discuss that fateful day's events. With Peter Esser and the American pilot comparing flight logs after the war and relating that information to Peter Düttmann, he noticed that his flight log had the dates supposedly incorrectly labbeld: the P-51 should have been on the 18th while his Yak-3 was therefore on the 20th![46] This strange calculation by Düttmann, using Obfhr. Peter Esser's genuine victory to justify his clerical error,[47] becomes more bizarre when the American records are reviewed in detail.

On 20 March 1945, P-51 Mustangs of the 15th AF, 306 FW, 332 FG escorted B-24 Liberators of the 304th Bomber Wing to the Kralupy oil refinery in Czechoslovakia (Mission No.238). The total number of escorting P-51s was 177 Mustangs all from the 306 FW, while 142 P-38 Lightnings of the 305 FW escorted other 15th AF bombing raids.[48] The single loss suffered by the escorts was a 332 FG P-51B due to a mechanical problem.[49] Around 11:30 LT P-51B-5-NA Mustang (S/N: 43-7068, V-1650-7 engine number: V-323688, no nickname) had engine trouble which forced the pilot, F/O Newman Camay Golden (T-64636, 99th FS, 1919-1951, KIA in Korea) to leave his plane. He informed his flight about the problem and bailed out at 11:32 LT near Wels, Austria.[50]

It is now obvious that this Abschuss is nothing more then an overclaim for Lt. Peter Düttmann. The Wels aera is nearly 300 km west of Düttmann's reported Veszprém-W,-SW location. There was no other P-51 Mustang loss in the entire region while the time reported for the mechanical failure of the Mustang was over two hours before Lt. Düttmann's claim. The 2nd Panzer Army was located at the Western end of Lake Balaton not near Veszprém, meaning that the American bombers bypassed the airfield from which II./JG 52 opperated. Pilot Newman Camay Golden lost his life in 1951 therefore he could not have talked to Peter Esser in the 1980s as claimed by Düttmann. It is clear that several decades after the war Peter Düttmann had trouble remembering this day's events and confused similar situations with his personal combat experiences; correctly remembering such detailes after many decades is difficult. However, the poor attempt to bridge the two dates (18th and 20th March 1945) together in order to reconcile his P-51 claim is suspicious, only moreso because Düttmann held an apparent appitie for claiming new types of aircraft for his Abschussliste.[51] This claim, rightfully not confirmed, was Lt. Peter Düttmann's sole P-51 Mustang of the war which turns out to be an overclaim.

Conclusion

Overall Lt. Peter Düttmann's victory claims over Hungary were far from accurate. Out of his original 42 claims, only 11 were victories or potential victories. Interestingly one of his nine unconfirmed claims seems to be a potential victory on 31 October 1944.

46 Klinnert, *Peter Düttmann "Bonifazius*, p. 194.
47 Esser's Mustang was P-51C-10-NT, S/N: 43-25120, nickname: 'Ski Snoot', flown by 1Lt James R. White (POW). This was the only Mustang shot down over Hungary on 18 March 1945.
48 Kevin Mahoney, *Fifteenth Air Force Against the Axis: Combat Missions over Europe during World War II* (Plymouth: Scarecrow Press Inc, 2013). p. 364
49 Mahoney, *Fifteenth Air Force Against the Axis*, p. 364
50 MACR 13126. Local time in Ausrtia was the same as in Hungary.
51 Markus Ewald, Falk Klinnert, *Heinz Ewald "Esau": Wo Wir Sind Ist Immer Oben* (Leipzig: Fips-Druck, 1998), p. 185.

7

Heinz Ewald (1922-2002)

Born on 1 September 1922, the twenty-one year old Heinz Ewald joined 6./JG 52 in late 1943. He was downed multiple times and was seriously wounded in Romania on 24 June 1944 in combat with P-51 Mustangs of the 15th AF. After three months of recovering from his injuries, Lt. Heinz Ewald traveld from the hospital in Bad Wiesse to Kraków, Poland, reporting to JG 52 Kommandore Hermann Graf, after which he flew across the High Tatras to Nagyrábé in Hungary.[1] For about two months he belonged to 7./JG 52, then on 15 February 1945 he took command of 6./JG 52. On 3 April 1945 he was shot down again by P-51 Mustangs near Vienna. On 20 April 1945 he was awarded the Ritterkreuz. Finishing the war with 84 aerial victories and many unconfirmed victories, flying 396 combat sorties,[2] Lt. Ewald also flew several time as the wingman of Gerhard Barkhorn 122 times. Heinz Ewald passed away on 14 March 2002.[3]

Lt. Heinz Ewald's claims are compiled from the following sources listed in order of heaviest reliance:

- Luftwaffe Aces: claims and bibliographies, Vol. 2
- Die Geschichte der II. Gruppe des Jagdgeschwaders 52: Offizielle Ausgabe der Traditionsgemeinschaft JG 52
- Heinz Ewald "Esau": Wo Wir Sind Ist Immer Oben
- Tony Woods – Eastern Front Vol 4. 1944. Jul – Dec, Issue 1

All the lists are congruent for the dates and aircraft types, however the numbering of the claims is different in the Mathews & Foreman publication as unconfirmed claims are left unnumbered. The claim number appearing in the Mathews & Foreman publication has been used.

6 October 1944 (Friday)
Ewald's 29th: OVERCLAIM, Yak-11 at 13:01 LT at Nagyrábé at 3500m, Anerk: Nr. 435

Soviet 5 VA single-engine fighter losses on 6 October 1944				
Regiment:	**Type:**	**c/n:**	**Pilot:**	**Details:**
192 IAP	La-5F	39214394	P. A. Charushnikov	Temesgyarmat, CL, 10:45 LT*
486 IAP	La-5FN	39212241	N. M. Chernishev+	Békés, 13:25 LT, 12 Fw 190s
486 IAP	La-5FN	39211147	A. P. Kononov	Békéscsaba, 14:10 LT, 8 Fw 190s
31 GvIAP	Yak-1B	36162	I. D. Brizhnik	Tótkomlós flak, CL, ~12:30 LT

* The Soviet record writes 11:45 (Moscow time.) Temesgyarmat is now located in Romania and called Giarmata which is only one hour behind Moscow time. During the war a large part of Transsylvania (Erdély) returned to Hungary through the Second Vienna Award. In 1944 it was part of Hungary again, meaning it was two hours' time behind Moscow time, so

1 Ewald, Klinnert, *Heinz Ewald "Esau*, p. 113.
2 Ewald, Klinnert, *Heinz Ewald "Esau*, p. 203.
3 Andrew-Johannes Mathews and John Foreman, *Luftwaffe Aces*, Vol. 1, p. 294.

the exact time of the crash-landing is uncertian. It could be either 09:45, or 10:45 local time – depending on the calculated time zones.

On 6 October 1944 Lt. Heinz Ewald claimed his very first victory over Hungary near Nagyrábé, which when verified turns out to be an overclaim since none of the 5 VA single-engine fighter losses match his claim in time or location. The only Yakovlev loss of the day was Gv.Lt. Ivan Demianovich Brizhnik's Yak-1B (c/n: 36162, engine: 415-1180) which was hit by flak over Tótkomlós and belly landed at Battonya-W, 1 km. Between 11:55-13:05 LT six Yak-1Bs, led by Gv.Capt. Ivan Ivanovich Demkin covered Soviet ground troops in the Orosháza area when Brizhnik's plane was hit by flak. The plane was written off but its pilot remained unhurt.[4] It is possible that Lt. Heinz Ewald damaged a Yak-3 (in his terminology a 'Yak-11') of the 150 GvIAP which flew several reconnaissance sorties during the day in the Békéscsaba area. On 1 October 1944 the 5 VA had only eighteen new Yak-3 fighters: seventeen in the 13 GvIAD and one in the 6 GvIAD.[5] None of these units, however, suffered any losses during the day. With the newly arriving planes, the number of the Yak-3s of the 5 VA kept increasing.[6]

28 October 1944 (Saturday)

Ewald's *unconfirmed claim:* OVERCLAIM, Boston at around 14:20 LT

Soviet 5 VA A-20 Boston loss on 28 October 1944				
Regiment:	**Type:**	**c/n:**	**Pilot:**	**Details:**
453 BAP	A-20G-15	42-54244*	L. Y. Sedov+	Büdszentmihály, to HUN Bf 109

* On 01.10.1944 the 5 VA had a total of 39 A-20G-15s. Lt. Sedov's A-20G was one of them.

Early in the afternoon on 28 October 1944 a 453 BAP, 2nd Sq. A-20G-15-DO Boston (S/N: 42-54244, R-2600-23 engines: 42-154202 and 42-154304) was attacking German military transports in the Nyíregyháza-Mezőkövesd-Tokaj-Miskolc area. The crew's last radio signal was received at 13:40 LT after which they disappeared without a trace. The exact details of their last moments are unknown, but they were most likely lost in air combat with Bf 109 fighters as both Lt. Heinz Ewald (7./JG 52) and Hungarian Szeverényi Kálmán hdgy. (101/7. FS) Bf 109 aces claimed a Boston bomber in the same area. The plane crashed at Büdszentmihály (now Tiszavasvári), exploded and burned. The entire crew of the plane perished:[7]

Lt. Leonid Yefimovich Sedov pilot, flight-commander (+)
St.Lt. Vasilii Yosifovich Naidenov navigator/bombardier (+)
St.Sgt. Sergei Sergeevich Lebedev radioman/aerial gunner (+)
Sgt. Kapitalina Fedorovna Vlasova (female) aerial gunner (+)

Lt. Heinz Ewald took off from the Taktakenéz airfield near Büdszentmihály (now Tiszavasvári) after an 'alarmstart' for a marauding Boston. Following the mission he reported a Boston claimed around 14:20 LT,[8] thought it should be noted that the 14:20 LT was actually the start time of this mission rather than the claim time, and Lt. Ewald landed eight minutes later at 14:28 LT.[9] In his flight logbook Lt. Ewald mentions this event in passing and acknowledges the victory as one for a Hungarian pilot.[10]

During this same time Hungarian ace Szeverényi Kálmán hdgy. of 101/7. FS also attacked the Boston which became his official aerial victory, a Boston III, and was acknowledged by Ewald. The exact details of the incident are unknown, both pilots probably hit the very same plane, but it was officially credited to Szeverényi Kálmán hdgy. (1920-1945, Bf 109G-6, coded 'V.3+91', WNr.: 166488).[11]

4 TsAMO RF: fu. 327, inv. 4999, f. 177, p. 27, Operations review of 3 GvIAK for October 1944, 6 GvIAD combat loss entry for 6 October 1944.
5 This single Yak-3 was flown by Gv.Maj. Boris Nikolaevich Eremin (HSU, 6 GvIAD HQ) c/n: 1729212, VK-105Pf2 engine: 412-190 built on 26 June 1944 in Saratov, Russia in Factory No.292.
6 The 6 GvIAD received new Yak-3s, including: 310197, 310306, 0529212, 1229237, 4529235, while the 13 GvIAD got 310212, 310255, 310274, 310275, 310291, 310293, 310305, 310310, 310312, 310315 and 310317.
7 TsAMO RF: fu. 20208, inv. 1, f. 17, p. 299, Combat diary (losses) of 218 BAD, entry for 28 October 1944.
8 Barbas, *Die Geschichte der II. Gruppe des Jagdgeschwaders 52*, p. 369.
9 Stenge Csaba, *Elfelejtett Hősök* 2nd Ed. (Budapest: HM Zrínyi kiadó, 2016), p. 237.
10 Csaba, *Elfelejtett Hősök*, p. 237.
11 Csaba, *Elfelejtett Hősök*, pp. 234, 237.

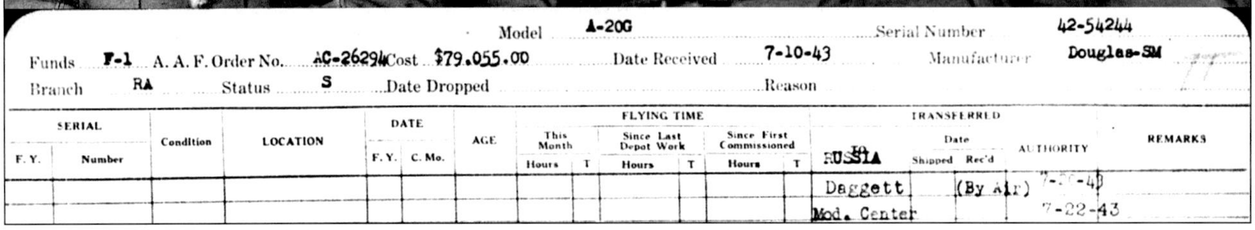

Model A-20G Serial Number 42-54244

Funds F-1 A. A. F. Order No. AC-26294 Cost $79,055.00 Date Received 7-10-43 Manufacturer Douglas-SM

Branch RA Status S Date Dropped Reason

Serial F. Y.	Serial Number	Condition	Location	Date F. Y.	Date C. Mo.	Age	Flying Time This Month Hours	T	Since Last Depot Work Hours	T	Since First Commissioned Hours	T	Transferred	Date Shipped	Rec'd	Authority	Remarks
													RUSSIA				
													Daggett	(By Air)			
													Mod. Center		7-22-43		

(L-R) Hungarian Bf 109G-6 ace Szeverényi Kálmán hdgy. (1920-1945) and his victims on 28 October 1944 at Büdszentmihály: Lt. Leonid Yefimovich Sedov pilot (1923-1944) and St.Lt. Vasilii Yosifovich Naidenov navigator/bombardier (1917-1944). Below is the Individual Aircraft Record Card of their downed A-20G-15-DO Boston, S/N: 42-54244. (Photos: Szeverényi Ferenc, Tatiana Evgenevna and AAIR)

This Boston was built by Douglas on 10 July 1943 in Santa Monica, CA, USA. It was delivered to the Soviet Union under the Lend Lease agreement via the 'ALSIB' (Alaska-Siberia) Northern delivery route through Great Falls (Montana, U.S.A.), Edmonton then Whitehorse (Canada), Ladd Field (Alaska, U.S.A.) and Krasnoyarsk (USSR).[12]

Beside Lt. Sedov, several other 453 BAP crews carried out tactical bombing missions in the area, for example: Maj. Ivan Ivanovich Lisenko and Maj. Ivan Haritonovich Lozovenko over Miskolc, Lt. Ivan Aleksandrovich Malov over Mezőkövesd and St.Lt. Victor Gavrilovich Kochanov, who destroyed four enemy vehicles on the road.

31 October 1944 (Tuesday)

Ewald's 30th: VICTORY, Il-2 at 15:37 LT in the Kecskemét area

Ewald's 31st: VICTORY, LaGG-5 at 15:42 LT at Kecskemét-SW, 10 km

Soviet 5 Air Army aircraft losses on 31 October 1944 in Hungary				
Regiment:	**Type:**	**c/n:**	**Pilot:**	**Details:**
130 GvShAP	Il-2m3	8280	D. S. Popov MIA	Nagykőrös, flak, 14:00 LT, 8 Il-2s
130 GvShAP	Il-2m3	9788	A. N. Yeremeev+	Nagykőrös, flak, 14:00 LT, 8 Il-2s
131 GvShAP	Il-2m3	10752	A. N. Korchagin	Nagykőrös-S, 13:50 LT, 4 *Fw190s*
187 GvShAP	Il-2m3	12172	A.G. Lubishev MIA	Kecskemét-SE to fighters, '56'
190 GvShAP	Il-2m3	11035	A. F. Berezhovskii	Gyoma, LAC, Bf 109s, 13:55 LT
190 GvShAP	Il-2m3	1871479	N.A. Bachurin MIA	Kecskemét-SE, 13:55LT, 18 Bf 109s
190 GvShAP	Il-2m3	303830	P. D. Suhodolskii+	Kecskemét-SW,13:55LT, 18 Bf 109s
177 GvIAP	La-5F	39215187	P. Y. Morduhovich	Kecskemét-SW, 15:25LT, 2 Bf 109s
177 GvIAP	La-5FN	41210105	A. A. Kunshin MIA	Cegléd-Szolnok, strafing at 09:30 LT
452 BAP	A-20G	42-54006	P. I. Ivanov+	Bánréve flak to Ózd, in factory yard

12 Individual Aircraft Record Card (AAIR – Aviation Archaeological Investigation & Research)

St.Lt. Vasilii Nikolaevich Petrunko's crash-landed A-20G-10-DO Boston (453 BAP, 1st Sq., S/N: 42-53873, red '8', R-2600-23 engines: 42-175265, 42-106695) on the Debrecen airfield on 21 December 1944. Lt. Sedov's Boston lost on 28 October 1944 carried similar blue tail markings. (Photo: Boris V. Davidov)

On 31 October 1944 Lt. Heinz Ewald claimed an Il-2 and a La-5 shot down in the greater Kecskemét area. This day around 15:30 LT nine 187 GvShAP Il-2 Sturmoviks led by Gv.Capt. Sergei Alekseevich Feoktistov escorted by four La-5s attacked the roads in the Kecskemét area.[13] Upon leaving the target at 300m, the Soviet formation was ambushed by two Bf 109s and two *Fw 190s*.[14] During the attack pilot Ml.Lt. Andrey Grigorevich Lubishev and aerial gunner Sgt. Gennadiy Georgievich Konev became separated from their group and went missing around Kecskemét-SE. Their plane (Il-2m3 Sturmovik, c/n: 12172, AM-38F engine: 2511952, white '56') was reported to have probably been downed by a fighter, certianly by Heinz Ewald.

After downing the Il-2 Lt. Ewald gained altitude and went after the fighter escort.[15] Within minutes he downed a La-5F (c/n: 39215187, white '87', M-82F engine: 6504058) piloted by Gv.Capt. Pavel Yakovlevich Morduhovich, Sq. commander. Around *15:25 LT* a flight of four La-5s of the 177 GvIAP were on patrol over the Kecskemét-Nagykőrös area, where at 2000m the pair of Gv.Capt. Pavel Yakovlevich Morduhovich – Gv.Lt. Nikifor Semyonovich Abramov met two Bf 109s and two *Fw 190s* (the same enemy flight as described by the Il-2s). Morduhovich attacked the *Fw 190s*, while the Bf 109s got into his tail and hit him. He fell out of Abramov's sight who never saw or heard from his flight leader ever again.

Beside these incidents, six Yaks of the 31 GvIAP led by Gv.St.Lt. Valentin Yefimovich Shapiro were also involved in a dogfight at 4000m with four 'Fw 190's in the Kecskemét area, in which Gv.Ml.Lt. Ivan Grigorevich Parshutkin claimed a 'Fw 190's shot down at Kecskemét-SE, 8 km. This time the Soviet fighters suffered no losses.

13 The nine 187 GvShAP Il-2s on this mission were marked white 51, 54, 56, 57, 58, 59, 60, 97, and 98. The lead-plane (white '60') was flown by Gv.Capt. Feoktistov, while Ml.Lt. Lubishev (white '56') was shot down by Lt. Heinz Ewald. Combat register of the 187 GvShAP, entry for 31 October 1944 TsAMO RF: fu. 22416, inv. 222544c, f. 2, p. 77.

14 Probably all four fighters were Bf 109s.

15 It is possible that in fact Lt. Ewald's first claim this day was the La-5 at 15:37 LT and he downed the Il-2 afterwards at 15:42 LT.

St.Lt. Grigorii Kirillovich Denisenko (Deputy CO of the 235 ShAP's 2nd Sq.) and his aerial gunner on their famous 235 ShAP Il-2m3 (c/n: 1878488, white '14') before a mission. Since Il-2m3 No.1878488 is mentioned first only in the 1 January 1945 quarterly aircraft inventory of his unit and he crash-landed Il-2 No.9933 on 17 November 1944, his plane on the 1 November 1944 mission was probably still No.9933. (Photo: Fortepan / Vörös Hadsereg)

1 November 1944 (Wednesday)
Ewald's 32nd: POTENTIAL VICTORY, Yak-7 at 11:18 LT at Nagykőrös-E, 5200m
Ewald's 33rd: OVERCLAIM, Yak-7 at 11:23 LT at Nagykőrös-E, 5500m
Ewald's 34th: OVERCLAIM, Il-2 at 14:24 LT in the Nagykőrös area, 600m

Soviet 5 VA single-engine fighter and Il-2 losses on 1 November 1944				
Regiment:	**Type:**	**c/n:**	**Pilot:**	**Details:**
177 GvIAP	La-5F	39215336	E. I. Batyunya WIA	Szolnok, CL, HUN Bf 109 victory
177 GvIAP	La-5	*Unknown*	M. V. Danshin	*Later returned, AC not lost!*
235 ShAP	Il-2m3	10472	V. I. Astahov MIA	Törtel, after 13:00 LT to flak
73 GvIAP	Yak-9D	18166046	*Unknown, 1st Sq.*	*Combat damage, Yakovenko rep.*
73 GvIAP	Yak-1B	08175	A. Andrianov POW	Nagykőrös, 4500-6000m,8 Bf 109
85 GvIAP	Yak-1B	xx1xx	B. I. Gelkin, 1st Sq.	*Temporary loss, later returned*

On 1 November 1944 while escorting Ju 87s, Lt. Heinz Ewald claimed two 'Yak-7' fighters and one Il-2 shot down. His and Uffz. Gmelin's (7./JG 52) Il-2 claims at 600m near Nagykőrös at 14:24 and 14:27 LT were both overclaims (plane damages at best), while only one of his Yak claims can be deemed as a potential victory. This day between 4500-6000m over Nagykőrös eight Yak-1Bs and Yak-3s of the 73 GvIAP, led by Gv.Maj. Mihail Aleksandrovich Zuev and Gv.Lt.Col. Boris Nikolaevich Yeryomin, Dep. Div. Commander of 6 GvIAD fought a wild dogfight with eight Bf 109s, in which Gv.Lt. Aleksandr Semyonovich Andrianov, who tried to protect the leaders' Yak-3s, was shot down.[16] His Yak-1B (c/n: 08175, engine: 345-2353) went down in flames, but the seriously injured pilot bailed out and was later captured. Since the area matches, Lt. Heinz Ewalds first 'Yak-7' claim could be his sole potential victory for the day. Although Lt. Ewald and Uffz. Gmelin both claimed an Il-2 at 14:24 and 14:27 LT, the only lost Il-2 was Ml.Lt. Vladimir Ilyich Astahov's Il-2m3 of the 235 ShAP which went down to flak at Törtel from St.Lt. Grigorii Kirillovich Denisenko's six plane flight soon after 13:00 LT, therefore it is not a candidate for them.

13 November 1944 (Monday)
Ewald's 35th: OVERCLAIM, Yak-9 at 14:34 LT at Eger-E, -SE 40 km, 400m[17]

16 After 26 June 1944 Gv.Lt.Col. Boris Nikolaevich Yeryomin's famous plane was a Yak-3 (c/n: 1729212, VK-105PF2 engine: 412-190) which he received in Saratov from Ferapont Petrovich Golovatiy delivered to the front on 30 June 1944 and flew it during multiple sorties until VE-Day. Yeryomin received his first Yak-3 (c/n: 1001, white '10') in Saratov on 29 May 1944 in a ceremony, however he never flew it in combat.

17 14:54 LT around Budaörs according to *Die Geschichte der II. Gruppe des Jagdgeschwaders 52: Offizielle Ausgabe der Traditionsgemeinschaft JG 52.*

Soviet 5 VA permanent single-engine fighter losses on 13 November 1944				
Regiment:	**Type:**	**c/n:**	**Pilot:**	**Details:**
122 IAP	Yak-9M	2715382	N. M. Grishaev	Take-off accident (Külső-Kiritó)
149 GvIAP	Yak-1B	11186	A. T. Kotlyar POW	Jászberény, 13:55-14:50 LT
149 GvIAP	Yak-1B	*42178*	Stepanov, returned	Abony-N, 12:55 LT, 6 Bf 109s
150 GvIAP	Yak-3	3529218	N. A. Kireev, WIA	Ócsa, 08:41 LT, 6 Yak, 13 Bf 109s
150 GvIAP	Yak-9D	1815358	Nikolai S. Yegorov	Nagykáta, 11:54 LT, 8 Fw 190s
179 IAP	Yak-9M	2715317	Svistkov, returned	Jászberény flak to Újszász-E
179 IAP	Yak-9T	0215354	E. I. Teplishev MIA	Zsámbok-SW, 13:50LT 8 Bf 109s
177 GvIAP	La-5FN	41210201	B. G. Kalinin+	Újszász, 12:30 LT, air combat

On 13 November 1944 Lt. Heinz Ewald claimed a Yak-9 shot down at Eger-E,-SE approximatley 40 km at 14:34 LT. This day the aerial battles and losses took place about 80-100 km Eger-SW, in a completely different direction to his claim. This Yak-9 claim therefore had to be an overclaim over an unidentified fighter unless Lt. Ewald incorrectly recorded the location of this claim. Obgefr. Welz's (6./JG 52) Yak-9 claim over Buda at 14:30 LT also seems to be an overclaim. Although six 17 VA, 39 ORAP reconnaissance planes (4 Pe-2s, 2 Yak-9s) approached Budapest from the South, they suffered no losses and fighter units of the 5 VA did not operate over Budapest at all.

14 November 1944 (Tuesday)

Ewald's *unconfirmed claim*: POTENTIAL VICTORY, Yak-9 around 08:00 LT

Soviet 5 VA single-engine fighter losses on 14 November 1944				
Regiment:	**Type:**	**c/n:**	**Pilot:**	**Details:**
92 IAP	La-5FN	39213519	S. A. Matveev WIA	Jászberény-NW, 4-5 km, flak
92 IAP	La-5FN	39211212	N. A. Lopatkin MIA	*Repaired, lost on 23 January 1945*
92 IAP	La-5FN	39212944	V. M. Vihlyaev MIA	*Repaired, stayed in service*
92 IAP	La-5FN	39213431	A. Kuprianov MIA	*Repaired, lost on 24 March 1945*
122 IAP	Yak-1B	121xx	I. T. Blagoder	Il-2 escort, later returned, '12'
179 IAP	Yak-1B	xx1xx	V. N. Bocharov	*Földes, CL, 08:40LT to 6 Bf 109s*
151 GvIAP	Yak-1B	18199	N. V. Rogatin	Jászberény, 2500m to Bf 109s
151 GvIAP	Yak-9T	1715339	L. I. Toropov	Jászberény, 1000m to Bf 109s
151 GvIAP	Yak-9T	xx153xx	A. A. Morozov	*Tápiógyörgye to 6 fighters, repaired*

On 14 November 1944 Lt. Heinz Ewald had an unconfirmed Yak-9 claim around 08:00 LT which could be a potential aerial victory from the 151 GvIAP, stationing in Kunszentmárton. Later at around 08:40 LT, six 179 IAP Yak-1Bs led by Maj. Pyotr Terentevich Kovalenko escorted six 91 GvShAP Il-2m3 Sturmoviks led by Gv.Capt. Prosendeev to the Zsámbok area where they were ambushed by six Bf 109s. An Il-2 and Ml.Lt. Vasilii Nikolaevich Bocharov's Yak-1B were hit and Bocharov crash-landed on his airfield after returning home. His plane was seriously damaged and he was slightly injured. His Yak-1B was most likely claimed by Uffz. Männel's (7./JG 52) as a 'Yak-9' at 08:42 LT, differing only two minutes from the Soviet records!

16 November 1944 (Thursday)

Ewald's 36th: VICTORY, La-5 at 08:52 LT in the Jászberény area, ground level
Ewald's 37th: POTENTIAL VICTORY, Yak-9 at 11:46 LT at Jászberény-NW, 3200m
Ewald's 38th: VICTORY, Yak-9 at 11:51 LT at Gyöngyös-SW, 20 km, 2500m
Ewald's 39th: OVERCLAIM, Yak-9 at 14:03 LT at Karcag-N, -NE, 40 km, 5600m

Soviet 5 VA single-engine fighter losses on 16 November 1944				
Regiment:	**Type:**	**c/n:**	**Pilot:**	**Details:**
31 GvIAP	Yak-9D	2015370	V. A. Koptelov OK	Jászkisér-E, 12:20 LT, 6 Bf 109s
73 GvIAP	Yak-9D	2015315	A. S.Shuvalov MIA	Jászárokszállás, 4000 m, – missing
85 GvIAP	Yak-9D	2015329	Ismail S. Rulev+	Jászberény, 10:10,4000 m,8 Bf 109
122 IAP	Yak-1B	22183	M. I. Sapa unhurt	Külső-Kiritó, LAC at 15:20 LT
122 IAP	Yak-1B	06179	P. G. Artemev+	Hatvan-S, 12:00, 8 Fw 190, Bf 109
122 IAP	Yak-9M	2715305	B. A. Horkin WIA	Törökszentmiklós-SE at 12:00 LT
122 IAP	Yak-9T	2515332	A. M. Znamenev	Jászfényszaru-E at 12:30, 6 Bf 109
122 IAP	Yak-9T	2515396	I. C. Babanin MIA	Jászfényszaru-E at 12:20, Bf 109s
179 IAP	Yak-1B	12152	M. V. Meshkov	Tiszapüspöki, LAC at 13:55 LT
513 IAP	Yak-9T	1015328	G. D. Yarovoy+	Hatvan, after 10:52 LT, 4 *Fw 190s*
149 GvIAP	Yak-9M	3615389	V. A. Ustich WIA	Alsódabas-NE, ~09:10 LT, flak
150 GvIAP	Yak-3	1229217	S. G. Yefimenkov	Pécel, 15:15LT, 6 Bf 109,8 Fw 190
150 GvIAP	Yak-3	3429214	A. N. Agdantsev	Isaszeg, 13:42 LT, 8 Yak, 4 Bf 109
150 GvIAP	Yak-9D	2315371	G. Y. Bekkerman	Dogfight at Kóka, landing accident
177 GvIAP	La-5	*3921xxxx*	A. D. Dogadailo	*Damaged by Hungarian 101/3. FS.*
177 GvIAP	La-5	*3921xxxx*	G. M. Pyatakov	*Damaged by German Bf 109s*
178 GvIAP	La-5FN	39212952	B. V. Zhigulenkov+	Besenyszög-SE, 6 Bf 109, *~10:10*
192 IAP	La-5F	39214932	V. M. Olnev WIA	Nagykáta-NE, 14:00LT, 6 *Fw 190s*

On 16 November 1944 Lt. Heinz Ewald claimed a La-5 and three Yak-9 fighters shot down in the greater Jászberény area. His La-5 claim was most likely 178 GvIAP ace Gv.St.Lt. Boris Vasilevich Zhigulenkov (HSU) whose La-5FN crashed at Besenyszög-SE, 4 km near the Tisza river.[18] Between 09:45-10:35 LT five 178 GvIAP La-5s were covering Soviet ground troops in the Jászberény-Pusztamonostor-Jászárokszállás triangle. Gv.Capt. Kirill Alekseevich Yevstigneev (HSU) led three and Gv.St.Lt. Pyotr Romanovich Shetinin led two La-5s.[19] After multiple engagements with twelve Bf 109s and eight Fw 190s near Pusztamonostor the La-5s were attacked by another five Bf 109s. The Soviets, being already low on fuel and ammunition suddenly turned back and tried to pull the Messerschmitts over Soviet held territory to the South-South East. Near Besenyszög at only about 100m the sixth Bf 109 attacked Zhigulenkov from below. His La-5FN was hit, his right landing gear fell off and he probably received an incoming bullet to the head. His plane rolled over and exploded instantly on the bank of the Tisza River covering the surrounding area with its burning debris. Lt. Ewald wittnessed this from a very close range and the local Soviet troops also confirmed Zhigulenkov's fatal crash. Zhigulenkov's body was returned to the 178 GvIAP.[20] According to Ewald, he attacked a lone La-5 which had separated from its flight around 100m above the Front line, and when his ammunition struck, the Soviet fighter turned over to the right and crashed near the river bank scattering burning debris 40m from the impact point.[21] Although Ewald's claiming time does not exactly match the Soviet records, yet because all major details are the same, we can consider his La-5 claim an aerial victory.

Soon after this between 10:30-11:45 LT eight La-5s of the 177 GvIAP, led by regiment commander Gv.Col. Grigorii Mihailovich Pyatakov covered ground troops in the same Jászárokszállás-Pusztamonostor-Jászberény triangle. Four planes were led by Gv.Col. Pyatakov, the other four were led by Gv.St.Lt. Pyotr Stephanovich Olin. At 10:40 LT at approximately 3500m five kilometers South of Jászárokszállás they met nine Ju 87G Stukas and eight Bf 109s. The Bf 109s attacked Pyatakov's flight and damaged his pane, but was saved by Gv.St.Lt. Aleksei Dmitrievich Dogadailo who chased two Bf 109s away from Pyatakov. At 10:50 LT at 2500m six kilometers West of Heves another 'six' Bf 109s attacked the Lavochkins, this time four Bf 109s of the Hungarian 101/3. FS (Debrődy-Boldizsár and Tobak-Pintér). The Bf 109s led by ace Debrődy György fhdgy. used their altitude advantage to attack Gv.St.Lt. Pyotr Stephanovich Olin's flight head-on. Debrődy, who opened fire on Olin's La-5, got the impression that his smoking opponent was already finished-off and thus he did not

18 La-5FN (c/n: 39212952, ASh-82FN engine: 8213749, white '<★52') Source: TsAMO RF, f. 20511, inv. 1, f. 195, p. 78. Order No.0229 of 14 GvIAD (22.11.1944) on enrollment and cancellation of aircrafts and aircraft engines.

19 On 16 November 1944 Gv.Capt. Yevstigneev's 178 GvIAP 1st Sq. plane in which he claimed a Bf 109 over Jászárokszállás was probably his famous La-5, c/n: 3811414, engine: 6504396, white '<★14' which was sent to Odessa (76 OTTR) for repair on 18 November 1944 among other La-5s. Yevstigneev's next plane that he broke upon landing on the Dunakeszi (Alagivilla) airfield after a dogfight with Fw 190s on 17 February 1945 was La-5FN, c/n: 39211445, engine: 8212047, white '<★45'.

20 Combat log of the 14 GvIAD, TsAMO RF: fu. 20062, inv. 1, f. 32, p. 303.

21 Heinz Ewald, *ESAU: Heinz Ewald Als Jagdflieger Im Erfolgreichsten Jagdeschwader 1943-1945* (Coburg, Self-Published, 1980), pp. 102-103.

visually track him. Gv.St.Lt. Olin pulled up into a loop while being fired at by Pintér and Tobak hdgy. In the raging dogfight Gv.Ml.Lt. Igor Wilhelmovich Zemit claimed a Bf 109 which damaged Gv.St.Lt. Dogadailo's La-5.[22] Although both sides claimed several aerial victories, neither the Messerschmitts nor the Lavochkins permanently lost any planes in this battle which gradually moved in a WNW direction towards Hatvan, where Debrődy and a 513 IAP Yak-9T mutually shot each other down in a head-on attack. The Yak-9T blew up mid-air, while Debrődy's plane was shot up with 12.7mm bullets.[23] One of them passed through his abdomen but he managed to crash-land along the Hatvan railway-line and was rushed to the hospital, which ended his fighting career. The bullet which ricocheted back into his body was removed in 1967! He passed away in 1984 in Cortland, New York, USA.

Later during the day Lt. Heinz Ewald claimed two more Soviet Yak fighters which belonged to the same Soviet flight due to the close claiming times (11:46, 11:51 LT). The most likely candidates for this incident are Yak-1B and Yak-9M fighters of the 122 IAP. Around 12:00 LT six Il-2s, escorted by three 122 IAP Yak-1Bs and a Yak-9M,[24] were flying in the Hatvan area when over Csány (roughly Gyöngyös-SW, 20 km) four Bf 109s and four Fw 190s attacked them. Capt. Pyotr Grigorevich Artemev's Yak-1B and Ml.Lt. Boris Aleksandrovich Horkin's Yak-9M were shot down, while Artemev's wingman Ml.Lt. Ilya Yegorovich Kostenko (Yak-1B, c/n: 45170) claimed one *'Fw 190'*.

At 12:30 LT at 1200m another flight of four 122 IAP Yak-9s escorting the next group of six Il-2s into the Hatvan area met 16 Bf 109s. In the unfolding dogfight the Soviet formation was broken and individual planes tried to defend themselves in the intense chase. St.Lt. Anatolii Mihailovich Znamenev (white '32') and Ml.Lt. Ivan Constantinovich Babanin (white '96') were hit and went missing. Ml.Lt. Yosif Dmitrievich Nabeda (Yak-9M, c/n: 3215344, white '44')[25] and Ml.Lt. Victor Mitrofanovich Koltsov (Yak-9T, c/n: 1515342, white '2'),[26] each claimed a Bf 109 and returned to their airfield alone.

Later at 14:03 LT Lt. Ewald claimed his fourth victory of the day over a Yak-9, which does not match the reported Soviet losses. This claim could have been a damaged Yakovlev fighter of an unidentified regiment.

17 November 1944 (Friday)

Ewald's 40th: VICTORY, Yak-9 at 08:36 LT in the Jászberény area, ground level
Ewald's 41st: POTENTIAL VICTORY, Il-2 at 11:06 LT in the Gyöngyös area, 150m

Soviet 5 VA Il-2 Sturmovik and single-engine fighter losses on 17 November 1944				
Regiment:	**Type:**	**c/n:**	**Pilot:**	**Details:**
235 ShAP	Il-2m3	9933	G. K. Denisenko	Debrecen AB, flak, chrash-landed
90 GvShAP	Il-2m3	*10392*	I. P. Kurilov+	Gyöngyöshalász, 11:05 LT to Bf 109
90 GvShAP	Il-2m3	*11360*	V. A. Ivlev WIA	Jászladány-SW, 11:05 LT to Bf 109
90 GvShAP	Il-2m3	*1875681**	M. E. Sudorgin	Flew: 07:50-9:10 LT, walked back
90 GvShAP	Il-2m3	*1872699*	N. V. Halin	Csány, 11:05 LT to Bf 109
131 GvShAP	Il-2m3	12315	I. V. Derkachev	*Missing on a test flight, returned*
188 GvShAP	Il-2m3	10956	G. S. Tyurikov+	Nagyréde, 13:45 LT, 11 Il, 4 Bf 109s
122 IAP	Yak-9M	2715306	V. M. Boltachev+	Hort, 08:50 LT, 400m, *2 Fw 190s*
122 IAP	Yak-9M	2615394	V.N. Gaponov+	Hort, Bf 109, Lipfert at 13:20 LT
179 IAP	Yak-1B	02162	S. G. Purgin MIA	Csány-SE, 12:50 LT, 8 Bf 109s
149 GvIAP	Yak-1B	37191	V. P. Isupov	Kóka-E, 15:00 LT, 4 Fw, 2 Bf 109s
151 GvIAP	Yak-1B	17139	A.V. Noskov MIA	Dány-Tura, 09:40-10:50 LT, 3500m
178 GvIAP	La-5FN	39212821	Lt. Myakinin MIA	Missing, 4 La-5s covering airfield

* This wreck with AM-38F engine: 255981 was later used for spare parts to repair other Il-2s.

On 17 November 1944 Lt. Heinz Ewald claimed a Yak-9 and an Il-2 Sturmovik in the Jászberény and Gyöngyös areas. This day around 08:50 LT six 122 IAP Yaks led by Maj. Nikolai Pavlovich Gugnin were returning from a combat mission

22 Gv.Ml.Lt. Zemit was shot down by Bf 109s on 6 January 1945 in La-5FN, c/n: 39212616 but survived.

23 Debrődy's opponent was probably Lt. Georgii Dorofeevich Yarovoy (513 IAP, Yak-9T, c/n: 1015328), who went missing at Hatvan after 10:52 LT. Lt. Yarovoy was covering St.Lt. Grigorii Kirillovich Denisenko's six 235 ShAP Il-2s with his flight of four Yaks (Malikov, Kovalenko, Astashkevich, Yarovoy), when they met 16 *Fw 190s* at Hatvan. During the 3rd attack at around 11:00 LT he was downed by four *'Fw 190s'*. Note, the arriving Hungarian flight also consisted of four Bf 109s. (Debrődy, Boldizsár, Tobak, Pintér)

24 There was ongoing pressure for the Soviet ground crews to keep the returning and combat damaged planes in flying condition. Pilots flew the planes which were availabe at the moment.

25 Since Ml.Lt. Yosif Dmitrievich Nabeda lost this plane on 21 December 1944, it is assumed that he flew this plane on this mission as well.

26 Since Ml.Lt. Victor Mitrofanovich Koltsov lost this plane on 22 December 1944, it is assumed that he flew this plane on this mission as well.

when at 400m two *'Fw 190s'* surprised them in a frontal attack. Lt. Venyamin Mihailovich Boltachev's Yak-9M was hit, he pulled up sharply, went into a spin and struck the ground South of Hort. The pilot was killed and his plane (white '06') was completely destroyed. This was Lt. Heinz Ewald's legitimate Yak-9 aerial victory in the Hort-Jászberény area.

The other 122 IAP flight of six Yak-1Bs had more luck. While escorting six 92 GvShAP Il-2s to the Gyöngyös-Hort area between 07:58-09:18 LT and confronting six Bf 109s,[27] they claimed two Bf 109s shot down without suffering any losses. One Bf 109 was claimed by Ml.Lt. Evgenii Semyonovich Titov (Yak-1B, c/n: 32161, white '1').[28]

Later around 11:00 LT six 90 GvShAP Il-2 Sturmoviks led by Gv.Maj. Aleksandr Grigorevich Kuzin were attacked by six German Bf 109s in the Hort, Gyöngyös-SW area.[29] In the unfolding dogfight the Soviets lost three ground-attack planes, one probably to Heinz Ewald, but due to the small area and short timeframe their exact identities cannot be determined.

5 December 1944 (Tuesday)
Ewald's 42nd: OVERCLAIM, Yak-9 at 10:51 LT at Hatvan-SE, ground level
Ewald's 43rd: VICTORY, Yak-9 at 11:04 LT at Hatvan-SE, 400m
Ewald's 44th: OVERCLAIM, LaGG-5 at 13:34 LT at Hatvan-SE, 400m
Ewald's 45th: VICTORY, Yak-9 at 15:09 LT at Tura-W, 400m

Soviet 5 VA single-engine fighter losses on 5 December 1944

Regiment:	Type:	c/n:	Pilot:	Details:
122 IAP	Yak-9T	1615383	M. S. Yerko MIA	Erdőtarcsa, 10:12 LT to Hptm. Lipfert
122 IAP	Yak-9M	3015336	G. A. Ulanov	Heréd, 15:05 LT to Heinz Ewald
513 IAP	Yak-1B	20153	I. A. Guriev MIA	Erdőtarcsa, 11:00 LT to Heinz Ewald
151 GvIAP	Yak-3	1529219	Y.M. Ravikovich+	Ercsi, 14:00 LT, 8 Yaks, to *Fw 190s*
151 GvIAP	Yak-3	*Unknown*	A. A. Morozov	Ercsi area to Bf 109s and Fw 190s*
177 GvIAP	La-5F	39215215	P. S. Olin	*Stabilizator damage, repaired later*
177 GvIAP	La-5FN	39211776	N. L. Vereshak	To flak, his next La-5 was 41210115
177 GvIAP	La-5FN	39212384	I. G. Sklyarov	*Cylinder damage, repaired at base*
486 IAP	La-5FN	39212724	V. G. Snagovskii+	Ercsi, 11:55 LT, 2 La-5 vs. 6 *'Fw 190'*

* This is a questionable loss since the 13 GvIAD, 151 GvIAP record of the day does not mention it, only Morozov's personal record written on 26 April 1945 (TsAMO RF: fu. 33, inv. 690306, storage: 1237-41950045, p. 28b), the date of 5 December 1944 could just be a typo (This is the only known contradicting case).

On 5 December 1944 at 11:00 LT eight 513 IAP Yak-1B and Yak-9 fighters escorted twelve 809 ShAP Il-2 Sturmoviks in the Erdőtarcsa area at Hatvan-NW. At 1500m the Soviet planes encountered eight Bf 109s which hit Ml.Lt. Ivan Arhipovich Guriev's Yak-1B during the first attack. This Soviet fighter was downed by Lt. Heinz Ewald as his second Yak-9 claim of the day while the Il-2s suffered no losses. Later the same units repeated their attack in the Szirák area. This time six 513 IAP Yak-1Bs led by Capt. Ivan Akimovich Malikov Sq. commander escorted St.Lt. Mihail Constantinovich Fokin's eight 809 ShAP Il-2s, when at 13:35 LT at the altitude of 800m they met four Bf 109s and two *Fw 190s*. In the unfolding dogfight the Yak-1Bs downed a Bf 109 which went down near Szirák. Flight-leader Lt. Aleksandr Grigorevich Grigorev while defending the Il-2s repelled three attacks of the enemy fighters, therefore the Soviet formation suffered no losses.

At 15:05 LT four 122 IAP Yak fighters escorted ten Il-2 Sturmoviks at 2000m over Heréd (Hatvan-NW) when four Bf 109s attacked them. The hydraulic system of Lt. Georgii Aleksandrovich Ulanov's Yak-9M was shot out (c/n: 3015336, engine: 425-1016, white '36'), he belly-landed near Pusztamonostor at Hatvan-SE. The plane was lost but the pilot remained unhurt. This Yak-9 was Lt. Heinz Ewald's legitimate aerial victory at 15:09 LT at Tura-W.

Lt. Heinz Ewald's first Yak-9 and La-5 claims this day were overclaims. He probably hit one of the two damaged La-5s of the 177 GvIAP, which were escorting A-20G Bostons of the 218 BAD to Vác and one of the Yaks of the 331 IAD, which with some minor combat damages both returned to their bases.

27 In the 92 GvShAP combat diary there were eight Il-2 crews selected for this mission, but in fact only six of them flew it. (Yakurnov, Pashenko, Demianov, Sokolov, Ryabov, Poletaev, Timchenko and Vinokurov) Two of them probably returned early for various reasons.
28 Since Ml.Lt. Evgenii Semyonovich Titov lost this plane on 23 November 1944, it is assumed that he flew this plane on this mission as well.
29 According to their combat diary the six 90 GvShAP Il-2 crews flying this mission were: Kuzin, Ivlev, Halin, Novikov, Kurilov and Ivanov. Kurilov, Ivlev and Halin were downed by enemy fighters.

8 December 1944 (Friday)
Ewald's unconfirmed claim: OVERCLAIM, Yak-9 around 15:00 LT

Soviet 5 and 17 VA single-engine fighter losses on 8 December 1944				
Regiment:	**Type:**	**c/n:**	**Pilot:**	**Details:**
897 IAP	Yak-9T	0815363	V. I. Tichkov	Decs, ferry-flight acc. at 10:20 LT
897 IAP	Yak-9T	0715373	V. M. Kolyagin	Decs, TAC at 11:00 LT
513 IAP	Yak-1B	46155	V. I. Malishev+	Flak, overheated, exploded mid-air
178 GvIAP	La-5FN	39211331	P. A. Brizgalov	MIA, La-5 from 179 GvIAP: 9.44.
178 GvIAP	La-5FN	39211699	V. P. Muhin	*MIA, later returned*

On 8 December 1944 Lt. Heinz Ewald had an unconfirmed Yak-9 claim which turns out to be an overclaim as neither the 5 VA nor the 17 VA had any dogfight related Yakovlev loss. The only combat related Yakovlev loss was Lt. Victor Ivanovich Malishev's Yak-1B (513 IAP, c/n: 46155, engine: 335-2120) which was damaged by flak over the target. This day four Yak-1Bs escorted ten 809 ShAP Il-2s over Balassagyarmat at 1500m, where Lt. Malishev's Yak-1B was hit by flak around 15:10 LT. He turned back and reported that his engine coolant overheated to 125-130 degrees due to radiator damage, and then his plane suddenly exploded in mid-air killing him. No enemy fighters were involved in his loss. One of the escorted Il-2s (c/n: 1874477, AM-38F engine: 258123) broke upon landing, but pilot Ml.Lt. Mihail Afanasevich Tereshenko remained unhurt. Over Verőce at 2500m four 31 GvIAP Yak-1Bs battled with four Bf 109s, but they suffered no losses. Gv.St.Lt. Nikolai Zakharovich Vidrigan claimed one Bf 109 shot down which was confirmed by Gv.Ml.Lt. Kutsenko and Gv.Lt. Krivosheev. 179 IAP Yak-1B pair of Maj. Kostikov – St.Lt. Bocharov met two Bf 109s and downed both. Pilots of 73, 85 and 150 GvIAPs also battled with German planes, but according to their combat reports they were all Fw 190s.

11 December 1944 (Monday)
Ewald's 46th: VICTORY, Yak-9 at 11:56 LT at Budapest-SW 20 km, at 4500m

Soviet 5 and 17 VA single-engine fighter losses on 11 December 1944				
Regiment:	**Type:**	**c/n:**	**Pilot:**	**Details:**
267 IAP	Yak-1B	16168	A. I. Korzun	Yugoslavia-N, Bagatić-SE, 2 km
611 IAP	Yak-1B	26170	V. A. Shelkunov	Taszár, at take-off hit a vehicle
611 IAP	Yak-9T	0915336	B. A. Kovalevskii	Taszár, combat damages, CL
659 IAP	Yak-9D	2515335	N. S. Semikin WIA	Out of fuel after dogfight, CL
866 IAP	Yak-9T	1215373	M. L. Serdyuk+	615 ShAP Il-2 escort to Tapolca, lost at Marcali-Nagybajom
866 IAP	Yak-9T	1315325	A. Shamshik MIA	
178 Gv IAP	La-5FN	39213286	P. A. Brizgalov	*Missing, later returned, '<★86'*
486 IAP	La-5FN	39213272	*Unknown*	*Damaged in air combat, repaired*
149 GvIAP	Yak-1B	11179	A. A. Merzlenko+	Ercsi-N, 11:20 LT to Bf 109
151 GvIAP	Yak-9T	2415358	L. I. Toropov	Tököl-W, 5 km
122 IAP	Yak-9M	2515346	V. E. Stadnik	Jászberény, 14:50 LT, in accident

The events, as recalled by Lt. Ewald, for this day generally overlap with existing documents though there are a few inconsistencies with his story. Supposedly on the day that he was ordered to relocate from the Budaörs airfield to Csór, his aerial experience can be called a real 'dog-fight' by all means! It should be noted that the relocation date occurred a few days prior on 9 December 1944, however the story is interesting regardless and matches the Soviet loss records.

Packing up their gear and supplies, the pilots of II./JG 52 ate a lunch partly consisting of red cabbage before they mounted their machines and took off. As was common in all airforces at the time, unit pets were kept around and cared for throughout the war to normalize an otherwise non-normal way of life. The unit's dog 'Maxi' was taken in by Ewald and sat behind his seat in the cockpit. Suddenly an alarmstart occurred for enemy fighters and light bombers (Il-2s) on course for Budapest flying at roughly 5000m.[30] Ewald and his wingman climbed up to 5500m then pounced in the incoming enemy flight and Lt. Ewald hit the incoming lead plane.[31] Coming out of the strike and dodging incoming enemy bullets Ewald

30 Ewald, Klinnert, *Heinz Ewald "Esau"*, p. 145.
31 Ewald, Klinnert, *Heinz Ewald "Esau"*, p. 145.

became perplexed at the strange smell of red cabbage reeking in his cockpit, fully forgetting that he had taken along Maxi for the ride.[32] Taking the dog up to a heigh of several kilometers without access to fresh oxygen, into an attacking dive and intense combat, Ewald looked back and saw that poor Maxi had vomited red cabbage into the cockpit and was in a 'half-dead state'.[33] This account contradicts the altitude written in the microfilm rolls, though it is possible that without access to these original film rolls Heinz Ewald only remembered that he flew at an elevated altitude that day.

This day the crossing at Ercsi was part of the main focus of the Red Army, and as such their massive force was spotted by the Luftwaffe. According to German intelligence the Soviets were preparing to strike and cross the Danube South of Budapest on-mass with 520 vechicles in the Danube-Balaton area, 22 tanks Southeast of Balatonfőkajár, 7 tanks in the NW area of Ercsi. One bridge was under construction at Ercsi and another was being extended with pontoons on the rivershore, while five ferries were making constant crossings. To the East of the Danube and North of Budapest over 5600 vechiles were making their way towards the front on the roads and some 45 tanks were also spotted.[34] To cover such a force the VVS had a constant flow of ground cover missions in store for the day, with near round-the-clock coverage offered to the ground personell hence it is one of two of these covering flights that Lt. Ewald engaged with.

Between 10:45-11:45 LT two Yaks led by Gv.Lt. Andrey Andreevich Merzlenko covered another four Yaks flying a ground cover mission over Ercsi between the altitudes of 3000m to 3500m. At 11:20 LT the group was attacked by Bf 109s and leader Merzlenko was shot down falling North of Ercsi. Between 11:35-12:45 LT two 151 GvIAP Yak-9s and four Yak-1Bs led by Gv.St.Lt. Pavel Nikolaevich Parovin covered Soviet ground troops in the Ercsi-Baracska-Martonvásár triangle Southwest of Budapest. After being attacked, the Rogatin-Toropov pair made a 180-degree turn and separated from their flight by about 150-200m. Gv.Ml.Lt. Lev Ivanovich Toropov took the pair's lead position when they were suddenly ambushed by two Bf 109s. Gv.Ml.Lt. Toropov broke out to the left but was hit and his Yak-9T (c/n: 2415358, engine: 415-2116) burst into flames. He tried to crashland his doomed fighter, but the flames reached his cockpit and he had to abandon his plane. Toropov bailed out with his parachute slightly burned and landed at 5 kilometers West of Tököl between Százhalombatta and Martonvásár.[35] It is certain that Lt. Ewald actually shot down a Soviet fighter this day, and it is very likely that Toropov's Yak-9 became Lt. Heinz Ewald's legitimate aerial victory.

14 December 1944 (Thursday)
Ewald's 47th: POTENTIAL VICTORY, Il-2 at 10:25 LT at Székesfehérvár-W, -NW, 15 km (Jenő-N), 400m

Soviet 17 VA Il-2 Sturmovik losses on 14 December 1944				
Regiment:	**Type:**	**c/n:**	**Pilot:**	**Details:**
210 ShAP	Il-2m3	*1887403*	A. I. Dolgov	*Damaged by fighter, white '3'*
715 ShAP	Il-2m3	11551	Y. M. Timofeev+	Sank in Lake Balaton due to flak*
715 ShAP	Il-2m3	11429 **	Y. K. Berg+	Balatonkenese-NW, Sár-Hill, Bf
715 ShAP	Il-2m3	11565	M. I. Nuhalov+	Lost between Csór-Úrhida between 11:00-11:20 LT to JG 52 pilots, including Ewald and Pitzl.
715 ShAP	Il-2m3	11550	V. V. Burlutskii+	
715 ShAP	Il-2m3	18862106	A. Shashkin POW	
715 ShAP	Il-2m3	11553	I. I. Dolgov WIA	Szabadszállás at landing, Bf 109s
715 ShAP	Il-2m3	10958	A. G. Anisimov	Near Szabadszállás to Bf 109s

* This Il-2 with replacement AM-38F engine: 259059 was shot down at 11:03 LT over Balatonkenese, ditched in the lake and sank. The crew of Ml.Lt. Timofeev – Gv.St.Sgt. Udalov perished. Recovered in 1999, it is now on display in the Szolnok Aircraft Museum (RepTár). Although Lt. Worlitzsch also claimed this very plane, the damages to the engine indicate that it was downed by flak.

** Based on the available documents, some aircraft construction numbers cannot be matched to the lost aircrews with complete certainity.

Between 08:55-11:55 LT Il-2 Sturmoviks of the 715 and 989 ShAP attacked the Berhida, Csajág, Úrhida, Szabadbattyán, Balatonkenese, Ősi and Vilonya areas in multiple waves.

32 Ewald, Klinnert, *Heinz Ewald "Esau"*, p. 145.
33 Ewald, Klinnert, *Heinz Ewald "Esau"*, p. 146.
34 Aufklärungsubersicht 11.12.1944. TsAMO RF, f. 500, inv. 12472, f. 382, p. 126.
35 The small town of Martonvásár is famous for the Brunszvik Palace, the former estate of the music-loving Brunszvik family that Ludwig van Beethoven (1770-1827) visited many times in the early 1800s as his favorite getaway and where he composed many of his pieces, including his famous *Für Elise*. Hungary's first known Christmas tree (in 1824) and the establishment of the first kindergarten called 'Angel Garden' are also linked to the Brunszvik family. In January 1945 during the Konrad operations the Brunszvik Palace operated as a frontline hospital and as such survived the war.

American 'ALCLAD 24S-T' stamps on the tail section of Ml.Lt. Yakov Matveevich Timofeev's 715 ShAP Ilyushin Il-2m3 Sturmovik (c/n: 11551), downed into Lake Balaton on 14 December 1944 and recovered in 1999. This picture clearly shows that even some typical Soviet aircrafts, such as the Il-2 Sturmovik, were partially built using Lend-Lease raw materials. (Photo: Authors' collection)

(L-R) 715 ShAP airmen who flew the 14 December 1944 Székesfehérvár-W, Balatonkenese missions: Sq. commander Capt. Mihail Ivanovich Nuhalov, Sq. commander Capt. Aleksei Alekseevich Katkov, Lt. Ivan Illarionovich Dolgov pilot (after the war) and aerial gunner Gv.St.Sgt. Ivan Ivanovich Udalov (+), who was lost in Lake Balaton with Il-2m3, c/n: 11551. (Photos via Boris V. Davidov)

Between 10:58-11:10 LT Capt. Aleksei Alekseevich Katkov's nine yellow spinner Il-2s strafed the German vehicle concentration in Balatonkenese on the Eastern shore of Lake Balaton.[36] Their fighter escort was provided by six La-5 fighters of the 116 IAP. Since the Sturmoviks flew into a solid wall of German anti-aircraft fire over the shore, Capt. Katkov ordered his Il-2s into a defense circle over the water and gave orders to strafe and rocket the shore in turns.[37] The Il-2s attacked six times while German flak and the attacking fighters downed two of them during their second and third strikes. Ml.Lt. Yurii Constantinovich Berg's plane fell on Sár-Hill at Balatonkenese-NW and exploded on impact, while Ml.Lt. Yakov Matveevich Timofeev ditched into Lake Balaton.[38] His engine was hit by flak on the port side, the oil pressure dropped, and with a failing engine he was forced to ditch into the freezing lake approximately two kilometers from shore. The plane sunk and the crew tried to reach the German held shore, but with their heavy wet flight suits they never finished the journey. When their plane was recovered in May of 1999, the canopy was found open and both seats were empty.[39] Four other Il-2s were damaged by Hungarian and German Bf 109s of I./JG 53, but they all were able to return to Szabadszállás.

36 Capt. Katkov, Ml.Lt. Berg, Ml.Lt. Godiaev, Ml.Lt. Kurtsidze, St.Lt. Larin, Ml.Lt. Timofeev and others.

37 This day the 136 ShAD Il-2s fired 119 RS-82 wing mounted rockets on their targets. TsAMO RF, fu. 20541, inv. 1, f. 203, p. 7, Operations journal of 136 ShAD, entry for 14 December 1944.

38 TsAMO RF: fu. 20541, inv. 1, f. 195, p. 115, Combat diary (losses) of 136 ShAD, 715 ShAP, entry for 14 December 1944. (Ml.Lt. Yakov Matveevich Timofeev's plane.)

39 The plane left the assembly line of Factory No.1 on 12 April 1944. Its AM-38F engine (No.259059) was already a replacement engine that was built on 25 April 1944 and was installed on 15 July 1944. (TsAMO RF: fu. 370, inv. 6552, f. 126.) The numbers of the installed weapons during its loss in Lake Balaton were ПР290 and А3188 (23mm cannons), ДЕ140 (12.7mm) and КЖ172 (7.62mm) machine guns. The cannons were loaded mainly with 1944 and 1942 manufactured rounds from Ordnance Plants No.513 (Omsk) and 606 (Kemerovo) with headstamps 513-44, 606-42, 606-44 among others. The aircraft is now on display in the Szolnok Aircraft Museum (RepTár) in Hungary.

Gv.S-a Nina Arkadevna Altsibeeva (Photo: Женские авиаполки. История. Факты. Лица, vk.com)

The Soviet fighter escort lost one plane, Lt. Leonid Nikolaevich Sokolov's La-5FN (c/n: 39211276, white '76') which was downed by Horváth György hdgy. (Hungarian 102/1. FS) over Balatonakarattya. Two other La-5s were damaged during the dogfight (Lt. Zolotarskii and Ml.Lt. Aganin).[40] Kálmán István zls. (102/1. FS) claimed two, Lt. Joachim Worlitzsch and Uffz. Hommes (2./JG 53) claimed three more Il-2s in the Balatonkenese area, right in the Soviets' reported timeframe between 11:03-09 LT. Fhr. Hans Joachim Kawig's (5./JG 52) Yak-9 claim at 10:20 LT at 300m near Szabadbattyán was an overclaim, since this day the 17 VA lost no Yakovlev fighters at all (64 planes flew 72 reconnaissance and escort sorties for the 189 ShAD, claiming one *'Fw 190'* in the only dogfight without suffering any losses). However, it is possible, that Fhr. Kawig's 'Yak-9' was just a damaged Yak-3 from Capt. Aleksandr Pavlovich Frolov's 659 IAP reconnaissance pair, which was engaged in dogfight with enemy fighters over Polgárdi at 600m in which Capt. Frolov claimed one *'Fw 190'* near Nádasdladány. Yak-3, c/n: 1229215, white '12' was repaired by 15 December 1944. Later, on 21 December 1944 its airframe was lost when St.Lt. Mihail Aleksandrovich Fisenko crash-landed.

Between 11:00-11:20 LT, at the altitude of 200-400m Capt. Mihail Ivanovich Nuhalov's other nine red spinner Il-2 Sturmoviks attacked German transportation in the Székesfehérvár-WNW area. They were escorted by Capt. Anatolii Aleksandrovich Pantelkin's six 116 IAP La-5FN fighters. The Soviet planes were ambushed near the target by approximately 20 Bf 109s and 30 *Fw 190s*. In the unfolding intense dogfight three Il-2s were shot down (Capt. Mihail Ivanovich Nuhalov,[41] Lt. Vasilii Vasilevich Burlutskii,[42] and Ml.Lt. Aleksei Vasilevich Shashkin[43]), while Lt. Ivan Illarionovich Dolgov crash-landed near their airbase with 150 holes in his plane. Ml.Lt. Aleksei Grigorevich Anisimov successfully reached Szabadszállás and crash-landed on the airfield. His Il-2m3 was written off, while two others required major factory repairs.

Meantime, Sturmoviks of the 989 ShAP attacked Berhida, Polgárdi and Csajág without losses. Their aerial gunners repelled the attacks of some *'Fw 190's*.

So which of these Il-2s was claimed by Lt. Heinz Ewald over Jenő-N? The exact identiy of this plane remains unknown. Based on his reported area, this Il-2 belonged to Capt. Nuhalov's nine-plane flight, which indeed lost three Il-2s over the target. But Ewald, along with Fw. Pitzl, claimed his Sturmovik 35-55 minutes earlier than the actual battle, so perhaps his time was recorded incorrectly. If his time was correct, then he just damaged an Il-2 of another flight (perhaps from the 989 ShAP) which suffered no losses. However, since this cannot be proven, Ewalds Il-2 claim may be considered as a potential victory.

Despite of the significant losses in the Lake Balaton area, regiments of the 17 VA continued their reconnaissance sorties in the region. For instance, on 18 December 1944 between 10:20-11:45 LT Il-2m3 pair Lt. Chugunov – Ml.Lt. Turusov (995 ShAP, 1st Sq.) flew a photo-reconnaissance mission in the Székesfehérvár-Szabadbattyán area. North of Tác they received strong anti-aircraft fire. Il-2m3 (c/n: 1875188, AM-38F engine: 255264) was hit, Lt. Aleksei Terentevich Chugunov tried to get back to this base however his engine quit shortly thereafter and they belly-landed near Hantos, Sárbogárd-NE. Around 15:00 LT a Po-2 biplane was sent out to pick up the downed crew. The ferry pilot this time was 29 year old Nina Arkadevna Altsibeeva of the 306 ShAD HQ, who was a very experienced Po-2 pilot. Previously she flew in the famous 46 GvNBAP, the 'Night Witches', before she joined the 3rd Ukrainian Front on 23 July 1943. By April 1945 she

40 TsAMO RF: fu. 20259, inv. 1, f. 54, p. 30, Combat journal of 295 IAD, entry for 14 December 1944.
41 TsAMO RF: fu. 20541, inv. 1, f. 195, p. 114, Combat diary (losses) of 136 ShAD, 715 ShAP, entry for 14 December 1944. (Capt. Nuhalov's plane.)
42 TsAMO RF: fu. 20541, inv. 1, f. 195, p. 115, Combat diary (losses) of 136 ShAD, 715 ShAP, entry for 14 December 1944. (Lt. Burlutskii's plane.)
43 TsAMO RF: fu. 20541, inv. 1, f. 195, p. 115, Combat diary (losses) of 136 ShAD, 715 ShAP, entry for 14 December 1944. (Ml.Lt. Shashkin's plane.)

already completed 570 sorties during the Great Patriotic War. She looked for an apropriate landing spot when suddenly two low flying SG 10 Fw 190Fs ambushed her. Her plane was hit and she crash-landed in the woods from a very low altitude. Her Po-2 was lost (c/n: 5666, M-11 engine: 258173), but she survived the incident. Although this evacuation attempt failed, later all three crewmembers returned to their units.

22 December 1944 (Friday)
Ewald's 48th: POTENTIAL VICTORY, Il-2 at Csór, ~14:00 LT

Soviet 17 VA Il-2 Sturmovik losses on 22 December 1944				
Regiment:	**Type:**	**c/n:**	**Pilot:**	**Details:**
639 ShAP	Il-2m3	1876296	N. S. Baklanov	Pátka-SW, Bf 109s, crash-landed
639 ShAP	Il-2m3	18756101	M. E. Aksengor	Pátka-SW, Bf 109, Őcsény airfield
639 ShAP	Il-2m3	11249	M.P. Ratnikov+	Pátka-Zámoly, Bf 109s
639 ShAP	Il-2m3	1871698	V. T. Montrezor	Pátka-SW, Bf 109s
639 ShAP	Il-2m3	1876996	G. Semenov POW	Pátka-SW, Bf 109s
639 ShAP	Il-2m3	11271	M. A. Pletnev	Pátka-SW, Bf 109s
672 ShAP	Il-2m3	1871398	*M. A. Sizikov?*	*Damaged, repaired at airbase*
672 ShAP	Il-2m3	1870288	A. M. Kianovskii	Kecel, airbase accident at 12:10 LT
672 ShAP	Il-2m3	1872184	I. M. Baranov KIFA	Kecel, airbase accident at 12:10 LT
672 ShAP	Il-2m3	18763100	E. V. Vaitsitskii	Kecel, 15:00LT, burned at landing
672 ShAP	Il-2m3	9466	*A. V. Pernaki* *	*Flak damage, repaired at airbase*
672 ShAP	Il-2m3	*Unknown***	P. A. Kuzmin	Székesfehérvár flak, 13:00 at base
707 ShAP	Il-2m3	11649	N. P. Mironov	Székesfehérvár-N, 14:50, 2 Bf 109s
951 ShAP	Il-2m3	1883301	N. B. Baronin+	Csákvár-NE, 09:40LT, Flakpanzer
951 ShAP	Il-2m3	1873693	P. A. Marakulin+	Near Lake Velence, to Flakpanzer
951 ShAP	Il-2m3	1884401	G. P. Odnotsenov	Near L. Velence, Bf 109, 11:50 LT
951 ShAP	Il-2m3	11118	Y. P. Vaslyanin	Flak, parts salvaged by 367 BAO
995 ShAP	Il-2m3	1874686	A. I. Groshev ret.	Dinnyés-NW, 10:30 LT to Bf 109
995 ShAP	Il-2m3	1886603	N. S. Shepochkin	Gyulamajor, 10:30 LT to Bf 109
995 ShAP	Il-2m3	1875696	V. I. Seregin+	Zámoly-NE, 10:30 LT to flak

* This Il-2 with AM-38F engine: 254007 piloted by Lt. Aleksandr Vasilevich Pernaki was downed by Flakpanzer on 21 January 1945 near Dömsöd. Perhaps he flew it on 22 December as well.

** Without crew details the 672 ShAP mechanical records list a few Il-2 Sturmoviks lost to flak in late 1944, such as 9978, 1871288, 1875588 and 18766100. Perhaps it was one of them.

On 22 December 1944 Lt. Heinz Ewald claimed an Il-2 Sturmovik shot down over Csór at Székesfehérvár-NW. This day several Il-2s were lost to enemy fighters in the very same area, therefore this can be considered a potential aerial victory for him, with Ml.Lt. Nikolai Petrovich Mironov's Il-2m3 (c/n: 11649, AM-38F engine: 2510494) being a potencial canidate. The exact identity of his victim however cannot be specified.

2 January 1945 (Tuesday)
Ewald's 49th: OVERCLAIM, La-5 at 12:?? LT at Gran-S
Ewald's 50th: POTENTIAL VICTORY, Yak-9 at 12:?? LT at Gran-S

Soviet 5 and 17 VA permanent single-engine fighter losses on 2 January 1945				
Regiment:	**Type:**	**c/n:**	**Pilot:**	**Details:**
31 IAP	La-5FN	39211844	D. S. Kravtsov WIA	Dág, after 10:45 LT, 4 (8) *Bf 109s*
116 IAP	La-5	*Unknown*	A. I. Roy returned	Tata, 8 La-5, 8 Bf 109s, crash-landed
611 IAP	Yak-9M	2515318	G. S. Gladkii WIA	Bánhida, 12:20 LT, 6-8 *Fw 190s**
611 IAP	Yak-9M	2515334	P. Y. Dimov+	Tata-SE, 2 km, 10:55 LT** to Bf 109
659 IAP	Yak-9T	2515315	Y. A. Vinogradov	Makád-S, 2 km, 08:05 LT, 1500m
659 IAP	Yak-9D	16166093	I. P. Trusin WIA	Tata, 08:05 LT, 1500m, 8 Bf 109s
897 IAP	Yak-9T	0815352	V. E. Novikov+	Vereb-W, 11:30, 2000m, 4 Bf 109s
897 IAP	Yak-9T	0815357	V. M. Gorbunov	Tata, 12:20LT to 8 Bf 109s, CL
92 IAP	La-5UTI	39215298	Rodionov-Hramov+	Örkény, fatal training accident, 2+
177 GvIAP	La-5FN	41210115	N. L. Vereshak	Kecskemét-SE, CL, out of fuel
331 IAD	Yak-1B	26174	*N/A*	Scrapped due to wear and tear
122 IAP	Yak-1B	04168	V. A. Kuznetsov	Tinnye, 08:50 LT to 6 *'Fw 190s'*
122 IAP	Yak-9T	1615361	E. S. Titov+	Vácrátót area, 08:50 LT, 6 *'Fw 190s'*

* This Yak-9M (engine: 425-43) was transferred from 17 VA, 236 IAD to 288 IAD in September 1944 in Burgas, Bulgaria and was lost on 2 January 1945.

** This 17 VA, 288 IAD, 611 IAP, 2nd Sq. Yak-9M previously served in the 17 VA, 236 IAD, 117 GvIAP in the summer of 1944 and was lost on 2 January 1945.

On 2 January 1945 Lt. Heinz Ewald reported aerial victories over a Soviet La-5 and a Yak-9 fighter South of the Gran river. At 12:20 LT six 897 IAP Yak-9T fighters (armed with 37mm cannons) were hunting for German tanks and transport vehicles in the Tata area when they fell into a dogfight with eight Bf 109s. Lt. Vasilii Mihailovich Gorbunov's Yak-9T was hit and he crash-landed on his airfield. The plane's airframe was written-off, its engine was salvaged but Lt. Gorbunov remained unhurt. Around the same time Lt. Heinz Ewald also claimed a La-5 fighter in the same area. The 295 IAD lost two La-5s while six others were damaged in air combat. Since the circumstances of the two lost La-5s point to other Luftwaffe pilots (including Helmut Lipfert), Lt. Heinz Ewald's La-5 claim this time was probably just one of the six damaged La-5s.

3 January 1945 (Wednesday)
Ewald's 51st: POTENTIAL VICTORY, Yak-9 at Gran-S
Ewald's 52nd: POTENTIAL VICTORY, Yak-9 at ~9:00 LT at Gran-S
Ewald's 53rd: POTENTIAL VICTORY, La-5 at ~9:00 LT at Gran-S
Ewald's 54th: OVERCLAIM, Yak-3 at ~9:00 LT in the Bajna area
Ewald's 55th: POTENTIAL VICTORY, La-5 at ~14:00 LT in the Bajna area

Soviet 5 and 17 VA single-engine fighter losses on 3 January 1945				
Regiment:	**Type:**	**c/n:**	**Pilot:**	**Details:**
116 IAP	La-5	*Unknown*	V. M. Boltyan	Zsámbék, Bf 109s, CL Kakucs-NE
116 IAP	La-5F	39214687	V. N. Schwarz+	Zsámbék, 13:50 LT to 10 Bf 109s
116 IAP	La-5F	39214952	V. P. Popov	Tata, 6 Fw 190s, CL at Kakucs
116 IAP	La-5F	392150100	V. Novikov KIFA	Kiskunlacháza, TOA at 08:25 LT
116 IAP	La-5FN	3810811	I. D. Plankevich	Délegyháza RR station-E, repaired
116 IAP	La-5FN	39211114	*Unknown, returns*	Szalkszentmárton-S, 1.5 km, CL
116 IAP	La-5FN	39211713	N/A, *parking La-5*	Landing 210 ShAP Il-2 ran into it
116 IAP	La-5FN	39211873	A. A. Radchenko	Tata, flak, CL at Vértesacsa-W
164 IAP	La-5FN	3921*xxxx*	N. Dolnikov MIA	Tata-Bajót, 8 La-5, 18 Bf 109, CL
56 IAP	La-5FN	39211604	A. I. Zlatoverhii	Ferry flight accident at Szabadka
530 IAP	La-5FN	39210830	N. F. Belov	Székesfehérvár, ferry flight LAC

Soviet 5 and 17 VA single-engine fighter losses on 3 January 1945 (*continued*)				
611 IAP	Yak-1B	22167	P. M. Belyaev	Héreg flak, 10:10 LT, 5 *'Fw 190s'*
611 IAP	Yak-9T	1115372	N. A. Verbovitskii	Bajna flak, Dunaszekcső, 15:10LT
611 IAP	Yak-9T	1315342*	O. I. Shetinkin	Engine c/n: 415-1300
659 IAP	Yak-9D	16166064	M. G. Achitkov	Bicske area, CL on return
659 IAP	Yak-9D	17166003	N/A	Scrapped due to wear and tear
659 IAP	Yak-9D	17166040	N/A	Transferred to the 'NKAP'
659 IAP	Yak-9D	2015365	D. D. Kostin	Székesfehérvár, ferry flight acc.
897 IAP	Yak-9D	17166023	P. P. Karavai	*Agostyán, returned on 6 January*
122 IAP	Yak-9M	2715378	M. A. Nesterov	Heréd, LAC at 10:25 LT
150 GvIAP	Yak-3	1829217	Y. Verginskii+	13:50, shot by Bf 109 on parachute
178 GvIAP	La-5F	39214789	V. F. Mudretsov	Tóalmás-SW, 12:17 LT, 2 Bf 109s
178 GvIAP	La-5F	39215236	A. N. Proskurin	Fót-S, 8:55-9:50, Bajna-Esztergom
179 IAP	Yak-9T	1515326	V. A. Alekseev	Süttő area, 09:40 LT, 2 *'Fw 190's*

* The airframe was scrapped on 24 January 1945 due to wear and tear without its engine.

On 3 January 1945, as part of the Konrad operation, heavy dogfights continued in the Budapest-W,-NW area. This day Lt. Heinz Ewald claimed five aerial victories: four in the morning and one in the afternoon. The time of his first claim is unknown, but his second, third and fourth claims were reported *around* 09:00 LT. Between 08:55-09:50 LT eight 178 GvIAP La 5s were covering Soviet ground troops in the Bajót-Esztergom area, where Gv.Ml.Lt. Aleksei Nikitovich Proskurin's La-5F was hit. Proskurin turned back to Tóalmás and crossed the Danube, but suddenly his engine quit and hit a tree with his right wing, crash-landing 500m South of Fót. He was injured and his plane (c/n: 39215236, engine: 6504180, white '<★36') was written off. At 09:40 LT at 2500m eleven Yak-1Bs and Yak-9s of the 179 IAP, led by Maj. Vasilii Panteleimonovich Babiy escorted Il-2s of the 91 and 92 GvShAPs at South of the River Gran in the Süttő-Nyergesújfalu area along the Danube where they met four Bf 109s and six *Fw 190s*. Over the target two '*Fw 190s*' managed to shoot down Ml.Lt. Vasilii Aleksandrovich Alekseev's Yak-9T which went missing. Soon after this at 10:25 LT Lt. Mihail Andreevich Nesterov of 122 IAP returned to Heréd from a Gran-area railway-strafing mission with his damaged Yak-9M (c/n: 2715378, engine: 415-2077, white '78'). During landing he lost control of his already crippled plane and rolled into a bomb crater, flipped over and broke it beyond repair. Later in the afternoon at 13:50 LT at 2000m four 116 IAP La-5s, led by Lt. Aleksandr Aleksandrovich Chernih escorted Il-2s in the Bajna aera where they met approximatley ten Bf 109s. Ml.Lt. Vasilii Nikolaevich Schwarz's La-5 was hit, he crashed and was killed. Based on the available records these two La-5s and Yak-9s can be considered potential aerial victories for Lt. Heinz Ewald.

4 January 1945 (Thursday)

Ewald's 56th: OVERCLAIM, La-5 at ~10:00 LT at Gran-S

Soviet 5 and 17 VA single-engine fighter losses on 4 January 1945				
Regiment:	**Type:**	**c/n:**	**Pilot:**	**Details:**
530 IAP	La-5F	39215048	M. Y. Yefimov	Bicske-SE, 14:55 LT, to Bf 109s
530 IAP	La-5FN	39211920	F. F. Orlovskii	Bicske, 9:15LT, 8 Bf 109s to Cece
530 IAP	La-5FN	39211023	A. P. Dyakov+	Vasztély, 09:30 LT, 8 *Fw 190*
530 IAP	La-5FN	39211488	I. P. Vashenko	Martonvásár, 10:30 LT, 8 Bf 109s
530 IAP	La-5FN	39211399	A. Suhorukhov+	Tardos-Tarján, 11:12LT to Lipfert
611 IAP	Yak-1B	33192	M. F. Batarov WIA	Székesfehérvár, 08:20 LT, CL
897 IAP	Yak-9T	0915316	P. M. Krugov	Börgönd, accident at 09:00 LT
897 IAP	Yak-9D	1615391	N. K. Konovalov	Bicske, after 12:10 LT, 4 Bf 109s
897 IAP	Yak-9D	1615396	E. L. Samohvalov	Same, – pilot returned on the 6th
92 IAP	La-5FN	39213325	V. F. Panov	Ferihegy airport, LAC, 15:20 LT

On 4 January 1945 Lt. Heinz Ewald claimed a La-5 fighter shot down at Gran-S around 10:00 LT. This day the 5th and 17th Air Armies lost six Lavochkin fighters, but the time of loss and geographical location were too far from Lt. Ewald's claim, therefore we can consider it as an overclaim.

6 January 1945 (Saturday)
Ewald's 57th: VICTORY, La-5 at 13:00 LT at Bicske

Soviet 5 and 17 VA single-engine fighter losses on 6 January 1945				
Regiment:	**Type:**	**c/n:**	**Pilot:**	**Details:**
177 GvIAP	La-5FN	39212618	I. W. Zemit	Komárom, 13:10 LT, 6+3 Bf 109s, Zemit: '18', Pyatakov: '08'
177 GvIAP	La-7FN	45210208	G. M. Pyatakov	
178 GvIAP	La-5F	3811404	M. A. Zaitsev+	Páld, 13:35 LT, 6 Bf 109, '<★04'
6 GvIAD	Yak-1B	18158	N/A	Scrapped for wear and tear
897 IAP	Yak-1B	06163	G. I. Kondratiev	Székesfehérvár-SW, 14:00LT,flak
897 IAP	Yak-1B	05188	I. I. Motolikov	Szomor, 6 Bf 109s, 6 Fw 190s, CL
659 IAP	Yak-9D	13166042	A. D. Tsirkun	Kamenin, Bf 109s, 12:15-13:20LT

On 6 January 1945 at 13:05 LT six 177 GvIAP La-5s and La-7s, led by Gv.St.Lt. Ivan Grigorevich Sklyarov (HSU) approached Esztergom where they met four Bf 109s which attacked. The pair of Gv.St.Lt. Pyotr Stephanovich Olin and Gv.Ml.Lt. Igor Wilhelmovich Zemit broke out to the right and Gv.St.Lt. Olin claimed one of the Bf 109s, while the rest fled into the clouds. At 13:10 LT near Komárom six more Bf 109s confronted them. This time three Bf 109s attacked the Olin-Zemit duo from the clouds and Zemit's engine (No.: 829273) was damaged. En route home his engine gave up and some of his engine covers flew off. Gv.Ml.Lt. Zemit bailed out immediately, his plane fell in the Cs [*sic*! – *Csabdi*?] area at Bicske-N and burned. This Lavochkin became Lt. Heinz Ewald's legitimate aerial victory on 6 January 1945.

16 January 1945 (Tuesday)
Ewald's 58th: OVERCLAIM, La-5 at ~11:00 LT at Gran-S
Ewald's 59th: POTENTIAL VICTORY, Yak-9 at ~14:00 LT near Budapest

Soviet 5 and 17 Air Army single-engine fighter losses on 16 January 1945				
Regiment:	**Type:**	**c/n:**	**Pilot:**	**Details:**
31 IAP	La-5FN	*Unknown**	I. F. Philippov+	Sank in the Danube at ~14:00 LT
116 IAP	La-5FN	39210921	A. A. Chernih+	Buda, 15:40LT to Bf 109s
164 IAP	La-5	3921*xxxx*	I. F. Shukin unhurt	*Tinnye-Tököl, repaired, Bf 109s*
73 GvIAP	Yak-1B	40171	S. Y. Verblyudov	Budapest area, ~15:20LT, Bf 109s
659 IAP	Yak-3	2929217	N. I. Galkin MIA	Sárszentmihály, 14:10, 8 Bf 109s
659 IAP	Yak-3	3929218	M. A. Fisenko+	Perkáta, 14:10 LT, 8 Bf 109s
513 IAP	Yak-9D	19166068	A. K. Fokin	Balassagyarmat-S, 10:20LT, 2 Fw

* Ml.Lt. Philippov's missing 31 IAP La-5 was probably La-5FN, c/n: 39212801, or 39212034.

On 16 January 1945 Lt. Heinz Ewald claimed a La-5 and a Yak-9 fighter shot down. Comparing his claims to the lost Soviet fighters of the day, his La-5 claim seems to be an overclaim, but his Yak-9 claim around 14:00 LT near Budapest seems to be a potential aerial victory though he seems to have misidentified his opponent. The potencial victim was, in fact, a Lavochkin La-5 of the 31 IAP instead of a Yakovlev Yak-9.

In the early afternoon of 16 January 1945 Capt. Nikolai Mihailovich Skomorokhov along with Ml.Lt. Ivan Philippovich Philippov and other 31 IAP pilots were battling over the Buda and Pilis Mountains while Luftwaffe aircraft were delivering supplies to the encircled German-Hungarian garrison of Budapest. In the very intense dogfight Lt. Philippov claimed a Bf 109 over Pilisvörösvár, while Capt. Skomorokhov claimed four enemy planes: two Ju 52 cargo planes and two Bf 109s. The Ju 52s crashed at Tarján and Pilisszentkereszt, while the Bf 109s went down near Dömös and Pilisszentkereszt. Since the Lavochkins' fuel and ammunition was already low, they headed for home. Capt. Skomorokhov landed safely on the Tököl airbase, but Ml.Lt. Philippov's La-5 was probably damaged and only one of his wheels came down. Since he also miscalculated his approach to the landing strip, he went around for another landing attempt from which he never returned.

This happened around 14:00 LT near Tököl at around 10 km South of Budapest. His landed comrades were still hopeful of his return and waited until the evening, then the next day, and then the day after. Philippov never returned. Finally, they sent out military divers into the cold Danube to search for some areas where La-5 remains were discovered, but the numbers of the recovered wrecks did not match Philippov's missing plane. They concluded that Ml.Lt. Philippov had crashed and disappeared in the Danube during his second landing attempt with his crippled fighter.

Considering Lt. Ewald's 'Yak-9' claim around 14:00 LT near Budapest, it is entirely possible that Ml.Lt. Philippov's damaged La-5, flying with only one wheel down fell to his guns while trying to land on the Tököl airbase on Csepel Island. In January 1945 with poor visibility, it is possible that Lt. Ewald misidentified his opponent and downed Ml.Lt. Philippov's La-5, instead of a his reported Yakovlev Yak-9. For all of these reasons we count his 'Yak-9' claim on 16 January 1945 a potential aerial victory.

19 January 1945 (Friday)

Ewald's 60th: POTENTIAL VICTORY, Il-2 at ~12:00 LT near Székesfehérvár

Soviet 17 VA Il-2 Sturmovik losses on 19 January 1945				
Regiment:	**Type:**	**c/n:**	**Pilot:**	**Details:**
210 ShAP	Il-2m3	11096	N. V. Patrin	Tác flak to Ercsi-S
715 ShAP	Il-2m3	11436	P. R. Murashko	Tököl, 1 wheel landing, -engine repair
715 ShAP	Il-2m3	1887803	M.A. Melnikov MIA	Szabadbattyán flak at 12:15 LT, CL
989 ShAP	Il-2m3	10178	A. A. Sidorenko	Szabadbattyán flak, CL, crew returned
672 ShAP	Il-2m3	1872290	L. D. Osipov+	Tác-Falubattyán, 14:00 LT to flak
951 ShAP	Il-2m3	1881301	M. I. Ribak	Seregélyes, flak, 14:15, CL set on fire
995 ShAP	Il-2m3	1877386	I. B. Nepochelov	Polgárdi, 12:45 LT, 10 *Fw 190s*, CL
995 ShAP	Il-2m3	1870387	A. Chugunov MIA	Battyán flak, 11:20 LT, CL at Tác-N
995 ShAP	Il-2m3	10513	N. V. Kobilyatskii	Polgárdi, 12:45 LT, 10 *Fw 190s*, Tác
995 ShAP	Il-2m3	9974	I. V. Tselishev MIA	Lake Velence, 11:20 LT, flak, missing
615 ShAP	Il-2m3	188100106	N/A	Börgönd-N, had no time to evacuate
615 ShAP	Il-2m3	18874106	N/A	Börgönd-N, had no time to evacuate
639 ShAP	Il-2m3	11289	K. K. Vasyuk MIA	Aba, Bf 109s, pilot bailed out
639 ShAP	Il-2m3	11267	H. M. Musin	Aba, Bf 109s, CL, crew returned

On 19 January 1945 around 12:00 LT Lt. Heinz Ewald claimed an Il-2 shot down near Székesfehérvár. This day the ground attack planes of the 17 VA suffered heavy losses to enemy fighters and anti-aircraft fire. Fourteen Il-2s were lost to various reasons. Even though his victim cannot be determined for certain, it is very likely to have been one of the 189 or 306 ShAD Il-2 Sturmoviks that were lost to enemy fighters in the Aba-Székesfehérvár-Polgárdi-Lake Velence areas. This time the Soviet ground attack planes provided aerial support to the struggeling Soviet armoured forces, which suffered heavy losses in the Székesfehérvár-SW, -SE areas.[44]

20 January 1945 (Saturday)

Ewald's 61st: POTENTIAL VICTORY, Boston at ~16:00 LT in the Veszprém area

Soviet 17 VA Douglas A-20 Boston losses on 20 January 1945				
Regiment:	**Type:**	**S/N:**	**Pilot:**	**Details:**
449 BAP	A-20B	41-3564	A. Krivtsov	Szabadbattyán to Fadd, 16:07 LT, 2 Bf 109s
449 BAP	A-20G	42-53865	N. Korotkov	Polgárdi, 16:00 LT, 6 Bf 109s, CL at Udvari
449 BAP	A-20G	43-21264	K. Gapanovich	Polgárdi, 15:30 LT, CL at Sásd-S, '4'

On 20 January 1945 Lt. Heinz Ewald shot down a Soviet A-20 Boston bomber in the Veszprém area North of Lake Balaton. Due to the weather conditions only a few Bostons of the 449 BAP bombed Polgárdi and Szabadbattyán losing three planes. Although the 'Veszprém area' is not a very specific location because at least two 449 BAP A-20 Bostons

44 For example a convoy of the 1 GvMK, 9 GvTBr was ambushed by Panthers of I./Pz.Rgt.24 South of Sárpentele and lost several M4A2(76)W Shermans, including U.S.A. 3081206/'958'.

Lt. Constantin Matveevich Gapanovich's A-20G Boston in Teslin, Canada enroute to the Soviet Union. Below 449 BAP officers are debriefing in front of one of the regiment's A-20 Bostons. Note the regiment's bomb dropping seagul emblem on the plane. (L-R:) Lt. Constantin Matveevich Gapanovich, Capt. Chernyavskii, Lt. Fridman, St.Lt. Grigorenko, Capt. Kozlov, Lt. Gazenko, and St.Lt. Shevkunov (HSU). (Photo: Capt. N. Gavrilov in the 15 November 1944 issue of 'Защитник Отечества', Soviet Second World War frontline newspaper.

were downed by Bf 109 fighters around 16:00 LT one of the three planes and crews could be Lt. Heinz Ewald's potential aerial victory:

449 BAP, *1st* Sq. A-20B-DL (S/N: 41-3564, engines: 42-149484, 42-26674):[45]
 Ml.Lt. Andrey Ignatevich Krivtsov pilot (unhurt)
 Ml.Lt. Vasilii Ivanovich Tolochko navigator (wounded)
 C-a Vyacheslav Mihailovich Trubachev radioman (wounded)
 Sgt. Ivan Ivanovich Kudryashov gunner (wounded)
449 BAP, 3rd Sq. A-20G-10-DO (S/N: 42-53865, engines: 43-103819, 43-103778):[46]
 Lt. Nikolai Alekseevich Korotkov pilot (unhurt)
 Lt. Nikolai Leontievich Simeisinov navigator (unhurt)
 C-a Stephan Fedorovich Gudkov radioman (unhurt)
 Sgt. Sergei Aleksandrovich Grishin gunner (MIA)
449 BAP, 2nd Sq. A-20G-40-DO (S/N: 43-21264, engines: 43-105321, 43-105435):[47]
 Lt. Constantin Matveevich Gapanovich pilot (+)
 Lt. Vladimir Petrovich Kushnarenko navigator (+)
 Sgt. Mihail Vasilevich Kirpichkov radioman (+)
 Sgt. Vasilii Ivanovich Kashenkov gunner (MIA)

During delivery to the Soviet Union on 30 March 1944, A-20G-40-DO Boston (S/N: 43-21264) piloted by 1Lt George C. Davis (0-502420, 3 O.T.U. HQ.) suffered minor landing accident on the icy landing strip of Teslin, Yukon Territory in Canada. After a repair, it continued its journey through Alaska to the Soviet Union:[48]

45 TsAMO RF: fu. 20224, inv. 2, f. 61, pp. 5, 18-19, Combat diary (losses) of 244 BAD, entry for 20 January 1945. (Ml.Lt. Krivtsov's plane.)
46 TsAMO RF: fu. 20224, inv. 2, f. 61, pp. 5, 20-21, Combat diary (losses) of 244 BAD, entry for 20 January 1945. (Lt. Korotkov's plane.)
47 TsAMO RF: fu. 20224, inv. 2, f. 61, pp. 5, 20-21, Combat diary (losses) of 244 BAD, entry for 20 January 1945. (Lt. Gapanovich's plane.)
48 Report of Aircraft Accident (AAIR – Aviation Archaeological Investigation & Research, USA.)

These days beside the fighters, the German anti-aircraft artillery also caused serious losses to the Soviet formations. For example on 25 January 1945 eighteen A-20 Bostons of the 260 BAP, led by St.Lt. Fedor Ilyich Kizim, escorted by eight fighters attacked 15 tanks in the Baracska and ten tanks in the Pettend areas. During their bomb run over Ferenc-major at 2000m at 12:14 LT an 88mm flak shell hit St.Lt. Nikolai Fedorovich Shapovalov 2nd Sq. flight-leader's A-20C-10-DO Boston (S/N: 42-33302) which went into a tailspin and crashed at Baracska-SW, killing its entire crew.[49]

22 January 1945 (Monday)

Ewald's 62nd: POTENTIAL VICTORY, La-5 at 13:??LT in the Székesfehérvár area
Ewald's 63rd: POTENTIAL VICTORY, La-5 at 13:?? LT in the Székesfehérvár area
Ewald's 64th: OVERCLAIM, La-5 in the Székesfehérvár area
Ewald's 65th: OVERCLAIM, La-5 in the Székesfehérvár area

Soviet 5 and 17 VA single-engine fighter losses on 22 January 1945				
Regiment:	**Type:**	**c/n:**	**Pilot:**	**Details:**
116 IAP	La-5FN	41210109	V. M. Boltyan	Sukoró, 6 Bf 109s, CL at Tököl
116 IAP	La-5FN	39212516	I. D. Plankevich POW	Pusztaszabolcs, recce. pair, both lost & captured at 09:55 LT to 8 Bf 109s
116 IAP	La-5FN	39211687	G.K. Zolotarskii POW	
164 IAP	La-5FN	39215251	V. S. Svistelnikov	Pázmánd-E to Málik József, Bf 109
164 IAP	La-5	*Unknown*	K. S. Shelkanov WIA	*Damaged by Bf 109s, returned*
530 IAP	La-5FN	39211521	A. N. Yakovlev+	Székesfehérvár, 13:35 LT to Bf 109s
611 IAP	Yak-9T	0815355	N. A. Verbovitskii	Bugyi, Hungarian Bf 109 (Máthé)
659 IAP	Yak-9D	16166062	N. A. Morozov	Kiskunlacháza, take off accident
897 IAP	Yak-1B	03193	I. I. Motolikov	Székesfehérvár, 8:30 LT, 6 Bf 109s
31 GvIAP	Yak-9D	2015396	A. M. Zhelobanov	Returned, broke upon landing
96 OKRAP	Yak-9D	1515390	A. A. Arefiev MIA	Missing, dogfight at 09:45 LT

On 22 January 1945 Lt. Heinz Ewald claimed no less than four La-5 fighters in the Székesfehérvár area. His first two La-5s were reported sometime after 13:00 LT, so the third and fourth La-5s had to be claimed sometime after those. This day the 17 VA lost five La-5s: two lost at 09:55 LT in the morning, a third lost to Málik József hdgy., Hungarian Bf 109 ace at Vál-S, Pázmánd-E, and the fourth and fifth losses were probably Heinz Ewald's victories. At 13:30 LT six 530 IAP La-5s escorted 13 Il-2s of the 707 ShAP in the Székesfehérvár-NW area, when at 800m four II./JG 52 Bf 109s attacked them. Soon after this another two JG 52 Bf 109s attacked the La-5 pair of Maj. Zolotoverhii–Ml.Lt. Yakovlev from the altitude of 1000m, setting Ml.Lt. Anatolii Nikolaevich Yakovlev's La-5FN on fire which fell five kilometers North of Székesfehérvár. The Soviet pilot was killed. The dogfight continued, which resulted the loss of three II./JG 52 Bf 109G-14s: WNr.510915, 510845/Steins+ and 510859/Wagner. Maj. Aleksandr Ivanovich Zolotoverhii shot a Bf 109 down at five kilometers North of Székesfehérvár, Ml.Lt. Pavel Fedorovich Panyushkin over Csiribpuszta and Maj. Nikolai Fedorovich Krasnov (HSU) ten kilometers North of Székesfehérvár.[50] There was a sixth, 164 IAP, La-5 which was damaged in air combat by six Bf 109s during a 306 ShAD Il-2 escort mission to Mór. The pilot, Ml.Lt. Kuzma Sergeevich Shelkanov successfully returned to his airbase with injuries to his leg. He was almost certainly hit by Lt. Heinz Ewald too near Székesfehérvár, but his plane was an overclaim for Heinz Ewald.[51]

30 January 1945 (Tuesday)

Ewald's 66th: POTENTIAL VICTORY, La-5 at 13:?? LT in the Budapest area

49 TsAMO RF: fu. 20224, inv. 2, f. 61, pp. 5, 8, 45-47, Combat diary (losses) of 244 BAD, entry for 25 January 1945 (St.Lt. Shapovalov's plane).

50 Maj. Krasnov (HSU) was killed in the morning of 29 January 1945 in a landing accident after experiencing engine trouble en route home from a ground cover mission. After touching the icy ground West of Szabadszállás, his 530 IAP, 3rd Sq. La-5FN (c/n: 39211314, ASh-82FN engine: 829030, white '14') slid 350m on the ground and flipped over. Maj. Krasnov was seriously injured in the accident and became stuck in the cockpit. The first person who got to his plane was aerial gunner Ml.Sgt. Boris Antonovich Solodchenko whose nearby crash-landed Boston (S/N: 41-3648) was among the three lost 260 BAP planes (41-3189, 41-3648, 42-86671) on 8 December 1944; Solodchenko walked for an hour across the snowy farmlands in order to help him. By the time he found the wreck and cut a hole in the right side of the flipped La-5, Maj. Krasnov was already dead. Solodchenko observed that Krasnov shot through the side of his plane in order to escape but could not and ultimately bled to death. He was later buried in Odessa.

51 TsAMO RF: fu. 20541, inv. 1, f. 83, p. 131, Operations journal of 295 IAD, entry for 22 January 1945.

Soviet 5 and 17 VA single-engine fighter losses on 30 January 1945				
Regiment:	**Type:**	**c/n:**	**Pilot:**	**Details:**
31 IAP	La-5FN	39211156	M. S. Derevnin+	Taksony, ~11:00 LT, 6 Bf 109s
31 IAP	La-5FN	39211768	I. M. Dudarev MIA	Csiribpuszta, ~13:25 LT, Bf 109s
56 IAP	La-5FN	392124100	A. P. Smirnov	*Madocsa, CL, 16:25 LT, repaired*
897 IAP	Yak-9D	1815393	I. A. Prozorov WIA	Szigetfalu, 13:25 LT, CL, Bf 109s
31 GvIAP	Yak-9D	2015360	A. M. Zhelobanov	*Budapest area to fighters, returned*

On 30 January 1945 between 13:05-13:45 LT, four 31 IAP La-5s (Smirnov, Popov, Dudarev and Tsikin), led by St.Lt. Oleg Nikolaevich Smirnov covered Soviet ground troops in the Kápolnásnyék, Lake Velence-E areas, where they met six Bf 109s and four '*Ju 88s*'. Lt. Mihail Dmitrievich Tsikin who downed a Bf 109 warned Lt. Ilya Martemyanovich Dudarev about an attacking Bf 109, but it was too late and Dudarev was hit. He pulled up sharply, rolled over to the right, bailed out at 4000m and landed on enemy held territory. He was taken prisoner while his La-5FN (c/n: 39211768, ASh-82FN engine: 8212330, white '68') fell in the Csiribpuszta area. Later he was executed for his two escape attempts. Dudarev's plane could be Lt. Ewald's legitimate La-5 aerial victory on 30 January 1945. But beside the 31 IAP, this day was tragic for the 235 ShAP as well when eight of their Il-2s attacked the Southern shore of Lake Velence. After 15:00 LT over Gárdony the very intense anti-aircraft fire hit Maj. Ivan Lazarevich Mogilchak's Il-2. Mogilchak was one of the most successful and most decorated Il-2 pilot of his regiment, whose Il-2m3 (c/n: 1882603, AM-38F engine: 259630) crossed the Danube and crash-landed near Dunaharaszti at Budapest-S. Maj. Mogilchak (HSU) was burned badly and died of his wounds two weeks later on 14 February 1945.

2 February 1945 (Friday)

Ewald's 67th: OVERCLAIM, La-5 at 15:00 LT in the Székesfehérvár area

Temporary Soviet 5 and 17 VA single-engine fighter losses on 2 February 1945				
Regiment:	**Type:**	**c/n:**	**Pilot:**	**Details:**
31 GvIAP	Yak-9D	2015390	*Unknown*	*Armament damage, repaired*
530 IAP	La-5	Unknown	D. I. Trubitsin WIA	*Damaged by Bf 109s, landed OK*

On 2 February 1945 Lt. Heinz Ewald claimed a Lavochkin La-5 fighter shot down in the Székesfehérvár area which was an overclaim. On 2 February the 17 VA had no fighter losses at all, rather only three 707 ShAP Il-2 Sturmoviks failed to return from combat missions.[52] Their details are known, but they were not related to Lt. Ewald's action. In the afternoon La-5s of the 530 and 848 IAPs, while escorting 244 BAD A-20 Bostons, engaged in combat with Bf 109s in the Szabadbattyán and Székesfehérvár areas indeed but neither the La-5s nor the Bostons suffered losses.

At 15:40 LT at 4000m four La-5s (Smirnov-Gushin, Orlovskii-Trubitsin) led by St.Lt. Aleksandr Petrovich Smirnov escorted thirteen 449 BAP A-20 Bostons led by Capt. Grigorii Petrovich Lisenko and Maj. Dmitrii Sergeevich Yegorkin at 3400m in the Szabadbattyán area. Here, the Soviet bombers were attacked by eight to twelve Bf 109s. The attack on the lead-bomber was intercepted by the pair of flight-leader St.Lt. Smirnov and his wingman Ml.Lt. Gushin who claimed a Bf 109 over Szabadbattyán. The La-5s managed to keep the fighters away from the bombers, while wingman Ml.Lt. Vasilii Nikolaevich Gushin shot down another Bf 109 that was positioning behind St.Lt. Smirnov saving his leader's life. This Bf 109 fell at Szabadbattyán-E, 5 km. Ml.Lt. Dmitrii Ivanovich Trubitsin's La-5 was damaged in air combat, he left his flight and returned to his airfield alone where he landed safely. This damaged La-5 was the only Lavochkin 'loss' within the 17th Air Army, which was probably claimed later by Lt. Heinz Ewald. One A-20 Boston, flown by Lt. Nikolai Alekseevich Korotkov was damaged by fighters more seriously, losing the right engine and the hydraulic system, while both gunners (Gudkov and Ismailov) were slightly injured.[53] This Boston was perhaps Lt. Korotkov's A-20G-20-DO Boston (S/N: 42-86710, built on 23 August 1943) which after repairs he later crash-landed on 6 March 1945 at Mohács-SW in Hungary during their mission to Donji Miholjac, Croatia. Three other bombers suffered minor damages, but none of them were lost as they all returned to the airbase safely.

4 February 1945 (Sunday)

Ewald's 68th: VICTORY, La-5 in the Székesfehérvár area, ~ 16:00 LT

Ewald's 69th: VICTORY, La-5 in the Székesfehérvár area, ~ 16:00 LT

52 Il-2m3 No.18854108: Lt. P. Orlov, No.11364: Ml.Lt. G. Dorokhov, No.305015: Ml.Lt. V. Polikarpov.

53 TsAMO RF: fu. 20224, inv. 1, f. 44, p. 95, Operations report of 449 BAP, entry for 2 February 1945.

Soviet 17 VA single-engine fighter losses on 4 February 1945				
Regiment:	**Type:**	**c/n:**	**Pilot:**	**Details:**
116 IAP	La-5FN	39212113	K. I. Kurenkov+	Kiskunlacháza, 09:55, at take off
848 IAP	La-5FN	39212754	B. P. Lazarev MIA	Sárkeresztes-W, 2 km, 16:00 LT, 2000m, flak, Bf 109s vs. 6 La-5s
848 IAP	La-5F	39215046	V. Z. Voronov MIA	
288 IAD	Yak-9T	1115393	N/A	Scrapped, regular wear and tear

On 4 February 1945 at 16:00 LT six 848 IAP La-5s attacked enemy positions in the Sárkeresztes-W, Székesfehérvár-NW area, where at 2000m they engaged in combat with German Bf 109s. The Soviets lost two planes with both of their pilots reported missing. Due to the match in location, time, and Soviet accounts, Ml.Lt. Vladimir Zaharovich Voronov's and Ml.Lt. Boris Dmitrievich Lazarev's 848 IAP La-5s were Heinz Ewald's legitimate aerial victories.[54] Two 31 IAP La-5FNs were also written off by 4 February 1945 but their incidents took place a few days earlier (c/n: 39211156 and 39211768).

1 March 1945 (Thursday)

Ewald's 70th: OVERCLAIM, P-51 Mustang in the Székesfehérvár area, around 13:00 LT, 2800m

15th AF aircraft losses on 1 March 1945 in Hungary*				
Group:	**Type:**	**S/N:**	**Pilot:**	**Details:**
325 FG	P-51D-15-NA	44-15480	Frederick J. Wulfe	Hajmáskér, 318th FS, black '59'
449 BG	B-24J-200-CO	44-41218	W. R. Farrington+	Ácsteszér, 5+, 4 executed, 1 POW
460 BG	B-24J-5-FO	42-51536	Foy E. Moudy	Pécs, landed successfully, red 'A'
460 BG	B-24J-20-FO	44-48862	Rodney C. Anspach	Győr, 18 km, red 'I'
460 BG	B-24L-10-FO	44-49693	Charles Thornburg	Landed near Pécs, white 'S'
465 BG	B-24J-20-FO	44-48861	William J. Smith	Pécs, landed successfully, red 'Y'
484 BG	B-24L-15-FO	44-49936	William K. Sutton	Kurd-NW, 5 POW, red '79'

* MACR 12508, 12517, 12711, 12712, 12745, 12747 and 12813. Researcher Mohos Nándor et al.

By March 1945 I./JG 53 often flew alongside II./JG 52 for various missions. Lipfert recalls some of this day's events: *Lt. Ewald and his Schwarm ran into eight of these American [P-51] fighters north of Lake Balaton. Ewald may well have had a score to settle with the Americans because they had fired at him in his parachute over Romania. For whatever reason, he attacked without regard to position. He damaged a Mustang, which dove away trailing black smoke …* [55] Obfhr. Peter Esser of 1./JG 53 recalled the events of this day. He remembers that after retuning from a mission lead by Hptm. Lipreft, the other JG 53 pilots encountered Ewald along with a few JG 52 pilots and engaged in a mock dogfight.[56] After they left, Ewald encountered about twenty Mustangs and made one claim while Fw. Pitzel (1./JG 53) also shot one down.[57] The Mustang pilot was brought back to the base later on.[58] The 5th SS Panzer Division 'Wiking' occupying the Székesfehérvár area also recorded their observations of this afternoon from the ground: eight Spitfires [*sic!*] at 2800m at 14:26 LT with fourteen B-24 Liberators at 6000m traveling from the North to the Southwest over Lake Balaton, a few more Liberators were spotted a little later in the area.[59] Engaging with these aircraft, Ewald made a claim over a P-51 Mustang at around 13:00 LT [sic].[60]

Heinz Ewald recalls the following series of events for the day, which differ slightly from the above accounts. Beginning with an alarmstart leading Fw. Eduard Pitzel, Uffz. Gerd Hauter and Uffz. Anton Kellmeier, Lt. Ewald climbed up above the Székesfehérvár area to look for the intruders.[61] Spotting what he believed to be over twenty American aircraft he ordered Fw. Pitzel to climb up in order to attack from a dive, whereafter he prepaired for an attack when suddenly Pitzel dove down and managed to shoot down a Mustang.[62] Ewald confirmed Fw. Pitzel's claim and congratulated him, later

54 TsAMO RF: fu: 17 VA, inv. 6531, f: 37, p. 520, Combat diary (losses) of 194 IAD, 848 IAP, entry for 4 February 1945.

55 Helmut Lipferf, Werner Gribig, *The War Diary of Hauptmann Helmut Lipfert: JG 52 on the Russian Front 1943-1945* (Atglen, Pennsylvania: Schiffer publishing, 1993), p. 153.

56 Jochen Prien, *Jagdeschwader 53: A History of the "Pik As" Geschwader January 1944 – May 1945* (Atglen, Pennsylvania: Shiffer Publishing Ltd., 1998), p. 858.

57 Fw. Eduard Pitzel was part of Ewalds flight this afternoon even though he was technically a pilot of I./JG 53. As mentioned, JG 52 and 53 pilots flew mixed missions by the spring of 1945 owing to the dim future of JG 53.

58 Prien, *Jagdeschwader 53*, p. 858.

59 5 SS Panzer Division Wiking Ic, Ic-Tagesmeldung vom 1.3.1945, TsAMO RF fu. 500, inv. 12493, f. 56. p. 18.

60 Barbas, *Die Geschichte der II. Gruppe des Jagdgeschwaders 52*, p. 371.

61 Ewald, *ESAU'*, p.114.

62 Ewald, *ESAU*, p.114.

spotting an opened parachute floating down to the earth.[63] Now the Americans were flying approximately 2800m over Lake Balaton and one Mustang managed to damage Ewald's engine.[64] Continuing the dogfight, Lt. Ewald managed to land hits on a Mustang, later a few more, causing what he saw as an eruption in the Mustangs nose putting the plane into a dive trailing brown smoke.[65] Ewald also recalls that the pilot in the parachute was Sergeant Wuws [sic] from Chicago who spent half a day with the Luftwaffe pilots as he was taken prisoner.[66]

Now seen from the American side, on 1 March 1945 heavy bomber formations of the 15th USAAF bombed Austrian targets in the Moosbierbaum area. Returning home, many critically damaged planes unable to return to their Southern Italian airbases turned East with their escort in order to reach the Soviet lines. Crossing over the Lake balaton area their fighter escort tried to keep the German fighters away from the distressed bombers. One of them was a North American P-51D (S/N: 44-15480, V-1650-7 engine: V-326826, black '59', nickname: 'SHU-SHU') which was shot down by Bf 109s near Hajmáskér, West of Székesfehérvár.[67] The pilot 1Lt Frederick J. Wulfe (0-513279) bailed out and was captured.

Lt. Ewald's account for 1 March 1945 strongly suggests that Fw. Pitzel was the pilot actually responsible for the only shot down Mustang over Hungary that day. Based on Hptm. Lipreft's account, Ewald only mamaged to damage the P-51 which may be accurate as not a single Mustang was lost over that day.[68] Heinz Ewalds sole Mustang claim of his fighter pilot career is an overclaim.

8 March 1945 (Thursday)

Ewald's *unconfirmed claim*: POTENTIAL VICTORY, Il-2 in the Székesfehérvár area around 16:00 LT

Soviet 5 and 17 Air Army Il-2 losses on 8 March 1945				
Regiment:	**Type:**	**c/n:**	**Pilot:**	**Details:**
615 ShAP	Il-2m3	18896106	M. A. Solodov	Bugac puszta, flak at 15:30 LT
615 ShAP	Il-2m3	18845124	P. P. Nikitin	Nagybajom flak, CL at Kaposvár-W
639 ShAP	Il-2m3	18865107	A. P. Shubin+	Fekete(?) flak at 15:00 LT, Enying-S
951 ShAP	Il-2m3	9957	G. Odnotsenov+	Seregélyes-NW, flak at 11:00 LT
989 ShAP	Il-2m3	10016	I. S. Gorkin	Belsőbáránd flak, scrapped, '7'
715 ShAP	Il-2m3	11465	C. E. Philippov	*Soponya dogfight, repaired, '12'*
715 ShAP	Il-2m3	*12965*	P. I. Ratushnuk	Soponya, crashed at Hercegfalva,'22'
989 ShAP	Il-2m3	11467	Leoncio Hernans	Belsőbáránd flak, 11:30 LT, CL, '38'
989 ShAP	Il-2m3	11560	I. Buryakovskii	Káloz, 15:50 LT to Hung. Bf 109
131 GvShAP	Il-2m3	12350	A. I. Zenin	*Flak damage, repaired at the base*
131 GvShAP	Il-2m3	1876367	V. K. Gaidash	*Flak damage, repaired at the base*
131 GvShAP	Il-2m3	12616	V. P. Evgrafov	Seregélyes-NW dogfight ~14:00 LT
131 GvShAP	Il-2m3	18833115	M. N. Lahtanov	Dogfight ~14:00 LT, CL near Makád
166 GvShAP	Il-2m3	1879095	G. I. Neminusii+	Novi Sad area, crashed
188 GvShAP	Il-2m3	11041	Unknown, 1st Sq.	*Combat damage, Il-2 repaired*
188 GvShAP	Il-2m3	11893	I. G. Bannih	*Combat damage, Il-2 repaired*
188 GvShAP	Il-2m3	18892115	Unknown, 3rd Sq.	*Combat damage, Il-2 repaired*

On 8 March 1945 Lt. Heinz Ewald claimed an unconfirmed Il-2 shot down around 16:00 LT in the Székesfehérvár area. During their second mission of the day between 15:50-16:44 LT seven 715 ShAP Il-2 Sturmoviks, led by Maj. Aleksandr Yulevich Zabludovskii, escorted by Capt. Anatolii Aleksandrovich Pantelkin's eight 116 IAP La-5s attacked enemy tanks and supply vehicles in the Szabadbattyán-Tác-Csősz-Soponya area at Székesfehérvár-SW. The Il-2s delivered 12 FAB-100 (GP) and 1050 PTAB bombs.[69] Over the target at 1500m, the Soviet planes noticed four Bf 109s and two *Fw 190s* which immediately went into an attack as the Sturmoviks left their target. St.Lt. Ratushnuk's Il-2m3, which dropped 280 PTAB bombs was hit and crash-landed at Hercegfalva-S, 2 km. The crew of St.Lt. Pavel Yosifovich Ratushnuk and

63 Ewald, *ESAU*, p.114.
64 Ewald, *ESAU*, p.114.
65 Ewald, *ESAU*, p.115.
66 Ewald, *ESAU*, p.115.
67 MACR 12517 and Veress Csaba, *A balatoni csata* (Veszprém: Veszprém megyei Nyomda Vállalat, 1976), p. 169.
68 Lipfert, Gribig, *The War Diary of Hauptmann Helmut Lipfert*, p. 153.
69 The seven 715 ShAP Il-2 Sturmoviks were No.'1' (c/n: 11928, Maj. Zabludovskii, 210 PTAB), '38' (St.Lt. Murashko, 280 PTAB), '17' (Ml. Lt. Godyaev, 280 PTAB), '22' (St.Lt. Ratushnuk, 280 PTAB), '12' (St.Lt. Philippov, 4 FAB-100), '11' (Ml.Lt. Pirogov, 4 FAB-100) and '39' (c/n: 11813, Capt. Kochergin, 4 FAB-100). Il-2 No.12 was damaged, while No.'22' failed to return from combat mission.

The wrecks of 715 ShAP Il-2m3, c/n: 11465 on the airfield of Trauersdorf, Austria on 17 April 1945. (Photo: Boris V. Davidov)

Sgt. Vasilii Nikolaevich Fominih aerial gunner returned to their airbase on 9 March 1945. The other damaged plane was St.Lt. Constantin Yegorovich Philippov's Il-2m3, but it successfully returned to its airbase, where it was later repaired. It was finally lost in Trauersdorf, Austria on 17 April 1945 in a training landing accident.[70]

We certainly do not know for sure if Lt. Heinz Ewald was involved in this particular fighter attack or if he hit Il-2 No.'22' and not No.'12', which ultimately survived the battle. Yet because we have no evidence which disproves this posibility, it is permissible to count this unconfirmed Il-2 claim as a potential aerial victory for Lt. Ewald.

11 March 1945 (Sunday)
Ewald's 71st: OVERCLAIM, Yak-9, ~ 15:00 LT

Soviet 17 VA single-engine fighter losses on 11 March 1945				
Regiment:	**Type:**	**c/n:**	**Pilot:**	**Details:**
611 IAP	Yak-9M	3315386	N. N. Kutsenko+	Simontornya-SE, 14:25 LT to Bf 109
866 IAP	Yak 3	310233	A. D. Piorunskii	Sárbogárd, at 3000m to Lipfert
866 IAP	Yak-3	*310xxx*	N. G. Surnev	*Simontornya, damaged by Lipfert*
866 IAP	Yak-3	*310xxx*	T. K. Gatitskii	*Dogfight at 15:00 LT, later returned*
164 IAP	La-5FN	39214947	P. M. Taikov	Burned on its airfield due to flak
530 IAP	La-5FN	39211581	G. F. Lesnyak	Bugac puszta-NW, take-off acc.
56 IAP	La-5FN	39211638	G. I. Dunaev	Őcsény, CL, ferry-flight accident

On 11 March 1945 Lt. Heinz Ewald claimed a Yak-9 fighter shot down. However, due to the significant time difference between all the Soviet single engine fighter losses of the 17 VA and Ewlad's claim, this Yak-9 is an overclaim.

13 March 1945 (Tuesday)
Ewald's 72nd: POTENTIAL VICTORY, Il-2 at 10:00LT near Székesfehérvár
Ewald's 73rd: VICTORY, La-5 in the Székesfehérvár area, ~16:00 LT
Ewald's 74th: OVERCLAIM, La-5 in the Székesfehérvár area, ~16:00 LT

Soviet aircraft losses on 13 March 1945 over Hungary				
Regiment:	**Type:**	**c/n:**	**Pilot:**	**Details:**
210 ShAP	Il-2m3	11584	V. T. Harchenko	Öregmajor-NW, flak, 15:10 LT, '33'
210 ShAP	Il-2m3	1887403	I. M. Mitrahovich	Rácalmás-SW, 12:00 LT, CL, '3'
210 ShAP	Il-2m3	*18886119*	N. S. Esaulenko	*AC not lost, flak, repaired,* '17'

70 715 ShAP Il-2m3 (c/n: 11465, AM-38F engine: 257468, No.'12') was finally lost on 17 April 1945 in Trauersdorf, Austria during a training flight landing accident at 16:06 LT when Ml.Lt. Fyodor Romanovich Pivnenko ran into a parking 951 ShAP Il-2m3 (c/n: 13574, AM-38F engine: 2516298), which was assigned to the 951 ShAP only three days prior from the 17 VA reserve. Ml.Lt. Pivnenko's Il-2 broke in half right at its fuselage number '12'. Both planes were write-offs, their engines were salvaged, but the accident was brought to a courtmarshal for investigation.

639 ShAP	Il-2m3	18858106, 11503	P. F. Vorobiev WIA	Őcsény, flak at 14:20 LT
639 ShAP	Il-2m3		I. E. Geiher MIA	Balatonszabadi, flak, 14:20 LT
672 ShAP	Il-2m3	18870106	N. A. Pribilov	*Baracska, flak, 17:30 LT, CL, rep.**
672 ShAP	Il-2m3	1875499	E. V. Vaitsitskii	*Gárdony, flak, CL, repaired.*
672 ShAP	Il-2m3	11221	N. M. Barsuk	*Agárd, flak, 13:00 LT, CL, repaired*
951 ShAP	Il-2m3	1877483	S. F. Tumashev+	Agárd flak, Agárd-E, 08:00 LT**
951 ShAP	Il-2m3	18854106	A. P. Pulnii+	Agárd flak to Csiribpuszta, 14:00 LT
989 ShAP	Il-2m3	18860124	V. D. Grabanchuk+	Seregélyes flak to Detrich, white '21'
989 ShAP	Il-2m3	*Unknown*	V. I. Biryukov	*Combat damages, repaired, '3'*
989 ShAP	Il-2m3	*Unknown*	V. A. Vasilevskii	*Combat damages, repaired, '29'*
989 ShAP	Il-2m3	*Unknown*	I. K. Buryakovskii	*Combat damages, repaired, '24'*
130 GShAP	Il-2m3	18836115	A. I. Proligin	Sárosd-SE at 11:20 LT, *Flakvierling*
131 GShAP	Il-2m3	12036	N. A. Titomirov	Nadap-NE, 10:26 LT, Bf 109s, CL
131 GShAP	Il-2m3	12206	F. I. Strelnikov	*Flak, CL at airbase, repaired*
131 GShAP	Il-2m3	12049	A. I. Zenin	Flak, *Fw 190s*, CL at base, scrapped
131 GShAP	Il-2m3	12632	V. N. Provalinskii	*Flak, CL at airbase, repaired*
131 GShAP	Il-2m3	1876367	I. P. Tsukanov	*Flak, CL at airbase, repaired*
190 GShAP	Il-2m3	*Unknown*	P. A. Davidov	Agárd flak, returned, later written-off
92 GvShAP	Il-2m3	*Unknown*	A. P. Kukovyakin	*Szolnok-NW, 10 km, CL, repaired*
92 GvShAP	Il-2m3	*Unknown*	V. S. Prusakov	*Tóalmás-E, 5 km, CL, repaired*
423 OAES	Po-2	4700	*Unknown*	Crash-landed, scrapped
116 IAP	La-5F	39215208	A. Radchenko MIA	Csiribpuszta, Il-2 escort 15:50 LT
866 IAP	Yak-3	310119	A. F. Balashov MIA	Sáregres, 15:30LT, 24 Fw, 16 Bf 109
897 IAP	Yak-3	310370	G. S. Eliseenkov***	17:05 LT, 2 Yak-3s over Fáncs, MIA
611 IAP	Yak-9M	3415323	S. A. Mazuhin+	Pákozd, 10:15 LT to Hptm. Lipfert
611 IAP	Yak-9M	3415305	M. A. Kamenetskii	Börgönd, 10:15 LT, flak to Pázmánd
513 IAP	Yak-9M	2815344	I. P. Isaichev	Újszász, crash-landed due to fighter
73 GvIAP	Yak-9D	2115372	V. M. Savchuk	Flak, engine salvaged by BAO
14 GvBAP	B-25DP	43-3733	A. G. Vasin+	Ádánd, flak at 17:45LT, tail: red '17'

* This Il-2 was repaired and shot down again on 7 May 1945 during a Znojmo mission with Ml.Lt. Vladimir Yegorovich Bershak's crew. The plane crash-landed at 12 kilometers North of Vienna.

** This Il-2 was transferred from the 995 ShAP to the 951 ShAP on 13 February 1945 with an American-made gun-camera (c/n: 23678) installed in it. The plane was downed by flak from the flight of 18 Il-2s and six 164 IAP La-5s.

*** This day the 897 IAP was assigned five new Yak-3s (c/n: 310052, 310348, 310366, 310370, 310377) and a Yak-9M (c/n: 3415353). Yak-3, c/n: 310370 was lost soon after its arrival during the very same day. The 867 BAO reported that VK-105PF-2 (Yak-3) engine No.422-51 is done, it can be picked up by the regiment. On the previous day the 897 IAP received a shipment of four Yak-3s (c/n: 310282, 310287, 310294, 310342) from the reserve of the 17 VA, while the 611 IAP received Yak-3, c/n: 310345. Source: TsAMO RF: fu. 20257, inv. 1, f. 95, p. 272, Report to the Head of the 'USM' Department of the 17 VA.

On 13 March 1945 Lt. Heinz Ewald claimed an Il-2 and two La-5 fighters shot down in the Székesfehérvár area.

At 09:43 LT eight Il-2s of 190 GvShAP, led by Gv.St.Lt. Nikolai Nikolaevich Strobikin attacked enemy tanks and trucks in the Agárd area, where they ran into intense anti-aircraft fire and enemy fighters. In the unfolding dogfight, without suffereing losses, they claimed one *'Fw 190'* shot down. Gv.St.Lt. Pyotr Antonovich Davidov's Il-2 was seriously damaged by flak and was written-off upon his return to base. Between 10:26-10:41 LT six 131 GvShAP Il-2s, led by Gv.Lt. Vasilii Nikitovich Provalinskii, escorted by six 92 IAP La-5s attacked the Gárdony, Csirip and Júliamajor areas near Lake Velence. Upon leaving the target, the Soviet planes encountered anti-aircraft fire near Seregélyes, while eight *'Fw 190s'* also attacked them. After their attacks, three Il-2s went down: Gv.Ml.Lt. Nikolai Arhipovich Titomirov's Il-2 crash-landed at Nadap-NE, 1.5 km in a forest,[71] Gv.Ml.Lt. Fedor Ivanovich Strelnikov's Il-2 crash-landed on its airbase and was written-off, later it was salvaged for spare parts. Gv.Ml.Lt. Aleksandr Ivanovich Zenin's Il-2 had the same fate. Gv.Ml.Lt. Tsukanov's and Gv.Lt. Vasilii Nikitovich Provalinskii s Il-2s were damaged by flak but returned to their airbase safely. One of the three lost Il-2s could be Heinz Ewald's legitimate Il-2 aerial victory. The Soviet fighter escort suffered no losses. The very intense anti-aircraft fire damaged fifteen Il-2s of the 7 and 12 GvShAD.[72]

Between 15:20-16:20 LT six La-5s of 116 IAP, led by Maj. Victor Pavlovich Shirokov escorted 136 ShAD Il-2 Sturmoviks in the Lake Velence area. After the first strike around 15:50 LT over Csiribpuszta Ml.Lt. Andrey Antonovich Radchenko separated from his flight and went missing in a dogfight with four *'Fw 190's*.[73] This single La-5 was a victory for Heinz Ewald, however his second La-5 claim does not correspond to any of the Soviet losses and must be deemed an overclaim.

Although they received their new Lavochkin La-7FN fighters only by the end of March 1945, pilots of 31 IAP continued their training for the new model.[74] It is interesting to note that this day twelve of their pilots flew sixteen practice flights with a total of 6.25 hours flight-time.

14 March 1945 (Wednesday)

Ewald's 75th: OVERCLAIM, Il-2 in the Székesfehérvár area, ~13:00LT
Ewald's 76th: VICTORY, Boston in the Székesfehérvár area, ~17:00 LT

Soviet 17 VA Douglas A-20 Boston and Il-2 losses on 14 March 1945				
Regiment:	**Type:**	**c/n:**	**Pilot:**	**Details:**
260 BAP	A-20B	41-3626	F. I. Larin	*Repaired on airfield, lost on 31 March*
260 BAP	A-20G	43-21603	P. T. Zaharov WIA	Tatárszentgyörgy, HUN Bf 109 victory
260 BAP	A-20G	43-9274	N. P. Pavlov	Zombor, 3 km, CL, tail: red '4'
260 BAP	A-20G	42-86706	K. A. Tsallagov	Sárosd-NE, 1 km, CL, exploded
260 BAP	A-20G	43-21904	A. K. Morozov	*Kiskunlacháza, air-combat, repaired*
449 BAP	A-20B	41-3643	Appolon P. Pavlov	CL at Szabadszállás, tail No.: white '8'
861 BAP	A-20G	42-53664	Ivan Y. Isachenko	*Gunners bailed out, plane returned, '7'*
861 BAP	A-20G	42-86876	E. I. Kropanev+	Sárosd-SE to JG 52 Bf 109s
861 BAP	A-20G	43-21519	V. N. Bahvalov+	Pálinkaházpuszta-W to Lt. Düttmann
210 ShAP	Il-2m3	*Unknown*	S. S. Elohov	*AC not lost, flak damage, repaired, '10'*
210 ShAP	Il-2m3	18886107	V. I. Lemeshkin	'29', LAC with an 897 IAP Yak-9*
210 ShAP	Il-2m3	18842110	Lev K. Vorobiev+	Seregélyes-SW, flak, 15:00 LT, '30'
210 ShAP	Il-2m3	11813	V. P. Godyaev	*AC not lost, flak damage, repaired, '39'*
210 ShAP	Il-2m3	12046	V. A. Leonov	*AC not lost, flak damage, repaired, '15'*
210 ShAP	Il-2m3	*18886119*	V. A. Tulenev	*AC not lost, flak damage, repaired, '17'*
210 ShAP	Il-2m3	11082	P. A. Taranovich	*AC not lost, flak damage, repaired, '8'*
615 ShAP	Il-2m3	11521	T. B. Kukaev+	Csiribpuszta, flak. 12 Il-2s, 6 La-5s
615 ShAP	Il-2m3	1874596	Ivan F. Brankov	Csiribpuszta-S, flak, 12 Il-2s, 6 La-5s
615 ShAP	Il-2m3	18801107	A. I. Zhigailo+	Csiribpuszta, flak. 12 Il-2s, 6 La-5s
672 ShAP	Il-2m3	12571	F. T. Mamontov+	Agárd-SE, 2 km , 17:25 LT, flak
672 ShAP	Il-2m3	1875688	P. S. Radchenko	Dinnyés, 2 Fw 190s, 14:35 LT, broken
672 ShAP	Il-2m3	1876788	Y. S. Makkoveev	Sukoró, dogfight, 17:10 LT
672 ShAP	Il-2m3	1877788	N. D. Botin+	Pákozd-S, in Lake Velence, 17:25 LT

71 TsAMO RF: fu. 22310, inv. 275171c, f. 12, pp. 75, 76, Operations journal of 131 GvShAP, entry for 13 March 1945.
72 TsAMO RF: fu: 20512, inv. 1, f. 126, p. 38, Operations journal of 3 GvShAK, entry for 13 March 1945.
73 TsAMO RF: fu: 20259, inv. 1, f. 88, p. 29, Operations journal of 295 IAD, entry for 13 March 1945.
74 On 29 March 1945 the regiments of the 295 IAD finally received their first thirty La-7FN fighters (c/n: 45211091, 45211117, 45211122, 45211128, 45211183, 45211191, 45211255, 45211314, 45211366, 45211671, 45211684, 45211707, 45211754, 45211779, 45211916, 45211917, 45211941, 45211953, 45211962, 45211986, 45211999, 45212009, 45212041, 45212066, 45212071, 45212078, 45212103, 45212135, 45212149, 45212166) beside their single, old La-7FN (c/n: 3811716) that they owned since the fall of 1944. From the Tököl airbase ten La-7s went to the 31 IAP at Várpalota, eleven to the 116 IAP and ten to the 164 IAP in Veszprém. These La-7FN fighters later participated in the air battles for Austria.

An A-20B Boston of the 449 BAP is flying over the Danube in early 1945. The regiment's bomb dropping seagull emblem beneath the pilot's cockpit is clearly visible. (Photo: Csanády-Nagyvárad-Winkler: A Magyar repülés története – Műszaki Könyvkiadó, Budapest, 1977, p. 267.)

Soviet 17 VA Douglas A-20 Boston and Il-2 losses on 14 March 1945 (*continued*)				
672 ShAP	Il-2m3	1889203	M. Golobokov+	Dinnyés-SE, 2 km, flak, 17:25 LT
707 ShAP	Il-2m3	18827109	V. I. Markov+	Őcsény airfield, accident, 16:44 LT
715 ShAP	Il-2m3	18881124	V. I. Kochergin	Sárosd-SE, 3.5 km, flak, white '4'
715 ShAP	Il-2m3	12332	Pirogov-Statsenko	Detric flak, 15:00 LT, CL at Ercsi, '33'
715 ShAP	Il-2m3	12293	I. V. Krasnoperov	Pusztaszabolcs-S, 3 km, white '18'
96 OKRAP	Il-2KR	11933	L. S.Kulikovskii+	Pákozd, 11:56 LT, lost to Lipfert
165 GShAP	Il-2m3	1871xxx**	K. Sidelnikov	Drávaszabolcs-NE, 4 Il-2s, 4 Bf 109s
989 ShAP	Il-2m3	18874124	N. M. Zaharov WIA	Vértesacsa-NW, 4 km , flak, '100'
989 ShAP	Il-2m3	*Unknown*	Leoncio V. Hernans	*Spanish pilot, damaged, white '26'*
989 ShAP	Il-2m3	*Unknown*	N. I. Pahai	*AC not lost, flak damage, repaired, '16'*
989 ShAP	Il-2m3	*Unknown*	V. A. Kabelkov	*AC not lost, flak damage, repaired, '27'*
989 ShAP	Il-2m3	12293	I. P. Krasnoperov	Pusztaszabolcs-S, dogfight, '18'
Unknown	Il-2m3	*Unknown*	*Unknown*	Seregélyes, destroyed by 210 ShAP***

* During landing at 15:30 LT a 897 IAP Yak-9 with damaged hydraulics and breaks piloted by Ml.Lt. Nikolai Kuzmich Konovalov could not stop at the end of the runway and ran into Ml.Lt. Valentin Ivanovich Lemeshkin's 210 ShAP Il-2m3 (c/n: 18886107) cutting it in half, fracturing the arm of Il-2 aerial gunner Ml.Sgt. Ivan Anisimovich Barannik. The Il-2 was written off, its engine was salvaged and the Yak-9 was repaired. Ml.Lt. Konovalov was killed in air combat on 10 April 1945 at 16:00 LT at Himberg, Austria at 4000m in his Yak-3 (c/n: 310052) where four 897 IAP Yaks battled with six Bf 109s.

** A 17 VA, 10 GvShAD, 165 GvShAP Il-2m3 Sturmovik, c/n: either 1871190, or 1871588.

*** This previously force landed and abandoned Il-2 was discovered and destroyed by the crew of Ml.Lt. Boris Mihailovich Troitskii pilot and Sgt. Kirill Kalinovich Dibrov aerial gunner flying 210 ShAP Il-2m3, No.'13' near Seregélyes over German-held territory.

On 14 March 1945 Lt. Heinz Ewald claimed an Il-2 and an A-20 Boston bomber shot down in the Székesfehérvár area. Since the time and location difference between his Il-2 claim and the lost Il-2s is too significant, his Il-2 claim seems to be an overclaim. His A-20 Boston claim, however, could be one of the eight lost A-20 Bostons, most likely St.Lt. Appolon Petrovich Pavlov's A-20B of the 449 BAP (S/N: 41-3643, R-2600-11 engines: 57124 and 57359, built on 28 December 1942 in Santa Monica, California, USA.)

This day at 16:42 LT fifteen A-20 Bostons of the 449 BAP, led by Capt. Dmitrii Sergeevich Yegorkin bombed Székesfehérvár from the altitude of 4000m. Upon leaving the target, the Soviet bombers were attacked by seven Bf 109 and two '*Fw 190*' fighters. Three Bf 109s opened fire on St.Lt. Pavlov's Boston which was hit, but they successfully escaped by losing altitude. At this time the radioman bailed out with his parachute and landed on Soviet held territory. The crippled Boston finally crossed the Danube and crash-landed near Szabadszállás:[75]

St.Lt. Appolon Petrovich Pavlov pilot (unhurt)
Lt. Ivan Nikolaevich Stroev navigator/bombardier (unhurt)
C-a Vasilii Mihailovich Bolotov radioman/gunner (WIA)
Sgt. Aleksandr Andreevich Sitnikov gunner (died in the hospital)

The plane burned and was written off in the 18 March 1945 mechanical report of the 244 BAD. The Boston's armament consisted of two 12.7mm KB, two 12.7mm Berezin BS and two 7.62mm KB machine guns.

16 March 1945 (Friday)
Ewald's 77th: OVERCLAIM, Yak-3 between 16-17:00 LT in the Székesfehérvár area

Soviet 17 VA single-engine fighter losses on 16 March 1945				
Regiment:	**Type:**	**c/n:**	**Pilot:**	**Details:**
611 IAP	Yak-9M	Unknown*	N. G. Yegorihin	*Ercsi-N, 16:30 LT, repaired*
659 IAP	Yak-3	310220	V. A. Korotkevich	Csór, A-20 escort, ~14:40 LT

* Either c/n: 27153100 or 3315348.

On 16 March 1945 Lt. Heinz Ewald claimed a 'Yak-3' fighter shot down in the Székesfehérvár area. This time his opponent was most likely Ml.Lt. Nikolai Vasilevich Yegorihin (611 IAP, Yak-9M), who was covering Soviet ground troops in the Pátka-Székesfehérvár area. Around 16:40 LT his flight met four groups of eight '*Fw 190s*'. He was hit and force landed at Ercsi-N, approximately 10 km near Tököl. He returned to his unit on 17 March 1945. His Yak-9 was repaired therefore it was an overclaim for Lt. Heinz Ewald.

Conclusion

Lt. Heinz Ewald claimed 53 aerial victories during his service time in Hungary. He claimed his first victory in the country on 6 October 1944 and the last one on 16 March 1945, which covers a significant part of his combat career between his 29th and 77th claims. During this time period he also had four unconfirmed claims (28 October, 14 November, 8 December 1944 and 8 March 1945) of which two are potential victories. He had thirteen single and six double daily victories/potential victories. His most sucessful day over Hungary was on 3 January 1945 with four potential victories. It is interesting to note that Ewlad's 28 October 1944 and 1 March 1945 claims, both of which were left unconfirmed, do involve him damaging aircraft though there were not shot down by him.

75 TsAMO RF: fu. 20224, inv. 2, f. 61, pp. 148, 152, 153, 162, Combat diary (losses) of 244 BAD, entries for 14 March 1945. (St.Lt. Appolon Petrovich Pavlov's plane.)

8

Friedrich Haas (1924-1945)

Born on 20 January 1924. Lt. Friedrich Haas joined JG 52 in the Soviet Union in the fall of 1943 at only nineteen years old. He took over the command of 5./JG 52 on 1 Februay 1945.[1] Of his documented claims, Friedrich Haas made 15 over Hungary between 16 October and 21 December 1944 consisting of nine Yak-9s, two La-5s, two Il-2s and two Yak-11s [*sic*]. It is thought that he had a total of around 74 claims by the time of his death,[2] though there is no concrete evidence to prove this. On 9 April 1945 he was shot down by Soviet fighters over Wien-Stockerau, Austria in his Bf 109G-14, *white* (?) '2'.[3] He bailed out at low altitude but hit the tail section of his plane and was killed at the age of twenty-one.[4] Posthumously he was awarded the Ritterkreuz on 26 April 1945.[5] The theorized tally of 74 claims could be the reason for Haas becoming the recipient of the Ritterkreuz award.

Friedrich Haas' claims are compiled from the following sources listed in order of heaviest reliance:

- Luftwaffe Aces: claims and bibliographies, Vol. 2
- Die Geschichte der II. Gruppe des Jagdgeschwaders 52: Offizielle Ausgabe der Traditionsgemeinschaft JG 52
- Tony Woods – Eastern Front Vol 4. 1944. Jul – Dec, Issue 1

All the lists are congruent for the dates and aircraft types, however the numbering of the claims is different in the Mathews and Foreman publication as unconfirmed claims are left unnumbered. The claim number appearing in the same has been used. Unfortunately, none of Lt. Friedrich Haas' 1945 claims are known in any detail, therefore the Authors do not attempt to verify them.

16 October 1944 (Monday)

Haas' 36th: POTENTIAL VICTORY, Yak-11 at Nagyvárad (Oradea) -NW, 10 km at 16:07 LT, 3500m, Anerk: Nr. 609

Soviet 5 VA single-engine fighter losses on 16 October 1944				
Regiment:	**Type:**	**c/n:**	**Pilot:**	**Details:**
178 GvIAP	La-5FN	392121142	Y. Y. Gukalin +	Szeghalom-SW to four Bf 109s
179 IAP	Yak-9M	2715334	D. Maksimenkov +	Torda-NE, flak, KIFA at 13:50 LT

This day between 15:10-16:20 LT La-5s of the 178 GvIAP, led by Gv.St.Lt. Pyotr Romanovich Setinin were covering Soviet ground forces in the Berettyóújfalu area. At 15:45 LT near Derecske they were ambushed by four Bf 109s, which attacked them from the clouds and hit Gv.Ml.Lt. Evgenii Efremovich Gukalin's La-5FN (c/n: 392121142 [*sic*!]). Although he escaped the battle, he reported that he was hit and was bleeding badly. Near his airfield at Szeghalom, his damaged plane went into a dive and crashed killing him. Although his final moments are unknown, it is likely that he lost consciousness

1 Barbas, *Die Geschichte der II. Gruppe des Jagdgeschwaders 52*, p. 286.
2 Andrew-Johannes Mathews and John Foreman, *Luftwaffe Aces: Biographies and Victory Claims*, Vol. 2 (Surrey: Red Kite, 2014), p. 446, and Barbas, *Die Geschichte der II. Gruppe des Jagdgeschwaders 52*, p. 200.
3 Correspondence with Matti Salonen (7 April 2021)
4 Barbas, *Die Geschichte der II. Gruppe des Jagdgeschwaders 52*, p. 199.
5 Mathews and Foreman, *Luftwaffe Aces*, Vol. 2, p. 446.

shortly before his La-5FN uncontrollably struck the ground. Due to the time and distance differences loosely matching each other, this claim could be a potential aerial victory for Lt. Haas, even if the downed aircraft and his reported victim were of two different models. The misidentification in this case could be the result of the poor visibility while fighting around the cloud layers.

The other 5 VA fighter loss this day was Lt. Dmitrii Nikolaevich Maksimenkov's Yak-9M which was damaged by flak during his mission. Upon return to his airfield at Torda-NE at 13:50 LT, Lt. Maksimenkov lost control of his damaged aircraft at 200m during his third landing attempt, crashed into the ground and was killed. The time of this tragedy and the circumstances of his loss prove that his Yak-9M could not have been related to Lt. Haas' actions.

18 OCTOBER 1944 (WEDNESDAY)

Haas' 37th: OVERCLAIM, Yak-11 at Debrecen-S, 35 km at 12:03 LT, 2500m, Anerk: Nr. 328

<table>
<tr><th colspan="5">Soviet 5 VA single-engine fighter losses on 18 October 1944</th></tr>
<tr><th>Regiment:</th><th>Type:</th><th>c/n:</th><th>Pilot:</th><th>Details:</th></tr>
<tr><td>149 GvIAP</td><td>Yak-7B</td><td>5315329</td><td>A. A. Sokolov</td><td rowspan="2">Hajdúszoboszló-S, Szeghalom-SW, 14:10 – 15:15 LT, in dogfight</td></tr>
<tr><td>149 GvIAP</td><td>Yak-9D</td><td>17166057</td><td>R. I. Kolechkin</td></tr>
<tr><td>149 GvIAP</td><td>Yak-9D</td><td>17166071</td><td>P. I. Kozlov</td><td>Derecske, 14:40 – 16:10 LT</td></tr>
<tr><td>486 IAP</td><td>La-5F</td><td>39214770</td><td>F. I. Nikonorenkov+</td><td>Nagylak, 14:13 LT, KIFA</td></tr>
<tr><td>178 GvIAP</td><td>La-5F</td><td>39214628</td><td>G. E. Karnauhov</td><td>Damaged in dogfight, repaired</td></tr>
</table>

On 18 October 1944 Lt. Friedrich Haas claimed a Yak-11 (Yak-3) at Debrecen-S at 12:03 LT, but because of the significant time difference between the four fighter losses of the 5 VA they should be considered as overclaims. Between 14:10-15:15 LT, 149 GvIAP Yaks led by Gv.St.Lt. Ryazhankin covered the ground troops in the area when they engaged in dogfights with six Fw 190s and four Bf 109s. Gv.Ml.Lt. Aleksandr Antonovich Sokolov and Gv.Ml.Lt. Ruvim Ivanovich Kolechkin went missing, while Gv.St.Lt. Pyotr Ivanovich Kozlov was shot down during the next mission at Hajdúszoboszló-S, 5 km and landed safely with his parachute. Ml.Lt. Philipp Ilyich Nikonorenkov's M-82F engine (486 IAP, La-5F) had mechanical problems. In order to avoid ditching in the small river over which he was flying, he made a sharp turn, rolled over and crashed right into the ground, leading to his instant death. Since smaller flights of 13 GvIAD were covering Soviet ground forces in the Debrecen-Derecske area all day, it is possible that Lt. Haas damaged one of their planes which finally could return to its base where it later got repaired. There are no Soviet losses which support Haas' claim for this day.

19 October 1944 (Thursday)

Haas' 38th: OVERCLAIM, LaGG-5 at Debrecen-S,-SW, 15 km at 10:21 LT, 1500m

<table>
<tr><th colspan="5">Soviet 5 VA single-engine fighter losses on 19 October 1944</th></tr>
<tr><th>Regiment:</th><th>Type:</th><th>c/n:</th><th>Pilot:</th><th>Details:</th></tr>
<tr><td>178 GvIAP</td><td>La-5FN</td><td>39212311</td><td>F.G. Semenov MIA</td><td>Debrecen-W, 11:25 LT to fighters</td></tr>
<tr><td>92 IAP</td><td>La-5FN</td><td>39211101</td><td>G. G. Tokarev MIA</td><td>Debrecen-N, 13:10 LT, 4 Bf 109s</td></tr>
</table>

On this day at 10:21 LT Lt. Friedrich Haas claimed a La-5 fighter at Debrecen-S,-SW. Unless his reported time and relative position to Debrecen is incorrect, his La-5 claim this time was an overclaim.[6] Between 10:45-12:05 LT six 178 GvIAP La-5s led by Gv.Capt. Fedor Georgievich Semenov (HSU) covered the ground troops in the Debrecen-Hajdúszovát area. At 11:25 LT between 1500-2000m became engaged in aerial combat with eight Fw 190s and four Bf 109s. Later another four Fw 190s and Bf 109s joined the battle. The La-5s attacked the Fw 190s, but Semenov's La-5FN (c/n: 39212311, ASh-82FN engine: 822951, white '<★11') was hit. He bailed out with his parachute at Debrecen-W, 8 km over enemy held territory and fell into captivity from which he never returned (Note that the 3 GvIAK summary report gives the wrong c/n for Gv.Capt. Fedor Georgievich Semenov's lost La-5FN: 39212331).[7]

Later at 13:10 LT at 1800m four 92 IAP La-5s, led by St.Lt. Aleksandr Pavlovich Soluyanov escorted eight 130 GvShAP Il-2s in the Debrecen-N area, where four Bf 109s tried to attack the Il-2s. The pair of Soluyanov and Tokarev intercepted the attack and downed one Bf 109. The remaining three Bf 109s turned against the La-5 pair of St.Lt. Matyushenko that Soluyanov and Tokarev immediately tried to defend. At this point one Bf 109 broke out and turned back onto the Il-2s. Soluyanov, performing a sharp turn to try to catch him right away, while his wingman Lt. Gavriil Grigorevich Tokarev was left alone with the remaining two Bf 109s. The Bf 109s took advantage of the sudden opportunity and downed Tokarev's

6 TsAMO RF: fu. 20062, inv. 1, f. 33, p. 174, Operations journal of 178 GvIAP, entry for 19 October 1944.
7 TsAMO RF: fu. 327, inv. 4999, f. 177, p. 27, Operations review of 3 GvIAK for October 1944, entry for 19 October 1944.

La-5FN (c/n: 39211101, ASh-82FN engine: 8213517, white '01'). The escorted Il-2s suffered no losses. Although Tokarev never returned, some details were preserved about his activity over the next few months. A previously downed 150 GvIAP Yak-9T pilot, Gv.Ml.Lt. Aleksandr Nikitovich Sisko,[8] was able to return from captivity and reported to his interrogators that in the Budapest hospital where the captured and injured Soviet airmen were treated, he met with Gv.Ml.Lt. Nikolai Matveevich Knut (a downed Yak-3 pilot),[9] Gv.Lt. Ivan Ivanovich Fyodorov (a downed B-25 Mitchell navigator),[10] and Lt. Gavriil Grigorevich Tokarev. Later when the ground forces of the 2nd Ukrainian Front approached Budapest these individuals were evacuated to Győr in Western Hungary, where on 21 December 1944 they escaped from the hospital.[11] They hid in a nearby house to escape the Germans searching for them. Sisko ran downstairs and hid in some hay while Tokarev ran upstairs. At this time Sisko heard two shots and never heard or saw Tokarev again. He believed Tokarev was either executed on the spot or was re-captured and taken to a camp from which he never returned.

30 October 1944 (Monday)
Haas' 39th: POTENTIAL VICTORY, LaGG-5 at Szolnok-E, 20 km at 300m at 14:09 LT, Anerk: Nr. 934.

Soviet 5 VA single-engine fighter losses on 30 October 1944				
Regiment:	**Type:**	**c/n:**	**Pilot:**	**Details:**
279 IAD	La-5F	39213362	Unknown	Szolnok, CL after a dogfight
31 GvIAP	Yak-1B	21151	E. V. Yerofitskii	Kecskemét area, flak, 13:50 LT
151 GvIAP	Yak-9T	1415399	A. V. Kozlov	Tiszaföldvár-E, Bf 109, ~11:40 LT, CL

On 30 October 1944 Lt. Friedrich Haas claimed a La-5 fighter at 20 kilometers East of Szolnok, which could correspond to the lost 279 IAD fighter which crash-landed that day after air combat. Since its details are currently unknown his claim can be considered as a potential aerial victory. On the Soviet side La-5s of the 192 IAP were escorting two reconnaissance Il-2 Sturmoviks in the Kecskemét area where they met ten Bf 109s. In the wild dogfight Ml.Lt. Afanasii Ivanovich Kudryavtsev claimed a Bf 109 shot down, while the Il-2s suffered no losses. At the same time four La-5s of the 92 IAP were escorting eight 132 GvShAP Il-2s to the Tiszaföldvár area, where they fell into air combat with eight Fw 190s. St.Lt. Ivan Alekseevich Yegorov claimed an Fw 190 shot down near Tiszaföldvár, while Maj. Nikolai Grigorevich Butoma claimed another one at Szolnok-E. Hungarian Bf 109 ace Kálmán István zls. (102/1. FS) claimed a La-5 in the Szolnok – Rákóczifalva area.

1 November 1944 (Wednesday)
Haas' 40th: OVERCLAIM, Yak-9 at Kecskemét-E at 13:47 LT, 2500m

Soviet 5 VA single-engine fighter losses on 1 November 1944				
Regiment:	**Type:**	**c/n:**	**Pilot:**	**Details:**
177 GvIAP	La-5F	39215336	E. I. Batyunya WIA	Szolnok, to Hungarian Bf 109
177 GvIAP	La-5	*Unknown*	M. V. Danshin	*Later returned, AC not lost!*
73 GvIAP	Yak-9D	18166046	*Unknown, 1st Sq.*	*Damaged, repaired on its airfield*
73 GvIAP	Yak-1B	08175	A. S. Andrianov	Lakitelek-NW to 8 Bf 109s
85 GvIAP	Yak-1B	xx1xx	B. I. Gelkin	*Later returned, AC not lost!*

On 1 November 1944 Lt. Friedrich Haas claimed a Yak-9 shot down at Kecskemét-E at 13:47 LT. This day the only possible Soviet fighter loss in this area was Gv.Lt. Aleksandr Semyonovich Andrianov's Yak-1B, which was probably downed by Lt. Peter Düttmann (see discussion in the Lt. Peter Düttmann chapter). Therefore this Yak 9 claim for Lt. Haas might have been a damaged Soviet fighter but could not have been a permanent Soviet loss.

8 Gv.Ml.Lt. Sisko was downed by Hptm. Lipfert on 24 October 1944 in Yak-9T (c/n: 1015348).

9 Gv.Ml.Lt. Knut was downed by Hptm. Fritz Schröter (Stab I./SG 10, Fw 190F) at 13:30 LT on 27 October 1944 in Yak-3 (c/n: 3929212) at Nyíregyháza-E at 300m.

10 Gv.Lt. Fyodorov was the navigator of downed 337 AP DD B-25J Mitchell (S/N: 43-27803, red '83') lost on 26/27 August 1944 near Sombor, Yugoslavia with Golovatenko's crew.

11 In the night of 22/23 December 1944 the railway station of Győr was hit hard by B-25 Mitchells of the Soviet 18 VA. On 21 December 1944 Soviet Mitchells flew reconnaissance sorties over the city to prepare their upcoming attack. The Soviet pilots probably used the ensuing alarm and chaos for their escape from the hospital.

23 November 1944 (Thursday)

Haas' 41st: OVERCLAIM, Yak-9 in the Atkár area at 08:38 LT, 800m

Haas' 42nd: OVERCLAIM, Il-2 at Miskolc-S, -SE, 30 km at 11:46 LT, 500m

Soviet 5 and 17 VA single-engine fighter and Il-2 losses on 23 November 1944				
Regiment:	**Type:**	**c/n:**	**Pilot:**	**Details:**
122 IAP	Yak-1B	32161	E. S. Titov	TOA at 08:40 LT, unhurt
513 IAP	Yak-1B	*29156 45168*	Y. A. Gopchenko	Kál-S, 15 km, 10:38 LT, 6 *'Fw 190'*
513 IAP	Yak-1B		P. P. Kuyanov+	Atkár, 10:38 LT to Helmut Lipfert
187 GvShAP	Il-2m3	12260	B. D. Grilev POW	Hatvan-NE, Bf 109, 11:20 LT, '57'
187 GvShAP	Il-2m3	*Unknown*	V. M. Afanasiev	*Nagykőrös, Bf 109s, '59', repaired*
187 GvShAP	Il-2m3	*Unknown*	V. V. Fedorenko	*Zsámbok-NE, flak, '98', repaired*
210 ShAP	Il-2m3	10982	N. V. Potapov +	Beli Manastir-E to 2 Bf 109s
995 ShAP	Il-2m3	9493 10146 1875972 1879583	I. D. Kornev MIA	Majs, 8 Il-2s, 2 La-5s vs. 15 Bf 109s
995 ShAP	Il-2m3		A. A. Horunin MIA	Majs-Töttös, 8 Il-2s and 2 164 IAP La-5s vs. Flak and ~15 Bf 109s
995 ShAP	Il-2m3		N. K. Kuzmin MIA	
995 ShAP	Il-2m3		V. M. Zaitsev WIA	Batina, 8 Il-2s, 2 La-5s vs. 15 Bf 109s
897 IAP	Yak-1B	15193	V. V. Kravchuk +	Matty-N, Ilka-farm, flak, 13:35 LT*
116 IAP	La-5FN	39211303 39211628	Kuznetsov	CL near its airfield after a dogfight
116 IAP	La-5FN		A. Y. Trusov	CL due to broken right landing gear

* Maj. Vladimir Valentinovich Kravchuk was strafing German motorcycles on the Siklós road when he crashed at the Ilka-farm along the highway and blew up, its engine flew 200m and landed at the forest. The pilot's body was unrecognizable, however his photo ID booklet found by Hungarian policemen in his pocket remained intact and contained two photos showing two beautiful teenage girls, one with the pilot himself. (Kovács József (14) witness via researcher Nagy Gábor).

On 23 November 1944 at 08:38 LT Lt. Friedrich Haas claimed a Soviet Yak-9 fighter shot down in the Atkár area. This day serious air battles took place here indeed in which one Yak-1B crashed killing its pilot Ml.Lt. Kuyanov, but this event took place two hours later at 10:38 LT (in Soviet records at 12:38 Moscow time) and it was downed by Hptm. Lipfert, therefore this claim of Lt. Haas is an overclaim. Lt. Haas' second claim of the day, an Il-2 Sturmovik at 11:46 LT at Miskolc-S, -SE, 30 km can not be verified either. This day ground forces of the Soviet 27th Army were hit hard by German artillery fire in the Miskolc-NNW area. Il-2 crews of the 264 ShAD were assigned the task to neutralize the German artillery. Il-2 flights of 4-6 planes including Sq. CO. St.Lt. Vladimir Stephanovich Zarubin of 451 ShAP hammered the German artillery positions throughout the day from a height of approximately 1200m, however none of the three ground attack regiments (235, 451, 809 ShAP) suffered any aircraft losses.[12]

5 DECEMBER 1944 (TUESDAY)

Haas' 43rd: OVERCLAIM, Yak-9 at Tura-W at 08:57 LT,[13] 500m

Haas' 44th: OVERCLAIM, Il-2 at Gyöngyös-E at 09:00 LT, 200m

Soviet 5 VA aircraft losses on 5 December 1944				
Regiment:	**Type:**	**c/n:**	**Pilot:**	**Details:**
177 GvIAP	La-5F	39215215	P. S. Olin	*Stabilizator damage, repaired later*
177 GvIAP	La-5FN	39211776	N. L. Vereshak	To flak, his next La-5 was 41210115.
177 GvIAP	La-5FN	39212384	I. G. Sklyarov	*Cylinder damage, repaired at base*
486 IAP	La-5FN	39212724	V. G. Snagovskii+	Ercsi, 11:55 LT, 2 La-5, 6 *'Fw 190'*
151 GvIAP	Yak-3	1529219	Y. M. Ravikovich+	Ercsi, Danube-crossing, 14:00, Ju 87
151 GvIAP	Yak-3	*Unknown*	A. A. Morozov	Ercsi area to Bf 109s, Fw 190s*
122 IAP	Yak-9M	3015336	G. A. Ulanov WIA	Heréd, 15:05 LT to Heinz Ewald
122 IAP	Yak-9T	1615383	M. S. Yerko MIA	Erdőtarcsa, 10:12 LT to Lipfert

12 TsAMO RF: fu: 20525, inv: 1, f: 26, p. 37, Combat journal of 5 ShAK, entry for 23 November 1944.

13 08:54 LT according to Tony Woods, O.K.L. Fighter Claims: Reich, West and Südfront, Aug to Dec 1944. Vol. I

Soviet 5 VA aircraft losses on 5 December 1944 (*continued*)				
513 IAP	Yak-1B	20153	I. A. Guriev MIA	Erdőtarcsa, 11:00 LT to Heinz Ewald
452 BAP	A-20G-15	42-54220	I. P. Chugunov	Abony, Belicei-farm, due to flak
453 BAP	A-20G-10	42-53860	P. P. Sklyarov	Szolnok to Bf 109s, 1st (red) Sq.
130 GvShAP	Il-2m3	*Unknown*	V. A. Kukushkin	*Damaged by 6 Fw 190s, 3 Bf 109s between 13:40-14:50 LT, repaired*
130 GvShAP	Il-2m3	*Unknown*	Gv.Maj. Krilov	

* This is a questionable loss since the 13 GvIAD, 151 GvIAP record of the day does not mention it, only Morozov's personal record written on 26 April 1945, the date of 5 December 1944 could just be a typo. This is the only known contradicting case. TsAMO RF: fu. 33, inv. 690306, storage: 1237-41950045, p. 28b.

On 5 December 1944, Lt. Friedrich Haas claimed a Soviet Yak-9 fighter at Tura-W at 08:57 LT and an Il-2 Sturmovik at Gyöngyös-E at 09:00 LT only three minutes apart from each other (both were probably from the very same wave). By the end of the day the 5 VA summary report listed the following losses: two La-5s and an A-20G Boston were shot down by enemy fighters, one A-20G Boston was downed by flak, while two La-5s, two Yak-3s and five *Yak-1Bs* [*sic*!] were missing due to unspecified reasons. Later these numbers were corrected by the more detailed regiment reports, as some of their planes later returned to their bases from different locations where they landed after their mission. Note, that none of the 5 VA units reported Il-2 losses that day. Based on the reported times, geographical locations and Soviet aircraft losses, neither Haas', nor Fhr. Hans Joachim Kawig's (5./JG 52) 09:05 LT Il-2 claim can be verified as aerial victories.

11 December 1944 (Monday)
Haas' 45th: OVERCLAIM, Yak-9 at 09:58 LT, 800m
Haas' 46th: OVERCLAIM, Yak-9 at Budapest-N,-NE, 10 km at 10:03 LT, 1000m

Soviet 5 and 17 VA single-engine fighter losses on 11 December 1944				
Regiment:	**Type:**	**c/n:**	**Pilot:**	**Details:**
267 IAP	Yak-1B	16168	A. I. Korzun	Yugoslavia-N (Bagatić-SE, 2 km)
611 IAP	Yak-1B	26170	V. A. Shelkunov	Taszár, hit a fuel truck at take-off
611 IAP	Yak-9T	0915336	B. A. Kovalevskii	Taszár, combat damages, CL
659 IAP	Yak-9D	2515335	N. S. Semikin WIA	Out of fuel after dogfight, CL
866 IAP	Yak-9T	1215373	M. L. Serdyuk+ and A. Shamshik MIA	615 ShAP Il-2 escorts, lost near Devecser and Nagybajom
866 IAP	Yak-9T	1315325		
178 GvIAP	La-5FN	39213286	P. A. Brizgalov	*Missing, later returned*
486 IAP	La-5FN	39213272	*Unknown*	*Damaged in air combat, repaired*
149 GvIAP	Yak-1B	11179	A. A. Merzlenko+	Ercsi-N, 11:20 LT to Bf 109
151 GvIAP	Yak-9T	2415358	L. I. Toropov	Tököl-W, 5 km to Heinz Ewald
122 IAP	Yak-9M	2515346	V. E. Stadnik	Jászberény, 14:50 LT, in accident

On 11 December 1944 Lt. Friedrich Haas claimed two Yak-9 fighters five minutes apart at 09:58 and 10:03 LT at Budapest-N,-NE, 10-15 km. This morning between 07:40-08:15 LT two 866 IAP Yak-3s took off from the Taszár airbase for a reconnaissance mission to the Tapolca airfield across Lake Balaton, where they discovered 30 single-engine and 15 twin-engine planes.[14] Lt.Col. Aleksandr Stephanovich Chugunov immediately went down to ground level and by strafing the airfield he set a Ju 52/3m transport plane on fire. Based on their intelligence report, between 10:15-10:40 LT 6+4 Yak-9s, led by Capt. Aleksandr Dmitrievich Doroshenko (866 IAP) and Capt. Constantin Leontevich Chernogor (611 IAP) escorted Il-2s of the 615 ShAP back to Tapolca to destroy the discovered aircraft. The Il-2s also attacked the railway station of Devecser, where the Yak-9s battled with four Bf 109s. Capt. Pizunskii claimed one Bf 109 for the loss of Ml.Lt. Mihail Lukich Serdyuk's Yak-9T which went missing near Tapolca. Although Ml.Lt. Serdyuk's Yak-9T was lost only a few minutes after Lt. Haas' claims at around 10:30 LT, the distance between his crash and Haas' claiming locations was approximately 150 km! For the successful attack the 615 ShAP paid with six of their Il-2s. Four planes returned later, but two were permanent losses. Lt. Yurii Harlampievich Markoch's Il-2m3 (c/n: 18867106) crashed at Pusztamiske-E and Lt.

14 On 8 October 1944 the 866 IAP received one brand new Yak-3 from Saratov (c/n: 2029215), on 10 October 1944 three more from Tbilisi (c/n: 310055, 310081, 310220). On 11 December 1944 two of these Yak-3s flew to Tapolca. Later all of them were transferred to the 17 VA, 288 IAD, 659 IAP.

Avtandil Mihailovich Turkadze's plane (c/n: 18891106) went down near Devecser. Ml.Lt. Aleksei Petrovich Shamshik's Yak-9T was lost even further away from Tapolca near Nagybajom at Lake Balaton-SSW, also during an Il-2 escort mission, therefore none of these two Yak-9Ts could be Lt. Haas' victims. This was the case with all lost 5 and 17 VA fighters of the day: either the time of their loss or the location of their crash (or sometimes both) were too distant from Lt. Haas' claims therefore both of them are considered overclaims. But beside Lt. Haas, Obfhr. Steins and Uffz. Welz (6./JG 52) also claimed Yak-9s at Lake Velence-N at 11:07 and 11:09 LT. Here Yak-9s of the 611 IAP escorted Il-2s of the 189 ShAD. Although no Soviet fighter crashed in the claiming area, a Yak-9T piloted by Ml.Lt. Boris Aleksandrovich Kovalevskii crash-landed on the Taszár airbase during its second landing attempt due to combat damages. The engine was salvaged, but the airframe was written off, therefore it can be considered an aerial victory for either Obfhr. Steins or Uffz. Welz.

20 December 1944 (Wednesday)
Haas' 47th: OVERCLAIM, Yak-9 in the Seregélyes area at 09:08 LT, 500m
Haas' 48th: POTENTIAL VICTORY Yak-9 at Dunaújváros-NW, 15 km at 09:11 LT, 400m

Soviet 17 VA single-engine fighter losses on 20 December 1944				
Regiment:	**Type:**	**c/n:**	**Pilot:**	**Details:**
116 IAP	La-5F	39215145	F. I. Razyuk MIA	Székesfehérvár area, 15:00 LT
611 IAP	Yak-9T	2515331	N. V. Negorohin	Varasd, lost orientation in the dark
611 IAP	Yak-9T	1315359	*Unknown*	Crash-landed, engine salvaged

On 20 December 1944, within three minutes of each other, Lt. Friedrich Haas claimed two Yak-9 fighters. Based on their location the fighters were part of the 17 VA's 288 Fighter Division. He claimed his first Yak-9 near Seregélyes at 09:08 LT, the second one at Dunaújváros-NW, 15 km at 09:11 LT. This day between 08:45 – 09:45 LT six Yaks of the 611 IAP led by Capt. Mihail Fedorovich Batarov were covering Soviet ground troops in the Börgönd (Seregélyes-N) – Szabadbattyán areas where at around 09:10 LT they became engaged in dogfights with six JG 52 Bf 109s. During the chase, Ml.Lt. Nikolai Vasilevich Negorohin became separated from his group and headed for home but through navigational error he landed at Novi Sad in Serbia instead of his own airfield. After being refilled around 16:00 LT he tried to fly over to Madocsa, but he lost orientation again. This time he followed the Drava river instead of the Danube. Ml.Lt. Negorohin reached Varasd (*Varaždin*, Croatia) where in the dark during his landing he slid into a church. With the help of the local resistance, he crossed the frontline and returned to his unit on 1 February 1945. Combat records which do not specify the c/n of his aircraft say it was a Yak-1B, however the 288 IAD mechanical report gives c/n: 2515331 for the missing plane on 20 December 1944 as a Yak-9T with engine: 342-108. Based on the mechanical records of 20 December 1944 the 611 IAP lost another crash-landed Yak-9T as well, which was written off without its engine. This implies that it belly-landed on or near its own airfield and its engine remained in good enough condition to be salvaged. Although its pilot was not specified in the mechanical records and the combat reports do not mention the missing pilot. Given the known information from various documents it is most likely that Yak-9T c/n: 1315359 was damaged in the dogfight around Dunaújváros which translates into a potential victory for Lt. Haas. Beside Lt. Haas, a Fw 190F-8 pair of 2./SG 10 was also successful this day. Near Baja at 10:10 LT at the altitude of 50m Gefr. Kath downed a Soviet Po-2/U-2 biplane of the 57th Army, 589 OAES (Po-2, c/n: 7133, M-11 engine: 06066) which crash-landed and burned on the ground. Pilot Lt. Serafim Petrovich Nehaenko was wounded, but his passenger remained unhurt.

21 December 1944 (Thursday)
Haas' 49th: OVERCLAIM, Yak-9 in the Seregélyes area at 13:14 LT, 800m
Haas' 50th: OVERCLAIM, Yak-9 in the Seregélyes area at 13:14 LT, 800m

Soviet 17 VA single-engine fighter losses on 21 December 1944				
Regiment:	**Type:**	**c/n:**	**Pilot:**	**Details:**
31 IAP	La-5UTI	39212156	V. F. Chirkin	Kiskunlacháza, LAC at 10:15 LT
611 IAP	Yak-9M	2715322	A. D. Kaftanov +	Székesfehérvár-SE, to Bf 109*
611 IAP	Yak-9T	2515378	P. V. Belyaev	Flak, CL on own territory
659 IAP	Yak-9DD	0115311	D. D. Kostin MIA	Pécs, MIA
659 IAP	Yak-3	1229215	M. A. Fisenko	*Production defect, crash-landed*
659 IAP	Yak-9DD	0115315	I. I. Soshnikov MIA	*Pécs, not a combat related loss*
897 IAP	Yak-9D	17166031	N.A. Posuyko POW	At Bicske on recce., 2 *Fw 190s*

897 IAP	Yak-1B	06151	*Unknown*	Lost in not combat related LAC

* Ml.Lt. Kaftanov was downed in the morning between 09:40 – 11:05 LT by Hungarian Bf 109 ace, Máthé László fhdgy. (102/1. FS) at Székesfehérvár-SE, confirmed by the German 7/35. Air Observation Station.

During the early afternoon on 21 December 1944 at 13:14 LT Lt. Friedrich Haas claimed two Soviet Yak-9 fighters in the Seregélyes area within the same minute! Since no Soviet fighter regiments reported any aircraft losses that would fit the time or location criteria as per Haas' account, these two claims should be considered as overclaims.

Conclusion

Lt. Friedrick Haas' known claims over Hungary match the Soviet loss reports the least among all the II./JG 52 pilots in this book. Out of his fifteen known claims over Hungary only three may be considered potential aerial victories. Based on the available documents he does not have a single claim entry which can be positively verified as a full victory over Hungary. It is noteworthy that most of his overclaims were for Yakovlev models: eight Yak-9s and one 'Yak-11'. A theory about the reason for the significant Yak-9 overclaiming will be discussed later in this book.

9

Erich Hartmann (1922-1993)

Born on 19 April 1922, Erich Alfred Hartmann would join the Luftwaffe's 7./JG 52 on 10 October 1942 in Russia.[1] Due to his youthful appearance and attitude, his superiors nicknamed him 'Bubi', meaning little boy, which was fitting as the hot-headed Hartmann was still only twenty years old and had much to learn. Oblt. Walter Krupinski said the following: *'He appeared not much more than a mere baby. So young and full of life. As he walked away from me that first day I thought to myself, "Such a young face".'*[2] Günther Rall also stated similar things: '*what a young boy – a baby.*'[3] Hartmann's personal tactic of see-decide-attack-reverse was used extensively throughout his career, refined overtime and learned in part from former leaders.[4] Surprise attacks were first introduced to Hartmann from then Oberfeldwebel Eduard Rossmann,[5] flying extremely close before shooting at the enemy was picked up from the encouragement of then Oberleutnant Walter Krupinski.[6] Both these tactics required great flying skills and nerves to pull off. Erich Sommavilla explains: *A diving approach at high speed to a point beneath the enemy, a close-range burst from below by an 'expert', and the Russian blew apart in the air, while the victor used his speed advantage to return to a safe altitude in seconds … That was the secret of the 'experts' of II/JG 52.*[7]

Married to his wife Ursula Paetsch on 9 September 1944,[8] Erich Hartmann returned from leave and joined 4./JG 52 on 1 October 1944 to fight over Hungary for the next few months.[9] As Staffelkapitän of 4./JG 52, Hartmann enjoyed relatively high 'success' over the country despite the spartan outfit of II./JG 52 at the time.[10] However this 'success' seems to have been intertwined with misfortune as Hartmann downed a friendly Fw 190 over the country, moments before Lt. Heinz Ewald 'Esau' could warn the Hauptmann of the tragic misidentification.[11] On the 28 of December, Gruppenkommandeur Barkhorn authorized special leave for Hartmann to travel home from 29 December 1944 till 8 January 1945 to see his expecting wife,[12] however this reunion was cut short after only four days and he was required to return back to Hungary.[13] After Maj. Barkhorn left his position as Gruppenkommondeur on 16 January 1945, Erich Hartmann took over this position as the temporary Kommondeur.[14] From 29 January 1945 Erich Hartmann was given the command of I./JG 53, a position he would leave on 14 February 1945.[15] Afterward he would hand over this position to Helmut Lipfert and go on to lead I./JG 52 as Gruppenkommandeur outside of Hungary at the specific request

1 Mathews and Foreman, *Luftwaffe Aces*, Vol. 2, p. 485.
2 Raymond Toliver, Trevor Constable, *The Blond Knight of Germany* (Blue Ridge Summit, Pennsylvania: Aero, 1985), p. 52.
3 Toliver, Constable, *The Blond Knight of Germany*, p. 53.
4 Toliver, Constable, *The Blond Knight of Germany*, p. 46.
5 Toliver, Constable, *The Blond Knight of Germany*, p. 43.
6 Toliver, Constable, *The Blond Knight of Germany*, p. 54.
7 Jochen Prien, *Jagdeschwader 53*, p. 848.
8 Barbas, *Das vergessene As*, p. 174.
9 Mathews and Foreman, *Luftwaffe Aces*, Vol. 2, p. 485.
10 Prien, *Jagdeschwader 53*, p. 847.
11 Correspondence with Bernd Barbas (27 October 2021). This tragic incident most likely occurred in the fall/winter 1944. The court martial was apparently put off until after the war but never materialized.
12 Page 23 in Erich Hartmann's paybook, this entry has been crossed out in red ink.
13 Toliver, Constable, *The Blond Knight of Germany*, p. 155.
14 Mathews and Foreman, *Luftwaffe Aces*, Vol. 2, p. 485.
15 Page 4 in Erich Hartmann's paybook.

Bes.: Hptm. Hartmann,Kdr.d.I./J.G.52, erzielte heute seinen 35o.Luftsieg.

Erich Hartmann's 350 claim as written in the special information section in the operation report for 17 April 1945.* Interesting to note is the word 'Luftsieg', not written besides other claims on the document. *Via Johannes Matthews.

of JG 52 Geschwaderkommodore Hermann Graf. Erich Hartmann engaged in 825 aerial combats and flew 1404/5 flights throughout the war.[16]

Misconceptions and Myths versus Reality

Owing to the fact that Erich Hartmann is credited with the most aerial claims during the Second World War, his story has attracted an aurora of attention that, over time, has unfortunately skewed the truth in order to dramatize history. As the highest claiming fighter ace the world has ever seen, it is fitting that in this chapter a portion of the misconceptions and myths surrounding Erich Hartmann should be dispelled, not only to clarify his story, but to also showcase how similar misconceptions of history pertaining to other prominent pilots may have occurred.

Never Lost a Wingman

After engaging in 825 combats during the war, there is some confusion as to whether Erich Hartman ever lost a wingman. In a good-will meeting between Allied and Axis fighter pilots in 1961 Erich Hartmann stated the following in his broken English: *The teamwork is the number one if you are a really good fighter pilot. Because one man in the air is most time lost. And I am really proud that in all of my combats I never lost a wingman.*[17] Attempting to adhere to the never-lose-a-wingman rule taught by his former mentors,[18] Erich Hartmann did have a wingman shot down late in the war. Major Günther Capito, a former bomber pilot, was shot down by Soviet Airacobra fighters while flying as Hartmann's wingman on 7 March 1945.[19] Capito bailed out of his damaged aircraft at a height of around 70m but managed to survive the incident.[20] In an interview later in his life, Hartmann retold the story: *'I only lost one wingman, Günther Capito, a former bomber pilot, but this was due to his inexperience with fighters, but he survived.'*[21] What is certain from these statements is the following: Hartmann lost a wingman shot down under his leadership though he never had a wingman die under his direct command.

Seven Mustangs

In battling the Americans, Erich Hartmann redressed a technical disadvantage by skill and experience, and downed seven of the formidable Mustangs, whose demise was confirmed.[22] Erich Hartmann supposedly claimed four of these Mustangs on 24 June 1944,[23] however this is the first indication that his P-51 claims are exaggerated by post-war writtings. Mustang pilot Capt. Arthur Charles Fiedler of 15th AF, 325 FG, 317 FS (1923-2016) states otherwise: *I was on the June 24th mission and only 1 P-51 was lost on the Ploesti mission. The other loss was on an Air Sea Rescue escort mission* [last sighted at Pesaro Italy].[24] These were the only P-51 combat losses suffered by the 306th FW during the day.[25] The Luftwaffe claim microfilms also show that Hartmann only had one confirmed P-51 claim on the 24th, not four as written in his biography,[26] with only two Mustang claims officially recorded in surviving documentation.[27] Seven Mustang claims, let alone seven 'confirmed' mustang claims, are one of the first myths surrounding Erich Hartmann, most likely propagated by the works *Holt Hartmann vom Himmel!* and *The Blond Knight of Germany*.

---

16 Some 1,404 according to *Holt Hartmann von Himmel!* and 1,405 according to *The Blond Knight of Germany*.
17 The Museum of Flight Seattle Washington, Goodwill Meeting, American Fighter Aces Association and Luftwaffe Fighter Pilots' Association (Part 2 of 3) Recording Date: May 1961 <https://digitalcollections.museumofflight.org/assets/Transcripts/2002-02-13_AV_002_02.pdf> (accessed 1 April 2021).
18 Toliver, Constable, *The Blond Knight of Germany*, p. 56.
19 Via Matti Salonen. Maj. Capito was flying a Bf 109 G-10 (WNr. 612723) of Stab I./JG 52
20 Barbas, *Die Geschichte der I. Gruppe des Jagdgeschwaders 52*, p. 279.
21 Final Interview with Erich Hartmann, MigFlug, 2016 <https://migflug.com/jetflights/final-interview-with-erich-hartmann/> (accessed 16 April 2021).
22 Toliver, Constable, *The Blond Knight of Germany*, p. 174.
23 Toliver, Constable, *The Blond Knight of Germany*, p. 165.
24 *Arthur Fiedler, 12 O'Clock High.net, Erich Hartmann vs. P-51* (6 May 2009) <http://forum.12oclockhigh.net/showthread.php?t=16&highlight=Hartmann+P-51&page=2> (accessed 13 October 2021).
25 MACR 6077 and 6178.
26 Tony Woods O.K.L Fighter Claims, *Eastern Front* [*Ostfront*] January-June 1944, Issue I.
27 Mathews and Foreman, *Luftwaffe Aces*, pp. 485-492.

Black Devil of the South

The legend of the Black Devil began when Erich had a black nose painted on his aircraft, a distinctive pattern shaped like tulip petals. His fighter was easily distinguishable in combat, and the Soviet flyers quickly realized that the pilot of this black-marked German fighter was a foe to be avoided. He never missed. The feared but as yet otherwise unidentified German pilot was nicknamed "Black Devil of the South" by the Russians ... Red pilots encountering and identifying the Black Devil's distinctively marked aircraft quickly left the scene of battle.[28] The mythical presence of such a plane over the battlefield is simply a legend not based in reality.

The ability for enemy pilots to notice a dark tulip paint scheme on a plane during or before an engagement is highly unlikely as German planes were already painted in dark colors; their nose cones were painted in dark colors and often had oil or smoke streaks around the engine areas. Due to Erich Hartmann's relatively poor ability – that is compared to his total claims – to actually destroy the enemy, as will be outlined within this chapter, there was no need for Soviet pilots to pay any special attention to Hartmann, if they could even identify this plane, as he was of no greater threat than the other excellent pilots around him.

As such, the nickname *Black Devil of the South* is extremely unlikely to have been used by any of Erich Hartmann's enemies. The origin of the nickname is more likely to have come from the German side, either through wartime propaganda or from post war material in which case, again, it was not used by the Soviets he fought against. Interestingly many other German aces received nicknames from their own side. Hans-Ulrich Rudel was nicknamed *Adler der Ostfront* (Eagle of the Eastern front), Walter Nowotny was nicknamed *Tiger vom Wolchowstroj* (Tiger of Wolchowstroj), Hans-Joachim Marseille was nicknamed *Stern von Afrika* (Star of Africa), and Johannes Wiese nicknamed the *Lion of Kuban*. Erich Hartmann's *Black Devil of the South* follows many of the same naming patterns, moreover all these names bestow glorious or endearing titles. Soviet aviators did not nickname unknown enemy pilots so amicably. Moreover, the names used would follow the standard titles used for such enemies, they would all be labeled as fascists (*фашист*), and still furthermore nicknames could be even explicitly vulgar, as the reader may imagine.

Bounty on Hartmann

There have also been legends created around a bounty placed on Erich Hartmann. According to the first as found in Hartmann's biography, sometime in the second half of 1943 a bounty was placed on his head: *'He was cutting a swath through their formations, and most of the Black Devil's victories were over single-engined fighters. A price of ten thousand rubles was placed on the Black Devil's head. The Russian pilot who could bring him down would win fame, glory and wealth.'*[29] The second legend comes from a supposed American P-51 Mustang fighter pilot named Lawrence Thompson, who states that in 1945 the bounty offered by Stalin was 50,000 dollars [sic!].[30] To date, there has yet to surface any credible information which alludes to a bounty placed specifically on Hartmann's head, or of a bounty this large for him. Contrary to the above claims, two Soviet orders found in archives help both explain why the tales are fictional and how such a legend could have been concocted in the first place.

Firstly, it is known that Soviet pilots would receive standard monetary rewards for the destruction of enemy aircraft. Order No. 0299 dated 19 August 1941 issued by Stalin outlines that fighter pilots would receive 1,000 Rubles for each enemy aircraft shot down in air combat.[31] Therefore the bounty placed specifically on Hartmann most likely originated from the overly creative interpretation, or rather misinterpretation, of Soviet VVS reward orders, and it is very likely that the number was inflated either purposefully or through lack of understanding. Such exaggeration was apparently typical of fighter pilots, as conveyed by Lt. Peter Düttmann: *My wife was very careful because of the fighter slang, she knew there was some possibility of exaggeration.*[32]

Secondly, Order No. 0294 dated 8 October 1943, under heading XIII.20.г titled '*For the sinking of an enemy destroyer or submarine*' states that pilots and navigators would receive 10,000 Rubles.[33] As this was decreed late in 1943, Hartmann's account given in his biography matches more closely to this order, however, the reward explicitly states that it was to be given for the destruction of a destroyer or submarine, not for the destruction of enemy aircraft, let alone a specific pilot.

Erich Hartmann's claims are compiled from the following sources listed in order of heaviest reliance:

- Luftwaffe Aces: claims and bibliographies, Vol. 2
- Die Geschichte der II. Gruppe des Jagdgeschwaders 52: Offizielle Ausgabe der Traditionsgemeinschaft JG 52
- Tony Woods – Eastern Front Vol 4. 1944. Jul – Dec, Issue 1

28 Toliver, Constable, *The Blond Knight of Germany*, pp. 78-79.
29 Toliver, Constable, *The Blond Knight of Germany*, p. 79.
30 Pentti Kurkinen, Erich Hartmann ,*The World's Top Ace of All Time, Finnish Virtual Pilots Association* <http://www.virtualpilots.fi/hist/WW2History-ErichHartmann.html> (accessed 20 March 2021).
31 Order of the People's Commissar of Defense of the USSR. TsAMO RF: fu. 299, inv. 161, f. 1, p. 191.
32 Peter Düttmann, *Itärintaman hävittäjäsotaa* (Helsinki: Koala-Kustannus, 2002), p. 141.
33 TsAMO RF: fu. 4, inv. 12, f. 105, pp. 502-518.

- Jagdeschwader 53: A History of the "Pik As" Geschwader, January 1944-May 1945, Vol. 3.
- Die Geschichte der I. Gruppe des Jagdgeschwaders 52: Offizielle Ausgabe der Traditionsgemeinschaft JG 52

All above lists contain differences in claim dates and aircraft types; the known differences have been included and assessed within this chapter. The claim number appearing in the Mathews & Foreman publication has been used.

27 October 1944 (Friday)

Hartmann's 304th: OVERCLAIM, Yak-9 at 10:16 LT at Nyíregyháza-SE at 2500m
***possible claim: OVERCLAIM, Il-2**[34]

Soviet 5 VA permanent single-engine fighter losses on 27 October 1944				
Regiment:	**Type:**	**c/n:**	**Pilot:**	**Details:**
207 OKRAP	Yak-9D	19166066	A. M. Rozhkov+	Took off for a recon. mission near Nyíregyháza. Later both were MIA
207 OKRAP	Yak-9D	19166078	K. V. Saiego MIA	
150 GvIAP	Yak-3	3929212	N. M. Knut POW	Nyíregyháza-E, 13:42 LT, I./SG 10
192 IAP	La-5FN	39213433	S. F. Gukov POW	Kecskemét-NW, 13:55 LT to flak
513 IAP	Yak-1B	20150	N/A	Destroyed on Debrecen airfield at 06:10 LT by 6 Fw190s, 6 Bf 109s
513 IAP	Yak-9M	2515338	A. P. Kutuzov+	

On 27 October 1944 at 10:16 LT Hptm. Erich Hartmann claimed a Yak-9 near Nagykálló in Eastern Hungary at Nyíregyháza-SE. This was his very first victory claim over the country and first after his return from a period of leave. This day the Soviet 5 VA lost three Yakovlev fighters and a single Il-2 in air combat to enemy fighters. According to the Soviet records two 207 OKRAP Yak-9Ds and an Il-2KR went missing without a trace, while a 150 GvIAP Yak-3 (c/n: 3929212, engine: 412-200, white '39') was lost in air combat with four Bf 109s and sixteen Fw 190s at Nyíregyháza-S at 13:42 LT. Gv.Ml.Lt. Nikolai Matveevich Knut bailed out of his aircraft with burns and was later taken as prisoner. His plane was probably shot down by Hptm. Fritz Schröter (Stab. I./SG 10, Fw 190F-8) around 13:30 LT. In a separate flight another 207 OKRAP Il-2KR piloted by Maj. Nikolai Petrovich Zubko was damaged by two Bf 109s at 10:36 LT, but he was able to successfully return to Romania.[35] The fact that the c/n of this Il-2KR was not recorded also indicates that the plane remained in combat service and was not written-off as a combat loss.[36] Between 12:17 and 12:21 LT Hptm. Lipfert and Obfhr. Steins claimed a full reconnaissance flight consisting of an Il-2 and its fighter escort of two Yaks shot down in the Büdszentmihály-S area at Nyíregyháza-W. These planes must have been the destroyed 207 OKRAP planes which went missing without a trace since there was nobody left on the Soviet side to report the incident. There were no other Soviet fighter losses in the area during the day.

One source suggests that Erich Hartmann made another claim made this day over an Il-2 for which the date may have also been 29 October. As previously described only one was lost over Hungary on the 27th, namely the one destroyed by Hptm. Helmut Lipfert at 12:17 LT, while another one was damaged in the air. The damaged Il-2KR from 207 OKRAP, piloted by Maj. Nikolai Petrovich Zubko, escaped two ambushes from two Bf 109s at 10:36 LT while flying between 2000 and 1800m whereafter it successfully managed to return to its base. It is possible that Erich Hartmann was responsible for causing the damage, however the plane was not destroyed and its c/n was not recorded therefore it cannot be counted as a victory. Another option could be one of the two damaged 451 ShAP Il-2s hit during the 1st Fliegerkorps attack on Debrecen airfield on the morning of 27 October, however at these were damaged aircraft not losses (see Helmut Lipfert chapter for details). On the 29th only one Il-2 was lost over Hungary, namely a 190 GvShAP Il-2m3 (c/n: 18893113) piloted by Gv.Ml.Lt. Nikolai Leontievich Solodovnikov and aerial gunner Gv.C-a Constantin Andreevich Mironov, that was brought down probably by flak around Izsák-Kecskemét roughly 190 kilometers from the Nyíregyháza-SE area. Izsák-Kecskemét is close to the Danube and south of Budapest, therefore it was not in the operational area of II./JG 52 which was at this time stationed in Taktakenéz.

The first victory claims made by Hartmann upon his return to combat are therefore overclaims. The fighter on the 27th was shot down by another pilot, while the Il-2 claim was either also shot down by another pilot or was most likely destroyed by flak while flying in a distant operational area.

34 Barbas, *Die Geschichte der II. Gruppe des Jagdgeschwaders 52*, p. 369. This claim only appears in this list and in not present in the *Chef für Ausz. und Dizsiplin Luftwaffen-Personalamt L.P. [A] V* microfilms. The claim's date is marked as uncertain occurring on either the 27 or 29 October 1944. It is labelled claim number 305 in the publication and does not increase Hartmann's final tally beyond 352.

35 The 207 OKRAP was divided into three reconnaissance groups. The 2nd group, led by Maj. Zubko moved to Torda (Turda) on 14 October 1944.

36 Beside four Po-2s (c/n: 5979, 640440, 640433, 640920) and seven Omsk-built Yak-9Ds, the 207 OKRAP had the following sixteen Il-2s between 1 October and 26 December 1944: 7414, 10197, 10224, 10546, 10739, 10948, 10979, 11264, 11297, 11414, 11415, 11482, 11505, 11577, 11612, and 302360. C/n: 10948 was shot down by Hptm. Helmut Lipfert, thus one of the others was perhaps damaged/claimed by Hptm. Erich Hartmann on the 27th though was never destroyed.

31 October 1944 (Tuesday)
Hartmann's 305th: OVERCLAIM, 'Yak-7' at 15:30 LT at Ladánybene-S at 2000m

Soviet 5 VA permanent single-engine fighter losses on 31 October 1944				
Regiment:	**Type:**	**c/n:**	**Pilot:**	**Details:**
177 GvIAP	La-5F	39215187	P. Y. Morduhovich	Kecskemét-NW,15:25,2000m,2 Bf 109
177 GvIAP	La-5FN	41210105	A. A. Kunshin MIA	Cegléd-Szolnok at 09:25 LT, strafing

Hptm. Erich Hartmann's next claim over Hungary was a Yak-7 fighter near Ladánybene. Although there was a Soviet fighter loss (a La-5F) in the area indeed, it was claimed and almost certainly destroyed by Hptm. Heinrich Sturm. As there was no other matching Soviet fighter loss in entire 5 VA, this kill must be considered as an overclaim.

1 November 1944 (Wednesday)
Hartmann's 306th: OVERCLAIM, LaGG-5 at 14:35 LT at Abony-NW at 2500m

Soviet 5 VA aircraft losses in Hungary on 1 November 1944				
Regiment:	**Type:**	**c/n:**	**Pilot:**	**Details:**
48 BAP	A-20G	*Unknown*	I. A. Bolsakov	*Flak damage, repaired at base*
452 BAP	A-20G	*Unknown*	L. M. Kakulia	*Landed at Vinga, Ro., returned later*
452 BAP	A-20G-1	42-53754	A. Y. Polonskii	Tiszakécske to Málnássy hdgy., '5'
452 BAP	A-20G-10	42-53947	L. N. Velikanov	*Kálmán zls. to Tiszaalpár, repaired*
177 GvIAP	La-5F	39215336	E. Batyuna WIA	*Pottyondy László szds. near Szolnok*
177 GvIAP	La-5	*Unknown*	M. V. Danshin	*Later returned, AC not lost!*
235 ShAP	Il-2m3	10472	V. I. Astahov	Törtel, flak, 12:50 LT, 6 Il-2s
73 GvIAP	Yak-1B	08175	Andrianov POW	Lakitelek-NW, at 4500-6000m
73 GvIAP	Yak-9D	18166046	?, 1st Squadron	*Combat damage, repaired at base*
85 GvIAP	Yak-1B	xx1xx	B. I. Gelkin MIA	*Later returned, aircraft not lost!*
511 ORAP	Pe-2	*16/153*	E. L. Panchenko	1st Sq., *combat damages*, 2 fighters*

* On 1 November 1944 a 511 ORAP Pe-2 piloted by St.Lt. Evgenii Leontevich Panchenko flew a photo-reconnaissance sortie over Budapest. En route home it was attacked by two persistent SG 2 Fw 190F-8s though over Cegléd one of the attackers was shot down (Stfw. Herbert Hellinger, Uffz. Wolfgang Böttcher, or Ofw. Hermann Glaser). The Pe-2 was probably the same one which was retired between 1-15 November 1944 due to combat damages (wear and tear).

On 1 November 1944 two flights of 18 A-20G Bostons of the 5 VA, 218 BAD, 48 and 452 BAPs bombed the railway station of Cegléd. First, at 12:58 LT the 48 BAP dropped their bombs and returned to Arad without any losses. Their formation was led by Maj. Vasilii Pavlovich Koliy, escorted by eight La-5s of the 177 GvIAP, led by regiment commander Gv.Col. Grigorii Mihailovich Pyatakov. At 13:06 LT at 2400m they were followed by two groups of nine Bostons of the 452 BAP, led by Maj. Aleksei Andreevich Panichkin flying without fighter escort.[37] While leaving the target they were countered by approximately ten Bf 109 fighters of the Hungarian 102 FG near Abony. In this moment the Soviet bomber crews could depend on only the defense fire of their aerial gunners. The very intense anti-aircraft fire damaged two A-20G Bostons which fell behind their formation and soon were finished off by the Bf 109s. Ml.Lt. Aron Yosifovich Polonskii's A-20G-1-DO (S/N: 42-53754, engines: 42-154008, 42-154041, white '5', built on 15 April 1943 in Santa Monica, CA, USA) was downed by Málnássy Ferenc hdgy. (102/2. FS) and crash-landed at Gyomaendrőd-W, 6 km in a wetland and became a total loss. This was Ml.Lt. Polonskii's very first, but not final combat mission. Ml.Lt. Lev Nikolaevich Velikanov's A-20G-10-DO (S/N: 42-53947, engines: 42-174974, 42-174895, built on 22 May 1943 in Santa Monica, CA, USA) was downed by Kálmán István zls. (102/1. FS) and crash-landed at Tiszaalpár. This plane was repaired and permanently lost probably to Soviet flak at 21:56 LT on 15 April 1945 and crash-landed near Erzsébetmajor (Miloslavov), Slovakia with Lt. Constantin Trofimovich Sayutin's crew. After attacking the Bostons the Hungarians also engaged the eight 177 GvIAP La-5s West of Szolnok and downed one of them. Therefore Hptm. Erich Hartmann's La-5 claim this day near Abony at 14:35 LT was an overclaim because the only lost La-5 was already downed by Hungarian Bf 109 ace Pottyondy László

37 Maj. Koliy's command plane was probably his famous A-20G-15-DO, S/N: 42-54255, while Maj. Panichkin's plane was probably A-20G-1-DO, S/N: 42-53768 that he lost on 21 December 1944 in Debrecen. A-20G, S/N: 42-54255 survived the war and was still in service on 1 July 1945.

452 BAP pilot Ml.Lt. Aron Yosifovich Polonskii's A-20G-1-DO Boston (S/N: 42-53754) with Soviet and Romanian airmen in the fall of 1944. This plane was downed on 1 November 1944 during the Cegléd mission by Hungarian Bf 109 ace, Málnássy Ferenc hdgy. (102/2. FS) over Újkécske (Tiszakécske) and crashed at Gyomaendrőd-W. (Photo: Bernád Dénes)

szds. (102/2. FS) near Szolnok shortly after 13:00 LT.[38] The pilot, Gv.Ml.Lt. Evgenii Ivanovich Batyuna, crash-landed his damaged plane on his airfield suffering only minor injuries from two shrapnels wounds to his right side. His damaged La-5F (c/n: 39215336, engine: 6504268, white '36') was sent back for a major factory repair to the Soviet Union. During the battle 23 A-20G Bostons of the 453 BAP, led by Lt.Col. Yakov Prokofievich Prokofiev bombed Abony at 13:00 LT without losses. This day's particular claim for Erich Hartmann is also briefly mentioned within a captured AOK 6 KTB currently held within the TsAMO RF archives as his 306 Luftsieg dated 1 November 1944.[39]

7 November 1944 (Tuesday)
Hartmann's 307th: OVERCLAIM, Yak-7 at 13:35 LT at Mende at 1000m

Soviet 5 VA permanent single-engine fighter losses on 7 November 1944				
Regiment:	**Type:**	**c/n:**	**Pilot:**	**Details:**
92 IAP	La-5FN	39211227	M. A. Kazanovskii	Szarvas-SE, 15:00 LT, 800m, '27'
150 GvIAP	Yak-3	3229214	E. A. Pyankov WIA	Lajosmizse, 12:19LT, 1400m, 4 '*Fw*'

Hptm. Erich Hartmann's 'Yak-7' victory on 7 November 1944 at 13:35 LT near Mende (Budapest-E, ~30 km) was an overclaim. The time and location differences of both 5 VA fighter losses this day were too significant to be deemed legitimate aerial victories for Hartmann. The only lost 5 VA Yakovlev fighter this day, a 150 GvIAP Yak-3 piloted by Gv.Lt. Evgenii Andreevich Pyankov, was shot down by Oblt. Hubert Pohl (1./SG 10, Fw 190F-8) between Lajosmizse and Sári at 12:25 LT at 1000m.

13 November 13, 1944 (Monday)
Hartmann's 308th: POTENTIAL VICTORY, Yak-9 at 14:10 LT at 5000m
Hartmann's 309th: OVERCLAIM, Yak-9 at 14:15 LT at 4200m
Hartmann's 310th: POTENTIAL VICTORY, Yak-9 at 14:25 LT at 4000m
Hartmann's 311th: VICTORY, Yak-9 at 14:30 LT at Jászberény-SE at 3500m

38 Csaba, *Elfelejtett Hősök*, pp. 157, 161.
39 Auszug aus Tagesabschlussmeldung I.Flg.Korps v. 1.11.44, TsAMO fu. 500, inv. 12472, f. 345, p. 178.

Soviet 5 VA permanent single-engine fighter losses on 13 November 1944				
Regiment:	**Type:**	**c/n:**	**Pilot:**	**Details:**
122 IAP	Yak-9M	2715382	N. M. Grishaev	Take-off accident (Külső-Kiritó)
149 GvIAP	Yak-1B	11186	A. Kotlyar POW	At Jászberény, 13:55-14:50 LT
149 GvIAP	Yak-1B	42188	Stepanov, returned	At Abony-N, 12:55 LT, 6 Bf 109s
149 GvIAP	Yak-9D	3615390	O. D. Kadagidze	Ferry flight accident near Karcag
150 GvIAP	Yak-3	3529218	N. A. Kireev WIA	At Ócsa, 8:41LT, 6 Yaks, 13 Bf 109s
150 GvIAP	Yak-9D	1815358	N. S. Yegorov	At Nagykáta, 11:54 LT, 8 Fw 190s
179 IAP	Yak-9M	2715317	A. A. Svistkov	Jászberény flak, CL at Újszász-E
179 IAP	Yak-9T	0215354	E. Teplishev MIA	Zsámbok-SW at 14:30 LT, 8 Bf 109s
177 GvIAP	La-5FN	41210201	B. G. Kalinin+	Újszász to Halasi Sándor (Bf 109)

On 13 November 1944 between 14:10-14:25 LT Hptm. Erich Hartmann claimed three Yak-9s shot down in the greater Jászberény area. Between 13:55-14:50 LT, two flights of four Yaks of 149 GvIAP, led by Gv.St.Lt. Vladimir Mihailovich Kalchenko and Gv.Lt. Otar Demidovich Kadagidze met eight *'Fw 190s'* at 3000m which then proceeded to attack the roads 5 km South of Jászberény. Kalchenko downed a Bf 109, but then a pair of Bf 109s hit Gv.Ml.Lt. Aleksandr Titovich Kotlyar's Yak-1B. Kotlyar crash-landed on enemy held territory and was captured alive though he had suffered heavy fragmentation in both of his hands and was held in hospital until 18 June 1945. He returned to his unit on 20 June 1945. After the war Gv.Ml.Lt. Kotlyar stayed with the Soviet Air Force and flew several jets.

A 149 GvIAP reconnaissance pair of Gv.Lt Andrey Andreevich Merzlenko and Gv.Ml.Lt. Vladimir Victorovich Konopko was patrolling over Vác flying at 2500m where they met six Bf 109s. During the unfolding dogfight Merzlenko claimed a Bf 109. The Soviet flight later returned to Kocsér (Kecskemét-NE) safely without suffering any losses. At 14:30 LT near Jászberény four 179 IAP Yak-9 fighters escorted six Il-2 Sturmoviks at 500m when four Bf 109s attacked them. The Yaks intercepted the attackers, while St.Lt. Bocharov and Ml.Lt. Teplishev claimed two Bf 109s. After their strike another four Bf 109s joined the battle. Ml.Lt. Evgenii Ivanovich Teplishev's Yak-9T (c/n: 0215354, engine: 345-2906) was hit and crash-landed near Zsámbok.[40] This plane was Hartmann's second legitimate aerial victory of the day.

The other 179 IAP loss this day was a Yak-9M (c/n: 2715317, engine: 425-384), which – according to Soviet records – was hit by flak near Jászberény. The pilot, Lt. Aleksei Alekseevich Svistkov crash-landed at Újszász-E, 5 km. Since the exact time of this loss, which would exclude the possibility that it was downed by Erich Hartmann by means of a quick ambush

13.11.44г. Гв.ст.л-т КОТЛЯР невернулся с боевого задания из р-на Пуста Моноштор. Самолет Як-1 № 11186.

A Yak-1B fighter of the 149 GvIAP and Gv.Ml.Lt. Aleksandr Titovich Kotlyar's Yak-1B loss entry. (Photo: Boris V. Davidov and TsAMO RF: fu. 327, inv. 4999, f. 178, p. 35, Operations review of 3 GvIAK for November 1944, entry for 13 November 1944.)

40 TsAMO RF: fu. 20292, inv. 1, f. 6, p. 476, Operations journal of 331 IAD, entry for 13 November 1944.

Gv.Ml.Lt. Aleksandr Titovich Kotlyar (1923-2003) (Photos: Viktor Kotlyar)

from a direction that the Soviets did not see, is not known, the Authors consider this Yak-9 as a potential aerial victory for Erich Hartmann.

There were two other big aerial battles in the Jászberény-Pusztamonostor-Kóka area, but the Soviets suffered no losses in any of them. Between 12:45-13:50 LT four Yak-1Bs and two Yak-9s of the 151 GvIAP (Shokurov-Kozlov, Bondarenko, Dudin, Torubalko and Hvostov) were covering Soviet ground forces between 2500-4000m when they encountered eight Bf 109s. The Soviet pilots, led by Gv.St.Lt. Fyodor Yakovlevich Shokurov attacked the Bf 109s and Shokurov, Torubalko and Hvostov each claimed a Bf 109 shot down. Soon after this, between 14:30-15:10 LT, eight Yak-3s of the 150 GvIAP (red nosed 'Sword Group') led by Gv.Lt.Col. Anton Dmitrievich Yakimenko covered Soviet troops in the same area. This time the Soviet fighters formed two flights of four planes at the altitudes of 4000 and 4500m. Over Tápióbicske, they met six Bf 109s coming head-on escorting sixteen Fw 190s flying below. In the unfolding dogfight the Soviet upper flight claimed three Bf 109s (Yakimenko, Shamenkov and Sergeev), while the lower flight claimed two Fw 190s (Leonov, Lapshin) without any losses of their own. It is possible that Fw. Karl Richter (6./SG 2, Fw 190F-8, WNr.: 933301, yellow '10') was killed in this dogfight.

The above events mean that even if Erich Hartmann was involved in one of these two battles and accidentally misreported the claim-times, the Soviets lost no aircraft whatsoever, therefore Hartmann's fourth Yak-9 claim of the day must be considered an overclaim.

14 November 1944 (Tuesday)

Hartmann's 312th: OVERCLAIM, LaGG-5 at 11:35 LT at Jászberény-NW at 2000m

Hartmann's 313th: POTENTAIL VICTORY, LaGG-5 at 11:45 LT at Szolnok-N, -NW, 35 km (Jászberény-NW) at 800m

Soviet 5 VA single-engine fighter losses on 14 November 1944				
Regiment:	**Type:**	**c/n:**	**Pilot:**	**Details:**
92 IAP	La-5FN	39213519	S. A. Matveev WIA	Jászberény-NW, '92', 11:20 LT
92 IAP	La-5FN	39211212	N.A. Lopatkin MIA	*Repaired, lost on 23 January 1945*
92 IAP	La-5FN	39212944	V. Vihlyaev MIA	*Repaired, stayed in service*
92 IAP	La-5FN	39213431	A. Kuprianov MIA	*Repaired, lost on 24 March 1945*
151 GvIAP	Yak-9T	1715339	L. I. Toropov	MIA, *AC not lost!*
151 GvIAP	Yak-1B	18199	N. V. Rogatin	MIA, *AC not lost!*
151 GvIAP	Yak-9T	*?(Not lost!)*	A. A. Morozov	*Tápiógyörgye, force landed, Bf 109*
122 IAP	Yak-1B	121xx	I. T. Blagoder	*White '12', flak, AC not lost!*
179 IAP	Yak-1B	*?(Not lost!)*	V. N. Bocharov	*08:40 LT, damaged by 6 Bf 109s*

On 14 November 1944 the aerial battles continued in the Jászberény-Hatvan-Zsámbok area. In the morning at 11:20 LT six 92 IAP La-5s were escorting two groups of eight 130 GvShAP Il-2s, led by Gv.Capt. Solomentsev and Palagin in the Jászdózsa – Tarnaörs area, where they met two *'Fw 190's.*[41] Hptm. Erich Hartmann opened fire on one of the La-5s which was then damaged but managed to escape his attack therefore resulting in an overclaim. Shortly thereafter at the altitude of 800m the engine of La-5FN (c/n: 39213519, ASh-82FN engine: 82131600, white '92'), piloted by Ml.Lt. Sergei

41 TsAMO RF: fu. 20512, inv. 1, f. 86, p. 144, Operations journal of 3 GvShAK for November 1944, entry for 14 November 1944.

Alekseevich Matveev was hit, the pilot received injuries to his head and lost consciousness.[42] Between 100 and 50m he regained consciousness, took control and successfully crash-landed on Soviet controlled territory at Jászberény-NW, 4-5 km. The pilot survived the crash, but his plane was written-off. This is a potential victory as the Soviet and German given times loosely match each other, however the account of the battle and location match more closely.

Gv.Ml.Lt. Yak pilots Toropov and Rogatin were marked as MIA, however the permanent loss of their planes does not appear in the documentation of either the regimental nor corps materials while they both are documented as flying missions in mid-December 1944. The lack of evidence proving the permanent loss of their Yaks suggests that they later returned to service.

16 November 1944 (Thursday)

Hartmann's 314th: POTENTIAL VICTORY, Yak-9 at 8:45 LT at Gödöllő-E, 4000m

Hartmann's 315th: OVERCLAIM, Yak-9 at 08:50 LT at Tóalmás at 1000m

Soviet 5 and 17 VA aircraft losses on 16 November 1944				
Regiment:	**Type:**	**c/n:**	**Pilot:**	**Details:**
188 GvShAP	Il-2m3	1878963	*Unknown*	*Flak, fighters, repaired on airfield*
188 GvShAP	Il-2m3	11091	Aleksandrov	Kecskemét air raid, destroyed
190 GvShAP	Il-2m3	1875556	*Nemchin/Valyuk?*	LAC, Bekkerman's Yak-9 ran in it
92 GvShAP	Il-2m3	10294	Kovalev unhurt	Kunt?, landed, '71', 11:45, Bf 109
92 GvShAP	Il-2m3	303933	V. E. Bizhko	Farmos, 3 km, '74', 11:45, Bf 109s
92 GvShAP	Il-2m3	303925	M. P. Sadohin	Kuns ... '75', 11:45 LT, Bf 109s
92 GvShAP	Il-2m3	10618	N. P. Konyukhov	Kóka, '83', 12:28 LT, Bf 109
92 GvShAP	Il-2m3	11360	Bocharov unhurt	Tóalmás-E, '99', 11:45 LT, Bf 109
207 OKRAP	Il-2KR	*Unknown*	N. A. Voronin WIA	*~150 hits from a Bf 109, repaired*
165 GvShAP	Il-2m3	*187xxxx*	M. I. Surnin +	Apatin area, missing
995 ShAP	Il-2m3	1870786	I. V. Tselishev	Madaras, CL, ferry flight acc.
260 BAP	*A-20B*	*41-3626*	F. I. Larin	*Missing, later returned in service*
897 IAP	Yak-9T	0815350	V. N. Fukin	Gospodinci, CL, ferry flight acc.
31 GvIAP	Yak-9D	2015370	V. A. Koptelov OK	Jászkisér-E, 12:20LT, 6 Bf 109s
73 GvIAP	Yak-9D	2015315	A.S. Shuvalov MIA	Jászárokszállás, 4000 m, – missing
85 GvIAP	Yak-9D	2015329	Ismail S. Rulev+	Jászberény, 10:10,4000 m,8Bf 109
122 IAP	Yak-1B	22183	M. I. Sapa unhurt	Külső-Kiritó, LAC at 15:20 LT
122 IAP	Yak-1B	06179	P. G. Artemev+	Hatvan-S, 12:00, 8 Fw190, Bf 109
122 IAP	Yak-9M	2715305	B. A. Horkin WIA	Törökszentmiklós-SE at 12:00 LT
122 IAP	Yak-9T	2515332	A. M. Znamenev	Jászfényszaru-E at 12:30, 6 Bf 109
122 IAP	Yak-9T	2515396	I. C. Babanin MIA	Jászfényszaru-NE at 12:20, Bf 109
179 IAP	Yak-1B	12152	M. V. Meshkov	Tiszapüspöki, LAC at 13:55 LT
513 IAP	Yak-9T	1015328	G. D. Yarovoy+	Hatvan, 10:52LT, 16 (4) *Fw190s*
149 GvIAP	Yak-9M	3615389	V. A. Ustich WIA	Alsódabas-NE, flak at ~09:10 LT
150 GvIAP	Yak-9D	2315371	G. Y. Bekkerman	Dogfight at Kóka, landing accident
150 GvIAP	Yak-3	1229217	S. G. Yefimenkov	Pécel, 15:15LT, 6 Bf 109, 8 Fw190
150 GvIAP	Yak-3	3429214	A. N. Agdantsev	Dány, 13.42LT, 8 Yak-3,4 Bf 109s
177 GvIAP	La-5	*3921xxxx*	A. D. Dogadailo	*Damaged by Hungarian 101/3. FS.*
177 GvIAP	La-5	*3921xxxx*	G. M. Pyatakov	*Damaged by German Bf 109s*
178 GvIAP	La-5FN	39212952	B. V. Zhigulenkov+	Besenyszög-SE, 6 Bf 109, ~*10:10*
192 IAP	La-5F	39214932	V. M. Olnev WIA	Nagykáta-NE, 14:00LT, 6 *Fw 190s*
4 GvBAK	C-47A	42-24140	P. T. Alekseenko*	Szeged-NW to Fw. Pilz, 6./SG 10

42 TsAMO RF: fu. 20249, inv. 1, f. 25, p. 46, Operations journal of 279 IAD for November 1944, entry for 14 November 1944.

* 5 GvAD DD C-47A-50-DL was forced to ground level by Fw. Erich Pilz (6./SG 10, Fw 190F-8) at Szeged-NW. Skilled pilot Gv.Capt. Pyotr Timofeevich Alekseenko crash-landed the burning plane at Szeged-NW, but his high-ranking passenger Gv.Col. Pavel Ivanovich Kondratev, Div. CO, died of his wounds in field hospital No.5202 the same day. Note the aircraft's AC card is wrong as it was not a RAAF plane!

Pilots of the 73 GvIAP in front of one of their Yak-9D fighters. Note the regiment's white lightning-bolt marking on the fuselage. 1st one from the left in the front is Gv.Ml.Lt. Shuvalov (MIA), the 4th is Gv.Capt. Fomichev, flight-leader. (Photo: Units and planes, <http://ava.org.ru/iap/73g.htm)

On 16 November 1944 ten Yaks of the 73 GvIAP, led by Gv.Lt.Col. Porfirii Afanasevich Mikhailyuk and Gv.Capt. Pyotr Petrovich Fomichev were covering soviet troops in the Jászberény – Pusztamonostor – Jászárokszállás triangle at 4000m. Over Jászárokszállás the Savchuk-Shuvalov pair separated from their group and Gv.Ml.Lt. Alekandr Stephanovich Shuvalov went missing. The radio connection was stable and no dogfights were reported. It is possible that Erich Hartmann downed him at 08:45 LT at Gödöllő-E by means of a surprise attack thus resulting in no radio warning from the Soviet pilot.

Around this time six Yak-9s of the 150 GvIAP, led by Gv.St.Lt. Dmitrii Artemevich Ovsyannikov (wingman: Gv.Lt. Fedor Lavrentevich Zimin) were covering Soviet ground forces in the Jászberény area. Over Kóka located just west of Tóalmás they met fifteen Fw 190s, escorted by ten Bf 109s. In the unfolding dogfight Gv.St.Lt. Grigorii Yakovlevich Bekkerman claimed one Bf 109 by firing a long burst from 100m down to 60m away from the enemy, which was confirmed by Gv.Ml.Lt. Pavel Fedorovich Kalistiy and Victor Ivanovich Zhigalin. Soon after this Bekkermann's Yak-9D was also hit. He left the battle and headed for home. At the base at around 09:00 LT a newly landed and likewise damaged 190 GvShAP Il-2m3 from Taranenko's flight became stuck on the wet landing strip due to flat tires right when Bekkerman was landing, and his Yak-9D ran into the stuck Il-2. Although Bekkerman survived the accident with minor injuries, his Yak-9D (c/n: 2315371, engine: 415-2206) was a total loss. On 22 November 1944 the damaged Il-2 (c/n: 1875556, AM-38F engine: 2510064) was transferred to the 38 OTTR and on 28 November 1944 it was erased from the 190 GvShAP's aircraft inventory. It is entirely possible that Bekkerman's plane was damaged by Hptm. Erich Hartmann at 08:50 LT at 1000m in the Tóalmás area, but because it returned safely to its airfield and was lost in a completely independent landing accident, this is another overclaim for Erich Hartmann. All other planes in Bekkerman's flight returned to Kecskemét and landed safely. After returning Nosov, Shishkin and Ovsyannikov claimed two Fw 190s and a Bf 109 as shot down.

17 November 1944 (Friday)

Hartmann's 316th: OVERCLAIM, Boston III at 14:25 LT at Ócsa at 2000m

Soviet 5 VA A-20 Boston losses on 17 November 1944				
Regiment:	**Type:**	**S/N:**	**Pilot:**	**Details:**
453 BAP	A-20G-10	42-53956	N. Danielyan WIA	Ócsa, Pottyondy László's victim, '2'
453 BAP	A-20G-15	42-54223	V. K. Yurchenko	Kevermes-S, weather, mech. failure

On 17 November 1944 A-20G Bostons of the 452 and 453 BAPs bombed the city center and Western edge of Budapest. Three A-20G Bostons dropped 36 FAB-100 type bombs on their targets. Upon leaving Budapest and flying South, they were attacked over Csepel Island by six Bf 109s from the Budaörs airfield (Budapest-SW). This time Hptm. Erich Hartmann and his Hungarian Bf 109 ace friend, Pottyondy László szds. (102/2. FS) flew together and started to pursue the leaving intruders. Interestingly, Pottyondy szds. was the leader and Hptm. Hartmann was his wingman. During their first strike Pottyondy szds. scored several hits on the fuselage and wings of Lt. Norayr Sumbatovich Danielyan's A-20G Boston (453 BAP, 1st Sq., S/N: 42-53956, ~red '2', engines: 42-82884 and 42-174979, built on 24 May 1943), which tried to escape into the clouds above. During his second and final strike Pottyondy szds. opened fire on the right engine (No: 42-174979) of the Boston, which then immediately burst into flames. The burning plane rapidly lost altitude and crash-landed near Ócsa.[43] The Bf 109s were not completely satisfied with the result and strafed the belly-landed bomber no less than four times. Either still in the air, or already on the ground the navigator and the radioman-gunner lost their lives due to the hostile bullets. The wounded pilot, Lt. Danielyan deputy Sq. commander and his aerial gunner were able to leave the burning plane and survived the incident. The plane was a complete loss and the two killed crewmen were buried at Bugyi-N, 6 km:

Lt. Norayr Sumbatovich Danielyan pilot (WIA, head injuries)
St.Lt. Georgii Nikolaevich Rizhkov bombardier/navigator (KIA)
C-a Aleksandr Nikolaevich Vigovskii radioman/gunner (KIA)
Ml.Sgt. Pavel Alekseevich Kopilov gunner (WIA)

(L-R:) Hptm. Erich Hartmann (4./JG 52), Pottyondy László szds. (102/2. FS) and Lt. Norayr Sumbatovich Danielyan (453 BAP, 1st Sq.). Below is Maj. Ivan Ivanovich Lisenko's crash-landed 453 BAP A-20G Boston (S/N: 42-53961, red '1') on the Debrecen airfield on 21 December 1944 where the 218 BAD lost five(!) Bostons during takeoff in the windy, dusty weather.* (Photos: Hartmann & Pottyondy from 'Magyar Szárnyak', Vol. 1, December 1944, Lt. Norayr Sumbatovich Danielyan and Maj. Lisenko's Boston: B. Davidov.) (*The 453 BAP, 1st (red) Sq. lost four A-20G Bostons in tail wind take off accidents: 42-53961 (Maj. Lisenko, red '1'), 42-54012 (Lt. Malov, red '5'), 42-53873 (St.Lt. Petrunko, red '8') and 43-21674 (Ml.Lt. Zhuchkov, red '?'). The 452 BAP lost two A-20Gs: Maj. Panichkin's Boston (42-53768) was taking off right above the blast of 43-21674, when one of the four FAB-250 bombs went off, while 42-54013 (Capt. Zinin, red '1') was downed by German flak at Ipolyszakállas (Ipeľský Sokolec, Slovakia).)

43 TsAMO RF: fu. 20208, inv. 1, f. 17, p. 349, Combat diary (losses) of 218 BAD, entry for 17 November 1944.

Since Pottyondy szds. striked first and gave a more detailed and accurate report of his claim (which agreed with the Soviet survivors' testimony of the burning right engine which forced their plane down), this bomber became Pottyondy's confirmed aerial victory at 14:30 LT.[44] Hptm. Erich Hartmann's Boston III claim at Budapest-SE, 25 km was probably just a duplicate of this victory as the Soviets lost only one bomber during the mission. Perhaps he claimed it because he shot at it on the ground or he attacked one of the other 452 or 453 BAP A-20G Bostons which also reported fighter attacks at 2000-2100m in the Budapest-S area, but then returned to their base safely:[45]

Beside the Budapest missions, individual Bostons flew tactical bombing missions to Ercsi, Dunaföldvár, Perkáta, Seregélyes and Székesfehérvár.[46] They suffered no losses. The other lost A-20G this day crashed at Kevermes-S roughly 200 km from Budapest during a mechanical and weather related ferry flight accident. Capt. Vasilii Kirillovich Yurchenko's crew was unhurt. For these reasons Hartmann's Boston III claim on 17 November 1944 is considered an overclaim.

21 November 1944 (Tuesday)

Hartmann's 317th: OVERCLAIM, La-5

On 21 November 1944 Hptm. Erich Hartmann supposedly claimed a La-5 victory claim, but the units within the entire Soviet 5 VA reported no single engine fighter losses over Hungary, therefore this entry is overclaim. One source establishes that II./JG 52 did not fly this day due to poor weather conditions.[47] Two points written in the Soviet 5 VA diary entry for this same day also confirmation the German reports: *4. ACTIONS OF THE OPPONENT'S AVIATION. No enemy aviation actions were observed. 5. SUMMARY OF MILITARY ACTIONS FOR THE DAY. In total for 21.11.44 one c/b.* [sortie] *was flown for weather reconnaissance and to bomb the enemy forces in BUDAPEST. One A-20G sortie. Flight 1.31* [time, hours. minutes]. *Dropped 15 FAB-100. Results of the bombardment were not observed due to poor weather conditions. No loss.*[48] Further confirmation may be found in Army Group South's daily meteorological report for the day stating that the temperature was around 7 °C with fog and rain.[49] Other weather reports mention overcast cloud layers at a height of 150-300m with light rain, fog and sometimes thick fog, temperatures between 4-10 °C and limited visibility of only 2-4 km.[50] Luftflotte 4 did not fly any ground attack sorties,[51] furthermore none if it's air units were employed during the fight due to bad weather.[52] As such, the genuine nature of Hartmann's 21 November claim is highly suspicious. Claim lists which do contain this date relied on materials such as personal letters sent by Hartmann to his loved ones or original biographical works to establish this claim's date.[53]

22 November 1944 (Wednesday)

Hartmann's 318th: OVERCLAIM, Il-2
Hartmann's 319th: OVERCLAIM, Il-2
Hartmann's 320th: OVERCLAIM, Yak-9 at 11:40 LT at Csány at 3500m
Hartmann's 321st: VICTORY, La-5 at 11:45 LT at Hatvan-SE at 4500m
Hartmann's 322nd: OVERCLAIM, Il-2
Hartmann's 323rd: OVERCLAIM, Il-2
*** One Yak-3 claimed in exchange for an Il-2[54]**

Soviet 5 and 17 VA aircraft losses on 22 November 1944				
Regiment:	**Type:**	**c/n:**	**Pilot:**	**Details:**
149 GvIAP	Yak-9	*Unknown*	A. A. Merzlenko	*Missing, later returned*
149 GvIAP	Yak-9	*Unknown*	I. I. Sadovoy	*Missing, later returned*

44 Stenge, B. Csaba, *Elfelejtett Hősök* [*Forgotten Heroes*] (Budapest: HM Zrínyi kiadó, 2016), 2nd edition, pp. 157, 162.
45 TsAMO RF: fu. 20208, inv. 1, f. 23, p. 96, Combat journal of 218 BAD, 2nd Ukrainian Front for November 1944, entry for 17 November 1944.
46 The Bostons over Székesfehérvár (453 BAP, 1st Sq., Maj. Ivan Ivanovich Lisenko with 12 FAB-100 bombs), over Ercsi (452 BAP, Lt. Yurii Vladimirovich Sukhov) and over Dunaföldvár (452 BAP, Lt. Pyotr Mihailovich Kovzalov) all returned to their airfields successfully. Over Dunaföldvár at 2000m Kovzalov's plane was attacked by four Hungarian Bf 109s, including Buday Lajos őrm., whose claim at Solt-NE, 5km was an overclaim since Kovzalov fled into the clouds and returned to his airbase successfully. Lt. Sukhov's Boston was also attacked by three Bf 109s over Ercsi, but he also returned to his base safely, just like Capt. Pavel Arsentevich Zhalibo and Maj. Yevgenii Yefimovich Stroganov who both survived the attacks of nine Bf 109s at 14:20 LT at 2100m at Budapest-S, 10km, claiming one Bf 109.
47 Barbas, *Die Geschichte der II. Gruppe des Jagdgeschwaders 52*, p. 174.
48 Combat log of 5 VA units for November 1944. TsAMO RF: fu. 327, inv. 4999, f. 227, p. 81.
49 NARA T311/R160/7210104.
50 Ic/Lw Wetterübersicht vom 21.11.1944 (H.Gr.Süd.) TsAMO RF Fu. 500, inv. 12472, f. 371, pp. 172, 181.
51 Számvéber Norbert, *Páncélosok A Budapesti Csatában-1944. Október 29-1945. Február 13*, (Hungary: Jaffa Kiadó, 2018), pp. 814-815.
52 NARA T311/R160/7210102.
53 Correspondence with Johannes Mathews (18 February 2021). The claim in question may be found in the work *Holt Hartmann vom Himmel!*
54 Barbas, *Die Geschichte der II. Gruppe des Jagdgeschwaders 52*, p. 370. Instead of four Il-2s this list states three Il-2s, one Yak-9, La-5 and a Yak-3.

Soviet 5 and 17 VA aircraft losses on 22 November 1944 (*continued*)				
151 GvIAP	Yak-1B	xx1xx	A. F. Yurchenko	*Missing, later returned*
151 GvIAP	Yak-1B	xx1xx	I. I. Lyashin*	*Missing, later returned*
151 GvIAP	Yak-1B	xx1xx	K. A. Hranovskii	*Missing, later returned*
207 OKRAP	Yak-9D	191660*xx*	A. F. Streltsov**	*Damaged by Hartmann, repaired*
177 GvIAP	La-5FN	39211746	V.A. Kovrigin WIA	11:50 LT, Hatvan area, 2 Bf 109s
178 GvIAP	La-5F	3811303	I. E. Sereda	*Missing, later returned, '<⊠03'*
809 ShAP	Il-2m3	1878785	Polunin – Kuptsov	*'Lost' at Csány-NE, flak, repaired*
187 GvShAP	Il-2m3	*Unknown*	I. F. Dovgopolov	*Nagykáta, Fw 190, repaired, '82'*
1001 OSNAP	Po-2/S-2	942328	N. A. Lobirev KIFA	Mezőberény-SW, in an accident
659 IAP	Yak-9D	2015306	Y. A. Vinogradov	Missing, Reg. CO's plane 14 times
897 IAP	Yak-9T	0815335	N. K. Konovalov	Harkány-SE, engine trouble, CL
989 ShAP	Il-2m3	1875997	*Unknown*	Topali, Serbia to flak

* Gv.Ml.Lt. Ivan Ivanovich Lyashin was shot down again on 16 April 1945 around 18:00 LT by 8 *Fw 190s* near Ždánice, Czech Rep. in his new Yak-9U (c/n: 42166063, engine: 437-716), but later returned.

** Lt. Streltsov's Yak-9D's c/n is uncertian since it was only damaged and not destroyed by Erich Hartmann. The 207 OKRAP, however, had four Yak-9Ds (19166070, 19166074, 19166092, 19166096), which were listed in both of the 1 October 1944 and 1 January 1945 quarterly aircraft inventory reports, therefore they were potential candidates for Lt. Streltsov's damaged plane on 22 November 1944.

On 22 November 1944 Hptm. Erich Hartmann claimed one Yak-9, one La-5 and four Il-2s shot down in air combat although unfortunately there is little information on most of these claims and on when they occurred. According to an account by I./JG 53 pilot Obfw. Erich Sommavilla whose unit shared airfields with II./JG 52, *'Once Hartmann even waggled his wings six times to indicate that he had scored six victories in one mission'*.[55] This account suggest that all six claims were made in a single mission, therefor the claim times available this day offer a hint as to when the others were possibly made. One source suggests that a Yak-3 was claimed in exchange for one of the Il-2s, however all the Yak fighters reported were later repaired or returned meaning none were permanetly lost. No Yak-3 fighter could have been claimed by Erich Hartmann this day.

By the end of the 22 November, the Soviet 5 VA in its summary reported the following losses: one La-5 was downed in dogfight, one Il-2 was downed by flak, one Il-2, two Yak-9s and three Yak-1Bs failed to return from combat missions. Since some of these planes later returned to combat service, they were not listed among the permanent losses by their respective units.[56]

This day two flights of six Yaks from the 151 GvIAP were escorting two 511 ORAP Pe-2Rs on their photo-reconnaissance mission to Jászberény, Hatvan, Budapest, Székesfehérvár, Siófok, Esztergom, Paks and Szekszárd. After completing their tasks, both Pe-2s returned to their base successfully but three Yak-1B fighters piloted by Gv.St.Lt. Aleksei Fedorovich Yurchenko, Gv.Ml.Lt. Ivan Ivanovich Lyashin and Gv.Ml.Lt. Constantin Alekseevich Hranovskii failed to return from their mission. Since they were not permanent losses, they all returned later to the 151 GvIAP.[57]

Between 11:20-12:00 LT four Yak-9Ds of the 207 OKRAP were also flying a photo-reconnaissance mission in the Aszód-Ecséd-Hatvan area, where at 11:40 LT they met four *'Fw 190s'* with which they engaged in a brief dogfight. During the battle Lt. Aleksei Philippovich Streltsov's engine and radiator was hit, he left the battle, returned home and landed safely. His Yak-9D was repaired the next day on 23 November 1944 by Mech.Lt. Vladimir Matveevich Grishkin and his fellow mechanics. Reviewing the daily reports, there is little question that this plane was damaged by Hptm. Erich Hartmann at 11:40 LT. Hartmann's claimed model, the reported time and area[58] point towards Streltsov's Yak-9D. However, as it often happened, Hartmann did not verify the loss of his opponent and after scoring a few 'impressive' hits, his opponent eventually escaped. Although this Yak-9 became Erich Hartmann's 320th official victory, the Soviet fighter was back in the sky in only one day!

La-5FN of 177 GvIAP (c/n: 39211746, engine: 8212292, white '46') was flying at 3500m near Hatvan when two Bf 109s jumped GvSt.Lt Kovrigin from the sun, his plane was hit and burst into flames.[59] He bailed out with his parachute

55 Prien, *Jagdeschwader 53*, p. 848.
56 TsAMO RF: fu. 240, inv. 2779, f. 1213, p. 86, Operations journal of the 5th Air Army units for November 1944, entry for 22 November 1944.
57 TsAMO RF: fu. 20511, inv. 1, f. 80, p. 33, Operations journal of 3 GvIAK for November 1944, entry for 22 November 1944.
58 Csány is next to Hatvan located just east, south-east.
59 TsAMO RF: fu. 20511, inv. 1, f. 82, p. 607, Operations journal of 14 GvIAD for November 1944, entry for 22 November 1944.

and landed two kilometres East from the Jászfényszaru train station with injuries to his leg and was taken to hospital.[60] This La-5FN was Hptm. Erich Hartmann's confirmed aerial victory at 11:45 LT over Jászfényszaru-NNE (~Gyöngyös-SW, 20 km).

La-5F of 178 GvIAP (c/n: 3811303, white '<★03'), piloted by Gv.Lt. Igor Emelyanovich Sereda[61] (temporarily) failed to return from a combat mission. It was not a permanent loss as it was later returned to its unit.

At 10:22 LT eight Il-2s of 187 GvShAP, led by Gv.Capt. Sergei Alekseevich Feoktistov, escorted by four La-5s were attacking ground targets in the Verseg-Nagykökényes area.[62] During the attack Il-2m3 (white '82') was hit by flak. The pilot Gv.Ml.Lt. Ivan Fjodorovics Dovgopolov made a 180 degree turn and headed for home. In just a few minutes four '*Fw 190's* attacked the crippled Sturmovik, which after gradually losing altitude and trailing smoke crash-landed near Nagykáta. Later the plane was repaired and returned to combat service which is why its c/n was not mentioned in the combat report. If Erich Hartmann was one of the attacking four fighters misidentified by the Soviets as 'Fw 190s', then this Il-2 is another overclaim for him. The flight of six 451 ShAP Il-2s which was also attacked by enemy fighters in the Miskolc area returned to their airfield without losses. Il-2m3 (c/n: 1878785) of the 809 ShAP was not so lucky: it was downed by flak and crash-landed at Csány-NE, 7 km.[63] The plane was repaired, its crew of Lt. Fedor Stepanovich Polunin and Semyon Semenovich Kuptsov returned to their regiment. This plane was lost again – this time permanently – on 20 March 1945 flying for the 451 ShAP, crash-landing after a combat mission at the Tóalmás-N airfield. The pilot, Ml.Lt. Dmitrii Mihailovich Volosyankin, suffered serious injuries.[64]

Reviewing the air events of 22 November 1944 it is clear that Erich Hartmann could have had a single La-5 victory at 11:45 LT, while all of his five other claims were overclaims. Interestingly, later on the night of 22/23 November 1944 the British RAF carried out its very last bombing mission against targets in Hungary suffering the loss of six planes.[65]

23 November 1944 (Thursday)
Hartmann's 324th: OVERCLAIM, Yak-3
Hartmann's 325th: OVERCLAIM, Yak-9
Hartmann's 326th: OVERCLAIM, Yak-9
Hartmann's 327th: OVERCLAIM, Yak-9
Hartmann's 328th: POTENTIAL VICTORY, Yak-9

Permanent Soviet 5 VA aircraft losses on 23 November 1944				
Regiment:	**Type:**	**c/n:**	**Pilot:**	**Details:**
122 IAP	Yak-1B	32161	E. S. Titov unhurt	Take off accident at 08:40 LT, '1'
513 IAP	Yak-1B	29156	Y. A. Gopchenko	Lost at Kál-S, 10:38 LT, 6 Bf 109s
513 IAP	Yak-1B	45168	P. P. Kuyanov +	Lost at Atkár, 10:38 LT, 6 Bf 109s
187 GvShAP	Il-2m3	12260	B. D. Grilev	*Hatvan-NE,* Bf 109, 11:20 LT, '57'

On 23 November 1944 Hptm. Erich Hartmann claimed five Yak-9 fighters shot down. This day the 5 VA permanently lost only three Yak-1B fighters: one in a take-off accident and two in dogfights at 10:38 LT. The first lost Yak-1B this day was Ml.Lt. Evgenii Semyonovich Titov's 122 IAP, 2nd Sq. Yak-1B (c/n: 32161, engine: 355-1983, white '1') which was lost in an airfield accident at 08:40 LT. He veered to the right during takeoff early and the right wing touched the ground. The plane crashed, but the pilot remained unhurt. His plane was written-off, but his engine was reused later. At 10:38 LT six 513 IAP Yak-1Bs were escorting six Il-2s of the 809 ShAP in the Rózsaszentmárton area where they met six '*Fw 190s*'. Four attacked the Yaks, two the Il-2s. Ml.Lt. Yakov Alekseevich Gopchenko's radiator was hit and he force landed at Kál-S, 15 km. The plane was not subject to repair, but the pilot remained unhurt. This plane could be Hptm. Erich Hartmann's potential aerial victory. The other 513 IAP Yak-1B, piloted by Ml.Lt. Pavel Petrovich Kuyanov (KIA) fell behind his formation at the beginning of the dogfight and was shot down immediately by Hptm. Helmut Lipfert at 10:40 LT over

60 TsAMO RF: fu. 20511, inv. 1, f. 82, p. 607, Operations journal of 14 GvIAD for November 1944, entry for 22 November 1944.
61 TsAMO RF: fu. 20062, inv. 1, f. 33, p. 188, Operations journal of 178 GvIAP for November 1944, entry for 22 November 1944.
62 The eight 187 GvShAP Il-2 Sturmoviks were: Feoktistov/60, Makarov/50, Nechiporuk/54, Grilev/57, Zatevahin/58, Afanasev/59, Turapin/52, Dovgopolov/82.
63 TsAMO RF: fu. 20525, inv. 1, f. 26, p. 34, Operations journal of 5 ShAK for November 1944, entry for 22 November 1944.
64 TsAMO RF: fu. 20177, inv. 1, f. 46, p. 138, Operations journal of 264 ShAD for 1945, entry for 20 March 1945.
65 The last British target in Hungary was the Szombathely airfield near the Austrian border. Six bombers of the RAF 205 BG failed to return to their bases in Southern-Italy: Liberator Mk. VI. (SAAF 34 Sq.: KH204 'C' and EW235 'M'), Wellington Mk. X. (37 Sq.: LP547 'S' lost at Felsőjánosfa, LP574 'U' at Pördeföld e, 40 Sq.: LP732 'O' at Kőszegpaty) and Halifax Mk. II. (614 Sq.: JP323 'I' at Bagodvitnyéd), while a seventh plane, Halifax Mk. II. (614 Sq.: JP321 'V') returned with major damages.

Atkár, located nearby. Since only these three single-engine fighters were lost in the 5 VA on 23 November 1944, this means that Hptm. Erich Hartmann could have only one Yak-1B victory and four overclaims.[66]

24 November 1944 (Friday)
Hartmann's 329th: OVERCLAIM, Yak-9
Hartmann's 330th: OVERCLAIM, Il-2
Hartmann's 331st: OVERCLAIM, Yak-9
Hartmann's 332nd: OVERCLAIM, Yak-9

Soviet 5 and 17 VA single-engine fighter losses on 24 November 1944				
Regiment:	**Type:**	**c/n:**	**Pilot:**	**Details:**
85 GvIAP	Yak-9D	1515335	*Unknown, 1st Sq.*	*Combat damage, repaired on base*
31 IAP	La-5FN	39211822	M. T. Savchenko	Lost orientation at Szeged-N, CL
31 IAP	La-5FN	39211241	A. I. Berezin	Lost orientation at Szeged-NW, CL
31 IAP	La-5FN	39211747	Y. P. Butenko	Lost orientation at Szeged-NE, CL

On 24 November 1944 Hptm. Erich Hartmann claimed one Il-2 and three Yak-9s, though no microfilm entries are present from this day until 5 December 1944. The 5 VA lost neither Il-2s, nor Yakovlev fighters. Only the 85 GvIAP reported air combat damages to one of their Yak-9D fighters which was repaired on its airbase.[67] The 17 VA lost three 31 IAP La-5FN fighters in landing accidents near Szeged along the Southern border while three Po-2s and two S-2s were destroyed on the Madaras airfield by four strafing Fw 190s. None of these planes were lost to Hptm. Erich Hartmann, just like the two 17 VA Il-2 Sturmoviks (Lt. Chizhov, 672 ShAP and Ml.Lt. Patsenko, 707 ShAP), which were lost to German flak over the territory of former Yugoslavia. Patsenko crash-landed at Monostorszeg-SW, 4 km (Bački Monoštor), while Chizhov crashed at Popovac-S, 2 km (Baranyabán). One list does not have any entries for this date.[68]

5 December 1944 (Tuesday)
Hartmann's 333rd: OVERCLAIM, LaGG-5 at 13:20 LT at Hatvan-SE at 1200m
Hartmann's 334th: OVERCLAIM, LaGG-5 at 13:25 LT at Erdőtarcsa-E at 1000m

Soviet 5 VA single-engine fighter losses on 5 December 1944				
Regiment:	**Type:**	**c/n:**	**Pilot:**	**Details:**
177 GvIAP	La-5F	39215215	P. S. Olin	*Stabilizator damage, repaired later*
177 GvIAP	La-5FN	39211776	N. L. Vereshak	To flak, his next La-5: 41210115
177 GvIAP	La-5FN	39212384	I. G. Sklyarov	*Cylinder damage, repaired at base*
486 IAP	La-5FN	39212724	V. G. Snagovskii+	Ercsi, 11:55 LT, 2 La-5, 6 '*Fw 190*'
151 GvIAP	Yak-3	1529219	Y.M. Ravikovich+	Ercsi, Danube-crossing, 14:00, Ju 87
151 GvIAP	Yak-?	*Unknown*	A. A. Morozov	Ercsi area to Bf 109s, Fw 190s*
122 IAP	Yak-9M	3015336	G. A. Ulanov WIA	Heréd, 15:05 LT to Heinz Ewald
122 IAP	Yak-9T	1615383	M. S. Yerko MIA	Erdőtarcsa, 10:12 LT to Lipfert
513 IAP	Yak-1B	20153	I. A. Guriev MIA	Erdőtarcsa, 11:00 LT to Heinz Ewald

* This is a questionable loss since the 13 GvIAD, 151 GvIAP record of the day does not mention it, only Morozov's personal record written on 26 April 1945. The date of 5 December 1944 could just be a typo. This is the only known contradicting case. (TsAMO RF: fu. 33, inv. 690306, storage: 1237-41950045, p. 28b)

On 5 December 1944 Hptm. Erich Hartmann claimed two La-5 fighters at 13:20 and 13:25 LT in the Hatvan-Erdőtarcsa areas. This day the 5 VA lost two La-5 fighters indeed, but the first La-5 was lost right before noon near Ercsi at the Danube crossing where its pilot Ml.Lt. Vladimir Grigorevich Snagovskii went missing. The other one, piloted by

66 By the end of the day the 5 VA reported the loss of two Yak-1Bs lost to enemy fighters, while two Il-2s and a Pe-2 failed to return from combat mission. The Pe-2 and one of the two Il-2s were only temporary losses because in November the 511 ORAP lost only one Pe-2 (c/n: 16/153) due to wear and tear between 1-15 November 1944 and the Il-2 (187 GvShAP, Fyodorenko/98) has been repaired after belly-landing. A third 187 GvShAP Il-2 (Afanasev/59) belly landed near its base and a Yak-1B was broken in a take-off accident.

67 TsAMO RF: fu. 33, inv. 690306, storage: 1306-41999401, p. 47, Personal records of 6 GvIAD personnel, entry for Gv.St.Sgt. Nil Stephanovich Bogachev aircraft mechanic of 85 GvIAP, 1st Sq. on 20 May 1945.

68 Barbas, *Die Geschichte der II. Gruppe des Jagdgeschwaders 52*, p. 370.

Gv.Ml.Lt. Nikolai Lukyanovich Vereshak went missing around 14:15 LT in a dogfight with Bf 109s of II./JG 51 during their A-20 Boston escort mission to Vác. Between 13:30 and 14:35 LT eight La-5s of 177 GvIAP led by Gv.Capt. Ivan Grigorevich Sklyarov (HSU) escorted 18 453 BAP A-20G Bostons (Prokofiev, Lisenko, Sklyarov, Anohin, Storchilo, Saratovskii, Petrunko, Danielyan and others) to Vác.[69] Both groups of nine Bostons were protected by four La-5s. At 14:05 LT at 2000m the Soviet formation was attacked by ten JG 51 Bf 109, six attacked from above, four from below. Gv.Capt. Sklyarov defended his bombers and repelled the attack of two Bf 109s, downing one of them at three kilometers South-East of Rád, though one cylinder from his radial engine was shot. Gv.St.Lt. Anatolii Fedorovich Muhin also downed a Bf 109 which went down in flames at five kilometers South-East of Rád. The dogfight continued and at 14:15 LT Gv.Ml.Lt. Nikolai Lukyanovich Vereshak separated from his group and went missing. The 177 GvIAP also reported two of their La-5s damaged in air combat, however both of them returned to their base safely where they were later repaired.[70] Since the Bostons and their La-5 fighter escort were still warming up their engines, lining up and taxiing out for the mission on their airfields when Hptm. Erich Hartmann claimed his La-5 'victories', it is evident that both of his La-5 kills this day were overclaims on another La-5 unit, which suffered no losses.

9 December 1944 (Saturday)
Hartmann's 335th: OVERCLAIM, Yak-9 at 13:10 LT at Martonvásár at 2000m
Hartmann's 336th: OVERCLAIM, Yak-9 at 13:20 LT at Ráckeresztúr-NE at 2000m

Soviet 5 and 17 VA single-engine fighter losses on 9 December 1944				
Regiment:	**Type:**	**c/n:**	**Pilot:**	**Details:**
150 GvIAP	Yak-3	2329218	L. G. Kamanyan	Kiskunlacháza LAC after 14:50LT
513 IAP	Yak-9D	19166063	A. K. Fokin WIA	LAC due to soft soil at ~*13:50 LT*
513 IAP	Yak-9T	2515361	V. P. Fedosov	Tiszanána, flak, 13:50 LT, 1500m
178 GvIAP	La-5FN	39212523	Ml.Lt.Maltsev MIA	Szanda-Becske-Terény, covering 'Pliev-Group': 09:00-9:40, 10:20-11:00, 13:00-13:40, 14:20-15:00.
178 GvIAP	La-5FN	39212631	F. G. Semenov MIA	
178 GvIAP	La-5FN	39213235	Ml.Lt. Ges MIA	
659 IAP	Yak-9D	16166070	V. V. Smirnov MIA	Il-2 escort to Úrhida, missing
659 IAP	Yak-9D	1515310	A. D. Bugrov	Paks-SW, 6 km, mech. failure, CL
866 IAP	Yak-9T	1015341	A. T. Belyaev	Engine failure during take off, CL

On 9 December 1944 Hptm. Erich Hartmann claimed two Yak-9 victories at 13:10 and 13:20 LT in the Martonvásár and Ráckeresztúr-NE area. This day at 14:50 LT and at 1000m two Yak-3s along with two Yak-9s of the 150 GvIAP were covering Soviet ground troops in the Ercsi-Baracska area when they met about twenty Fw 190s attacking the front line. Gv.Lt. Ivan Frolovich Shamenkov downed a 'Fw 190' during the unfolding dogfight which crashed near Baracska. Gv.St.Lt. Savelii Vasilevich Nosov downed two Fw 190s at Kisvelence-SE.[71] Gv.Ml.Lt. Lev Gerasimovich Kamanyan was covering his leader Gv.St.Lt. Nikolai Sergeevich Yegorov's attack on a Fw 190, which went down near Baracska, but his Yak-3 (c/n: 2329218, engine: 422-304) was also hit. Losing altitude rapidly, Kamanyan crash-landed 3 km from his airfield with a dying engine. The Yak-3 was a complete write off, but Kamanyan survived the crash.[72] This crash took place more than 1.5 hours after Hartmann's second claim of the day. The 149 GvIAP also fought with four '*Fw 190s*' in the Ercsi area when four Yaks led by Gv.St.Lt. Boris Fedorovich Kozulin covered the Danube river-crossing.[73] The Soviet fighters suffered no losses and Gv.St.Lt. Kozulin claimed one 'Fw 190'. In addition to these dogfights, at 13:50 LT six Il-2s of the 809 ShAP, escorted by four Yak-9s of the 513 IAP attacked ground targets in the Csömör-Veresegyház area at Budapest-SE. Over Csömör at 1500m St.Lt. Vasilii Pavlovich Fedosov's Yak-9T (c/n: 2515361, engine: 435-327) was hit by flak. The Soviet fighter lost altitude and crash-landed near Tiszanána. During landing Capt. Aleksandr Kuzmich Fokin's Yak-9D (c/n: 19166063, engine: 415-897) nosed into the ground due to the wet and soft soiled landing strip, suffering bruising to his hands while

69 By 5 December 1944 Lt. Norayr Sumbatovich Danielyan recovered from his 17 November 1944 injuries and flew two missions; one to Esztergom and the other one to Vác.
70 TsAMO RF: fu. 20062, inv. 1, f. 33, p. 249, Operations journal of 177 GvIAP, entry for 5 December 1944.
71 The 5 VA received two factory marked '12' Yak-3s from Tbilisi, Georgia (310212, 310312) on 18 April 1945 which were assigned to the 150 GvIAP on 26 April 1945. One of them became Nosov's famous red nosed 'Sword Group' Yak-3 with marking '12' and both were still listed in the unit's 1 July 1945 aircraft inventory. Nosov's earlier planes, however, are unknown. The 6 GvIAD, 85 GvIAP also received a '12' marked Yak-3 on 29 April 1945 (c/n: 1229237), but it was from Saratov, similar to the 236 IAD, 267 IAP's Yak-3 yellow '12' (1229213) which was already in service in October, 1944. It was flown by Lt.Col. Shirov and handed over in April 1945 to the new Yugoslav Air Force along with 1029213 and 1129213.
72 TsAMO RF: fu. 20059, inv. 1, f. 23, p. 305, Operations journal of 13 GvIAD, entry for 9 December 1944.
73 Gv.St.Lt. Kozulin, leading his flight of six Yaks was downed by four Fw 190s and two Bf 109s on 26 December 1944 at around 14:30 LT with his Yak-1B (c/n: 44191, engine: 767-41) over Szakállas at 2500m and crash-landed near Verseg.

protecting his face. Further to the North a 31 GvIAP Yak reconnaissance pair led by Gv.Lt. Anatolii Yakovlevich Rogov was surveying German railway traffic in the Esztergom, Szőny, Komárom, Ács, Kisbér areas along the Danube, but they reported no encounter with enemy fighters. As such in all cases of permanent or temporary Soviet fighter losses of the day, the time and/or location differences are too great to be considered potential candidates for Hartmann's claims.

4 February 1945 (Sunday)
Hartmann's 337th: OVERCLAIM, Yak-9 in the Sárkeresztes-Mór area

Soviet 5 and 17 VA single-engine fighter losses on 4 February 1945				
Regiment:	**Type:**	**c/n:**	**Pilot:**	**Details:**
92 IAP	La-5FN	39212054	M. P. Dimakov	*Enying, 13:25 LT, 1500m, repaired**
31 GvIAP	Yak-9D	1515321	I. A. Yangaev WIA	Budapest-W, dogfight over Csepel, 12:50 LT, 4500m, 8 Bf 109s, 6 Yaks
31 GvIAP	Yak-9D	2015350	P. Y. Vidanov+	
31 GvIAP	Yak-9D	*Unknown*	*?, flight-leader*	*Gun damages in dogfight, repaired*
73 GvIAP	Yak-1B	01174	N. P. Katushkin	*Damaged fuel system, repaired*
73 GvIAP	Yak-9D	1515364	Pavel F. Urban	*Hydr. damaged by Bf 109, repaired*
178 GvIAP	La-5FN	39213685	Igor E. Sereda unh.	Székesfehérvár flak, Budapest crash
179 GvIAP	La-7FN	45210566	I. N. Lebedev+	Buda, flak over Castle strongholds
116 IAP	La-5FN	39212113	K. Kurenkov KIFA	Kiskunlacháza, LAC, ran in a truck
848 IAP	La-5FN	39212754	B. P. Lazarev MIA	Sárkeresztes-W, 2 km, ~16:00 LT, 2000m, 6 La-5s, vs. 10 Bf 109s**
848 IAP	La-5F	39215046	V. Z. Voronov MIA	
288 IAD	Yak-9T	1115393	N/A	Scrapped, regular wear and tear***

* Four 92 IAP La-5FNs escorted two 131 GvShAP reconnaissance Il-2s (12505/Kovalerskii and 12623/Zubov) to the Polgárdi-Enying area. Combat with 14 Fw 190s and Bf 109s over Enying at 1500m. Both Il-2s were shot down and Dimakov's La-5FN was also hit. After return he crash-landed on his airfield while his plane was subject to medium repair.

** Hartmann's action was linked to the Bostons and their Yak fighter escort's attack which took place around 14:00 LT. The two 848 IAP La-5s at 16:00 LT in the very same Sárkeresztes-W area were lost in different events.

*** In February 1945 the 288 IAD lost 2 Yak-1Bs, 2 Yak-3s, 1 Yak-9D and on 4 February a Yak-9T. On this day they also received 11 Yak-3s from the c/n range of 310072 – 310271. The division's total resupply of the month was 25 Yak-3s (between 310060 – 310271), 22 Yak-9Ms (between 2715313 – 3515326), 1 Yak-9DD (0115345) and 3 Po-2s (3868, 6691, 7327 from the 993 NBAP).

In early February for a brief period of time, 1 February – 14 February 1945, Hptm. Erich Hartmann served as the acting Kommandeur of I./JG 53 based in Veszprém. His main duties included ordering the unit's planes to be painted a grey-white color to conceal their profiles against the wintery landscape,[74] most likely as a protective measure for the many close support escort missions being flown to help the ground forces during this time. His entry into I./JG 53 was hoped to spur new zeal for fighting as Obfhr. Peter Esser remembered: *'We young fighter pilots had very high expectations after having had so little contact with the enemy of late'*,[75] however it turned out to be somewhat lackluster as Lt. Arno Fischer of I./JG 53 recalls: *'He only flew with us a few times – anyway why should he? He had the highest decoration and the war was long lost. Many of us were therefore a little disappointed, but he was essentially correct: why sacrifice men and material when there was nothing more to be gained.'*[76] Hartmann's only combat mission with I./JG 53 was therefore to be flown of 4 February 1945.[77]

Taking off on a free hunt sortie with Erich Sommavilla he claimed a Yak-9 out of a '*large number*' of fighters which were escorting '*about 20 Boston twin-engined bombers*' in the Székesfehérvár area.[78] According to Sommavilla's statement, when they saw the bombers, Hartmann ordered nearby Bf 109s to attack while he went after the fighters. Unfortunately, no further German details are known about this event therefore it is challenging, though not impossible, to compare Hartmann's claim to the Soviet records. According to mission reports for the day, the 260 and 861 BAPs of the 17 VA attacked this region, while their fighter escort was provided by six Yak-3s of the 659 IAP and four La-5s of the 164 IAP.

In the 17 VA sector in the afternoon, two groups of seven 861 BAP A-20 Bostons led by Capt. Aleksandr Semyonovich Zolotarev and two groups of nine 260 BAP A-20 Bostons led by Capt. Kizim and Maj. Makkeev bombed the 150mm

74 Prien, *Jagdeschwader 53*, p. 850.
75 Prien, *Jagdeschwader 53*, p. 850.
76 Prien, *Jagdeschwader 53*, p. 850.
77 Prien, *Jagdeschwader 53*, p. 851.
78 Prien, *Jagdeschwader 53*, p. 850.

Pilot Lt. Vladimir Ivanovich Bogdanov of the 861 BAP, 1st (red) Sq., based on his medal and service history in the spring of 1945 with his plane, most likely A-20B Boston, S/N: 41-3529, red '2'. (Photo: 861 BAP memorial exhibition, School No.212, Moscow, Russia)

Hummel batteries of I./Pz.Art.Reg.73 and the maintenance-supply section of the heavy 'Feldherrnhalle' Division at Sárkeresztes.[79] The Soviet aerial support was much needed since the German Panzer units destroyed an extremely large number of Soviet tanks in the Székesfehérvár-Zámoly-Sárkeresztes area. The 1st Guards-Mechanized Corps alone lost over thirty M4A2(76)W Sherman tanks north of Székesfehérvár, mainly to Panthers of I./Pz.Rgt.24, SS-Pz.Rgt.3 'Totenkopf' and Tiger IIs of s.Pz.Abt.503.[80]

At 13:35 LT flying at 600m approximately ten minutes before the arrival of the first bomber wave, the lead plane of the 861 BAP appeared above the airfield of the 659 IAP in order to pick up the fighter escorts which had a smaller fuel capacity for the mission. This way by taking off from an airfield near the frontline they could save their fuel for air combat rather than burn it up during a long and uneventful flight alongside the bombers. Within ten minutes of flying at 2000-2500m the bombers arrived and crossed the frontline with their six 659 IAP Yak-3 fighters, led by Capt. Nikolai Vasilevich Salamatov.[81] Soon after this at 3000m, the Soviet formation was attacked by six and later by approximately twelve Bf 109s. The Yak-3s protected the bombers so effectively that the Bf 109s could not get close enough for serious attacks. During the very intense dogfight Lt. Anatolii Grigorevich Ivanov saved Ml.Lt. Buykevich's life by repelling the attack of a Bf 109 over Csákberény. Because of this, it is quite possible that Ml.Lt. Anton Constantinovich Buykevich's Yak-3 was attacked and later claimed by Hptm. Erich Hartmann as his 337th Yak-9 victory.[82] Ml.Lt. Buykevich however returned to his airbase and landed safely. The only Soviet loss during the entire mission, beside three slightly damaged 861 BAP A-20B Bostons (S/N: 41-3529 '2', 41-3605 '★', 41-3637 '16'), was Lt. Vladimir Fedorovich Shuvaev's A-20G-36-DO Boston (S/N: 43-10075, 861 BAP, 2nd Sq.) which was hit by flak, left its formation and turned to the East. Two Soviet fighters joined the crippled bomber, which was later finished off by six *'Fw 190s'* near Zsámbék at Budapest-W.[83] The other Yak-3 group which fought

79 Dr. Számvéber Norbert, *Kard a pajzs mögött* (Veszprém: PeKo Publishing Kft., 2013), p. 399.

80 Aussenstelle bei H. Gr. Süd, 13.2.45. The turret numbers of the examined lost Soviet M4A2(76)W Shermans were 104, 106 and 127 in the 18th Guards-Tank Regiment, 214 and 216 in the 19th Guards-Tank Regiment, 301, 302, 304, 306, 307, 308, 312, 314, 315, 321, 324, 328, 329, 330, 331, 332, 333, 334 and 335 in the 20th Guards-Tank Regiment, 901, 910, 926, 929, 949, 951, 955, 958, 965 and 969 in the 9th Guards-Tank Brigade. They were built in the summer/fall of 1944 as part of the 'U.S.A. 308*xxxx*' Sherman-batch in Grand Blanc, MI, USA, eg.: 'U.S.A. 3080513', 'U.S.A. 3080807' and 'U.S.A. 3081116.'

81 At this time the 659 IAP had the following six Yak-3s: No.1711, 2015, 310037, 310055, 310081 and 310220. Hptm. Erich Hartmann probably attacked and later claimed one of them over Csákberény. All of their other fighters were different Yak-9 models. 1711 was originally Maj. Koldunov's (866 IAP) very first Yak-3 that he flew between 22 September and 11 November 1944 before it was transferred to the 659 IAP.

82 TsAMO RF: fu. 370, inv. 6518, f. 340, pp. 798-799, Operations review of 288 IAD for February 1945, entry for 4 February 1945.

83 TsAMO RF: fu. 20224, inv. 1, f. 44, p. 122, Operative report of 861 BAP, entry for 4 February 1945.

in the area was Capt. Aleksandr Ivanovich Koldunov's eight-plane flight which covered Soviet ground troops in the Zámoly area around 13:05 LT.[84]

Just before the A-20 Bostons of the 260 BAP reached Sárkeresztes, Lt. Vasilii Alekseevich Tushnov flying A-20B (S/N: 41-3626) experienced engine trouble, left his formation and landed at Szabadszállás. His formation was escorted by four La-5s of the 164 IAP which during the upcoming dogfight repelled the attacks of the Hungarian 101/4. and 101/5. FS Bf 109s. Thus, the Hungarians could only damage two of the bombers at Székesfehérvár-S and Kunszentmiklós-E for the loss of one of their fighters. The Bf 109 crashed and pilot Molnár Lajos őrm. was killed (101/4. FS, Hungarian-built Bf 109G-14, WNr.: 511026). Two other Hungarian Bf 109s suffered minor damages.[85]

989 ShAP Il-2m3 (c/n: 11532, white '27'), piloted by Lt. Ivan Alekseevich Dzhanaev was shot down by two *Fw 190s* attacking from the sun over the Kiskunlacháza airfield. The plane belly landed and was written off, gunner Sgt. Angilenko was seriously injured.

In the 5 VA sector flights of two, three, four, and six Il-2s of the 7 and 12 GvShAD attacked the Pz.Art.Rgt. 'Feldhernhalle' Hummel self-propelled artillery positions in the Tabán Park as well as the anti-aircraft artillery positions of the Citadel Fort on Gellért Hill continuously throughout the day. They took off, emptied their magazines into the strongholds, landed, re-armed and repeated this all over again. The 187 GvShAP alone flew 35 sorties against the Tabán Park and 43 sorties against the Citadel and Gellért Hill. Here between 12:15-12:20 LT the Il-2 pair of Gv.Lt. Andrey Makkeevich Nechiporuk (Il-2, white '60') and Gv.Ml.Lt. Pavel Trofimovich Zhukovskii (Il-2, white '51') noticed something (perhaps some enemy vehicles) during the approach to the Citadel and after altering course, from 1200m to 400m they attacked the last houses of Rezeda Street right on the edge of the park surrounding the Citadel. They fired two hundred 23mm cannon, four hundred ShKAS rounds, dropped six 50kg and two 250kg bombs. The villa at 11 Rezeda Street was hit, killing local resident geologist Hanuszik Elemér (47). Il-2s of the 130 and 131 GvShAPs, beside some reconnaissance sorties in the Komárom and Lake Velence area, also concentrated their attacks on the Tabán Park and Gellért Hill. Il-2s of the 188 GvShAP attacked targets No.97 and 126 in the triangle of the Sas, Gellért and Castle Hills. Il-2s of the 90 and 91 GvShAPs on the other hand attacked targets in the Buda Castle, mainly with FAB-100 HE bombs.

But beside the Il-2s, fifty-two A-20G Bostons of the 218 BAD also bombed the central and governmental districts of Buda in sixty sorties, including the Buda Royal Castle Target No.100, the Pz.Art.Rgt. 'Feldhernhalle' Hummel self-propelled artillery positions in the Tabán Park and the Citadel on Gellért Hill. Their fighter escort was provided by Yakovlev fighters of the 6 GvIAD. Here five Yak-9s and one Yak-1B of the 73 GvIAP, taking off from Erdőtarcsa led by Gv.Lt. Pyotr Nikitovich Svezhentsev, escorting twelve Il-2m3 Sturmoviks got into combat with twelve German Bf 109s over Buda. In the very effective defensive fighting the Yaks repelled all attacks of the Bf 109s, so neither the Il-2s, nor the fighters themselves suffered any combat losses. Only Gv.Lt. Pavel Fedorovich Urban's Yak-9D and Gv.Ml.Lt Katushkin's Yak-1B suffered combat damages, while Gv.Lt. Anatolii Ivanovich Kuznetsov claimed a Bf 109 shot down at Budapest-SW. Gv.Lt. Mihail Nikolaevich Gamsheev (85 GvIAP) also claimed a Bf 109 at Pesthidegkút-E at 11:35 LT, while Gv.St.Lt. Fyodor Stephanovich Vetchinin a I./SG 10 Fw 190 at Budapest-N.[86] Later in the dark, as part of the Budapest airlift, at least five more DFS 230 gliders landed successfully in the Vérmező Park in Budapest with their desperately needed supplies for the German-Hungarian garrison left within the city, while one of the transport planes was shot down just outside of Budapest (Ju 52/3mg5e of 11./TG 3, WNr.: 7083, coded: 4V+FV, piloted by Uffz. Heinrich Auf der Heide, MIA).

Ironically, it was the 5 VA which lost two Yak-9s in the Budapest area, not near Sárkeresztes, which both belonged to the 31 GvIAP. Yak-9D (c/n: 1515321, engine: 345-2705) from a flight of six Yaks, piloted by Gv.Lt. Ivan Andreevich Yangaev was patrolling at about 5 km Budapest-W.[87] At 12:50 LT at 4500m they met eight Bf 109s near the Csepel Island. In the sudden dogfight the plane was hit and crash-landed at Rákoscsaba. The pilot was injured and taken to hospital in Isaszeg.[88] A Yak-9D was also lost at 12:50 LT in the same dogfight with pilot Gv.Ml.Lt. Pyotr Yakovlevich Vidanov listed as missing.[89] Since none of these Yak-9s were shot down by Hptm. Erich Hartmann, his 337th victory was another overclaim.

8 May 1945 (Tuesday)

Hartmann's 352nd: OVERCLAIM, Yak-9 around 9:00 LT over Brünn at 4000m[90]

84 At the end of January 1945 the 866 IAP received the following Tbilisi-built Yak-3s that Capt. Koldunov and his pilots flew during the following weeks: c/n 310011, 310012, 310062, 310077, 310128, 310137, 310143, 310155, 310173, 310175, 310190, 310207, 310210, 310228, 310233, 310086, 310123, 310165.

85 Punka György, *A 'Messzer': Bf 109-ek a Magyar Királyi Honvéd Légierőben* (Budapest: KÓDEX GMK, 1995), p. 76 and Luft. GQM 1945.

86 The Fw 190F-8 victim of Gv.St.Lt. Vetchinin (85 GvIAP, 2nd Sq., Yak-1B) could be Ofw. Ernst Selzer (WNr.: 931023 '<', I./SG 10), or Obltn. Ferdinand Kerstin (WNr.: 588449, yellow '7', 3./SG 10).

87 The 3 GvIAK summary report gives incorrect construction numbers: 6015318 and 1715319 instead of Yak-9D, c/n: 1515221, engine: 345-2705 and 2015350, engine: 415-1514.

88 TsAMO RF: fu. 327, inv. 4999, f. 290, pp. 157, Combat journal of 3 GvIAK, entry for 4 February 1945.

89 TsAMO RF: fu. 327, inv. 4999, f. 290, pp. 157, Combat journal of 3 GvIAK, entry for 4 February 1945.

90 The book *The Blond Knight of Germany* mentions 12,000 ft, while other sources state 4000m. In an interview with SAMISDAT in 1991 Erich Hartman was asked at which altitudes he would use his oxygen mask. In response to the question he stated: '4000m – 12,000 feet', therefore Hartmann equated these two altitudes as equal which is why there is a discrepancy in some sources. It should be noted that 4000m is actually slightly greater than 13,100ft.

Although Erich Hartmann's final and perhaps most symbolic 352nd victory claim was not made over Hungary, due to its historical significance in terms of aviation achievements the Authors felt that it should also be analyzed in this chapter. On 8 May 1945, JG 52 *Geschwaderkommodore* Herman Graf was visited by an officer around 08:00 who appeared from a Fi 156 Storch relaying that the war was lost and that the unconditional surrender has been signed.[91] Graf thereafter issued his final military order, requiring Hartmann to fly a reconnaissance mission to find out how far the Soviet advance was from the Deutsch Brod airfield. The day would be filled with emotion and the mission would span from 08:30 until 09:20 LT. Taking off, Erich Hartmann used the main road as a line of reference to fly to the nearest population center of Brünn.[92] During the mission at around 09:00 LT over Brünn (Brno in today's Czech Republic) Maj. Erich Hartmann claimed a Soviet Yak-9 fighter as he later recalled: *'I was filled with hate, and when I saw the Russians I only had one thing in my mind: He must go down!'*[93] After the war, Hartmann reportedly referred to this final claim with anguished feelings by saying *'I have one victory too many'*.[94] Most publications state the opponents were comprised of a formation of eight Yaks with the combat taking place directly over the city of Brünn. Hartmann, flying with an unknown wingman,[95] spotted the 'loose gaggle' of eight Yaks and struck one plane that was conducting aerobatic maneuvers over the city.[96] Some contemporary Authors liberally exercised their creative writing freedom regarding this event and according to them, certainly not according to historical fact, Hartmann downed this Yak-9 in a surprise attack in the very moment when the Soviet pilot was making a war-end *'victory salute to the Red Army on the ground'*,[97] while the shocked Soviet infantrymen gazed at the burning wreck plummeting towards the city.[98] After the attack Hartmann spotted twelve aircraft flying in a tight formation some distance away which he recognized as P-51 Mustangs, and keen not to become a victim during the final day of the war retreated without further engagement back towards the Deutsch Brod airfield.[99] Upon glancing back he noticed that the Soviet and American fighters had begun to engage each other: *'Once again the USAAF and the Red Air Force had mistaken each other's identity. YAKs and Mustangs were whirling in a savage dogfight over Brünn. Erich saw no aircraft go down, but he had no intention of going back to assess the damage the two Allies were doing to each other. The situation was not without humor.'*[100] Returning back to Deutsch Brod Hartmann was informed by Herman Graf that the war was lost and the decision was made to destroy the unit's aircrafts, then to walk into American captivity.[101] Allegedly Hartmann wanted to complete this destruction personally, he mounted his parked Messerschmitt one final time and shot out the remaining rounds from his nose mounted cannon in one long burst aimed at the grounded aircrafts, this caused an explosion in his plane which threw Hartmann out of the cabin.[102] More elaborate information about the day's events are missing as the remaining JG 52 documents were seized and confiscated by American troops of the 90th Infantry Division later that same day.[103]

Beginning with the American side of this account, there is no information which shows that such an engagement with Soviet aircraft took place on 8 May 1945 over Brno. By 8 May 1945 the American Third Army lead by General Patton halted within the Czechoslovak boarder while his XIX TAC's 10th Reconnaissance Group made contact and claimed a few German planes near Pilsen,[104] however Pilsen is over 200 km West of Brno. These successes were from the Group's 15th TAC reconnaissance Sq. downing two Fw 109s which modern archaeological digs suggest fell outside of Pilsen in the vicinities North of Nadryby and West of Nynice.[105] Flying a few missions on the 8 May, the 10th RG's 162nd TAC reconnaissance Sq. flew over Western Czechoslovakia around Horšovský Týn (roughly 260 km West of Brno) and claimed two Fw 190s.[106] The Group's 12th TAC reconnaissance Sq. downed a final Fw 190 around Regensburg Germany at 20:00 LT.[107] All other encounters with enemy aircraft were identified as German not Soviet, and efforts to escort these few enemy planes to Allied

91 Christer Bergström, *Graf and Grislawski: A Pair of Aces* (Hamilton, Montana: Eagles Editions Ltd., 2003), p.253.
92 Toliver, Constable, *The Blond Knight of Germany*, p. 175.
93 Bergström, *Graf and Grislawski*, p.253.
94 Bergström, *Graf and Grislawski*, p.253.
95 Correspondence with Johannes Mathews (18 February 2021), Bernd Barbas (14 March 2021) and Christer Bergström (1 July 2021). Even with the assistance of these respected authors the name of the mysterious wingman remains unknown.
96 Toliver, Constable, *The Blond Knight of Germany*, pp. 175-176.
97 Toliver, Constable, *The Blond Knight of Germany*, p. 176.
98 D. Hind, D. and P. Nicolaides, Ace of Aces: Erich Hartmann the Blond Knight of Germany, *Open Journal of Social Sciences*, 8, (2002) 383-406. doi: 10.4236/jss.2020.83034.
99 Toliver, Constable, *The Blond Knight of Germany*, p. 176.
100 Toliver, Constable, *The Blond Knight of Germany*, p. 176.
101 Destruction of the airfields military equipment had already begun a day earlier. Aleš Janda, Tomáš Poruba, *Luftwaffe Over Czech Territory – 1945: Messerschmitt Bf 109s of JG 52 in Deutsch Brod* (Hradec Králové: JaPo Publishing, 2004), p. 8.
102 Barbas, *Die Geschichte der I. Gruppe des Jagdgeschwaders 52*, p. 284.
103 Christer Bergström, *Graf and Grislawski*, p. 259.
104 David Spires, *Air Power for Patton's Army: The XIX Tactical Air Command in the Second World War* (Washington, DC: Air Force History and Museums Program, 2002), p. 289.
105 Pavel Krejčí, *Focke-Wulf Fw 190 Pilot, Jednotka? Nadryby okr. Plzeň-sever 8.5.1945*, Letecká Badatelna, (2015), <http://www.leteckabadatelna.cz/havarie-a-sestrely/detail/306/> and <http://www.leteckabadatelna.cz/havarie-a-sestrely/detail/305/> (accessed 1 March 2021).
106 Thomas Ivie, *Aerial Reconnaissance: The 10th Photo Recon Group in World War II* (Fallbrook, California: Aero Publishers Inc, 1981), p. 170.
107 Ivie, *Aerial Reconnaissance*, pp. 168-170.

controlled airfields was carried out throughout the day within the U.S. area of operations.[108] The U.S. Ninth Air Force's IX and XIX TACs both flew demonstration and relocation flights in Germany and Austria while the Eight and Twelfth Air Forces were not present in the Czechoslovakian sector,[109] and the Fifteenth Air Force flew no operations on V-E Day at all.[110] As no records highlight engagement with Soviet aircraft, let alone an entire flight of twelve P-51 Mustangs fighting Soviet aircrafts, Hartmann's recollection that such an engagement occurred cannot be considered accurate.

Returning focus to the Red Army, here too a battle against Americans cannot be found, and this is not due to the prevelent notion that such encouters are deliberately withheld from public access. Previous examples of Allied classes such as between a P-38 Lightning and Soviet Airacobras over Kiev in June 1944,[111] P-38s and Yak-9s over Niš on 7 November 1944,[112] and P-51s, B-17s, B-24s against Yaks around the Oder River on 18 March 1945 are well documented and available.[113] If these examples, of which many hold more serious implications than the event described in Hartmann's biography, are available, why would there be a lack of documentation for Hartmann's event except for the precise reason that such an event never occurred. American and Soviet aircraft did, however, fly peacefully alongside each other on 8 May. In the 16 VA sector flying as escorts to American planes bringing German officials to sign the act of unconditional surrender, 18 Yak-9s commanded by Maj. M. N. Tyulkin of 515 IAP (193 IAD, 13 IAK) escorted the Allied planes from Stendal along the Elbe River to Tempelhof Airport in Berlin, some 430km NW of Brno.[114]

Based on all available Soviet records Erich Hartmann's final claim was also an overclaim. The area and the city of Brno itself were taken on 26 April 1945 by the ground forces of the 2nd Ukrainian Front, covered by its 5 VA. On 8 May 1945 the 5 VA reported only a single combat loss, an Il-2 (c/n: 12854, AM-38F engine: 2512856) from the 90 GvShAP piloted by Gv.Ml.Lt. Pyotr Vasilevich Osipov who remained unhurt and on 9 May 1945 returned to his unit. His gunner, Gv.S-a Pavel Vasilevich Prohorov was taken to hospital with leg injuries. Between 13:15-14:17 LT six 90 GvShAP Il-2s, led by Gv.Maj. Anatolii Ivanovich Fedulov, escorted by four 122 IAP Yak-9s attacked ground targets at Moravské Budějovice (Brno-SW, 60km) when Osipov's plane was downed by flak, therefore his plane could not be Hartmann's victim over Brno at 09:00 LT. The other 90 GvShAP Il-2 (c/n: 12888, AM-38F engine: 2514204) crash-landed near their airfield immediately after take-off due to engine failure. All other 5 VA losses of the day were just temporary plane damages, or scrapped, retired planes due to previous events. Eight 179 IAP Yak-1Bs, however, were right in the air between Znojmo and Brno when Hartmann claimed his Yak-9 victory over the city. Here four Yaks escorted Gv.Capt. Aleksei Nikolaevich Shedogubov's six 91 GvShAP Il-2s to Únanov (Znojmo-N) between 08:55-09:42 LT and another four escorted Gv.St.Lt. Nikolai Semyonovich Alferev's six 92 GvShAP Il-2s to Třeštice (Brno-W, 80km) between 08:13-09:15 LT. Both flights, however, returned to their airbase safely without any air events or losses. The next loss of the 331 IAD occurred only on 18 May 1945 near Kopčany when Lt. Victor Mitrofanovich Koltsov accidentaly hit the ground during a shooting practice with his 122 IAP Yak-9M (c/n: 5215324, engine: 445-378) and was instantly killed.

Soviet 5 VA temporary and permanent aircraft losses on 8 May 1945				
Regiment:	**Type:**	**c/n:**	**Pilot:**	**Details:**
90 GvShAP	Il-2m3	12854	P. V. Osipov	Flak at Kadov, CL, plane burned
90 GvShAP	Il-2m3	12888	N. I. Ivanov	*From 43 ZShAP, TOA, repaired*
92 GvShAP	Il-2m3	9884	*Unknown*	*Flak damage, used for spare parts*
92 GvShAP	Il-2m3	1874799	Y. Karpitskii, '95'	Flak on 7 May, for parts on 8 May
85 GvIAP	Yak-3	4529235	*Unknown, 1st Sq.*	*Radiator damage, repaired at base*

108 Thomas Ivie, *Aerial Reconnaissance: the 10th Photo Recon Group in World War II* (Fallbrook: Aero Publishers Inc, 1981), p. 170 and Spires, *Air Power for Patton's Army*, p. 289.
109 *USAAF Worldwide Operations Chronology: May 1945, Air Crew Remembered* <http://www.aircrewremembered.com/USAAFCombatOperations/May.45.html>, accessed 1 March 2021.
110 Kevin Mahoney, *Fifteenth Air Force Against the Axis: Combat Missions over Europe During World War II* (Plymouth: Scarecrow Press Inc, 2013), p. 400.
111 TsAMO RF: fu. 20538, inv. 1, f. 42, p. 39, Combat log of the 9 IAK PVO.
112 TsAMO RF: fu. 20257, inv. 1, f. 42, p. 391, Combat log of the 288 IAD.
113 TsAMO RF: fu. 368, inv. 6476, f. 499, p. 66, Combat log of the 16 VA for the month of March 1945.
114 Combat log of the 16 VA for May 1945, TsAMO RF, fu. 368, inv. 6476, f. 509, p.30.

Reported single-engine fighter losses on 8 May 1945 in the 5 VA area		
Unit:	**Reported:**	**Closest, or other losses, etc.:**
5 VA	No losses[a]	1 (90 GvShAP) Il-2 lost to flak. Osipov-Prosov crew at Kadov
6 GvIAD	No losses[b]	2 May 1945: Yak-1B, c/n: 39174 at Viskov, Gv.Ml.Lt. Kutsenko
85 GvIAP	No losses[c]	*Damaged Yak-3 (c/n: 4529235), oil-radiator repaired at airbase*
13 GvIAD	No losses[d]	No combat loss in the entire month of May 1945
14 GvIAD	No losses[e]	No combat loss in the entire month of May 1945
279 IAD	No losses[f]	192, 486 IAPs escorting Il-2s of 12 GvShAD without losses
331 IAD	No losses[g]	179 IAP Yak-1B, c/n: 18177 burned while refuelling on 7 May
3 GvIAK	No losses[h]	The 31 GvIAP lost 1 Yak-1B on 2 May 1945. (Kutsenko MIA)
207 OKRAP	No losses[i]	Had 5 Yak-9Ds in 2nd Sq. on 1 May 1945. No losses in May
9 Corps PVO	No losses[j]	Covering the Brno-S area
87 Div. PVO	No losses[k]	Covering the Brno-N area

a. TsAMO RF: fu. 327, inv. 4999, f. 300, p. 38, Operations journal of the 5th Air Army units for May 1945, entry for 8 May 1945.
b. TsAMO RF: fu. 327, inv. 4999, f. 271, p. 333b, Operations report of the 3 GvIAK staff, entry for 8 May 1945.
c. TsAMO RF: fu. 20036, inv. 1, f. 56, p. 30, Combat report of 85 GvIAP, 6 GvIAD, 5th Air Army, 2nd Ukrainian Front for May 1945, entry for 8 May 1945.
d. TsAMO RF: fu. 20511, inv. 1, f. 118, p. 281, Operations journal of 13 GvIAD, entry for 8 May 1945.
e. TsAMO RF: fu. 20062, inv. 1, f. 43, p. 153, Operations journal of 14 GvIAD staff, entry for 8 May 1945.
f. TsAMO RF: fu. 20057, inv. 1, f. 55, p. 658, Operations journal of 12 GvShAD, entry for 8 May 1945. 92 IAP La-5s escorted Il-2s of the 187 GvShAP and 486 IAP La-7s escorted Il-2s of the 188 GvShAP without any losses. Gv.Ml.Lt. Polyanskii (188 GvShAP) landed elsewhere, but later returned to his airbase.
g. TsAMO RF: fu. 20292, inv. 1, f. 15, p. 674, Operations journal of 331 IAD, entry for 8 May 1945.
h. TsAMO RF: fu. 327, inv. 4999, f. 271, p. 333, Operations report of the 3 GvIAK staff, entry for 8 May 1945.
i. TsAMO RF: fu. 327, inv. 4999, f. 290, pp. 384-387, Operations review of 207 OKRAP, entry for 8 May 1945.
j. TsAMO RF: fu. 13607, inv. 20368, f. 798, p. 7, Combat log of the 9th Corps PVO, entry for 8 May 1945.
k. TsAMO RF: fu. 13644, inv. 20258, f. 25, p. 61, Combat log of the 87th Division PVO, entry for 8 May 1945.

The 8 May 1945 summary report of the 3 GvIAK containing nine fighter regiments of the Soviet 6th, 13th and 14th Guards-Fighter Divisions stationing around Brno adds that on this day the enemy *(Luftwaffe)* had no air activities except for two Bf 109s which tried to counteract the combat mission of the Soviet reconnaissance planes in the Znojmo area. It must be noted that Znojmo is about 50 km SW from Brno! This in tandem with the previously mentioned American reports further proves that the members of the two nations did not come into contact with each other on that day. Only these two Bf 109s were seen in the air in the area. The Soviet fighter-activity on 8 May 1945 in the Brno area was as follows:[115]

6 GvIAD (31, 73, 85 GvIAPs: 92 sorties with a total of 55.46 hours flight-time. On reconnaissance: 4 Yaks in 4 sorties with a total of 3.5 hours flight-time, no losses.[116]

13 GvIAD (149, 150, 151 GvIAPs: 60 sorties with a total of 44.10 hours flight-time. (Neither reconnaissance sorties, nor losses.)

14 GvIAD (177, 178, 179 GvIAPs: 88 sorties with a total of 62.57 hours flight-time. On reconnaissance: 4 La-7s in 4 sorties with a total of 3.5 hours flight-time, no losses.[117]

The maximum number of Yakovlev fighters which did make contact with the Luftwaffe on 8 May 1945 could have only been the four reconnaissance Yaks and not eight as written in Hartmann's biography. Besides, such a high number of aircraft flying reconnaissance missions would alert the enemy and hinder the ability to conduct reconnaissance. All other Soviet fighter sorties were flown as escorts to A-20G or Il-2m3 ground attack aircraft, for airfield relocation assignments or training flights which would not occur over the front line.[118] In the Soviet regiment-level documents of the 177 GvIAP, four La-7s belonging to the 2nd and 3rd Sq. also flew reconnaissance missions this day. In the early morning of 8 May 1945

115 TsAMO RF: fu. 327, inv. 4999, f. 271, p. 333, Operations report of the 3 GvIAK staff, entry for 8 May 1945.
116 TsAMO RF, fu. 20036, inv. 1, f. 56, p. 73, Combat report of 31 GvIAP for 1-10 May 1945, entry for 8 May 1945. Two Yak-1s and two Yak-9s of 31 GvIAP, led by Gv.R-y Morozov on reconnaissance between 08:15-09:15 LT in the Moravský Krumlov and Pohořelice areas between Brno and Znojmo.
117 Two pairs of 177 GvIAP La-7s from Brno. (TsAMO RF: fu. 22400, inv. 223841c, f. 1, p. 118.)
118 Two Yak-3s for instance escorted four A-20Gs of the 453 BAP which droped 500,000 leaflets.

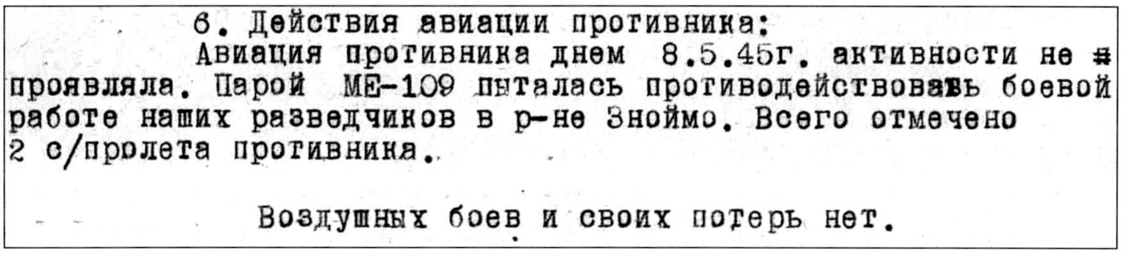

6. Действия авиации противника:
Авиация противника днем 8.5.45г. активности не # проявляла. Парой МЕ-109 пыталась противодействовать боевой работе наших разведчиков в р-не Зноймо. Всего отмечено 2 с/пролета противника.

Воздушных боев и своих потерь нет.

The German aerial activity in the Znojmo area on 8 May 1945. (TsAMO RF: fu. 20511, inv. 1, f. 117, p. 158, Operations journal of 3 GvIAK, entry for 8 May 1945.)

at 06:30 LT a La-7 pair of the 177 GvIAP's 2nd Squadron took off for a reconnaissance flight in the Boskovice, Svitavy, Velké Meziříčí, Moravské Budějovice, Znojmo and Ivancice areas; they returned without losses. The second La-7 pair of the 177 GvIAP, 3rd Sq. repeated this mission at 11:30 LT; they also returned without a scratch. The other 5 VA Fighter Division that flew reconnaissance sorties this day was the 6 GvIAD. Their regiment-level documentation describes that four Yaks of the 31 GvIAP flew four sorties in the Moravský Krumlov and Pohořelice areas, right between Znojmo and Brno with a total flight-time of 3.5 hours. The first Yakovlev pair (a Yak-1B and a Yak-9D) of the 1st Sq. took off at 08:15 LT and returned safely at 09:15 LT.[119] Their pilots were Gv.R-y Fotii Yakovlevich Morozov and Gv.Lt. Grigorii Vasilevich Krivosheev. Over Tulešice, at Moravský Krumlov-W they warned the advancing 6th Guards Tank Army's 9th Guards Mechanized Corps' M4A2 Sherman tank column that they had just spotted German tanks preparing for an ambush by firing off red signal flares from their aircraft. If the two observed Bf 109s were in fact those of Hartmann's flight around 09:00 LT, then Hartmann had to meet and attack Morozov's and Krivosheev's returning Yaks from the 31 GvIAP. No other Soviet reconnaissance aircraft were in the air at that time when the two Bf 109s were reported, only Morozov and Krivosheev. Hartmann's mission time also very closely matches the Soviet mission-time between 08:15 and 09:15 LT, however only two Yaks were flying, and both returned to their airbase safely. If the reported Bf 109 pair was not Hartmann's flight, then Hartmann could not have met other Soviet planes, and as such he could not have shoot down anything. No other Soviet planes observed any German aircraft, only the ones on reconnaissance who suffered no losses. The Soviets lost no single-engine fighters in the entire Brno area on 8 May 1945. This is confirmed by the line added after the second paragraph of the 3 GvIAK report: 'No air combat and no losses.'

It is now clear that Hartmann could not shoot down a Soviet fighter from the 5 VA which controlled the entire aera around Brno. If, somehow, he still encountered their planes then perhaps he damaged a Yak-3 (c/n: 4529235) of the 85 GvIAP, potentially causing the minor damage to its radiator. However, this is extremely unlikely and is not an aerial victory but another overclaim.

In order to rule out any speculation that Hartmann might have encountered Soviet planes from one of the other nearby Air Armies, the Authors list their losses as well. Soviet 8 VA which was covering the ground forces of the 4th Ukrainian Front North of the 2nd Ukrainian Front on 8 May 1945 reported the following losses:[120]

One 8 VA, 10 GvIAD, 113 GvIAP La-7FN (c/n: 45211829, white '29'), escorting six Il-2s, piloted by Gv.Ml.Lt. Mihail Fedorovich Polivenok was downed by flak in the Krzhelov area between 12:00-13:10 LT.[121]

One 8 VA, 10 GvIAD, 112 GvIAP Yak-3 (c/n: 0829227, white '8') was lost in a mid-air collision at seven kilometers North of Olomouc at 800m with an Il-2m3 from 224 ShAD, 565 ShAP (c/n: 9816) between 08:00-08:50 LT.[122] Pilot Gv.Lt. Ilya Fedorovich Kuzin was killed.[123] During this mission six Yak-3s, led by Gv.Capt. Verenikin, including the pair of Raskoshnii-Kuzin (Kuchik), escorted eight 565 ShAP Il-2m3s in the Olomouc area when the fatal accident happened. Following his leader St.Lt. Raskoshnii, Gv.Lt. Kuzin was unable to see the Il-2 beneath him due to haze and smoke as he was turning left and collided with the Sturmovik right where the aerial gunner was sitting, breaking the plane in half before falling and burning on the ground, however the Il-2 pilot was able to jump out with his parachute. Upon returning from this mission another 565 ShAP Il-2 (c/n: 10529) piloted by Ml.Lt. Grigorii Timofeevich Neminushii crash-landed but was later repaired.

One 8 VA, 224 ShAD, 996 ShAP Il-2m3 (c/n: 18845111) failed to return from a combat mission. Its pilot, Ml.Lt. Aleksandr Pavlovich Gubarenko went missing.[124]

119 In the spring of 1945 when the 85 GvIAP was re-armed with newer Yak-3s (eg.: 1229237) their Yak-9s were transferred to the 31 and 73 GvIAPs. On 25 August 1945 Gv.Ml.Lt. Gennadiy Nikitovich Kochetov flew one of these Yak-9Ds (31 GvIAP, c/n: 1015304, white '4') when he deserted from Czechoslovakia to Dübendorf, Switzerland. This plane arrived in the 31 GvIAP on 2 April 1945.
120 TsAMO RF: fu. 346, inv. 5755, f. 243, p. 33, Operations journal of 8th Air Army, entry for 8 May 1945.
121 TsAMO RF: fu. 346, inv. 5755, f. 229, p. 178b, Operations journal of 10 GvIAD staff for April and 1-11 May 1945, entry for 8 May 1945.
122 TsAMO RF: fu. 20211, inv. 1, f. 42, p. 296, Operations journal of 224 ShAD, entry for 8 May 1945.
123 TsAMO RF: fu. 346, inv. 5755, f. 229, pp. 178b-179, Operations journal of 10 GvIAD staff for April and 1-11 May 1945, entry for 8 May 1945.
124 TsAMO RF: fu. 20211, inv. 1, f. 42, p. 297, Operations journal of 224 ShAD, entry for 8 May 1945.

One 8 VA, 227 ShAD, 637 ShAP Il-2m3 piloted by Ml.Lt. Georgii Demyanovich Podoinitsin (+) was lost 12 kilometers North of Olomouc. Beside the Il-2s, the 8 VA also lost three brand new 571 ShAP Ilyushin Il-10s: 1892604/G. V. Titov, 1890604/V. I. Prishepa and 1893203/G. P. Kupaigorodskii.

One 8 VA, 321 BAD, 13 GvBAP Douglas A-20G-1-DO Boston (S/N: 42-53622) piloted by Gv.Lt. Stepan Mihailovich Dubrovin caught fire in the air and crashed in flames. Its crew bailed out successfully.

North of the 4th Ukrainian Front, the 1st Ukrainian Front was advancing covered by the 2 VA. This was the only Soviet Air Army which lost 'real' Yak-9 fighters in the greater area. A 53 IAP Yak-9M was lost at Görlitz-NW to flak (approximately 240 km from Brno). The pilot, St.Lt. Pyotr Romanovich Korolev was killed. The other lost Yak-9M was from the 355 IAP. It was lost over Görlitz, Germany to flak (approximately 240 km from Brno). The pilot, Ml.Lt. Aleksandr Dmitrievich Alifatev was also killed. The 2 VA lost additional Il-2s from the 621 and 948 ShAPs to flak as well, but they were not in combat with German fighters.[125] Here too the losses were far from the claimed location of Brno, while the cause of destruction was anti-aircraft fire.

And finally, the 17 VA fighting South of Brno (mainly in Austria), covering the ground forces of the 3rd Ukrainian Front had no combat loss on 8 May 1945 at all.[126]

Those skeptical might say that by the end of the war the remaining Luftwaffe victory records were written down incorrectly and perhaps Hartmann's final victory was claimed on 7 May 1945 but was mistakenly written down as 8 May. If this were the case, and by bending history in order to make this theory more viable, we also assess the 7 May losses and flight information. Again, starting with the American part of the story, the Ninth Air Force's 10th RG's 162nd TAC reconnaissance Sq. conducted flyby missions over Austrian POW camps in Lienz, Spittal, Klagenfurt, Wulfsberg, and Libnitz.[127] The Eight Air Force dropped supplies and leaflets over the Netherlands and Germany, the Twelfth Air Force flew reconnaissance missions over the Austrian Alps, and the Fifteenth Air Force dropped supplies in Yugoslavia.[128] Once again the engagement of USAAF P-51 Mustangs and Soviet Yaks over Brno can be shown to never have occurred.

On 7 May 1945 the 5 VA lost only one burned down Yak-1B fighter (179 IAP, c/n: 18177) at 21:25 LT at Lužice airfield during a fuel-refilling service accident. Their other loss was a La-7FN fighter (192 IAP, c/n: 45212545, white '45') which was lost at 18:20 LT during landing after an Il-2 escort mission to Miroslav. The pilot, Ml.Lt. Aleksandr Gerasimovich Spirin was unhurt. Both planes were lost well into the afternoon, in non-combat related incidents, and on their respective airfields, not in morning combat at 4000m over Brno.

The 17 VA lost only two Il-2 Sturmoviks on 7 May 1945: one Il-2m3 in Austria (672 ShAP, c/n: 18870106, AM-38F engine: 259397 with the Ml.Lt. Vladimir Yegorovich Bershak crew),[129] the other one over the downtown of Miroslav to flak. (715 ShAP, c/n: 12656, AM-38F engine: 2516962, white '25') The crew of Ml.Lt. Pyotr Vasilevich Kravtsev and Nikolai Fedorovich Chertov was killed.[130] In this mission between 09:30-09:45 LT, twenty-nine Il-2s of the 715 ShAP,[131] led by Capt. Evgenii Romanovich Ignatov in Il-2m3, white '29', escorted by twelve La-5s of the 31 IAP were attacking German army vehicles in the Miroslav area.[132] There is no other option with which to verify Erich Hartmann's final claim. A last and very extreme option, if his final claim was not just a fictious story fueled by emotional revenge to compensate for the lost war, may be that as the German war machine was completely collapsing Erich Hartmann downed an escaping German plane over Brno in a 'friendly fire' incident that he misidentified as a Soviet Yak-9. Because the Luftwaffe documentation at the end of the war ceased to exist, recall operation Feuertod, the Authors cannot verify the validity of this option. What is certain is that in the final hours of the war many German pilots tried to fly over and surrender to the Western Allies in order to escape the much feared and otherwise unavoidable Soviet captivity. One could also question the reliability of the German verification system that was in place by early 1945, let alone on 8 May 1945?

Inconsistencies in the Hartmann claims list

Due to the disappearance of Hartmann's second logbook containing his claims from late 1943 till the end of the war, his performance over Hungary had to be derived from other sources written by different authors post-war and in some cases though the personal letters Hartmann sent home to his loved ones. As there is no single original claims list in which all this information can be found, different versions of Erich Hartmann's 352 claims have been published leading to inconsistencies. The Authors of this book have analyzed the most complete lists within this chapter. However in addition to these complete

125 TsAMO RF: fu. 20515, inv. 1, f. 45, p. 221, Operations journal of 3 ShAK, entry for 8 May 1945.
126 TsAMO RF: fu. 370, inv. 6518, f. 445, pp. 25-31, Operations journal of 17th Air Army for May, 1945, entry for 8 May 1945.
127 Ivie, *Aerial Reconnaissance*, p. 170.
128 *USAAF Worldwide Operations Chronology: May 1945, Air Crew Remembered* <http://www.aircrewremembered.com/USAAFCombatOperations/May.45.html> (accessed 1 March 2021).
129 TsAMO RF: fu. 20541, inv. 1, f. 104, p. 73, Operations journal of 306 ShAD, entry for 7 May 1945.
130 TsAMO RF: fu. 20174, inv. 1, f. 37, p. 459, Operations report of 715 ShAP, entry for 7 May 1945.
131 According to the 715 ShAP mission report, their 29 tail/fuselage tactical numbers were: white 1, 2, 3, 5, 6, 7, 8, 9, 11, 12, 13, 14, 15, 18, 19, 21, 22, 25, 26, 27, 28, 29, 30, 31, 32, 35, 37, 39 and 40.
132 TsAMO RF: fu. 22926, inv. 188593c, f. 2, p. 98b, Combat report of 715 ShAP staff, entry for 7 May 1945.

lists, official German documents captured by the Soviets which now reside in Russian archives bring to light new pieces of information which challenge what was known about the dates and numbering for some of Hartmann's claims. At least three such documents contained within a KTB of AOK 6 for December 1944 differ in both the dates and in the numbering of claims. These were written by a liaison officer from Luftflotte 4 attached to AOK 6 responsible for the documentation of the aerial events and on informing AOK 6 of the Luftwaffe's successes. As the documents were written at a detached level from II./JG 52 there is some chance that the dates presented within the documents are backdated or incorrect. According to the captured German KTB, Erich Hartmann reached 328 Luftsieg on 23 December 1944.[133] One day later he had reached 331 Luftsieg.[134] On the 25 of December Erich Hartmann made five claims and reached 336 Luftsieg.[135] These discrepancies cannot be meaningfully assessed as the documents do not indicate the specific aircraft type or the time when the claims were made.

CONCLUSION

Erich Hartmann was a very skilled and brave fighter pilot who flew an extremely high number of operational missions over several long years of the war. Given the available claims over Hungary his combat performance, compared to the alure of his famous 352 kills once analyzed and compared to Soviet aircraft losses, may be summarized as unreliable and unlikely. The Authors noticed similar results outside of Hungary as demonstrated by his 352nd claim on 8 May 1945 among others. The question arises: what is the probability that his accuracy would have changed simply by crossing a nation's wartime border?

Reviewing his 34 victory claims over Hungary,[136] Erich Hartmann managed to achieve seven victories or potential victories which results in a claiming accuracy just above 21%. Debate over how many aircrafts were actually shot down by Erich Hartmann has captivated many historians and aviation enthusiast, however a definite answer cannot be given until an original claim-list documenting all 352 victory claims surfaces. Until such a historical artifact becomes known and a careful verification of individual claims found within is performed, Erich Hartmann cannot be credited with the most verified victories in history. With his excellent flying ability there is little doubt that Hartmann could hit his opponents, however there is a significant difference between hitting a plane and destroying it. There is also a wide range of public opinion on how he was made the 'superhero' of the Luftwaffe. Some say he was simply a liar who only wanted personal glory. It is a known fact that high claiming aces received exceptional public treatment due to their achievements. Others say his favorite tactic of see-decide-attack-reverse made him unable to properly observe the results of his actions. The Bf 109 was notorious for its poor visibility rearwards, something a boom-and-zoom attack would only further reduce. This model of aircraft was also the only German mainline fighter which never received a bubble-type canopy by the end of the war. Hartmann may have reported his claims honestly with good will to the best of his abilities but was physically limited by the visibility from his plane. Others say there was political pressure on him and on his unit to maintain the combat moral of the Luftwaffe by producing a 'superhero'. Since the Authors were obviously not present when Hartmann filed his claims, they cannot and do not want to be the judge in this question. It is up to the Respected Reader to consider the above detailed analysis and form their own opinion about this question of '*why?*': why is there such a significant difference between Erich Hartmann's claims and verified Soviet losses when other successful Luftwaffe pilots withstand this test using the very same documents?

Another question remains: if not Erich Hartmann, then who was the most successful fighter pilot in human history? For the sake of both military and aviation history, this designation and recognition is still owed to someone!

133 Luftlage 24.12.1944 TsAMO RF: fu. 500, inv. 12472, f. 382, p. 375.
134 Nachmeldung zur Luftlage 24.12.1944 TsAMO RF: fu. 500, inv. 12472, f. 382, p. 393.
135 Luftlage 25.12.1944 TsAMO RF: fu. 500, inv. 12472, f. 382, pp. 394a-394b.
136 Discounting the claim entry for 21 November 1944 which could not have occurred due to poor weather over Hungary effectively grounding all combat flights. This erroneous claim most likely originated from the biography *Holt Hartmann vom Himmel!* which contains the faulty entry. The additional claim entry for 26 October 1944 has been retained.

10

Helmut Lipfert (1916-1990)

Born on 6 August 1916 Helmut Lipfert joined the Luftwaffe in 1941 and was assigned to 6./JG 52 on 16 December 1942 in Russia. At twenty-six years of age he was an 'old' pilot compared to many of his comrades.[1] He became commander of the 6./JG 52 on 6 September 1943. He crash-landed multiple times before he claimed his first aerial victory over Hungary on 17 October 1944. On 14 February 1945 he became the last commander of I./JG 53, a position which he never felt fully comfortable in. His final claim over Hungary was a Yak-9 on 21 March 1945 and his last claim was a Yak-9 on 16 April 1945. Hptm. Helmut Lipfert had 203 confirmed claims along with many unconfirmed.[2] After at least 687 combat sorties during the war,[3] he passed away on 10 August 1990.[4]

Helmut Lipfert's claims are compiled from the following sources listed in order of heaviest reliance:

- Luftwaffe Aces: claims and bibliographies, Vol. 2
- Die Geschichte der II. Gruppe des Jagdgeschwaders 52: Offizielle Ausgabe der Traditionsgemeinschaft JG 52
- Jagdeschwader 53: A History of the "Pik As" Geschwader, January 1944-May 1945, Vol. 3.
- The War Diary of Hauptmann Helmut Lipfert: JG 52 on the Russian Front 1934-1945
- Tony Woods – Eastern Front Vol 4. 1944. Jul – Dec, Issue 1

All above lists contain occasional differences in aircraft types, along with unclaimed victories;[5] the known differences have been included and assessed within this chapter. The claim number appearing in the Mathews & Foreman publication has been used.

17 October 1944 (Tuesday)

Lipfert's 143rd: VICTORY, 'Yak-11' at 10:38 LT at Hosszúpályi-SE, 3 km, 3000m

Soviet 5 VA permanent single-engine fighter losses on 17 October 1944				
Regiment:	**Type:**	**c/n:**	**Pilot:**	**Details:**
73 GvIAP	Yak-1B	38147	G. I. Malyavin+	Hósszúpályi, 10:38 LT to Bf 109s
92 IAP	La-5FN	39212976	N. A. Lopatkin	Ferry-flight accident at Kisszénás
192 IAP	La-5F	3810526	V. I. Mokridin MIA	Debrecen, 15:25LT, 2 Fw 190s, MIA

1 Lipfert, Gribig, *The War Diary of Hauptmann Helmut Lipfert*, p. 11.
2 Some 200 confirmed and around 30 unconfirmed according to Mathews and Foreman, *Luftwaffe Aces: Biographies and Victory claims*, Vol. 2, p. 758.
3 Lipfert, Gribig, *The War Diary of Hauptmann Helmut Lipfert*, p. 181.
4 Mathews and Foreman, *Luftwaffe Aces*, p. 758.
5 These few unclaimed victories are described in Lipfert's autobiography and have corresponding identifiable Soviet losses. Why these claims were not officially filed remains a mystery.

6. 17.10.44г. на самолете ЯК-1 № 38147 летчик гв л-нт Малявин сбит в воздушном бою.самолет и летчик погиоли

Gv.Lt. Grigorii Ivanovich Malyavin's loss-entry in the 73 GvIAP records. (TsAMO RF: fu. 20036, inv. 1, f. 56, p. 114, Combat and non-combat related operation of the 73 GvIAP for the time period of 20 September 1944 – 10 May 1945, entry for 17 October 1944.)

At 10:38 LT on 17 October 1944, Hptm. Helmut Lipfert claimed a *'Yak-11'* fighter at Hosszúpályi, fifteen kilometers Southeast of Debrecen. Between 10:55-11:25 LT, seven Yak-1Bs and one Yak-9 of the 73 GvIAP led by Gv.Capt. Nikolai Pavlovich Katushkin engaged fourteen Fw 190s and six Bf 109s. When the German fighter-bombers spotted the Soviet planes they immediately dropped their bomb load in a field and entered into dogfights at an altitude of 3000m. The Messerschmitt's also engaged and Lipfert opened fire on a Yak-1B over Hosszúpályi, downing it. The pilot, Gv.Lt. Grigorii Ivanovich Malyavin (1922-1944), was not able to leave his plane and perished. This Yak-1B was Lipfert's first confirmed aerial victory over Hungary, recorded under the proprietary designation of 'Yak-11'.

In the same area over Derecske between 13:00-13:30 LT four Yak-3s of the 150 GvIAP met four Bf 109s from which Gv.Lt. Yurii Nikolaevich Verginskii (probably in c/n: 1829217, white '18') downed one Bf 109 from the distance of only 20m. Another Bf 109 was claimed by Gv.St.lt. Sergei Ivanovich Konovalov West of Derecske. The Yak-3s returned to their airfield without any losses.

Right at the same time as Helmut Lipfert's Yak-1B victory, between 09:55-11:35 LT eight Il-2 Sturmoviks of the 873 ShAP led by St.Lt. Mihail Stephanovich Osipenko,[6] escorted by four 192 IAP La-5s from Tótkomlós, attacked Újtelep (the Northern railway station of Derecske) where they were ambushed by two Bf 109s. During the unfolding dogfight the German fighters damaged St.Lt. Mihail Stephanovich Osipenko's plane (c/n: 1879479, AM-38F engine: 253501, aerial gunner Vardo Ivanovich Mamisashvili) of the 3rd Squadron which force landed at six to eight kilometers West of Békéscsaba, soon after being repaired it returned to combat service. Later, between 14:10-15:20 LT another seven 873 ShAP Il-2s led by Capt. Aleksei Vasilevich Dolgih, escorted by four 192 IAP La-5s, attacked the Törökszentmiklós-NE area. During the attack the German anti-aircraft artillery damaged Capt. Dolgih's Il-2 (c/n: 11033), who limped back to his airbase and later also had his Il-2 repaired.[7]

21 October 1944 (Saturday)

Lipfert's 144th: VICTORY, LaGG-5 at 10:52 LT at Öcsöd-SE, 6 km, 700m

Soviet 5 VA permanent single-engine fighter losses on 21 October 1944				
Regiment:	**Type:**	**c/n:**	**Pilot:**	**Details:**
192 IAP	La-5F	39214225	A. S. Sukoviants	Szentes-SE, 10:25 LT, 8 *Fw 190s*
486 IAP	La-5FN	39213343	V. Grushkin WIA	Gyomaendrőd, 11:05 LT, *Fw 190s*

On 21 October 1944 at 1500m four La-5s and two Il-2s were flying a reconnaissance mission in the Mezőtúr-Túrkeve area. Around 11:05 LT they were attacked by six *'Fw 190s'*, of which Hptm. Lipfert was one of the pilots. Lipfert shot down Ml.Lt. Vasilii Mihailovich Grushkin's La-5FN (c/n: 39213343, ASh-82FN engine: 82131308, white '43') near Öcsöd. The wounded pilot belly landed six kilometers Northwest of Gyomaendrőd and was taken to the hospital of 442 BAO.

23 October 1944 (Monday)

Lipfert's 145th: VICTORY, Il-2 at 15:31 LT at Szolnok-SE, 1 km, 1000m
Lipfert's 146th: VICTORY, Il-2 at 15:32 LT at Szolnok-NE, 1 km, 1000m

Soviet 5 VA permanent Il-2 Sturmovik losses on 23 October 1944				
Regiment:	**Type:**	**c/n:**	**Pilot:**	**Details:**
131 GvShAP	Il-2m3	10620	A. Lapinskii POW	Szolnok-E, 15:32 LT to Lipfert
131 GvShAP	Il-2m3	302820	V. I. Kralkin+	Szolnok-E, 15:31 LT to Lipfert
131 GvShAP	Il-2m3	1873563	V. P. Zubov	Returned to airbase, *major repair*
132 GvShAP	Il-2m3	18753100	S. D. Pilipets KIFA	14:35LT, take off accident, burned

On 23 October 1944 at 15:25 LT, six (3x2) 131 GvShAP Il-2m3 Sturmoviks, piloted by Derkachev-Zinchenko, Zubov-Klevtsov and Kralkin-Lapinskii attacked the German Tisza river-crossing East of Szolnok. The Il-2s strafed German

6 The eight Il-2 pilots were: Osipenko, Korkotsenko, Osetrov, Tyurikov, Anukhin, Kopilov, Ivanishev and Sviridov. TsAMO RF: fu. 22418, inv. 0222525c, f. 4, p. 76, Operations journal of 873 ShAP for May-December 1944, entry for 17 October 1944.

7 The seven Il-2 pilots were: Dolnih, Dyachenko, Stupak, Andreev, Aleksandrov, Suhih and Demakov. TsAMO RF: fu. 22418, inv. 0222525c, f. 4, p. 77, Operations journal of 873 ShAP for May-December 1944, entry for 17 October 1944.

armour and transport targets in the Eastern side of the city, when ten *'Fw 190's* attacked them. Flying in from the North, Helmut Lipfert and his wingman Ofhr. Steins made a 90-degree turn to get behind the Soviet ground attack planes and began firing from a range of only 30-50 meters, managing to shoot down two Il-2m3 within one minute of each other just East of Szolnok.[8] Armed with a 30mm cannon, Lipfert fired only ten rounds of cannon and thirtyfive rounds of machine-gun ammunition.[9]

The first Il-2m3 piloted by Lt. Vitalii Ivanovich Kralkin exploded mid-air after Lipfert's attack using his 30mm cannon, flying right through the debris. Both pilot Lt. Vitalii Ivanovich Kralkin and aerial gunner Mihail Semyonovich Babailov were killed.[10]

Immediately after Lipfert opened fire on the second Il-2m3 the aircraft lost its tail section and crashed. The pilot, Gv.Lt. Aleksei Kirillovich Lapinskii bailed out successfully and survived the crash, but his aerial gunner Gv.Ml.Sgt. Pyotr Alekseevich Filippov went down with the disintegrated plane.[11]

The 7 GvShAD's other twelve Il-2s, which at this time also attacked Szolnok, were luckier, their fighter escort of four 92 IAP La-5s repelled all attacks of approximately twenty enemy fighters while Maj. Nikolai Grigorevich Butoma claimed one Fw 190 shot down East of Szolnok.

24 October 1944 (Tuesday)
Lipfert's 147th: VICTORY, Yak-7 at 9:22 LT at Fehértó-NW, 1 km, low level

Soviet 5 VA permanent single-engine fighter losses on 24 October 1944				
Regiment:	**Type:**	**c/n:**	**Pilot:**	**Details:**
150 GvIAP	Yak-9T	1015348	A. N. Sisko WIA	Újfehértó, 4 Yak-9 vs. 6 Bf 109s

On 24 October 1944 at 08:50 LT four Yak-9s of the 150 GvIAP led by Gv.Ml.Lt. Sisko took off from Gospodski Dvor to cover Soviet ground troops in the Nyíregyháza-S area. Over Újfehértó they fell into combat with six Bf 109s. Dogfighting for about three minutes, Gv.Ml.Lt. Aleksandr Nikitovich Sisko disappeared into the clouds where Helmut Lipfert shot him down. After bailing out and opening his parachute, Aleksandr Nikitovich Sisko was captured and taken to a hospital. He later escaped from the hospital and on 25 December 1944 crossed the frontline near Székesfehérvár to return to his own side.

27 October 1944 (Friday)
Lipfert's UNCLAIMED POTECNIAL GROUND VICTORY, Yak fighter on Debrecen airfield
Lipfert's 148th: VICTORY, Il-2 at 12:17 LT at Büdszentmihály-SW, 6 km, 1200m
Lipfert's 149th: VICTORY, Yak-7 at 12:21 LT at Büdszentmihály-S, 11 km, 800m

Soviet 5 VA aircraft losses on 27 October 1944				
Regiment:	**Type:**	**c/n:**	**Pilot:**	**Details:**
207 OKRAP	Il-2KR	10948	M. P. Lanskii+	Józsefháza-NE, 1200m to Bf 109
207 OKRAP	Yak-9D	19166066	A. M. Rozhkov+	Both missing to Steins & Lipfert at 12:18 and 12:21 LT
207 OKRAP	Yak-9D	19166078	K.V. Sapego MIA	
150 GvIAP	Yak-3	3929212	N. M. Knut POW	Nyíregyháza-S, to Stab. I./SG 10
192 IAP	La-5FN	39213433	S. F. Gukov POW	Kecskemét-NW, 8 km, lakeshore
513 IAP	Yak-9M	2515338	A. P. Kutuzov+	Destroyed during an attack on the Debrecen airfield. *(Seven Po-2s and two 451 ShAP Il-2s were also damaged, one Po-2 at 18:15 LT by a Hs 126, Ml.Lt. N. Efremov+)*
513 IAP	Yak-1B	20150	N/A	
930 NBAP	Po-2/U-2	8257	N/A	
930 NBAP	Po-2/U-2	127107*	N/A	
930 NBAP	Po-2/U-2	167109	N/A	
392 NBAP	Po-2/U-2	*Unknown*	A. P. Shishkanov	*Szeghalom, LAC, broken, repaired*

* Crew chief of 930 NBAP Po-2, white '8' (c/n: 127107, M-11 engine: 4120753) was mechanic C-a Nikon Semyonovich Podzherei who served this plane for 31 combat sorties before its loss on the Debrecen airfield on 27 October 1944.

8 Lipfert, Gribig, *The War Diary of Hauptmann Helmut Lipfert*, p. 142.
9 Lipfert, Gribig, *The War Diary of Hauptmann Helmut Lipfert*, p. 143.
10 TsAMO RF: fu. 20039, inv. 1, f. 22, p. 181, Operations journal of 7 GvShAD staff for October 1944, entry for 23 October 1944.
11 TsAMO RF: fu. 20039, inv. 1, f. 22, p. 181, Operations journal of 7 GvShAD staff for October 1944, entry for 23 October 1944.

According to his personal diary, the assigned crew of his plane was pilot Lt. Mihail Aleksandrovich Nikolaev and navigator/bombardier Ml.Lt. Mihail Yakovlevich Kireev who both survived the bombardment as they were not in their plane.

For the morning of 27 October 1944, a large German aerial raid was planned against the Soviets with II./JG 52 to partake in the attack on Debrecen airfiled. Lipfert recalls that the *staffel* leaders were prepaird for the attack the previous night including himself (6./JG 52), Maj. Barkhorn (stab II./JG 52), Hptm. Hartmann (4./JG 52) and Hptm. Sturm (5./JG 52).[12] The 1st Fliegercorps sent a total of 139 aircraft on the attack with the airfield being an important target for the raid as German intelligence estimated 170 Soviet aircraft to be stationed in Debrecen.[13] The Soviets observed the first flight of enemy aircraft approaching at 6:10LT consisting of 6 Bf 109s and 6 Fw 190s.[14] Once the attack was over, the German's reported 25-30 aircraft set on fire, 10-15 aircraft damamged by bombs or gunfire, five aircraft shot down in the air of which three were over the airfiled itself, along with 50 trucks, 20 covered vehicles and six ferry boats(!) were also destroyed.[15]

According to the initial 5 VA daily report, the enemy attack on the Debrecen airfield destroyed three Po-2, three planes were damaged, another fifteen aircrafts suffered only minor damages while a single Yak-9 went MIA after taking off.[16] The more accurate divisional and regimental reports offer more complete information regarding the losses suffered during the raid. During the unexpected dawn attack at 06:30 LT two 513 IAP Yaks and three 930 NBAP Po-2s were destroyed, while seven 930 NBAP, three 18 TAP Po-2s and two 451 ShAP Il-2s were significantly damaged. The attacking planes flew to the South and with a wide left turn struck the Debrecen airfield from the East then later repeated the attack from the West as well.[17] Hptm. Lipfert, flying a few meters above the ground, opened fire from about 100m on a parked Yakovlev fighter and with a short burst he set it on fire. As he looked back the Soviet fighter was already on fire and estimated that around twelve aircraft were left buring on the airfield after the attack was over.[18] It must be pointed out that Lipfert's assessment of the damage inflicted on the Soviet's is very close to the actual number of machines lost by the 5 VA over Debercen that day (five destroyed, twelve damaged and one MIA).

The Yak claimed to be set ablaze by Lipfert had to be one of the two destroyed planes of 513 IAP, most likely c/n: 20150 as no pilot was reported harmed during the incident, meaning the aircraft was probably parked on the tarmac unoccupied at the time of its destruction. The other Yak loss was therefore certainly the single MIA aircraft which managed to take off that morning as a pilot is recorded to have been lost as well. Based on the Soviet records Hptm. Lipfert's unclaimed *am Boden* claim may be confirmed as a potential victory. As the other ground claims are not known, it may only be assumed that Lipfert was responsible for the destruction of the Yak-1B, though the described events strongly suggest that Lipfert's actions were responsible for the parked Yakovlev loss. If new information regarding the German claims this day are discovered in the future, a more detailed analysis may be undertanken to discover what happed that fateful morning.

Il-2KR, yellow '1' (c/n: probably 7414) of 207 OKRAP on an airfield before a combat sortie. *The yellow '1' is outlined in either dark blue or black paint. (Photo: Units and planes, <http://ava.org.ru/rap/207.htm>) (*According to their plane-inventory, between 1 October and 26 December 1944 the 207 OKRAP had the following sixteen Il-2s: c/n 7414, 10197, 10224, 10546, 10739, 10948, 10979, 11264, 11297, 11414, 11415, 11482, 11505, 11577, 11612, and 302360. Il-2KR, c/n: 10948 was shot down by Hptm. Lipfert on 27 October 1944 with its AM-38F engine: 256676 and was written off by 3 November 1944.)

12 Lipfert, Gribig, *The War Diary of Hauptmann Helmut Lipfert*, p. 132.
13 The attack consisted of 71 Fw 190, 15 Ju 87, 7 Hs 129, 34 Bf 109 fighter and 12 Bf 109 reconnaissance aircraft. Verb.Kdo. der Luftflotte 4 zum A.O.K. 6, 27.10.1944. TsAMO RF: fu. 500, inv. 12472, f. 345, p. 67.
14 Operations Journal of 5 VA for October 1944. TsAMO RF: fu. 327, inv. 4999, f. 225, p. 99.
15 Verb.Kdo. der Luftflotte 4 zum A.O.K. 6, 27.10.1944. TsAMO RF: fu. 500, inv. 12472, f. 345, p. 67.
16 Operations Journal of 5 VA for October 1944. TsAMO RF: fu. 327, inv. 4999, f. 225, pp. 99-100.
17 Lipfert, Gribig, *The War Diary of Hauptmann Helmut Lipfert*, p. 132.
18 Lipfert, Gribig, *The War Diary of Hauptmann Helmut Lipfert*, p. 143.

Testing of the guns on Yak-3 (c/n: 310317) before its assignment to the 5 VA around 12 April 1945. On 1 July and 1 September 1945 it was still serving in the 149 GvIAP. Note the large factory applied (Tbilisi-style) digits on the fuselage. (Photo: B. V. Davidov)

Later that morning after 10:15 LT, Il-2KR reconnaissance planes escorted by Yak-9D fighters of the 207 OKRAP surveyed enemy traffic on the roads in the Csap, Mátészalka, Nyírmeggyes, Vásárosnamény, Nyíregyháza, Büdszentmihály, Nyírbátor areas. At 10:25 LT four 331 IAD Yak-1B fighters fought a pair of Bf 109s at Nyíregyháza-NE without any results.[19] It was probably these very same two Bf 109s opened fire on Maj. Nikolai Petrovich Zubko's Il-2KR twice at 10:36 LT between 1800-2000m, however Zubko was able to return to his airbase in Romania.

Another 207 OKRAP Il-2KR and its Yak-9D fighter escorts were not so lucky: they went missing after a dogfight with Helmut Lipfert near Büdszentmihály. Later in the early afternoon a ground unit, 3./Flak-Abt.375 of 15 Flakdivison,[20] recorded the following in the areas of Taktakenéz (II./JG 52's airfield at the time) and Taktaharkány: *12:14 – 12:15 hours, 1 Il-2, 2 LaGG* [sic!], *2200 m, bomb dropped in direction 9, no damage reported.*[21] Returning from his flight which began at 11:25LT, Helmut Lipfert recalled the following: *'I was about 20 kilometers from the field when Ewald reported that he was about to land, but he had not finished his transmission when the ground station called: Six one from Garden Fence, one Furniture Van and two Indians over Picnic Ground at Hanni 1,000. Try and shoot the fellows down if you can, they've discovered our base.*[22] Lipfert and his wingman Steins attacked one of the two escorting Yak-9Ds which were flying roughly 500m above the Sturmovik shooting a fighter down over Józsefháza-S at 12:21 LT.[23] Lipfert now focused in on the Sturmovik, firing from a distance of only 60m with his machineguns then later his cannon,[24] downing the Il-2KR at 1200m over Józsefháza-NE (Büdszentmihály-SW) killing both pilot Ml.Lt. Mihail Petrovich Lanskii and observer St.Lt. Lev Dmitrievich Sinev. Lipfet noted that *The Il-2 bobbed and weaved so that I had difficulty scoring even a few hits, but at least the fire from the rear gunner had stopped. His machine-gun pointed straight up in the air,*[25] indicating that his fire had probably killed St.Lt. Sinev while the Sturmovik was still flying.

Shortly after this victory, when Lipfert's shells struck home, the Yak-9 lost almost its entire wing as it crashed in a ditch along the road.[26] This plane was either Ml.Lt. Aleksandr Mihailovich Rozhkov's, or St.Lt. Constantin Vasilevich Sapego deputy squadron commander's missing Yak-9D. The other Yak-9D, downed by Obfhr. Steins at 12:18 LT crashed in the area West of Büdszentmihály. Following this long and challenging dogfight, Steins ran out of fuel and made a force landing, however his damaged Bf 109 was repaired in two days.

During that day over Nyíregyháza, six 150 GvIAP Yak-3s met sixteen Fw 190s and four Bf 109s. In the unfolding dogfight Gv.St.Lt. Aleksandr Nikolaevich Agdantsev opened fire on a Fw 190 and firing from 50 to 30m downed it. The Soviet fighters suffered no losses. One La-5FN (c/n: 39213286) arrived to 178 GvIAP from ВОШВБ (Higher Officer School of Air Combat).

13 November 1944 (Monday)

Lipfert's 150th: OVERCLAIM, Yak-3[27] at 12:45 LT at Jászberény-SE, 9 km, 4000m

19 TsAMO RF: fu. 20525, inv. 1, f. 25, p. 35, Combat journal of 5 ShAK for the time period of 1-31 October 1944, entry for 27 October 1944.

20 3./Flak-Abt.375 was stationed around the bridge at Tiszafüred and at Tiszabábolna armed with two 8.8cm and three 2cm Flak cannons. 15. Flakdivision (mot) Abt. Ia op 2, Flaklagemeldung vom 27.10.1944. TsAMO RF: fu. 500, inv. 12472, f. 345, p. 70a.

21 15. Flakdivision (mot) Abt. Ia op 2, Flaklagemeldung vom 27.10.1944. TsAMO RF: fu. 500, inv. 12472, f. 345, p. 70b.

22 Lipfert, Gribig, *The War Diary of Hauptmann Helmut Lipfert*, p. 144.

23 Lipfert, Gribig, *The War Diary of Hauptmann Helmut Lipfert*, p. 145.

24 Lipfert, Gribig, *The War Diary of Hauptmann Helmut Lipfert*, p. 146.

25 Lipfert, r Gribig, *The War Diary of Hauptmann Helmut Lipfert*p. 145.

26 Lipfert, Gribig, *The War Diary of Hauptmann Helmut Lipfert*, p. 147.

27 Claimed to be a Yak-9 which is actually more accurate. See Lipfert and Gribig, *The War Diary of Hauptmann Helmut Lipfert*, p. 179.

Soviet 5 VA single-engine fighter losses on 13 November 1944				
Regiment:	**Type:**	**c/n:**	**Pilot:**	**Details:**
122 IAP	Yak-9M	2715382	N. M. Grishaev	Take-off accident (Külső-Kiritó)
149 GvIAP	Yak-9M	3615390	O. T. Kadagidze*	*Missing in dogfight, retuned later*
149 GvIAP	Yak-1B	11186	A. T. Kotlyar POW	Jászberény, 13:55-14:50 LT
149 GvIAP	Yak-1B	42188	Stepanov, returned	Abony-N, 12:55 LT, 6 Bf 109s
150 GvIAP	Yak-3	3529218	N. A. Kireev, WIA	Ócsa, 08:41 LT, 6 Yak, 13 Bf 109s
150 GvIAP	Yak-9D	1815358	N. S. Yegorov	Nagykáta, 11:54 LT, 8 Fw 190s
179 IAP	Yak-9M	2715317	Svistkov, returned	Újszász-E (flak at Jászberény)
179 IAP	Yak-9T	0215354	E. I. Teplishev MIA	Zsámbok-SW, 13:50 LT, 8 Bf 109s
177 GvIAP	La-5FN	41210201	B. G. Kalinin+	Újszász to Halasi Sándor (Bf 109)

* Gv.Lt. Otar Demidovich Kadagidze ran out of fuel and crash-landed this same plane again on 12 March 1945 on a non-combat mission. The engine (No: 432-77) was salvaged but the airframe was written off, Kadagidze was unhurt. After March 1945 his Regiment CO, Gv.Lt.Col. Matvei Ivanovich Zotov flew Yak-3 (c/n: 310315, white '15') until the end of the war.

On 13 November 1944 at 12:55 LT eight 149 GvIAP Yaks were flying above the Jászberény area at 3000m when six JG 52 Bf 109s attacked them from the sun. The hydraulic-system of Ml.Lt. Stepanov's Yak-1B (c/n: 42188, or *42187*) was hit and he crash-landed twenty kilometers North of Abony with one wheel down within Soviet lines. The aircraft's right wheel snapped and the propeller was bent, Ml.Lt. Stepanov returned to his unit on the same day without his plane. His Yak-1B was hit and claimed by Hptm. Lipfert as a 'Yak-3', although it was handed over to 76 OTER on 14 November 1944 and was still in this unit's inventory on 1 January 1945. Tempting as it may be to consider this a victory, the Yak landed within Soviet lines and was operational after the crash, moreover L. V. Blatt Nr. 18/41 clearly states that *'Destruction means burnt out or destroyed so that the aircraft is of no further use to the enemy (destruction has been documented or has been removed so that the enemy cannot repossess it.*'[28] Obfhr. Steins' (6./JG 52) 'Yak-11' claim over Tápiószőlős at 09:06 LT at 4000m also seems to be an overclaim.

16 November 1944 (Thursday)
Lipfert's 151st: VICTORY, 'Yak-11' at 12:39 LT at Tura-W, 5 km, 1500m

Soviet 5 VA single-engine fighter losses on 16 November 1944				
Regiment:	**Type:**	**c/n:**	**Pilot:**	**Details:**
31 GvIAP	Yak-9D	2015370	V. A. Koptelov OK	Jászkisér-E, 12:20 LT, 6 Bf 109s
73 GvIAP	Yak-9D	2015315	A. S.Shuvalov MIA	Jászárokszállás, 4000m, – missing
85 GvIAP	Yak-9D	2015329	Ismail S. Rulev+	Jászberény, 10:10 LT, 8 Bf 109s
122 IAP	Yak-1B	22183	M. I. Sapa unhurt	Külső-Kiritó, LAC at 15:20 LT
122 IAP	Yak-1B	06179	P. G. Artemev+	Hatvan-S, 12:00, 8 Fw 190, Bf 109
122 IAP	Yak-9M	2715305	B. A. Horkin WIA	Törökszentmiklós-SE at 12:00 LT
122 IAP	Yak-9M	2515332	A. M. Znamenev	Hatvan-S area, 12:30, 16 Bf 109s
122 IAP	Yak-9M	2515396	I. C. Babanin MIA	Hatvan-SE area, 12:20, 16 Bf 109s
179 IAP	Yak-1B	12152	M. V. Meshkov	Tiszapüspöki, LAC at 13:55 LT
513 IAP	Yak-9T	1015328	G. D. Yarovoy+	At Hatvan, 10:52LT, 4 *Fw 190*
149 GvIAP	Yak-9M	3615389	V. A. Ustich WIA	Alsódabas-NE, ~09:10 LT, flak
150 GvIAP	Yak-3	1229217	S. G. Yefimenkov	Pécel, 15:15LT, 6Bf 109, 8 Fw 190
150 GvIAP	Yak-3	3429214	A. N. Agdantsev	Isaszeg, 13:42LT, 8 Yak, 4 Bf 109
150 GvIAP	Yak-9D	2315371	G. Y. Bekkerman	Dogfight at Kóka, landing accident
177 GvIAP	La-5	*3921xxxx*	A. D. Dogadailo	*Damaged by Hungarian 101/3. FS.*
177 GvIAP	La-5	*3921xxxx*	G. M. Pyatakov	*Damaged by German Bf 109s*

28 Hugh Morgan, Jürgen Seibel, *Combat Kill: The Drama of Aerial Warfare in World War 2 and the Controversy Surrounding Victories* (Somerset: PSL, 1997), p. 181.

A crash-landed 92 GvShAP Il-2m3 Sturmovik (c/n: 13982, white '79') in Moldavia on 18 December 1945. Note the white edge tail markings of the 5 VA, 4 GvShAD regiments. (Photo: TsAMO RF via Boris Davidov)

Soviet 5 VA single-engine fighter losses on 16 November 1944 (*continued*)				
178 GvIAP	La-5FN	39212952	B. V. Zhigulenkov+	Besenyszög-SE, 6 Bf 109, ~*10:10*
192 IAP	La-5F	39214932	V. M. Olnev WIA	Nagykáta-NE, 14:00LT, 6 *Fw 190*

On 16 November 1944 at 12:20 LT four 122 IAP Yak-9s escorted six 92 GvShAP Il-2 Sturmoviks in the Hatvan-S area at 1200m when sixteen JG 52 Bf 109s attacked. In the uneven fight the Soviet fighter escort's formation was broken resulting in duels between single planes. Soon Ml.Lt. Yosif Dmitrievich Nabeda claimed one Bf 109 then he returned to his base alone as his wingman St.Lt. Znamenev went missing. Ml.Lt. Ivan Constantinovich Babanin was shot down in his Yak-9M, white '96', at around 12:20 LT with no one witnessing what happened to him. It is possible that he fell to the guns of Obgefr. Welz (6./JG 52) at 1200m at Hatvan-S as a 'Yak-11'. Based on the proximity of the claim time, St.Lt. Anatolii Mihailovich Znamenev's Yak-9M, white '32', was shot down by Hptm. Helmut Lipfert over Tura (Hatvan-SW) at 12:30LT. One of the six Il-2s was also shot down by the Bf 109s. Sgt. Nikolai Pavlovich Konyukhov's and Sgt. Anatolii Petrovich Petrov's 92 GvShAP Il-2m3 Sturmovik (c/n: 10618, white '83') went down in flames near Kóka killing its entire crew.

17 November 1944 (Friday)
Lipfert's 152nd: VICTORY, Il-2 at 11:05 LT at Jászberény-S, 6 km, 600m
Lipfert's 153rd: VICTORY, Il-2 at 11:10 LT at Jászberény-NW, 3 km, 400m
Lipfert's 154th: VICTORY, Yak-7[29] at 13:20 LT at Hort (Jászberény-NW, 3 km), 600m

Soviet and Romanian Air Force losses on 17 November 1944 in Hungary				
Regiment:	**Type:**	**c/n:**	**Pilot:**	**Details:**
235 ShAP	Il-2m3	9933	G. K. Denisenko	Debrecen AB, flak, chrashlanded
90 GvShAP	Il-2m3	*10392*	I. P. Kurilov+	Gyöngyöshalász, 11:05 LT, Bf 109
90 GvShAP	Il-2m3	*10618*	V. A. Ivlev WIA	Jászladány-SW, 11:05 LT, Bf 109
90 GvShAP	Il-2m3	*11360*	M. E. Sudorgin	Walked back without his plane
90 GvShAP	Il-2m3	*1872699*	N. V. Halin	Csány, 11:05 LT to Bf 109s
131 GvShAP	Il-2m3	12315	I. V. Derkachev	*Missing on a test flight, returned**
188 GvShAP	Il-2m3	10956	G. S. Tyurikov+	Nagyréde, 13:45 LT, 11 Il-2, 4 Bf
122 IAP	Yak-9M	2715306	V. Boltachev+	Hort, 08:50 LT, 400m, 2 Fw 190s
122 IAP	Yak-9M	2615394	V. N. Gaponov+	Hort, Bf 109, Lipfert at 13:20 LT
179 IAP	Yak-1B	02162	S. G. Purgin MIA	Csány-SE, 12:50 LT, 8 Bf 109s
149 GvIAP	Yak-1B	37191	V. P. Isupov	Kóka-E, 15:00 LT, 4 Fw, 2 Bf 109s
151 GvIAP	Yak-1B	17139	A. V. Noskov MIA	Dány-Tura, 09:40-10:50 LT, 3500m
178 GvIAP	La-5FN	39212821	Lt. Myakinin MIA	Missing, 4 La-5s covering airfield
164 IAP	La-5FN	*39211933*	I. D. Novikov	Bácsalmás, LAC due to Fw 190s
164 IAP	La-5FN	*39212007*	V. S. Svistelnikov	Bácsbokod, CL due to Fw 190s

29 Il-2 acording to Die Geschichte der II. Gruppe des Jagdgeschwaders 52: Offizielle Ausgabe der Traditionsgemeinschaft JG 52, p. 370.

Soviet and Romanian Air Force losses on 17 November 1944 in Hungary (*continued*)				
97 GvNBAP	Po-2/U-2	7352	A. V. Styazhkov	Felsőszentiván, 09:20, 2 '*Bf 109s*'
453 BAP	A-20G-10	42-53956	N. Danielyan WIA	Ócsa, HUN Pottyondy's victim
453 BAP	A-20G-15	42-54223	V. K. Yurchenko	Kevermes-S, weather, mech. failure
Grupul 8 Asalt, Esc.74	Ju 87D-5	141379	Victor Zizda + Const. Pietraru +	Tószeg-SW to Soviet La-5(!) in a friendly-fire incident, wreck found
Grupul 8 Asalt, Esc.74	Ju 87D	*Unknown*	Nicolae Stan WIA Cons. Bleanda WIA	Kengyel, Bagimajor to La-5(!)** in a friendly-fire incident, scrapped

* Il-2, c/n: 12315 was damaged by flak over Kőbánya-W on 2 January 1945 and was sent to 704 PARM.

** On 17 November 1944 six Romanian Ju 87D 'Stukas' returned from their Budapest-S dive-bombing mission when Soviet Lavochkin La-5s misidentified their nationality due to the recent German 'Stuka' attacks in the area and attacked them. In the tragic friendly-fire incident all six 'Stukas' were hit. Two became permanent losses, while the other four (which force landed at Tószeg, Jászkarajenő, Szolnok-S, 8 km and on the Szolnok airfield) were later repaired.

On 17 November 1944 the heavy dogfights continued between Soviet and German-Hungarian planes in the Hatvan-Gyöngyös-Jászberény area. At 11:05 LT six Il-2s of the 90 GvShAP (Kuzin, Ivlev, Halin, Novikov, Kurilov and Ivanov), led by Gv.Maj. Aleksandr Grigorevich Kuzin, escorted by six Yak-9s of the 122 IAP were attacked by Bf 109s in the Hort area. Lipfert opened fire on an Il-2 which caught fire and crashed near Jászárokszállás. Although pilot Gv.Capt. Ivan Prokofevich Kurilov bailed out with his parachute, he died of his wounds two hours after landing. The aerial gunner, Pyotr Mihailovich Ananev, survived the crash and returned to his unit on 20 November 1944. Immeadietly after Lipfert attacked a second Il-2m3 which then crash-landed in the Jászladány-SW area. The plane was written-off, the injured crew consisting of Gv.Ml.Lt. Vasilii Andreevich Ivlev and Vasilii Gavrilovich Petrunin returned to their unit the following day. Finally, between 12:50-14:00 LT four Yak-1Bs (Drozzhikov/22, Kostenko/45, Erko/8, Pugin/5) and two Yak-9Ms (Stadnik/90, Gaponov/94) of the 122 IAP led by Capt. Drozzhikov escorted six Il-2s of the 90 GvShAP at 700m in the Gyöngyös area.[30] After completing their task they turned to Szolnok when Ml.Lt. Victor Nikolaevich Gaponov left his group and went missing. His Yak-9M (c/n: 2615394, engine: 425-455, white '94') was downed at 13:20 LT by Helmut Lipfert in the Hort, Gyöngyös-W area. The Soviet fighters followed the Il-2s back to their base after their attack except for Gaponov who turned around to check the results of their action, when Hptm. Lipfert caught him from below. Lipfert and his wingman Steins did not allow the Yak to turn back to the East to follow his formation, rather they kept him turning for his life at around 300m [sic!] -wasting time and fuel- until he started to trail black smoke and prepared for landing. Near the ground he applied power again and made a last attempt to escape. This final attempt failed and Lipfert saw that the plane touched the ground, skidd through two large haystacks and immediately burst into flames.[31] Lipfert and Steins circled above the

Ml.Lt. Victor Nikolaevich Gaponov (Photo: Gaponov family)

30 The six 90 GvShAP pilots were: Lyadskii, Malev, Lopatin, Lyashenko, Pryazhennikov and Averyanov.

31 Lipfert, Gribig, *The War Diary of Hauptmann Helmut Lipfert*, p. 149.

downed Yak for a few minutes and saw that the canopy did not open and that flames slowly consumed the plane. Fulfilling his military duty, Ml.Lt. Gaponov made the ultimate sacrifice for his homeland at the age of 21. His family, even as late as in 2013, tried to find old witnesses through a local newspaper and contacted the Szolnok Aircraft Museum to find out what happened to their loved one back in 1944.

Finally in the South Fw 190s attacked the Szeged airfield where they became engaged in air combat with Lavochkin La-5s of the 17 VA, 31 IAP that recently moved to Hungary from Yugoslavia. During the dogfight the Soviet pilots claimed two Fw 190s. Ml.Lt. Aleksei Vasilevich Artemov claimed one plane at Szeged-NW, 7 km, Lt. Pyotr Mihailovich Mitrofanov at Szeged-NW, 9 km. While covering the Soviet river crossing on the Danube, La-5s of 164 IAP got into dogfights with probably these same Fw 190s. St.Lt. Ivan Dmitrievich Novikov claimed one plane at Bácsbokod-N, while he and Lt. Vasilii Vasilevich Svistelnikov crash-landed after the mission due to combat damages.

23 November 1944 (Thursday)
Lipfert's 155th: VICTORY, Yak-9 at 10:40 LT at Atkár-SE, 3 km, 800m

<table>
<tr><th colspan="5">Soviet 5 VA permanent single-engine fighter losses on 23 November 1944</th></tr>
<tr><th>Regiment:</th><th>Type:</th><th>c/n:</th><th>Pilot:</th><th>Details:</th></tr>
<tr><td>122 IAP</td><td>Yak-1B</td><td>32161</td><td>E. S. Titov unhurt</td><td>Take off accident at 08:40 LT</td></tr>
<tr><td>513 IAP</td><td>Yak-1B</td><td rowspan="2">29156, 45168</td><td>Y. A. Gopchenko</td><td>Kál-S, 15 km, 10:38 LT, 6 'Fw 190'</td></tr>
<tr><td>513 IAP</td><td>Yak-1B</td><td>P. P. Kuyanov+</td><td>Atkár, 10:38 LT to Helmut Lipfert</td></tr>
</table>

On 23 November 1944 at 10:38 LT six Yaks of the 513 IAP (Malikov, Astashkevich, Gopchenko, Kuyanov and two others) covered six Il-2s of the 809 ShAP in the Rózsaszentmárton area and met six *'Fw 190s'*. Four of them attacked the Yaks, two the Il-2s. After leaving the target Ml.Lt. Pavel Petrovich Kuyanov fell behind his formation and was shot down immediately. His plane fell and crashed near Atkár (Rózsaszentmárton-SE) killing its pilot.

5 December 1944 (Tuesday)
Lipfert's 156th: VICTORY, Yak-9 at 10:30 LT at Hatvan-SE, 5 km, 1500m

Soviet 5 VA single-engine fighter losses on 5 December 1944				
Regiment:	**Type:**	**c/n:**	**Pilot:**	**Details:**
122 IAP	Yak-9T	1615383	M. S. Yerko MIA	Erdőtarcsa, 10:12 LT to Lipfert
122 IAP	Yak-9M	3015336	G. A. Ulanov	Heréd, 15:05 LT, to Heinz Ewald
513 IAP	Yak-1B	20153	I. A. Guriev MIA	Erdőtarcsa, 11:00 LT to Heinz Ewald
151 GvIAP	Yak-3	1529219	Y. Ravikovich+	Ercsi, 14:00 LT, 8 Yaks, to *Fw 190s*
151 GvIAP	Yak-?	*Unknown*	A. A. Morozov	Ercsi area to Bf 109s, Fw 190s*
177 GvIAP	La-5FN	39211776	N. L. Vereshak	Lost to flak, white '76'
177 GvIAP	La-5FN	39212384	I. G. Sklyarov	*Cylinder damage, repaired at base*
177 GvIAP	La-5F	39215215	P. S. Olin	*Stabilizator damage, repaired later*
486 IAP	La-5FN	39212724	V. Snagovskii+	Ercsi, 11:55 LT, 2 La-5, 6 *Fw 190s*

* This is a questionable loss. Since the 13 GvIAD 151 GvIAP record of the day does not mention it, only Morozov's personal record written on 26 April 1945 (TsAMO RF: fu. 33, inv. 690306, storage: 1237-41950045, p. 28b), the date of 5 December 1944 could just be a typo (this is the only known contradicting case).

On 5 December 1944 at 10:12 LT at 1500m six Yak-9s of the 122 IAP escorted ten Il-2s into the Erdőtarcsa area. Over their target, the Soviet planes were attacked by eight Bf 109s, four attacked the Il-2s while four the fighters. During the unfolding dogfight the Bf 109s shot down Ml.Lt. Mihail Semyonovich Yerko's Yak-9T, white '83', which crashed near Hatvan, at Erdőtarcsa-SE. The Soviet pilot went missing. His plane was most likely shot down by Hptm. Helmut Lipfert.

Beside the multiple waves of the 4 GvShAD Il-2s, A-20Gs of the 218 BAD also bombed the German lines in the Erdőtarcsa area. The Soviet aerial support was much needed as anti-tank guns and JPz.IVs of SS-Pz.Jg.Abt.4 halted Dmitry Fedorovich Loza's 46th Guards-Tank Brigade's advancing Shermans and knocked out seven of them. 5 December 1944 was the first day when the brand new 76mm Soviet Shermans suffered heavy losses in Hungary. During their way on the road between Heréd and Vanyarc Shermans of the 1st battalion ran into concentrated anti-tank fire. They tried to find cover along the road but sank in the wet and swampy fields literally becoming 'sitting ducks' for the German guns. The following day the battle continued with further losses.[32]

The other 122 IAP flight was luckier in the air: six of their Yak-1Bs escorting six Il-2s of the 264 ShAD got into aerial battle with six Bf 109s in which Ml.Lt. Victor Mitrofanovich Koltsov, Capt. Aleksandr Grigorevich Klyuev and Capt. Mihail Yakovlevich Storozhenko each claimed a Bf 109 shot down without suffering any losses. The third flight of four 122 IAP Yak-9s, escorting ten Il-2s battled five Bf 109s. Here Ml.Lt. Boris Aleksandrovich Sumskoi claimed one of those shot down.

Beside the heavy battles around Erdőtarcsa, extremely heavy dogfights developed in the skies around Ercsi (Budapest-S) over the new Danube river-crossing of the Soviet 46th Army, where the Soviets began their push West of the Danube. The plan was to make a rapid move to the North with strong armoured forces and by joining forces of the 2nd Ukrainian Front advancing from the East, encircling the Hungarian capital Budapest. The operation was extremely difficult costing the Soviets thousands of lives and lots of equipment.[33] The Luftwaffe regularly showed up over the area to strike and bomb the pontoon bridges and the developing West-bank bridgehead. Hundreds fell and disappeared in the cold river upon the fighter-bomber attacks of Fw 190s. In this critical situation the fighters of the 5 VA were given the task of providing aerial support to the crossing ground forces, to repel and destroy every enemy aircraft that was approaching the bridgehead. Due to the limited fuel capacity of the Soviet fighters, they flew in smaller groups over the aera in a rotating manner. When the planes were low on fuel, they returned to their base for refueling while the next flight protected the area. The Soviet pilots flew multiple sorties during the day while often confronting formations of the enemy.

During one of these dogfights a flight of four 150 GvIAP Yak-3s partolled the Ercsi area. Southwest of Ercsi they intercepted twelve Junkers Ju 88G night fighters /bombers of NJG 6 escorted by six Bf 109s which attacked the Soviet forces in the Kaposvár, Szekszárd, Székesfehérvár-S areas. Pair-leader Gv.St.Lt. Aleksei Ivanovich Proskurin, with the cover of his wingman Gv.Lt. Yuri Dmitrievich Orlov, immediately opened fire on a Ju 88 and it shot down over Göböljárás North of Iváncsa. The Ju 88G started to lose altitude and finally crashed in the middle of Lake Balaton in the line of Balatonföldvár with Oblt. Helmut Buder's crew onboard en route back home to the airfield of Vát, Szombathely-E.[34] Yak-3 pair of Gv.Lt. Ivan Nikitovich Tabakov was also called to the Ercsi-Ráckeve area where they met six Fw 190s and two Bf 109s.[35] Despite being outnumbered – by their estimations 4:1 by the enemy – they went into an attack. From a distance of 50m Tabakov opened fire on one of the Fw 190s which crashed near Ercsi, while his wingman claimed one of the Bf 109s. Flying at the altitude of 1000m, the other Yak-3 pair of Efremenko-Mironchenko (149 GvIAP) also intercepted two strafing Bf 109s over the Ercsi bridgehead. Gv.Lt. Ilya Fedorovich Efremenko opened fire on one of the Bf 109s from a distance of 50m and shot it down, while Gv.St.Lt. Victor Pavlovich Ryazhankin from his flight of four 149 GvIAP Yaks downed a Fw 190 from the distance of only 40-50m. Gv.Maj. Salva Nesterovich Kiriya and Gv.Capt. Yegor Vasilevich Vasilevskii from the 151 GvIAP each claimed a Fw 190.[36] Despite the heavy non-stop combat over the Ercsi bridgehead it is entirely possible that many of these Soviet claims were only damaged planes, not real victories. However, Ercsi was not the only bridgehead where forces of the 3rd Ukrainian Front were moving over to the West side of the Danube. They crossed the Danube at Mohács and in Croatia as well whose forces were advancing to the North towards Lake Balaton and Székesfehérvár. During their push on 5 December 1944 near Keszőhidegkút the 18 Tank Corps' 170th Tank Brigade's T-34/85, No.'502' collapsed a small bridge over the Kapos canal which fell into the water and sank. The driver, St.Sgt. Aleksei Vasilevich Truhachev could not get out from the sunken tank in time and tragically drowned.

9 December 1944 (Saturday)
Lipfert's 157th: VICTORY, Il-2 at 15:05 LT at Csajág-SW, 2 km, 1200m

32 Lost 2nd Ukr. Front, 9 GvMK, 46 GvTBr M4A2 Sherman tanks: U.S.A. 3080762/'3', 3080791/'5', 3080561/'7', 3080929/'9', 3080311/'11', 3080241/'13', 3080330/'17', 3056452/'21', 3038972/'25', etc.

33 The total number of Soviet casualties during the entire Ercsi operation totaled between 3700-4000 men.

34 The plane was a Ju 88G-1 of 7./NJG 6, marked '2Z+BR', WNr.: 714628. The crew of Buder-Jentsch-Böhler was KIA. The wrecks of the plane were found in 1995 as the tip of its vertical stabilizer was only 1.5m under the surface. The restored plane is now on display in Berlin as the only known Junkers Ju 88G-1 night fighter in the world, while some of its original parts were retained in the Szolnok Aircraft Museum.

35 Gv.Lt. Ivan Nikitovich Tabakov (150 GvIAP, 1st Squadron) was shot down and killed in a dogfight on 20 February 1945 at 11:15 LT in his Yak-3 (c/n: 2129219, white '21') as Reg. CO Yakimenko's (Yak-3, white '360') wingman.

36 Gv.Capt. Yegor Vasilevich Vasilevskii was downed by error by Soviet flak on 17 April 1945 after 18:00 LT while leading his eight Yak-9s against eight Bf 109s and 24 Fw 190s, claiming two of them. He gave the command to his group, left the battle and crash-landed his 151 GvIAP Yak-9U (c/n: 42166074, engine: 427-100) at Rapovice, Cz. The plane was scrapped, Vasilevskii remained unhurt.

Soviet 5 and 17 VA Il-2 Sturmovik losses on 9 December 1944				
Regiment:	**Type:**	**c/n:**	**Pilot:**	**Details:**
187 GvShAP	Il-2m3	11010	G. V. Miheichev	Ercsi-SW, CL, flak, fighters, '74'
188 GvShAP	Il-2m3	303021	*Unknown, 1st Sq.*	*Combat damages, repaired at base*
451 ShAP	Il-2m3	11412	N. S. Pavlyutin	Ground acc. with a landing Po-2
989 ShAP	Il-2m3	10301	V. Veretelnikov MIA	Csajág-Úrhida-SW, flak, Bf 109s

On 9 December 1944 around 14:30 LT six 989 ShAP Il-2s attacked ground targets in the Csajág-Úrhida area. After the attacks the planes encountered twelve Bf 109s and anti-aircraft artillery fire. Flying over Csajág, the Bf 109s attacked flight-commander Lt. Mihail Ivanovich Sintsov's Il-2 (c/n: probably 11607, white '17'), but his aerial gunner St.Sgt. Sergei Ivanovich Dolgov managed to repel all attacks. While the escorting 659 IAP Yak-9Ds were chasing the enemy fighters, Helmut Lipfert managed to shoot down one of the unprotected Il-2s. The Il-2 crashed, its pilot Ml.Lt. Vasilii Ivanovich Veretelnikov and aerial gunner Grigorii Nikolaevich Bezrukov went missing.

11 December 1944 (Monday)
Lipfert's 158th: VICTORY, Pe-2 at 14:53 LT at Balatonkenese (Balaton-SE, 5 km), 4500m

Soviet 17 VA Pe-2 and Il-2 Sturmovik losses on 11 December 1944				
Regiment:	**Type:**	**c/n:**	**Pilot:**	**Details:**
39 ORAP	Pe-2R	6/235	V. R. Elohov+, 3+	In Lake Balaton at Balatonkenese
615 ShAP	Il-2m3	18891106	A. M. Turkadze	Lókút-SE, 2nd Sq.
615 ShAP	Il-2m3	18867106	Y. H. Markoch+	Pusztamiske-E to Bf 109s
615 ShAP	Il-2m3	188100106	V. N. Kotov	*Later returned, 2nd Sq.*
615 ShAP	Il-2m3	18843111	F. N. Kligun	*Later returned, 2nd Sq.*
615 ShAP	Il-2m3	18897106	I. F. Brankov	*Later returned, 3rd Sq.*
615 ShAP	Il-2m3	10496	D. S. Gnatchenko	*Later returned, 2nd Sq.*
707 ShAP	Il-2m3	1873594	V. M. Efimov+	Gospođinci, out of fuel, crashed
715 ShAP	Il-2m3	11404	I. S. Voinov	Szabadbattyán-E, 10:14 to Bf 109
989 ShAP	Il-2m3	11535	P. T. Kaplienko	Székesfehérvár-S,11:36 to Bf 109

On 11 December 1944 Pe-2s and Yak-9s of 39 ORAP flew reconnaissance missions in the Lake Velence, Lake Balaton, Veszprém, Tapolca and Seregélyes areas. Lt. Vladimir Radionovich Elohov's Pe-2R (c/n: 6/235, engine: 345-1391 and 415-1996) was photographing enemy activities in the Lake Balaton area when Hptm. Lipfert and his wingman, Uffz.

Crew of 39 ORAP Pe-2 (c/n: 6/235) that Hptm. Lipfert downed over Lake Balaton on 11 December 1944. The pilot, Vladimir Radionovich Elohov is sitting on the left. (Photo: Rad, Moscow)

Gerhard Brandecker spotted them patrolling over the lake.[37] The Pe-2 crew sent their last radio message signaling that they

37 TsAMO RF: fu. 370, inv. 6518, f. 343, p. 204, Operations journal of 39 ORAP for December, 1944, entry for 11 December 1944.

17 VA, 189 ShAD, 639 ShAP, 2nd Sq. pilot, Lt. Mihail Efimovich Aksengor in the cockpit of his Il-2m3 Sturmovik (probably No.'19') before a mission. On 22 December 1944 his Il-2m3 (c/n: 18756101, AM-38F engine: 258460) was seriousely damaged by JG 52 fighters just North of Székesfehérvár and was lost on the Madocsa airfield during crash landing. His plane was a potential victim of Hptm. Helmut Lipfert as his 159th aerial victory. (Photo: Capt. N. Gavrilov in the 17 VA's daily frontline newspaper called: 'Защитник отечества' (Defender of the Fatherland)

completed their task at 14:30 LT and were never heard from again. Hptm. Lipfert was already on his way back home when he spotted the lonely Pe-2 flying westbound over Lake Balaton at about 5000m. The two German Bf 109s approached the unsuspecting Soviet plane from below. When they got close to the plane, the Soviets realized the danger and dived and turned in order to escape back East. Tishenko's tracers passed Lipfert's cockpit at close range but were not able to suppress Lipfert's cannon fire. Only two of Lipfert's 30mm cannon shells hit the Soviet plane yet these were enough to destroy it.[38] The Pe-2 exploded mid-air, its debris falling over the lake West of Balatonkenese and killing its entire crew.

Lt. Vladimir Radionovich Elohov pilot (№125886, +)
Lt. Ivan Efimovich Uhvatov observer (№125866, +)
St.Sgt. Victor Sergeevich Tishenko radioman/gunner (+)

At the same time Il-2s of the 189 ShAD, escorted by Yak-9s of the 866 IAP, attacked Tapolca at Lake Balaton-N,-NW; Il-2s of the 136 ShAD attacked the Székesfehérvár area. The remains of Lt. Elohov's Pe-2 were recovered from Lake Balaton in September of 1994 with its left wingtip now on display in the Szolnok Aircraft Museum.

22 December 1944 (Friday)
Lipfert's 159th: POTENTIAL VICTORY, Il-2 at 9:37LT at Székesfehérvár-N, 6 km

Soviet 17 VA Il-2 Sturmovik losses on 22 December 1944				
Regiment:	**Type:**	**c/n:**	**Pilot:**	**Details:**
639 ShAP	Il-2m3	1876296	N. S. Baklanov	Pátka-SW, Bf 109s, crash-landed
639 ShAP	Il-2m3	18756101	M. E. Aksengor	Pátka-SW, Bf 109, Madocsa, CL
639 ShAP	Il-2m3	*11249*	M. P. Ratnikov+	Pátka-Zámoly to Bf 109s
639 ShAP	Il-2m3	*1871698*	V. T. Montrezor	Pátka-SW to Bf 109s
639 ShAP	Il-2m3	*1876996*	G. Semenov POW	Pátka-SW to Bf 109s
639 ShAP	Il-2m3	11271	M. A. Pletnev	Pátka-SW to Bf 109s
672 ShAP	Il-2m3	1871398	*Sizikov?*	*Damaged, repaired at airbase*
672 ShAP	Il-2m3	1870288	A. M. Kianovskii	Kecel, airbase accident at 12:10LT
672 ShAP	Il-2m3	1872184	I. M. Baranov KIFA	Kecel, airbase accident at 12:10LT
672 ShAP	Il-2m3	18763100	E. V. Vaitsitskii	Kecel, 15:00LT, burned at landing
672 ShAP	Il-2m3	1879466	*Unknown*	*Flak damage, repaired at airbase*
672 ShAP	Il-2m3	*Unknown*	P. A. Kuzmin	Székesfehérvár flak, 13:00, at base
707 ShAP	Il-2m3	11649	N. P. Mironov	Székesfehérvár-N, 14:50, 2 Bf 109
951 ShAP	Il-2m3	1883301	N. B. Baronin+	Csákvár-NE, 09:40 LT, Flakpanzer

38 Lipfert, Gribig, *The War Diary of Hauptmann Helmut Lipfert*, p. 153.

Pilots of 639 ShAP (L-R): Lt. Aleksandr Nikitovich Starshinov of the 3rd (white) squadron and Lt. Ivan Petrovich Razin (1922-1996, HSU) of the 1st (red) squadron with his aerial gunner, St.Sgt. Ilya Stephanovich Ivanov. Taking off from Madocsa with eight Il-2s to targets at Galambospuszta, Lt. Razin crash-landed his flak damaged Il-2m3 (c/n: 1884001, probably No.'5', AM-38F engine: 257919) on the Kiskunlacháza airfield on 25 January 1945. On 20 March 1945 on his 85th Il-2 combat mission he was almost shot down by flak over Szabadbattyán.* Lt. Starshinov crash-landed at least two Il-2s in Hungary: c/n: 11109 (AM-38F engine: 257966) at Dunaföldvár-N on 18 January 1945 and c/n: 11139 (AM-38F engine: 258798) at Paks on 3 February 1945. (Photos: Capt. N. Gavrilov in the 22 June 1945 issue of the 17 VA's daily frontline newspaper: 'Защитник отечества' (Defender of the Fatherland) (*TsAMO RF: fu. 33, inv. 793756, storage 40, record 150027484, p. 26, Personal records, entry for pilot Lt. Ivan Petrovich Razin of 639 ShAP, entry for 20 March 1945, signed by Lt.Col. Tsurkan, commander of 639 ShAP on 2 April 1945.)

Soviet 17 VA Il-2 Sturmovik losses on 22 December 1944 (*continued*)				
951 ShAP	Il-2m3	1873693	P. Marakulin+	Near L. Velence to Flakpanzer
951 ShAP	Il-2m3	1884401	G. P. Odnotsenov	Near L. Velence, Bf 109, 11:50 LT
951 ShAP	Il-2m3	11118	Y. P. Vaslyanin	Flak, AM-38F No.257973 salvaged
995 ShAP	Il-2m3	*1874686*	A. I. Groshev ret.	Dinnyés-NW, 10:30 LT to Bf 109
995 ShAP	Il-2m3	*1886603*	N. S. Shepochkin	Gyulamajor, 10:30 LT to Bf 109
995 ShAP	Il-2m3	*1875696*	V. I. Seregin+	Zámoly-NE, 10:30 LT to flak

On 22 December 1944 six Ilyushin Il-2m3s of 639 ShAP took off from Őcsény to attack German armour and artillery targets in the Székesfehérvár-N, Pátka area. Although the Soviet formation was successful in carrying out its task, the fire of the German anti-aircraft artillery and Bf 109 fighters destroyed them shortly afterwards. Some planes crashed in the target area at Székesfehérvár-N,-NE, others crash-landed at various locations and were scrapped later. Based on the available mission records, one of them could be Hptm. Lipfert's legitimate aerial victory in the Székesfehérvár area, but due to the multiple options the exact identity of his 639 ShAP victim cannot be determined.

23 December 1944 (Saturday)

Lipfert's 160th: VICTORY, Yak-9 at 10:48 LT at Enying-S, 7 km

Soviet 17 VA single-engine fighter losses on 23 December 1944				
Regiment:	**Type:**	**c/n:**	**Pilot:**	**Details:**
611 IAP	Yak-9M	2515324	G. A. Alaverdov	Pátka, Bf 109s, crashed at Taszár AB
659 IAP	Yak-9D	1915323	N. V. Salamatov	Moha-N, Bf 109s, crashed at base
39 ORAP	Yak-9D	16166055	V. Dementev WIA	Madocsa to 6 Bf 109s, scrapped
31 IAP	La-5F	3810933	V.N. Yakovlev+	Vál-Baracska, Bf 109s, Fw 190s
164 IAP	La-5F	39214786	N. V. Mozgov	Bellye, lost orientation, CL

On 23 December 1944 Yakovlev fighters of 17 VA, 288 IAD, 611 IAP covered Soviet ground forces in the Pátka area. En route home to Taszár airbase at Lake Balaton-S, near Enying, the Soviet fighters were attacked by Bf 109s where a Yak-9M (c/n: 2515324, engine: 425-111) was damaged. The Yak-9M crash-landed at Taszár airbase and was written off, but pilot Ml.Lt. Georgii Artemovich Alaverdov remained unhurt.

Not far from Enying over Csajág, Yak-9D pair of Lt. Nikolai Nikolaevich Ribakov and Ml.Lt. Vladimir Dementevich Dementev of 39 ORAP, 3rd Squadron fought a fierce dogfight with six Bf 109s. The Soviet reconnaissance-pair patrolled at 200m in the Lake Balaton – Lake Velence area when six Bf 109s attacked them. During the first strike two Bf 109s separated from the group and re-positioned for a second strike. The remaining four Bf 109s concentrated their attack on Ml.Lt. Dementev's plane (Yak-9D, c/n: 16166055, engine: 415-373) which injured the pilot and seriously damaged his plane. Ml.Lt. Dementev went down to ground level and at around 20m he claimed one of the Bf 109s of the first pair and then returned to Madocsa. His damaged plane was not subject to repair and was finally scrapped.[39] After this the 39 ORAP had 14 Pe-2s, 8 Yak-9s and 3 Po-2s left. Since both battles took place near each other it is difficult to tell which Yak-9 fell to Hptm. Lipfert's guns, but because both planes were permanently lost, Hptm. Lipfert's Yak-9 claim for 23 December 1944 can be verified as a confirmed aerial victory.

24 December 1944 (Sunday)
Lipfert's 161st: OVERCLAIM, Il-2 at 14:25 LT at Seregélyes-N, 2 km

Soviet 5 and 17 VA Il-2 Sturmovik losses on 24 December 1944				
Regiment:	**Type:**	**c/n:**	**Pilot:**	**Details:**
615 ShAP	Il-2m3	11571	A. N. Kudryavtsev	Szár, flak to Adony-S, 10:55 LT
615 ShAP	Il-2m3	*Unknown*	V. A. Guk WIA	Bodajk
639 ShAP	Il-2m3	11274	S. K. Palva	*Pátka, flak to Őcsény, repaired*
672 ShAP	Il-2m3	1876188	*Unknown*	*Combat damage, repaired at base*
672 ShAP	Il-2m3	1889801	N. N. Dyakonov+	Szabadszállás, flak, LAC, 08:30 LT
707 ShAP	Il-2m3	11368	G. V. Valuev	Bodajk flak, 16:20 LT, missing
707 ShAP	Il-2m3	11132	S. T. Gudkov	Zámoly flak, 16:02 LT, Sárbogárd
707 ShAP	Il-2m3	10270	N. I. Punkevich	Söréd-Bodajk, 11:07 LT, missing
707 ShAP	Il-2m3	11350	A.N. Denisenko '23'	Bodajk, Bf 109, Szekszárd, 11:03 LT
995 ShAP	Il-2m3	10170	M. S. Akopian	Csákberény flak to Baglyas-W, 09:22
995 ShAP	Il-2m3	1871394	L. A. Kosobian	Érsckcsanád, TOA at 07:34 LT, '17'
131 GvShAP	Il-2m3	1872385	S. I. Allenov+	Rákóczifalva-N, 08:30 LT, KIFA
188 GvShAP	Il-2m3	8860	Y. P. Tsukerov WIA	Explosion of two bombs at take off
188 GvShAP	Il-2m3	1875470	Gv.St.Lt. Shevelev	Flak damages, repaired on airfield
235 ShAP	Il-2m3	10403	K. A. Nadezhdin	Near target, 14:05 LT, to 4 fighters
90 GvShAP	Il-2m3	10337	P. K. Fesenko	Nagyoroszi-N, 11:00 LT, 6 Fw 190s
90 GvShAP	Il-2m3	10941	I. M. Lyashenko+	Nagykőrös-E, 8./SG10-Goetze, 11:05
92 GvShAP	Il-2m3	9977	V. A. Bocharov, '70'	Szakállas, 12:45 LT, in mid-air-coll. '85' was hit by flak & flew into '70'
92 GvShAP	Il-2m3	10125	I. G. Kovalev+, '85'	

On 24 December 1944 at 14:25 LT Hptm. Helmut Lipfert reported an Il-2 shot down 2 km North of Seregélyes, Székesfehérvár-S. This location was right in the middle of the operational area of the 17 VA, 189 ShAD Il-2 regiments attacking the Bodajk-Zámoly-Csákvár area from the South. Although these regiments (615, 639, 707 ShAP) flew missions throughout the day, none of the 17 VA Il-2 regiments reported permanent Il-2 losses this time of the day. The 615 ShAP daily combat report however reveals that after leaving its target of Bodajk-Sárkeresztes at around 14:00 LT, deputy commander of the 3rd squadron Lt. Nikolai Andreevich Troshilov observed two Bf 109s attacking an Il-2 which was wearing the '25 лет Башкирии' inscription on its fuselage. The damaged plane which was losing altitude and trailing black smoke crossed Székesfehérvár and kept flying low towards the South. More details could not be observed due to the smoke and the poor December visibility in the afternoon. From this combat report we also know that this plane was Lt. Vladimir Afanasevich Guk's 1st Sq. Il-2m3, with which the severely wounded crew landed saftely on their Madocsa-S airfield.[40] Since the plane was later repaired, no c/n was recorded. Lt. Guk was later shot down and killed by flak in the Prater-SE area in Vienna, Austria on 10 April 1945 in his Il-2m3, c/n: 11233. For these reasons Hptm. Lipfert's Il-2 claim on this day should be considered an overclaim. The attack on the Bodajk-Fehérvárcsurgó area between 13:48-14:00 LT was carried out by fifteen Il-2s of the 615 ShAP led by Lt. Vitaliy Mihailovich Frolov. The fighter escort was provided by six Yaks of the 897 IAP, led by Capt. Daniil Gavrilovich Barchenkov. The Soviet fighter escort suffered no losses. The opponents at 13:50 LT were reported to be eleven Bf 109s flying at 800m which lost two fighters at Fehérvárcsurgó-S, 3 km to Capt. Daniil Gavrilovich Barchenkov. One of them could be Bf 109G-6, WNr.: 441028, yellow '8' (Uffz. Fritz Grabbert+, 5./JG 52).

39 Ml.Lt. Dementev later flew Yak-9R (c/n: 07-013) and Yak-9M (c/n: 3415301) in which he died on 22 March 1945 in a landing accident at Jakabszállás airfield afer returning from combat mission.

40 TsAMO RF: fu. 22823, inv. 209365c, f. 2, pp. 159-160, Operations report of 615 ShAP staff, entry for 24 December 1944. Also at TsAMO RF: fu. 33, inv. 690306, Storage 1457, record 39489430, p. 65, Personal records of 189 ShAD personnel, entry for pilot Lt. Vladimir Afanasevich Guk of 615 ShAP, entry for 24 December 1944, signed on 17 January 1945.

25 December 1944 (Monday)
Lipfert's 162nd: VICTORY, Yak-9 at 12:08 LT at Székesfehérvár-NW, 9 km
Lipfert's 163rd: VICTORY, Yak-9 at 12:15 LT at Mór-SE, 3 km

Soviet 17 Air Army permanent single-engine fighter losses on 25 December 1944*				
Type:	c/n:	Mission(LT)	Pilot:	Details:
Yak-9M 611 IAP	2715376	11:05-11:55 Zámoly, Moha	G. Alaverdov WIA	Székesfehérvár-N, crash-landed, Bf 109s
	2715372 2715374		A. T. Fadeev	Dinnyés, Batarov's 7 Yak, vs. 4 Bf 109
		11:40-12:30 Csákvár, Moha, Zámoly	Ivan I. Aleshkin	Székesfehérvár-N, crash-landed, Bf 109s
Yak-9T 611 IAP	1115364		Dmitrii Gavrilovich Kirichenko+	Csákvár-Zámoly, Churilin's wingman Engine: 345-253, written off by 27th
Yak-1B 611 IAP	05193 14177 15150		N.N. Kutsenko WIA	Zámoly, Bf 109, bailed out, burned
		14:55-15:45 Székesfehérvár	Boris Aleksandrovich Yavlyukhin	Székesfehérvár-N, 8km, CL to 4 Bf 109s, returned on 27 December 1944
	44172		Capt. Konstantin L. Chernogor KIA	Csala, led by Capt. Batarov, 8 Yak, vs. 4 Bf 109, Maj. Isaenko flew 41 times
Yak-9D 659 IAP	16166065	Mór, Il-2 escort	Pavel A. Gorlach MIA	Vértesszőlős, during 189 ShAD Il-2 escort to Mór, missing
Yak-9D	16166092	Börgönd	?, 96 OKRAP	Later returned, engine: 415-124
La-5FN 56 IAP	39211251	A-20 escort 13:06-07 LT	A.V. Rogachev+	Smederevo-S, Serbia. The A-20 lost orientation, the two La-5s force landed
	39211606		F. I. Romanenkov	
La-5 164 IAP	39214786 41210113	18 Il-2 escort 13:00-14:00	R. I. Alekseenko B. I. Shilov	4 La-5s, led by Capt. Zaitsev. Separated from the group, went missing. No flak.

* On 25 December 1944 the 17 VA also removed 14 old Yak-1Bs from combat service due to wear and tear (02176, 03170, 05158, 09171, 13150, 14180, 19157, 32152, 33151, 35157, 40152, 41166, 47147, 48158). These planes were not repaired due to the large number of incoming Yak-3s, waiting for being distributed among the fighter regiments in the 17 VA reserve.

On Christmas day, 25 December 1944, heavy dogfights developed between German and Soviet fighters in the Zámoly, Székesfehérvár and Mór areas. Between 11:40-12:30 LT six 611 IAP Yak-1B and Yak-9 (Capt. Churilin – Kirichenko, Rizhov – Aleshkin, Kutsenko – Yegorov), led by Capt. Churilin covered Soviet ground troops in the Csákvár-Zámoly-Moha area. Dogfights erupted when ten Bf 109s attacked from above with a significant speed advantage. In the battle Helmut Lipfert downed a Yak-9M and a Yak-9T at 12:08 and 12:15 LT respectively near Székesfehérvár and Mór. First Lt. Nikolai Nikolaevich Kutsenko's, then Ml.Lt. Ivan Ivanovich Aleshkin's plane was shot down. Kutsenko bailed out and landed among Soviet troops with severe burns while Aleshkin belly landed safely and returned to his own unit. The

A downed 611 IAP Yak-1B, white '20' near Székesfehérvár, Hungary in January 1945. Tail markings of the 611 IAP were similar to the ones used by 236 IAD, because until 19 September 1944 the regiment belonged to 236 IAD. However, on 19 September 1944 in Burgas, Bulgaria, the 611 IAP was transferred to the 288 IAD, making it a significant four-regiment division within the 17 VA, soon to enter into Hungary. The 236 IAD with its three remaining regiments (267 IAP, 117, 168 GvIAP) moved to Yugoslavia. Their surviving planes at the end of the war were handed over to the newly organized Yugoslavian Air Force. (Photo: Karai Sándor, Hungarian war correspondent)

Messerschmitts regained altitude and during their second attack the commander, Capt. Churilin, lost his wingman. Ml.Lt. Dmitrii Gavrilovich Kirichenko's Yak-9T (c/n: 1115364) went down in flames in the Zámoly-NW, Mór area.

Beside the Bf 109s of II./JG 52, Fw 190Fs of 3./SG 10 were also successful this day. At 12:20 LT at Zsámbék-E Oblt. Norbert Schmitt downed a Soviet 'R-5' biplane. This plane was in fact a Po-2 of the 17 VA, 282 OAPS (c/n: 14821, M-11 engine: 00532) which – according to Soviet records – was attacked by six enemy fighters during landing near Zsámbék at *12:25* LT and was set on fire after coming to a stop. The plane burned, but pilot Ml.Lt. Vasilii Fedotovich Afanasev and his passenger Maj. Konratev both survived the incident.

2 January 1945 (Tuesday)

Lipfert's 164th: POTENTIAL VICTORY, LaGG-5 at 11:15 LT at Bodmér-E

Lipfert's 165th: VICTORY, Yak-9 at 11:45 LT at Vereb-E, 4 km

Soviet 17 VA single-engine fighter losses on 2 January 1945				
Regiment:	**Type:**	**c/n:**	**Pilot:**	**Details:**
31 IAP	La-5FN	39211844	D.S. Kravtsov WIA	Dág, after 10:45 LT, 4 *Bf 109s*
116 IAP	La-5	*Unknown*	A. I. Roy returned	Tata, 8 La-5, Bf 109s, crash-landed
116 IAP	La-5	*Unknown*	A. N. Belkin WIA	*Damaged in dogfight, returned**
611 IAP	Yak-9T	2515318	G. S. Gladkii WIA	Bánhida, 12:20 LT, 6-8 *Fw 190s*
611 IAP	Yak-9T	2515334	P. Y. Dimov+	Tata-SE, 2 km, 10:55 LT
659 IAP	Yak-9T	2515315	Y. A. Vinogradov	Makád-S, 2 km, 08:05 LT, 1500m
659 IAP	Yak-9D	16166093	I. P. Trusin WIA	Tata, 08:05 LT, 1500m, 8 Bf 109s
897 IAP	Yak-9T	0815352	V. E. Novikov+	Vereb-W, 11:30, 2000m, 4 Bf 109s
897 IAP	Yak-9T	0815357	V. M. Gorbunov	Tata, 12:20LT, 8 Bf 109s, on airfield

* A total of six 295 IAD La-5s were damaged in dogfights, but all returned and were repaired later. (TsAMO RF: fu. 20541, inv. 1, f. 83, p. 77.)

On 2 January 1945 La-5s of 17 VA, 295 IAD fought heavy dogfights with German-Hungarian fighters in the Tata-Neszmély Bicske-Budapest area. Two La-5s were shot down (Maj. Kravtsov and Ml.Lt. Roy), six others including Capt. Aleksandr Nikitovich Belkin (wounded, 116 IAP) were damaged in air combat.

Maj. Dmitrii Stephanovich Kravtsov (1916-1996, HSU in his 31 IAP Lavochkin La-5FN, c/n: 39211844, ASh-82FN engine: 8212412, white '44') with his flight of four La-5s (Kravtsov, Tsikin, Kalinin and Soloviev) escorted eighteen Il-2s in the Budapest-NW area when eight Bf 109s attacked them. At 10:45 LT the attack of four of the Bf 109s separated him from his group and downed him over Dág, Budapest-NW. The Soviet pilot bailed out but was seriously injured.

St.Lt. Victor Victorovich Vitkovich with his 17 VA, 288 IAD, 897 IAP Yakovlev Yak-3 in Austria, 1945. On 2 January 1945 he claimed an Fw 190 South of Tolna with his previous Yak-9. This Yak-3, however, was assigned to the 897 IAP only by 26 April 1945 from factory No.31 and was still in the 897 IAP by 1 July 1945. Note the large typical factory No.31-applied fuselage number (the last two digits of the plane's c/n: 310518.) In February-March 1945 St.Lt. Vitkovich temporarily flew in the 659 IAP as well. (Photo: Dmitri Karlenko)

Ml.Lt. Aleksei Ignatevich Roy as a member of a flight of eight La-5s led by Capt. Polikarp Andreevich Kalchenko was covering Soviet ground troops in the Tata area. He was downed by enemy fighters, crash-landed unhurt and retuned to his base the next day. Unfortunately neither the location, nor the exact time of his crash is known, but Bodmér, Helmut Lipfert's reported victory area, was right on the flight-path of these La-5s between Tata and their Budapest-S airfields.[41] Thus we can count this claim as a potential victory for Hptm. Lipfert.

Later during the day, Hptm. Lipfert downed an 897 IAP Yak-9T near Vereb, which crashed at Pátka, Zámoly-SE 3 km, at around 11:30 LT. The pilot, flight-commander Ml.Lt. Vasilii Ermolaevich Novikov was buried in Pátka.

4 January 1945 (Thursday)
Lipfert's 166th: POTENTIAL VICTORY, Il-2 at 08:26 LT at Tarján-S, 6 km
Lipfert's 167th: POTENTIAL VICTORY, Il-2 at 08:28 LT at Tarján-SW, 5 km
Lipfert's 168th: VICTORY, Yak-9 at 10:41 LT at Bicske-NW, 6 km
Lipfert's 169th: VICTORY, LaGG-5 at 11:12 LT at Tardos-SW, 1 km

Soviet 17 VA Il-2 and single-engine fighter losses on 4 January 1945				
Regiment:	**Type:**	**c/n:**	**Pilot:**	**Details:**
210 ShAP	Il-2m3	18704106	I. A. Balakin	Bajna, downed by Bf 109s, '36'
210 ShAP	Il-2m3	12054	S. M. Kolobkov	Bia-W, flak, '5'
210 ShAP	Il-2m3	10967	L. A. Philippovich	Bicske-W, '30'
210 ShAP	Il-2m3	12052	N. I. Sokolov	Csepel-N, 1 km, flak, '7'
210 ShAP	Il-2m3	10987	L. K. Vorobiev	Kiskunlacháza, flak, CL, '15'
210 ShAP	Il-2m3	304836	V. V. Ivanov	Mány-N, CL, '2'
210 ShAP	Il-2m3	18853106	I. M. Pavlov	Mány-NW, CL,'35',crew returned
210 ShAP	Il-2m3	11425	N. P. Ivanov*	Bajót-E, to Bf 109s at Bajna, '24'
210 ShAP	Il-2m3	10930	*V. K. Mihailyuk*	*Combat damages, repaired, '210'*
639 ShAP	Il-2m3	1870197	I. Y. Tarabrin	*Tarján, flak, – repaired*
639 ShAP	Il-2m3	*Unknown*	K. A. Gusev	Bánhida, flak, crash at Börgönd
639 ShAP	Il-2m3	*11262*	A. I. Kozhin	Bánhida, flak to Székesfehérvár
672 ShAP	Il-2m3	1871398	?, returned	*Damaged in combat, – repaired*
707 ShAP	Il-2m3	304822	S. V. Pigalev	Martonvásár, crash-landed
715 ShAP	Il-2m3	11511	N. I. Soroka MIA	Budapest-SW, flak, '15'
715 ShAP	Il-2m3	11536	N.D. Moskvitchev+	Sárisáp-W, 08:22 LT, '21', Bf 109
951 ShAP	Il-2m3	1874287	N. A. Samoilov	Héreg-NW, 08:00LT, MIA
951 ShAP	Il-2m3	1870194	M. P. Petrakov	Héreg-NW, 08:05 LT, flak at 200m
989 ShAP	Il-2m3	10430	I. A. Dzhanaev	Bajna, Bf 109, Herceghalom,'20'
989 ShAP	Il-2m3	11413	M. K. Artazian	Kiskunlacháza, Bf 109, '38'
989 ShAP	Il-2m3	12515	N. A. Bachurin	*Combat damages, repaired, '28'*
166 GvShAP	Il-2m3	1873995	A. P. Dudkin+	Bačka Palanka, flak at 10:36 LT, crash in mid-air collision
166 GvShAP	Il-2m3	*Unknown*	P. I. Buzrukov+	
530 IAP	La-5F	39215048	M. Y. Yefimov	Bicske-SE, 14:55 LT, to Bf 109s
530 IAP	La-5FN	39211920	F. F. Orlovskii	Bicske, Bf 109, crashed at Cece
530 IAP	La-5FN	39211023	A. P. Dyakov+	Vasztély, 09:30 LT, 8 *Fw 190*
530 IAP	La-5FN	39211488	I. P. Vashenko	Martonvásár, 10:30 LT, 8 Bf 109
530 IAP	La-5FN	39211399	A. S. Suhorukhov+	Tardos-Tarján, 11:12LT to Lipfert
611 IAP	Yak-1B	33192	M. F. Batarov WIA	Székesfehérvár, 08:20 LT, CL
897 IAP	Yak-9T	0915316	P. M. Krugov	Börgönd, accident at 09:00 LT
897 IAP	Yak-9D	1615391	N. K. Konovalov	Bicske, after 12:10 LT, 4 Bf 109s
897 IAP	Yak-9D	1615396	E. L. Samohvalov	Same, returned on 6 January 1945

* The 'PL-3M' parachute numbers of the crew of Lt. N. P. Ivanov and Ml.Lt. D. E. Rizhkov were 01096 and 5566. Ivanov later returned from captivity, but Rizhkov was killed in the crash.

41 TsAMO RF: fu. 20541, inv. 1, f. 83, pp. 77-78, Operations journal of 295 IAD, entry for 2 January 1945.

At 08:26 and 08:28 LT Helmut Lipfert shot down two Sturmoviks which were attacking ground targets in the Tarján-Bajna area. This day Il-2 formations of the 136 and 306 ShADs suffered very heavy losses around Bajna while trying to provide aerial support for the ground forces of the 18 Tank Corps which was in heavy combat with the 3rd SS-Pz.Div. 'Totenkopf'. Checking the Soviet loss records of the day, we can see that the 210 ShAP suffered the heaviest losses: eight of their Il-2s failed to return to their Kiskunlacháza airbase. However, these planes were lost hours later between 11:08-12:20 LT during their large twenty-two plane mission led by Capt. Sivkov, Capt. Prohorov, St.Lt. Esaulenko and Lt. Markov flight-leaders. The fighter escort was provided by six La-5s of the 116 IAP. The Soviet planes were attacked over the target by approximately fourty Fw 190s and ten to fifteen Bf 109s leading to their heavy losses. Besides the 210 ShAP, the 715, 951 and 989 ShAPs also lost Il-2s in the same area: the 951 ShAP lost two Il-2s to flak, the 989 ShAP lost two Il-2s to enemy fighters. Unfortunately, the exact time of the 989 ShAP losses are not yet known, though it is very likely that these planes (*No.'20' and '38')* were downed by Hptm. Lipfert at 08:26 and 08:28 LT in the same area. The damaged planes were finally lost at Herceghalom and at the Kiskunlacháza airbase during landing. The seven-plane flight of 715 ShAP lost an Il-2 at 08:22LT at Sárisáp-W to five Bf 109s and five *Fw 190s* while attacking an enemy column on the road. The incident was witnessed and confirmed by the Soviet 110th (T-34/85, '4xx') Tank Brigade. Their other plane went down at Csepel, Budapest-S to flak. The 639 ShAP lost three Il-2s to flak over Tarján which finally crashed at Tarján, Börgönd and Székesfehérvár.

Helmut Lipfert's third victory on 4 January 1945 at 10:41 LT was a Yak-9 from the 897 IAP near Bicske. On this day after 10:10 LT, Yak-9s of the 897 IAP were covering Soviet ground troops in the Bicske area. The planes were attacked by four Bf 109s and two of the Yaks were shot down. One of them was Ml.Lt. Nikolai Kuzmich Konovalov's Yak-9D (c/n: 1615391, VK-105PF engine: 415-676). Its pilot bailed out with his parachute and landed safely. The other loss was St.Lt. Egor Lukyanovich Samohvalov's Yak-9D (c/n: 1615396, engine: 415-521) whose pilot returned to his regiment on 6 January 1945. Since both losses took place close to each other, it cannot be determined which of the two planes was Lipfert's legitimate aerial victory.

The other substantial aerial battle of the day between Soviet Yaks and German Bf 109s took place over the Perbál area. While covering Soviet ground troops at 11:10 LT near Bicske, eleven 659 IAP Yaks led by Lt.Col. Vasilii Mefodevich

A 210 ShAP Il-2m3 Sturmovik (c/n: 18853106, AM-38F engine: 259316, No.'35', St.Lt. Ivan Mihailovich Pavlov and Sgt. Kirill Kalinovich Dibrov crew) on the Kiskunlacháza airfield. On 4 January 1945 this regiment suffered catastrophic losses during its Bajna mission. Eight Il-2m3s (including this one) failed to return from combat mission. (Photo: Units and planes, <http://ava.org.ru/shap/210.htm>)

Il-2m3 Sturmoviks of 17 VA, 136 ShAD, 989 ShAP are taxiing to take-off on the Kiskunlacháza airfield at Budapest-S in early 1945. *On 4 January 1945 Hptm. Helmut Lipfert downed two of these planes (No.'20' and '38') in the Bajna-Tarján area. Below are the potential victims of his claims: (L-R) St.Lt. Mnatsakan Karpovich Artazian (KIA) and Lt. Ivan Alekseevich Dzhanaev, who returned to his unit successfully. Lt. Dzhanaev was later killed by flak on 17 March 1945 in his new Il-2 (c/n: 12515, No.'28') near Moha. (Photos: Georgii Zelma and Boris V. Davidov) (*'Borrowed' 989 ShAP Il-2m3 Sturmovik No.'15' (c/n: 11531, AM-38F engine: 258770) was downed by flak on 16 March 1945 in a 210 ShAP formation with the Ml.Lt. Mihail Semyonovich Luchkovskii crew onboard. Based on their camouflage and long flat tail wheel fairings both planes were built at Factory No.1 with c/n: 1xxxx. Spanish 989 ShAP pilot Lt. Celestino Martínez Fierros' lost Il-2 on 9 March 1945 at Soponya looked similar, except his fuselage number was '19' and its spinner was white.

Smeshkov (CO of 659 IAP) fought against twelve Bf 109s over Perbál. Lt.Col. Smeshkov opened fire on one of the Bf

109s from the distance of only 50m and downed it at Perbál-N, 3 km.[42] Capt. Ilya Mihailovich Pavlovskii, Capt. Andrey Antonovich Kopichenko and Ml.Lt. Nikolai Ivanovich Galkin each claimed a Bf 109 near Nagykovácsi, Perbál-NE, 2 and 6 km.[43] Altough some of these Soviet claims were probably overclaims, Lt. Ludwig Düll's Bf 109G-14/AS (WNr.: 782779, DB 605 engine: 00710416, white '2') of 5./JG 51 was likely lost in this battle.[44]

Helmut Lipfert's final victory of the day was a 530 IAP La-5FN (c/n: 39211399, white '99'), piloted by Ml.Lt. Aleksei Stepanovich Suhorukov. At 11:20 LT six La-5s of 530 IAP escorted fourteen Il-2s of 639 ShAP in the Tardos-Tarján area when Lipfert caught him. In his autobiography, Lipfert describes this victory in detail. Exhausted, he and his wingman Sepp Prokoph flew back to Nagyigmánd when they met a group of Il-2s and La-5s. This time the Soviet fighter cover was so tight that they could not get close to the Il-2s so they decided to fly back home. They left the Soviets, but one La-5 pilot insisted on chasing after them. The situation became more and more serious as the La-5 pilot was as skilled as Lipfert in every aspect.[45] Lipfert was forced into a duel, in which he finally pursued the La-5 in an upright position where he could hit him hard. Then he flew very close to the Soviet plane on the right and saw that the Soviet pilot had slid the hood back and was lying in the right corner of the cockpit. His blood coloured the fuselage red all the way back to the tail. The plane then nosed down and the rest was entirely up to gravity. The downed La-5, with its lifeless pilot, struck the ground South of Tarján near a forest. The view shocked Lipfert so much, that he immediately regretted this victory and could not shoot down other Soviet planes for awhile until he was forced to. Since Suhorukhov separated from his group and Hptm. Lipfert hit him from down below, some records indicate he was downed by flak.[46]

8 January 1945 (Monday)
Lipfert's 170th: VICTORY, Boston at 14:13 LT at Székesfehérvár-SE, 5 km
Lipfert's 171st: VICTORY, Boston at 14:18 LT at Székesfehérvár-NW, 2 km
Lipfert's UNCLAIMED POTENTIAL VICTORY, Boston at Székesfehérvár

Soviet 17 VA permanent A-20 Boston bomber losses on 8 January 1945				
Regiment:	**Type:**	**S/N:**	**Pilot:**	**Details:**
449 BAP	A-20B-DL	41-2937	V. M. Vetlov 4+	Börgönd, single, 600m 14:13 LT
449 BAP	A-20G-36	43-21588	V. A. Kruglov 4+	Börgönd, 14:18 LT, pilot hit tail
449 BAP	A-20G-30	43-9596	N. N. Larionov OK	Székesfehérvár, crash-landed, '3'

On 8 January 1945 at 13:50 LT A-20B-DL Boston (S/N: 41-2937, 17 VA, 244 BAD, 449 BAP) took off from Madocsa airfield in southern Hungary to lead the attack on the German armour concentration at Borbálamajor, in the Székesfehérvár-N area. This Boston had arrived over the Börgönd airfield approximately five minutes before the main wave of Capt. Nikolai Vasilevich Kozlov's bombers in order to pick up the fighter escort by circling over the airfield at 600m. The Yaks of the 288 IAD just started their take off, when Hptm. Lipfert and his wingman Josef Prokoph, from their flight of sixteen Bf 109s, surprised them. Chasing the Boston over the airflied, with a few precise bursts, Lipfert sent the Boston into the ground.[47] The plane exploded; its entire crew perished:[48]

Lt. Victor Mihailovich Vetlov pilot (№104164, +)
Lt. Victor Matveevich Ionov bombardier (№104174, +)
St.Sgt. Yosif Isaevich Tolmatskii gunner/radioman (+)
Sgt. Vasilii Fedorovich Burtsev gunner (+)

The plane was built in Santa Monica, CA, USA on 21 June 1942. Order No.: W 535-AC-15948, price: $97.502.00 (USD), left the U.S. on 7 November 1942 via Florida, Puerto Rico, Brazil, Atlantic, Nigeria, Egypt, Iran, Soviet Union. Its final armament was three 12.7mm and three 7.62mm machine guns. Engine numbers: 42-36247, 43-57293.

42 Lt.Col. Vasilii Mefodevich Smeshkov inherited his Saratov-built Yak-3 (c/n: 1711) from Capt. Aleksandr Ivanovich Koldunov (866 IAP) on 15 November 1944 and flew it until 9 March 1945. Between 4-30 April 1945 it was flown by Capt. Victor Aleksandrovich Shukin (659 IAP). On 7 November 1944 during the infamous American-Soviet friendly fire incident over Niš, Yugoslavia, Yak-3 (c/n: 1711) was Capt. Koldunov's plane. In the incident the Soviets lost two Yak-9T (c/n: 2415351: Krivonogih+, 1215370: Zhestovskii) and a Yak-9M (c/n: 2715396: Shipulin+) fighter for the 'success' over 82 FG P-38J (43-28662: Coulson+) and P-38L (44-24035: Brewer+). On 10 October 1944 the 288 IAD had only the following Yak-3s: 1215, 1515, 1711, 2917, 3918, 4516, 2015, 310055, 310081 and 310220, – some of them participated in the Niš incident.
43 TsAMO RF: fu: 20257, inv: 1, f: 46, pp. 86-87, Operations journal of 288 IAD for January 1945, entry for 4 January 1945.
44 Information kindly provided by Matti Salonen Luftwaffe researcher.
45 Lipfert, Gribig, *The War Diary of Hauptmann Helmut Lipfert*, p. 154.
46 TsAMO RF: fu. 370, inv. 6518, f. 207, p. 387, Operations journal of 194 IAD for January 1945, entry for 4 January 1945.
47 Lipfert, Gribig, *The War Diary of Hauptmann Helmut Lipfert*, p. 156.
48 TsAMO RF: fu.: 244 BAD, inv.: 2, f.: 61, pp. 5, 10-11, Combat diary (losses) of 244 BAD, entry for 8 January 1945.

Hptm. Lipfert's 173rd victim still in Bulgaria, in the fall of 1944. This very attractive A-20B Boston (S/N: 41-2937, Douglas c/n: 5267, nickname: 'За Победу!' / 'For Victory!') belonged to the Soviet 17th Air Army, 244 Bomber Division, 449th Bomber Regiment. (Photo: Carl-Fredrik Geust collection)

Hptm. Lipfert's 174th victim was an A-20G-36-DO Boston (S/N: 43-21588) from the approaching bomber wave coming from Madocsa; these bombers took off at 13:53 LT.

Lipfert recalls the following: *'In spite of my long time at the front as a fighter pilot I had never before seen so many Russians in the air. And how they defended themselves! I seleced a Boston and shot it up as best I could. Unfortunately my cannon jammed again – how often this happened in such situation! The machine in fromt of me was capable of absorbing a lot of punishment and I was so excited that my aim was poor. Finally the Russian in front of me began to burn and sheared away from the formation. A little while later he went down in flames.'*[49] Lipfert downed it only five minutes after he hit the first Boston. The bomber flipped on its side, crashed right beside the airfield and exploded killing its entire crew:[50]

Lt. Valentin Aleksandrovich Kruglov pilot (№104814, +)
Lt. Ivan Daniilovich Kudryavtsev bombardier (№104226, +)
Sgt. Ivan Ivanovich Shikov gunner/radioman (+)
Sgt. Anatolii Grigorevich Sestakov gunner (+)

Pilot Lt. Kruglov still could leave his plane but hit the vertical stabilizer, lost consciousness and fell to the ground without opening his parachute. His body was found a distance from the plane. The two gunners burned in the wreck. The plane was built in Santa Monica, CA, USA on 27 February 1944. Douglas c/n.: 21235, Order No.: AC 32732, price: $97.502.00 (USD) Left the U.S. on 20 April 1944 via the ALSIB (Alaska-Siberia) delivery route. Its final armament was five 12.7mm machine guns. Comrades of the killed bomber crews took the bodies back to Madocsa, where they were buried on 12 January 1945 with a proper military ceremony.

During the subsequent dogfight a third 449 BAP A-20 Boston was also shot down (A-20G-30-DO, S/N: 43-9596, '3', built on 11 December 1943 in Santa Monica, CA, USA), which crash-landed near Székesfehérvár. Lt. Nikolai Nikitovich Larionov's crew survied the incident and returned to their unit.[51] The cause of its destruction seems to have actually been Helmut Lipreft again, though it seems he never officially claimed this third bomber! Lipreft recalls: *'I soon had the next machine in front of me and fired again. This one, too, showed the effects of my fire. Unfortunately I couldn't watch to see what became of it, as one look behind was enough to spot several enemy fighters* ... [no fighters were claimed] ... *The sky appeared to be empty, but down below we saw three downed aircraft which were still burning fiercely.'*[52] Humbly, Lipfert wrote: *'I had shot down two*

49 Lipfert, Gribig, *The War Diary of Hauptmann Helmut Lipfert*, p. 157.
50 TsAMO RF: fu.: 20224, inv.: 2, f.: 61, pp. 5, 14-15, Combat diary of 244 BAD, entry for 8.1.1945.
51 TsAMO RF: fu.: 244 BAD, inv.: 2, f.: 61, pp. 5, 12-13, Combat diary (losses) of 244 BAD, entry for 8 January 1945.
52 Lipfert, Gribig, *The War Diary of Hauptmann Helmut Lipfert*, p. 157.

Wrecks of a blown up 449 BAP A-20G Boston in Hungary. This A-20G-20-DO Boston (S/N: 42-86673, engines: 103281, 107161, built on 23 August 1943) hit trees during take-off at the Pápa airfield on 5 April 1945, fell back to the ground and blew up. Pilot Lt. Pyotr Osipovich Zhigankov and bombardier Lt. Ivan Nikolaevich Stroev were killed instantly. (Photo: Boris V. Davidov)

of them the third must have been Prokoph's.[53] However, Prokoph did not make any claims on 8 January 1945 with II./JG 52 over Hungary, though one source states that he may have had a single claim with I./JG 53 in Hungary sometime in 1945 without specifying any details.[54] This single claim surely could not have been a Boston on 8 January 1945 as Prokoph was not yet with I./JG 53, moreover the known flight times of the 'Pik-As' Geschwader were: 08:15-09:15 LT, 10:00-10:35 LT, 11:45-13:00 LT and 14:40-15:45 LT.[55]

14 January 1945 (Sunday)

Lipfert's 172nd: VICTORY, Yak-3 at 12:11 LT at Muzsla-NW, 2 km

Lipfert's 173rd: VICTORY, Yak-3 at 14:36 LT at Muzsla-SW, 1 km

Soviet 5 and 17 VA single-engine fighter losses on 14 January 1945				
Regiment:	**Type:**	**c/n:**	**Pilot:**	**Details:**
179 GvIAP	La-7FN	45210490	V. S. Pishelko	Budapest, 14:25 LT, HUN Bf 109
179 GvIAP	La-7FN	45210495	A. A. Ivanov+	Budapest, HUN Bf 109, Kovács J.
85 GvIAP	Yak-1B	42174	*Unknown*	Crash-landed, scrapped
85 GvIAP	Yak-1B	17157	N/A	Scrapped due to wear and tear
31 GvIAP	Yak-9D	2115368	N. P. Bezuglii	Muzsla, Bf 109, 11:55-12:30 LT
31 GvIAP	Yak-9D	1615342	A. Stadnichenko	Muzsla, Bf 109, 14:20-15:35 LT
48 GvORAP	Yak-9D	13166009	F. M. Volkov	Mindszent, CL in bad weather, 13:20
530 IAP	La-5	*Unknown*	*Unknown*	*LAC, ran into an A-20B, repaired**
611 IAP	Yak-9T	0815377	P. I. Mordovskii	Küngös-E to Veszprém flak, burned
611 IAP	Yak-9DD	0115334	D. D. Kostin	Zámoly, 15:15 LT, in frontal attack

* At 12:55 LT at 1900m 8+7 449 BAP A-20 Bostons bombed Esztergom-Tábor where A-20B Boston, S/N: 41-2802, piloted by Ml.Lt. Nikolai Fedotovich Bakanev was damaged by two Bf 109s. After return the Boston crash-landed on its nose wheel and engines, slipped off the runway and stopped in about 100m. In this moment a fast landing 530 IAP La-5,

53 Lipfert, Gribig, *The War Diary of Hauptmann Helmut Lipfert*, p. 157.
54 Prien, *Jagdeschwader 53*, p. 1149.
55 Prien, *Jagdeschwader 53*, p. 847.

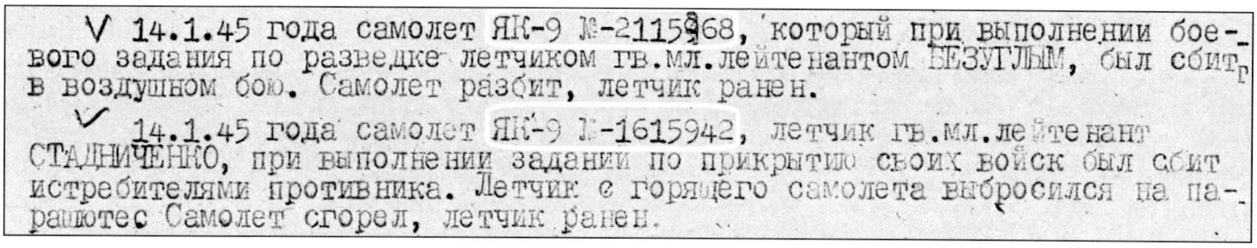
V 14.1.45 года самолет ЯК-9 №-2115968, который при выполнении боевого задания по разведке летчиком гв.мл.лейтенантом БЕЗУГЛЫМ, был сбит в воздушном бою. Самолет разбит, летчик ранен.

✓ 14.1.45 года самолет ЯК-9 №-1615942, летчик гв.мл.лейтенант СТАДНИЧЕНКО, при выполнении задании по прикрытию своих войск был сбит истребителями противника. Летчик с горящего самолета выбросился на парашютес Самолет сгорел, летчик ранен.

which was returning from a 189 ShAD Il-2 escort mission ran into the stopped plane. The A-20B became a complete loss, but the La-5 was later repaired.

On 14 January 1945 between 11:55-12:30 LT a reconnaissance Yak-1B and Yak-9D pair from 31 GvIAP piloted by Gv.Ml.Lt. Borovoy and Bezuglii patrolled the Tata-Komárom-Szomor area where at 2800m they met two Fw 190s. Borovoy unsuccessfully attacked them, but when they pulled up two Bf 109s got behind their tails and hit Bezuglii's Yak-9D. The Soviet fighter caught fire and fell in the Marcelháza-NE area, Hungary (now Marcelová, Slovakia). The wounded pilot bailed out successfully and was taken to a hospital. The other reconnaissance pair of 31 GvIAP was more successful: near Komárom at 2000m they met a pair of Bf 109s. Gv.Ml.Lt. Yangaev opened fire from a distance of 200m on one of them. The Bf 109 burst into flames and went down in the Nagyigmánd-SE area. Two hours later between 14:20-15:35 LT three 31 GvIAP Yak-9Ds and three Yak-3s led by Maj. Aleksei Mihailovich Reshetov covered Soviet ground troops in the Köbölkút, Hungary area (now Gbelce, Slovakia) where at 3000m four Bf 109s attacked them. Gv.Ml.Lt. Aleksei Efimovich Stadnichenko was hit he bailed out from his burning plane which crashed three kilometers West of Esztergom near Muzsla Hungary (now Mužla, Slovakia). Tragically, when he left his plane, some burning fuel spilled on him and his parachute burned up in the air, he hit the ground in an almost free fall state.

Helmut Lipfert once again saw it correctly, some Yak-3s were present in the dogfight, but the summary loss-report of 31 GvIAP for 1944-1945 clearly shows that those two Yak fighters that he claimed were Yak-9Ds, not Yak-3s.[56] Note the typo in c/n 1615942: there was no Factory No.159 building Yak-9 fighters, only Factory No.153 in Novosibirsk. Therefore the correct c/n was 1615342 or 1642 in short form. Other records state that Stadnichenko was killed, not wounded during the dogfight.[57]

Meanwhile in the South over Budapest, after 07:30 LT six 235 ShAP Il-2s escorted by two 513 IAP Yak-9s attacked the central districts of the city in the Deák Square, Károly Boulevard and the (main) City Hall areas. Their attack was repeated by six Il-2s of the 451 ShAP, also escorted by two 513 IAP Yak-9s. The Il-2 attacks continued with the 91, 92, 130, 131, 187, 188 and 190 GvShAP, which targeted objects on the Buda side and central bridges over the Danube. Il-2 formations of the 17 VA's 210, 715, 989 and 951 ShAP also strafed the Chain Bridge and the Elizabeth Bridge in Budapest.

The Royal Castle in Buda, as the main stronghold and headquarters of the Budapest garrison, was bombed multiple times by A-20G Bostons of the 218 BAD. At 13:09 LT at 2000m seven Bostons of the 453 BAP led by Maj. Lozovenko crossed the Danube North of Budapest and over Pilisvörösvár started their bomb run on the Buda Castle with their 91 FAB-100 bombs. During this manouver Hungarian Bf 109s arriving from the West intercepted and attacked them. Bf 109 ace Pottyondy László szds. (101/8. FS) opened fire on St.Lt. Grigorii Rodionovich Voevodin's A-20G Boston (S/N: 42-

Crash-landed Yak-1B of the 31 GvIAP, 2nd Sq. at Erdőtarcsa, Hungary on 17 January 1945. At 08:15 LT the Yakovlev was returning from a weather reconnaissance sortie when in poor visibility its left wing hit a vehicle of the 85 GvIAP moving along the landing stripe. The driver, Sgt. Philipp Efimovich Gorkovets was killed in the accident. The plane (c/n: 26175, engine: 422-422) was written off, but the pilot Gv.Capt. Ivan Ivanovich Demkin remained unhurt. (Photo: Boris V. Davidov)

56 TsAMO RF: fu. 20036, inv. 1, f. 56, p. 110, Operations summary of 31 GvIAP for the time period between 20 September 1944 – 10 May 1945, entry for 14 January 1945.

57 TsAMO RF: fu. 33, inv. 11458, f. 727, p. 103, Permanent officer losses of the 5 VA for January 1945, entry for 14 January 1945.

54166, 2nd Sq.)[58] flying as 'Tail-end Charlie' on the right in Capt. Ivan Haritonovich Lozovenko's formation.[59] Pottyondy szds. struck three times. His storming shells damaged the Boston's right wing, the hydraulic-system and the suspension of the nose-wheel. St.Lt. Voevodin forced his crippled bomber in an escape-dive and jettisoned his bombs into the Danube as he tried to flee Eastwards. Finally, with approximately 120 holes in his plane, he crash-landed his Boston on its nose wheel in a field at Rákospalota-NE, 2.5 km on Soviet controlled territory. The plane was inspected by Soviet mechanics, who verified that both of its cockpits (F-1, F-2) and the fuselage were deformed, so they removed it from the plane-inventory of the 218 BAD in their 15 January 1945 mechanical report. The crew survived the battle, but both gunners got injured:

St.Lt. Grigorii Rodionovich Voevodin pilot (unhurt)
Ml.Lt. Vladimir Illarionovich Ruban navigator (unhurt)
St.Sgt. Vasilii Stepanovich Kochev radioman-gunner (leg injury)
Gv.Ml.Sgt. Denis Leontievich Baranov aerial gunner (head injury)

In the afternoon at 14:25 LT Hungarian Bf 109s battled again with Soviet planes over Budapest in which Kovács János hdgy. downed Gv.Ml.Lt. Artemii Artemevich Ivanov's 179 GvIAP La-7FN (c/n: 45210495, engine: 82131905, white '95'), falling in downtown Pest killing its pilot. Gv.St.Lt. Valerii Semyonovich Pishelko's La-7FN (c/n: 45210490, engine: 82131853, white '90') was also hit but managed to escape the fire. En route home over Szentmártonkáta-W his engine finally quit, he bailed out successfully and returned to his unit. Budapest was covered with smoke and haze, transportation and military movements were limited or impossible due to the constant attacks of the Soviet Air Force. As the daily report described:

The enemy planes bombed in formations and the fighters strafed the streets with their onboard weapons. They caused severe losses and ignited large fires.[60]

Despite of the heavy dogfights and the Soviet fighter presence over Budapest WNW areas, the Luftwaffe persisted in sending Ju 52 transport planes over the city in order to deliver the desperately needed medical, food and military supplies to the encircled Budapest-garrison. Although in the evening hours they could avoid the attacks of the Soviet daytime fighters, the transports became easy prey for Soviet anti-aircraft artillery which was waiting for them around the city, especially on the heights of the Buda-hills. This night a 11./TG 3 Ju 52/3m ('4V+FV', WNr.: 6333) became one of their victims. The Junkers was hit by the 2nd battery of the Soviet 1654 AP PVO and fell in the forest North of Zugliget where it damaged one of the 76.2mm ZiS-3 anti-tank guns of the Soviet 627th Artillery Regiment's 2nd division.[61] One crewmember, Fw. Wilhelm Schneck radioman was captured alive.

16 January 1945 (Tuesday)

Lipfert's 174th: OVERCLAIM, LaGG-5 at 12:17 LT at Budaörs-N, 3 km

Soviet 17 VA single-engine fighter losses on 16 January 1945				
Regiment:	**Type:**	**c/n:**	**Pilot:**	**Details:**
31 IAP	La-5FN	3921*xxxx*	I. F. Philippov+	Tát, 13:50 LT, Bf 109, in Danube
116 IAP	La-5FN	39210921	A. A. Chernih+	Buda, 15:40 LT, Bf 109s
164 IAP	La-5	3921*xxxx*	I. F. Shukin unhurt	*Tinnye-Tököl, repaired, Bf 109s*
659 IAP	Yak-3	2929217	N. I. Galkin MIA	Sárszentmihály, 14:10, 8 Bf 109s
659 IAP	Yak-3	3929218	M. A. Fisenko+	Perkáta, 14:10 LT, 8 Bf 109s

On 16 January 1945 La-5s of 164 IAP covered 136 ShAD Il-2 Sturmoviks in the Tát-Bajna region at Budapest-NW. On their way the La-5s encountered two Fw 190s and four Bf 109s. St.Lt. Anatolii Ivanovich Volodin claimed a Fw 190 over Tinnye, but one of their La-5s was also damaged. Pilot Lt. Ivan Fedotovich Shukin decided to return and land on the closer Soviet held airbase of Tököl instead of his own airbase at Kiskunlacháza. His La-5 was not lost. They repaired it at Tököl and later it flew back to Kiskunlacháza. The exact time of this event is unknown, but because it was not lost and this is the only remaining option in the Budaörs-Tinnye area, for Helmut Lipfert, it is an overclaim. The other two La-5s (Chernih and Philippov) were lost later in the afternoon therefore they could not be victims of Lipfert's action.

58 St.Lt. Voevodin's lost A-20G-15-DO Boston (S/N: 42-54166, R-2600-23 engines: 42-154229, 42-175195) was built on 25 June 1943 and was delivered to the Soviet Union by way of Alaska. (AAIR) Engine No.42-175195 was salvaged from Lt. Malov's crashed A-20G after 21 December 1944 and got re-installed on St.Lt. Voevodin's A-20G Boston, S/N: 42-54166. (TsAMO RF: fu. 20208, inv. 1, f. 46, pp. 45-47)

59 Maj. Lozovenko was KIFA on 16 April 1945 at Bábolnapuszta, Hungary in his A-20G, S/N: 42-53927.

60 Ungváry Krisztián, *Budapest ostroma* (Budapest: Corvina, 2005), 5th Ed, p. 132.

61 The Junkers nearly fell on top of the gun! TsAMO RF: fu. 11667, inv. 1, f. 8, p. 25, Combat log of the 627th Art. Reg., entry for 14 January 1945.

This day Il-2s attacked target-object No.99, 100, 102-104, 128 and 132 in Budapest. Beside the 31, 116 and 164 IAP La-5s, German fighters attacked the Il-2 formations as well. Over Zugliget in the Buda-hills at 14:40 LT at 1000m two Fw 190s challenged the 190 GvShAP Il-2 pair of Gv.St.Lt. Korneichuk and Gv.Ml.Lt. Nemchin. This time the Soviet gunners were more successful and downed one of the attackers, probably Uffz. Gerhard Pütz's Fw 190F-8 (8./SG 10, WNr.: 582393, black '4'). At 2000m four Hungarian Fw 190Fs attacked St.Lt. Storchilo's 453 BAP A-20G Boston formation, which was about to bomb Budapest. Although Storchilo's Boston was hit, aerial gunner Sgt. Grigorii Semyonovich Malihin (453 BAP A-20G, S/N: 42-53998) managed to claim one Fw 190 shot down over the Eastern suburbs of the city. This plane was probably Majoross István's damaged Fw 190F-8 (102/1. FBS), which flipped over upon landing at Kemenesszentpéter after returning from a combat mission. At the same time 31 IAP and 178 GvIAP La-5s encountered and destroyed several TG.2, TG.3 and TG.4 Junkers Ju 52/3m transport planes at Budapest-WNW which carried supplies to the encircled German-Hungarian defenders of Budapest.[62] Mixed Yak-1B and Yak-9 flight of six 179 IAP Yaks led by Capt. Boris Semyonovich Lednev battled a large group of Junkers Ju 87 Stukas north of Esztergom, claiming four of them, suffering no losses.

22 January 1945 (Monday)
Lipfert's 175th: POTENTIAL VICTORY, La-5 at 13:24 LT at Székesfehérvár-NE, 10 km

Soviet 5 and 17 VA single-engine fighter losses on 22 January 1945				
Regiment:	**Type:**	**c/n:**	**Pilot:**	**Details:**
116 IAP	La-5FN	41210109	V. M. Boltyan	LAC after dogfight, six Bf 109s
116 IAP	La-5FN	39212516	I. D. Plankevich	Adony-Pusztaszabolcs, 9:55 LT, 8 Bf 109s, both recc. pilots captured
116 IAP	La-5FN	39211687	G. K. Zolotarskii	
164 IAP	La-5F	39215251	V. S. Svistelnikov	Pázmánd-E, crash-landed to Bf 109
164 IAP	La-5	*Unknown*	K. S. Shelkanov	*Damaged by Bf 109s, returned*
530 IAP	La-5FN	39211521	A. N. Yakovlev+	Székesfehérvár, 13:35 LT, Bf 109
897 IAP	Yak-1B	03193	I. I. Motolikov	Székesfehérvár, 8:30 LT, 6 Bf 109s
611 IAP	Yak-9T	0815355	N. A. Verbovitskii	Bugyi, Hungarian Bf 109 (Máthé)
659 IAP	Yak-9D	16166062	N. A. Morozov	Kiskunlacháza, take off accident
96 OKRAP	Yak-9D	1515390	A. A. Arefiev MIA	Missing, dogfight at 09:45 LT
31 GvIAP	Yak-9D	2015396	A. M. Zhelobanov	Returned, broke upon landing

On 22 January 1945 La-5s of 295 IAD covered 136 and 306 ShAD Il-2s in the Székesfehérvár area. Near '*Sariko*' *(Sárkeszi?)* a flight of five Il-2s and four La-5s were attacked by six Bf 109s. Ml.Lt. Vasilii Maksimovich Boltyan's plane, white '09', was hit and crash landed on his own airfield upon returning and burned. Lt. Vasilii Savelevich Svistelnikov's plane (164 IAP, La-5F, c/n: 39215251, M-82F engine: 65033094, white '51') was also hit by Bf 109s and crash-landed at Pázmánd-E. The plane was written off, but the pilot was unhurt. One of them could be Hptm. Helmut Lipfert's victim near Székesfehérvár as a potential aerial victory.

27 January 1945 (Saturday)
Lipfert's 176th: VICTORY, Il-2 at 14:45 LT at Adony-NW, 7 km

Soviet 17 VA Il-2 Sturmovik losses on 27 January 1945				
Regiment:	**Type:**	**c/n:**	**Pilot:**	**Details:**
615 ShAP	Il-2m3	304934	N. N. Palevich	Előszállás, 1 km, crash-landed, flak
672 ShAP	Il-2m3	1875688	*Unknown, 3rd Sq.*	*Combat damage, repaired*
951 ShAP	Il-2m3	1876398	V. A. Filonovich+	Gróf-N, 2 km, 14:50 LT, 4 *Fw 190*
951 ShAP	Il-2m3	11594	B. A. Drobinin	Adony-E, crash-landed at 14:50 LT

On 26-27 January 1945 the Soviet 23 Tank Corps launched a concentrated counter-attack East of Lake Velence. The 3rd Tank Brigade attacked Vereb, the 39th Tank Brigade attacked Pázmánd while the 135th Tank Brigade attacked Pettend.

62 During the 16 January 1945 Budapest-airlift operations the Luftwaffe has lost several Ju 52/3m cargo planes, including '8T+FN' (WNr.641033), '8T+?U' (WNr.5441), 'G6+BU' (WNr.641229), 'G6+DU' (WNr.640190) and 'G6+GU' (WNr.131068). Hungarian Ju 52/3m 'S.2+14' (WNr.: 901137) was destroyed during take-off on the Pápa airfield by exploding bombs dropped by 449 BAP A-20 Bostons, while 'S.2+18' (WNr.: 901141) was lost when a landing Fw 190F ran into it.

Scrapping of a destroyed 39 TBr T-34/85 (<Г> 67) with flame-cutters in March 1948. This tank was lost on 27 March 1945 near Bőnyrétalap and was scrapped along with many others by Mühlenkampf József. (Photo: Rabi Lenke)

However, after a short advance all brigades were halted by strong German defence fire. Since in just a few hours the Soviets lost more than 60 tanks(!), Il-2 formations of the 10 ShAK were put into action despite the poor weather conditions to provide immediate aerial support to the struggeling Soviet armoured forces – whatever was left of them.[63] Their formations in the air were countered by Bf 109s, including fighters of II./JG 52.

At approximately 14:45 four *'Fw 190s'* opened fire on the seven-plane flight of the 951 ShAP, which was returning from their ground attack mission to Gróf-tanya, East of Lake Velence. Hptm. Helmut Lipfert's projectiles hit Lt. Boris Afanasevich Drobinin's Il-2m3 (c/n: 11594, AM-38F engine: 259602) which crash-landed 1 km North of Makád on Csepel Island, right across from Adony. Although their plane was permanently written off by 8 February 1945 the crew of Lt. Drobinin and St.Sgt. Bragin returned to their unit on 28 January 1945 unhurt. The crew of the other lost Il-2 was not so fortunate: Lt. Vsevolod Alekseevich Filonovich's plane crashed North of Gróf-tanya and both crewmen were killed.[64] The remaining five Il-2s landed safely at Szabadszállás. The question remains: who shot down this Il-2, since Hptm. Lipfert claimed only one, could it have been Uffz. Albert Burggraf of 1./JG 53?[65]

22 February 1945 (Thursday)

Lipfert's 177th: VICTORY, LaGG-5 at 14:00 LT at Bart

Lipfert's 178th: VICTORY, Yak-3 at 16:25 LT at Bina

63 The 3 TBr attacked Vereb from the direction of Vál and Kajászószentpéter and lost four burned out T-34/85s: No.4110037 ('<B> B-153'), 4110083 ('<B> B-155'), 4110035 ('<B> B-151') and 4110013 ('<B> B-156') to Panthers of I./Pz.Rgt.24 which also destroyed two M4A2(76)W Shermans of the 1 GvMK, 9 GvTBr, including U.S.A. 30116426 ('959'). The 39 TBr attacked Pázmánd and lost 11 burned out T-34/85s East of the village. The 135 TBr which managed to break into Pettend along the Balaton-Budapest railway line became trapped and almost completely destroyed by only four Tiger IIs of s.Pz.Abt.509 which arrived from Kápolnásnyék under the cover of the morning fog. (They lost T-34/85, No.'<Д> 03, 04, 05, 06, 14, 19, 45, 46, 48, 49, 50, 51, 55, 56, 60', etc.) Ofw. Gustav Neuhaus (2./s.Pz.Abt. 509) destroyed 15, Fw. Bauer (in Tiger II., No.'133') 13, Fw. Kollmannsberger 11 and Hptm. Hans-Jürgen Burmester two T-34/85s. In close combat the tanks and panzer-grenadiers of I./Pz.Rgt.24, 3rd SS-Pz.Div. and I./SS-Pz.Gren.Rgt.23 'Norge' destroyed another 22 Soviet tanks. The total number of the burned out 23 TK T-34/85s on 26-27 January 1945 in the Vereb-Pettend area was 54 (!), plus another 14 knocked out and beside the 1 GvMK M4A2 Shermans the heavy 1443 SAP lost three ISU-122s of which one burned out. The Germans lost a Tiger B (s.Pz.Abt.509), six Panther Ausf. Gs (I./Pz.Rgt.24), a StuG.III, a JPz.IV (SS-Pz.Jg.Abt.3), a Tiger Ausf. E (9./SS-Pz.Rgt.3, '924'), etc., – mainly in the Baracska area.

64 In December 1944-January 1945 the 951 ShAP erased the following PL-3M parachutes from their parachute inventory: PL-3M, No.20425 (Filonovich), 56913, 5414, 270, 18605, 0154, 46175, 36238, ?873, 23109 (Baronin), 44157 (Vorobiev), 21418 (Marakulin), 20690 (Yadrihinskii), 4608 (Odnotsenov), 6211 (Ufimtsev), 22187 (Pivoshenko), 0387 (Pogudin), 4260 (Petrakov), 38677 (Prohorov), 20941 (Samoilov), 20546 (Boldin), 20625 (Vaslyanin), 14240, or 32167 (Solovey).

65 Prien, *Jagdeschwader 53*, p. 1149.

War-weary Ilyushin Il-2m3 Sturmovik No.'31' of 17 VA, 306 ShAD, 951 ShAP after returning from a combat mission. This very durable plane just received new combat damages. (Photo: 306 ShAD memorial exhibition, School No.1265, Moscow, Russia)

Soviet 5 VA permanent single-engine fighter losses on 22 February 1945				
Regiment:	Type:	c/n:	Pilot:	Details:
178 GvIAP	La-5FN	39212527	V. F. Pogodin WIA	Bina-Kicsind, ~16:25 LT, Bf 109s
179 GvIAP	La-7FN	45210640	I. E. Pinko WIA	Bart-Ebed, 13:45 LT to Bf 109s

On 22 February 1945 between 13:45-14:30 LT, six La-7s of 179 GvIAP patrolled at 2000m over Libád, Hungary (now Ľubá, Slovakia) when Bf 109s attacked them. The pair of Gv.Lt. Fyodor Alekseevich Snigirev deputy Sq. commander and Gv.Ml.Lt. Ivan Erofeevich Pinko immediately broke out to the left, but Pinko was already hit. He bailed out with second degree burns from his La-7 (c/n: 45210640, ASh-82FN engine: 82131965, white '40') and landed on the front line near Ebed, Hungary (now Obid, Slovakia) at Bart (Bruty)-SE. He was picked up by Soviet tank crews who rushed him to hospital. The La-7s kept fighting the Bf 109s and Gv.Capt. Pavel Vladimirovich Supronov, Sq. commander claimed one.

Later, between 15:55-16:55 LT eight 178 GvIAP La-5s led by Gv.St.Lt. Pyotr Romanovich Setinin covered Soviet ground troops in the Bina (now Bíňa, Slovakia) – Kicsind (now Malá nad Hronom, Slovakia) area where at around 16:25LT two pairs of Bf 109s attacked them from the sun. One of them hit Gv.Ml.Lt. Vladimir Fedorovich Pogodin's La-5FN (c/n: 39212527, ASh-82FN engine: 8213249, white '<★27') from a distance of 100m. Pogodin bailed out with his parachute and landed at Kicsind-NE 3 km and was taken to hospital.

This day Hptm. Helmut Lipfert misidentified both of his victims: his 'LaGG-5' was in fact a La-7FN and his 'Yak-3' was a La-5FN. His reported times and locations, however, matched the Soviet loss records:

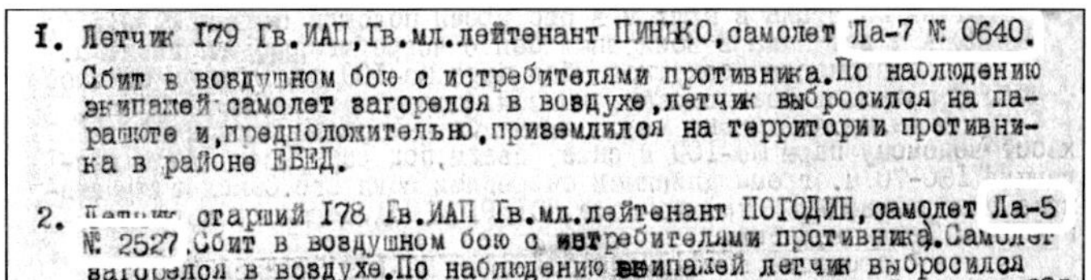

1. Летчик 179 Гв.ИАП, Гв.мл.лейтенант ПИНЬКО, самолет Ла-7 № 0640.
Сбит в воздушном бою с истребителями противника. По наблюдению экипажей самолет загорелся в воздухе, летчик выбросился на парашюте и, предположительно, приземлился на территории противника в районе ЕБЕД.

2. Летчик старший 178 Гв.ИАП Гв.мл.лейтенант ПОГОДИН, самолет Ла-5 № 2527. Сбит в воздушном бою с истребителями противника. Самолет загорелся в воздухе. По наблюдению экипажей летчик выбросился на парашюте и приземлился на нашей территории в районе выс. 285 что 3 км. сев.-вост. КИЧИНД.

Gv.Ml.Lt. Ivan Erofeevich Pinko's and Gv.Ml.Lt. Vladimir Fedorovich Pogodin's loss entry in the 14 GvIAD records. (TsAMO RF: fu. 20062, inv. 1, f. 43, p. 57, Operations journal of 14 GvIAD staff, entry for 22 February 1945.)

25 February 1945 (Sunday)
Lipfert's 179th: VICTORY, Yak-9 at 10:53 LT at Zvolen (Altsohl)-S, 15 km
Lipfert's UNCLAIMED VICTORY, Bf 109 after 14:00LT, Altsohl area

Soviet 5 VA permanent single-engine fighter losses on 25 February 1945				
Regiment:	**Type:**	**c/n:**	**Pilot:**	**Details:**
513 IAP	Yak-9M	2615337	A. G. Ananev+	Zvolen (Zólyom)-S, six 'Fw 190' at 2000 m
513 IAP	Yak-9T	2015385	A. A. Ribalko+	
Romanian Grupul 9 V.	Bf 109G-6	166248	T. Dârjan+	Detva-NW, 14:00 LT, yellow '9'
Romanian Grupul 9 V.	Bf 109G-6	166169	P. C. Cantacuzino	Detva-NW, shortly after T. Dârjan, possibly to SG2 or SG10, red '2'
Romanian Grupul 9 V.	Bf 109G-6	Unknown	L. Manu	Altsohl- Zv Slatina-W area, after 14:00 LT to Bf 109s, yellow '2'

On 25 February 1945 four Yak-9s of 513 IAP escorted six Il-2s of 451 ShAP over Pliešovce, Zvolen-S. Flying at 2000m the soviet formation was attacked by six *'Fw 190s'*. Ananev and Ribalko were shot down, one of them by Hptm. Lipfert. Il-2 (c/n: 10963, AM-38F engine c/n: 253905, piloted by Lt. Ivan Fedorovich Grigorev) crash-landed upon return to Tóalmás-N.[66]

In the afternoon around 14:00 LT near Zvolen, Hptm. Lipfert shot down a Romanian Bf 109 as well, which crashed at Detva-NW, but was not officially documented by him due to the lack of witnesses. However, an account of the battle is written in his autobiography for 24 February 1945 [sic!]. The date recalled by Lipreft is incorrect as the Romanian Air Force did not loose any Bf-109's except on the 25th. On 22 February the Romanians did not fly combat missions as they were planning for a 'large' raid for the 25th, on the 23rd an armed Bf-109 pair took part in reconnassiance and a few Ju-87s attacked ground target, on the 24th there was again no air activity this time due to bad weather.[67] On 25 February 1945 the Romanians opened the day with Ju-88A attacks covered by fighter escorts beginning at 09:30 then more flights in the early afternoon,[68] attacks which are mentioned in Lipferts autobiography as the following: *The infantry informed us that the last attacks had been flown by German aircraft which we had supplied to the Rumanians: Ju 88s, He 111s and Bf 109s.*[69]

According to the Soviet 5 VA, on 25 February the Romanian Air Force did in fact lose one Bf 109, while other two Bf 109s and a Ju 88 belly landed. The Romanian pilot Adj. av. Traian Dârjan was killed while his Bf 109G-6 (Escadrila 47, Grupul 9 Vânătoare, WNr.: 166248, yellow '9') was a complete loss.[70] Traian Dârjan was the last AAR ace to be shot down and killed in aerial combat.[71] Lipfert recalls: *After the first shots at the Romanian he immediately tried to dive away in the direction of the enemy lines ... The other Romanian separated from his companion but did not come to his aid. Afterward I maintained an especially close watch behind and contunied firing at the Me in front of me. It was already smoking heavily and then suddenly it crashed into a hill. There was no fire.*[72] Adj. av. Dârjan was actually killed before his plane stopped on the hill, having been almost decapitated by one of Lipfert's machine gun bullets; Dârjan flew over 150 combat missions and had twelve claims to his name.[73]

8 March 1945 (Thursday)
Lipfert's 180th: VICTORY, Il-2 at 14:10 LT at Sapolce (Soponya?)**-W, 6 km**

Soviet 5 and 17 VA Il-2 losses on 8 March 1945				
Regiment:	**Type:**	**c/n:**	**Pilot:**	**Details:**
615 ShAP	Il-2m3	18896106	M. A. Solodov	Bugac puszta, CL, flak at 15:30 LT
615 ShAP	Il-2m3	18845124	P. P. Nikitin	Nagybajom flak, CL at Kaposvár-W
639 ShAP	Il-2m3	18865107	A. P. Shubin+	Fekete(?) flak at 15:00 LT, Enying-S
951 ShAP	Il-2m3	9957	G. Odnotsenov+	Seregélyes-NW, flak at 11:00 LT *
989 ShAP	Il-2m3	10016	I. S. Gorkin	Belsőbáránd flak, scrapped, '7'

66 TsAMO RF: fu. 20177, inv. 1, f. 46, p. 110, Operations journal of 264 ShAD, entry for 25 February 1945.
67 Correspondence with Dénes Bernád (31 March, 2021)
68 Dénes Bernád, *Rumanian Air Force: The Prime Decade, 1938-1947* (Carrolton, Texas: Squardon/Signal publications, 1999), p. 37.
69 Lipfert, Gribig, *The War Diary of Hauptmann Helmut Lipfert*, p. 164.
70 Dénes Berná, *Rumanian Aces of World War 2* (Oxford: Osprey, 2003), p. 65.
71 Berná, *Rumanian Aces of World War 2*, p. 65.
72 Lipfert, Gribig, *The War Diary of Hauptmann Helmut Lipfert*, pp. 164-165.
73 Dénes Bernád, *Rumanian Air Force: The Prime Decade, 1938-1947* (Carrolton, Texas: Squardon/Signal publications, 1999), p. 40.

Soviet 5 and 17 VA Il-2 losses on 8 March 1945 (*continued*)				
715 ShAP	Il-2m3	*12965*	P. I. Ratushnuk	Soponya, crashed: Hercegfalva,'22'
989 ShAP	Il-2m3	11467	Leoncio Hernans	Belsőbáránd flak, 11:30 LT, CL, '38'
989 ShAP	Il-2m3	11560	I. Buryakovskii	Káloz, 15:50LT, Bf109, repaired,'30'
131 GvShAP	Il-2m3	12350	A. I. Zenin	*Flak damage, repaired at the base*
131 GvShAP	Il-2m3	1876367	V. K. Gaidash	*Flak damage, repaired at the base*
131 GvShAP	Il-2m3	12616	V. P. Evgrafov	Seregélyes-NW, 1 km in dogfight
131 GvShAP	Il-2m3	18833115	M. N. Lahtanov	*Seregélyes-Makád, Bf 109s, repaired*
166 GvShAP	Il-2m3	187xxxx	G. I. Neminusii+	Novi Sad, crashed
188 GvShAP	Il-2m3	11041	*Unknown, 1st Sq.*	*Combat damage, Il-2 repaired*
188 GvShAP	Il-2m3	11893	I. G. Bannih	*Combat damage, Il-2 repaired*
188 GvShAP	Il-2m3	18892115	*Unknown, 3rd Sq.*	*Combat damage, Il-2 repaired*

* The numbers of the assigned 'PL-3M' type parachutes of the Lt. German Petrovich Odnotsenov (HSU) and St.Sgt. Stephan Pavlovich Ufimtsev crew were 19256 and 38162 (their TT and Nagant numbers were also recorded.)

On 8 March 1945, between 13:52-14:02 LT six Il-2m3 Sturmoviks of the 130 GvShAP and six Il-2s of the 131 GvShAP led by Maj. Victor Mihailovich Samodelkin, escorted by six 92 IAP La-5s of St.Lt. Nikolai Alekseevich Matyushenko, strafed ground targets in the Soponya-Seregélyes-S area. Their aerial support was much needed as on the ground – despite of the massive Soviet resistance – as Panthers followed by Pz.IVs of SS-Pz.Rgt. 9 'Hohenstaufen' and SS-Pz.Rgt. 2 'Das Reich', leading the German offensive along the Eastern shore of the Sárvíz canal, broke deep into the defense lines of the Soviet 18 Tank Corps West of Sárosd and destroyed several T-34/85 tanks and heavy ISU-122S self-propelled guns.[74] The Soviets' BM-13 Katyusha, 122, 152 and 203mm heavy artillery, 82 and 120mm mortar fire, combined with their armoured forces tried to stop, or at least slow down the German advancing towards Simontornya. The desperate battle continued for the next few days and nights.[75] Over the target the Soviet planes met six German fighters which chased them to approximately six kilometers east of Seregélyes. The Axis fighters, which included Hptm. Lipfert, opened fire on the second wave of Il-2s containing six planes. First Evrafov's then Lahtanov's plane was shot down. Gv.Ml.Lt. Vasilii Petrovich Evgrafov's Il-2m3 crashed at Korcsma-E (Seregélyes-E, 5 km), Gv.Ml.Lt. Matvei Nikolaevich Lahtanov's damaged Il-2m3 crossed the Danube and crash-landed East of Makád on the Southern tip of Csepel Island.

11 March 1945 (Sunday)

Lipfert's 181st: VICTORY, Yak-3 at 10:35 LT at Sárbogárd-SW, 6 km

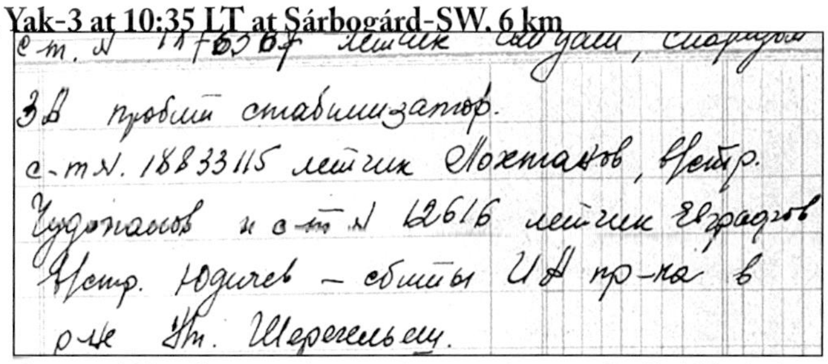

List of lost, or damaged Il-2 Sturmoviks as written in the 131 GvShAP's daily summary report for 8 March 1945, including Hptm. Helmut Lipfert's victim.* (*TsAMO RF: fu. 22310, inv. 275171c, f. 12, p. 62, Operations journal of 131 GvShAP, entry for 8 March 1945.)

74 On 8 March 1945 the 110 TBr lost six T-34/85s West of Sárosd (Chassis No./Turret marking/Crew): 412836/'406'/Cherkasov, 412928/'407'/Gorokhov, 4120466/'409'/Grigorenko, 4110247/'412'/Ibrahimov+, 412915/'414'/Potapov and 412511/'447'/Ilin. The 363 GvTSAP lost five ISU-122S SPGs of which two burned out (41224/'301'/Katkov and 41222/'303'/Kosinov+). On 21 March 1945 they lost an ISU-152 (41264/'401'/Malishev) to a Pz.Rgt.6 StuG at Seregélyes-SW, which also burned out.

75 On 9 March 1945 the 110 TBr lost T-34/85, 4120890/'410'/Kopilov. On 14 March 1945 the 170 TBr lost four T-34/85s at Seregélyes-NE (4121531/'536', 4121616/'544', 4121591/'545', 0412228/'575'). On 19 March 1945 the 20 GvTP lost a burned out M4A2(76) W Sherman (U.S.A. 3080508/'3xx'). Between 20-22 March 1945 the 110 and 181 TBr lost T-34/85 No.412597/'442', 412356/'448', 410486/'639', 412652/'643', 412238/'661', 4121023/'667', 412914/'413', 412926/'404', 4120930/'403', 4801/'660', 412920/'411', 4121519/'421' and 4121543/'423'. On 10 March 1945 at Sáregres the 1951 SAP lost five SU-100 SPGs (41178/'419', 41195/'415', 411103/'416', 411132/'408', 411135/'410') while between 12-14 March 1945 at Cece and Simontornya the 1953 SAP lost eight SU-100s (41184/'480', 411157/'473', 411106/'466', 41181/'479', 411148/'468', 41193/'465', 411161/'462' and 411162/'463'). On 13-14 March at Seregélyes-NE the 1438 SAP lost six SU-76M SPGs (411591/'B-946', 411012, 410150, 411700, 411697, 411693). At Simontornya the 209 SABr lost a Harley-Davidson 42WLA recon. motorcycle (HD679183 / U.S.A. 679183) and a T48/SU-57 halftrack (U.S.A. 4021593), while at Henrikmajor the 1 GvMBr lost an M3A1 Scout Car (U.S.A. 6089987/'146'/Shiller) – just to mention a few.

Lipfert's 182nd: OVERCLAIM, Yak-3 at 14:05 LT at Siófok-S, 9-10 km

Soviet 17 VA single-engine fighter losses on 11 March 1945				
Regiment:	Type:	c/n:	Pilot:	Details:
611 IAP	Yak-9M	3315386	N. N. Kutsenko+	Simontornya-SE, 14:25 LT to Bf 109
866 IAP	Yak-3	310233	A. D. Piorunskii	Sárbogárd, at 3000m to Lipfert
866 IAP	Yak-3	310xxx	N. G. Surnev	Simontornya, damaged by Lipfert
866 IAP	Yak-3	310xxx	T. K. Gatitskii	Dogfight at 15:00 LT, later returned
164 IAP	La-5FN	39214947	P. M. Taikov	Burned on its airfield due to flak
530 IAP	La-5FN	39211581	G. F. Lesnyak	Bugac puszta-NW, take-off acc.
56 IAP	La-5FN	39211638	G. I. Dunaev	Őcsény, CL, ferry-flight accident

On 11 March 1945 regiments of 288 IAD covered A-20 Bostons of 244 BAD and ground troops in the Cece-Simontornya-Sárbogárd-Aba-Enying areas. At 15:15 LT at 3100m a battle erupted between 16 Bf 109s, Capt. Kizim's 18 A-20 Bostons and Lt. Laguta's five 659 IAP Yak-9s. Lt. Vladimir Andreevich Malishev's 260 BAP A-20G (S/N: 43-10068) was shot down by two Bf 109s.[76] The Boston caught fire and spun down in flames at Ernőmajor, Seregélyes-SE killing its entire crew. Especially heavy battles were unfolding in the Sárkeresztúr area where the Germans destroyed numerous Soviet tanks.[77] Above them in the air several dogfights occured during the day with about four to eight Bf 109s engaging in each. Between 10:10-11:25 LT at 3000m eight Yak-3s of 866 IAP led by Capt. Bondar flew in the Sárkeresztúr-Sárbogárd area. At 10:35 LT they engaged in combat with four Bf 109s. Two Bf 109s were claimed by the Yaks while one Yak-3 (c/n: 310233, engine: 432-265, arrived on 24 January 1945) was hit by Hptm. Lipfert. The damaged Yak-3 still could return to its base where it crashed but the pilot, Capt. Aleksandr Danilovich Piorunskii, was unhurt.

Between 13:00-14:00 LT six Yak-3s of 611 IAP, led by regiment commander Lt.Col. Nikolai Fedorovich Isaenko,[78] covered Soviet ground troops in the Sárkeresztúr-Sárbogárd area. At 13:25 LT at 3500m over Aba they met eight Bf 109s. Maj. Aleksei Pavlovich Churilin went into the attack first and from the distance of only 15-20m downed a Bf 109 which fell at Felsőtarnóca. At 13:30 LT at 4500m Lt.Col. Isaenko went into the attack and firing from 50 to 40m downed another Bf 109, which crashed four kilometers East of Mezőszentgyörgy. At 13:32 LT at 3000m Maj. Pyotr Mihailovich Moshin opened fire on a Bf 109 from 30m and downed it at Sárszentágota. Finally St.Lt. Ivan Ivanovich Soshnikov claimed a Bf 109 from 20m over Enying.[79] By checking the records it is entirely possible that the Soviet fighters engaged in air combat with Bf 109s of the Hungarian 101/1. and 101/3. fighter squadrons which lost two Messerschmitts in the Sárbogárd area indeed. Sgt. Bárány József (in Bf 109G-14, WNr.: 511869, 'W-1+15', who returned) and Ens. Asztalos Károly (in Bf 109G-14, WNr.: 610576, 'W-1+99', who went missing). A third Bf 109G-10 (WNr.: 610951) was only damaged (25%) and

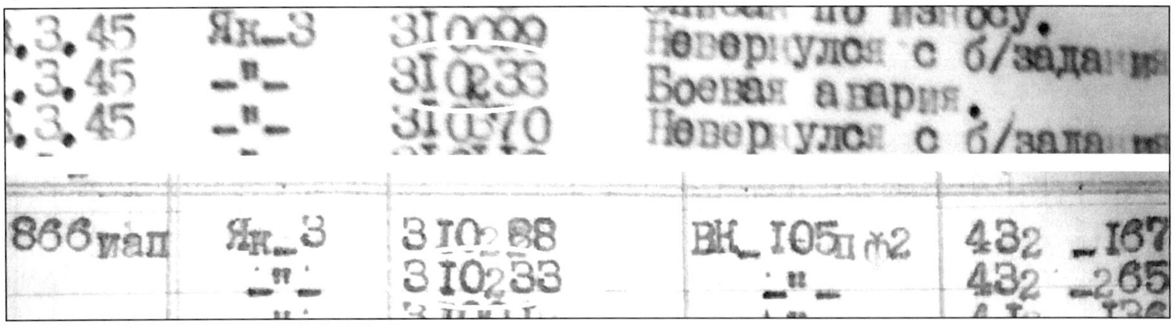

Capt. Piorunskii's Yak-3 in the aircraft loss summary list of the 288 IAD for March 1945. This plane was downed by Helmut Lipfert on 11 March 1945. (TsAMO RF: fu. 20257, inv. 1, f. 95, p. 309)

76 This sortie was one of Lt. Nikolai Afanasevich Laguta's last Yak-9 sorties, since on 19 March 1945 he was assigned Yak-3, c/n: 310081, white '81' that he flew 20 times until April 1945. This Yak-3 originally arrived in 866 IAP on 10 October 1944 from Tbilisi. Later it was transferred to the 659 IAP where it became Lt. Laguta's personal plane. It survived the war and was listed in all three quarterly reports of the 288 IAD in 1945 (1 January, 1 April and 1 July 1945).

77 For example the Soviet 110th Tank Brigade lost T-34/85 No.4120942/'461'/Savva+, 4120944/'467' and 4120945/'466'. The 181st Tank Brigade lost T-34, #311551/'625' and 4100753/'663'/Politko. The 18th Guards Tank Regiment lost two Fisher-built M4A2(76)W Shermans: U.S.A. 3080649/'130'/L-R engines: 671112597, 671112674/Gv.Ml.Lt. Victor Ivanovich Shishkanov and USA 3080899/'139'/ L-R engines: 671111700, 671113781/Gv.Lt. Mihail Ananevich Erastov (WIA).

78 Lt.Col. Nikolai Fedorovich Isaenko flew two Yak-3s in 1945: c/n: 310123 from Tbilisi (28 times) and c/n: 2229235 from Saratov (11 times). His plane on 11 March 1945 had to be one of them.

79 TsAMO RF: fu. 20257, inv. 1, f. 46, p. 364, Operations journal of 288 IAD, entry for 11 March 1945.

landed at Székesfehérvár. This means that the Soviet fighters shot down two and overclaimed two Bf 109s, however due to the relatively small area it is impossible to tell who overclaimed and who had authentic aerial victories.

Between 13:25-14:30 LT at 4000m eight Yak-3s of 866 IAP led by Capt. Aleksandr Alekseevich Bondar covered ground troops at Cece. At 13:40 LT combat ensued with about fifty Fw 190s and twenty Bf 109s in groups of eight and twelve in the Simontornya area. St.Lt. Nikolai Grigorevich Surnev claimed two Bf 109s and a Fw 190, but was eventually hit – most likely by Hptm. Lipfert – at 14:05 LT. Surnev could still return to his base with severely damaged wings, tail-section, radiator and cabling. The damaged Yak-3 underwent a major repair by St.Mech.Lt. Fyodor Akakievich Blohin's mechanics and returned to combat service, therefore it cannot be sonsidered a verified aerial victory.

At 14:25 LT over Cece six 611 IAP Yaks also battled with eight Bf 109s. In the unfolding dogfight Lt. Nikolai Nikolaevich Kutsenko's Yak-9M was shot down at Simontornya-SE, 4 km and struck the ground vertically with such a high speed that its engine-block was later found disintegrated six meters deep in the ground. An old witness, who led the researchers to the exact crash site, recalled that the Soviet pilot bailed out successfully but was murdered in the air by an enemy fighter on his open parachute. First he was buried beside the church in Pálfa, later in Simontornya. His recovered engine was No.425-1449, his installed weapons were ИП-731 and МП-250 (44 г. Мч 75, М250ч).

Over Cece at 3000m 39 ORAP Yak-9 reconnaissance pair of Capt. Pavlov and Lt. Nicholskii received anti-aircraft fire but they returned to their base unhurt.

13 March 1945 (Tuesday)
Lipfert's 183rd: VICTORY, Yak-7 at 10:13 LT at Pákozd-S, 1 km

Soviet 5 and 17 VA permanent single-engine fighter losses on 13 March 1945				
Regiment:	**Type:**	**c/n:**	**Pilot:**	**Details:**
866 IAP	Yak-3	310119	A. F. Balashov MIA	Sáregres, 15:30 LT, 24Fw,16 Bf 109s
897 IAP	Yak-3	310370	G. S. Eliseenkov	17:05 LT, 2 Yak-3s over Fáncs, MIA
611 IAP	Yak-9M	3415323	S. A. Mazuhin+	Pákozd, 10:15 LT to Lipfert
611 IAP	Yak-9M	3415305	M. A. Kamenetskii	Börgönd, 10:15 LT, flak to Pázmánd
513 IAP	Yak-9M	2815344	I. P. Isaichev	Újszász, crash-landed due to fighter
73 GvIAP	Yak-9D	2115372	V. M. Savchuk	Lost to flak, engine salvaged
116 IAP	La-5F	39215208	A. Radchenko MIA	Csiribpuszta, Il-2 escort, 15:50 LT

On 13 March 1945, around 10:15 LT, Yak-9s of the 611 IAP attacked the Börgönd area. Combat was recored with eight to ten *'Fw 190s'*. Lt. Semyon Afanasevich Mazuhin was lost to Hptm. Lipfert near Pákozd, at Börgönd-NNE at 10:13LT. The other 611 IAP plane, Lt. Moisei Aronovich Kamenetskii's Yak-9M, was hit by small calibre flak and crash-landed at Pázmánd enroute home. In the battle Lt. Pyotr Constantinovich Rochagov claimed two *'Fw 190*'s.

Between 14:50-15:55 LT four Yak-3s of 866 IAP, led by Capt. Aleksandr Ivanovich Koldunov attacked enemy positions between Káloz and Szilasbalhás (now Mezőszilas) at Simontornya-NW. At 15:15 LT at 800m over Sáregres they met three groups of Fw 190s which were flying under the cover of sixteen Bf 109s. Koldunov immediately attacked the first group of the Fw 190s and downed one of them over Mezőszilas. Capt. Koldunov went into a second attack and downed a second Fw 190 from the second group, which exploded mid-air and fell Northwest of Igar. St.Lt. Stepan Georgievich Shamonov also claimed a Fw 190 which went down West of Igar. During the battle Ml.Lt. Aleksandr Fedorovich Balashov separated from his group and went missing.

On the same day Yak-3 reconnaissance pair of Lt. Guriev – Ml.Lt. Belyaev of 866 IAP met eight Bf 109s. In the unfolding dogfight Ml.Lt. Aleksandr Timofeevich Belyaev claimed a Bf 109 shot down.

14 March 1945 (Wednesday)
Lipfert's 184th: VICTORY, LaGG-5 at 12:07 LT at Székesfehérvár-SE, 10 km
Lipfert's 185th: VICTORY, Il-2 at 12:11 LT at Pákozd-W, 1 km

Soviet 5 and 17 VA Il-2 and single-engine fighter losses on 14 March 1945				
Regiment:	**Type:**	**c/n:**	**Pilot:**	**Details:**
116 IAP	La-5FN	39212869	A. A. Pantelkin+	Sárkeresztúr-E to fighter, HSU, '69'
164 IAP	La-5FN	39210653	Ivan F. Shukin	Accident, belly landed
164 IAP	La-5FN	39210906	V. F. Buldigin	Accident, belly landed
164 IAP	La-5FN	39211637	A.Yozhitskii POW	Székesfehérvár, lost to Lipfert
210 ShAP	Il-2m3	18842110	Lev K. Vorobiev+	Seregélyes-W, flak, '30'
210 ShAP	Il-2m3	18886107	V. I. Lemeshkin	*897 IAP Yak-9 ran into it, repaired*
267 IAP	Yak-1B	*11166*	Yankovich+	Slankamen, flew into ground object
611 IAP	Yak-9M	3315348	Kamenetskii MIA	Székesfehérvár-N, covering Soviet ground forces, returned
611 IAP	Yak-9M	27153100	Kovalevskii MIA	
611 IAP	Yak-1B	22163	*Unknown*	*Missing, later in service again*
611 IAP	Yak-1B	46185	G. P. Cherevko	Jászberény, lost in dark, bailed out
288 IAD	Yak-1B	48185	N/A	Scrapped due to wear and tear
897 IAP	Yak-9	*Unknown*	N. K. Konovalov	*Ran into a 210 ShAP Il-2, repaired*
615 ShAP	Il-2m3	11521	T. B. Kukaev+	Csiribpuszta, flak. 12 Il-2, 6 La-5
615 ShAP	Il-2m3	1874596	Ivan F. Brankov	Csiribpuszta-S, flak, 12 Il-2, 6 La-5
615 ShAP	Il-2m3	18801107	A. I. Zhigailo+	Csiribpuszta, flak. 12 Il-2, 6 La-5
672 ShAP	Il-2m3	12571	F. T. Mamontov+	Agárd-SE, 2 km , 17:25 LT, flak
672 ShAP	Il-2m3	1875688	P. S. Radchenko	Dinnyés, 2 Fw 190, 14:35LT, broken
672 ShAP	Il-2m3	1876788	Y. S. Makkoveev	Sukoró, dogfight, 17:10 LT
672 ShAP	Il-2m3	1877788	N. D. Botin+	Pákozd-S, in Lake Velence, 17:25 LT
672 ShAP	Il-2m3	1889203	M. Golobokov+	Dinnyés-SE, 2 km, flak, 17:25 LT*
707 ShAP	Il-2m3	18827109	V. I. Markov+	Őcsény airfield, accident, 16:44 LT
715 ShAP	Il-2m3	18881124	V. I. Kochergin	Sárosd-SE, 3.5 km, flak, white '4'
715 ShAP	Il-2m3	12332	G. N. Pirogov	Detric flak, CL at Ercsi, '33'
715 ShAP	Il-2m3	12293	I. P. Krasnoperov	Pusztaszabolcs-S, 3 km, white '18'
96 OKRAP	Il-2KR	11933	L. S.Kulikovskii+	Pákozd, 11:56 LT, lost to Lipfert
96 OKRAP	Yak-9M	3415313	O. A. Tihomirov	Sárkeresztúr, flak
165 GvShAP	Il-2m3	1871xxx	K. Sidelnikov	Drávaszabolcs-NE, 4 Il-2, 4 Bf 109
989 ShAP	Il-2m3	18874124	N. Zaharov	Vértesacsa-NW, 4 km , flak, '100'
989 ShAP	Il-2m3	*Unknown*	L. V. Hernans	Spanish pilot, *damaged*, white '26'
Unknown	Il-2m3	*Unknown*	*Unknown*	Seregélyes, destroyed by 210 ShAP
235 ShAP	Il-2m3	18818123	*Unknown*	*Combat damages, repaired*
131 GvShAP	Il-2m3	12342	G. N. Borisov	*Damaged by fighter, repaired, 1st Sq.*
131 GvShAP	Il-2m3	1876367	I. P. Tsukanov	*Damaged by flak, repaired, 1st Sq.*
131 GvShAP	Il-2m3	1873774	A. M. Skleptchuk	*Damaged by flak, repaired, 2nd Sq.*
188 GvShAP	Il-2m3	303945	*Unknown, 1st Sq.*	*Combat damages, repaired***
207 OKRAP	Il-2KR	11505	N/A	Scrapped
207 OKRAP	Yak-9D	19166096	*Unknown*	Combat loss to flak
179 IAP	Yak-1B	28161	N/A	Scrapped due to wear and tear
92 IAP	La-5FN	39213380	V. I. Andreev	*Vecsés, LAC, propeller damage****

* This Il-2 arrived to the 672 ShAP on 1 February 1945 from the main reserve of the 17 VA.

** Scrapped by 4 May 1945.

*** The plane landed on a bad spot and stopped on its nose. It was repaired in one hour.

14 March 1945 was definitely one of the harder days for the 17 VA crews during the War. Continuous missions, several dogfights and an unusually high rate of losses were occuring throughout the day. The events became even more complex when damaged American planes crossed the battlefield seeking safety on the Soviet side.[80]

At 11:45 LT, twelve 306 ShAD Il-2s escorted by six 164 IAP La-5s, led by Capt. Ivan Dmitrievich Novikov, took off from Tököl airbase South of Budapest to attack ground targets in the Székesfehérvár area. At the altitude of 1000m the Soviet formation was attacked by eight *'Fw 190'*s over the target area. One of the attackers was Hptm. Lipfert who downed a *'LaGG-5'* at 12:07 LT. This plane was Lt. Anatolii Victorovich Yozhitskii's La-5FN (c/n: 39211637, ASh-82FN engine: 8211279, white '37'). Yozhitskii bailed out successfully from his plane at around 150m and was captured by nearby German tank crews. He spent the night in their HQ, was sent to Veszprém, then to Bratislava, where he escaped with Capt. Maksimov (136 ShAD) and Capt. Chekurin (4 GvShAD), crossed the Vág river and returned to his own side by 30 March 1945

Lipfert's next victim of the day was 96 OKRAP Il-2KR around 11:56 LT, 1000m at Pákozd near Lake Velence. This artillery spotter-reconnaissance Il-2 was attacked by enemy fighter Northwest of Lake Velence. Pilot Ml.Lt. Leonid Semyonovich Kulikovskii was killed and buried two kilometers Northwest of Pákozd. His observer Lt. Vasilii Ivanovich Romashin bailed out successfully and survived the crash with minor injuries.

Between 14:53-15:03 LT ten 715 ShAP Il-2s escorted by six 116 IAP La-5s, led by Maj. Anatolii Aleksandrovich Pantelkin (HSU), attacked about twenty enemy tanks and forty vehicles in the Seregélyes area where they met four Bf 109s and two *Fw 190s*.[81] The enemy planes attacked from the sun. One of the two *'new model Fw 190'*s' hit the closest La-5 (Maj. Pantelkin's La-5FN, c/n: 39212869, ASh-82FN engine: 8213627, white '69') from 50m which burst into flames, went into a 45-degree dive and hit the ground Southeast of Aba killing its pilot instantly. The attacker left the battle immediately after his victory and flew back to German controlled territory.[82] The other hit La-5 was flown by Ml.Lt. Ivan Pavlovich Antonov, who after claiming a Bf 109 over two kilometers Northwest of Seregélyes successfully returned to his airbase.

17 March 1945 (Saturday)

Lipfert's 186th: VICTORY, Il-2 at 16:15 LT at Lake Velence

Soviet 17 VA Il-2 losses on 17 March 1945				
Regiment:	**Type:**	**c/n:**	**Pilot:**	**Details:**
210 ShAP	Il-2m3	18818116	N. S. Esaulenko	Pátka, Bf 109s at 500m, white '2'
615 ShAP	Il-2m3	1873298	N. I. Panasyuk*	Decs-NW, engine issue at 09:52 LT
615 ShAP	Il-2m3	303434	F. N. Kligun	Őcsény, take off accident, 16:10 LT
615 ShAP	Il-2m3	11219	P. P. Nikitin**	Lake Velence, after 16:00 LT, Bf 109
639 ShAP	Il-2m3	12108	I. Y. Tarabrin	Őcsény, LAC, – forgot the wheels
639 ShAP	Il-2m3	1889403	I. Y. Tarabrin+	Székesfehérvár-S in Lake Sós to flak
672 ShAP	Il-2m3	1889303	P. F. Senikov	Sárkeresztes-NE, flak, no repair
989 ShAP	Il-2m3	12515	I. A. Dzhanaev+	Moha, flak at 700m, 17:32 LT, '28'
989 ShAP	Il-2m3	*Unknown*	N. F. Bakanov	*Combat damages, repaired, '3'*
165 GvShAP	Il-2m3	18753xx	*Unknown*	*Flak damage, repaired*
165 GvShAP	Il-2m3	18871114	I. D. Pavlov+	Nard, Croatia, flak, 14:17 LT

* In June 1945 Ml.Lt. Nikolai Ivanovich Panasyuk, pilot of the 1st Sq. flew Il-2m3, white '3'.

** In June 1945 Capt. Pyotr Petrovich Nikitin (CO of 1st Sq.) flew Il-2m3, white '1'.

80 325 FG P-51D Mustangs force landed or were lost at Bia and Ozora (44-13430 and 44-63360), a 2 BG B-17G at Tata (44-6428) and a 464 BG B-24L at Pécs (44-49713) – all in the middle of intense dogfights fought in the air. Similar events occurred more and more often as the front lines moved to the West.

81 At 14:32 LT twelve 715 ShAP Il-2s led by Il-2 No.29/Murashko took off for this mission to Seregélyes, but two of them (white No.10/Elohov and 38/Ratushnuk) returned early. Thus the attack was carried out only by ten Il-2s, which formed two groups of five planes. (White 4, 8, 13, 15, 17, 18, 29, 30, 33 and 39.) No.18/Krasnoperov was downed by four Bf 109s from the second group. No.30/Vorobiev, as well as No.33/Pirogov were shot down by flak, while four others (39/Gadiaev, 15/Leonov, 17/Tulenev and 8/Taranovich) were damaged by flak. Vorobiev's plane was 'borrowed' from the 210 ShAP for the mission. No.4/Kochergin returned though was downed during the next mission of the day. The Soviet 116 IAP fighter escort lost one plane near the target (No.69/Pantelkin). Source: TsAMO RF: fu. 22926, inv. 188593s, f. 2, p. 26, 715 ShAP Mission Report, entry for 14 March 1945.

82 According to the Soviet report Maj. Pantelkin's attacker was a 'new Fw 190 model' with a longer nose and liquid-coolant system. This was probably a wrong observation, since the Fw 190D-9 never flew over Hungary. Perhaps it was a new Bf 109 model that they misidentified in the air, especially because small mixed Bf 109 and Fw 190 flights were usually not deployed in the area.

After 16:00 LT this day seven 615 ShAP Il-2s continued straffing German tanks and artillery targets in the Székesfehérvár-SW area when they were attacked by twelve Bf 109s and six Fw 190s. Three of them, including Hptm. Lipfert, attacked Capt. Nikitin's Il-2 and damaged his engine. The engine (AM-38F, No.259196) lost power and the plane ditched into Lake Velence aproximately 300m from the North-West shore. St.Lt. Bersenev's escorting six 848 IAP La-5 fighters reported that the crew (Squadron commander pilot Capt. Pyotr Petrovich Nikitin and aerial gunner Gv.Sgt. Dmitry Sergeevich Apalkov) abandoned their plane in about 1.5m deep water and probably exited the lake by wandering through the reeds present in the Northern shoreline.

20 March 1945 (Tuesday)
Lipfert's 187th: VICTORY, Il-2 at 15:33 LT at Székesfehérvár-SE, 3-4 km
Lipfert's 188th: VICTORY, Il-2 at 15:41 LT at Várpalota-SW, 2-3 km
Lipfert's UNCLAIMED POTENTIAL VICOTRY, Il-2

Soviet 17 VA Il-2m3 Sturmovik losses on 20 March 1945				
Regiment:	**Type:**	**c/n:**	**Pilot:**	**Details:**
210 ShAP	Il-2m3	11082	P. A. Taranovich	Gúttamási-NW to Lipfert, white '8'
210 ShAP	Il-2m3	1871797	A. D. Belyashin+	Öskü-NE, in a swamp, white '23'
639 ShAP	Il-2m3	*Unknown*	I. P. Razin	*Szabadbattyán flak, later repaired*
672 ShAP	Il-2m3	1871188	F. M. Dadyushko	Csákberény-E, 15:30 LT to Lipfert
715 ShAP	Il-2m3	18810118	G. N. Domnin+	Söréd, 15:38 LT, Lipfert, white '21'
951 ShAP	Il-2m3	11623*	V. M. Staritskii+	Tác-NE, 2 km, flak, 600 m
989 ShAP	Il-2m3	10200	G. P. Mirnii+	Csákberény, 10:22 LT, flak, wh.'22'
989 ShAP	Il-2m3	*Unknown*	E. A. Gorshunov	*Combat damages, repaired, '2'*
989 ShAP	Il-2m3	18802121	N. I. Pahai	*Combat damages, repaired, '23'*

* According to the January 1945 weapon inspection report the S/N of the installed weapons on this plane were ГА-250, ГО-255 (23mm VYa-23s), БФ-120 (7.62mm ShKAS) and XC-642 (12.7mm UBT).

20 March 1945 was among one of Hptm. Lipfert's most successful, yet most unusual, days during the Second World War. A war correspondent interviewed him on the Veszprém airbase after offering Lipfert two bottles of wine. Right after the interview and after consuming the liquid courage, Lipfert took off for marauding Il-2s in the Várpalota area. Later he admitted that the consumed alcohol had a fair share in his success, because it suppressed his fear, so that he challenged the Soviets in a way that otherwise he would have never done.[83] This time he engaged Il-2s of the 672, 715 and 210 ShAPs of the Soviet 17 VA.

First at 15:30 LT he attacked a flight of nine Il-2s of the 672 ShAP. Lipfert dived under the formation, then by pulling up opened fire on the last Il-2. He hit the engine so well that the heavy ground attack plane simply sheared away from its formation in a shallow dive, flying on its failing engine (AM-38F, No.4509681) to later crash-land East of Csákberény on Soviet controlled territory. Its crew, pilot Ml.Lt. Fyodor Mihailovich Dadyushko and aerial gunner Sgt. Vasilii Sergeevich Morchkov were slightly injured. A few minutes later Lipfert went into the second attack on the Il-2s flying at around 3000m.[84] This time he attacked the formation of the 715 ShAP, which, between 14:45-16:12 LT was led by Lt.Col. Aleksandr Vasilevich Samohin in Il-2m3, c/n: 13522, white '36', flew 23 sorties in the Székesfehérvár-N area.[85] This time he chose an Il-2 from the first 'troika'. He opened fire and shot it down. The plane disintegrated in the air and crashed near Söréd at 15:38 LT. Its crew, pilot Ml.Sgt. Gennadiy Nikitovich Domnin and aerial gunner Evgenii Consantinovich Shmyakov were killed. The soviet fighter escort of eight 164 IAP La-5s, flying at 3000m failed to protect the Il-2s because they entered into combat tragically late.

By the time Lipfert went into his third attack the air was full of fighters – all Soviet – therefore he found himself alone. With his consumed alcohol still calling the shots and without a sense of fear he closed in on his third Il-2 (most likely 210 ShAP Il-2m3, c/n: 11082, white '8'), which left the group and turned back from the Öskü area with light flak damages in its left aileron. Lipfert opened fire and shot it down with the aircraft's wings and fuselage ablaze.[86] The Il-2 disintegrated in the air and crashed at Gúttamási-NW, but the crew of pilot Ml.Lt. Pyotr Alekseevich Taranovich and wounded aerial gunner

83 Lipfert, Gribig, *The War Diary of Hauptmann Helmut Lipfert*, p. 170.
84 Lipfert, Gribig, *The War Diary of Hauptmann Helmut Lipfert*, p. 169.
85 The 23 715 ShAP Il-2m3 Sturmoviks between 14:45-16:12 LT in the Székesfehérvár area were white 1, 2, 7, 8, 9, 10, 12, 13, 14, 15, 17, 18, 19, 20, 21, 22, 25, 26, 29, 30, 33, 36 and 38.
86 Lipfert, Gribig, *The War Diary of Hauptmann Helmut Lipfert*, p. 170.

Il-2m3, white '38' of the 715 ShAP with officers. On 20 March 1945 715 ShAP Il-2m3 No.'38' was flown by Gv.Ml.Lt. Ivan Mihailovich Degtyarev pilot and Ml.Sgt. Vasilii Philippovich Bobrov aerial gunner who successfully returned to their airbase. (Photo: Units and planes, <http://ava.org.ru/shap/715.htm>)

St.Sgt. Victor Constantinovich Ogarkov successfully bailed out and returned to their unit.[87] Lipfert recalls: *'I flew toward the command post from an altitude of about 500 meters in order to indicate my three kills by waggling my wings'*.[88] The Soviet loss report written on 24 March 1945 mentiones that between 15:47-15:52 LT five 210 ShAP Il-2s attacked the Öskü-Berhida area at 900m when an Il-2m3 (c/n: 1871797) was shot down by flak and by six *Fw 190* and four Bf 109 fighters. The other damaged plane, Il-2 (c/n: 11082), left the formation only after this crash and was heading for Gúttamási where four *'Fw 190'*s finally downed it. The time and area seem to match Lipfert's unclaimed Sturmovik victory. The question is why did the Soviets report four fighters? Why did Lipfert, who recalled the events accurately and who wrote that he made three victories, only have two claims recorded? Maybe it was just an overclaim? We might never get to know the answers to these questions. What we know for sure is that all the above listed Il-2 Sturmoviks were permanently lost on 20 March 1945, with Helmut Lipfert playing a very large part in their destruction.

21 March 1945 (Wednesday)
Lipfert's 189th: VICTORY, La-5 at 11:58 LT at Lake Balaton-E
Lipfert's 190th: VICTORY, 'Yak-5'[Sic!] at 15:30 LT at Felsőgalla-SW, 6 km

Soviet 5 and 17 VA permanent single-engine fighter losses on 21 March 1945				
Regiment:	**Type:**	**c/n:**	**Pilot:**	**Details:**
164 IAP	La-5F	39214179	V.G. Puzirenko MIA	Polgárdi, 07:20, 8 La, 23 Il-2, 4 Fw
164 IAP	La-5FN	39211401	V. M. Larichev MIA	Polgárdi, 07:20, 8 La, 23 Il-2, 4 Fw
31 IAP	La-5FN	39211435	A. V. Artemov WIA	Csákvár, 18:28 LT, LAC, '35'
848 IAP	La-5FN	39213018	K. Y. Vasilev+	In Lake Balaton near Alsóörs, '18'
611 IAP	Yak-9M	3215307	A. A. Aleshkin+	Bakonycsernye-S, 11:00, 8 *Fw 190*
897 IAP	Yak-9M	3415317	A. K. Klavdiev WIA	Bicske-E, 2 km, flak, 6 Yak-9s
179 IAP	Yak-9M	4515340	V. Y. Ragulin+	Felsőgalla, 15:30LT to Hptm. Lipfert

87 TsAMO RF: fu. 20174, inv. 1, f. 37, p. 258, Operations report of 210 ShAP staff for March 1945, entry for 20 March 1945.
88 Lipfert, Gribig, *The War Diary of Hauptmann Helmut Lipfert*, p. 170.

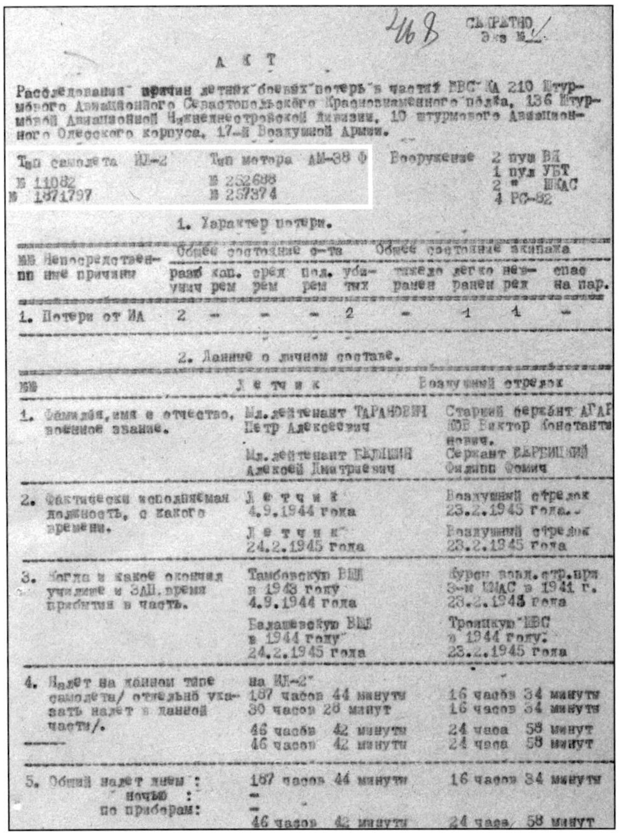

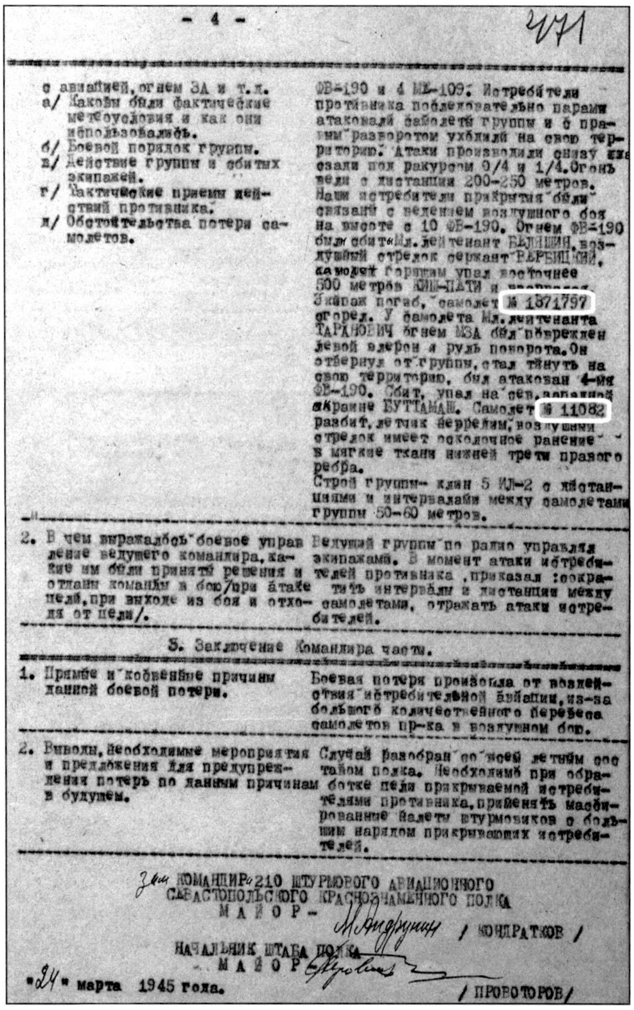

The first and the fourth page of Soviet loss report of the two 210 ShAP Il-2s lost on 20 March 1945 at Öskü and Gúttamási, Hungary with specified aircraft construction and AM-38F engine numbers. Il-2m3 (c/n: 11082) was probably shot down by Hptm. Helmut Lipfert. (TsAMO RF: fu. 20174, inv. 2, f. 42, pp. 468-471.)

On 21 March 1945 Hptm. Lipfert scored his last two victories in the Hungarian sky. He first downed a La-5 fighter over Lake Balaton. This was 848 IAP La-5FN (c/n: 39213018, engine: 82131264, white '18') of St.Lt. Constantin Yakovlevich Vasilev (+, deputy Sq. CO). At 12:00 LT in the vicinity of Balatonkenese, six 848 IAP La-5s escorted 17 Il-2s of 707 ShAP (led by St.Lt. Balashov) when eight Bf 109s attacked them. The Vasilev-Honenev pair tried to protect the Il-2s but Vasilev was hit and abandoned his plane over the lake. The Il-2 crews observed an open parachute over Lake Balaton between 1000-500m. What happened to Vasilev after this is a mystery. He could have died of hypothermia, his wounds, or his enemies waiting for him on the shore. Either way he made the ultimate sacrifice for his homeland at the age of 24. The remains of his plane were recovered from the Eastern end of Lake Balaton in the early 1950s.

This event is almost certianly linked to Lipfert's account of his *'LaGG-5'* shot down over Lake Balaton whose pilot bailed out into the water on 17 March 1945 [sic!].[89] After unsuccessfully attacking Il-2s over the Northern end of Lake Balaon, Lipfert saw an enemy fighter directly 500m above.[90] He reported that only a few cannon hits were necessary for the *LaGG-5* to disintergrate in the air, while the Soviet pilot began to swim towards the Geman held shoreline after sucessfully bailing out into the water.[91] The Soviets most likely could not follow up with Vasilev as he had either been captured by the Germans or had died in the cold waters of the lake.

Hptm. Lipfert's very last aerial victory over Hungary, which he recorded as a 'Yak-5'[Sic!], was Lt. Victor Yakovlevich Ragulin's Yak-9M at Felsőgalla (Tatabánya-SE). This time the Yak-9 pair of Maj. Kostikov – Lt. Ragulin were flying a reconnaissance mission in the Ács area when eight *'Fw 190's* attacked them. The recconasiance pair turned back and tried to avoid any direct confrontation with the fighters. Soon after this at 15:30 LT another twelve *'Fw 190's* joined the battle and hit Ragulin's plane. Maj. Mihail Mihailovich Kostikov could return to his base but Lt. Ragulin went missing.

89 Lipfert, Gribig, *The War Diary of Hauptmann Helmut Lipfert*, pp. 168-169.
90 Lipfert, Gribig, *The War Diary of Hauptmann Helmut Lipfert*, p. 168.
91 Lipfert, Gribig, *The War Diary of Hauptmann Helmut Lipfert*), p. 169.

Conclusion

Based on his wartime records and memoires, Hptm. Helmut Lipfert had extraordinary flying and observation skills and was exceptional amongst all fighter aces of the Luftwaffe during the Second World War. He was one of the braver – or more daring – German fighter aces who tended to verify the actual results of his actions before leaving the battlefield, witnessing the burning wrecks of the planes that he claimed. This honest approach, which was obviously extremely dangerous in the final years of the war, made him one of the top and most reliable German fighter aces whose records passed the tests of not only the German, but the Soviet military records as well.

11

Heinrich Sturm (1920-1944)

Born on 12 June 1920, Heinrich Sturm joined JG 52 in the summer of 1941. He claimed his first aerial victory, a Soviet Pe-2 on 18 October 1941 just a few months after he turned 21 years old. Later he served as a fighter-school instructor until November 1942, when he returned to frontline service. On 1 September 1943 he officially took command of 4./JG 52 and was awarded the *Ritterkreuz* on 26 March 1944. After recovering from wounds he returned in August 1944 to operations and took command of 5./JG 52 where he claimed his first aerial victory over Hungary on 18 October 1944. By the time of his death on 22 December 1944 on the airfield of Csór where his landing gear accidentally hit a truck, he had 123 aerial victories though his former wingmen estimated a somewhat higher number of over 125.[1] He claimed his last 13 victories over Hungary. Sturm also seemingly had the very last OKL/RLM confirmed claim of the Luftwaffe remaining on record.[2]

Heinrich Sturm's claims are compiled from the following sources listed in order of heaviest reliance:

- Luftwaffe Aces: claims and bibliographies, Vol. 1
- Die Geschichte der II. Gruppe des Jagdgeschwaders 52: Offizielle Ausgabe der Traditionsgemeinschaft JG 52
- Tony Woods – Eastern Front Vol 4. 1944. Jul – Dec, Issue 1

All the lists are congruent for the dates and aircraft types. The claim number appearing in the Mathews & Foreman publication has been used.

18 October 1944 (Wednesday)

Sturm's 111th: VICTORY, Yak-7 at 15:29 LT[3] at Mikepércs-N (Debrecen-S) at 4000m, Anerk: Nr. 929

Soviet 5 VA single-engine fighter losses on 18 October 1944				
Regiment:	**Type:**	**c/n:**	**Pilot:**	**Details:**
149 GvIAP	Yak-7B	5315329	A. A. Sokolov	Hajdúszoboszló-S, Szeghalom-SW, 14:10 – 15:15 LT, in dogfight
149 GvIAP	Yak-9D	17166057	R. I. Kolechkin	
149 GvIAP	Yak-9D	17166071	P. I. Kozlov WIA	Derecske-W, 14:40 – 16:10 LT
486 IAP	La-5F	39214770	F. I. Nikonorenkov+	Nagylak, KIFA at 14:13 LT
178 GvIAP	La-5F	39214628	G. E. Karnauhov	*Damaged in dogfight, repaired*

On 18 October 1944 Hptm. Sturm claimed a Soviet Yak-7 fighter at 'Miki Peres'-N (correct location: Mikepércs-N) at 15:23 LT. Between 14:40 and 16:10 LT five 149 GvIAP Yaks led by Sq. commander Gv.Capt. Mihail Stephanovich Fateev covered the Soviet ground troops in the Hajdúszoboszló-Debrecen-Derecske triangle. During their patrol, the Soviet fighters spotted two *'Fw 190s'* and began to follow them. Since they were called back to their airbase over the radio at this time they left the battle and headed for home. All turned for home except Gv.St.Lt. Pyotr Ivanovich Kozlov who kept chasing the Germans alone and was soon shot down. His Omsk-built Yak-9D (c/n: 17166071, engine: 415-151) caught fire

1 Andrew-Johannes Mathews and John Foreman, *Luftwaffe Aces: Biographies and Victory claims*. Vol. 4 (Surrey: Red Kite, 2014), p. 1293.
2 Tony Woods, O.K.L. Fighter Claims: Reich, West and Südfront, Aug to Dec 1944. Vol. I. It was #938.
3 15:23 LT according to Tony Woods, O.K.L. Fighter Claims: Reich, West and Südfront, Aug to Dec 1944. Vol. I

and he bailed out with his parachute. Having been seriously injured in the air he landed near Derecske. Soon after landing a patrol of eight German and Hungarian troops approached and ordered him to surrender. At this moment Kozlov grabbed his pistol and instead of surrendering he opened fire on the patrol. When he ran out of bullets, he was taken prisoner right away. For his aggressive action the angered troops beat him badly and questioned him about his unit and airbase. He refused to cooperate with his captors who then took his documents and beat him again to the point where he lost consciousness. After a very hard and painful day he was rescued by advancing Soviet tank crews who took him to field hospital No.2308, which he was able to leave by 11 January 1945. After 5 February 1945 he worked as ground personnel with the 5 VA. His Yak-9D was downed by Hptm. Heinrich Sturm as one of his legitimate aerial victories.

20 October 1944 (Friday)
Sturm's 112th: POTENTIAL VICTORY, LaGG-5 at 07:59 LT at Szolnok-E, 30 km at 7000m, Anerk: Nr. 930

Soviet 5 VA single-engine fighter losses on 20 October 1944 in Hungary				
Regiment:	**Type:**	**c/n:**	**Pilot:**	**Details:**
73 GvIAP	Yak-1B	38151	G. F. Harchenko	Csanádapáca, 14:40 LT, 2 *Fw 190s*
85 GvIAP	Yak-1B	17157	*Unknown, 1st Sq.*	*Engine replacement, SOC on 14.01.45.*
85 GvIAP	Yak-9D	2015398	*Unknown*	CL, scrapped
92 IAP	La-5FN	39213223	N. F. Grevtsov	Missing. 08:10 LT to Fw 190s, Bf 109s
92 IAP	La-5FN	39212966	I. S. Bemov WIA	Bombed at Szarvas Fl.Pl. at 08:00LT*

* The Szarvas airfield was bombed by Hungarian Me 210Ca-1s and as such the 132 GvShAP lost four Il-2m3 Sturmoviks (c/n: 1870276, 1870780, 1878476, 1879279).

On 20 October 1944 Hptm. Sturm claimed a Soviet La-5 fighter shot down in the Szolnok-E area. This day around 08:00 LT at 2000m four 92 IAP La-5s, led by St.Lt. Ivan Petrovich Maslov were escorting six Il-2s in the Szolnok area where they engaged in aggressive aerial combat with approximately twelve Bf 109s which forced them to return to their base without completing their mission. On the way home, the Soviets met seven Ju 88s and another twenty Bf 109s and Fw 190s which had just bombed their airfield South of Szarvas.[4] During the unfolding dogfight Ml.Lt. Nikolai Fedorovich Grevtsov, flying his eighth combat mission during the war, separated from his group and went missing. About the same time on the ground a nearby explosion destroyed Ml.Lt. Ivan Sergeevich Bemov's La-5FN, while the Soviet pilot received minor shrapnel injuries to his head. Since the time and the reported area both closely match Hptm. Sturm's LaGG 5 claim – thought the altitude of 7000m does not (perhaps this was a clerical error?) – Ml.Lt. Nikolai Fedorovich Grevtsov's lost La-5FN can be considered Sturm's potential aerial victory.

29 October 1944 (Sunday)
Sturm's 113th: OVERCLAIM, LaGG-5 at 14:35 LT at Szolnok-NE, 25 km at 1500m, Anerk: Nr. 931
Sturm's 114th: OVERCLAIM, Il-2 at 14:36 LT at Szolnok-SW at 1000m, Anerk: Nr. 932

Soviet 5 VA Il-2 and single-engine fighter losses on 29 October 1944 in Hungary				
Regiment:	**Type:**	**c/n:**	**Pilot:**	**Details:**
486 IAP	La-5FN	39213394	V. G. Pletnev	Jászszentlászló, to Kecskemét flak
190 GvShAP	Il-2m3	18893113	N. Solodovnikov	MIA in the Kecskemét area

On 29 October 1944 at 14:35 and 14:36 LT Hptm. Sturm claimed a La-5 and an Il-2 victory one minute apart from each other in the Szolnok-Törökszentmiklós area. The only lost La-5 this day was Lt. Vasilii Gerasimovich Pletnev's La-5FN at 14:50 LT, which was hit by flak over Kecskemét and crashed near Jászszentlászló which is too great a distance from Szolnok and Törökszentmiklós to be considered a possible victim (four La-5s were escorting two reconnaissance Il-2s over Izsák-Kecskemét between 600 and 800m). This was the case with Sturm's Il-2 claim as well. Between 12:25-13:00 LT two groups of eight 190 GvShAP Il-2m3 Sturmoviks attacked the German artillery positions in the Izsák-Kecskemét area.[5] Gv.Ml.Lt. Nikolai Leontevich Solodovnikov failed to return from the combat mission as the only 5 VA Il-2 loss of the day. Since the reported times and the regions were too far from Hptm. Sturm's victory claims for both of these aircrafts should be considered overclaims.

4 The reported Ju 88s were in fact Hungarian Messerschmitt Me 210Ca-1s of the 102/1., 102/2. FBS.
5 TsAMO RF: fu: 20512, inv: 1, f: 90, p. 249, Operations journal of 231 ShAD covering the 2nd Ukrainian Front, entry for 29 October 1944.

31 October 1944 (Tuesday)
Sturm's 115th: OVERCLAIM, LaGG-5 at 15:18 LT at Kecskemét-N, Anerk: Nr. 935
Sturm's 116th: POTENTIAL VICTORY, Il-2 at 15:23 LT in the Kecskemét area, Anerk: Nr. 936
Sturm's 117th: POTENTIAL VICTORY, LaGG-5 at 15:26 LT at Kecskemét-N, Anerk: Nr. 937
Sturm's 118th: OVERCLAIM, Il-2 at 15:28 LT at Kecskemét-W, Anerk: Nr. 938

Soviet 5 VA aircraft losses on 31 October 1944 in Hungary				
Regiment:	**Type:**	**c/n:**	**Pilot:**	**Details:**
130 GvShAP	Il-2m3	8280	D. S. Popov MIA	Nagykőrös, flak, 14:00 LT, 8 Il-2s
130 GvShAP	Il-2m3	9788	A. N. Yeremeev+	Nagykőrös, flak, 14:00 LT, 8 Il-2s
131 GvShAP	Il-2m3	10752	A. N. Korchagin	Nagykőrös-S, 13:50 LT, 4 *Fw190s*
187 GvShAP	Il-2m3	12172	A.G. Lubishev MIA	Kecskemét-SE, lost to fighters, '56'
190 GvShAP	Il-2m3	11035	A. F. Berezhovskii	Gyoma, LAC, Bf 109s, 13:55 LT
190 GvShAP	Il-2m3	1871479	N.A. Bachurin MIA	Kecskemét-SE, 13:55LT, 18 Bf 109s
190 GvShAP	Il-2m3	303830	P. D. Suhodolskii+	Kecskemét-SW,13:55LT, 18 Bf 109s
177 GvIAP	La-5F	39215187	P. Y. Morduhovich	Kecskemét-SW, 15:25LT, 2 Bf 109s
177 GvIAP	La-5FN	41210105	A. A. Kunshin MIA	Cegléd-Szolnok, strafing at 09:30 LT
452 BAP	A-20G	42-54006	P. I. Ivanov+	Bánréve flak to Ózd, factory yard

On 31 October 1944 between 15:18 and 15:28 LT Hptm. Heinrich Sturm claimed two Il-2s and two LaGG-5 fighters shot down in the Kecskemét area. That day at 15:25 LT four La-5s of the 177 GvIAP were patrolling over the Kecskemét-Nagykőrös-Lajosmizse triangle, where at 2000m they engaged in air combat with two *'Fw 190's* and two Bf 109s. Gv.Capt. Pavel Yakovlevich Morduhovich and his wingman Gv.Lt. Abramov attacked the *'Fw 190s'*, while the Bf 109 pair got into Morduhovich's tail. Gv.Lt. Abramov broke away immediately and did not see or hear from his leader over the radio ever again.[6] Since the area matches and there was only one minute (!) between his claim and the Soviet loss report, this La-5F certainly seems to be Hptm. Heinrich Sturm's authentic aerial victory. However, a problem arises as Hptm. Erich Hartmann's 305th claim also matches this location and time of day. This problem is rectified through the examination of a few pieces of information about both claims. Firstly, Hptm. Sturm's claim time is only one minute apart from the Soviet reported loss time while Hptm. Hartmann made his claim five minutes later at 15:30 LT. Secondly, Sturm received official confirmation from the RLM (Anerk: Nr. 937), while Hartmann's claim did not though it was recorded in the microfilms. Thirdly, Erich Hartmann claimed a Yak-7, not a La-5 that Gv.Capt. Morduhovich flew during this mission while Hptm. Sturm claimed the correct aircraft type.

Hptm. Sturm's first La-5 claim of the day however is a completely different story. Since Morduhovich's La-5 was the only lost 5 VA La-5 in the afternoon at 15:25 LT, Hptm. Sturm's other La-5 claim at 15:18 LT had to be an overclaim.

For Hptm. Sturm's Il-2 claims of the day Gv.Ml.Lt. Andrey Grigorevich Lubishev's and Sgt. Gennadiy Georgievich Konev's Il-2 (white '56') seems to be an appropriate candidate, as after leaving their target near Kecskemét they left their group and went missing, presumably lost to enemy fighters.[7] Between 14:45-16:12 LT nine 187 GvShAP Il-2 Sturmoviks, led by Gv.Capt. Sergei Alekseevich Feoktistov escorted by four 177 GvIAP La-5s attacked the Lajosmizse-Kerekegyháza-Tatárszentgyörgy triangle at Kecskemét-NW, when two *'Fw 190s'* and two Bf 109s ambushed them and Gv.Ml.Lt. Lubishev's Il-2 went missing.

Hptm. Sturm's second Il-2 claim does not match the Soviet loss records. Although by the end of the day the 5 VA has reported 11 missing Il-2s (beside an A-20G Boston and two La-5s),[8] only seven of them were permanent losses while the remaining four later returned to combat service.

6 TsAMO RF: fu. 20062, inv. 1, f. 33, p. 157, Operations journal of 177 GvIAP, 14 GvIAD, entry for 31 October 1944.
7 The nine 187 GvShAP Il-2s were flown by Gv.Capt. Feoktistov/60, Makarov/98, Turapin/97, Nechiporuk/54, Zhukovskii/51, Grilev (Il-2 No.12260, '57'), Afanasev/59, Lubishev (Il-2 No.12172, '56'), Zatevahin/58. TsAMO RF: fu. 22416, inv. 0222544c, f. 2, p. 77, Combat register of the 187 GvShAP for April-December 1944, entry for 31 October 1944.
8 TsAMO RF: fu. 327, inv. 4999, f. 225, p. 118, Operations journal of the 5 VA for October 1944, entry for 31 October 1944.

2 November 1944 (Thursday)
Sturm's 119th: POTENTIAL VICTORY, Yak-9 at 11:35 LT at Nagykőrös-N, -NW, 30 km (Nyáregyháza-SW)

Soviet 5 VA single-engine fighter losses on 2 November 1944 in Hungary				
Regiment:	**Type:**	**c/n:**	**Pilot:**	**Details:**
192 IAP	La-5FN	39211287	V. M. Kashintsev	Kunszentmárton, 11:40 LT to flak
486 IAP	La-5FN	3921xx09	*Unknown*	*Flak damage, repaired, '09'*
31 GvIAP	Yak-9D	19166064	P. I. Chervinskii WIA	Ócsa-SE, CL, ~12:00 LT, *Fw 190s*
31 GvIAP	Yak-9D	1615309	A. N. Sirenko+	Albertirsa-W to *Dány* in dogfight
73 GvIAP	Yak-1B	15343	*Unknown*	*Combat damage, repaired at base*
73 GvIAP	Yak-9D	xx15343	*Unknown*	*Combat damage, repaired at base*
92 IAP	La-5FN	39212206	A. I. Belov	Ciborháza-SE, 3km, CL to flak*
92 IAP	La-5FN	39213295	I. A. Yegorov	Ciborháza-SE, 3km, flak, 14:30 LT

* The plane and engine were delivered to a scrapping yard in Odessa by 38 OTTR on 30 November 1944.

On 2 November 1944 at 11:35 LT Hptm. Sturm claimed a Soviet Yak-9 fighter shot down in the Nyáregyháza-SW area. This day around noon, six 31 GvIAP Yak-9s were covering Soviet ground troops in the Örkény-N area, where at around 1500m they met eight Ju 87 Stukas, fifteen Fw 190s and nine Bf 109s. While Yak-9D pilot Gv.Ml.Lt. Pavel Yosifovich Chervinskii repelled the attack of the enemy fighters on his leader, he was hit by two 'Fw 190s'. The leader of the 'Fw 190' pair set his engine on fire from a very short distance of approximately fifteen meters. He immediately went into a dive to escape followed by the two fighters down to ground level. Chervinskii finally ditched his burning plane in a shallow swamp right beside the forest of Újhartyán at Ócsa-SE. The enemy fighters strafed his plane on the ground two times which was very close to the actual frontline to ensure its destruction. The Yak-9D (31 GvIAP, 3rd Sq., c/n: 19166064, engine: 415-1978) burned out while Chervinskii received injures to his left leg. A local Hungarian hunter/forest ranger Mr. Kozma rushed to his help. He took him into his remote house in the forest where he treated his wounds and hid him. Soon afterwards the frontline passed the area and tank columns of the Soviet 4th Mechanized Corps were moving on the nearby Nagykőrösi road towards Budapest. Chervinskii left the house and waved to the Soviet tanks moving on the road with a white bra that he took from Mr. Kozma's house in order to get their attention. The tankmen took Chervinskii in and put the white bra on the tank's main gun as a 'trophy'. The Soviet aviator returned to his unit with the help of the Soviet 4th Mechanized Corps the next day. He was so thankful to the Kozma couple for saving his life that in the summer of 1972 -promoted to a Major General of Aviation- he returned to the area of his crash landing, visited the Kozma's and thanked them again. They kept in touch until as late as 1989.[9] After 1966 Chervinskii was deputy commander, later commander

31 GvIAP, 3rd Squadron pilot Gv.Ml.Lt. Pavel Yosifovich Chervinskii in his Yak-9D with the fuselage inscription 'От трудящихся Ростова – фронту' ('From the workers of Rostov to the front'), downed by Hptm. Heinrich Sturm on 2 November 1944 at Ócsa-Újhartyán. Below is the loss entry for his Yak-9D (c/n: 19166064) in the records of the 5th Air Army, 3rd GvIAK, entry for 2 November 1944: TsAMO RF: fu. 327, inv. 4999, f. 178, p.42. (Photo: Units and planes, <http://ava.org.ru/iap/31g.htm> (accessed 4 September 2021)

9 Collected memoires of local residents kindly provided by regional historian Félix Gábor.

of the Foreign (Air Force) Servicemen's Training Centre in Frunze, Kyrgyz SSR. Although Chervinskii's crash time and Hptm. Sturm's claiming time do not exactly match and another 31 GvIAP pilot, Gv.Ml.Lt. Aleksandr Nikolaevich Sirenko, was also shot down MIA in the aerial battle, the precisely matching area and Chervinskii's memoires suggest that his Yak-9D was Hptm. Heinrich Sturm's legitimate aerial victory. Gv.Ml.Lt. Aleksandr Nikolaevich Sirenko's Yak-9D probably crashed near Dány, Budapest-E as it is written in the brief 2 November 1944 telegram of the Royal Hungarian Police: *'Dány (Pest county): 1 single-engine Russian fighter crashed, its pilot has died.'*[10]

23 November 1944 (Thursday)
Sturm's 120th: VICTORY, Il-2 at 11:21 LT at Gyöngyös-SW, 20 km at 700m
Sturm's 121st: OVERCLAIM, Il-2 at 11:22 LT at Gyöngyös-SW, 20 km at 700m

Soviet 5 VA Il-2 Sturmovik losses on 23 November 1944				
Regiment:	**Type:**	**c/n:**	**Pilot:**	**Details:**
187 GvShAP	Il-2m3	12260	B. D. Grilev POW	*Hatvan-NE,* Bf 109, 11:20 LT, '57'
187 GvShAP	Il-2m3	*Unknown*	V. M. Afanasiev	*Nagykőrös, Bf 109s, '59', repaired*
187 GvShAP	Il-2m3	*Unknown*	V. V. Fedorenko	*Zsámbok-NE, flak, '98', repaired*

On 23 November 1944 at 11:21 and 11:22 LT Hptm. Sturm claimed two Soviet Il-2m3 Sturmoviks shot down one minute apart from each other in the Hatvan-S area. His opponent this time was the nine-plane flight of the 187 GvShAP, led by Gv.Capt. Sergei Alekseevich Feoktistov which was attacked by enemy fighters at 11:20 LT.[11] During the long and very intense dogfight the Soviets lost one plane, while a few others were badly damaged, including the one that Oblt. Paul Linxen (5./JG 52) claimed at 11:19 LT at Hatvan-E. Since Hptm. Sturm's first Il-2 claim is only one minute(!) apart from the single permanently lost 5 VA Il-2 of the day, this suggests that Il-2m3 (c/n: 12260, AM-38F engine: 2512489, white '57'), piloted by Gv.Ml.Lt. Boris Dmitrievich Grilev was Hptm. Heinrich Sturm's confirmed aerial victory. His other Il-2 claim was probably one of the two damaged Il-2s: Gv.Ml.Lt. Vasilii Mihailovich Afanasev's white '59', or Gv.St.Lt. Vladimir Vladimirovich Fedorenko's white '98', which later returned to combat service, thus cannot be considered as a verified aerial victory.

22 December 1944 (Friday)
Sturm's unconfirmed: POTENTAIL VICTORY in the Csór area
Sturm's unconfirmed: POTENTIAL VICTORY in the Csór area

Soviet 17 VA aircraft losses on 22 December 1944				
Regiment:	**Type:**	**c/n:**	**Pilot:**	**Details:**
611 IAP	Yak-1B	18193	P. M. Belyaev	Aba, to Hun. Bf 109, ~14:00 LT
611 IAP	Yak-9T	*Unknown*	A. I. Salnikov	*Flak, CL on airfield, repaired**
639 ShAP	Il-2m3	1876296	N. S. Baklanov	Pátka-SW, Bf 109s, crash-landed
639 ShAP	Il-2m3	18756101	M. E. Aksengor	Pátka-SW, Bf 109, Madocsa, CL
639 ShAP	Il-2m3	11249	M. P. Ratnikov+	Pátka-Zámoly, Bf 109s
639 ShAP	Il-2m3	1871698	V. T. Montrezor	Pátka-SW to Bf 109s
639 ShAP	Il-2m3	1876996	G. Semenov POW	Pátka-SW to Bf 109s
639 ShAP	Il-2m3	11271	M. A. Pletnev	Pátka-SW to Bf 109s
659 IAP	Yak-9D	16166036	A. E. Andreev+	Vereb, Hung. Fw 190F, ~12:30 LT
672 ShAP	Il-2m3	1871398	*M. A. Sizikov?*	*Damaged, repaired at airbase*
672 ShAP	Il-2m3	1870288	A. M. Kianovskii	Kecel, airbase accident at 12:10LT
672 ShAP	Il-2m3	1872184	I. M. Baranov KIFA	Kecel, airbase accident at 12:10LT
672 ShAP	Il-2m3	18763100	E. V. Vaitsitskii	Kecel, 15:00 LT, burned at landing
672 ShAP	Il-2m3	1879466	*Unknown*	*Flak damage, repaired at airbase*

10 Dr. Pataky, Iván: *Air events in Hungary according to the reports/telegrams of the Royal Hungarian Police, 1944*, Part III (A repüléstörténeti konferencia közleményei, 1998), p. 174.

11 The nine 187 GvShAP Il-2s between 10:43-12:20 LT were flown by Gv.Capt. Feoktistov/60, Makarov/50, Nechiporuk/96, Grilev/57, Zhukovskii/51, Afanasev/59, Turapin/52, Fyodorenko/98 and Ribalchenko/71. TsAMO RF: fu. 22416, inv.0222544c, f. 2, p. 84, Combat register of the 187 GvShAP for April-December 1944, entry for 23 November 1944.

Soviet 17 VA aircraft losses on 22 December 1944 (*continued*)				
672 ShAP	Il-2m3	*Unknown*	P. A. Kuzmin	Székesfehérvár flak, 13:00, at base
707 ShAP	Il-2m3	11649	N. P. Mironov	Székesfehérvár-N, 14:50, 2 Bf 109s
897 IAP	Yak-9D	16166099	N. I. Hlebantsov	Zámoly area, 6 Bf 109s, 9-10 LT
897 IAP	Yak-9D	0815357	*Unkown*	MIA, written off this day**
951 ShAP	Il-2m3	1883301	N. B. Baronin+	Csákvár-NE, 09:40 LT, Flakpanzer
951 ShAP	Il-2m3	1873693	P. A. Marakulin+	Near Lake Velence to Flakpanzer
951 ShAP	Il-2m3	1884401	G. P. Odnotsenov	Near L. Velence, Bf 109, 11:50 LT
951 ShAP	Il-2m3	11118	Y. P. Vaslyanin	Flak, parts salvaged by 367 BAO
995 ShAP	Il-2m3	1874686	A. I. Groshev ret.	Dinnyés-NW, 10:30 LT to Bf 109s
995 ShAP	Il-2m3	1886603	N. S. Shepochkin	Gyulamajor, 10:30 LT to Bf 109s
995 ShAP	Il-2m3	1875696	V. I. Seregin+	Zámoly-NE, 10:30 LT to flak

* Ml.Lt. Salnikov's Yak-9T was damaged by small calibre anti-aircraft artillery fire and crash-landed on its airbase. Pilot injured, his plane was repaired by aircraft mechanic C-a Georgii Borisovich Dyubin.

** Found in the mechanical loss report for 897 IAP. The loss probably occurred on one of the previous days and was removed from inventory on 22 December 1944 after the plane did not return from combat.

On 22 December 1944 just before his fatal accident, Hptm. Sturm claimed two aircraft shot down in the Csór area. Although the exact time, plane model and location details of his claims remain unknown, one small piece of remaining evidence allows for near certain verification of his claims: the time of Hptm. Heinrich Sturm's death.

Returning from a successful mission where he claimed two enemy aircraft, it was established that the 5./JG 52's Abschuss tally was now at 899 and that one lucky pilot would now be able to claim the 900th victory.[12] As Staffel captain of 5./JG 52, Hptm. Sturm wished to be this lucky pilot.[13] After landing he quickly boarded another aircraft and prepared for takeoff in the hopes of claiming another victory, however during the process of taking off his aircraft's wheels struck the top of a truck crossing the Csór airfield.[14] Hptm. Sturm's aircraft crashed and was engulfed in flames. The time of this accident and the death of Heinrich Sturm was 10:50 LT.[15]

Since Hptm. Sturm died before a proper documentation of his claims could be written there is no certainty about the timing, or aircraft type he claimed to be victorious over, though a detailed analysis of the morning's events partly make up for the lack of German documentation. Due to the timing of his death, Sturm's claims must have occurred before 10:50 LT, almost certainly around 10:30 LT or earlier (Sturm would need to return to his base from his first mission, land, mount a new aircraft and prepare for takeoff). This greatly reduces the group of his potential victims down to a few aircraft.

His first sortie was flown in the Székesfehérvár-N area, not far from his Csór airfield. Here the Soviet ground forces moved rapidly to the North in an effort to close and complete the blockade around Budapest from the West and met strong German resistance. In the concentrated German armour and artillery fire the Soviet 18th Tank Corps and the 7th Mechanized Corps alone lost 61 tanks![16] It is not hard to understand that in this critical situation the struggling Soviet ground forces immediately requested strong aerial support and air cover from their 17 VA, which with continuous Il-2 attacks pounded German artillery and armour in the Székesfehérvár-N area throughout the day.

There was also some Soviet fighter action in the morning around the Székesfehérvár area. Four Yaks from 611 IAP flew a ground cover mission led by Lt.Col. Isaenko from 09:45-10:40 LT around Székesfehérvár and engaged with three Bf 109s at 10:10 LT at 2500m, but suffered no losses. Between 09:00-10:00 LT four Yaks of 897 IAP escorted Il-2s to the Zámoly-Pátka area and fought against six Bf 109s at 800m, they suffered the loss of Ml.Lt. Nikolai Ivanovich Hlebantsov (KIA) with his Omsk-built Yakovlev Yak-9D (c/n: 16166099, engine: 345-2030 with RSI-4 radio system).[17]

12 This account is interesting as the final documented *Anerkennung* number given by the OKL/RLM to 5./JG 52 was for Sturm himself (#938) on 31 October and was thus actually higher than 900!

13 Lipfert, Gribig, *The War Diary of Hauptmann Helmut Lipfert,* p. 152.

14 Lipfert, Gribig, *The War Diary of Hauptmann Helmut Lipfert*, p. 152.

15 Bernd Barbas, *Die Geschichte der II. Gruppe des Jagdgeschwaders 52: Offizielle Ausgabe der Traditionsgemeinschaft JG 52* (Überlingen: Self-published, 2003), p. 323. Lt. Sturm was in Bf 109G-6/U4 WNr: 442036 at the time of his death.

16 The 7 MK lost 19 T-34/85s (Vashurin, Sitiy, Soloviev, etc.) and two 78 GvTTP IS-2 heavy tanks of which one burned out. The 18 TK lost one 363 GvTSAP ISU-122 and 40 T-34/85s, of which 30 burned out. The heaviest losses were recorded by its 110th Tank Brigade at Pázmánd-NW, which lost one knocked out T-34/85 tank, while 19 others burned out. (Saburov, Melnikov, Savchenko, Pryamitsin, Korzh, Butorin, Tereshenko, Mihailov, etc.) The 18 TK, 170 TBr (Shubin, Firsov, Aleksashin, etc.) and 181 TBr (Bondarchuk, Druzhinin, Strashkov, etc.) lost nine and three burned out T-34/85 tanks respectively, while they each had four other tanks knocked out.

17 TsAMO RF: fu. 20257, inv. 1, f. 42, p. 467 says it was a Yak-9T, but that is incorrect. It was a D model.

Экз.№ 5

А К Т

РАССЛЕДОВАНИЯ ПРИЧИН ЛЕТНЫХ БОЕВЫХ ПОТЕРЬ В ЧАСТЯХ ВВС КА
951 АВИАПОЛКА.306 АВИАДИВИЗИИ.17 ВОЗДУШНОЙ АРМИИ.
ТИП САМОЛЕТА ИЛ-2 №№ 4401,3698.ТИП МОТОРА АМ-38Ф.

I. ХАРАКТЕР ПОТЕРИ

Detail of the combined 951 ShAP loss report of Lt. German Petrovich Odnotsenov's (HSU, KIA on 8 March 1945 in Il-2m3, c/n: 9957) and Ml.Lt. Pavel Alekseevich Marakulin's Il-2m3 Sturmoviks on 22 December 1944. Odnotsenov's plane (c/n: 1884401) was downed by German Bf 109s, while Marakulin's plane was hit by a Flakpanzer. (Source: TsAMO RF: fu. 370, inv. 6531, f. 14, p. 28.)

The other Yak-9D this day was downed by Hungarian 102/1. VB. oszt. Fw 190F-8 fighter-bombers between Vereb and Lovasberény. At 12:20 LT four Fw 190, led by Lévay Győző szds. escorted Hans-Ulrich Rudel's nine[18] 10.(Pz)/StG 2 Ju 87G-2 'Stukas' during their attack at 100m on the 7th Mechanized Corp's advancing T-34/85 tanks, when four 659 IAP Yak-9s, led by Lt. Semyon Nikitovich Nikitin intercepted them. The Fw 190s[19] immediately went into action and during the dogfight Kázár László fhdgy. hit Ml.Lt. Arsenii Emelyanovich Andreev's Yak-9D which separated from its group, burst into flames, blew into pieces and fell in the Vereb area.[20]

As Hptm. Sturm made his claims just prior to his death, his victims could not have fallen to his guns any earlier then 10:00 LT and almost certainly around 10:30LT, greatly reducing the potential candidates. Around 10:30 LT the only losses were Il-2s of the 995 and 639 ShAPs who flew in and around the Pátka-Zámoly-Lake Velence areas, East of Csór. Since so many Il-2s were shot down by enemy fighters in the Csór-E – Pátka area, Hptm. Sturm's two unconfirmed victory claims on 22 December 1944, due to the lack of documentation owing to his death, seem to be legitimate aerial victories, however their exact identities cannot be determined. As such these claims can only be deemed as potential victories, though it is nearly certain that Hptm. Heinrich Sturm actually downed two enemy aircrafts on his final mission.

Conclusion

Hptm. Sturm, commander of 5./JG 52 during his 2-3 months of service time in Hungary claimed thirteen aerial victories of which eight were verifiable victories or potential victories, while the remaining five were overclaims. This is approximately 63% accuracy which represents a fair average among the fighter pilots of the Eastern Front.

18 The Yak-9 pilots mentioned only eight Ju 87 'Stukas', probably because one Ju 87G-2 (WNr.: 490200, 'T6+AU', pilot Fhr. Bernhard Pietruschka and aerial gunner Uffz. Willibald Gaumer) had already been shot down near Kőhányáspuszta at Csákvár-NW by 31 IAP La-5 ace, St.Lt. Victor Vasilevich Kirilyuk.

19 Fw 190F-8 pairs of Lévay Győző szds., Kishady Gábor fhdgy. and Kázár László fhdgy., Sipos János őrm.

20 TsAMO RF: fu. 20257, inv. 1, f. 42, p. 466, Journal of Operations of 288 IAD, entry for 22 December 1944.

Final Conclusions

The top eight fighter aces of II./JG 52 had a total of 245 Abschüsse over Hungary of which 137 were victories or potential victories.[1] Of these, 108 were overclaims where the opponents were not permanently destroyed representing a 56 percent claiming accuracy. The most successful and reliable claimer was Hptm. Helmut Lipfert with 48 victories/potential victories representing an astonishing claiming accuracy of over 92 percent! Based on the analysis in this book the least reliable II./JG 52 claimer over Hungary was Lt. Friedrich Haas, who had only three potential victories with a 20 percent reliability. The records show that out of the 246 total claims analyzed within this book, only one claim can be proven to have been falsely written about postwar, while only two overclaims may be considered to have been possibly made with dishonest intents.[2]

Pilot	Pilots total victory srcore*	Total claims in Hungary (Victories / potential victories, confirmed and unconfirmed total)	Overclaims in Hungary (confirmed and uncoinfirmed)	Unconfirmed claims in Hungary (victories and overclaims)	Days with one V/PV in Hungary	Days with two V/PVs in Hungary	Days with three V/PVs in Hungary	Days with four V/PVs in Hungary	Days with five V/PVs in Hungary	Accuracy of claims (confirmed and uncoinfirmed) over Hungary (% rounded up)
Barkhorn, Gerhard	301	28 (22)	6	-	-	3	1	2	1	79%
Batz, Wilhelm	237	8 (7)	1	-	-	2	1	-	-	88%
Düttmann, Peter	150	42 (11)	31	9	8	-	1	-	-	27%
Ewald, Heinz	84	53 (32)	21	4	13	6	1	1	-	60%
Haas, Friedrich	50	15 (3)	12	-	3	-	-			20%
Hartmann, Erich	352	34** (7)	27	-	4	-	1	-	-	22%
Lipfert, Helmut	203	52 (48)	4	4	16	8	4	1	-	93%
Sturm, Heinrich	123	13 (8)	5	-	4	2	-	-	-	62%
Total	**1500**	**245 (138)**	**107**	**17**	**48**	**21**	**9**	**4**	**1**	**56%**

* According to the pilots themselves, see Luftwaffe Aces: Biographies and Victory Claims volumes 1, 2 & 4 for corrected/documented totals.

** False claim on 21.11.1944 not included, 8.5.1945 claim not included.

While reviewing these numbers one should keep in mind that they are all relative. Obviously, a pilot who happened to shoot down only three enemy planes with 100 percent accuracy was much less successful overall than the one who claimed one hundred enemy planes with only 30 percent accuracy; the first pilot destroyed three while the second one destroyed thirty. Certainly, the poor results do not mean that overclaiming was the 'speciality' of II./JG 52 or the Luftwaffe itself. VVS,

1 Including Lipfert's four unclaimed entries discussed within his respective chapter. Hartmann's false 21 November 1944 claim and 8 May 1945 claim are not included.

2 False claim: Erich Hartmann's La-5 claim on 21 November 1944. Potentially dishonest overclaims: Peter Düttmann's P-51 claim on 20 March 1945 and Erich Hartmann's Yak-9 claim on 8 May 1945.

RAF and USAAF fighter pilots overclaimed as well, sometimes with even higher rates. By examining the types of aircraft overclaimed over Hungary, a theory as to why many overclaims occurred may be made.

Pilot	Number of overclaims in Hungary	Yakovlev (Yak-1B, -7, -9, -11)	Yakovlev Yak-3 (all metal)	Lavochkin models (La-5, La-7)	Ilyushin Il-2 Sturmovik	Douglas A-20 Boston	Petlyakov Pe-2	Misc. (P-51, 'MiG-3')
Barkhorn	6	1	-	1	2	1	1	-
Batz	1	-	-	-	1	-	-	-
Düttmann	31	11	4	4	9	-	-	3
Ewald	22	6	3	8	2	1	-	1
Haas	12	9	-	1	2	-	-	-
Hartmann	27	15	2	4	5	1	-	-
Lipfert	4	-	2	1	1	-	-	-
Sturm	5	-	-	2	3	-	-	-
Total	**107**	**42**	**11**	**21**	**25**	**3**	**1**	**4**
Percent (%)	**100%**	**39.3%**	**10.3%**	**19.6%**	**23.4%**	**2.8%**	**0.9%**	**3.7%**

The abover numbers speak for themselves. Roughly half of the overclaims made by the top II./JG 52 aces over Hungary were Yakovlev fighters, while the Lavochkin and Ilyushin models made up a little over twenty-percent each, while the remaining few percentages are comprised of other aircraft. Yakovlevs were overclaimed almost twice as often as any other type, but why? Their presence in the fighter regiments do not explain this phenomenon, especially if one takes a look at the 17 VA which was the main opponent in 1945. Comparing the Yakovlev and Lavochkin aircraft inventories on first days of January, February and March,[3] then subracting the 236 IAD's Yaks operating in Yugoslavia (not the operational area of II./JG 52), the Lavochkins outnumbered the Yakovlev fighters by 1.35 in January, 2.14 in February and 1.72 in March. If one looks at the specific example of March 1945 when the last large-scale German offensive of the war took place (Operation Spring Awakening), the relative lack of Yakovlev losses further opposes the Yak-Abschuss-Phenomenon. The 17 VA, which bore the main combat pressure in March 1945 in the Lake Balaton area, had only one Yakovlev fighter division in Hungary (288 IAD) comprised of four fighter regiments (611, 659, 866, 897 IAPs). Their potential air combat related losses (dogfight + missing) amounted to only 24, while the final number of Yak losses for the entire month of March was 31 (flak + accidents + wear and tear included).[4] This explains why a large portion of the German Yakovlev victories were simply overclaims in the Balaton area during March and most likely even earlier. The temporary air activity of the 5 VA in the area was very minimal.

Fuselage canvas repair of a damaged 611 IAP Yak-9T fighter on a frontline airfield. (Photo: Dmitrii Karlenko)

3 Horváth Gábor, *Bostonok a Magyar Égen és Földben 1944-1945*, (Self-published: Szolnok, 2013), p. 23.
4 4 Yak-1B, 8 (Tbilisi-built) Yak-3, 6 Yak-9D, 2 Yak-9DD, 8 Yak-9M and 3 Yak-9T. Source: TsAMO RF: fu. 20257, inv. 1, f. 95, p. 309, Checklist (c/n list) of lost aircrafts of the 288 IAD in March 1945.

Combat damage on a Yakovlev fighter in Hungary in the winter of 1944-1945 from the 5 VA, 6 GvIAD. The explosion caused by incoming ammunition always takes the path of the least resistance, namely the canvas, rather than the metal geodesic structure. Perhaps this plane was also wrongly credited to one of the JG 52 aces. (Photo: Boris V. Davidov)

The answer to the Yak-Abschuss-Phenomenon may lay in the structural design of the Yakovlev fighters. A very large part of these aircrafts (excluding the Yak-3 and the Yak-9U) were built with metal frames covered by sheets of canvas, similar in principle to the well known British Vickers Wellington bomber. The fuselages of the Yak-1B, -7B, -9D, -9DD, -9M, -9T and -9R models were all made of geodesic metal frame, covered by canvas. This was an inexpensive and extremely durable structure, which could take several hits without suffering critial damages. A hit Yak-1, -7, -9 could look very 'visual' by losing large parts of the fuselage skin or have large parts burn off without suffering critical damages to the wings or its control surfaces. This could give the opponent pilot the false impression of an explosion, serious fire or obvious aerial victory. If the ambush lasted only for a few seconds, such 'visual' damages could be interpreted incorrectly. These damaged planes could recover by diving away and returning to base, while the victory list on the opponent's side continued to grow. The repair of the canvas was easy, fast and inexpensive allowing the plane to return to the air within just a few hours.

The overclaiming over the Hungarian skies by II./JG 52, in addition to being proven by archival documents, is believable precisely because it is expected. The fighter-vs-fighter overclaiming which makes up over 70 percent of cases assessed within this book are expected due to the inherent danger each pilot faced if they risked staying in the combat zone to thoroughly observe their 'kill'. This type of overclaiming was not exclusive to the Eastern Front, as on the Western Front there was also a *huge disparity – sometimes to a factor of one to eight – between Allied* [loss] *records and German claims when dealing with fighter vs. fighter combats.*[5] In many cases the enemy opponents were indeed hit, however their ultimate fate was not destruction. It is interesting to note that the Luftwaffe pilots experienced frequent run-ins with Soviet reconnaissance aircraft, possibly more so then what was previously thought. There was also a large presence of Soviet reconnaissance aircraft over Hungary as in addition to the Il-2KRs, A-20 Bostons, Yak-9Rs and Yak-9Ds, all available Pe-2s and Pe-3s were used in the reconnaissance role.

But how do the successes of these eight pilots fit in to the overall picture of the air war over the Eastern Front? Below is an analysis of the accuracy of confirmed claims made over Hungary by the eight II./JG 52 pilots assessed in this book. Accuracy of claims within the surviving microfilms are compared to the confirmed claims within the pilot's chapter to provide a theorized total victory count based one the total number claims commonly attributed to the pilot (actual claim counts are constantly being revised as new information is discovered). Although the theorized victories are imperfect as they are derived from a sample of claims, they provide an interesting assessment of the possible number of enemy aircraft actually destroyed by the pilots.

5 Jean-Yves Lorant, Richard Goyat, *Jagdeschwader 300 "Wilde Sau": A Chronicle of a Fighter Arm Geschwader in the Battle for Germany*. Vol. 1 (Hamilton, Montana: Eagle Edition Ltd., 2005), p. viii.

Ace:	Barkhorn	Batz	Düttmann	Ewald	Haas	Hartmann	Lipfert	Sturm
Microfilm claims	7	-	21	19	15	19	16	11
V/PV	6	-	6	12	3	6	15	6
Accuracy	86%	-	29%	63%	20%	32%	94%	55%
Confirmed Claims in Chapter	28	8	33	49	15	34***	48	13
V/PV	22	7	10	30	3	7	44	8
Accuracy	79%	88%	31%	61%	20%	21%	92%	62%
Claim by Pilots*	301	237	150	84	50	352	203	123
Theorized Real Victories	238-259	N/A**	44-47	51-53	~10	74-113	187-191	68-77

* According to the pilots themselves, see Luftwaffe Aces: Biographies and Victory Claims, Vols. 1, 2 & 4 for corrected/ documented totals.

** Inadequate information for theorized range.

*** Claim for 21 November 1944 has not been included.

How do the individual accuracies of these eight pilots compare against the overall accuracy of late-war aerial combat over the Eastern Front? If one takes the year 1944 as a basis for comparison, then the accuracy of the eight pilots drops below the average accuracy for the entire German military forces on the Eastern Front for the 1944 period.[6] This difference may be the result of the poor visibility conditions the fall and winter months and/or the dire need for successes to boost morale. The very raw nature of Eastern Front combat may also partly explain why the accuracy is relatively low, with multiple sorites flown day-after-day leading to exhaustion, nervous breakdowns and poor observations.

OKL Data for Soviet Combat Losses in 1944*						
January	February	March	April	May	June	July
912	845	1,028	1,408	1,117	1,602	1,708
August	September	October	November	December	**Total****	
1,689	1,157	1,692	354	719	**14,231**	

* 'According to reports from the Luftflottenkommandos and the Army units. Raw figures'. NARA T321/R92/0000398.

** This total is conservative as slides 0000334 and 0000383 state 18,699 for the same year!

Soviet Data for Soviet Combat Losses in 1944*					
ADD/18 VA	GVF	PVO	VVS -KA	VVS -VMF	**Total**
554	79	131	7,861	910	**9,535**

* Carl-Fredrik Geust, Gennadiy Petrov. Lend-Lease aircraft in Russia: Red Stars Vol. 4. (Finland: Apali Oy, 2002), pp. 185-187; Советская авиация в Великой Отечественной войне 1941-1945 гг. в цифрах, М., 1962 (Главный штаб Военно-воздушных сил. Экз. №34), chapters 1,6.

Accuracy of German Claims for 1944 in the East	**Accuracy of Confirmed Claims within Chapters**
14,231 claims for 9,535 Soviet losses	227 confirmed claims for 131 Soviet losses
67%	**58%**

Other German claims totals provide different though comparable results suggesting that an average claiming accuracy for the Germans over Soviet aircraft lies somewhere around seventy percent.[7] The eight pilots in this book were unable to, on average, keep in line with the German average. Below are listed the victories and potential victories of the eight II./JG 52 pilots with the corrected aircraft models. This list also includes all victories or potential victories resulting from unconfirmed or unclaimed claims over Hungary:

6 Note that the 1944 basis statistic includes claims from non-airborne units such flak, Soviet combat losses also included losses attributed to flak and other factors.

7 Using different German claims totals for the Eastern Front, an accuracy percentage of 71% is achieved. Of the 13,390 claims 9,952 were attributed to Luftflottes 1,4,6 and Kdr.Gen.Finland with an additional 3,438 attribute to Flak. AIR 40/1397, A.D.I.(K) Report No. 351/1945. G.A.F. Operations, Claims and Losses, 1944-Feb. 1945, appendices VI, VII, VIII.

Pilot	V	PV	Yak	La	Il-2	Boston	Pe-2	Bf 109	Victories
Barkhorn	6	16	10	5	7	-	-	-	22
Batz	-	7	-	1	5	1	-	-	7
Düttmann	2	9	2	3	5	1	-	-	11
Ewald	13	19	11	12	7	2	-	-	32
Haas	-	3	1	2	-	-	-	-	3
Hartmann	2	5	5	2	-	-	-	-	7
Lipfert	40	8	19	8	16	3	1	1	48
Sturm	2	6	2	2	4	-	-	-	8
Total:	**66**	**72**	**50**	**35**	**44**	**7**	**1**	**1**	**138**

Despite the obvious reduction in combat sucesses these pilots achived once victories are verified, their accomplishments continue to top the charts of combat aviation history. Since achieving this many, or more aerial victories in modern warfare is impossible, it is almost certain that the highest number of verified aerial victories scored by the top fighter aces of the Second World War will never be exceeded. May it never happen again!

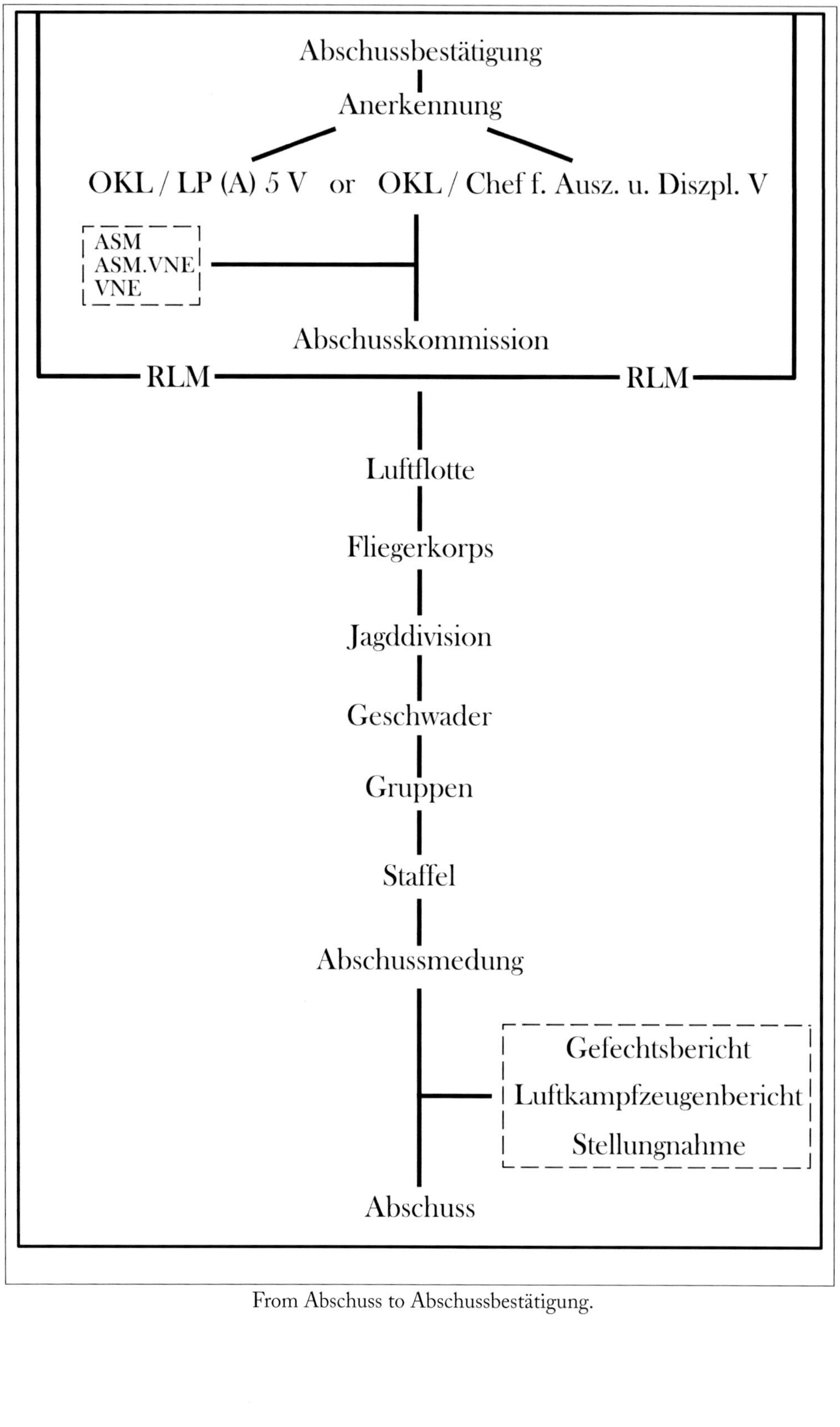

From Abschuss to Abschussbestätigung.

II./52 Jagdgeschwader Gefechtsstand, den 1.2.1945

A b s c h u s s

einer La-5 am 29.1.1945

Abschusszeit: 12.30 Uhr

im Raum B u d a p e s t

Pl.Qu. coordinate

d u r c h

Hauptmann F i r s t n a m e L a s t N a m e , unit

wird als

22. Abschuss des Schützen,
432. Abschuss der staffel,
2450. Abschuss der Gruppe,

zur Anerkennung eingereicht.

Major und Gruppenkommandeur.

Inhalt:
1. Abschussmeldung,
2. Gefechtsbericht des Schützen,
3. Luftkampfzeugen bericht,
4. Stellungnahme.

The cover page for a ficticious claim package. Note the general information describing the claim, the request for confirmation and the attached documents within the package.

Anlage 1
zu Nr. 431

....
(Truppenteil) (Ort Datum)

Abschußmeldung, Zerstörungsmeldung

1. Zeit (Tag, Stunde, Miunte) und Gegend des Absturzes: ....

   Höhe: ....
2. Durch wen ist Abschuß / Zerstörung erfolgt? ....
3. Flugzeugtyp des abgeschossenen Flugzeuges: ....
4. Staatsangehörigkeit des Gegners: ....

   Werknummern bzw. Kennzeichen: ....
5. Art der Vernichtung: ....
   a) Flammen mit dunkler Fahne, Flammen mit heller Fahne;
   b) Einzelteil weggeflogen, abmontiert (Art der Teile erläutern), auseinandergeplatzt;
   c) zur Landung gezwungen (diesseits oder jenseits der Front, glatt bzw. mit Bruch);
   d) jenseits der Front am Boden in Brand geschossen.
6. Art des Aufschlages (nur wenn dieser beobachtet werden konnte):
   a) diesseits oder jenseits der Front;
   b) senkrecht, flachem Winkel, Aufschlagbrand, Staubwolke;
   c) nicht beobachtet warum nicht? ....
7. Schicksal der Insassen (tot, mit Fallschirm abgesprungen, nicht beobachtet).
8. Gefechtsbericht des Schützen ist in der Anlage beigefügt.
9. Zeugen:
   a) Luft: ....
   b) Erde: ....
10. Anzahl der Angriffe, die auf das feindliche Flugzeug gemacht wurden: ....
11. Richtung, aus der die einzelnen Angriffe erfolgten: ....
12. Entfernung, aus der der Abschuß erfolgte: ....
13. Takt. Position aus der der Abschuß angesetzt wurde: ....
14. Ist einer der feindlichen Bordschützen kampfunfähig gemacht worden? ....
15. Verwandte Munitionsart: ....
16. Munitionsverbrauch: ....
17. Art und Anzahl der Waffen, die bei dem Abschuß gebraucht wurden: ....
18. Typ der eigenen Maschine (z. B. Me 109 E mit 2 Kanonen und 2 MG.): ....
19. Weiteres taktisch oder technisch Bemerkenswertes ....
20. Treffer in der eigenen Maschine: ....
21. Beteiligung weiterer Einheiten (auch Flak): ....

....
(Unterschrift)

Zu Ziffer 5–7 ist Zutreffendes zu unterstreichen.

2143a

V. N. E. **A. S. M.** **Ohne Zeugen!**

An example of a blank Abschussmeldung. Note 'Anlage 1 zu Nr. 431' in the top corner, referring to the main claiming regulation, Ziffer 431-directive 55270/41. The stamps below the form were used to indicate problems with the Abschussmeldung.

First Name, Last Name, Hauptmann
unit

Befehlsstelle, 29. 1. 45

Gefechtsbericht des Schützen

Start: 29.1.45 um 12.00 Uhr.
Auftrag: Alarmstart nach Budapest.
Landung: 12.45 Uhr.

Description

Abschussort: Im Raum Budapest.
Abschusszeit: 29.1.45 um 12.30 Uhr.
Abschusshöhe: 1800 m.

....

First Name, Last Name, Hauptmann
unit

Befehlsstelle, 29. 1. 45

Luftkampfzeugenbericht

Start: 29.1.45 um 12.00 Uhr.
Auftrag: Alarmstart nach Budapest.
Landung: 12.45 Uhr.

Witness description

Abschussort: Im Raum Budapest.
Abschusszeit: 29.1.45 um 12.30 Uhr.
Abschusshöhe: 1800 m.

....

Unit

Gefechtsstelle, 30. 1. 45

S t e l l u n g n a h m e .

Statement

Major und Gruppen-Kdeur.

Examples of the additional supportive documents required for recognition of the claim.

Der Reichsminister der Luftfahrt
und Oberbefehlschaber der Luftwaffe
Luftwaffenpersonalamt
Az. 29 Nr. /44 ((A)5, V) ⓘ

Berlin, den

An

Der ....

wird der Abschuß eines ....

.... am ....

durch ....

....

....

als .... Luftsieg der Staffel / Gruppe } anerkannt

I.A.

ⓘ

Printed until late May 1944

Der Reichsminister der Luftfahrt
und Oberbefehlschaber der Luftwaffe
Luftwaffenpersonalamt
Az. 29 Nr. /44 ((A)5, V)

Printed until late July 1944

Der Reichsminister der Luftfahrt
und Oberbefehlschaber der Luftwaffe
Chef f. Ausz. u. Diszpl. (V)
Az. 29 Nr. /44

Printed from August 1944

Oberkommando der Luftwaffe
Chef f. Ausz. u. Diszpl. (V)
Az. 29 Nr. /44

Altered beginning mid-December 1944

Oberkommando der Luftwaffe
L.P. - ~~Chef f.~~ Ausz. u. Diszpl. (V) -
Az. 29 Nr. /44

Example of a blank Abschussbestätigung. Note how the various certificate headings reflect the restructuring of recognition departments.

5. SS Panzer Division
W i k i n g
I c

Div.Gef.Stand, 1. 3.1945

<u>Ic-Tagesmeldung vom 1. 3.1945</u>

***

<u>Luftlage:</u>

Geringe feindliche Nachtfliegertätigkeit und am Tages geringe feindliche Luftaufklärung. 14.26 Uhr 8 Spitfire kreisend in 2800 m Höhe am Südrand Stuhlweißenburg, dabei 14 Liberators von Norden nach Südrwesten fliegend, Höhe 6000 m, 14.28 Uhr 4 Liberator mit angehängten Lastenseglern und 14.29 Uhr 4 Liberator mit angahängten Lastenseglern in gleicher Rightung.

Extract from a 5 SS Panzer Division intelligence report documenting the aerial activities above the division the day Lt. Heinz Ewald claimed a P-51 Mustang. Note that the report misidentifies the enemy fighters as Spitfires.

Ic-Tagesmeldung vom 22.12.1944.

***

Fliegerverbände:
Im Raum des III.Pz.Korps:
639. Schlachtflieger Rgt. durch 1 abgeschossenen Flieger.
770. Schlachtflieger Rgt. - 189. Schlachtflieger-Div. durch
2 abgeschossene Flieger.
879. Aufkl.Rgt. der 17. Luftarmee durch Besatzung einer abgeschos-
senen Jak 9.

Extract from a ground intelligence report describing the aerial activity between lakes Balaton and Velence the morning Hptm. Hernrich Sturm lost his life. The Soviet losses differ from the claims in this report. Note the attempt to identify the enemy units. Corrected units are 707 ShAP and 897 IAP.

VOL

2.11.44

A u s z u g a u s

Tagesabschlussmeldung I.Flg.Korps v.1.11.44

***

Abschüsse: 17 Flugzeuge mit Zeugen, 1 Flgz. ohne Zeugen.
Major Barkhorn 274. Luftsieg.
Hptm. Hartmann 306. Luftsieg.
Lt. Duattmann 5 Flugzeuge Abgeschossen, 123 . Luftsieg.

Extract from a VOL report made for the ground units. II./JG 52 claims seem to have made the headlines this day (1.11.44). Note that Lt. Düttmann's name is incorrelty spelt.

VOL **Luftlage 24.12.1944**

***

8 Flugzeuge abgeschossen.
Besonderes: Am 23.12. erzielte Hptm. Hartmann seinen
328. Luftsieg, Oberstlt. Rudel flog seinen 2400 Feind-
flug.

Extract from a VOL report made on 24.12.1944. Hptm. Hartmann's previous claim has made it into the special remarks section of the report. No further details are given about this 'Luftsieg'.

VOL

25.12.1944

<u>Nachmeldung zur Luftlage 24.12.1944</u>

***

<u>Abschüsse:</u> 19 Flugzeuge mit Zeugen, 2 Flugzeuge ohne Zeugen, 7 weitere Flugzeuge wirksam beschossen. Hptm. Hartmann 331. Luftsieg.

Extract from a VOL report describing aerial successes for 24.12.1944. Hptm. Hartmann has made another 'Luftsieg'

VOL 25.12.1944

L u f t l a g e 25.12.1944

***

B e s o n d e r e s: Hauptmann Hartmann 5 Abschüsse, 336.Luft-seig, Major Barkhorn 4 Abschüsse, 289. Luftseig.

Extract from a VOL report for 25.12.1944 with an interesting special remarks section: Both Hptm. Hartmann and Maj. Barkhorn have made multiple claims. If the report is not backdated then the confirmation of these claims happened extremely quickly. No further details are available for these claims.

Bibliography

Archival Sources

Центральный архив Министерства обороны Российской Федерации (ЦАМО РФ)
[Central Archive of the Ministry of Defence of the Russian Federation – TsAMO RF], Podolsk, Russia; various archival funds numbering from 33-22444.
Суворовский натиск [Suvorov onslaught] – Newspaper of the 2nd Ukrainian Front
Советский воин [Soviet Warrior] – Newspaper of the 3rd Ukrainian Front
Советский пилот [Soviet Pilot] – Newspaper of the 5th Air Army
Защитник Отечества [Defender of the Fatherland] – Newspaper of the 17th Air Army
AAIR (Aviation Archaeological Investigation & Research) Rohnert Park, California, USA – Individual Aircraft Record Cards for Soviet Lend-Lease aircrafts over Hungary in 1944-1945
Missing Air Crew Reports (MACRs) of lost 15th AF planes in Central-Europe in 1945
NARA (National Archives and Records Administration) Washington DC, USA – various archival sources
Various issues of Hungarian wartime military magazine: Magyar Szárnyak [Hungarian Wings], 1944

Books & Articles

Aders, Gebhard, *History of the German Night Fighter Force 1917-1945* (London: Jane's Publishing Company, 1997)
Archer, Lee and Nevenkin, Kamen, *Panzerwrecks: 20: Ostfront 3* (Sussex: Panzerwrecks, 2016)
Barbas, Bernd, *Das vergessene As – Der Jagdflieger Gerhard Barkhorn* (Osnabrück: Luftfahrtverlag-Start, 2014)
Barbas, Bernd, *Die Geschichte der II. Gruppe des Jagdgeschwaders 52* (Überlingen: Self-published, 2003)
Bergström, Christer, *Graf and Grislawski: A Pair of Aces* (Hamilton, Montana: Eagles Editions Ltd., 2003)
Bernád, Dénes, *Rumanian Aces of World War 2* (Oxford: Osprey, 200)
Bernád, Dénes, *Rumanian Air Force: The Prime Decade, 1938-1947* (Carrolton, Texas: Squardon/Signal publications, 1999)
Bikov, Mihail Yurevich, Асы Великой Отечественной – Самые результативные
летчики *1941-1945* (Москва, 2007)
Boog, Horst, *Die Deutsche Luftwaffenführung 1935-1945. Führungsprobleme, Spitzengliederung, Generalstabsausbildung* (Stuttgart: Deutsche Verlags-Ansalt, 1982)
Boiten, Theo, *Nachtjagd – Combat Archive, 1943 Part 1* (Red Kite, 2018)
Davtyan, S. M., Пятая воздушная (Военно-исторический очерк боевого пути 5-й
воздушной армии в годы Великой Отечественной войны*)* (М.: Воениздат, 1990)
Dilip, Sarkar, How the Spitfire Won the Battle of Britain. Kindle
Düttmann, Peter, *Itärintaman hävittäjäsotaa* (Helsinki: Koala-Kustannus Helsinki Aviation books, 2002)
Erik, Mombeeck and Gòralczyk, Maciej, *Luftwaffe Gallery 6: Luck Fate and Destiny* (La Porte d Hoves Belgium: ASBL La Porte d Hoves, 2020)
Eriksson, Patrick, *Alarmstart East: The German Fighter Pilot's Experience on the Eastern Front 1941-1945*, Kindle
Evdokimov, G. P: *300* вылетов за линию фронта (Ижевск: Удмуртия, 1979)
Ewald, Heinz, *ESAU. Heinz Ewald Als Jagdflieger im erfolgreichsten Jagdgeschwader 1943 – 1945* (Coburg: Self-published, 1980)
Ewald, Markus and Klinnert, Falk, *Heinz Ewald "Esau": Wo Wir Sind Ist Immer Oben* (Leipzig: Fips-Druck, 1998)
Galland, Adolf, *The First and the Last: the Rise and Fall of the German Fighter Forces, 1938-1945* (New York: Ballantine Books, 1969)
General Staff of the Air Force, No. 34: Советская авиация в Великой Отечественной войне *1941-1945.* (в цифрах, 1962)
Geust, Carl-Fredrik and Petrov Gennadiy, *Lend-Lease aircraft in Russia: Red Stars Vol. 4.* (Tampere, Finland: Apali Oy, 2002)
Horváth, Gábor, *Bostonok a magyar égen és földben, 1944-1945* (Szolnok: Self-published, 2013)
Isaenko, Nikolai Fedorovich, Вижу противника*!* (Политиздат, 1981)
Ivie, Thomas, *Aerial Reconnaissance: the 10th Photo Recon Group in World War II* (Fallbrook: Aero Publishers Inc, 1981)
Janda, Aleš and Poruba, Tomáš, *Luftwaffe Over Czech Territory – 1945: Messerschmitt Bf 109s of JG 52 in Deutsch Brod* (JaPo Publishing, 2004)
Klinnert, Falk, *Peter Düttmann "Bonifazius": Wir Kämpften In Einsamen Höhen* (Leipzig: Fips-Druck, 2002)
Kurowski, Franz, *Major Wilhelm Batz – Vom Fluglehrer zum Schwerterträger* (Flechsig Verlag, 2008)

Lipfert, Helmut and Gribig, Werner, *The War Diary of Hauptmann Helmut Lipfert: JG 52 on the Russian Front 1943-1945* (Atglen, Pennsylvania: Schiffer Publishing Ltd., 1993)
Lorant, Jean-Yves and Goyat, Richard, *Jagdeschwader 300 "Wilde Sau": A chronicle of a fighter arm geschwader in the battle for Germany. Vol. 1* (Hamilton, Montana: Eagle Edition Ltd., 2005)
Magó, Károly, *Szolnok repüléstörténete 1945-ig* (RepTár Szolnok Nkft: Szolnok, 2018)
Mahoney, Kevin, *Fifteenth Air Force Against the Axis: Combat Missions over Europe during World War II* (Plymouth: Scarecrow Press Inc, 2013)
Maier, Georg, *Drama between Budapest and Vienna. The Final Battles of the 6. Panzer-Armee in the East – 1945*, (Winnipeg, Manitoba: J. J. Fedorowicz Publishing Inc., 2004)
Manrho, John and Putz, Ron, *Bodenplatte The Luftwaffe's Last Hope: The Attack on Allied Airfields New Year's Day 1945* (Sussex: Hikoki Publications, 2004)
Matthews, Andrew Johannes and Foreman, John, *Luftwaffe Aces: Biographies and Victory Claims, Vol. 1, A-F* (Surrey: Red Kite, 2015)
Matthews, Andrew Johannes and Foreman, John, *Luftwaffe Aces: Biographies and Victory Claims, Vol. 2, G-L* (Surrey: Red Kite, 2015)
Matthews, Andrew Johannes and Foreman, John, *Luftwaffe Ace: Biographies and Victory Claims, Vol. 4, S-Z* (Surrey: Red Kite, 2015)
Medved, Nikolaevich and Khazanov, Dmitry, Пикирующий бомбардировщик Пе-*2*. "Пешка", ставшая ферзем, (Москва: Эксмо, 2007)
Morgan, Hugh and Seibel, Jürgen, *Combat Kill – The drama of aerial warfare in World War 2 and the controversy surrounding victories* (Somerset: Patrick Stephens Limited, 1997)
Nevenkin, Kamen, *Fortress Budapest: The Siege of the Hungarian Capital, 1944-45 Vol. 1* (Keszthely: PeKo Publishing, 2020)
Nevenkin, Kamen, *Take Budapest!: The Struggle for Hungary, Autumn 1944*, Kindle
Dr. Norbert, Számvéber, Kard a pajzs mögött (Veszprém: PeKo Publishing, 2013
Dr. Norbert, Számvéber, *Páncélosok A Budapesti Csatában – 1944. Október 29-1945. Február 13* (Hungary: Jaffa Kiadó, 2018)
Dr. Pataky, Iván, *Repülőesemények Magyarországon a csendőrségi jelentések alapján 1944 – III. Rész* (A repüléstörténeti konferencia közleményei, 1998)
Dr. Pataky, Iván – Rozsos, László – Sárhidai, Gyula, *Légi háború Magyarország felett II*
(Zrínyi, 1992)
Pawlas, Karl, *Luftfahrt International: Blohm & Voss BV 138, Vol. 11 Sept.-Okt. 1975* (Publizistisches Archiv: Nürnberg, 1975)
Prien, Jochen, *Jagdeschwader 53: A History of the "Pik As" Geschwader, January 1944-May 1945, Vol. 3* (Atglen, Pennsylvania: Schiffer Publishing, 1998)
Punka, György, *A Messzer. Bf 109-ek a Magyar Királyi Honvéd Légierőben* (Budapest, OMIKK, 1995)
Punka, György, *Hungarian Aces of World War 2* (Oxford, Osprey Publishing, 2004)
Reschke, Willi, *Jagdgeschwader 301/302 'Wilde Sau': In Defense of the Reich with the Bf 109, Fw 190 and Ta 152* (Atglen, Pennsylvania: Schiffer Millitary History, 2005)
Seidl, Hans, *Stalin's Eagles: An Illustrated Study of the Soviet Aces of World War II and Korea* (Atglen, Pennsylvania: Schiffer Publishing Ltd., 1998)
Stenge, B. Csaba, *Elfelejtett hősök – A magyar királyi honvéd légierők ászai a második világháborúban* (HM Zrínyi kiadó, 2016)
Skomorokhov, Nikolai Mihailovich – Burlyai, N. N. – Guchok, V. M. and others, *17-я*
воздушная армия в боях от Сталинграда до Вены (М., Воениздат, 1977)
Smirnov, Boris Aleksandrovich, Небо моей молодости (М.: Воениздат, 1990)
Spires, David, *Air Power for Patton's Army: The XIX Tactical Air Command in the Second World War.* (USA. 2002)
Szidnainé Dr. Csete, Ágnes, *A 125 éves Budapesti Állat- és Növénykert története* (Budapest, Athenaeum Nyomda, 1991)
Tálosi, Zoltán, *Háborús évek (1941-1945) – Légiesemények és harcok Tolna megyében. (2nd edition)* (Szekszárd: Wosinsky Mór Megyei Múzeum, 2016)
Tobak, Tibor, *Pumák földön-égen. Háttér Kiadó* (Budapest, 1989)
Toliver, Raymond and Constable, Trevor, *The Blond Knight of Germany* (Blue Ridge Summit, Pennsylvania: Aero, 1985)
Ungváry, Krisztián, *Budapest ostroma*n (Budapest: Corvina, 2005)
Veress, D. Csaba, *A Balatoni csata* (Veszprém: Veszprém Megyei Nyomdaipari Vállalat, 1976)
Veress, D. Csaba, *Magyarország hadikrónikája 1944-1945. Vol. 2* (Militaria, Budapest, 2002)
William, Green and Swanborough, Gordon, *Flying Review International 1965-66: Vol. 21, December 1965* (London: Purnell LTD., 1965)

Correspondence & Interviews

Dr. B. Stenge, Csaba (Hungary)
Barbas, Bernd (Germany)
Barnaky, Péter (Hungary)
Bergström, Christer (Sweden)
Bernád, Dénes (Hungary)
Davidov, Boris Vladimirovich (Russia)
DeMarco, Joe (USA)

Félix, Gábor (Hungary)
Geust, Carl-Fredrik (Finland)
Golovin, Dmitry (Uzbekistan)
Horváth, Péter (Hungary)
Katona József (Hungary)
Kotlyar, Viktor (Belarus)
Légrády Lajos (Hungary)
Magó, Károly (Hungary)
Mahr, Jan (Czech Republic, +2013)
Malov, Ivan Aleksandrovich (Russia)
Mamedov, Vitaly Olegovich (Russia)
Matthews, Andrew Johannes (United Kingdom)
Nagy, Gábor (Hungary)
Nikolaev, Andrey Evgenevich (Russia)
Pálffy, Sándor (Hungary)
Punka, György (Hungary)
Rabi, Lenke (Hungary)
Dr. Reisner, Markus (Austria)
Salonen, Matti (Finland)
Dr. Számvéber, Norbert (Hungary)
Tálosi, Zoltán (Hungary)
Dr. Theo, Boiten (Netherlands)
Ungváry, Krisztián (Hungary)
Webb, Cameron (Canada)
Zavesiczky, Ottó (Canada, +2006)

Electronic Sources

Авиаторы Второй мировой [Aviators of the Second World War]:
<http://allaces.ru/sssr/struct/main.php> – Structure of the Soviet Air Armies over Hungary in 1944-1945
Женские авиаполки. История. Факты. Лица. (*Women's Air Regiments. History. Facts. Faces*) vk.com
Ace of Aces: Erich Hartmann the Blond Knight of Germany <https://www.researchgate.net/publication/340177048_Ace_of_Aces_Erich_Hartmann_the_Blond_Knight_of_Germany> Erich Hartmann May 8
Die Schließung von Überlieferungslücken am Beispiel des Schriftgutes der Luftwaffe 1933-1945 ('The Closing of Gaps in Returned Collections Using the Documentation of the Luftwaffe 1933-1945 as an Example')
<http://www.lwag.org/reference/fla001.pdf> Information on Luftwaffe
Erich Hartmann – The World's Top Ace of All Time
<http://www.virtualpilots.fi/hist/WW2History-ErichHartmann.html) – Erich Hartmann Interview
Focke-Wulf Fw 190 Pilot, Jednotka? Nadryby okr. Plzeň-sever 8.5.1945
<http://www.leteckabadatelna.cz/havarie-a-sestrely/detail/305/> – Recovered Luftwaffe aircraft
Goodwill Meeting, American Fighter Aces Association and Luftwaffe Fighter Pilots Association (Part 2 of 3)
<https://digitalcollections.museumofflight.org/assets/Transcripts/2002-02> 13_AV_002_02.pdf) – Pilot discussions
Hartmann's claims disputed: An Over-view of Dimitri Khazanov's article in *Le Fana* with comments by Jean-Yves Lorant and Hans Ring
<https://web.archive.org/web/20070209153845/http://members.aol.com/falkeeins/Sturmgruppen/hartmannclaims.html> Discussion on Erich Hartmann (last accessed 5 September 2021)
Határon túli magyar helységnévszótár <http://sebok2.adatbank.transindex.ro/>
Sebők, László: Location and settlement names of Historical Hungary
Luftwaffe and Allied Air Forces Discussion Forum 12 O'Clock High! (http://forum.12oclockhigh.net/) – Discussions and threads
Magyar Roncskutató Egyesület [Hungarian Wreck Research Association]:
<http://www.roncskutatok.hu/> Aircraft recoveries in Hungary
Tony Wood's Combat Claims & Casualties Lists
<http://don-caldwell.we.bs/jg26/claims/tonywood.htm> – Luftwaffe claims over Hungary in late 1944
Units and Planes <http://ava.org.ru/> Photos and regiment markings of Soviet air units during the Great Patriotic War
USAAF Worldwide Operations Chronology, May 1945
<https://www.aircrewremembered.com/USAAFCombatOperations/May.45.html> USAAF missions